FIRESIDE

The
Most
of
P. G. Wodehouse

A FIRESIDE BOOK
Published by Simon & Schuster
New York London Toronto Sydney Tokyo Singapore

ISBN 0-671-20349-5
Library of Congress Catalog Card Number 60-12584
Manufactured in the United States of America
     25   26   27   28   29   30

✿ Contents

✿ The Drones Club

✿ Mr. Mulliner

✿ Stanley Featherstonehaugh Ukridge

✿ Lord Emsworth

✿ The Golf Stories

✿ Jeeves

✿ Quick Service: The Complete Novel

Introducing the gentlemen of

The Drones Club

An assortment of Eggs, Beans and Crumpets—including the most reluctant bachelor of them all, Freddie Widgeon.

"Do you know," said a thoughtful Bean, "I'll bet that if all the girls Freddie Widgeon has loved and lost were placed end to end—not that I suppose one could do it—they would reach halfway down Piccadilly."

"Further than that," said the Egg. "Some of them were pretty tall."

✿ *Fate*

IT WAS THE HOUR of the morning snifter, and a little group of Eggs and Beans and Crumpets had assembled in the smoking room of the Drones Club to do a bit of inhaling. There had been a party of sorts overnight, and the general disposition of the company was toward a restful and somewhat glassy-eyed silence. This was broken at length by one of the Crumpets.

"Old Freddie's back," he observed.

Some moments elapsed before any of those present felt equal to commenting on this statement. Then a Bean spoke.

"Freddie who?"

"Freddie Widgeon."

"Back where?"

"Back here."

"I mean, back from what spot?"

"New York."

"I didn't know Freddie had been to New York."

"Well, you can take it from me he has. Or else how," argued the Crumpet, "could he have got back?"

The Bean considered the point.

"Something in that," he agreed. "What sort of a time did he have?"

"Not so good. He lost the girl he loved."

"I wish I had a quid for every girl Freddie Widgeon has loved and lost," sighed an Egg wistfully. "If I had, I shouldn't be touching you for a fiver."

"You aren't," said the Crumpet.

The Bean frowned. His head was hurting him, and he considered that the conversation was becoming sordid.

"How did he lose his girl?"

"Because of the suitcase."

"What suitcase?"

"The suitcase he carried for the other girl."

"What other girl?"

"The one he carried the suitcase for."

The Bean frowned again.

"A bit complex, all this, isn't it?" he said. "Hardly the sort of stuff, I mean, to spring on personal friends who were up a trifle late last night."

"It isn't really," the Crumpet assured him. "Not when you know the facts. The way old Freddie told me the story it was as limpid as dammit. And what he thinks—and what I think, too—is that it just shows what toys we are in the hands of Fate, if you know what I mean. I mean to say, it's no good worrying and trying to look ahead and plan and scheme and weigh your every action, if you follow me, because you never can tell when doing such-and-such won't make so-and-so happen—while, on the other hand, if you do so-and-so it may just as easily lead to such-and-such."

A pale-faced Egg with heavy circles under his eyes rose at this point and excused himself. He said his head had begun to throb again and he proposed to step round to the chemist on the corner for another of his dark-brown pick-me-ups.

"I mean to say," resumed the Crumpet, "if Freddie—with the best motives in the world—hadn't carried that suitcase for that girl, he might at this moment be walking up the aisle with a gardenia in his buttonhole and Mavis Peasemarch, only daughter of the fifth Earl of Bodsham, on his arm."

The Bean demurred. He refused to admit the possibility of such a thing, even if Freddie Widgeon had sworn off suitcases for life.

"Old Bodders would never have allowed Mavis to marry a bird of Freddie's caliber. He would think him worldly and frivolous. I don't know if you are personally acquainted with the Bod, but I may tell you that my people once lugged me to a week end at his place and not only were we scooped in and shanghaied to church twice on the Sunday, regardless of age or sex, but on the Monday morning at eight o'clock—eight, mark you—there were family prayers in the dining room. There you have old Bodders in a nutshell. Freddie's a good chap, but he can't have stood a dog's chance from the start."

"On the contrary," said the Crumpet warmly. "He made his presence felt right from the beginning to an almost unbelievable extent, and actually clicked as early as the fourth day out."

"Were Bodders and Mavis on the boat, then?"

"They certainly were. All the way over."

"And Bodders, you say, actually approved of Freddie?"

"He couldn't have been more all over him, Freddie tells me, if Freddie had been a Pan-Anglican Congress. What you overlook is that Bodsham—living, as he does, all the year round in the country— knew nothing of Freddie except that one of his uncles was his old school friend, Lord Blicester, and another of his uncles was actually a bishop. Taking a line through them, he undoubtedly regarded Freddie as a pretty hot potato."

The Bean seemed shaken, but he put another point.

"What about Mavis, then?"

"What about her?"

"I should have thought Freddie would have been the last bloke she would have considered hitching up with. I've seen her in action down at Peasemarch, and you can take it from me that she is very far from being one of the boys. You needn't let it get about, of course, but that girl, to my certain knowledge, plays the organ in the local church and may often be seen taking soup to the deserving villagers with many a gracious word."

The Crumpet had his answer to this, too.

"She knew nothing of Freddie, either. She liked his quiet, saintly manner and considered that he had a soul. At any rate, I can assure you that everything went like a breeze. Helped by the fact that the sea was calm and that there was a dashed fine moon every night, old Freddie shoved his nose past the judge's box at 10:45 P.M. on the fourth day out. And when next morning he informed old Bodsham that he had now a son to comfort his declining years, there was not a discordant note. The old boy said that he could wish no better husband for his daughter than a steady, respectable young fellow like Freddie, and they arrived in New York a happy and united family."

The only thing in the nature of a flaw that Freddie found in New York, he tells me, was the fact that the populace, to judge from the daily papers, didn't seem to be so ideally happy in its love life as he was. What I mean to say, he wanted smiling faces about him, so to speak, and it looked to him as if everybody in the place were cutting up their wives and hiding them in sacks in the Jersey marshes or else putting detectives on to them to secure the necessary evidence.

It saddened him, he tells me, when he opened his illustrated tabloid of a morning, to have to try to eat eggs and bacon while gazing at a photograph of Mae Belle McGinnis, taken when she was not looking her best because Mr. McGinnis had just settled some domestic dispute with the meat ax.

Also, there seemed to him far too much of all that stuff about Sugar Daddies being Discovered in Love Nest As Blizzard Grips City.

However, when you are the guest of a great nation, you have to take the rough with the smooth. And there appears to be no doubt that, despite all the marital unrest around him, Freddie at this juncture was indisputably in the pink. I've never been engaged myself, so I know nothing of the symptoms at first hand, but Freddie tells me that the way it takes a fellow is to make him feel as if he were floating on a fleecy cloud, high up in the air, and only touching the ground at odd spots.

Most of the time, he says, he just hovered over New York like some winged thing. But occasionally he would come down and emerge from the ether, and on one of these rare occasions he found himself wandering in the neighborhood of Seventy-second Street, somewhere on the West Side.

And just in front of him was a girl lugging a dashed great heavy suitcase.

Now, I want you to follow me very closely here. This is where Freddie stands or falls. He was pretty eloquent at this point, when he told me the story; and, as far as I am concerned, I may say fearlessly that I dismiss him without a stain on his character. I consider his motives to have been pure to the last drop.

One of the things that being engaged does to you, you must remember, is to fill you to the gills with a sort of knightly chivalry. So Freddie tells me. You go about the place like a Boy Scout, pouncing out on passers-by and doing acts of kindness to them. Three times that day Freddie had chased seedy-looking birds up side streets and forced cash on them. He had patted four small boys on the head and asked them if they meant to be President some day. He had beamed benevolently on the citizenry till his cheeks ached. And he was still full of the milk of human kindness and longing to assist some less fortunate fellow traveler along the road of Life, when he saw this girl in front of him, staggering under the weight of the suitcase.

Now, although the impulse to help her with her burden was intense, he tells me that, if she had been a pretty girl, he would have resisted it. His sense of loyalty to Mavis was so great that he was right off pretty girls. They were the only persons he had excluded from his beaming operations. Toward them, in spite of all that milk of human kindness, he had been consistently aloof and austere. The cold face. The unwobbly eye. Something seemed to tell him that Mavis would prefer it so.

But this girl before him was not pretty. She was distinctly plain. Even ugly. She looked as if she might be a stenographer selected for some business magnate by his wife out of a number of competing applicants. And, such being so, he did not hesitate. Already the suitcase seemed to be giving the poor little thing a crick in the back, and it was as if he heard Mavis's voice in his ear, whispering: "Go to it!"

He ambled up like a courtly mustang.

"Excuse me," he said. "May I help you with that apparatus of yours?"

The girl gave him a keen look through her spectacles, and either thought he was thoroughly to be trusted, or didn't. At any rate, she passed over the bag.

"And now where?" asked Freddie.

The girl said she lived in Sixty-ninth Street, and Freddie right-hoed, and they set off. And presently they came to a brownstone building, in which she had Flat B on the fourth floor.

Well, of course, you may say that, having deposited female and suitcase at their destination, old Freddie should have uttered a brief, courteous "Pip-pip!" and legged it. And very possibly you are right. But consider the facts. The flat, as I have indicated, was four flights up. There was no lift, so he had to hoof it up all those stairs. It was a warm day. And the suitcase appeared to be packed with sheet iron or something.

I mean to say, by the time he had reached Journey's End, he was in sore need of a spot of repose. So, rightly or wrongly, he didn't biff off, but sort of collapsed into a chair and sat there restoring his tissues.

The girl, meanwhile, prattled in friendly vein. As far as Freddie can recall her remarks, her name was Myra Jennings. She was employed in the office of a wholesale silk importer. She had just come back from the country. The photograph over the sideboard was her mother's, who lived in Waterbury, Connecticut. The girl friend with whom she shared the flat was away on her vacation. And all that sort of thing, don't you know. I mean, pleasant gossip from the home.

She had just begun to tell him that, though she yielded to no one in her admiration for Ronald Colman, she couldn't help saying that William Powell had a sort of something that kind of seemed to place him sort of even higher in a girl's estimation, when there occurred one of those interruptions which, I understand, are always happening in New York.

If you're a native, you hardly notice them. You just look over your shoulder and say "Oh, ah?" and go on trying to get Los Angeles on the radio.

But Freddie, being new to the place, was a little startled. Because you see, what happened was that just as they were sitting there, chatting of this and that, there was a sudden crash. The door of the hallway which opened onto the landing outside was burst open. And in surged an extraordinarily hefty bloke with a big mustache. He wore a bowler hat. Behind him came a couple of other birds, also hefty and similarly bowler-hatted.

"Ah!" said Bloke A, in a satisfied sort of voice.

Freddie did a bit of gaping. He was a good deal on the nonplused side. He supposed, as his head began to clear, that this was one of those cases of "Bandits Break into House and Rob Two."

"Seems to me," said the Bloke, addressing his associate Blokes, "this case is open and shut."

The other two nodded.

"That's right," said one.

"Open and shut," said the other.

"Yes," said the Bloke, summing up. "That's about what it is. Open *and* shut."

Miss Jennings, who had been dusting the photograph of her mother, now appeared to notice for the first time that she had visitors. She spoke as follows:

"What in the world do you think you're doing?"

The Bloke lit a cigar. So did his associates. Two cigars.

"That's all right, Mrs. Silvers," he said.

"Sure, it's all right," said the other two.

"You boys are witnesses," said the Bloke.

"Sure, we're witnesses," said the other two.

"You can give evidence that we found Mrs. Silvers alone in her apartment with this pie-faced cluck."

"Sure, we can give evidence that we found her alone in her apartment with this pie-faced cluck."

"Then that's all right," said the Bloke contentedly. "That is all her husband will want to know. It makes the thing open and shut."

And it came home to Freddie with a sickening thud that these fellows were not, as he had supposed, a holdup gang, but detectives. He ought to have recognized them from the start, he tells me, by the bowler hats. What had misled him was the fact that at the outset they weren't smoking cigars. When they started smoking cigars, the scales fell from his eyes.

He gulped a bit. In fact, he gulped rather more than a bit. He realized now what his mistaken sense of knightly chivalry had made him stumble into. The soup, no less. With the best intentions, meaning only to scatter light and sweetness on every side, he had become a Sugar Daddy Surprised in Love Nest.

The female of the species, however, appeared unwilling to take this thing lying down. Her chin was up, her shoulders were squared, she had both feet on the ground, and she looked the troupe steadily in the eye through her spectacles.

"Just for fun," she said, "tell me where you fellows think you are?"

"Where do we think we are?" said the Bloke. "That's all right where we think we are. We're in Flat 4A. And you're Mrs. Silvers. And I'm from the Alert Detective Agency. And I'm acting under instructions from your husband. Laugh that off!"

"I will," said the girl. "I'm not Mrs. Silvers. I haven't a husband. And this isn't Flat A, it's Flat B."

The Bloke gasped. He reminded Freddie of his Uncle Joseph, the time he swallowed the bad oyster. The same visible emotion.

"Don't tell me we've busted into the wrong flat?" he said pleadingly.

"That's just what I am telling you."

"The wrong flat?"

"The wrong flat."

There was a pause.

"I'll tell you what it is," said one of the assistant blokes, a pretty acute chap, quick in the uptake. "We've been and busted into the wrong flat."

"That's it," said the other. "The wrong flat."

Well, they were very decent about it, Freddie tells me. They didn't take off their hats, and they went on smoking their cigars, but they paid for the door. And presently the party broke up, the Bloke protesting to the last that this was the first mistake he had made in twenty years.

Having had a hearty laugh with the Jennings over the whole amusing episode, Freddie hopped into a taxi and started off for Forty-sixth Street, for he was lunching with old Bodsham and Mavis at the Ritz-Carlton and a bit late already. All the way down there, he was chuckling to himself at the thought of what a capital story he had to tell them. Put him one up, he thought it would.

You see, if there was a snag in the wholehearted joy of being engaged to Mavis Peasemarch, it was the fact that, when in the society of herself and father, he occasionally found the going a bit sticky as regarded conversation.

Freddie, as you know, is a bird who, when the conditions are right, can be the life and soul of the party. Shoot a few stiffish cocktails into him and give him his head in the matter of sprightly anecdotes and the riper kind of Limerick, and he will hold you spellbound. But, cut off from these resources, he frequently found himself a trifle tongue-tied when taking a bite with old Bodsham.

And, as no fellow likes to feel that his future father-in-law is beginning to regard him as a loony deaf-mute, he welcomed the opportunity of showing himself a gay and gifted raconteur.

If the story of his morning's adventure, told as he proposed to tell it, didn't have the old boy hiccupping and wiping the tears from his eyes, he would be jolly well dashed.

And the same applied to Mavis.

"Capital! Capital! Ah, Van Sprunt, this is my son-in-law-to-be, Frederick Widgeon. A most entertaining young fellow. Get him to tell you his story about the detectives in the wrong flat. You'll die laughing. We all think very highly of Frederick Widgeon."

And all that sort of thing, I mean. What? I mean to say, you follow his reasoning.

Well, he didn't get a chance to spring the story over the melon and powdered ginger, because old Bodsham was rather holding the floor a bit on the subject of iniquitous Socialist attacks on the House of Lords. Then, with the *côtelettes* and mashed, Mavis started to haul up her slacks about the Soul of America. In fact, it wasn't till the coffee had arrived that he secured a genuine opening.

"I say," said Freddie, catching the Speaker's eye at this juncture, "a most awfully funny thing happened to me this morning. Make you scream. You'll burst your corsets."

And, lighting a carefree cigarette, he embarked upon the narrative.

He told it well. Looking back, he says, he can't remember when he has ever done more justice to a yarn, squeezed the last drop of juice out of it with a firmer hand, if you know what I mean. The grave, intent faces of his audience, he tells me, only spurred him on to further efforts. He approved of their self-restraint. He realized that they realized that a story like this was not the sort of story to fritter away with giggles. You saved yourself up for the big howl at the finish.

And then suddenly—he couldn't tell just when—there stole over him a sort of feeling that the *conte* wasn't getting across quite so big as he had hoped. There seemed to him to be a certain definite something in the atmosphere. You know how it is when you strike a cold audience. Old Bodsham was looking a little like a codfish with something on its mind, and there was an odd kind of expression in Mavis's eye.

When he had finished, there was a longish silence. Mavis looked at old Bodsham. Old Bodsham looked at Mavis.

"I don't quite understand, Frederick," said Mavis at length. "You say this girl was a stranger?"

"Why, yes," said Freddie.

"And you accosted her in the street?"

"Why, yes," said Freddie.

"Oh?" said Mavis.

"I was sorry for her," said Freddie.

"Oh?" said Mavis.

"In fact, you might say that my heart bled for her."

"Oh?" said Mavis.

Old Bodsham let his breath go in a sort of whistling sigh.

"Is it your practice, may I ask," he said, "to scrape acquaintance in the public streets with young persons of the opposite sex?"

"You must remember, father," said Mavis, in a voice which would have had an Eskimo slapping his ribs and calling for the steam heat, "that this girl was probably very pretty. So many of these New York girls are. That would, of course, explain Frederick's behavior."

"She wasn't!" yipped Freddie. "She was a gargoyle."

"Oh?" said Mavis.

"Spectacled to bursting point and utterly lacking in feminine allure."

"Oh?" said Mavis.

"And when I saw her frail form bowed down by that dashed great suitcase . . . I should have thought," said Freddie, injured, "that, having learned the salient facts, you would have fawned on me for my bighearted chivalry."

"Oh?" said Mavis.

There was another silence.

"I must be going, father," said Mavis. "I have some shopping to do."

"Shall I come with you?" said Freddie.

"I would prefer to be alone," said Mavis.

"I must be going," said old Bodsham. "I have some thinking to do."

"Thinking?" said Freddie.

"Thinking," said old Bodsham. "Some serious thinking. Some extremely serious thinking. Some very serious thinking indeed."

"We will leave Frederick to finish his cigarette," said Mavis.

"Yes," said old Bodsham. "We will leave Frederick to finish his cigarette."

"But listen," bleated Freddie. "I give you my honest word she looked like something employed by the government for scaring crows in the cornfields of Minnesota."

"Oh?" said Mavis.

"Oh?" said old Bodsham.

"Come, father," said Mavis.

And old Freddie found himself alone, and not feeling so frightfully good.

Now, it was Freddie's practice—and a very prudent practice, too—to carry on his person, concealed in his hip pocket, a small but service-able flask full of the true, the blushful Hippocrene. Friends whom he had made since his arrival in New York had advocated this policy, pointing out that you never knew when it would come in useful. His first act, accordingly, after the two Vice-Presidents of the Knicker-bocker Ice Company had left him and he had begun to thaw out a bit, was to produce this flask and take a quick, sharp snort.

The effect was instantaneous. His numbed brain began to work. And presently, after a couple more swift ones, he saw daylight.

The whole nub of the thing, he perceived clearly, was the personal appearance of the girl Jennings. In the matter of her loved one's acts of chivalry toward damsels in distress, a fiancée holds certain definite views. If the damsels he assists are plain, he is a good chap and deserves credit. If they are pretty, he is a low hound who jolly well gets his ring and letters back by the first post.

Obviously, then, his only course was to return to Sixty-ninth Street, dig up the Jennings, and parade her before Mavis. Her mere appear-ance, he was convinced, would clear him completely.

Of course, the thing would have to be done delicately. I mean to say, you can't just go to a comparatively strange female and ask her to trot round to see a friend of yours so that the latter can ascertain at first hand what a repellently unattractive girl she is. But Freddie, now full of the juice, fancied he could work it all right. All it wanted was just a little tact.

"Yoicks!" said Freddie to himself. "Hark for'ard!" And, in his opinion, that about summed it up.

It was a lovely afternoon as Freddie got into his taxi outside the Ritz and tooled uptown. Alighting at Sixty-ninth Street, he braced himself with a visible effort and started the long climb up the four flights of stairs. And presently he was outside the door of Flat 4B and tootling on the bell.

Nothing happened. He tootled again. He knocked. He even went so far as to kick the door. But there were no signs of human occupa-tion, and after a bit he was reluctantly forced to the conclusion that the Jennings was out.

Freddie had not foreseen this possibility, and he leaned against the wall for a space, thinking out his next move. He had just come to the conclusion that the only thing to do was to edge away for the nonce and have another pop later on, when a door opposite opened and a female appeared.

"Hullo," said this bird.

"Hullo," said Freddie.

He spoke, he tells me, a little doubtfully, for a glance had shown him that this woman was not at all the kind of whom Mavis would have approved. A different species altogether. Her eyes were blue and totally free from spectacles. Her teeth were white and even. Her hair was a beautiful gold.

Judging by her costume, she seemed to be a late riser. The hour was three-thirty, but she had not yet progressed beyond the negligee and slippers stage. That negligee, moreover, was a soft pink in color and was decorated throughout with a series of fowls of some kind. Lovebirds, Freddie tells me he thinks they were. And a man who is engaged to be married and who, already, is not any too popular with the bride-to-be, shrinks—automatically, as it were—from blue-eyed, golden-haired females in pink negligees picked out with ultramarine lovebirds.

However, a fellow has to be civil. So, having said "Hullo!" he threw in a reserved, gentlemanly sort of smile for good measure.

He assures me that it was merely one of those aloof smiles which the Honorary Secretary of a Bible Class would have given the elderly aunt of a promising pupil; but it had the effect of encouraging the contents of the negligee to further conversation.

"Looking for someone?" she asked.

"Why, yes," said Freddie. "I suppose you couldn't tell me when Miss Jennings will be in?"

"Miss who?"

"Jennings."

"What name?"

"Jennings."

"How do you spell it?"

"Oh, much in the usual way, I expect. Start off with a J and then a good many n's and g's and things."

"Miss Jennings, did you say?"

"That's right. Jennings."

"I'll tell you something," said the female frankly. "I've never seen any Miss Jennings. I've never heard of any Miss Jennings. I don't know who she is. She means literally nothing in my life. And I'll tell you something else. I've been breaking my back for half an hour trying to open my living-room window, and do you think I can do it? No, sir! What do you advise?"

"Leave it shut," said Freddie.

"But it's so warm. The weather, I mean."

"It *is* warm," agreed Freddie.

"I'm just stifling. Yes, sir. That's what I am. Stifling in my tracks."

At this point, undoubtedly, old Freddie should have said "Oh?" or "Well, best o' luck!" or something on that order, and buzzed off. But once a fellow drops into the habit of doing acts of kindness, he tells me, it's dashed difficult to pull up. The thing becomes second nature.

So now, instead of hoofing it, he unshipped another of those polished smiles of his, and asked if there was anything he could do.

"Well, it's a shame to trouble you. . . ."

"Not at all."

"I hate to impose on you. . . ."

"Not—a—tall," said Freddie, becoming more *preux* every moment. "Only too pleased."

And he trotted after her into the flat.

"There it is," said the female. "The window, I mean."

Freddie surveyed it carefully. He went over and gave it a shake. It certainly seemed pretty tightly stuck.

"The way they build these joints nowadays," observed the female, with a certain amount of severity, "the windows either won't open at all or else they drop out altogether."

"Well, that's life, isn't it?" said Freddie.

The thing didn't look any too good to him, but he buckled to like a man, and for some moments nothing was to be heard in the room but his tense breathing.

"How are you getting on?" asked the female.

"I've a sort of rummy buzzing in my head," said Freddie. "You don't think it's apoplexy or something?"

"I'd take a rest if I was you," said his hostess. "You look warm."

"I *am* warm," said Freddie.

"Take your coat off."

"May I? Thanks."

"Your collar, too, if you like."

"Thanks."

The removal of the upholstery made Freddie feel a little better.

"I once knew a man who opened a window in a Pullman car," said the female.

"No, really?" said Freddie.

"Ah, what a man!" sighed the female wistfully. "They don't make 'em like that nowadays."

I don't suppose she actually intended anything in the way of a slur or innuendo, if you know what I mean, but Freddie tells me he felt a bit stung. It was as if his manly spirit had been challenged. Setting his teeth, he charged forward and had another go.

"Try pulling it down from the top," said the female.

Freddie tried pulling it down from the top, but nothing happened.

"Try wiggling it sideways," said the female.

Freddie tried wiggling it sideways, but his efforts were null and void.

"Have a drink," said the female.

This seemed to old Freddie by miles the best suggestion yet. He sank into a chair and let his tongue hang out. And presently a brimming glass stole into his hand, and he quaffed deeply.

"That's some stuff I brought away from home," said the female.

"From where?" said Freddie.

"Home."

"But isn't this your home?"

"Well, it is now. But I used to live in Utica. Mr. Silvers made this stuff. About the only good thing he ever did. Mr. Silvers, I mean."

Freddie pondered a bit.

"Mr. Silvers? Don't I seem to know that name?"

"I wish I didn't," said the female. "There was a palooka, if you want one."

"A what?"

"A palooka. Mr. Silvers. Slice him where you like, he was still baloney."

The rather generous nature of the fluid he was absorbing was making Freddie feel a bit clouded.

"I don't altogether follow this. Who is Mr. Silvers?"

"Ed Silvers. My husband. And is he jealous? Ask me!"

"Ask who?"

"Ask *me*."

"Ask you what?"

"I'm telling you. I left him flat, because he didn't have no ideals."

"Who didn't?"

"Mr. Silvers."

"Your husband?"

"That's right."

"Ah!" said Freddie. "Now we've got it straight."

He quaffed again. The foundation of the beverage manufactured by Mr. Silvers seemed to be neat vitriol, but, once you had got used to the top of your head going up and down like the lid of a kettle with boiling water in it, the effects were far from unpleasant. Mr. Silvers may not have had ideals, but he unquestionably knew what to do when you handed him a still and a potato.

"He made me very unhappy," said the female.

"Who did?"

"Mr. Silvers."

"Mr. Silvers made you unhappy?"

"You're darn tooting Mr. Silvers made me unhappy. Entertaining his low suspicions."

Freddie was shocked.

"Did Mr. Silvers entertain low suspicions?"

"He certainly did."

"Mr. Ed Silvers?"

"That's right."

"I bet that made you unhappy."

"You never said a truer word."

"You poor little thing," said Freddie. "You poor little Mrs. Silvers."

"Mrs. Ed Silvers."

"You poor little Mrs. Ed Silvers. I never heard anything so dashed monstrous in my life. May I pat your hand?"

"You bet your lavender spats you may pat my hand."

"I will," said Freddie, and did so.

He even went further. He squeezed her hand. His whole attitude toward her, he tells me, was that of a brother toward a suffering sister.

And at this moment the door flew open, and a number of large objects crashed in. Without any warning the air had suddenly become full of bowler hats.

Freddie, gazing upon them, was conscious of an odd feeling. You know that feeling you sometimes feel of feeling you're feeling that something has happened which has happened before. I believe doctors explain it by saying that the two halves of the brain aren't working strictly on the up-and-up. Anyway, that was how Freddie felt at this point. He felt he had seen those bowler hats before—perhaps in some previous existence.

"What ho!" he said. "Callers, what?"

And then his brain seemed to clear—or the two halves clicked together, or something—and he recognized the Bloke who had interrupted his *tête-à-tête* with Miss Myra Jennings that morning.

Now the last time Freddie had seen this Bloke, the latter had been bathed in confusion. You pictured his embarrassment. He was now looking far cheerier. He had the air of a bloke in a bowler hat who has won through to his objective.

"We're in, boys," he said.

The two subsidiary Blokes nodded briefly. One of them said: "Sure, we're in." The other said: "Hot dog!"

The head Bloke scrutinized Freddie closely.

"Well, I'm darned!" he exclaimed. "If it isn't you again! Boys," he said, a note of respect creeping into his voice, "take a good slant at this guy. Eye him reverently. The swiftest worker in New York. Mark how he flits from spot to spot. You can't go anywhere without finding him. And he hasn't even got a bicycle."

Freddie saw that it was time to draw himself up to his full height and put these fellows in their place. He endeavored to do so, but something seemed to prevent him.

"Let me explain," he said.

The Bloke sneered visibly.

"Are you going to tell us we are in the wrong flat again?"

"My answer to that," said Freddie, "is yes—and no."

"What do you mean, yes and no? This is Flat 4A."

"True," said Freddie. "That point I yield. This *is* Flat 4A. But I assure you, on the word of an English gentleman, that this lady is a complete stranger to me."

"Stranger?"

"A complete and total stranger."

"Oh?" said the Bloke. "Then what's she doing sitting in your lap?"

And Freddie, with acute astonishment, perceived that this was indeed so. At what point in their conversation it had occurred, he could not have said, but Mrs. Ed Silvers was undeniably nestling on the spot indicated. It was this, he saw now, which had prevented him a moment ago drawing himself up to his full height.

"By Jove!" he said. "She is, isn't she?"

"She certainly is."

"Well, well!" said Freddie. "Well, well, well!"

You could have knocked him down with a feather, and he said as much.

Mrs. Silvers spoke.

"Listen," she said. "As Heaven is my witness I never saw this man before."

"Then what's he doing here?"

"Opening the window."

"It's shut."

"I know it's shut."

"Open *and* shut," said the Bloke. "Like this case. Eh, boys?"

"Ah!" said one of the boys.

"Uh-huh," said the other.

The Bloke eyed Mrs. Silver severely.

"You ought to be ashamed of yourself, lady," he said. "Such goings on. I'm shocked. That's what I am. Shocked. And the boys are shocked, too."

Freddie was able to rise now, for the female had ceased to roost. He got up, and would have towered above the Bloke, only it so happened that the latter was about six inches taller.

"You are aspersing a woman's name," he said.

"Eh?"

"Don't attempt to evade the issue," said Freddie, giving him a haughty glance. "You are aspersing a woman's name, and—what makes it worse—you are doing it in a bowler hat. Take off that hat," said Freddie.

The Bloke stared at him blankly. He was probably on the point of explaining that detectives' hats don't take off, when Freddie—injudiciously, in my opinion—got him in the right eye with one of the nicest wallops you could wish to see.

And after that, Freddie tells me, things got a bit mixed. He is conscious of having done his best, but he thinks he must have had rather the worse of the exchanges, because some little time later he became aware that he was in a prison cell and that one of his ears had swollen to the proportions of a medium-sized cauliflower. Also the black eye and the bees swarming in the head.

And scarcely had he coughed up the fifty dollars to the Clerk of the Court next morning when, coming out into the open and buying a paper, he found the events of the previous afternoon splashed over half a column of the very periodical which, he knew, old Bodsham was in the habit of reading with his morning Java and egg.

And, to show you how overwrought the poor chap must have been, Freddie had actually omitted to take the elementary precaution of giving a false name. He had even gone to the extraordinary length of revealing his middle one—which, though I don't think we should hold it against him, is Fotheringay.

Well, that finished it. Rightly or wrongly, Freddie decided not to wait for the full returns. There was a boat starting back for England that night, and he leaped aboard it without having ascertained from a personal interview what old Bodsham and Mavis thought of the episode. He is a pretty intuitive chap, Freddie, and he was content to guess.

So now he's back, and more or less soured and morose. He was saying some pretty harsh things about Woman this morning, some very harsh things.

And I happen to know that, as the boat docked at Southampton, an extraordinarily pretty girl standing beside him stumbled and dropped her vanity bag. And Freddie, instead of springing to her aid, just folded his arms and looked away with a somber frown. He says that damsels in distress from now on must seek elsewhere for custom, because he has retired from business.

This fact, he tells me, cannot be too widely known.

⚙ *Tried in the Furnace*

THE ANNUAL smoking concert of the Drones Club had just come to an end, and it was the unanimous verdict of the little group assembled in the bar for a last quick one that the gem of the evening had been item number six on the program, the knockabout cross-talk act of Cyril ("Barmy") Fotheringay-Phipps and Reginald ("Pongo") Twistleton-Twistleton. Both Cyril, in the red beard, and Reginald, in the more effective green whiskers, had shown themselves, it was agreed, at the very peak of their form. With sparkling repartee and vigorous byplay they had gripped the audience from the start.

"In fact," said an Egg, "it struck me that they were even better than last year. Their art seemed to have deepened somehow."

A thoughtful Crumpet nodded.

"I noticed the same thing. The fact is, they passed through a soul-testing experience not long ago and it has left its mark upon them. It also dashed nearly wrecked the act. I don't know if any of you fellows are aware of it, but at one time they had definitely decided to scratch the fixture and not give a performance at all."

"What!"

"Absolutely. They were within a toucher of failing to keep faith with their public. Bad blood had sprung up between them. Also pique and strained relations. They were not on speaking terms."

His hearers were frankly incredulous. They pointed out that the friendship between the two artists had always been a byword or whatever you called it. A well-read Egg summed it up by saying that they were like Thingummy and what's-his-name.

"Nevertheless," insisted the Crumpet, "what I am telling you is straight, official stuff. Two weeks ago, if Barmy had said to Pongo: 'Who was that lady I saw you coming down the street with?' Pongo would not have replied: 'That was no lady, that was my wife'—he would simply have raised his eyebrows coldly and turned away in a marked manner."

It was a woman, of course (proceeded the Crumpet) who came between them. Angelica Briscoe was her name, and she was the daughter of the Rev. P. P. Briscoe, who vetted the souls of the local peasantry at a place called Maiden Eggesford down in Somersetshire. This hamlet is about half a dozen miles from the well-known resort, Bridmouth-on-Sea, and it was in the establishment of the Messrs. Thorpe and Widgery, the popular grocers of that town, that Barmy and Pongo first set eyes on the girl.

They had gone to Bridmouth partly for a splash of golf, but principally to be alone and away from distractions, so that they would be able to concentrate on the rehearsing and building-up of this cross-talk act which we have just witnessed. And on the morning of which I speak they had strolled into the Thorpe and Widgery emporium to lay in a few little odds and ends, and there, putting in a bid for five pounds of streaky bacon, was a girl so lovely that they congealed in their tracks. And, as they stood staring, she said to the bloke behind the counter:

"That's the lot. Send them to Miss Angelica Briscoe, The Vicarage, Maiden Eggesford."

She then pushed off, and Barmy and Pongo, feeling rather as if they had been struck by lightning, bought some sardines and a segment of certified butter in an overwrought sort of way and went out.

They were both pretty quiet for the rest of the day, and after dinner that night Pongo said to Barmy:

"I say, Barmy."

And Barmy said:

"Hullo?"

And Pongo said:

"I say, Barmy, it's a bally nuisance, but I'll have to buzz up to London for a day or two. I've suddenly remembered some spots of business that call for my personal attention. You won't mind my leaving you?"

Barmy could scarcely conceal his bracedness. Within two minutes of seeing that girl, he had made up his mind that somehow or other he must repair to Maiden Eggesford and get to know her, and the problem which had been vexing him all day had been what to do with the body—viz. Pongo's.

"Not a bit," he said.

"I'll be back as soon as I can."

"Don't hurry," said Barmy heartily. "As a matter of fact, a few days' layoff will do the act all the good in the world. Any pro will tell you that the worst thing possible is to overrehearse. Stay away as long as you like."

So next morning—it was a Saturday—Pongo climbed on to a train, and in the afternoon Barmy collected his baggage and pushed off to the Goose and Grasshopper at Maiden Eggesford. And, having booked a room there and toddled into the saloon bar for a refresher with the love light in his eyes, the first thing he saw was Pongo chatting across the counter with the barmaid.

Neither was much bucked. A touch of constraint about sums it up.

"Hullo!" said Barmy.

"Hullo!" said Pongo.

"You here?"

"Ycs. You here?"

"Yes."

"Oh."

There was a bit of a silence.

"So you didn't go to London?" said Barmy.

"No," said Pongo.

"Oh," said Barmy.

"And you didn't stick on at Bridmouth?" said Pongo.

"No," said Barmy.

"Oh," said Pongo.

There was some more silence.

"You came here, I see," said Pongo.

"Yes," said Barmy. "I see *you* came here."

"Yes," said Pongo. "An odd coincidence."

"Very odd."

"Well, skin off your nose," said Pongo.

"Fluff in your latchkey," said Barmy.

He drained his glass and tried to exhibit a lighthearted non-chalance, but his mood was somber. He was a chap who could put two and two together and sift and weigh the evidence and all that sort of thing, and it was plain to him that love had brought Pongo also to this hamlet, and he resented the fact. Indeed, it was at this instant, he tells me, that there came to him the first nebulous idea of oiling out of that cross-talk act of theirs. The thought of having to ask a beastly, butting-in blighter like Reginald Twistleton-Twistleton if he was fond of mutton broth and being compelled to hit him over the head with a rolled-up umbrella when he replied "No, Mutt and Jeff," somehow seemed to revolt his finest feelings.

Conversation rather languished after this, and presently Pongo excused himself in a somewhat stiff manner and went upstairs to his room. And it was while Barmy was standing at the counter listening in a distrait kind of way to the barmaid telling him what cucumber did to her digestive organs that a fellow in plus fours entered the bar and Barmy saw that he was wearing the tie of his old school.

Well, you know how it is when you're in some public spot and a stranger comes in wearing the old school tie. You shove a hasty hand over your own and start to sidle out before the chap can spot it and grab you and start gassing. And Barmy was just doing this when the barmaid uttered these sensational words:

"Good evening, Mr. Briscoe."

Barmy stood spellbound. He turned to the barmaid and spoke in a hushed whisper.

"Did you say 'Briscoe'?"

"Yes, sir."

"From the Vicarage?"

"Yes, sir."

Barmy quivered like a jelly. The thought that he had had the amazing luck to find in the brother of the girl he loved an old school-mate made him feel boneless. After all, he felt, as he took his hand away from his tie, there is no bond like that of the old school. If you meet one of the dear old school in a public spot, he meant to say, why, you go straight up to him and start fraternizing.

He made a beeline for the chap's table.

"I say," he said, "I see you're wearing a . . ."

The chap's hand had shot up to his tie with a sort of nervous gesture, but he evidently realized that the time had gone by for protective measures. He smiled a bit wryly.

"Have a drink," he said.

"I've got one, thanks," said Barmy. "I'll bring it along to your table, shall I? Such a treat meeting someone from the dear old place, what?"

"Oh, rather."

"I think I'd have been a bit after your time, wouldn't I?" said Barmy, for the fellow was well stricken in years—twenty-eight, if a day. "Fotheringay-Phipps is more or less my name. Yours is Briscoe, what?"

"Yes."

Barmy swallowed a couple of times.

"Er . . . Ah . . . Um . . . I think I saw your sister yesterday in Bridmouth," he said, blushing prettily.

So scarlet, indeed, did his countenance become that the other regarded him narrowly, and Barmy knew that he had guessed his secret.

"You saw her in Bridmouth yesterday, eh?"

"Yes."

"And now you're here."

"Er—yes."

"Well, well," said the chap, drawing his breath in rather thoughtfully.

There was a pause, during which Barmy's vascular motors continued to do their bit.

"You must meet her," said the chap.

"I should like to," said Barmy. "I only saw her for a moment buying streaky bacon, but she seemed a charming girl."

"Oh, she is."

"I scarcely noticed her, of course, but rather attractive she struck me as."

"Quite."

"I gave her the merest glance, you understand, but I should say at a venture that she has a great white soul. In fact," said Barmy, losing his grip altogether, "you wouldn't be far out in describing her as divine."

"You must certainly meet her," said the chap. Then he shook his head. "No, it wouldn't be any good."

"Why not?" bleated Barmy.

"Well, I'll tell you," said the chap. "You know what girls are. They have their little enthusiasms and it hurts them when people scoff at them. Being a parson's daughter, Angelica is wrapped up at present in the annual village School Treat. I can see at a glance the sort of fellow you are—witty, mordant, ironical. You would get off one of your devastating epigrams at the expense of the School Treat, and, while she might laugh at the wit, she would be deeply wounded by the satire."

"But, I wouldn't dream . . ."

"Ah, but if you didn't, if you spoke approvingly of the School Treat, what then? The next thing that would happen would be that she would be asking you to help her run it. And that would bore you stiff."

Barmy shook from stem to stern. This was better even than he had hoped.

"You don't mean she would let me help her with the School Treat?"

"Why, you wouldn't do it, would you?"

"I should enjoy it above all things."

"Well, if that's the way you feel, the matter can easily be arranged. She will be here any moment now to pick me up in her car."

And, sure enough, not two minutes later there floated through the open window a silvery voice, urging the fellow, who seemed to answer to the name of "Fathead," to come out quick, because the voice did not intend to remain there all night.

So the fellow took Barmy out, and there was the girl, sitting in a two-seater. He introduced Barmy. The girl beamed. Barmy beamed. The fellow said that Barmy was anxious to come and help with the School Treat. The girl beamed again. Barmy beamed again. And presently the car drove off, the girl's last words being a reminder that the binge started at two sharp on the Monday.

That night, as they dined together, Barmy and Pongo put in their usual spot of rehearsing. It was their practice to mold and shape the act during meals, as they found that mastication seemed to sharpen their intellect. But tonight it would have been plain to an observant spectator that their hearts were not in it. There was an unmistakable coolness between them. Pongo said he had an aunt who complained of rheumatism, and Barmy said, Well, who wouldn't? And Barmy said his father could not meet his creditors, and Pongo said, Did he want to? But the old fire and sparkle were absent. And they had relapsed into a moody silence when the door opened and the barmaid pushed her head in.

"Miss Briscoe has just sent over a message, Mr. Phipps," said the barmaid. "She says she would like you to be there a little earlier than two, if you can manage it. One-fifteen, if possible, because there's always so much to do."

"Oh, right," said Barmy, a bit rattled, for he had heard the sharp hiss of his companion's indrawn breath.

"I'll tell her," said the barmaid.

She withdrew, and Barmy found Pongo's eyes resting on him like a couple of blobs of vitriol.

"What's all this?" asked Pongo.

Barmy tried to be airy.

"Oh, it's nothing. Just the local School Treat. The vicar's daughter here—a Miss Briscoe—seems anxious that I should drop round on Monday and help her run it."

Pongo started to grind his teeth, but he had a chunk of potato in his mouth at the moment and was hampered. But he gripped the table till his knuckles stood out white under the strain.

"Have you been sneaking round behind my back and inflicting your beastly society on Miss Briscoe?" he demanded.

"I do not like your tone, Reginald."

"Never mind about my tone. I'll attend to my tone. Of all the bally low hounds that ever stepped you are the lowest. So this is what the friendship of years amounts to, is it? You crawl in here and try to cut me out with the girl I love."

"Well, dash it . . ."

"That is quite enough."

"But, dash it . . ."

"I wish to hear no more."

"But, dash it, I love her, too. It's not my fault if you happen to love her, too, is it? I mean to say, if a fellow loves a girl and another fellow loves her, too, you can't expect the fellow who loves the girl to edge out because he happens to be acquainted with the fellow who loves her, too. When it comes to Love, a chap has got to look out for his own interests, hasn't he? You didn't find Romeo or any of those chaps easing away from the girl just to oblige a pal, did you? Certainly not. So I don't see . . ."

"Please!" said Pongo.

A silence fell.

"Might I trouble you to pass the mustard, Fotheringay-Phipps," said Pongo coldly.

"Certainly, Twistleton-Twistleton," replied Barmy, with equal hauteur.

It is always unpleasant not to be on speaking terms with an old friends. To be cooped up alone in a moldy village pub with an old friend with whom one has ceased to converse is simply rotten. And this is especially so if the day happens to be a Sunday.

Maiden Eggesford, like so many of our rural hamlets, is not at its best and brightest on a Sunday. When you have walked down the main street and looked at the Jubilee Watering Trough, there is nothing much to do except go home and then come out again and walk down the main street once more and take another look at the Jubilee Watering Trough. It will give you some rough idea of the state to which Barmy Fotheringay-Phipps had been reduced by the end of the next day when I tell you that the sound of the church bells ringing for evensong brought him out of the Goose and Grasshopper as if he had heard a fire engine. The thought that at last something was going to happen in Maiden Eggesford in which the Jubilee Watering Trough *motif* was not stressed, stirred him strangely. He was in his pew in three jumps. And as the service got under way he began to feel curious emotions going on in his bosom.

There is something about evening church in a village in the summertime that affects the most hard-boiled. They had left the door open, and through it came the scent of lime trees and wallflowers and the distant hum of bees fooling about. And gradually there poured over Barmy a wave of sentiment. As he sat and listened to the First Lesson he became a changed man.

The Lesson was one of those chapters of the Old Testament all about how Abimelech begat Jazzbo and Jazzbo begat Zachariah. And, what with the beauty of the words and the peace of his surroundings, Barmy suddenly began to become conscious of a great remorse.

He had not done the square thing, he told himself, by dear old Pongo. Here was a chap, notoriously one of the best, as sound an egg as ever donned a heliotrope sock, and he was deliberately chiseling him out of the girl he loved. He was doing the dirty on a fellow whom he had been pally with since their Eton jacket days—a bloke who time and again had shared with him his last bar of almond-rock. Was this right? Was this just? Would Abimelech have behaved like that to Jazzbo or—for the matter of that—Jazzbo to Zachariah? The answer, he could not disguise it from himself, was in the negative.

It was a different, stronger Barmy, a changed, chastened Cyril Fotheringay-Phipps, who left the sacred edifice at the conclusion of the vicar's fifty-minute sermon. He had made the great decision. It would play the dickens with his heart and probably render the rest of his life a blank, but nevertheless he would retire from the unseemly struggle and give the girl up to Pongo.

That night, as they cold-suppered together, Barmy cleared his throat and looked across at Pongo with a sad, sweet smile.

"Pongo," he said.

The other glanced distantly up from his baked potato.

"There is something you wish to say to me, Fotheringay-Phipps?"

"Yes," said Barmy. "A short while ago I sent a note to Miss Briscoe, informing her that I shall not be attending the School Treat and mentioning that you will be there in my stead. Take her, Pongo, old man. She is yours. I scratch my nomination."

Pongo stared. His whole manner changed. It was as if he had been a Trappist monk who had suddenly decided to give Trappism a miss and become one of the boys again.

"But, dash it, this is noble!"

"No, no."

"But it is! It's . . . well, dash it, I hardly know what to say."

"I hope you will be very, very happy."

"Thanks, old man."

"Very, very, very happy."

"Rather! I should say so. And I'll tell you one thing. In the years to come there will always be a knife and fork for you at our little home. The children shall be taught to call you Uncle Barmy."

"Thanks," said Barmy. "Thanks."

"Not at all," said Pongo. "Not at all."

At this moment, the barmaid entered with a note for Barmy. He read it and crumpled it up.

"From Her?" asked Pongo.

"Yes."

"Saying she quite understands, and so forth?"

"Yes."

Pongo ate a piece of cheese in a meditative manner. He seemed to be pursuing some train of thought.

"I should think," he said, "that a fellow who married a clergyman's daughter would get the ceremony performed at cut rates, wouldn't he?"

"Probably."

"If not absolutely on the nod?"

"I shouldn't wonder."

"Not," said Pongo, "that I am influenced by any consideration like that, of course. My love is pure and flamelike, with no taint of dross. Still, in times like these, every little helps."

"Quite," said Barmy. "Quite."

He found it hard to control his voice. He had lied to his friend about that note. What Angelica Briscoe had really said in it was that it was quite all right if he wanted to edge out of the School Treat, but that she would require him to take the Village Mothers for their Annual Outing on the same day. There had to be some responsible person with them, and the curate had sprained his ankle tripping over a footstool in the vestry.

Barmy could read between the lines. He saw what this meant. His fatal fascination had done its deadly work, and the girl had become infatuated with him. No other explanation would fit the facts. It was absurd to suppose that she would lightly have selected him for this extraordinarily important assignment. Obviously it was the big event of the village year. Anyone would do to mess about at the School Treat, but Angelica Briscoe would place in charge of the Mothers' Annual Outing only a man she trusted . . . respected . . . loved.

He sighed. What must be, he felt, must be. He had done his conscientious best to retire in favor of his friend, but Fate had been too strong.

I found it a little difficult (said the Crumpet) to elicit from Barmy exactly what occurred at the annual outing of the Village Mothers of Maiden Eggesford. When telling me the story, he had the air of a man whose old wound is troubling him. It was not, indeed, till the fourth cocktail that he became really communicative. And then, speaking with a kind of stony look in his eye, he gave me a fairly comprehensive account. But even then each word seemed to hurt him in some tender spot.

The proceedings would appear to have opened in a quiet and orderly manner. Sixteen females of advanced years assembled in a motor coach, and the expedition was seen off from the Vicarage door by the Rev. P. P. Briscoe in person. Under his eye, Barmy tells me, the Beauty Chorus was demure and docile. It was a treat to listen to their murmured responses. As nice and respectable a bunch of mothers, Barmy says, as he had ever struck. His only apprehension at this point, he tells me, was lest the afternoon's proceedings might possibly be a trifle stodgy. He feared a touch of ennui.

He needn't have worried. There was no ennui.

The human cargo, as I say, had started out in a spirit of demureness and docility. But it was amazing what a difference a mere fifty yards of the high road made to these Mothers. No sooner were they out of sight of the Vicarage than they began to effervesce to an almost unbelievable extent. The first intimation Barmy had that the binge was going to be run on lines other than those which he had anticipated was when a very stout Mother in a pink bonnet and a dress covered with bugles suddenly picked off a passing cyclist with a well-directed tomato, causing him to skid into a ditch. Upon which, all sixteen mothers laughed like fiends in hell, and it was plain that they considered that the proceedings had now been formally opened.

Of course, looking back at it now in a calmer spirit, Barmy tells me that he can realize that there is much to be said in palliation of the exuberance of these ghastly female pimples. When you are shut up all the year round in a place like Maiden Eggesford, with nothing to do but wash underclothing and attend Divine Service, you naturally incline to let yourself go a bit at times of festival and holiday. But at the moment he did not think of this, and his spiritual agony was pretty pronounced.

If there's one thing Barmy hates it's being conspicuous, and conspicuous is precisely what a fellow cannot fail to be when he's in a motor coach with sixteen women of mature ages who alternate between singing ribald songs and hurling volleys of homely chaff at passers-by. In this connection, he tells me, he is thinking particularly of a Mother in spectacles and a Homburg hat, which she had pinched from the driver of the vehicle, whose prose style appeared to have been modeled on that of Rabelais.

It was a more than usually penetrating sally on the part of this female which at length led him to venture a protest.

"I say! I mean, I say. I say, dash it, you know. I mean, dash it," said Barmy, feeling, even as he spoke, that the rebuke had not been phrased as neatly as he could have wished.

Still, lame though it had been, it caused a sensation which can only be described as profound. Mother looked at Mother. Eyebrows were raised, breath drawn in censoriously.

"Young man," said the Mother in the pink bonnet, who seemed to have elected herself forewoman, "kindly keep your remarks to yourself."

Another Mother said: "The idea!" and a third described him as a kill-joy.

"We don't want none of *your* impudence," said the one in the pink bonnet.

"Ah!" agreed the others.

"A slip of a boy like that!" said the Mother in the Homburg hat, and there was a general laugh, as if the meeting considered that the point had been well taken.

Barmy subsided. He was wishing that he had yielded to the advice of his family and become a curate after coming down from the University. Curates are specially trained to handle this sort of situation. A tough, hard-boiled curate, spitting out of the corner of his mouth, would soon have subdued these mothers, he reflected. He would have played on them as on a stringed instrument—or, rather, as on sixteen stringed instruments. But Barmy, never having taken orders, was helpless.

So helpless, indeed, that when he suddenly discovered that they were heading for Bridmouth-on-Sea he felt that there was nothing he could do about it. From the vicar's own lips he had had it officially that the program was that the expedition should drive to the neighboring village of Bottsford Mortimer, where there were the ruins of an old abbey, replete with interest; lunch among these ruins; visit the local museum (founded and presented to the village by the late Sir Wandesbury Pott, J.P.); and, after filling in with a bit of knitting, return home. And now the whole trend of the party appeared to be toward the Amusement Park on the Bridmouth pier. And, though Barmy's whole soul shuddered at the thought of these sixteen Bacchantes let loose in an Amusement Park, he hadn't the nerve to say a word.

It was at about this point, he tells me, that a vision rose before him of Pongo happily loafing through the summer afternoon amidst the placid joys of the School Treat.

Of what happened at the Amusement Park Barmy asked me to be content with the sketchiest of outlines. He said that even now he could not bear to let his memory dwell upon it. He confessed himself perplexed by the psychology of the thing. These mothers, he said, must have had mothers of their own and at those mothers' knees must have learned years ago the difference between right and wrong, and yet . . . Well, what he was thinking of particularly, he said, was what occurred on the Bump the Bumps apparatus. He refused to specify exactly, but he said that there was one woman in a puce mantle who definitely seemed to be living for pleasure alone.

It was a little unpleasantness with the proprietor of this concern that eventually led to the expedition leaving the Amusement Park and going down to the beach. Some purely technical point of finance, I understand—he claiming that a Mother in bombazine had had eleven rides and only paid once. It resulted in Barmy getting lugged into the brawl and rather roughly handled—which was particularly unfortunate, because the bombazined Mother explained on their way down to the beach that the whole thing had been due to a misunderstanding. In actual fact, what had really happened was that she had had twelve rides and paid twice.

However, he was so glad to get his little troupe out of the place that he counted an eye well blacked as the price of deliverance, and his spirits, he tells me, had definitely risen when suddenly the sixteen mothers gave a simultaneous whoop and made for a sailing boat which was waiting to be hired, sweeping him along with them. And the next moment they were off across the bay, bowling along before a nippy breeze which, naturally, cheesed it abruptly as soon as it had landed them far enough away from shore to make things interesting for the unfortunate blighter who had to take to the oars.

This, of course, was poor old Barmy. There was a man in charge of the boat, but he, though but a rough, untutored salt, had enough sense not to let himself in for a job like rowing this Noah's Ark home. Barmy did put it up to him tentatively, but the fellow said that he had to attend to the steering, and when Barmy said that he, Barmy, knew how to steer, the fellow said that he, the fellow, could not entrust a valuable boat to an amateur. After which, he lit his pipe and lolled back in the stern sheets with rather the air of an ancient Roman banqueter making himself cozy among the cushions. And Barmy, attaching himself to a couple of oars of about the size of those served out to galley slaves in the old trireme days, started to put his back into it.

For a chap who hadn't rowed anything except a light canoe since he was up at Oxford, he considers he did dashed well, especially when you take into account the fact that he was much hampered by the Mothers. They would insist on singing that thing about "Give yourself a pat on the back," and, apart from the fact that Barmy considered that something on the lines of the "Volga Boat Song" would have been far more fitting, it was a tune it was pretty hard to keep time to. Seven times he caught crabs, and seven times those sixteen Mothers stopped singing and guffawed like one Mother. All in all, a most painful experience. Add the fact that the first thing the females did on hitting the old Homeland again was to get up an informal dance on the sands and that the ride home in the quiet evenfall was more or less a repetition of the journey out, and you will agree with me that Barmy, as he eventually tottered into the saloon bar of the Goose and Grasshopper, had earned the frothing tankard which he now proceeded to order.

He had just sucked it down and was signaling for another, when the door of the saloon bar opened and in came Pongo.

If Barmy had been less preoccupied with his own troubles he would have seen that Pongo was in poorish shape. His collar was torn, his hair disheveled. There were streaks of chocolate down his face and half a jam sandwich attached to the back of his coat. And so moved was he at seeing Barmy that he started ticking him off before he had so much as ordered a gin and ginger.

"A nice thing you let me in for!" said Pongo. "A jolly job you shoved off on me!"

Barmy was feeling a little better after his ingurgitations, and he was able to speak.

"What are you talking about?"

"I am talking about School Treats," replied Pongo, with an intense bitterness. "I am talking about seas of children, all with sticky hands, who rubbed those hands on me. I am talking . . . Oh, it's no good your gaping like a diseased fish, Fotheringay-Phipps. You know dashed well that you planned the whole thing. Your cunning fiend's brain formulated the entire devilish scheme. You engineered the bally outrage for your own foul purposes, to queer me with Angelica. You thought that when a girl sees a man blindfolded and smacked with rolled-up newspapers by smelly children she can never feel the same to him again. Ha!" said Pongo, at last ordering his gin and ginger.

Barmy was stunned, of course, by this violent attack, but he retained enough of the nice sense of propriety of the Fotheringay-

Phippses to realize that this discussion could not be continued in public. Already the barmaid's ears had begun to work loose at the roots as she pricked them up.

"I don't know what the dickens you're talking about," he said, "but bring your drink up to my room and we'll go into the matter there. We cannot bandy a woman's name in a saloon bar."

"Who's bandying a woman's name?"

"You are. You bandied it only half a second ago. If you don't call what you said bandying, there are finer-minded men who do."

So they went upstairs, and Barmy shut the door.

"Now, then," he said. "What's all this drivel?"

"I've told you."

"Tell me again."

"I will."

"Right ho. One moment."

Barmy went to the door and opened it sharply. There came the unmistakable sound of a barmaid falling downstairs. He closed the door again.

"Now, then," he said.

Pongo drained his gin and ginger.

"Of all the dirty tricks one man ever played on another," he began, "your sneaking out of that School Treat and letting me in for it is one which the verdict of history will undoubtedly rank the dirtiest. I can read you now like a book, Fotheringay-Phipps. Your motive is crystal clear to me. You knew at what a disadvantage a man appears at a School Treat, and you saw to it that I and not you should be the poor mutt to get smeared with chocolate and sloshed with newspapers before the eyes of Angelica Briscoe. And I believed you when you handed me all that drip about yielding your claim and what not. My gosh!"

For an instant, as he heard these words, stupefaction rendered Barmy speechless. Then he found his tongue. His generous soul was seething with indignation at the thought of how his altruism, his great sacrifice, had been misinterpreted.

"What absolute rot!" he cried. "I never heard such bilge in my life. My motives in sending you to that School Treat instead of me were unmixedly chivalrous. I did it simply and solely to enable you to ingratiate yourself with the girl, not reflecting that it was out of the question that she should ever love a popeyed, pimply-faced poop like you."

Pongo started.

"Pop-eyed?"

"Pop-eyed was what I said."

"Pimply-faced?"

"Pimply-faced was the term I employed."

"Poop?"

"Poop was the expression with which I concluded. If you want to know the real obstacle in the way of any wooing you may do now or in the years to come, Twistleton-Twistleton, it is this—that you entirely lack sex appeal and look like nothing on earth. A girl of the sweet, sensitive nature of Angelica Briscoe does not have to see you smeared with chocolate to recoil from you with loathing. She does it automatically, and she does it on her head."

"Is that so?"

"That is so."

"Oh? Well, let me inform you that in spite of what has happened, in spite of the fact that she has seen me at my worst, there is something within me that tells me that Angelica Briscoe loves me and will one day be mine."

"Mine, you mean. I can read the message in a girl's shy, drooping eyes, Twistleton-Twistleton, and I am prepared to give you odds of eleven to four that before the year is out I shall be walking down the aisle with Angelica Fotheringay-Phipps on my arm. I will go further. Thirty-three to eight."

"What in?"

"Tenners."

"Done."

It was at this moment that the door opened.

"Excuse me, gentlemen," said the barmaid.

The two rivals glared at the intruder. She was a well-nourished girl with a kind face. She was rubbing her left leg, which appeared to be paining her. The staircases are steep at the Goose and Grasshopper.

"You'll excuse me muscling in like this, gentlemen," said the barmaid, or words to that effect, "but I happened inadvertently to overhear your conversation, and I feel it my duty to put you straight on an important point of fact. Gentlemen, all bets are off. Miss Angelica Briscoe is already engaged to be married."

You can readily conceive the effect of this announcement. Pongo biffed down into the only chair, and Barmy staggered against the wash-hand stand.

"What!" said Pongo.

"What!" said Barmy.

The barmaid turned to Barmy.

"Yes, sir. To the gentleman you were talking to in my bar the afternoon you arrived."

Her initial observation had made Barmy feel as if he had been punched in the wind by sixteen Mothers, but at this addendum he was able to pull himself together a bit.

"Don't be an ass, my dear old barmaid," he said. "That was Miss Briscoe's brother."

"No, sir."

"But his name was Briscoe, and you told me he was at the Vicarage."

"Yes, sir. He spends a good deal of his time at the Vicarage, being the young lady's second cousin, and engaged to her since last Christmas!"

Barmy eyed her sternly. He was deeply moved.

"Why did you not inform me of this earlier, you chump of a barmaid? With your gift for listening at doors you must long since have become aware that this gentleman here and myself were deeply enamored of Miss Briscoe. And yet you kept these facts under your hat, causing us to waste our time and experience the utmost alarm and despondency. Do you realize, barmaid, that, had you spoken sooner, my friend here would not have been subjected to nameless indignities at the School Treat. . . ."

"Yes, sir. It was the School Treat that Mr. Briscoe was so bent on not having to go to, which he would have had to have done, Miss Angelica insisting. He had a terrible time there last year, poor gentleman. He was telling me about it. And that was why he asked me as a particular favor not to mention that he was engaged to Miss Briscoe, because he said that, if he played his cards properly and a little secrecy and silence were observed in the proper quarters, there was a mug staying at the inn that he thought he could get to go instead of him. It would have done you good, sir, to have seen the way his face lit up as he said it. He's a very nice gentleman, Mr. Briscoe, and we're all very fond of him. Well, I mustn't stay talking here, sir. I've got my bar to see to."

She withdrew, and for some minutes there was silence in the room. It was Barmy who was the first to break it.

"After all, we still have our Art," said Barmy.

He crossed the room and patted Pongo on the shoulder.

"Of course, it's a nasty knock, old man. . . ."

Pongo had raised his face from his hands and was fumbling for his cigarette case. There was a look in his eyes as if he had just wakened from a dream.

"Well, *is* it?" he said. "You've got to look at these things from every angle. Is a girl who can deliberately allow a man to go through the horrors of a School Treat worth bothering about?"

Barmy started.

"I never thought of that. Or a girl, for that matter, who could callously throw a fellow to the Village Mothers."

"Remind me some time to tell you about a game called 'Is Mr. Smith at Home?' where you put your head in a sack and the younger generation jab you with sticks."

"And don't let me forget to tell you about that Mother in the puce mantle on the Bump the Bumps."

"There was a kid called Horace . . ."

"There was a Mother in a Homburg hat . . ."

"The fact is," said Pongo, "we have allowed ourselves to lose our sober judgment over a girl whose idea of a mate is a mere 'Hey, you,' to be ordered hither and thither at her will, and who will unleash the juvenile population of her native village upon him without so much as a pang of pity—in a word, a parson's daughter. If you want to know the secret of a happy and successful life, Barmy, old man, it is this: Keep away from parsons' daughters."

"Right away," agreed Barmy. "How do you react to hiring a car and pushing off to the metropolis at once?"

"I am all for it. And if we're to give our best on the evening of the eleventh *prox.* we ought to start rehearsing again immediately."

"We certainly ought."

"We haven't any too much time, as it is."

"We certainly haven't. I've got an aunt who complains of rheumatism."

"Well, who wouldn't? My father can't meet his creditors."

"Does he want to? My uncle Joe's in very low water just now."

"Too bad. What's he doing?"

"Teaching swimming. Listen, Pongo," said Barmy, "I've been thinking. You take the green whiskers this year."

"No, no."

"Yes, really. I mean it. If I've said it to myself once, I've said it a hundred times—good old Pongo simply must have the green whiskers this year."

"Barmy!"

"Pongo!"

They clasped hands. Tried in the furnace, their friendship had emerged strong and true. Cyril Fotheringay-Phipps and Reginald Twistleton-Twistleton were themselves again.

❀ *The Amazing Hat Mystery*

A BEAN was in a nursing home with a broken leg as the result of trying to drive his sports-model Poppenheim through the Marble Arch instead of round it, and a kindly Crumpet had looked in to give him the gossip of the town. He found him playing halma with the nurse, and he sat down on the bed and took a grape, and the Bean asked what was going on in the great world.

"Well," said the Crumpet, taking another grape, "the finest minds in the Drones are still wrestling with the great Hat mystery."

"What's that?"

"You don't mean you haven't heard about it?"

"Not a word."

The Crumpet was astounded. He swallowed two grapes at once in his surprise.

"Why, London's seething with it. The general consensus of opinion is that it has something to do with the Fourth Dimension. You know how things do. I mean to say, something rummy occurs and you consult some big-brained bird and he wags his head and says 'Ah! The Fourth Dimension!' Extraordinary nobody's told you about the great Hat mystery."

"You're the first visitor I've had. What is it, anyway? What hat?"

"Well, there were two hats. Reading from left to right, Percy Wimbolt's and Nelson Cork's."

The Bean nodded intelligently.

"I see what you mean. Percy had one, and Nelson had the other."

"Exactly. Two hats in all. Top hats."

"What was mysterious about them?"

"Why, Elizabeth Bottsworth and Diana Punter said they didn't fit."

"Well, hats don't sometimes."

"But these came from Bodmin's."

The Bean shot up in bed. "What?"

"You mustn't excite the patient," said the nurse, who up to this point had taken no part in the conversation.

"But, dash it, nurse," cried the Bean, "you can't have caught what he said. If we are to give credence to his story, Percy Wimbolt and Nelson Cork bought a couple of hats at Bodmin's—at *Bodmin's,* I'll trouble you—and they didn't fit. It isn't possible."

He spoke with strong emotion, and the Crumpet nodded understandingly. People can say what they please about the modern young man believing in nothing nowadays, but there is one thing every right-minded young man believes in, and that is the infallibility of Bodmin's hats. It is one of the eternal verities. Once admit that it is possible for a Bodmin hat not to fit, and you leave the door open for Doubt, Schism, and Chaos generally.

"That's exactly how Percy and Nelson felt, and it was for that reason that they were compelled to take the strong line they did with E. Bottsworth and D. Punter."

"They took a strong line, did they?"

"A very strong line."

"Won't you tell us the whole story from the beginning?" said the nurse.

"Right ho," said the Crumpet, taking a grape. "It'll make your head swim."

"So mysterious?"

"So absolutely dashed uncanny from start to finish."

You must know, to begin with, my dear old nurse (said the Crumpet), that these two blokes, Percy Wimbolt and Nelson Cork, are fellows who have to exercise the most watchful care about their lids, because they are so situated that in their case there can be none of that business of just charging into any old hattery and grabbing the first thing in sight. Percy is one of those large, stout, outsize chaps with a head like a watermelon, while Nelson is built more on the lines of a minor jockey and has a head like a peanut.

You will readily appreciate, therefore, that it requires an artist hand to fit them properly, and that is why they have always gone to Bodmin. I have heard Percy say that his trust in Bodmin is like the unspotted faith of a young curate in his bishop and I have no doubt that Nelson would have said the same, if he had thought of it.

It was at Bodmin's door that they ran into each other on the morning when my story begins.

"Hullo," said Percy. "You come to buy a hat?"

"Yes," said Nelson. "You come to buy a hat?"

"Yes." Percy glanced cautiously about him, saw that he was alone (except for Nelson, of course) and unobserved, and drew closer and lowered his voice. "There's a reason!"

"That's rummy," said Nelson. He, also, spoke in a hushed tone. "I have a special reason, too."

Percy looked warily about him again, and lowered his voice another notch.

"Nelson," he said, "you know Elizabeth Bottsworth?"

"Intimately," said Nelson.

"Rather a sound young potato, what?"

"Very much so."

"Pretty."

"I've often noticed it."

"Me, too. She is so small, so sweet, so dainty, so lively, so viv— what's the word?—that a fellow wouldn't be far out in calling her an angel in human shape."

"Aren't all angels in human shape?"

"Are they?" said Percy, who was a bit foggy on angels. "Well, be that as it may," he went on, his cheeks suffused to a certain extent, "I love that girl, Nelson, and she's coming with me to the first day of Ascot, and I'm relying on this new hat of mine to do just that extra bit that's needed in the way of making her reciprocate my passion. Having only met her so far at country houses, I've never yet flashed upon her in a topper."

Nelson Cork was staring.

"Well, if that isn't the most remarkable coincidence I ever came across in my puff!" he exclaimed, amazed. "I'm buying my new hat for exactly the same reason."

A convulsive start shook Percy's massive frame. His eyes bulged.

"To fascinate Elizabeth Bottsworth?" he cried, beginning to writhe.

"No, no," said Nelson soothingly. "Of course not. Elizabeth and I have always been great friends, but nothing more. What I meant was that I, like you, am counting on this forthcoming topper of mine to put me across with the girl I love."

Percy stopped writhing.

"Who is she?" he asked, interested.

"Diana Punter, the niece of my godmother, old Ma Punter. It's an odd thing, I've known her all my life—brought up as kids together and so forth—but it's only recently that passion has burgeoned. I now worship that girl, Percy, from the top of her head to the soles of her divine feet."

Percy looked dubious.

"That's a pretty longish distance, isn't it? Diana Punter is one of my closest friends, and a charming girl in every respect, but isn't she a bit tall for you, old man?"

"My dear chap, that's just what I admire so much about her, her superb statuesqueness. More like a Greek goddess than anything I've struck for years. Besides, she isn't any taller for me than you are for Elizabeth Bottsworth."

"True," admitted Percy.

"And, anyway, I love her, blast it, and I don't propose to argue the point. I love her, I love her, I love her, and we are lunching together the first day of Ascot."

"At Ascot?"

"No. She isn't keen on racing, so I shall have to give Ascot a miss."

"That's Love," said Percy, awed.

"The binge will take place at my godmother's house in Berkeley Square, and it won't be long after that, I feel, before you see an interesting announcement in the *Morning Post*."

Percy extended his hand. Nelson grasped it warmly.

"These new hats are pretty well bound to do the trick, I should say, wouldn't you?"

"Infallibly. Where girls are concerned, there is nothing that brings home the gravy like a well-fitting topper."

"Bodmin must extend himself as never before," said Percy.

"He certainly must," said Nelson.

They entered the shop. And Bodmin, having measured them with his own hands, promised that two of his very finest efforts should be at their respective addresses in the course of the next few days.

Now, Percy Wimbolt isn't a chap you would suspect of having nerves, but there is no doubt that in the interval which elapsed before Bodmin was scheduled to deliver he got pretty twittery. He kept having awful visions of some great disaster happening to his new hat; and, as things turned out, these visions came jolly near being fulfilled. It has made Percy feel that he is psychic.

What occurred was this. Owing to these jitters of his, he hadn't been sleeping any too well, and on the morning before Ascot he was up as early as ten-thirty, and he went to his sitting-room window to see what sort of a day it was, and the sight he beheld from that window absolutely froze the blood in his veins.

For there below him, strutting up and down the pavement, were a uniformed little blighter whom he recognized as Bodmin's errand boy and an equally foul kid in mufti. And balanced on each child's loathsome head was a top hat. Against the railings were leaning a couple of cardboard hatboxes.

Now, considering that Percy had only just woken from a dream in which he had been standing outside the Guildhall in his new hat, receiving the Freedom of the City from the Lord Mayor, and the Lord Mayor had suddenly taken a terrific swipe at the hat with his mace, knocking it into hash, you might have supposed that he would have been hardened to anything. But he wasn't. His reaction was terrific. There was a moment of sort of paralysis, during which he was telling himself that he had always suspected this beastly little boy of Bodmin's of having a low and frivolous outlook and being temperamentally unfitted for his high office; and then he came alive with a jerk and let out probably the juiciest yell the neighborhood had heard for years.

It stopped the striplings like a high-powered shell. One moment, they had been swanking up and down in a mincing and affected sort of way; the next, the second kid had legged it like a streak and Bodmin's boy was shoving the hats back in the boxes and trying to do it quickly enough to enable him to be elsewhere when Percy should arrive.

And in this he was successful. By the time Percy had got to the front door and opened it, there was nothing to be seen but a hatbox standing on the steps. He took it up to his flat and removed the contents with a gingerly and reverent hand, holding his breath for fear the nap should have got rubbed the wrong way or a dent of any nature been made in the gleaming surface; but apparently all was well. Bodmin's boy might sink to taking hats out of their boxes and fooling about with them, but at least he hadn't gone to the last awful extreme of dropping them.

The lid was O.K. absolutely; and on the following morning Percy, having spent the interval polishing it with stout, assembled the boots, the spats, the trousers, the coat, the flowered waistcoat, the collar, the shirt, the quiet gray tie, and the good old gardenia, and set off in a taxi for the house where Elizabeth was staying. And presently he was ringing the bell and being told she would be down in a minute, and eventually down she came, looking perfectly marvelous.

"What ho, what ho!" said Percy.

"Hullo, Percy," said Elizabeth.

Now, naturally, up to this moment Percy had been standing with bared head. At this point, he put the hat on. He wanted her to get the full effect suddenly in a good light. And very strategic, too. I mean to say, it would have been the act of a juggins to have waited till they were in the taxi, because in a taxi all toppers look much alike.

So Percy popped the hat on his head with a meaning glance and stood waiting for the uncontrollable round of applause.

And instead of clapping her little hands in girlish ecstasy and doing

spring dances round him, this young Bottsworth gave a sort of gurgling scream not unlike a coloratura soprano choking on a fishbone.

Then she blinked and became calmer.

"It's all right," she said. "The momentary weakness has passed.
Tell me, Percy, when do you open?"

"Open?" said Percy, not having the remotest.

"On the Halls. Aren't you going to sing comic songs on the Music
Halls?"

Percy's perplexity deepened.

"Me? No. How? Why? What do you mean?"

"I thought that hat must be part of the make-up and that you were
trying it on the dog. I couldn't think of any other reason why you
should wear one six sizes too small."

Percy gasped.

"You aren't suggesting this hat doesn't fit me?"

"It doesn't fit you by a mile."

"But it's a Bodmin."

"Call it that if you like. I call it a public outrage."

Percy was appalled. I mean, naturally. A nice thing for a chap to
give his heart to a girl and then find her talking in this hideous, flippant way of sacred subjects.

Then it occurred to him that, living all the time in the country, she
might not have learned to appreciate the holy significance of the name
Bodmin.

"Listen," he said gently. "Let me explain. This hat was made by
Bodmin, the world-famous hatter of Vigo Street. He measured me in
person and guaranteed a fit."

"And I nearly had one."

"And if Bodmin guarantees that a hat shall fit," proceeded Percy,
trying to fight against a sickening sort of feeling that he had been all
wrong about this girl, "it fits. I mean, saying a Bodmin hat doesn't
fit is like saying . . . well, I can't think of anything awful enough."

"That hat's awful enough. It's like something out of a two-reel
comedy. Pure Chas. Chaplin. I know a joke's a joke, Percy, and
I'm as fond of a laugh as anyone, but there is such a thing as cruelty
to animals. Imagine the feelings of the horses at Ascot when they
see that hat."

Poets and other literary blokes talk a lot about falling in love at first
sight, but it's equally possible to fall out of love just as quickly. One
moment, this girl was the be-all and the end-all, as you might say, of
Percy Wimbolt's life. The next, she was just a regrettable young
blister with whom he wished to hold no further communication. He

could stand a good deal from the sex. Insults directed at himself left him unmoved. But he was not prepared to countenance destructive criticism of a Bodmin hat.

"Possibly," he said coldly, "you would prefer to go to this bally race meeting alone?"

"You bet I'm going alone. You don't suppose I mean to be seen in broad daylight in the paddock at Ascot with a hat like that?"

Percy stepped back and bowed formally.

"Drive on, driver," he said to the driver, and the driver drove on.

Now, you would say that that was rummy enough. A full-sized mystery in itself, you might call it. But wait. Mark the sequel. You haven't heard anything yet.

We now turn to Nelson Cork. Shortly before one-thirty, Nelson had shoved over to Berkeley Square and had lunch with his godmother and Diana Punter, and Diana's manner and deportment had been absolutely all that could have been desired. In fact, so chummy had she been over the cutlets and fruit salad that it seemed to Nelson that, if she was like this now, imagination boggled at the thought of how utterly all over him she would be when he sprang his new hat on her.

So when the meal was concluded and coffee had been drunk and old Lady Punter had gone up to her boudoir with a digestive tablet and a sex novel, he thought it would be a sound move to invite her to come for a stroll along Bruton Street. There was the chance, of course, that she would fall into his arms right in the middle of the pavement; but if that happened, he told himself, they could always get into a cab. So he mooted the saunter, and she checked up, and presently they started off.

And you will scarcely believe this, but they hadn't gone more than halfway along Bruton Street when she suddenly stopped and looked at him in an odd manner.

"I don't want to be personal, Nelson," she said, "but really I do think you ought to take the trouble to get measured for your hats."

If a gas main had exploded beneath Nelson's feet, he could hardly have been more taken aback.

"M-m-m-m . . ." he gasped. He could scarcely believe that he had heard aright.

"It's the only way with a head like yours. I know it's a temptation for a lazy man to go into a shop and take just whatever is offered him, but the result is so sloppy. That thing you're wearing now looks like an extinguisher."

Nelson was telling himself that he must be strong.

"Are you endeavoring to intimate that this hat does not fit?"

"Can't you feel that it doesn't fit?"

"But it's a Bodmin."

"I don't know what you mean. It's just an ordinary silk hat."

"Not at all. It's a Bodmin."

"I don't know what you are talking about."

"The point I am trying to drive home," said Nelson stiffly, "is that this hat was constructed under the personal auspices of Jno. Bodmin of Vigo Street."

"Well, it's too big."

"It is not too big."

"I say it is too big."

"And I say a Bodmin hat cannot be too big."

"Well, I've got eyes, and I say it is."

Nelson controlled himself with an effort.

"I would be the last person," he said, "to criticize your eyesight, but on the present occasion you will permit me to say that it has let you down with a considerable bump. Myopia is indicated. Allow me," said Nelson, hot under the collar, but still dignified, "to tell you something about Jno. Bodmin, as the name apears new to you. Jno. is the last of a long line of Bodmins, all of whom have made hats assiduously for the nobility and gentry all their lives. Hats are in Jno. Bodmin's blood."

"I don't . . ."

Nelson held up a restraining hand.

"Over the door of his emporium in Vigo Street the passer-by may read a significant legend. It runs: 'Bespoke Hatter To The Royal Family.' That means, in simple language adapted to the lay intelligence, that if the King wants a new topper he simply ankles round to Bodmin's and says: 'Good morning, Bodmin, we want a topper.' He does not ask if it will fit. He takes it for granted that it will fit. He has bespoken Jno. Bodmin, and he trusts him blindly. You don't suppose His Gracious Majesty would bespeak a hatter whose hats did not fit. The whole essence of being a hatter is to make hats that fit, and it is to this end that Jno. Bodmin has strained every nerve for years. And that is why I say again—simply and without heat—this hat is a Bodmin."

Diana was beginning to get a bit peeved. The blood of the Punters is hot, and very little is required to steam it up. She tapped Bruton Street with a testy foot.

"You always were an obstinate, pigheaded little fiend, Nelson, even as a child. I tell you once more, for the last time, that that hat is too big. If it were not for the fact that I can see a pair of boots and part of a pair of trousers, I should not know that there was a human being under it. I don't care how much you argue, I still think you ought to be ashamed of yourself for coming out in the thing. Even if you didn't mind for your own sake, you might have considered the feelings of the pedestrians and traffic."

Nelson quivered.

"You do, do you?"

"Yes, I do."

"Oh, you do?"

"I said I did. Didn't you hear me? No, I suppose you could hardly be expected to, with an enormous great hat coming down over your ears."

"You say this hat comes down over my ears?"

"Right over your ears. It's a mystery to me why you think it worth while to deny it."

I fear that what follows does not show Nelson Cork in the role of a parfait gentil knight, but in extenuation of his behavior I must remind you that he and Diana Punter had been brought up as children together, and a dispute between a couple who have shared the same nursery is always liable to degenerate into an exchange of personalities and innuendos. What starts as an academic discussion on hats turns only too swiftly into a raking up of old sores and a grand parade of family skeletons.

It was so in this case. At the word "mystery," Nelson uttered a nasty laugh.

"A mystery, eh? As much a mystery, I suppose, as why your Uncle George suddenly left England in the year 1920 without stopping to pack up?"

Diana's eyes flashed. Her foot struck the pavement another shrewd wallop.

"Uncle George," she said haughtily, "went abroad for his health."

"You bet he did," retorted Nelson. "He knew what was good for him."

"Anyway, he wouldn't have worn a hat like that."

"Where they would have put him if he hadn't been off like a scalded kitten, he wouldn't have worn a hat at all."

A small groove was now beginning to appear in the paving stone on which Diana Punter stood.

"Well, Uncle George escaped one thing by going abroad, at any rate," she said. "He missed the big scandal about your Aunt Clarissa in 1922."

Nelson clenched his fists.

"The jury gave Aunt Clarissa the benefit of the doubt," he said hoarsely.

"Well, we all know what that means. It was accompanied, if you recollect, by some very strong remarks from the Bench."

There was a pause.

"I may be wrong," said Nelson, "but I should have thought it ill beseemed a girl whose brother Cyril was warned off the Turf in 1924 to haul up her slacks about other people's Aunt Clarissas."

"Passing lightly over my brother Cyril in 1924," rejoined Diana, "what price your cousin Fred in 1927?"

They glared at one another in silence for a space, each realizing with a pang that the supply of erring relatives had now given out. Diana was still pawing the paving stone, and Nelson was wondering what on earth he could ever have seen in a girl who, in addition to talking subversive drivel about hats, was eight feet tall and ungainly, to boot.

"While as for your brother-in-law's niece's sister-in-law Muriel . . ." began Diana, suddenly brightening.

Nelson checked her with a gesture.

"I prefer not to continue this discussion," he said frigidly.

"It is no pleasure to me," replied Diana, with equal coldness, "to have to listen to your vapid gibberings. That's the worst of a man who wears his hat over his mouth—he will talk through it."

"I bid you a very hearty good afternoon, Miss Punter," said Nelson.

He strode off without a backward glance.

Now, one advantage of having a row with a girl in Bruton Street is that the Drones is only just round the corner, so that you can pop in and restore the old nervous system with the minimum of trouble. Nelson was round there in what practically amounted to a trice, and the first person he saw was Percy, hunched up over a double and splash.

"Hullo," said Percy.

"Hullo," said Nelson.

There was a silence, broken only by the sound of Nelson ordering a mixed vermouth. Percy continued to stare before him like a man who has drained the wine cup of life to its lees, only to discover a dead mouse at the bottom.

"Nelson," he said at length, "what are your views on the Modern Girl?"

"I think she's a mess."

"I thoroughly agree with you," said Percy. "Of course, Diana Punter is a rare exception, but, apart from Diana, I wouldn't give you twopence for the modern girl. She lacks depth and reverence and has no sense of what is fitting. Hats, for example."

"Exactly. But what do you mean Diana Punter is an exception? She's one of the ringleaders—the spearhead of the movement, if you like to put it that way. Think," said Nelson, sipping his vermouth, "of all the unpleasant qualities of the modern girl, add them up, double them, and what have you got? Diana Punter. Let me tell you what took place between me and this Punter only a few minutes ago."

"No," said Percy. "Let me tell you what transpired between me and Elizabeth Bottsworth this morning. Nelson, old man, she said my hat—my Bodmin hat—was too small."

"You don't mean that?"

"Those were her very words."

"Well, I'm dashed. Listen. Diana Punter told me my equally Bodmin hat was too large."

They stared at one another.

"It's the Spirit of something," said Nelson. "I don't know what, quite, but of something. You see it on all sides. Something very serious has gone wrong with girls nowadays. There is lawlessness and license abroad."

"And here in England, too."

"Well, naturally, you silly ass," said Nelson, with some asperity. "When I said abroad, I didn't mean abroad, I meant abroad."

He mused for a moment.

"I must say, though," he continued, "I am surprised at what you tell me about Elizabeth Bottsworth, and am inclined to think there must have been some mistake. I have always been a warm admirer of Elizabeth."

"And I have always thought Diana one of the best, and I find it hard to believe that she should have shown up in such a dubious light as you suggest. Probably there was a misunderstanding of some kind."

"Well, I ticked her off properly, anyway."

Percy Wimbolt shook his head.

"You shouldn't have done that, Nelson. You may have wounded her feelings. In my case, of course, I had no alternative but to be pretty crisp with Elizabeth."

Nelson Cork clicked his tongue.

"A pity," he said. "Elizabeth is sensitive."

"So is Diana."

"Not so sensitive as Elizabeth."

"I should say, at a venture, about five times as sensitive as Elizabeth. However, we must not quarrel about a point like that, old man. The fact that emerges is that we seem both to have been dashed badly treated. I think I shall toddle home and take an aspirin."

"Me, too."

They went off to the cloakroom, where their hats were, and Percy put his on.

"Surely," he said, "nobody but a half-witted little pipsqueak who can't see straight would say this was too small?"

"It isn't a bit too small," said Nelson. "And take a look at this one. Am I not right in supposing that only a female giantess with straws in her hair and astigmatism in both eyes could say it was too large?"

"It's a lovely fit."

And the cloakroom waiter, a knowledgeable chap of the name of Robinson, said the same.

"So there you are," said Nelson.

"Ah, well," said Percy.

They left the club, and parted at the top of Dover Street.

Now, though he had not said so in so many words, Nelson Cork's heart had bled for Percy Wimbolt. He knew the other's fine sensibilities and he could guess how deeply they must have been gashed by this unfortunate breaking-off of diplomatic relations with the girl he loved. For, whatever might have happened, however sorely he might have been wounded, the way Nelson Cork looked at it was that Percy loved Elizabeth Bottsworth in spite of everything. What was required here, felt Nelson, was a tactful mediator—a kindly, sensible friend of both parties who would hitch up his socks and plunge in and heal the breach.

So the moment he had got rid of Percy outside the club he hared round to the house where Elizabeth was staying and was lucky enough to catch her on the front doorsteps. For, naturally, Elizabeth hadn't gone off to Ascot by herself. Directly Percy was out of sight, she had told the taximan to drive her home, and she had been occupying the interval since the painful scene in thinking of things she wished she had said to him and taking her hostess's dog for a run—a Pekingese called Clarkson.

She seemed very pleased to see Nelson, and started to prattle of this and that, her whole demeanor that of a girl who, after having been compelled to associate for a while with the Underworld, has at last found a kindred soul. And the more he listened, the more he wanted to go on listening. And the more he looked at her, the more he felt that a lifetime spent in gazing at Elizabeth Bottsworth would be a lifetime dashed well spent.

There was something about the girl's exquisite petiteness and fragility that appealed to Nelson Cork's depths. After having wasted so much time looking at a female Carnera like Diana Punter, it was a genuine treat to him to be privileged to feast the eyes on one so small and dainty. And, what with one thing and another, he found the most extraordinary difficulty in lugging Percy into the conversation.

They strolled along, chatting. And, mark you, Elizabeth Bottsworth was a girl a fellow could chat with without getting a crick in the neck from goggling up at her, the way you had to do when you took the air with Diana Punter. Nelson realized now that talking to Diana Punter had been like trying to exchange thoughts with a flagpole sitter. He was surprised that this had never occurred to him before.

"You know, you're looking perfectly ripping, Elizabeth," he said.

"How funny!" said the girl. "I was just going to say the same thing about you."

"Not really?"

"Yes, I was. After some of the gargoyles I've seen today—Percy Wimbolt is an example that springs to the mind—it's such a relief to be with a man who really knows how to turn himself out."

Now that the Percy *motif* had been introduced, it should have been a simple task for Nelson to turn the talk to the subject of his absent friend. But somehow he didn't. Instead, he just simpered a bit and said: "Oh no, I say, really, do you mean that?"

"I do, indeed," said Elizabeth earnestly. "It's your hat, principally, I think. I don't know why it is, but ever since a child I have been intensely sensitive to hats, and it has always been a pleasure to me to remember that at the age of five I dropped a pot of jam out of the nursery window on to my Uncle Alexander when he came to visit us in a deerstalker cap with ear flaps, as worn by Sherlock Holmes. I consider the hat the final test of a man. Now, yours is perfect. I never saw such a beautiful fit. I can't tell you how much I admire that hat. It gives you quite an ambassadorial look."

Nelson Cork drew a deep breath. He was tingling from head to foot. It was as if the scales had fallen from his eyes and a new life begun for him.

"I say," he said, trembling with emotion, "I wonder if you would mind if I pressed your little hand?"

"Do," said Elizabeth cordially.

"I will," said Nelson, and did so. "And now," he went on, clinging to the fin like glue and hiccupping a bit, "how about buzzing off somewhere for a quiet cup of tea? I have a feeling that we have much to say to one another."

It is odd how often it happens in this world that when there are two chaps and one chap's heart is bleeding for the other chap you find that all the while the second chap's heart is bleeding just as much for the first chap. Both bleeding, I mean to say, not only one. It was so in the case of Nelson Cork and Percy Wimbolt. The moment he had left Nelson, Percy charged straight off in search of Diana Punter with the intention of putting everything right with a few well-chosen words.

Because what he felt was that, though at the actual moment of going to press pique might be putting Nelson off Diana, this would pass off and love come into its own again. All that was required, he considered, was a suave go-between, a genial mutual pal who would pour oil on the troubled w's and generally fix things up.

He found Diana walking round and round Berkeley Square with her chin up, breathing tensely through the nostrils. He drew up alongside and what-hoed, and as she beheld him the cold, hard gleam in her eyes changed to a light of cordiality. She appeared charmed to see him and at once embarked on an animated conversation. And with every word she spoke his conviction deepened that of all the ways of passing a summer afternoon there were none fruitier than having a friendly hike with Diana Punter.

And it was not only her talk that enchanted him. He was equally fascinated by that wonderful physique of hers. When he considered that he had actually wasted several valuable minutes that day conversing with a young shrimp like Elizabeth Bottsworth, he could have kicked himself.

Here, he reflected, as they walked round the square, was a girl whose ear was more or less on a level with a fellow's mouth, so that such observations as he might make were enabled to get from point to point with the least possible delay. Talking to Elizabeth Bottsworth had always been like bellowing down a well in the hope of attracting the attention of one of the smaller infusoria at the bottom. It surprised him that he had been so long in coming to this conclusion.

He was awakened from this reverie by hearing his companion utter the name of Nelson Cork.

"I beg your pardon?" he said.

"I was saying," said Diana, "that Nelson Cork is a wretched little undersized blob who, if he were not too lazy to work, would long since have signed up with some good troupe of midgets."

"Oh, would you say that?"

"I would say more than that," said Diana firmly. "I tell you, Percy, that what makes life so ghastly for girls, what causes girls to get gray hair and go into convents, is the fact that it is not always possible for them to avoid being seen in public with men like Nelson Cork. I trust I am not uncharitable. I try to view these things in a broad-minded way, saying to myself that if a man looks like something that has come out from under a flat stone it is his misfortune rather than his fault and that he is more to be pitied than censured. But on one thing I do insist, that such a man does not wantonly aggravate the natural unpleasantness of his appearance by prancing about London in a hat that reaches down to his ankles. I cannot and will not endure being escorted along Bruton Street by a sort of human bacillus the brim of whose hat bumps on the pavement with every step he takes. What I have always said and what I shall always say is that the hat is the acid test. A man who cannot buy the right-sized hat is a man one could never like or trust. Your hat, now, Percy, is exactly right. I have seen a good many hats in my time, but I really do not think that I have ever come across a more perfect specimen of all that a hat should be. Not too large, not too small, fitting snugly to the head like the skin on a sausage. And you have just the kind of head that a silk hat shows off. It gives you a sort of look . . . how shall I describe it? . . . it conveys the idea of a master of men. Leonine is the word I want. There is something about the way it rests on the brow and the almost imperceptible tilt toward the southeast . . ."

Percy Wimbolt was quivering like an Oriental muscle dancer. Soft music seemed to be playing from the direction of Hay Hill, and Berkeley Square had begun to skip round him on one foot.

He drew a deep breath.

"I say," he said, "stop me if you've heard this before, but what I feel we ought to do at this juncture is to dash off somewhere where it's quiet and there aren't so many houses dancing the 'Blue Danube' and shove some tea into ourselves. And over the pot and muffins I shall have something very important to say to you."

"So that," concluded the Crumpet, taking a grape, "is how the thing stands; and, in a sense, of course, you could say that it is a satisfactory ending.

"The announcement of Elizabeth's engagement to Nelson Cork appeared in the *Press* on the same day as that of Diana's projected hitching up with Percy Wimbolt; and it is pleasant that the happy couples should be so well matched as regards size.

"I mean to say, there will be none of that business of a six-foot girl tripping down the aisle with a five-foot-four man, or a six-foot-two man trying to keep step along the sacred edifice with a four-foot-three girl. This is always good for a laugh from the ringside pews, but it does not make for wedded bliss.

"No, as far as the principals are concerned, we may say that all has ended well. But that doesn't seem to me the important point. What seems to me the important point is this extraordinary, baffling mystery of those hats."

"Absolutely," said the Bean.

"I mean to say, if Percy's hat really didn't fit, as Elizabeth Bottsworth contended, why should it have registered as a winner with Diana Punter?"

"Absolutely," said the Bean.

"And, conversely, if Nelson's hat was the total loss which Diana Punter considered it, why, only a brief while later, was it going like a breeze with Elizabeth Bottsworth?"

"Absolutely," said the Bean.

"The whole thing is utterly inscrutable."

It was at this point that the nurse gave signs of wishing to catch the Speaker's eye.

"Shall I tell you what I think?"

"Say on, my dear young pillow-smoother."

"I believe Bodmin's boy must have got those hats mixed. When he was putting them back in the boxes, I mean."

The Crumpet shook his head, and took a grape.

"And then at the club they got the right ones again."

The Crumpet smiled indulgently.

"Ingenious," he said, taking a grape. "Quite ingenious. But a little farfetched. No, I prefer to think the whole thing, as I say, has something to do with the Fourth Dimension. I am convinced that that is the true explanation, if our minds could only grasp it."

"Absolutely," said the Bean.

❁ *Noblesse Oblige*

ON THE usually unruffled brow of the Bean who had just entered the smoking room of the Drones Club there was a furrow of perplexity. He crossed pensively to the settee in the corner and addressed the group of Eggs and Crumpets assembled there.

"I say," he said, "in re Freddie Widgeon, do any of you chaps happen to know if he's gone off his rocker?"

An Egg asked what made him think so.

"Well, he's out in the bar, drinking Lizard's Breaths . . ."

"Nothing unbalanced about that."

"No, but his manner is strange. It so happens that at the seminary where he and I were educated they are getting up a fund for some new rackets courts, and when I tackled Freddie just now and said that he ought to chip in and rally round the dear old school, he replied that he was fed to the tonsils with dear old schools and never wished to hear anyone talk about dear old schools again."

"Rummy," agreed the Egg.

"He then gave a hideous laugh and added that, if anybody was interested in his plans, he was going to join the Foreign Legion, that Cohort of the Damned in which broken men may toil and die and, dying, forget."

"Beau Widgeon?" said the Egg, impressed. "What ho!"

A Crumpet shook his head.

"You won't catch Freddie joining any Foreign Legion, once he gets on to the fact that it means missing his morning cup of tea. All the same, I can understand his feeling a bit upset at the moment, poor old blighter. Tragedy has come into his life. He's just lost the only girl in the world."

"Well, he ought to be used to that by this time."

"Yes. But he also got touched for his only tenner in the world, and on top of that his uncle, old Blicester, has cut his allowance in half."

"Ah," said the Egg understandingly.

"It was at Cannes that it all happened," proceeded the Crumpet. "Old Blicester had been ordered there by his doctor, and he offered to take Freddie along, paying all expenses. A glittering prospect, of course, for there are few juicier spots than the south of France during the summer season; nevertheless, I warned the poor fish not to go. I told him no good could come of it, pointing out the unexampled opportunities he would have of making some sort of a bloomer and alienating the old boy, if cooped up with him at a foreign resort for a matter of six weeks. But he merely blushed prettily and said that, while nobody was more alive to that possibility than himself, he was jolly well going to go, because this girl was at Cannes."

"Who was this girl?"

"I forget her name. Drusilla something. Never met her myself. He described her to me, and I received the impression of a sort of blend of Tallulah Bankhead and a policewoman. Fascinating exterior, I mean to say, but full of ideas at variance with the spirit of modern progress. Apparently she sprang from a long line of bishops and archdeacons and what not, and was strongly opposed to all forms of gambling, smoking and cocktail drinking. And Freddie had made an excellent first impression on her owing to the fact that he never gambled, never smoked, and looked on cocktails as the curse of the age."

"Freddie?" said the Egg, startled.

"That was what he had told her, and I consider it a justifiable stratagem. I mean to say, if you don't kid the delicately nurtured along a bit in the initial stages, where are you?"

"True," said the Egg.

Well, that is how matters stood when Freddie arrived at Cannes, and as he sauntered along the Croisette on the fourth or fifth day of his visit I don't suppose there was a happier bloke in all that gay throng. The sun was shining, the sea was blue, the girl had promised to have tea with him that afternoon at the Casino, and he knew he was looking absolutely his best. Always a natty dresser, today he had eclipsed himself. The glistening trousers, the spotless shirt, the form-fitting blue coat . . . all these combined to present an intoxicating picture. And this picture he had topped off with a superb tie which he had contrived to pinch overnight from his uncle's effects. Gold and lavender in its general color scheme, with a red stripe thrown in for good measure. Lots of fellows, he tells me, couldn't have carried it off, but it made him look positively godlike.

Well, when I tell you that he hadn't been out on the Croisette ten minutes before a French bloke came up and offered him five hundred francs to judge a Peasant Mothers Baby Competition down by the harbor, where they were having some sort of local fête or jamboree in honor of a saint whose name has escaped me, you will admit that he must have looked pretty impressive. These knowledgeable Gauls don't waste their money on tramps.

Now, you might have thought that as old Blicester, the world's greatest exponent of the one-way pocket, consistently refused to slip him so much as a franc for current expenses, Freddie would have jumped at this chance of making a bit. But it so happened that he had recently wired to a staunch pal in London for a tenner and had received intimation that the sum would be arriving by that afternoon's post. He had no need, accordingly, for the gold the chap was dangling before his eyes. However, he was pleased by the compliment, and said he would most certainly look in, if he could, and lend the binge the prestige of his presence, and they parted on cordial terms.

It was almost immediately after this that the bird in the shabby reach-me-downs accosted him.

His watch having told him that the afternoon post would be in any minute now, Freddie, in his perambulations, had not moved very far from the Carlton, which was the hotel where he and his uncle and also the girl were stopping, and he was maneuvering up and down about opposite it when a voice at his elbow, speaking in that sort of surprised and joyful manner in which one addresses an old friend encountered in a foreign spot, said:

"Why, hullo!"

And, turning, he perceived the above-mentioned bird in the reach-me-downs as described. A tallish, thinnish chap.

"Well, well, well!" said the bird.

Freddie goggled at him. As far as memory served, he didn't know the blighter from Adam.

"Hullo," he said, playing for time.

"Fancy running into you," said the chap.

"Ah," said Freddie.

"It's a long time since we met."

"Absolutely," said Freddie, the persp. beginning to start out a bit on the brow. Because if there's one thing that makes a man feel a chump it is this business of meeting ancient cronies and not being able to put a name to them.

"I don't suppose you see any of the old crowd now?" said the chap.

"Not many," said Freddie.

"They scatter."

"They do scatter."

"I came across Smith a few weeks ago."

"Oh, yes?"

"T. T. Smith, I mean."

"Oh, T. T. Smith?"

"Yes. Not J. B. I hear J. B.'s gone to the Malay States. T. T.'s in some sort of agency business. Rather prosperous."

"That's good."

"You seem to be doing pretty well, yourself."

"Oh, fairly."

"Well, I'm not surprised," said the chap. "One always knew you would, even at school."

The word, Freddie tells me, was like a life belt. He grabbed at it. So this was a fellow he had known at school. That narrowed it down a lot. Surely now, he felt, the old brain would begin to function. Then he took another look at the chap, and the momentary exhilaration ebbed. He had not known him from Adam, and he still did not know him from Adam. The situation had thus become more awkward than ever, because the odds were that in the end this fellow was going to turn out to be someone he had shared a study with and ought to be falling on the neck of and swopping reminiscences of the time when old Boko Jervis brought the white rabbit into chapel and what not.

"Yes," said the chap. "Even then one could tell that you were bound to go up and up. Gosh, how I used to admire you at the dear old school. You were my hero."

"What!" yipped Freddie. He hadn't the foggiest that he had been anyone's hero at school. His career there hadn't been so dashed distinguished as all that. He had scraped into the cricket team in his last year, true; but even so he couldn't imagine any of his contemporaries looking up to him much.

"You were," said the chap. "I thought you a marvel."

"No, really?" said Freddie, suffused with coy blushes. "Well, well, well, fancy that. Have a cigarette?"

"Thanks," said the chap. "But what I really want is a meal. I'm right on my uppers. We aren't all like you, you see. While you've been going up and up, some of us have been going down and down. If I don't get a meal today, I don't know what I shall do."

Freddie tells me the thing came on him as a complete surprise. You might have supposed that a wary bird like him, who has been a member of this club since he came down from Oxford, would have known better, but he insists that he had absolutely no suspicion that a touch was in the air till it suddenly hit him like this. And his first impulse, he says, was to mumble something at the back of his throat and slide off.

And he was just going to when a sudden surge of generous emotion swept over him. Could he let a fellow down who had not only been at school with him but who, when at school, had looked upon him as a hero? Imposs., felt Freddie. There had been six hundred and forty-seven chaps at the old school. Was he to hand the callous mitten to the only one of those six hundred and forty-seven who had admired him? Absolutely out of the q., was Freddie's verdict. A *mille* was the dickens of a sum of money, of course—at the present rate of exchange a bit more than a tenner—but it would have to be found somehow. Noblesse oblige, he meant to say.

And just when the fervor was at its height he recollected this check which was arriving by the afternoon post. In the stress of emotion it had quite slipped his mind.

"By Jove!" he said. "Yes, I can fix you up. Suppose we meet at the Casino a couple of hours from now."

"God bless you," said the chap.

"Not at all," said Freddie.

It was with mixed feelings that he went into the hotel to see if the post had come. On the one hand, there was the solemn anguish of parting with a tenner which he had earmarked for quite a different end. On the other, there was the quiet chestiness induced by the realization that here he had been jogging along through the world, not thinking such a frightful lot of himself, and all the while in the background was this bloke treasuring his memory and saying to himself: "Ah, if we could all be like Freddie Widgeon!" Cheap at a tenner, he told himself, the sensation of spiritual yeastiness which this reflection gave him.

All the same, he wished the chap could have done with five, because there was a bookie in London to whom he had owed a fiver for some months now and recent correspondence had shown that this hellhound was on the verge of becoming a bit unpleasant. Until this episode had occurred, he had fully intended to send the man thirty bob or so, to sweeten him. Now, of course, this was out of the question. The entire sum must go unbroken to this old schoolfellow whose name he wished he could remember.

Spivis? . . . Brent? . . . Jerningham? . . . Fosway? . . .
No.
Brewster? . . . Goggs? . . . Bootle? . . . Finsbury? . . .
No.

He gave it up and went to the desk. The letter was there, and in it the check. The very decent johnnie behind the counter cashed it for him without a murmur, and he was just gathering up the loot when somebody behind him said "Ah!"

Now, in the word "Ah!" you might say that there is nothing really to fill a fellow with a nameless dread. Nevertheless, that is what this "Ah!" filled Freddie with. For he had recognized the voice. It was none other than that of the bookie to whom he owed the fiver. That is the trouble about Cannes in August—it becomes very mixed. You get your Freddie Widgeons there—splendid chaps who were worshiped by their schoolmates—and you also get men like this bookie. All sorts, if you follow me, from the highest to the lowest.

From the very moment when he turned and gazed into the fellow's steely eyes, Freddie tells me he hadn't a hope. But he did his best.

"Hullo, Mr. McIntosh!" he said. "You here? Well, well, well! Ha, ha!"

"Yes," said the bookie.

"I never thought I should run into you in these parts."

"You have," the bookie assured him.

"Come down here for a nice holiday, what? Taking a perfect rest, eh? Going to bask in the lovely sunshine and put all thoughts of business completely out of your head, yes?"

"Well, not quite all," said the bookie, producing the little black book. "Now, let me see, Mr. Widgeon. . . . Ah, yes, five pounds on Marmalade to cop in the second at Ally Pally. Should have won by the formbook, but ran third. Well, that's Life, isn't it? I think it comes to a little more than four hundred and fifty francs, really, but we'll call it four-fifty. One doesn't want any haggling among friends."

"I'm awfully sorry," said Freddie. "Some other time, what? I can't manage it just at the moment. I haven't any money."

"No?"

"I mean to say, I want this for a poor man."

"So do I," said the bookie.

And the upshot and outcome, of course, was that poor old Freddie had to brass up. You can't appeal to a bookie's better feelings, because he hasn't any. He pushed over the four hundred and fifty.

"Oh, very well," he said. "Here you are. And let me tell you, Mr. McIntosh, that the curse of the Widgeons goes with it."

"Right," said the bookie.

So there Freddie was with five hundred and fifty francs in his kick, and needing a thousand.

I must say I wouldn't have blamed him if, in these circs., he had decided to give a miss to the old school friend. Allowing fifty francs for lushing up the girl Drusilla at the tea table, he would in that case have had a cool five hundred with which to plunge into the variegated pleasures of Cannes in the summertime. A very nice sum, indeed.

But, though tempted, he was strong. This old admirer of his— Muttlebury? . . . Jukes? . . . Ferguson? . . . Braithwaite? . . . —had said that he needed a *mille,* and a *mille* he must have.

But how to raise the other five hundred? That was the prob.

For some moments he toyed with mad schemes like trying to borrow it from his uncle. Then it suddenly flashed upon him that the sum he required was the exact amount which the intelligent Gaul had offered him if he would come down to the jamboree by the harbor and judge the Peasant Mothers Baby Competition.

Now, Freddie's views on babies are well defined. He is prepared to cope with them singly, if all avenues of escape are blocked and there is a nurse or mother standing by to lend aid in case of sudden hiccups, retchings, or nauseas. Under such conditions he has even been known to offer his watch to one related by ties of blood in order that the little stranger might listen to the tick-tick. But it would be paltering with the truth to say that he likes babies. They give him, he says, a sort of gray feeling. He resents their cold stare and the supercilious and upstage way in which they dribble out of the corner of their mouths on seeing him. Eying them, he is conscious of doubts as to whether Man can really be Nature's last word.

This being so, you will readily understand that, even for so stupendous a fee as five hundred francs, he shrank from being closeted with a whole platoon of the little brutes. And I think it is greatly to his credit that after only the shortest of internal struggles he set his teeth, clenched his fists, and made for the harbor with a steady step. How different it would all have been, he felt wistfully, if he were being called upon to judge a contest of Bathing Belles.

There was the possibility, of course, that in the interval since he had met the intelligent Gaul the post of judge would have been filled. But no. The fellow welcomed him with open arms and led him joyfully into a sort of marquee place crowded with as tough-looking a bunch of mothers and as hard-boiled a gaggle of issue as anybody could wish to see. He made a short speech in French which was much too rapid for Freddie to follow, and the mothers all applauded, and the babies all yelled, and then he was conducted along the line, with all the mothers glaring at him in an intimidating way, as much as to warn him that if he dared give the prize to anybody else's off-

spring he had jolly well better look out for himself. Dashed unpleasant, the whole thing, Freddie tells me, and I see his viewpoint.

He kept his head, however. This was the first time he had ever
been let in for anything of this nature, but a sort of instinct told him
to adopt the policy followed by all experienced judges at these
affairs—viz. to ignore the babies absolutely and concentrate entirely
on the mothers. So many points for ferocity of demeanor, that is to
say, and so many for possibility of knife concealed in stocking, and
so on and so forth. You ask any curate how he works the gaff at the
annual Baby Competition in his village, and he will tell you that
these, broadly, are the lines on which he goes.

There were, it seemed, to be three prizes and about the first one
there could be no question at all. It went automatically to a heavyweight mother with beetling eyebrows who looked as if she had just
come from doing a spot of knitting at the foot of the guillotine. Just
to see those eyebrows, Freddie tells me, was to hear the heads dropping into the basket, and he had no hesitation, as I say, in declaring
her progeny the big winner.

The second and third prizes were a bit more difficult, but after
some consideration he awarded them to two other female plug-
uglies with suspicious bulges in their stockings. This done, he sidled
up to the intelligent Gaul to receive his wage, doing his best not to
listen to the angry mutterings from the losers which were already
beginning to rumble through the air.

The brand of English which this bird affected was not of the best,
and it took Freddie some moments to get his drift. When he did, he
reeled and came very near clutching for support at the other's
beard. Because what the Gaul was endeavoring to communicate
was the fact that, so far from being paid five hundred francs for his
services, Freddie was expected to cough up that sum.

It was an old Cannes custom, the man explained, for some rich
visiting milord to take on the providing of the prizes on this occasion, his reward being the compliment implied in the invitation.

He said that when he had perceived Freddie promenading himself
on the Croisette he had been so struck by his appearance of the most
elegant and his altogether of a superbness so unparalleled that he had
picked him without another look at the field.

Well, dashed gratifying, of course, from one point of view and a
handsome tribute to the way Freddie had got himself up that day; but
it was not long before he was looking in a tentative sort of manner at
the nearest exit. And I think that, had that exit been just a shade
closer, he would have put his fortune to the test, to win or lose it all.

But to edge out and leg it would have taken that ten seconds or so which make all the difference. Those mothers would have been on his very heels, and the prospect of sprinting along the streets of Cannes under such conditions was too much for him. Quite possibly he might have shown a flash of speed sufficient to shake off their challenge, but it would have been a very close thing, with nothing in it for the first hundred yards or so, and he could not have failed to make himself conspicuous.

So, with a heavy sigh, he forked out the five h., and tottered into the open. So somber was his mood that he scarcely heard the mutterings of the disappointed losers, who were now calling him an *espèce de* something and hinting rather broadly in the local *patois* that he had been fixed.

And the thing that weighed so heavily upon him was the thought that, unless some miracle occurred, he would now be forced to let down his old chum Bulstrode, Waters, Parsloe, Bingley, Murgatroyd, or whatever the blighter's name might be.

He had told the fellow to meet him outside the Casino—which in summer at Cannes is, of course, the Palm Beach at the far end of the Croisette—so he directed his steps thither. And jolly halting steps they were, he tells me. The urge to give the school chum his *mille* had now become with Frederick Widgeon a regular obsession. He felt that his honor was involved. And he shuddered at the thought of the meeting that lay before him. Up the chap would come frisking, with his hand outstretched and the light of expectation in his eyes, and what would ensue? The miss-in-baulk.

He groaned in spirit. He could see the other's pained and disillusioned look. He could hear him saying to himself: "This is not the old Widgeon form. The boy I admired so much in the dear old days of school would not have foozled a small loan like this. A pretty serious change for the worse there must have been in Frederick W. since the time when we used to sport together in the shade of the old cloisters." The thought was agony.

All the way along the Croisette he pondered deeply. To the gay throng around him he paid no attention. There were girls within a biscuit throw in bathing suits which began at the base of the spine and ended two inches lower down, but he did not give them so much as a glance. His whole being was absorbed in this reverie of his.

By the time he reached the Casino, he had made up his mind. Visionary, chimerical though the idea would have seemed to anybody who knew the latter and his views on parting with cash, he had resolved to make the attempt to borrow a thousand francs from his uncle. With this end, therefore, he proceeded to the baccarat rooms. The other, he knew, was always to be found at this hour seated at one of the three-louis chemmy tables. For, definite though the Earl of Blicester's creed was on the subject of his nephew gambling, he himself enjoyed a modest flutter.

He found the old boy, as expected, hunched up over the green cloth. At the moment of Freddie's arrival he was just scooping in three pink counters with a holy light of exaltation on his face. For there was nothing spacious and sensational about Lord Blicester's method of play. He was not one of those punters you read about in the papers who rook the Greek Syndicate of three million francs in an evening. If he came out one-and-sixpence ahead of the game, he considered his day well spent.

It looked to Freddie, examining the counters in front of his relative, as if the moment were propitious for a touch. There must have been fully five bobs' worth of them, which meant that the other had struck one of those big winning streaks which come to all gamblers sooner or later. His mood, accordingly, ought to be sunny.

"I say, Uncle," he said, sidling up.

"Get to hell out of here," replied Lord Blicester, not half so sunny as might have been expected. "Banco!" he cried, and a second later was gathering in another sixty francs.

"I say, Uncle . . ."

"Well, what is it?"

"I say, Uncle, will you lend me . . ."

"No."

"I only want . . ."

"Well, you won't get it."

"It's not for myself . . ."

"Go to blazes," said old Blicester.

Freddie receded. Though he had never really expected any solid results, his heart was pretty well bowed down with weight of care. He had shot his bolt. His last source of supply had proved a wash-out.

He looked at his watch. About now, the old schoolmate would be approaching the tryst. He would be walking—so firm would be his faith in his hero—with elastic steps. Possibly he would even be humming some gay air. Had he a stick? Freddie could not remember. But if he had he would be twirling it.

And then would come the meeting . . . the confession of failure . . . the harsh awakening and the brutal shattering of dreams. . . .

It was at this moment that he was roused from his meditations by the one word in the French language capable of bringing him back to the world.

"*Un mille.*"

It was the voice of the croupier, chanting his litany.

"*Cinquante louis à la banque. Un banco de mille.*"

I can't do the dialect, you understand, but what he meant was that somebody holding the bank had run it up to a thousand francs. And Freddie, waking with a start, perceived that a pile of assorted counters, presumably amounting to that sum, now lay in the center of the board.

Well, a thousand francs isn't much, of course, to the nibs at the big tables, but among the three-louis-minimum lizards if you run a bank up to a *mille* you make a pretty big sensation. There was quite a crowd round the table now, and over their heads Freddie could see that pile of counters, and it seemed to smile up at him.

For an instant he hesitated, while his past life seemed to flit before him as if he had been a drowning man. Then he heard a voice croak "*Banco*" and there seemed something oddly familiar about it, and he suddenly realized that it was his own. He had taken the plunge.

It was a pretty agonizing moment for old Freddie, as you may well imagine. I mean to say, he had bancoed this fellow, whoever he was, and if he happened to lose the *coup* all he would have to offer him would be fifty francs and his apologies. There would, he could not conceal it from himself, be the devil of a row. What exactly, he wondered, did they do to you at these French casinos if you lost and couldn't pay up? Something sticky, beyond a question. Hardly the guillotine, perhaps, and possibly not even Devil's Island. But something nasty, undoubtedly. With a dim recollection of a movie he had once seen, he pictured himself in the middle of a hollow square formed by punters and croupiers with the managing director of the place snipping off his coat buttons.

Or was it trouser buttons? No, in a mixed company like this it would hardly be trouser buttons. Still, even coat buttons would be bad enough.

And, if the moment was agonizing for Freddie, it was scarcely less so for his uncle, Lord Blicester. It was his bank which had been running up to such impressive proportions, and he was now faced with the problem of whether to take a chance on doubling his loot or to pass the hand.

Lord Blicester was a man who, when in the feverish atmosphere of the gaming rooms, believed in small profits and quick returns. He was accustomed to start his bank at the minimum, run it twice with his heart in his mouth, and then pass. But on the present occasion he had been carried away to such an extent that he had worked the kitty up to a solid *mille*. It was a fearful sum to risk losing. On the other hand, suppose he didn't lose? Someone in the crowd outside his line of vision had said "Banco!" and with a bit of luck he might be two *mille* up instead of one, just like that.

What to do? It was a man's crossroads.

In the end, he decided to take the big chance. And it was as the croupier pushed the cards along the table and the crowd opened up a bit to let the challenger get at them that he recognized in the individual leaning forward his nephew Frederick.

"Brzzghl!" gasped Lord Blicester. "Gor! Woosh!"

What he meant was that the deal was off because the young hound who had just come into the picture was his late brother's son Frederick Fotheringay Widgeon, who had never had a penny except what he allowed him and certainly hadn't a hundredth part of the sum necessary for cashing in if he lost. But he hadn't made himself clear enough. The next moment, with infinite emotion, Freddie was chucking down a nine and the croupier was pushing all old Blicester's hardearned at him.

It was as he was gathering it up that he caught the old boy's eye. The effect of it was to cause him to spill a hundred-franc counter, two louis counters, and a five-franc counter. And he had just straightened himself after picking these up, when a voice spoke.

"Good afternoon, Mr. Widgeon," said the girl Drusilla.

"Oh, ah," said Freddie.

You couldn't say it was a frightfully bright remark, but he considers it was dashed good going to utter even as much as that. In the matter of eyes, he tells me, there was not much to choose between this girl's and his uncle's. Their gazes differed in quality, it is true, because, whereas old Blicester's had been piping hot and had expressed hate, fury and the desire to skin, the girl Drusilla's was right off the ice and conveyed a sort of sick disillusionment and a loathing contempt. But as to which he would rather have met on a dark night down a lonely alley, Freddie couldn't have told you.

"You appear to have been lucky," said this Drusilla.

"Oh, ah," said Freddie.

He looked quickly away, and ran up against old Blicester's eye again. Then he looked back and caught Drusilla's. The whole situation, he tells me, was extraordinarily like that of an African explorer who, endeavoring to ignore one of the local serpents, finds himself exchanging glances with a man-eating tiger.

The girl was now wrinkling her nose as if a particularly foul brand of poison gas had begun to permeate the Casino and she was standing nearest it.

"I must confess I am a little surprised," she said, "because I was under the impression that you had told me that you never gambled."

"Oh, ah," said Freddie.

"If I remember rightly, you described gambling as a cancer in the body politic."

"Oh, ah," said Freddie.

She took a final sniff, as if she had been hoping against hope that he was not a main sewer and was now reluctantly compelled to realize that he was.

"I am afraid I shall not be able to come to tea this afternoon. Good-bye, Mr. Widgeon."

"Oh, ah," said Freddie.

He watched her go, knowing that she was going out of his life and that any chance of the scent of orange blossoms and the amble up the aisle with the organ playing "O perfect Love" was now blue round the edges; and it was as if there was a dull weight pressing on him.

And then he found that there was a dull weight pressing on him, viz. that of all the counters he was loaded down with. And it was at this point that it dawned upon him that, though he had in prospect an interview with old Blicester which would undoubtedly lower all previous records, and though a life's romance had gone phut, he was at least in a position to satisfy the *noblesse oblige* of the Widgeons.

So he tottered to the cashier's desk and changed the stuff into a pink note, and then he tottered out of the Casino, and was tottering down the steps when he perceived the school friend in the immediate offing, looking bright and expectant.

"Here I am," said the school friend.

"Oh, ah," said Freddie.

And with a supreme gesture of resignation he pressed the *mille* into the man's hand.

There was never any doubt about the chap taking it. He took it like a trout sucking down a May fly and shoved it away in a pocket at the back of his costume. But what was odd was that he seemed stupefied. His eyes grew round, his jaw fell, and he stared at Freddie in awe-struck amazement.

"I say," he said, "don't think I'm raising any objections or anything of that sort, because I'm not. I am heart and soul in this scheme of giving me a *mille*. But it's an awful lot, isn't it? I don't mind telling you that what I had been sketching out as more or less the sum that was going to change hands was something in the nature of fifty francs."

Freddie was a bit surprised too. He couldn't make this out.

"But you said you had to have a *mille*."

"And a meal is just what I'm going to have," replied the chap enthusiastically. "I haven't had a bite to eat since breakfast."

Freddie was stunned. He isn't what you would call a quick thinker, but he was beginning to see that there had been a confusion of ideas.

"Do you mean to tell me," he cried, "that when you said a *mille* what you meant was a meal?"

"I don't suppose anyone ever meant a meal more," said the chap. He stood awhile in thought. "Hors d'oeuvres, I think, to start with," he went on, passing his tongue meditatively over his lips. "Then perhaps a touch of clear soup, followed by some fish of the country and a good steak *minute* with fried potatoes and a salad. Cheese, of course, and he usual et ceteras, and then coffee, liqueur, and a cigar to wind up with. Yes, you may certainly take it as official that I intend to have a meal. Ah, yes, and I was forgetting. A bot. of some nice, dry wine to wash things down. Yes, yes, yes, to be sure. You see this stomach?" he said, patting it. "Here stands a stomach that is scheduled in about a quarter of an hour to get the surprise of its young life."

Freddie saw it all now, and the irony of the situation seemed to hit him like a bit of lead piping on the base of the skull. Just because of this footling business of having words in one language which meant something quite different in another language—a thing which could so easily have been prevented by the responsible heads of the French and English nations getting together across a round table and coming to some sensible arrangement—here he was deeper in the soup than he had ever been in the whole course of his career.

He tells me he chafed, and I don't blame him. Anybody would have chafed in the circs. For about half a minute he had half a mind to leap at the chap and wrench the *mille* out of him and substitute for it the fifty francs which he had been anticipating.

Then the old *noblesse oblige* spirit awoke once more. He might be in the soup, he might be a financial wreck, he might be faced with a *tête-à-tête* with his uncle, Lord Blicester, in the course of which the testy old man would in all probability endeavor to bite a piece out of the fleshy part of his leg, but at least he had done the fine, square thing. He had not let down a fellow who had admired him at school.

The chap had begun to speak again. At first, all he said was a

brief word or two revising that passage in his previous address which
had dealt with steak *minute*. A steak *minute,* he told Freddie,
had among its obvious merits one fault—to wit, that it was not as
filling as it might be. A more prudent move, he considered, and he
called on Freddie to endorse this view, would be a couple of chump
chops. Then he turned from that subject.

"Well, it was certainly a bit of luck running into you, Postlethwaite," he said.

Freddie was a trifle stymied.

"Postlethwaite?" he said. "How do you mean, Postlethwaite?"

The chap seemed surprised.

"How do you mean, how do I mean Postlethwaite?"

"I mean, why Postlethwaite? How has this Postlethwaite stuff
crept in?"

"But, Postlethwaite, your name's Postlethwaite."

"My name's Widgeon."

"Widgeon?"

"Widgeon."

"*Not* Postlethwaite?"

"Certainly not."

The chap uttered an indulgent laugh.

"Ha, ha. Still the same old jovial, merry, kidding Postlethwaite, I
see."

"I'm not the same old jovial, merry, kidding Postlethwaite," said
Freddie, with heat. "I never was the jovial, merry, kidding Postlethwaite."

The chap stared.

"You aren't the Postlethwaite I used to admire so much at dear
old Bingleton?"

"I've never been near dear old Bingleton in my life."

"But you're wearing an Old Bingletonian tie."

Freddie reeled.

"Is this beastly thing an Old Bingletonian tie? It's one I sneaked
from my uncle."

The chap laughed heartily.

"Well, of all the absurd mix-ups! You look like Postlethwaite and
you're wearing an O.B. tie. Naturally, I thought you *were* Postlethwaite. And all the time we were thinking of a couple of other
fellows! Well, well, well! However, it's all worked out for the best,
what? Good-bye," he added hastily, and was round the corner like a
streak.

Freddie looked after him dully. He was totting up in his mind the final returns. On the debit side, he had lost Drusilla whatever-her-name-was. He had alienated his uncle, old Blicester. He was down a tenner. And, scaliest thought of all, he hadn't been anybody's hero at school.

On the credit side, he had fifty francs.

At the Palm Beach Casino at Cannes you can get five Martini cocktails for fifty francs. Freddie went and had them.

Then, wiping his lips with the napkin provided by the management, he strode from the bar to face the hopeless dawn.

⚙ *Goodbye to All Cats*

As THE CLUB kitten sauntered into the smoking room of the Drones Club and greeted those present with a friendly miaow, Freddie Widgeon, who had been sitting in a corner with his head between his hands, rose stiffly.

"I had supposed," he said, in a cold, level voice, "that this was a quiet retreat for gentlemen. As I perceive that it is a blasted zoo, I will withdraw."

And he left the room in a marked manner.

There was a good deal of surprise, mixed with consternation.

"What's the trouble?" asked an Egg, concerned. Such exhibitions of the naked emotions are rare at the Drones. "Have they had a row?"

A Crumpet, always well informed, shook his head.

"Freddie has had no personal breach with this particular kitten," he said. "It is simply that since that week end at Matcham Scratchings he can't stand the sight of a cat."

"Matcham what?"

"Scratchings. The ancestral home of Dahlia Prenderby in Oxfordshire."

"I met Dahlia Prenderby once," said the Egg. "I thought she seemed a nice girl."

"Freddie thought so, too. He loved her madly."

"And lost her, of course?"

"Absolutely."

"Do you know," said a thoughtful Bean, "I'll bet that if all the girls Freddie Widgeon has loved and lost were placed end to end—not that I suppose one could do it—they would reach halfway down Piccadilly."

"Farther than that," said the Egg. "Some of them were pretty tall. What beats me is why he ever bothers to love them. They always turn him down in the end. He might just as well never begin. Better, in fact, because in the time saved he could be reading some good book."

"I think the trouble with Freddie," said the Crumpet, "is that he always gets off to a flying start. He's a good-looking sort of chap who dances well and can wiggle his ears, and the girl is dazzled for the moment, and this encourages him. From what he tells me, he appears to have gone very big with this Prenderby girl at the outset. So much so, indeed, that when she invited him down to Matcham Scratchings he had already bought his copy of *What Every Young Bridegroom Ought to Know*."

"Rummy, these old country-house names," mused the Bean. "Why Scratchings, I wonder?"

"Freddie wondered, too, till he got to the place. Then he tells me he felt it was absolutely the *mot juste*. This girl Dahlia's family, you see, was one of those animal-loving families, and the house, he tells me, was just a frothing maelstrom of dumb chums. As far as the eye could reach, there were dogs scratching themselves and cats scratching the furniture. I believe, though he never met it socially, there was even a tame chimpanzee somewhere on the premises, no doubt scratching away as assiduously as the rest of them. You get these conditions here and there in the depths of the country, and this Matcham place was well away from the center of things, being about six miles from the nearest station.

"It was at this station that Dahlia Prenderby met Freddie in her two-seater, and on the way to the house there occurred a conversation which I consider significant—showing, as it does, the cordial relations existing between the young couple at that point in the proceedings. I mean, it was only later that the bitter awakening and all that sort of thing popped up.

" 'I do want you to be a success, Freddie,' said the girl, after talking a while of this and that. 'Some of the men I've asked down here have been such awful flops. The great thing is to make a good impression on Father.'

" 'I will,' said Freddie.

" 'He can be a little difficult at times.'

" 'Lead me to him,' said Freddie. 'That's all I ask. Lead me to him.'

" 'The trouble is, he doesn't much like young men.'

" 'He'll like me.'

" 'He will, will he?'

" 'Rather!'

" 'What makes you think that?'

" 'I'm a dashed fascinating chap.'

" 'Oh, you are?'

"Yes, I am."

" 'You are, are you?'

" 'Rather!'

"Upon which, she gave him a sort of push and he gave her a sort of push, and she giggled and he laughed like a paper bag bursting, and she gave him a kind of shove and he gave her a kind of shove, and she said 'You *are* a silly ass!' and he said 'What ho!' All of which shows you, I mean to say, the stage they had got to by this time. Nothing definitely settled, of course, but Love obviously beginning to burgeon in the girl's heart."

Well, naturally, Freddie gave a good deal of thought during the drive to this father of whom the girl had spoken so feelingly, and he resolved that he would not fail her. The way he would suck up to the old dad would be nobody's business. He proposed to exert upon him the full force of his magnetic personality, and looked forward to registering a very substantial hit.

Which being so, I need scarcely tell you, knowing Freddie as you do, that his first act on entering Sir Mortimer Prenderby's orbit was to make the scaliest kind of floater, hitting him on the back of the neck with a tortoise-shell cat not ten minutes after his arrival.

His train having been a bit late, there was no time on reaching the house for any stately receptions or any of that "Welcome to Meadowsweet Hall" stuff. The girl simply shot him up to his room and told him to dress like a streak, because dinner was in a quarter of an hour, and then buzzed off to don the soup and fish herself. And Freddie was just going well when, looking round for his shirt, which he had left on the bed, he saw a large tortoise-shell cat standing on it, kneading it with its paws.

Well, you know how a fellow feels about his shirt front. For an instant, Freddie stood spellbound. Then with a hoarse cry he bounded forward, scooped up the animal, and, carrying it out onto the balcony, flung it into the void. And an elderly gentleman, coming round the corner at this moment, received a direct hit on the back of his neck.

"Hell!" cried the elderly gentleman.

A head popped out of a window.

"Whatever is the matter, Mortimer?"

"It's raining cats."

"Nonsense. It's a lovely evening," said the head and disappeared.

Freddie thought an apology would be in order.

"I say," he said.

The old gentleman looked in every direction of the compass, and finally located Freddie on his balcony.

"I say," said Freddie, "I'm awfully sorry you got that nasty buffet. It was me."

"It was not you. It was a cat."

"I know. I threw the cat."

"Why?"

"Well . . ."

"Dam' fool."

"I'm sorry," said Freddie.

"Go to blazes," said the old gentleman.

Freddie backed into the room and the incident closed.

Freddie is a pretty slippy dresser, as a rule, but this episode had shaken him, and he not only lost a collar stud but made a mess of the first two ties. The result was that the gong went while he was still in his shirtsleeves; and on emerging from his boudoir he was informed by a footman that the gang were already nuzzling their bouillon in the dining room. He pushed straight on there, accordingly, and sank into a chair beside his hostess just in time to dead-heat with the final spoonful.

Awkward, of course, but he was feeling in pretty good form owing to the pleasantness of the thought that he was shoving his knees under the same board as the girl Dahlia; so, having nodded to his host, who was glaring at him from the head of the table, as much as to say that all would be explained in God's good time, he shot his cuffs and started to make sparkling conversation to Lady Prenderby.

"Charming place you have here, what?"

Lady Prenderby said that the local scenery was generally admired. She was one of those tall, rangy, Queen Elizabeth sort of women, with tight lips and cold, *blanc-mange-y* eyes. Freddie didn't like her looks much, but he was feeling, as I say, fairly fizzy, so he carried on with a bright zip.

"Pretty good hunting country, I should think?"

"I believe there is a good deal of hunting near here, yes."

"I thought as much," said Freddie. "Ah, that's the stuff, is it not? A cracking gallop across good country with a jolly fine kill at the end of it, what, what? Hark for'ard, yoicks, tallyho, I mean to say, and all that sort of thing."

Lady Prenderby shivered austerely.

"I fear I cannot share your enthusiasm," she said. "I have the strongest possible objection to hunting. I have always set my face against it, as against all similar brutalizing blood sports."

This was a nasty jar for poor old Freddie, who had been relying on the topic to carry him nicely through at least a couple of courses. It silenced him for the nonce. And as he paused to collect his faculties, his host, who had now been glowering for six and a half minutes practically without cessation, put a hand in front of his mouth and addressed the girl Dahlia across the table. Freddie thinks he was under the impression that he was speaking in a guarded whisper, but, as a matter of fact, the words boomed through the air as if he had been a costermonger calling attention to his Brussels sprouts.

"Dahlia!"

"Yes, Father?"

"Who's that ugly feller?"

"Hush!"

"What do you mean, hush? Who is he?"

"Mr. Widgeon."

"Mr. Who?"

"Widgeon."

"I wish you would articulate clearly and not mumble," said Sir Mortimer fretfully. "It sounds to me just like 'Widgeon.' Who asked him here?"

"I did."

"Why?"

"He's a friend of mine."

"Well, he looks a pretty frightful young slab of damnation to me. What I'd call a criminal face."

"Hush!"

"Why do you keep saying 'Hush'? Must be a lunatic, too. Throws cats at people."

"Please, Father!"

"Don't say 'Please, Father!' No sense in it. I tell you he does throw cats at people. He threw one at me. Half-witted, I'd call him—if that. Besides being the most offensive-looking young toad I've ever seen on the premises. How long's he staying?"

"Till Monday."

"My God! And today's only Friday!" bellowed Sir Mortimer Prenderby.

It was an unpleasant situation for Freddie, of course, and I'm bound to admit he didn't carry it off particularly well. What he ought to have done, obviously, was to have plunged into an easy flow of small talk; but all he could think of was to ask Lady Prenderby if she was fond of shooting. Lady Prenderby having replied that, owing to being deficient in the savage instincts and wanton blood lust that went to make up a callous and coldhearted murderess, she was not, he relapsed into silence with his lower jaw hanging down.

All in all, he wasn't so dashed sorry when dinner came to an end.

As he and Sir Mortimer were the only men at the table, most of the seats having been filled by a covey of mildewed females whom he had classified under the general heading of Aunts, it seemed to Freddie that the moment had now arrived when they would be able to get together once more, under happier conditions than those of their last meeting, and start to learn to appreciate one another's true worth. He looked forward to a cozy *tête-à-tête* over the port, in the course of which he would smooth over that cat incident and generally do all that lay within his power to revise the unfavorable opinion of him which the other must have formed.

But apparently Sir Mortimer had his own idea of the duties and obligations of a host. Instead of clustering round Freddie with decanters, he simply gave him a long, lingering look of distaste and shot out of the French window into the garden. A moment later, his head reappeared and he uttered the words: "You and your dam' cats!" Then the night swallowed him again.

Freddie was a good deal perplexed. All this was new stuff to him. He had been in and out of a number of country houses in his time, but this was the first occasion on which he had ever been left flat at the conclusion of the evening meal, and he wasn't quite sure how to handle the situation. He was still wondering, when Sir Mortimer's head came into view again and its owner, after giving him another of those long, lingering looks, said: "Cats, forsooth!" and disappeared once more.

Freddie was now definitely piqued. It was all very well, he felt, Dahlia Prenderby telling him to make himself solid with her father, but how can you make yourself solid with a fellow who doesn't stay put for a couple of consecutive seconds? If it was Sir Mortimer's intention to spend the remainder of the night flashing past like a merry-go-round, there seemed little hope of anything amounting to a genuine *rapprochement*. It was a relief to his feelings when there suddenly appeared from nowhere his old acquaintance the tortoise-shell cat. It seemed to offer to him a means of working off his spleen.

Taking from Lady Prenderby's plate, accordingly, the remains of a banana, he plugged the animal at a range of two yards. It yowled and withdrew. And a moment later, there was Sir Mortimer again.

"Did you kick that cat?" said Sir Mortimer.

Freddie had half a mind to ask this old disease if he thought he was a man or a jack-in-the-box, but the breeding of the Widgeons restrained him.

"No," he said, "I did not kick that cat."

"You must have done something to it to make it come charging out at forty miles an hour."

"I merely offered the animal a piece of fruit."

"Do it again and see what happens to you."

"Lovely evening," said Freddie, changing the subject.

"No, it's not, you silly ass," said Sir Mortimer. Freddie rose. His nerve, I fancy, was a little shaken.

"I shall join the ladies," he said, with dignity.

"God help them!" replied Sir Mortimer Prenderby in a voice instinct with the deepest feeling, and vanished once more.

Freddie's mood, as he made for the drawing room, was thoughtful. I don't say he has much sense, but he's got enough to know when he is and when he isn't going with a bang. Tonight, he realized, he had been very far from going in such a manner. It was not, that is to say, as the Idol of Matcham Scratchings that he would enter the drawing room, but rather as a young fellow who had made an unfortunate first impression and would have to do a lot of heavy ingratiating before he could regard himself as really popular in the home.

He must bustle about, he felt, and make up leeway. And, knowing that what counts with these old-style females who have lived in the country all their lives is the exhibition of those little politenesses and attentions which were all the go in Queen Victoria's time, his first action, on entering, was to make a dive for one of the aunts who seemed to be trying to find a place to put her coffee cup.

"Permit me," said Freddie, suave to the eyebrows.

And bounding forward with the feeling that this was the stuff to give them, he barged right into a cat.

"Oh, sorry," he said, backing and bringing down his heel on another cat.

"I say, most frightfully sorry," he said.

And, tottering to a chair, he sank heavily onto a third cat.

Well, he was up and about again in a jiffy, of course, but it was too late. There was the usual not-at-all-ing and don't-mention-it-ing, but he could read between the lines. Lady Prenderby's eyes had rested on his for only a brief instant, but it had been enough. His standing with her, he perceived, was now approximately what King Herod's would have been at an Israelite Mothers Social Saturday Afternoon.

The girl Dahlia during these exchanges had been sitting on a sofa at the end of the room, turning the pages of a weekly paper, and the sight of her drew Freddie like a magnet. Her womanly sympathy was just what he felt he could do with at this juncture. Treading with infinite caution, he crossed to where she sat; and, having scanned the terrain narrowly for cats, sank down on the sofa at her side. And conceive his agony of spirit when he discovered that womanly sympathy had been turned off at the main. The girl was like a chunk of ice cream with spikes all over it.

"Please do not trouble to explain," she said coldly, in answer to his opening words. "I quite understand that there are people who have this odd dislike of animals."

"But, dash it . . ." cried Freddie, waving his arm in a frenzied sort of way. "Oh, I say, sorry," he added, as his fist sloshed another of the menagerie in the short ribs.

Dahlia caught the animal as it flew through the air.

"I think perhaps you had better take Augustus, Mother," she said. "He seems to be annoying Mr. Widgeon."

"Quite," said Lady Prenderby. "He will be safer with me."

"But, dash it . . ." bleated Freddie.

Dahlia Prenderby drew in her breath sharply.

"How true it is," she said, "that one never really knows a man till after one has seen him in one's own home."

"What do you mean by that?"

"Oh, nothing," said Dahlia Prenderby.

She rose and moved to the piano, where she proceeded to sing old Breton folk songs in a distant manner, leaving Freddie to make out as best he could with a family album containing faded photographs with "Aunt Emmy bathing at Llandudno, 1893," and "This is Cousin George at the fancy-dress ball" written under them.

And so the long, quiet, peaceful home evening wore on, till eventually Lady Prenderby mercifully blew the whistle and he was at liberty to sneak off to his bedroom.

You might have supposed that Freddie's thoughts, as he toddled upstairs with his candle, would have dwelt exclusively on the girl Dahlia. This, however, was not so. He did give her obvious shirtiness a certain measure of attention, of course, but what really filled his mind was the soothing reflection that at long last his patch and that of the animal kingdom of Matcham Scratchings had now divided. He, so to speak, was taking the high road while they, as it were, would take the low road. For whatever might be the conditions prevailing in the dining room, the drawing room, and the rest of the house, his bedroom, he felt, must surely be a haven totally free from cats of all descriptions.

Remembering, however, that unfortunate episode before dinner, he went down on all fours and subjected the various nooks and crannies to a close examination. His eye could detect no cats. Relieved, he rose to his feet with a gay song on his lips; and he hadn't got much beyond the first couple of bars when a voice behind him suddenly started taking the bass; and, turning, he perceived on the bed a fine Alsatian dog.

Freddie looked at the dog. The dog looked at Freddie. The situation was one fraught with embarrassment. A glance at the animal was enough to convince him that it had got an entirely wrong angle on the position of affairs and was regarding him purely in the light of an intrusive stranger who had muscled in on its private sleeping quarters. Its manner was plainly resentful. It fixed Freddie with a cold, yellow eye and curled its upper lip slightly, the better to display a long, white tooth. It also twitched its nose and gave a *sotto-voce* imitation of distant thunder.

Freddie did not know quite what avenue to explore. It was impossible to climb between the sheets with a thing like that on the counterpane. To spend the night in a chair, on the other hand, would have been foreign to his policy. He did what I consider the most statesmanlike thing by sidling out onto the balcony and squinting along the wall of the house to see if there wasn't a lighted window hard by, behind which might lurk somebody who would rally round with aid and comfort.

There was a lighted window only a short distance away, so he shoved his head out as far as it would stretch and said:

"I say!"

There being no response, he repeated:

"I say!"

And, finally, to drive his point home, he added:

"I say! I say! I say!"

This time he got results. The head of Lady Prenderby suddenly protruded from the window.

"Who," she inquired, "is making that abominable noise?"

It was not precisely the attitude Freddie had hoped for, but he could take the rough with the smooth.

"It's me. Widgeon, Frederick."

"Must you sing on your balcony, Mr. Widgeon?"

"I wasn't singing. I was saying 'I say'."

"What were you saying?"

" 'I say'."

"You say what?"

"I say I was saying 'I say.' Kind of a heart cry, if you know what I mean. The fact is, there's a dog in my room."

"What sort of dog?"

"A whacking great Alsatian."

"Ah, that would be Wilhelm. Good night, Mr. Widgeon."

The window closed. Freddie let out a heart-stricken yip.

"But I say!"

The window reopened.

"Really, Mr. Widgeon!"

"But what am I to do?"

"Do?"

"About this whacking great Alsatian!"

Lady Prenderby seemed to consider.

"No sweet biscuits," she said. "And when the maid brings you your tea in the morning please do not give him sugar. Simply a little milk in the saucer. He is on a diet. Good night, Mr. Widgeon."

Freddie was now pretty well nonplused. No matter what his hostess might say about this beastly dog being on a diet, he was convinced from its manner that its medical adviser had not forbidden it Widgeons, and once more he bent his brain to the task of ascertaining what to do next.

There were several possible methods of procedure. His balcony being not so very far from the ground, he could, if he pleased, jump down and pass a health-giving night in the nasturtium bed. Or he might curl up on the floor. Or he might get out of the room and doss downstairs somewhere.

This last scheme seemed about the best. The only obstacle in the way of its fulfillment was the fact that, when he started for the door, his roommate would probably think he was a burglar about to loot silver of lonely country house and pin him. Still, it had to be risked, and a moment later he might have been observed tiptoeing across the carpet with all the caution of a slack-wire artist who isn't any too sure he remembers the correct steps.

Well, it was a near thing. At the instant when he started, the dog seemed occupied with something that looked like a cushion on the bed. It was licking this object in a thoughtful way, and paid no attention to Freddie till he was halfway across No Man's Land. Then it suddenly did a sort of sitting high jump in his direction, and two seconds later, Freddie, with a drafty feeling about the seat of his trouserings, was on top of a wardrobe, with the dog underneath looking up. He tells me that if he ever moved quicker in his life it was only on the occasion when, a lad of fourteen, he was discovered by his uncle, Lord Blicester, smoking one of the latter's cigars in the library; and he rather thinks he must have clipped at least a fifth of a second off the record then set up.

It looked to him now as if his sleeping arrangements for the night had been settled for him. And the thought of having to roost on top of a wardrobe at the whim of a dog was pretty dashed offensive to his proud spirit, as you may well imagine. However, as you cannot reason with Alsatians, it seemed the only thing to be done; and he was trying to make himself as comfortable as a sharp piece of wood sticking into the fleshy part of his leg would permit, when there was a snuffling noise in the passage and through the door came an object which in the dim light he was at first not able to identify. It looked something like a penwiper and something like a piece of a hearthrug. A second and keener inspection revealed it as a Pekingese puppy.

The uncertainty which Freddie had felt as to the newcomer's status was shared, it appeared, by the Alsatian, for after raising its eyebrows in a puzzled manner it rose and advanced inquiringly. In a tentative way it put out a paw and rolled the intruder over. Then, advancing again, it lowered its nose and sniffed.

It was a course of action against which its best friends would have advised it. These Pekes are tough eggs, especially when, as in this case, female. They look the world in the eye, and are swift to resent familiarity. There was a sort of explosion, and the next moment the Alsatian was shooting out of the room with its tail between its legs, hotly pursued. Freddie could hear the noise of battle rolling away along the passage, and it was music to his ears. Something on these lines was precisely what that Alsatian had been asking for, and now it had got it.

Presently, the Peke returned, dashing the beads of perspiration from its forehead, and came and sat down under the wardrobe, wagging a stumpy tail. And Freddie, feeling that the All Clear had been blown and that he was now at liberty to descend, did so.

His first move was to shut the door, his second to fraternize with his preserver. Freddie is a chap who believes in giving credit where credit is due, and it seemed to him that this Peke had shown itself an ornament of its species. He spared no effort, accordingly, to entertain it. He lay down on the floor and let it lick his face two hundred and thirty-three times. He tickled it under the left ear, the right ear, and at the base of the tail, in the order named. He also scratched its stomach.

All these attentions the animal received with cordiality and marked gratification; and as it seemed still in pleasure-seeking mood and had plainly come to look upon him as the official Master of the Revels, Freddie, feeling that he could not disappoint it but must play the host no matter what the cost to himself, took off his tie and handed it over. He would not have done it for everybody, he says, but where this lifesaving Peke was concerned the sky was the limit.

Well, the tie went like a breeze. It was a success from the start. The Peke chewed it and chased it and got entangled in it and dragged it about the room, and was just starting to shake it from side to side when an unfortunate thing happened. Misjudging its distance, it banged its head a nasty wallop against the leg of the bed.

There is nothing of the Red Indian at the stake about a puppy in circumstances like this. A moment later, Freddie's blood was chilled by a series of fearful shrieks that seemed to ring through the night like the dying cries of the party of the second part to a first-class murder. It amazed him that a mere Peke, and a juvenile Peke at that, should have been capable of producing such an uproar. He says that a baronet, stabbed in the back with a paper knife in his library, could not have made half such a row.

Eventually, the agony seemed to abate. Quite suddenly, as if nothing had happened, the Peke stopped yelling and with an amused smile started to play with the tie again. And at the same moment there was a sound of whispering outside, and then a knock at the door.

"Hullo?" said Freddie.

"It is I, sir. Biggleswade."

"Who's Biggleswade?"

"The butler, sir."

"What do you want?"

"Her ladyship wishes me to remove the dog which you are torturing."

There was more whispering.

"Her ladyship also desires me to say that she will be reporting the affair in the morning to the Society for the Prevention of Cruelty to Animals."

There was another spot of whispering.

"Her ladyship further instructs me to add that, should you prove recalcitrant, I am to strike you over the head with the poker."

Well, you can't say this was pleasant for poor old Freddie, and he didn't think so himself. He opened the door, to perceive, without, a group consisting of Lady Prenderby, her daughter Dahlia, a few assorted aunts, and the butler, with poker. And he says he met Dahlia's eyes and they went through him like a knife.

"Let me explain . . ." he began.

"Spare us the details," said Lady Prenderby with a shiver. She scooped up the Peke and felt it for broken bones.

"But listen . . ."

"Good night, Mr. Widgeon."

The aunts said good night, too, and so did the butler. The girl Dahlia preserved a revolted silence.

"But, honestly, it was nothing, really. It banged its head against the bed . . ."

"What did he say?" asked one of the aunts, who was a little hard of hearing.

"He says he banged the poor creature's head against the bed," said Lady Prenderby.

"Dreadful!" said the aunt.

"Hideous!" said a second aunt.

A third aunt opened up another line of thought. She said that with men like Freddie in the house, was anyone safe? She mooted the possibility of them all being murdered in their beds. And though Freddie offered to give her a written guarantee that he hadn't the slightest intention of going anywhere near her bed, the idea seemed to make a deep impression.

"Biggleswade," said Lady Prenderby.

"M'lady?"

"You will remain in this passage for the remainder of the night with your poker."

"Very good, m'lady."

"Should this man attempt to leave his room, you will strike him smartly over the head."

"Just so, m'lady."

"But, listen . . ." said Freddie.

"Good night, Mr. Widgeon."

The mob scene broke up. Soon the passage was empty save for Biggleswade the butler, who had begun to pace up and down, halting every now and then to flick the air with his poker as if testing the limpomeness of his wrist muscles and satisfying himself that they were in a condition to ensure the right amount of follow-through.

The spectacle he presented was so unpleasant that Freddie withdrew into his room and shut the door. His bosom, as you may imagine, was surging with distressing emotions. That look which Dahlia Prenderby had given him had churned him up to no little extent. He realized that he had a lot of tense thinking to do, and to assist thought he sat down on the bed.

Or, rather, to be accurate, on the dead cat which was lying on the bed. It was this cat which the Alsatian had been licking just before the final breach in his relations with Freddie—the object, if you remember, which the latter had supposed to be a cushion.

He leaped up as if the corpse, instead of being cold, had been piping hot. He stared down, hoping against hope that the animal was merely in some sort of coma. But a glance told him that it had made the great change. He had never seen a deader cat. After life's fitful fever it slept well.

You wouldn't be far out in saying that poor old Freddie was now appalled. Already his reputation in this house was at zero, his name mud. On all sides he was looked upon as Widgeon the Amateur Vivisectionist. This final disaster could not but put the tin hat on it. Before, he had had a faint hope that in the morning, when calmer moods would prevail, he might be able to explain that matter of the Peke. But who was going to listen to him if he were discovered with a dead cat on his person?

And then the thought came to him that it might be possible not to be discovered with it on his person. He had only to nip downstairs and deposit the remains in the drawing room or somewhere and suspicion might not fall upon him. After all, in a super-catted house like this, cats must always be dying like flies all over the place. A housemaid would find the animal in the morning and report to G.H.Q. that the cat strength of the establishment had been reduced by one, and there would be a bit of tut-tutting and perhaps a silent tear or two, and then the thing would be forgotten.

The thought gave him new life. All briskness and efficiency, he picked up the body by the tail and was just about to dash out of the room when, with a silent groan, he remembered Biggleswade.

He peeped out. It might be that the butler, once the eye of authority had been removed, had departed to get the remainder of his beauty sleep. But no. Service and Fidelity were evidently the watchwords at Matcham Scratchings. There the fellow was, still practicing half-arm shots with the poker. Freddie closed the door.

And, as he did so, he suddenly thought of the window. There lay the solution. Here he had been, fooling about with doors and thinking in terms of drawing rooms, and all the while there was the balcony staring him in the face. All he had to do was to shoot the body out into the silent night, and let gardeners, not housemaids, discover it.

He hurried out. It was a moment for swift action. He raised his burden. He swung it to and fro, working up steam. Then he let it go, and from the dark garden there came suddenly the cry of a strong man in his anger.

"Who threw that cat?"

It was the voice of his host, Sir Mortimer Prenderby.

"Show me the man who threw that cat!" he thundered.

Windows flew up. Heads came out. Freddie sank to the floor of the balcony and rolled against the wall.

"Whatever is the matter, Mortimer?"

"Let me get at the man who hit me in the eye with a cat."

"A cat?" Lady Prenderby's voice sounded perplexed. "Are you sure?"

"Sure? What do you mean sure? Of course I'm sure. I was just dropping off to sleep in my hammock, when suddenly a great beastly cat came whizzing through the air and caught me properly in the eyeball. It's a nice thing. A man can't sleep in hammocks in his own garden without people pelting him with cats. I insist on the blood of the man who threw that cat."

"Where did it come from?"

"Must have come from that balcony there."

"Mr. Widgeon's balcony," said Lady Prenderby in an acid voice. "As I might have guessed."

Sir Mortimer uttered a cry.

"So might I have guessed! Widgeon, of course! That ugly feller. He's been throwing cats all the evening. I've got a nasty sore place on the back of my neck where he hit me with one before dinner. Somebody come and open the front door. I want my heavy cane, the one with the carved ivory handle. Or a horsewhip will do."

"Wait, Mortimer," said Lady Prenderby. "Do nothing rash. The man is evidently a very dangerous lunatic. I will send Biggleswade to overpower him. He has the kitchen poker."

Little (said the Crumpet) remains to be told. At two-fifteen that morning a somber figure in dress clothes without a tie limped into the little railway station of Lower Smattering on the Wissel, some six miles from Matcham Scratchings. At three-forty-seven it departed Londonwards on the up milk train. It was Frederick Widgeon. He had a broken heart and blisters on both heels. And in that broken heart was that loathing for all cats of which you recently saw so signal a manifestation. I am revealing no secrets when I tell you that Freddie Widgeon is permanently through with cats. From now on, they cross his path at their peril.

❦ *All's Well with Bingo*

A BEAN and a Crumpet were in the smoking room of the Drones Club having a quick one before lunch, when an Egg who had been seated at the writing table in the corner rose and approached them.

"How many 'r's' in 'intolerable'?" he asked.

"Two," said the Crumpet. "Why?"

"I am writing a strong letter to the committee," explained the Egg, "drawing their attention to the intolerable . . . Great Scott!" he cried, breaking off. "There he goes again!"

A spasm contorted his face. Outside in the passage a fresh young voice had burst into a gay song with a good deal of vo-de-o-de-o about it. The Bean cocked an attentive ear as it died away in the direction of the dining room.

"Who is this linnet?" he inquired.

"Bingo Little, blast him! He's always singing nowadays. That's what I'm writing my strong letter to the committee about—the intolerable nuisance of this incessant heartiness of his. Because it isn't only his singing. He slaps backs. Only yesterday he came sneaking up behind me in the bar and sloshed me between the shoulder blades, saying 'Aha!' as he did so. Might have choked me. How many 's's' in 'incessant'?"

"Three," said the Crumpet.

"Thanks," said the Egg.

He returned to the writing table. The Bean seemed perplexed.

"Odd," he said. "Very odd. How do you account for young Bingo carrying on like this?"

"Just *joie de vivre*."

"But he's married. Didn't he marry some female novelist or other?"

"That's right. Rosie M. Banks, authoress of *Only a Factory Girl, Mervyn Keene, Clubman, 'Twas Once in May,* and other works. You see her name everywhere. I understand she makes a packet with the pen."

"I didn't know married men had any *joie de vivre*."

"Not many, of course. But Bingo's union has been an exceptionally happy one. He and the other half of the sketch have hit it off from the start like a couple of lovebirds."

"Well, he oughtn't to slap backs about it."

"You don't know the inside facts. Bingo is no mere wanton back-slapper. What has made him that way at the moment is the fact that he recently had a most merciful escape. There was within a toucher of being very serious trouble in the home."

"But you said they were like a couple of lovebirds."

"Quite. But even with lovebirds circumstances can arise which will cause the female lovebird to get above herself and start throwing her weight about. If Mrs. Bingo had got on Bingo what at one time it appeared inevitable that she must get on him, it would have kept her in conversation for the remainder of their married lives. She is a sweet little thing, one of the best, but women are women and I think that there can be no doubt that she would have continued to make passing allusions to the affair right up to the golden wedding day. The way Bingo looks at it is that he has escaped the fate that is worse than death, and I am inclined to agree with him."

The thing started one morning when Bingo returned to the love nest for a bite of lunch after taking the Pekingese for a saunter. He was in the hall trying to balance an umbrella on the tip of his nose, his habit when at leisure, and Mrs. Bingo came out of her study with a wrinkled brow and a couple of spots of ink on her chin.

"Oh, there you are," she said. "Bingo, have you ever been to Monte Carlo?"

Bingo could not help wincing a little at this. Unwittingly, the woman had touched an exposed nerve. The thing he had always wanted to do most in the world was to go to Monte Carlo, for he had a system which couldn't fail to clean out the Casino, but few places, as you are probably aware, are more difficult for a married man to sneak off to.

"No," he said with a touch of moodiness. Then, recovering his usual sunny aplomb, "Look," he said. "Watch, old partner in sickness and in health. I place the umbrella so. Then, maintaining a perfect equilibrium . . ."

"I want you to go there at once," said Mrs. Bingo.

Bingo dropped the umbrella. You could have knocked him down with a toothpick. For a moment, he tells me, he thought that he must be dreaming some beautiful dream.

"It's for my book. I can't get on without some local color."

Bingo grasped the gist. Mrs. Bingo had often discussed this business of local color with him, and he had got the strength of it. Nowadays, he knew, if you are providing wholesome fiction for the masses, you have simply got to get your atmosphere right. The customers have become cagey. They know too much. Chance your arm with the *mise en scène,* and before you can say, "What ho," you've made some bloomer and people are writing you nasty letters, beginning, "Dear Madam: Are you aware . . ."

"And I can't go myself. There's the Pen and Ink Dinner on Friday, and on Tuesday the Writers Club is giving a luncheon to Mrs. Carrie Melrose Bopp, the American novelist. And any moment now I shall be coming to the part where Lord Peter Shipbourne breaks the bank. So do you think you could possibly go, Bingo darling?"

Bingo was beginning to understand how the Israelites must have felt when that manna started descending in the wilderness.

"Of course I'll go, old egg," he said heartily. "Anything I can—"

His voice trailed away. A sudden thought had come, biting into his soul like acid. He had remembered that he hadn't a bean to his name. He had lost every penny he possessed two weeks before on a horse called Bounding Beauty which was running—if you could call it running—in the two-thirty at Haydock Park.

The trouble with old Bingo is that he will allow his cooler judgment to be warped by dreams and omens. Nobody had known better than he that by the ruling of the formbook Bounding Beauty hadn't a chance; but on the eve of the race he had a nightmare in which he saw his Uncle Wilberforce dancing the rumba in the nude on the steps of the National Liberal Club and, like a silly ass, accepted this as a bit of stable information. And bang, as I say, had gone every penny he had in the world.

For a moment he reeled a bit. Then he brightened. Rosie, he reasoned, would scarcely expect him to undertake an irksome job like sweating all the way over to Monte Carlo without financing the tedious expedition.

"Of course, of course, of course," he said. "Yes, rather! I'll start tomorrow. And about expenses. I suppose a hundred quid would see me through, though two would be still better, and even three wouldn't hurt . . ."

"Oh, no, that's all right," said Mrs. Bingo. "You won't need any money."

Bingo gulped like an ostrich swallowing a brass doorknob.

"Not . . . need . . . any . . . money?"

"Except a pound or two for tips and so on. Everything is arranged. Dora Spurgeon is at Cannes, and I'm going to phone her to get you a room at the Hôtel de Paris at Monte Carlo, and all the bills will be sent to my bank."

Bingo had to gulp a couple more times before he was able to continue holding up his end of the dialogue.

"But I take it," he said in a low voice, "that you want me to hobnob with the international spies and veiled women and so forth and observe their habits carefully, don't you? This will run into money. You know what international spies are. It's champagne for them every time, and no half bots, either."

"You needn't bother about the spies. I can imagine them. All I want is the local color. An exact description of the Rooms and the Square and all that. Besides, if you had a lot of money, you might be tempted to gamble."

"What!" cried Bingo. "Gamble? Me?"

"No, no," said Mrs. Bingo remorsefully. "I'm wronging you, of course. Still, I think I'd sooner we did it the way I've arranged."

So there you have the position of affairs, and you will not be surprised to learn that poor old Bingo made an indifferent lunch, toying with the minced chicken and pushing the roly-poly pudding away untasted. His manner during the meal was distrait, for his brain was racing like a dynamo. Somehow he had got to get the stuff. But how? How?

Bingo, you see, is not a man who finds it easy to float a really substantial loan. People know too much about his financial outlook. He will have it in sackfuls some day, of course, but until he realizes on his Uncle Wilberforce—who is seventy-six and may quite easily go to par—the wolf, as far as he is concerned, will always be in or about the vestibule. The public is aware of this, and it makes the market sluggish.

It seemed to him, brooding over the thing, that his only prospect for the sort of sum he required was Oofy Prosser. Oofy, while not an easy parter, is a millionaire, and a millionaire was what he required. So round about cocktail time he buzzed off to the club, only to be informed that Oofy was abroad. The disappointment was so severe that he was compelled to go to the smoking room and have a restorative. I was there when he came in, and so haggard and fishlike was his demeanor that I asked him what was up, and he told me all.

"You couldn't lend me between twenty and twenty-five or, better still, thirty quid, could you?" he said.

I said, No, I couldn't and he heaved a long, low, quivering sigh.

"And so it goes on," he said. "That's life. Here I am with this unique opportunity of making a stupendous fortune, and crippled for lack of the essential capital. Did you ever hear of a chap called Garcia?"

"No."

"Skinned the Monte Carlo administration of a hundred thousand quid in his day. Ever hear of a chap called Darnborough?"

"No."

"Eighty-three thousand of the best was what he pocketed. Did you ever hear of a chap called Owers?"

"No."

"His winning streak lasted for more than twenty years. These three birds of whom I speak simply went to Monte Carlo and lolled back in their chairs with fat cigars and the Casino just thrust the money on them. And I don't suppose any of them had a system like mine. Oh, hell, oh, blast, oh, damn, a thousand curses!" said Bingo.

Well, there isn't much you can say when a fellow's in the depths like that. The only thing I could suggest was that he should put some little trinket up the spout temporarily. His cigarette case, for instance, I said, and it was then that I learned that that cigarette case of his is not the solid gold we have always imagined. Tin, really. And except for the cigarette case, it appeared, the only trinket he had ever possessed was a diamond brooch which, being in funds at the moment as the result of a fortunate speculation at Catterick Bridge, he had bought Mrs. Bingo for a birthday present.

It all seemed pretty hopeless, accordingly, so I merely offered him my heartfelt sympathy and another snootful. And next morning he steamed off on the eleven-o'clock express, despair in his soul and in his pocket a notebook, four pencils, his return ticket, and about three pounds for tips and so on. And shortly before lunch on the following day he was alighting at Monte Carlo station.

I don't know if you remember a song some years ago that went "Ti-um-ti-um-ti-um-ti-um, ti-um-ti-um-ti-ay," and then, after a bit more of that, finished up:

> *"Ti-um-ti-um-ti-um-ti-um,*
> *The curse of an aching heart."*

You don't hear it much nowadays, but at one time you were extraordinarily apt to get it shot at you by basses at smoking concerts and entertainments in aid of the Church Organ Fund in the old village hall. They would pause for a moment after the *"um"* and take a breath that came up from their anklebones, and then:

> *"It's the curse of an a-ching heart."*

Most unpleasant, of course, the whole thing, and I wouldn't have mentioned it, only the phrase absolutely puts in a nutshell the way poor old Bingo felt during his first two days at Monte Carlo. He had an aching heart, and he cursed like billy-o. And I'm not surprised, poor chap, for he was suffering severe torments.

All day long, though it was like twisting the knife in the wound, he would wander through the Rooms, trying out that system of his on paper; and the more he tried it out, the more ironclad it revealed itself. Simply couldn't lose.

By bedtime on the second night he found that, if he had been playing in hundred-franc chips, he would have been no less than two hundred and fifty pounds ahead—just like that. In short, there was all that stuff—his for the picking up, as you might say—and he couldn't get it.

Garcia would have got it. Darnborough would have got it. So would Owers. But he couldn't. Simply, mark you, for lack of a trifling spot of initial capital which a fellow like Oofy Prosser could have slipped him and never felt it. Pretty bitter.

And then, on the third morning, as he sat glancing through the continental New York *Herald* over the breakfast table, he saw a news item which brought him up in his chair with a jerk, choking over his coffee.

Among recent arrivals at the Hotel Magnifique at Nice, it said, were their serene highnesses, the Prince and Princess of Graustark, His Majesty the ex-King of Ruritania, Lord Percy Poffin, the Countess of Goffin, Major General Sir Everard Slurk, K.V.O., and Mr. Prosser.

Well, of course, it might be some other brand of Prosser, but Bingo didn't think so. A hotel where serene highnesses were to be found was just the place for which a bally snob like Oofy would have made a beeline. He rushed to the telephone and was presently in communication with the concierge.

"Hullo? Yes?" said the concierge. "This is the Hotel Magnifique. Hall porter speaking."

"Dites-moi," said Bingo. "Esker-vous avez dans votre hotel un monsieur nommé Prosser?"

"Yes, sir. Quite correct. There is a Mr. Prosser staying in the hotel."

"Est-il un oiseau avec beaucoup de . . . Oh, hell, what's the French for 'pimples'?"

"The word you are trying to find is *bouton*," said the concierge. "Yes, sir, Mr. Prosser is liberally pimpled."

"Then put me through to his room," said Bingo. And pretty soon he heard a sleepy and familiar voice hullo-ing.

"Hullo, Oofy, old man," he cried. "This is Bingo Little."

"Oh, God!" said Oofy, and something in his manner warned Bingo that it would be well to proceed with snakiness and caution.

There were, he knew, two things which rendered Oofy Prosser a difficult proposition for the ear biter. In the first place, owing to his habit of mopping it up at late parties, he nearly always had a dyspeptic headache. In the second place, his position as the official moneyed man of the Drones Club had caused him to become shy and wary, like a bird that's been a good deal shot over. You can't touch a chap like that on the telephone at ten in the morning. It would, he perceived, if solid results were to be obtained, be necessary to sweeten Oofy.

"I just this minute saw in the paper that you were in these parts, Oofy, old man. A wonderful surprise it was. Gosh, I said. Golly, I said. Dear old Oofy, I said. Well, well, well!"

"Get on with it," said Oofy. "What do you want?"

"Why, to give you lunch, of course, old chap," said Bingo.

Yes, he had made the great decision. That money which he had been earmarking for tips must be diverted to another end. It might lead to his having to sneak out of the hotel at the conclusion of his visit with his face scarlet and his ears hanging down, but the risk had to be taken. Nothing venture, nothing have.

At the other end of the telephone he heard a sort of choking gasp.

"There must be something wrong with this wire," said Oofy. "It sounds just as if you were saying you want to give me lunch."

"So I am."

"*Give* me lunch?"

"That's right."

"What, pay the bill?"

"Yes."

There was a silence.

"I must send this to Ripley," said Oofy.

"Ripley?"

"The 'Believe-it-or-not' man."

"Oh?" said Bingo. He was not quite sure that he liked Oofy's attitude, but he remained sunny. "Well, where and when? What time? What place?"

"We may as well lunch here. Come fairly early, because I'm going to the races this afternoon."

"Right," said Bingo. "I'll be on the mat at one sharp."

And at one sharp there he was, his little all in his pocket. His emotions, he tells me, as he drove in on the Monte Carlo–Nice bus, were mixed. One moment, he was hoping that Oofy would have his usual dyspeptic headache, because that would blunt his appetite and enable him to save something out of the wreck; the next, he was reminding himself that an Oofy with dull, shooting pains about the temples would be less likely to come across. It was all very complex.

Well, as it turned out, Oofy's appetite was the reverse of blunted. The extraordinary position in which he found himself—guest and not host to a fellow member of the Drones—seemed to have put an edge on it. It is not too much to say that from the very outset he ate like a starving python. The light, casual way in which he spoke to the headwaiter about hothouse grapes and asparagus froze Bingo to the marrow. And when—from force of habit, no doubt—he called for the wine list and ordered a nice, dry champagne, it began to look to Bingo as if the bill for this binge was going to resemble something submitted to Congress by President Roosevelt in aid of the American farmer.

However, though once or twice—notably when Oofy started wading into the caviar—he had to clench his fists and summon up all his iron self-control, he did not on the whole repine. Each moment, as the feast proceeded, he could see his guest becoming more and more mellow. It seemed merely a question of time before the milk of human kindness would come gushing out of him as if the dam had burst. Feeling that a cigar and liqueur ought just about to do the trick, Bingo ordered them; and Oofy, unbuttoning the last three buttons of his waistcoat, leaned back in his chair.

"Well," said Oofy, beaming, "this will certainly be something to tell my grandchildren. I mean, that I once lunched with a member of the Drones Club and didn't get stuck with the bill. Listen, Bingo, I'd like to do something for you in return."

Bingo felt like some great actor who has received his cue. He leaned forward and relighted Oofy's cigar with a loving hand. He also flicked a speck of dust off his coat sleeve.

"And what I'm going to do is this. I'm going to give you a tip. On these races this afternoon. Back Spotted Dog for the Prix Honoré Sauvan. A sure winner."

"Thanks, Oofy, old man," said Bingo. "That's splendid news. If you will lend me a tenner, then, Oofy, old boy, I'll put it on."

"What do you want me to lend you a tenner for?"

"Because, after I've paid the lunch bill, Oofy, old chap, I shan't have any money."

"You won't need any money," said Oofy, and Bingo wondered how many more people were going to make this blithering remark to him. "My London bookie is staying here. He will accommodate you in credit, seeing that you are a friend of mine."

"But doesn't it seem a pity to bother him with a lot of extra book-keeping, Oofy, old fellow?" said Bingo, flicking another speck of dust off Oofy's other coat sleeve. "Much better if you would just lend me a tenner."

"Joking aside," said Oofy, "I think I'll have another kümmel."

And it was at this moment, when the conversation appeared to have reached a deadlock, and there seemed no hope of finding a formula, that a stout, benevolent-looking man approached their table. From the fact that he and Oofy at once began to talk odds and figures, Bingo deduced that this must be the bookie from London.

"And my friend, Mr. Little," said Oofy, in conclusion, "wants a tenner on Spotted Dog for the Prix Honoré Sauvan."

And Bingo was just about to shake his head and say that he didn't think his wife would like him to bet, when the glorious Riviera sunshine, streaming in through the window by which they sat, lit up Oofy's face and he saw that it was a perfect mass of spots. A moment later, he perceived that the bookie had a pink spot on his nose and the waiter, who was now bringing the bill, a bountifully spotted forehead. A thrill shot through him. These things, he knew, are sent to us for a purpose.

"Right ho," he said. "A tenner at the current odds."

And then they all went off to the races. The Prix Honoré Sauvan was the three o'clock. A horse called Lilium won it. Kerry second, Maubourget third, Ironside fourth, Irresistible fifth, Sweet and Lovely sixth, Spotted Dog seventh. Seven ran. So there was Bingo owing ten quid to this bookie and not a chance of a happy ending unless the fellow would consent to let the settlement stand over for a bit.

So he buttonholed the bookie and suggested this, and the bookie said, certainly.

"Certainly," said the bookie. He put his hand on Bingo's shoulder and patted it. "I like you, Mr. Little," he said.

"Do you?" said Bingo, putting his hand on the bookie's and patting that. "Do you, old pal?"

"I do, indeed," said the bookie. "You remind me of my little boy Percy, who took the knock the year Worcester Sauce won the Jubilee Handicap. Bronchial trouble. So when you ask me to wait for my money, I say, of course I'll wait for my money. Suppose we say till next Friday?"

Bingo blenched a bit. The period he had had in mind had been something more along the lines of a year or eighteen months.

"Well," he said, "I'll try to brass up then . . . but you know how it is . . . you mustn't be disappointed if . . . this world-wide money shortage . . . circumstances over which I have no control . . ."

"You think you may not be able to settle?"

"I'm a bit doubtful."

The bookie pursed his lips.

"I do hope you will," he said, "and I'll tell you why. It's silly to be superstitious, I know, but I can't help remembering that every single bloke that's ever done me down for money has had a nasty accident occur to him. Time after time I've seen it happen."

"Have you?" said Bingo, beginning to exhibit symptoms of bronchial trouble like the late Percy.

"I have, indeed," said the bookie. "Time after time after time. It almost seems like some kind of fate. Only the other day there was a fellow with a ginger mustache named Watherspoon. Owed me fifty for Plumpton and pleaded the gaming act. And would you believe it, less than a week later he was found unconscious in the street—must have got into some unpleasantness of some kind—and had to have six stitches."

"Six!"

"Seven. I was forgetting the one over his left eye. Makes you think, that sort of thing does. Hoy, Erbut," he called.

A frightful plug-ugly appeared from nowhere, as if he had been a djin and the bookie had rubbed a lamp.

"Erbut," said the bookie, "I want you to meet Mr. Little, Erbut. Take a good look at him. You'll remember him again?"

The plug-ugly drank Bingo in. His eye was cold and gray, like a parrot's.

"Yus," he said. "Yus, I won't forget him."

"Good," said the bookie. "That will be all, Erbut. Then about that money, Mr. Little, we'll say Friday without fail, shall we?"

Bingo tottered away and sought out Oofy.

"Oofy, old man," he said, "it is within your power to save a human life."

"Well, I'm jolly well not going to," said Oofy, who had now got one of his dyspeptic headaches. "The more human lives that aren't saved, the better I shall like it. I loathe the human race. Any time it wants to stand in front of the Cornish Express, it will be all right with me."

"If I don't get a tenner by Friday, a fearful bounder named Erbut is going to beat me into a pulp."

"Good," said Oofy, brightening a little. "Capital. Splendid. That's fine."

Bingo then caught the bus back to Monte Carlo.

That night, he dressed for dinner moodily. He was unable to discern the bluebird. In three months from now he would be getting another quarter's allowance, but a fat lot of good that would be. In far less than three months, if he had read aright the message in Erbut's eyes, he would be in some hospital or nursing home with stitches all over him. How many stitches, time alone could tell. He fell to musing on Watherspoon. Was it, he wondered, to be his fate to lower that ginger-mustached man's melancholy record?

His thoughts were still busy with the stitch outlook, when the telephone rang.

"Hullo," said a female voice. "Is that Rosie?"

"No," said Bingo, and might have added that the future was not, either. "I'm Mr. Little."

"Oh, Mr. Little, this is Dora Spurgeon. Can I speak to Rosie?"

"She isn't here."

"Well, when she comes in, will you tell her that I'm just off to Corsica in some people's yacht. We leave in an hour, so I shan't have time to come over and see her, so will you give her my love and tell her I am sending the brooch back."

"Brooch?"

"She lent me her brooch when I left London. I think it's the one you gave her on her birthday. She told me to take special care of it, and I don't feel it's safe having it with me in Corsica—so many brigands about—so I am sending it by registered post to the Hôtel de Paris. Good-bye, Mr. Little. I must rush."

Bingo hung up the receiver and sat down on the bed to think this over. Up to a point, of course, the situation was clear. Dora Spurgeon, a muddleheaded poop if ever there was one, obviously supposed that Mrs. Bingo had accompanied him to Monte Carlo. No doubt Mrs. Bingo had gone to some pains in her telephone call to make it thoroughly clear that she was remaining in London, but it was no good trying to drive things into a head like Dora Spurgeon's by means of the spoken word. You needed a hammer. The result was that on the morrow that brooch which he had given Mrs. Bingo would arrive at the hotel.

So far, as I say, Bingo found nothing to perplex him. But what he could not make up his mind about was this: should he, after he had pawned the brooch, send the proceeds straight to that bookie? Or should he take the money and go and have a whack at the Casino?

Far into the silent night he pondered without being able to reach a decision, but next morning everything seemed to clarify, as is so often the way after a night's sleep, and he wondered how he could ever have been in doubt. Of course he must have a whack at the Casino.

The catch about sending the money to the bookie was that, while this policy would remove from his future the dark shadow of Erbut, it would not make for contentment and happiness in the home. When Mrs. Bingo discovered that he had shoved her brooch up the spout in order to pay a racing debt, friction would ensue. He unquestionably had a moral claim on the brooch—bought with his hard-earned money —the thing, you might say, was really his to do what he liked with— nevertheless, something told him that friction would ensue.

By going and playing his system he would avoid all unpleasantness. It was simply a matter of strolling into the Rooms and taking the stuff away.

And, as it turned out, he couldn't have paid off Erbut's bookie, anyway, because the local popshop would only give him a fiver on the brooch. He pleaded passionately for more, but the cove behind the counter was adamant. So, taking the fiver, he lunched sparingly at a pub up the hill, and shortly after two o'clock was in the arena, doing his stuff.

I have never been able quite to get the hang of that system of Bingo's. He has explained it to me a dozen times, but it remains vague. However, the basis of it, the thing that made it so frightfully ingenious, was that instead of doubling your stake when you lost, as in all these other systems, you doubled it when you won. It involved a lot of fancywork with a pencil and a bit of paper, because you had to write down figures and add figures and scratch figures out, but that, I gathered, was the nub of the thing—you doubled up when you won, thus increasing your profits by leaps and bounds and making the authorities look pretty sick.

The only snag about it was that in order to do this you first had to win, which Bingo didn't.

I don't suppose there is anything—not even Oofy Prosser—that has a nastier disposition than the wheel at Monte Carlo. It seems to take a sinister pleasure in doing down the common people. You can play mentally by the hour and never get a losing spin, but once you put real money up the whole aspect of things alters. Poor old Bingo hadn't been able to put a foot wrong so long as he stuck to paper punting, but he now found himself in the soup from the start.

There he stood, straining like a greyhound at the leash, waiting for his chance of doubling up, only to see all his little capital raked in except one solitary hundred-franc chip. And when with a weary gesture he bunged this on black, up came zero and it was swept away.

And scarcely had he passed through this grueling spiritual experience, when a voice behind him said, "Oh, there you are!" and, turning, he found himself face to face with Mrs. Bingo.

He stood gaping at her, his heart bounding about inside him like an adagio dancer with nettle rash. For an instant, he tells me, he was under the impression that this was no flesh and blood creature that stood before him, but a phantasm. He thought that she must have been run over by a bus or something in London, and that this was her specter looking in to report, as specters do.

"You!" he said, like someone in a play.

"I've just arrived," said Mrs. Bingo, very merry and bright.

"I—I didn't know you were coming."

"I thought I would surprise you," said Mrs. Bingo, still bubbling over with joyous animation. "You see, what happened was that I was talking to Millie Pringle about my book, and she said that it was no use getting local color about the Rooms, because a man like Lord Peter Shipbourne would never go to the Rooms—he would do all his playing at the Sporting Club. And I was just going to wire you to go there, when Mrs. Carrie Melrose Bopp trod on a bananaskin in the street and sprained her ankle, and the luncheon was postponed, so there was nothing to prevent me coming over, so I came. Oh, Bingo darling, isn't this jolly!"

Bingo quivered from cravat to socks. The adjective "jolly" was not the one he would have selected. And it was at this point that Mrs. Bingo appeared to observe for the first time that her loved one was looking like a corpse that has been left out in the rain for a day or two.

"Bingo!" she cried. "What's the matter?"

"Nothing," said Bingo. "Nothing. Matter? How do you mean?"

"You look . . ." A wifely suspicion shot through Mrs. Bingo. She eyed him narrowly. "You haven't been gambling?"

"No, no," said Bingo. He is a fellow who is rather exact in his speech, and the word "gambling," to his mind, implied that a chap had a chance of winning. All that he had done, he felt, had been to take his little bit of money and give it to the administration. You couldn't describe that as gambling. More like making a donation to a charity. "No, no," he said. "Rather not."

"I'm so glad. Oh, by the way, I found a letter from Dora Spurgeon at the hotel. She said she was sending my brooch. I suppose it will arrive this afternoon."

Bingo's gallant spirit was broken. It seemed to him that this was the end. It was all over, he felt, except the composition of the speech in which he must confess everything. And he was just turning over in his mind a few opening remarks, beginning with the words "Listen, darling," when his eye fell on the table, and there on black was a pile of chips, no less than three thousand, two hundred francs worth in all—or, looking at it from another angle, about forty quid. And as he gazed at them, wondering which of the lucky stiffs seated round the board had got ahead of the game to that extent, the croupier at the bottom of the table caught his eye and smirked congratulatingly, as croupiers do when somebody has won a parcel and they think that there is going to be something in it for them in the way of largess.

And Bingo, tottering on his base, suddenly realized that this piled-up wealth belonged to him. It was the increment accruing from that last hundred francs of his.

What he had forgotten, you see, was that though, when zero turns up, those who have betted on numbers, columns and what not get it in the neck, stakes on the even chances aren't scooped up—they are what is called put in prison. I mean, they just withdraw into the background for the moment, awaiting the result of the next spin. And, if that wins, out they come again.

Bingo's hundred francs had been on black, so zero had put it in prison. And then, presumably, black must have turned up, getting it out again. And, as he hadn't taken it off, it had of course stayed on black. And then, while he was immersed in conversation with Mrs. Bingo about brooches, the wheel, from being a sort of mechanical Oofy Prosser, had suddenly turned into a Santa Claus. Seven more times it had come up black, putting Bingo in the position in which that system of his ought to have put him—viz. of doubling up when he won. And the result, as I say, was that the loot now amounted to the colossal sum of forty quid, more than double what he required in order to be able to pay off all his obligations and look the world in the eye again.

The relief was so terrific that Bingo tells me he came within a toucher of swooning. And it was only as he was about to snatch the stuff up and trouser it and live happily ever after—he had, indeed, actually poised himself for the spring—that he suddenly saw that there was a catch. To wit, that if he did, all must be discovered. Mrs. Bingo would know that he had been gambling; she would speedily ascertain the source whence had proceeded the money he had been gambling with, and the home, if not actually wrecked, would unquestionably become about as hot for him as the inside of a baked potato.

And yet, if he left the doubloons where they were, the next spin might see them all go down the drain.

I expect you know the expression "A man's crossroads." Those were what Bingo was at, at this juncture.

There seemed just one hope—to make a face at the croupier and do it with such consummate skill that the other would see that he wanted those thirty-two hundred francs taken off the board and put on one side till he was at liberty to come and collect. So he threw his whole soul into a face, and the croupier nodded intelligently and left the money on. Bingo, he saw, was signaling to him to let the works ride for another spin, and he admired his sporting spirit. He said something to the other croupier in an undertone—no doubt "Quel homme!" or "Epatant!" or something of that kind.

And the wheel, which now appeared definitely to have accepted the role of Bingo's rich uncle from Australia, fetched up another black.

Mrs. Bingo was studying the gamesters. She didn't seem to think much of them.

"What dreadful faces these people have," she said.

Bingo did not reply. His own face at this moment was nothing to write home about, resembling more than anything else that of an anxious fiend in hell. He was watching the wheel revolve.

It came up black again, bringing his total to twelve thousand eight hundred.

And now at last it seemed that his tortured spirit was to be at rest. The croupier, having shot another smirk in his direction, was leaning forward to the pile of chips and had started scooping. Yes, all was well. At the eleventh hour the silly ass had divined the message of that face of his and was doing the needful.

Bingo drew a deep, shuddering breath. He felt like one who has passed through the furnace and, though a bit charred in spots, can once more take up the burden of life with an easy mind. Twelve thousand eight hundred francs . . . Gosh! It was over a hundred and fifty quid, more than he had ever possessed at one time since the Christmas, three years ago, when his Uncle Wilberforce had come over all Dickensy as the result of lemon punch and had given him a check on which next day he had vainly tried to stop payment. There was a frowst in the Rooms which you could have cut with a knife, but he drew it into his lungs as if it had been the finest ozone. Birds seemed to be twittering from the ceiling and soft music playing everywhere.

And then the world went to pieces again. The wheel had begun to spin, and there on black lay twelve thousand francs. The croupier, though he had scooped, hadn't scooped enough. All he had done was to remove from the board the eight hundred. On that last coup, you see, Bingo had come up against the limit. You can't have more than twelve thousand on an even chance.

And, of course, eight hundred francs was no use to him whatever. It would enable him to pay off Erbut and the bookie, but what of the brooch?

It was at this point that he was aware that Mrs. Bingo was saying something to him. He came slowly out of his trance with a where-am-I look.

"Eh?" he said.

"I said, 'Don't you think so?' "

"Think so?"

"I was saying that it didn't seem much good wasting any more time in here. Millie Pringle was quite right. Lord Peter Shipbourne would never dream of coming to a place like this. He would never stand the smell, for one thing. I have drawn him as a most fastidious man. So shall I go on to the Sporting Club . . . Bingo?"

Bingo was watching the wheel, tense and rigid. He was tense and rigid, I mean, not the wheel. The wheel was spinning.

"Bingo!"

"Hullo?"

"Shall I go on to the Sporting Club and pay our entrance fees?"

A sudden bright light came into Bingo's face, rendering it almost beautiful. His brow was bedewed with perspiration and he rather thought his hair had turned snowy white, but the map was shining like the sun at noon, and he beamed as he had seldom beamed before.

For the returns were in. The wheel had stopped. And once again black had come up, and even now the croupier was removing twelve thousand francs from the pile and adding them to the eight hundred before him.

"Yes, do," said Bingo. "Do. Yes, do. That'll be fine. Splendid. I think I'll just stick on here for a minute or two. I like watching these weird blokes. But you go on and I'll join you."

Twenty minutes later he did so. He walked into the Sporting Club a little stiffly, for there were forty-eight thousand francs distributed about his person, some of it in his pockets, some of it in his socks, and quite a good deal tucked inside his shirt. He did not see Mrs. Bingo at first; then he caught sight of her sitting over in the bar with a bottle of vittel in front of her.

"What ho, what ho," he said, lumbering up.

Then he paused, for it seemed to him that her manner was strange. Her face was sad and set, her eyes dull. She gave him an odd look, and an appalling suspicion struck him amidships. Could it be, he asked himself, was it possible that somehow, by some mysterious wifely intuition . . .

"There you are," he said. He sat down beside her, hoping that he wasn't going to crackle. "Er—how's everything?" He paused. She was still looking strange. "I've got that brooch," he said.

"Oh?"

"Yes. I—er—thought you might like to have it, so I—ah—nipped out and got it."

"I'm glad it arrived safely . . . Bingo!" said Mrs. Bingo.

She was staring somberly before her. Bingo's apprehension increased. He now definitely feared the worst. It was as if he could feel the soup plashing about his ankles. He took her hand in his and pressed it. It might, he felt, help. You never knew.

"Bingo," said Mrs. Bingo, "we always tell each other everything, don't we?"

"Do we? Oh, yes. Yes."

"Because when we got married, we decided that that was the only way. I remember your saying so on the honeymoon."

"Yes," said Bingo, licking his lips and marveling at the depths of fatheadedness to which men can sink on their honeymoons.

"I'd hate to feel that you were concealing anything from me. It would make me wretched."

"Yes," said Bingo.

"So if you had been gambling, you would tell me, wouldn't you?"

Bingo drew a deep breath. It made him crackle all over, but he couldn't help that. He needed air. Besides, what did it matter now if he crackled like a forest fire? He threw his mind back to those opening sentences which he had composed.

"Listen, darling," he began.

"So I must tell you," said Mrs. Bingo. "I've just made the most dreadful fool of myself. When I came in here, I went over to that table there to watch the play, and suddenly something came over me . . ."

Bingo uttered a snort which rang through the Sporting Club like a bugle.

"You didn't have a pop?"

"I lost over two hundred pounds in ten minutes. Oh, Bingo, can you ever forgive me?"

Bingo had still got hold of her hand, for he had been relying on the soothing effects of hanging on to it during the remarks which he had outlined. He squeezed it lovingly. Not immediately, however, because for perhaps half a minute he had felt so boneless that he could not have squeezed a grape.

"There, there!" he said.

"Oh, Bingo!"

"There, there, there!"

"You do forgive me?"

"Of course. Of course."

"Oh, Bingo," cried Mrs. Bingo, her eyes like twin stars, and damp ones at that, "there's nobody like you in the world."

"Would you say that?"

"You remind me of Sir Galahad. Most husbands——"

"Ah," said Bingo, "but I understand these sudden impulses. I don't have them myself, but I understand them. Not another word. Good gosh, what's a couple of hundred quid, if it gave you a moment's pleasure?"

His emotions now almost overpowered him, so strenuously did they call for an outlet. He wanted to shout, but he couldn't shout—the croupiers would object. He wanted to give three cheers, but he couldn't give three cheers—the barman wouldn't like it. He wanted to sing, but he couldn't sing—the customers would complain.

His eye fell on the bottle of vittel.

"Ah!" said Bingo. "Darling!"

"Yes, darling?"

"Watch, darling," said Bingo. "I place the bottle so. Then, maintaining a perfect equilibrium . . ."

✿ *Uncle Fred Flits By*

IN ORDER that they might enjoy their after-luncheon coffee in peace, the Crumpet had taken the guest whom he was entertaining at the Drones Club to the smaller and less frequented of the two smoking rooms. In the other, he explained, though the conversation always touched an exceptionally high level of brilliance, there was apt to be a good deal of sugar thrown about.

The guest said he understood.

"Young blood, eh?"

"That's right. Young blood."

"And animal spirits."

"And animal, as you say, spirits," agreed the Crumpet. "We get a fairish amount of those here."

"The complaint, however, is not, I observe, universal."

"Eh."

The other drew his host's attention to the doorway, where a young man in form-fitting tweeds had just appeared. The aspect of this young man was haggard. His eyes glared wildly and he sucked at an empty cigarette holder. If he had a mind, there was something on it. When the Crumpet called to him to come and join the party, he merely shook his head in a distraught sort of way and disappeared, looking like a character out of a Greek tragedy pursued by the Fates.

The Crumpet sighed. "Poor old Pongo!"

"Pongo?"

"That was Pongo Twistleton. He's all broken up about his Uncle Fred."

"Dead?"

"No such luck. Coming up to London again tomorrow. Pongo had a wire this morning."

"And that upsets him?"

"Naturally. After what happened last time."

"What was that?"

"Ah!" said the Crumpet.

"What happened last time?"

"You may well ask."

"I do ask."

"Ah!" said the Crumpet.

Poor old Pongo (said the Crumpet) has often discussed his Uncle Fred with me, and if there weren't tears in his eyes when he did so, I don't know a tear in the eye when I see one. In round numbers the Earl of Ickenham, of Ickenham Hall, Ickenham, Hants, he lives in the country most of the year, but from time to time has a nasty way of slipping his collar and getting loose and descending upon Pongo at his flat in the Albany. And every time he does so, the unhappy young blighter is subjected to some soul-testing experience. Because the trouble with this uncle is that, though sixty if a day, he becomes on arriving in the metropolis as young as he feels—which is, apparently, a youngish twenty-two. I don't know if you happen to know what the word "excesses" means, but those are what Pongo's Uncle Fred from the country, when in London, invariably commits.

It wouldn't so much matter, mind you, if he would confine his activities to the club premises. We're pretty broad-minded here, and if you stop short of smashing the piano, there isn't much that you can do at the Drones that will cause the raised eyebrow and the sharp intake of breath. The snag is that he will insist on lugging Pongo out in the open and there, right in the public eye, proceeding to step high, wide and plentiful.

So when, on the occasion to which I allude, he stood pink and genial on Pongo's hearthrug, bulging with Pongo's lunch and wreathed in the smoke of one of Pongo's cigars, and said: "And now, my boy, for a pleasant and instructive afternoon," you will readily understand why the unfortunate young clam gazed at him as he would have gazed at two-penn'orth of dynamite, had he discovered it lighting up in his presence.

"A what?" he said, giving at the knees and paling beneath the tan a bit.

"A pleasant and instructive afternoon," repeated Lord Ickenham, rolling the words round his tongue. "I propose that you place yourself in my hands and leave the program entirely to me."

Now, owing to Pongo's circumstances being such as to necessitate his getting into the aged relative's ribs at intervals and shaking him down for an occasional much-needed tenner or what not, he isn't in a position to use the iron hand with the old buster. But at these words he displayed a manly firmness.

"You aren't going to get me to the dog races again."

"No, no."

"You remember what happened last June."

"Quite," said Lord Ickenham, "quite. Though I still think that a wiser magistrate would have been content with a mere reprimand."

"And I won't—"

"Certainly not. Nothing of that kind at all. What I propose to do this afternoon is to take you to visit the home of your ancestors."

Pongo did not get this.

"I thought Ickenham was the home of my ancestors."

"It is one of the homes of your ancestors. They also resided rather nearer the heart of things, at a place called Mitching Hill."

"Down in the suburbs, do you mean?"

"The neighborhood is now suburban, true. It is many years since the meadows where I sported as a child were sold and cut up into building lots. But when I was a boy Mitching Hill was open country. It was a vast, rolling estate belonging to your great-uncle, Marmaduke, a man with whiskers of a nature which you with your pure mind would scarcely credit, and I have long felt a sentimental urge to see what the hell the old place looks like now. Perfectly foul, I expect. Still, I think we should make the pious pilgrimage."

Pongo absolutely-ed heartily. He was all for the scheme. A great weight seemed to have rolled off his mind. The way he looked at it was that even an uncle within a short jump of the looney bin couldn't very well get into much trouble in a suburb. I mean, you know what suburbs are. They don't, as it were, offer the scope. One follows his reasoning, of course.

"Fine!" he said. "Splendid! Topping!"

"Then put on your hat and rompers, my boy," said Lord Ickenham, "and let us be off. I fancy one gets there by omnibuses and things."

Well, Pongo hadn't expected much in the way of mental uplift from the sight of Mitching Hill, and he didn't get it. Alighting from the bus, he tells me, you found yourself in the middle of rows and rows of semi-detached villas, all looking exactly alike, and you went on and you came to more semidetached villas, and those all looked exactly alike, too. Nevertheless, he did not repine. It was one of those early spring days which suddenly change to midwinter and he had come out without his overcoat, and it looked like rain and he hadn't an umbrella, but despite this his mood was one of sober ecstasy. The hours were passing and his uncle had not yet made a goat of himself. At the Dog Races the other had been in the hands of the constabulary in the first ten minutes.

It began to seem to Pongo that with any luck he might be able to keep the old blister pottering harmlessly about here till nightfall, when he could shoot a bit of dinner into him and put him to bed. And as Lord Ickenham had specifically stated that his wife, Pongo's Aunt Jane, had expressed her intention of scalping him with a blunt knife if he wasn't back at the Hall by lunchtime on the morrow, it really looked as if he might get through this visit without perpetrating a single major outrage on the public weal. It is rather interesting to note that as he thought this Pongo smiled, because it was the last time he smiled that day.

All this while, I should mention, Lord Ickenham had been stopping at intervals like a pointing dog and saying that it must have been just about here that he plugged the gardener in the trousers seat with his bow and arrow and that over there he had been sick after his first cigar, and he now paused in front of a villa which for some unknown reason called itself The Cedars. His face was tender and wistful.

"On this very spot, if I am not mistaken," he said, heaving a bit of a sigh, "on this very spot, fifty years ago come Lammas Eve, I . . . Oh, blast it!"

The concluding remark had been caused by the fact that the rain, which had held off until now, suddenly began to buzz down like a shower bath. With no further words, they leaped into the porch of the villa and there took shelter, exchanging glances with a gray parrot which hung in a cage in the window.

Not that you could really call it shelter. They were protected from above all right, but the moisture was now falling with a sort of swivel action, whipping in through the sides of the porch and tickling them up properly. And it was just after Pongo had turned up his collar and was huddling against the door that the door gave way. From the fact that a female of general-servant aspect was standing there he gathered that his uncle must have rung the bell.

This female wore a long mackintosh, and Lord Ickenham beamed upon her with a fairish spot of suavity.

"Good afternoon," he said.

The female said good afternoon.

"The Cedars?"

The female said yes, it was The Cedars.

"Are the old folks at home?"

The female said there was nobody at home.

"Ah? Well, never mind. I have come," said Lord Ickenham, edging in, "to clip the parrot's claws. My assistant, Mr. Walkinshaw, who applies the anesthetic," he added, indicating Pongo with a gesture.

"Are you from the bird shop?"

"A very happy guess."

"Nobody told me you were coming."

"They keep things from you, do they?" said Lord Ickenham sympathetically. "Too bad."

Continuing to edge, he had got into the parlor by now, Pongo following in a sort of dream and the female following Pongo.

"Well, I suppose it's all right," she said. "I was just going out. It's my afternoon."

"Go out," said Lord Ickenham cordially. "By all means go out. We will leave everything in order."

And presently the female, though still a bit on the dubious side, pushed off, and Lord Ickenham lit the gas fire and drew a chair up.

"So here we are, my boy," he said. "A little tact, a little address, and here we are, snug and cozy and not catching our deaths of cold. You'll never go far wrong if you leave things to me."

"But, dash it, we can't stop here," said Pongo.

Lord Ickenham raised his eyebrows.

"Not stop here? Are you suggesting that we go out into that rain? My dear lad, you are not aware of the grave issues involved. This morning, as I was leaving home, I had a rather painful disagreement with your aunt. She said the weather was treacherous and wished me to take my woolly muffler. I replied that the weather was not treacherous and that I would be dashed if I took my woolly muffler. Eventually, by the exercise of an iron will, I had my way, and I ask you, my dear boy, to envisage what will happen if I return with a cold in the head. I shall sink to the level of a fifth-class power. Next time I came to London, it would be with a liver pad and a respirator. No! I shall remain here, toasting my toes at this really excellent fire. I had no idea that a gas fire radiated such warmth. I feel all in a glow."

So did Pongo. His brow was wet with honest sweat. He is reading for the Bar, and while he would be the first to admit that he hasn't yet got a complete toehold on the Law of Great Britain he had a sort of notion that oiling into a perfect stranger's semidetached villa on the pretext of pruning the parrot was a tort or misdemeanor, if not actual barratry or socage in fief or something like that. And apart from the legal aspect of the matter there was the embarrassment of the thing. Nobody is more of a whale on correctness and not doing what's not done than Pongo, and the situation in which he now found himself caused him to chew the lower lip and, as I say, perspire a goodish deal.

"But suppose the blighter who owns this ghastly house comes back?" he asked. "Talking of envisaging things, try that one over on your pianola."

And, sure enough, as he spoke, the front doorbell rang.

"There!" said Pongo.

"Don't say 'There!', my boy," said Lord Ickenham reprovingly. "It's the sort of thing your aunt says. I see no reason for alarm. Obviously this is some casual caller. A ratepayer would have used his latchkey. Glance cautiously out of the window and see if you can see anybody."

"It's a pink chap," said Pongo, having done so.

"How pink?"

"Pretty pink."

"Well, there you are, then. I told you so. It can't be the big chief. The sort of fellows who own houses like this are pale and sallow, owing to working in offices all day. Go and see what he wants."

"You go and see what he wants."

"We'll both go and see what he wants," said Lord Ickenham.

So they went and opened the front door, and there, as Pongo had said, was a pink chap. A small young pink chap, a bit moist about the shoulder blades.

"Pardon me," said this pink chap, "is Mr. Roddis in?"

"No," said Pongo.

"Yes," said Lord Ickenham. "Don't be silly, Douglas—of course I'm in. I am Mr. Roddis," he said to the pink chap. "This, such as he is, is my son Douglas. And you?"

"Name of Robinson."

"What about it?"

"My name's Robinson."

"Oh, *your* name's Robinson? Now we've got it straight. Delighted to see you, Mr. Robinson. Come right in and take your boots off."

They all trickled back to the parlor, Lord Ickenham pointing out objects of interest by the wayside to the chap, Pongo gulping for air a bit and trying to get himself abreast of this new twist in the scenario. His heart was becoming more and more bowed down with weight of woe. He hadn't liked being Mr. Walkinshaw, the anesthetist, and he didn't like it any better being Roddis Junior. In brief, he feared the worst. It was only too plain to him by now that his uncle had got it thoroughly up his nose and had settled down to one of his big afternoons, and he was asking himself, as he had so often asked himself before, what would the harvest be?

Arrived in the parlor, the pink chap proceeded to stand on one leg and look coy.

"Is Julia here?" he asked, simpering a bit, Pongo says.

"Is she?" said Lord Ickenham to Pongo.

"No," said Pongo.

"No," said Lord Ickenham.

"She wired me she was coming here today."

"Ah, then we shall have a bridge four."

The pink chap stood on the other leg.

"I don't suppose you've ever met Julia. Bit of trouble in the family, she gave me to understand."

"It is often the way."

"The Julia I mean is your niece Julia Parker. Or, rather, your wife's niece Julia Parker."

"Any niece of my wife is a niece of mine," said Lord Ickenham heartily. "We share and share alike."

"Julia and I want to get married."

"Well, go ahead."

"But they won't let us."

"Who won't?"

"Her mother and father. And Uncle Charlie Parker and Uncle Henry Parker and the rest of them. They don't think I'm good enough."

"The morality of the modern young man is notoriously lax."

"Class enough, I mean. They're a haughty lot."

"What makes them haughty? Are they earls?"

"No, they aren't earls."

"Then why the devil," said Lord Ickenham warmly, "are they haughty? Only earls have a right to be haughty. Earls are hot stuff. When you get an earl, you've got something."

"Besides, we've had words. Me and her father. One thing led to another, and in the end I called him a perishing old— Coo!" said the pink chap, breaking off suddenly.

He had been standing by the window, and he now leaped lissomely into the middle of the room, causing Pongo, whose nervous system was by this time definitely down among the wines and spirits and who hadn't been expecting this *adagio* stuff, to bite his tongue with some severity.

"They're on the doorstep! Julia and her mother and father. I didn't know they were all coming."

"You do not wish to meet them?"

"No, I don't!"

"Then duck behind the settee, Mr. Robinson," said Lord Ickenham, and the pink chap, weighing the advice and finding it good, did so. And as he disappeared the doorbell rang.

Once more, Lord Ickenham led Pongo out into the hall.

"I say!" said Pongo, and a close observer might have noted that he was quivering like an aspen.

"Say on, my dear boy."

"I mean to say, what?"

"What?"

"You aren't going to let these bounders in, are you?"

"Certainly," said Lord Ickenham. "We Roddises keep open house. And as they are presumably aware that Mr. Roddis has no son, I think we had better return to the old layout. You are the local vet, my boy, come to minister to my parrot. When I return, I should like to find you by the cage, staring at the bird in a scientific manner. Tap your teeth from time to time with a pencil and try to smell of iodoform. It will help to add conviction."

So Pongo shifted back to the parrot's cage and stared so earnestly that it was only when a voice said "Well!" that he became aware that there was anybody in the room. Turning, he perceived that Hampshire's leading curse had come back, bringing the gang.

It consisted of a stern, thin, middle-aged woman, a middle-aged man and a girl.

You can generally accept Pongo's estimate of girls, and when he says that this one was a pippin one knows that he uses the term in its most exact sense. She was about nineteen, he thinks, and she wore a black beret, a dark-green leather coat, a shortish tweed skirt, silk stockings and high-heeled shoes. Her eyes were large and lustrous and her face like a dewy rosebud at daybreak on a June morning. So Pongo tells me. Not that I suppose he has ever seen a rosebud at daybreak on a June morning, because it's generally as much as you can do to lug him out of bed in time for nine-thirty breakfast. Still, one gets the idea.

"Well," said the woman, "you don't know who I am, I'll be bound. I'm Laura's sister Connie. This is Claude, my husband. And this is my daughter Julia. Is Laura in?"

"I regret to say, no," said Lord Ickenham.

The woman was looking at him as if he didn't come up to her specifications.

"I thought you were younger," she said.

"Younger than what?" said Lord Ickenham.

"Younger than you are."

"You can't be younger than you are, worse luck," said Lord Ickenham. "Still, one does one's best, and I am bound to say that of recent years I have made a pretty good go of it."

The woman caught sight of Pongo, and he didn't seem to please her, either.

"Who's that?"

"The local vet, clustering round my parrot."

"I can't talk in front of him."

"It is quite all right," Lord Ickenham assured her. "The poor fellow is stone deaf."

And with an imperious gesture at Pongo, as much as to bid him stare less at girls and more at parrots, he got the company seated.

"Now, then," he said.

There was silence for a moment, then a sort of muffled sob, which Pongo thinks proceeded from the girl. He couldn't see, of course, because his back was turned and he was looking at the parrot, which looked back at him—most offensively, he says, as parrots will, using one eye only for the purpose. It also asked him to have a nut.

The woman came into action again.

"Although," she said, "Laura never did me the honor to invite me to her wedding, for which reason I have not communicated with her for five years, necessity compels me to cross her threshold today. There comes a time when differences must be forgotten and relatives must stand shoulder to shoulder."

"I see what you mean," said Lord Ickenham. "Like the boys of the old brigade."

"What I say is, let bygones be bygones. I would not have intruded on you, but needs must. I disregard the past and appeal to your sense of pity."

The thing began to look to Pongo like a touch, and he is convinced that the parrot thought so, too, for it winked and cleared its throat. But they were both wrong. The woman went on.

"I want you and Laura to take Julia into your home for a week or so, until I can make other arrangements for her. Julia is studying the piano, and she sits for her examination in two weeks' time, so until then she must remain in London. The trouble is, she has fallen in love. Or thinks she has."

"I know I have," said Julia.

Her voice was so attractive that Pongo was compelled to slew round and take another look at her. Her eyes, he says, were shining like twin stars and there was a sort of Soul's Awakening expression on her face, and what the dickens there was in a pink chap like the pink chap, who even as pink chaps go wasn't much of a pink chap, to

make her look like that, was frankly, Pongo says, more than he could
understand. The thing baffled him. He sought in vain for a solution.

"Yesterday, Claude and I arrived in London from our Bexhill
home to give Julia a pleasant surprise. We stayed, naturally, in the
boardinghouse where she has been living for the past six weeks.
And what do you think we discovered?"

"Insects."

"Not insects. A letter. From a young man. I found to my horror
that a young man of whom I knew nothing was arranging to marry
my daughter. I sent for him immediately, and found him to be quite
impossible. He jellies eels!"

"Does what?"

"He is an assistant at a jellied eel shop."

"But surely," said Lord Ickenham, "that speaks well for him. The
capacity to jelly an eel seems to me to argue intelligence of a high
order. It isn't everybody who can do it, by any means. I know if
someone came to me and said 'Jelly this eel!' I should be nonplused.
And so, or I am very much mistaken, would Ramsay MacDonald and
Winston Churchill."

The woman did not seem to see eye to eye.

"Tchah!" she said. "What do you suppose my husband's brother
Charlie Parker would say if I allowed his niece to marry a man who
jellies eels?"

"Ah!" said Claude, who, before we go any further, was a tall, drooping bird with a red soup-strainer mustache.

"Or my husband's brother, Henry Parker."

"Ah!" said Claude. "Or Cousin Alf Robbins, for that matter."

"Exactly. Cousin Alfred would die of shame."

The girl Julia hiccupped passionately, so much so that Pongo says
it was all he could do to stop himself nipping across and taking her
hand in his and patting it.

"I've told you a hundred times, Mother, that Wilberforce is only
jellying eels till he finds something better."

"What is better than an eel?" asked Lord Ickenham, who had been
following this discussion with the close attention it deserved. "For
jellying purposes, I mean."

"He is ambitious. It won't be long," said the girl, "before Wilberforce suddenly rises in the world."

She never spoke a truer word. At this very moment, up he came
from behind the settee like a leaping salmon.

"Julia!" he cried.

"Wilby!" yipped the girl.

And Pongo says he never saw anything more sickening in his life than the way she flung herself into the blighter's arms and clung there like the ivy on the old garden wall. It wasn't that he had anything specific against the pink chap, but this girl had made a deep impression on him and he resented her gluing herself to another in this manner.

Julia's mother, after just that brief moment which a woman needs in which to recover from her natural surprise at seeing eel-jelliers pop up from behind sofas, got moving and plucked her away like a referee breaking a couple of welterweights.

"Julia Parker," she said, "I'm ashamed of you!"

"So am I," said Claude.

"I blush for you."

"Me, too," said Claude. "Hugging and kissing a man who called your father a perishing old bottle-nosed Gawd-help-us."

"I think," said Lord Ickenham, shoving his oar in, "that before proceeding any further we ought to go into that point. If he called you a perishing old bottle-nosed Gawd-help-us, it seems to me that the first thing to do is to decide whether he was right, and frankly, in my opinion . . ."

"Wilberforce will apologize."

"Certainly I'll apologize. It isn't fair to hold a remark passed in the heat of the moment against a chap . . ."

"Mr. Robinson," said the woman, "you know perfectly well that whatever remarks you may have seen fit to pass don't matter one way or the other. If you were listening to what I was saying you will understand . . ."

"Oh, I know, I know. Uncle Charlie Parker and Uncle Henry Parker and Cousin Alf Robbins and all that. Pack of snobs!"

"What!"

"Haughty, stuck-up snobs. Them and their class distinctions. Think themselves everybody just because they've got money. I'd like to know how they got it."

"What do you mean by that?"

"Never mind what I mean."

"If you are insinuating—"

"Well, of course, you know, Connie," said Lord Ickenham mildly, "he's quite right. You can't get away from that."

I don't know if you have ever seen a bull terrier embarking on a scrap with an Airedale and just as it was getting down nicely to its work suddenly having an unexpected Kerry Blue sneak up behind it and bite it in the rear quarters. When this happens, it lets go of the Airedale and swivels round and fixes the butting-in animal with a pretty nasty eye. It was exactly the same with the woman Connie when Lord Ickenham spoke these words.

"What!"

"I was only wondering if you had forgotten how Charlie Parker made his pile."

"What are you talking about?"

"I know it is painful," said Lord Ickenham, "and one doesn't mention it as a rule, but, as we are on the subject, you must admit that lending money at two hundred and fifty per cent interest is not done in the best circles. The judge, if you remember, said so at the trial."

"I never knew that!" cried the girl Julia.

"Ah," said Lord Ickenham. "You kept it from the child? Quite right, quite right."

"It's a lie!"

"And when Henry Parker had all that fuss with the bank it was touch and go they didn't send him to prison. Between ourselves, Connie, has a bank official, even a brother of your husband, any right to sneak fifty pounds from the till in order to put it on a hundred to one shot for the Grand National? Not quite playing the game, Connie. Not the straight bat. Henry, I grant you, won five thousand of the best and never looked back afterwards, but, though we applaud his judgment of form, we must surely look askance at his financial methods. As for Cousin Alf Robbins . . ."

The woman was making rummy stuttering sounds. Pongo tells me he once had a Pommery Seven which used to express itself in much the same way if you tried to get it to take a hill on high. A sort of mixture of gurgles and explosions.

"There is not a word of truth in this," she gasped at length, having managed to get the vocal cords disentangled. "Not a single word. I think you must have gone mad."

Lord Ickenham shrugged his shoulders.

"Have it your own way, Connie. I was only going to say that, while the jury were probably compelled on the evidence submitted to them to give Cousin Alf Robbins the benefit of the doubt when charged with smuggling dope, everybody knew that he had been doing it for years. I am not blaming him, mind you. If a man can smuggle cocaine and get away with it, good luck to him, say I. The only point I am trying to make is that we are hardly a family that can afford to put on dog and sneer at honest suitors for our daughters' hands. Speaking for myself, I consider that we are very lucky to have the chance of marrying even into eel-jellying circles."

"So do I," said Julia firmly.

"You don't believe what this man is saying?"

"I believe every word."

"So do I," said the pink chap.

The woman snorted. She seemed overwrought.

"Well," she said, "goodness knows I have never liked Laura, but I would never have wished her a husband like you!"

"Husband?" said Lord Ickenham, puzzled. "What gives you the impression that Laura and I are married?"

There was a weighty silence, during which the parrot threw out a general invitation to join it in a nut. Then the girl Julia spoke.

"You'll have to let me marry Wilberforce now," she said. "He knows too much about us."

"I was rather thinking that myself," said Lord Ickenham. "Seal his lips, I say."

"You wouldn't mind marrying into a low family, would you, darling?" asked the girl, with a touch of anxiety.

"No family could be too low for me, dearest, if it was yours," said the pink chap.

"After all, we needn't see them."

"That's right."

"It isn't one's relations that matter; it's oneselves."

"That's right, too."

"Wilby!"

"Julia!"

They repeated the old ivy on the garden wall act. Pongo says he didn't like it any better than the first time, but his distaste wasn't in it with the woman Connie's.

"And what, may I ask," she said, "do you propose to marry on?"

This seemed to cast a damper. They came apart. They looked at each other. The girl looked at the pink chap, and the pink chap looked at the girl. You could see that a jarring note had been struck.

"Wilberforce is going to be a very rich man some day."

"Some day!"

"If I had a hundred pounds," said the pink chap, "I could buy a half share in one of the best milk walks in South London tomorrow."

"If!" said the woman.

"Ah!" said Claude.

"Where are you going to get it?"

"Ah!" said Claude.

"Where," repeated the woman, plainly pleased with the snappy crack and loath to let it ride without an encore, "are you going to get it?"

"That," said Claude, "is the point. Where are you going to get a hundred pounds?"

"Why, bless my soul," said Lord Ickenham jovially, "from me, of course. Where else?"

And before Pongo's bulging eyes he fished out from the recesses of his costume a crackling bundle of notes and handed it over. And the agony of realizing that the old bounder had had all that stuff on him all this time and that he hadn't touched him for so much as a tithe of it was so keen, Pongo says, that before he knew what he was doing he had let out a sharp, whinnying cry which rang through the room like the yowl of a stepped-on puppy.

"Ah," said Lord Ickenham. "The vet wishes to speak to me. Yes, vet?"

This seemed to puzzle the cerise bloke a bit.

"I thought you said this chap was your son."

"If I had a son," said Lord Ickenham, a little hurt, "he would be a good deal better-looking than that. No, this is the local veterinary surgeon. I may have said I *looked* on him as a son. Perhaps that was what confused you."

He shifted across to Pongo and twiddled his hands inquiringly. Pongo gaped at him, and it was not until one of the hands caught him smartly in the lower ribs that he remembered he was deaf and started to twiddle back. Considering that he wasn't supposed to be dumb, I can't see why he should have twiddled, but no doubt there are moments when twiddling is about all a fellow feels himself equal to. For what seemed to him at least ten hours Pongo had been undergoing great mental stress, and one can't blame him for not being chatty. Anyway, be that as it may, he twiddled.

"I cannot quite understand what he says," announced Lord Ickenham at length, "because he sprained a finger this morning and that makes him stammer. But I gather that he wishes to have a word with me in private. Possibly my parrot has got something the matter with it which he is reluctant to mention even in sign language in front of a young unmarried girl. You know what parrots are. We will step outside."

"*We* will step outside," said Wilberforce.

"Yes," said the girl Julia. "I feel like a walk."

"And you?" said Lord Ickenham to the woman Connie, who was

looking like a female Napoleon at Moscow. "Do you join the hikers?"

"I shall remain and make myself a cup of tea. You will not grudge us a cup of tea, I hope?"

"Far from it," said Lord Ickenham cordially. "This is Liberty Hall. Stick around and mop it up till your eyes bubble."

Outside, the girl, looking more like a dewy rosebud than ever, fawned on the old buster pretty considerably.

"I don't know how to thank you!" she said. And the pink chap said he didn't, either.

"Not at all, my dear, not at all," said Lord Ickenham.

"I think you're simply wonderful."

"No, no."

"You are. Perfectly marvelous."

"Tut, tut," said Lord Ickenham. "Don't give the matter another thought."

He kissed her on both cheeks, the chin, the forehead, the right eyebrow, and the tip of the nose, Pongo looking on the while in a baffled and discontented manner. Everybody seemed to be kissing this girl except him.

Eventually the degrading spectacle ceased and the girl and the pink chap shoved off, and Pongo was enabled to take up the matter of that hundred quid.

"Where," he asked, "did you get all that money?"

"Now, where did I?" mused Lord Ickenham. "I know your aunt gave it to me for some purpose. But what? To pay some bill or other, I rather fancy."

This cheered Pongo up slightly.

"She'll give you the devil when you get back," he said, with not a little relish. "I wouldn't be in your shoes for something. When you tell Aunt Jane," he said, with confidence, for he knew his Aunt Jane's emotional nature, "that you slipped her entire roll to a girl, and explain, as you will have to explain, that she was an extraordinarily pretty girl—a girl, in fine, who looked like something out of a beauty chorus of the better sort, I should think she would pluck down one of the ancestral battle-axes from the wall and jolly well strike you on the mazzard."

"Have no anxiety, my dear boy," said Lord Ickenham. "It is like your kind heart to be so concerned, but have no anxiety. I shall tell her that I was compelled to give the money to you to enable you to buy back some compromising letters from a Spanish *demi-mondaine*. She will scarcely be able to blame me for rescuing a fondly loved nephew from the clutches of an adventuress. It may be that she will feel a little vexed with you for a while, and that you may have to allow a certain time to elapse before you visit Ickenham again, but then I shan't be wanting you at Ickenham till the ratting season starts, so all is well."

At this moment, there came toddling up to the gate of The Cedars a large red-faced man. He was just going in when Lord Ickenham hailed him.

"Mr. Roddis?"

"Hey?"

"Am I addressing Mr. Roddis?"

"That's me."

"I am Mr. J. G. Bulstrode from down the road," said Lord Ickenham. "This is my sister's husband's brother, Percy Frensham in the lard and imported butter business."

The red-faced bird said he was pleased to meet them. He asked Pongo if things were brisk in the lard and imported butter business, and Pongo said they were all right, and the red-faced bird said he was glad to hear it.

"We have never met, Mr. Roddis," said Lord Ickenham, "but I think it would be only neighborly to inform you that a short while ago I observed two suspicious-looking persons in your house."

"In my house? How on earth did they get there?"

"No doubt through a window at the back. They looked to me like cat burglars. If you creep up, you may be able to see them."

The red-faced bird crept, and came back not exactly foaming at the mouth but with the air of a man who for two pins would so foam.

"You're perfectly right. They're sitting in my parlor as cool as dammit, swigging my tea and buttered toast."

"I thought as much."

"And they've opened a pot of my raspberry jam."

"Ah, then you will be able to catch them red-handed. I should fetch a policeman."

"I will. Thank you, Mr. Bulstrode."

"Only too glad to have been able to render you this little service, Mr. Roddis," said Lord Ickenham. "Well, I must be moving along. I have an appointment. Pleasant after the rain, is it not? Come, Percy."

He lugged Pongo off.

"So that," he said, with satisfaction, "is that. On these visits of mine to the metropolis, my boy, I always make it my aim, if possible, to spread sweetness and light. I look about me, even in a foul hole like Mitching Hill, and I ask myself—How can I leave this foul hole a

better and happier foul hole than I found it? And if I see a chance,
I grab it. Here is our omnibus. Spring aboard, my boy, and on our
way home we will be sketching out rough plans for the evening. If
the old Leicester Grill is still in existence, we might look in there. It
must be fully thirty-five years since I was last thrown out of the
Leicester Grill. I wonder who is the bouncer there now."

Such (concluded the Crumpet) is Pongo Twistleton's Uncle Fred
from the country, and you will have gathered by now a rough notion
of why it is that when a telegram comes announcing his impending
arrival in the great city Pongo blenches to the core and calls for a
couple of quick ones.

The whole situation, Pongo says, is very complex. Looking at it
from one angle, it is fine that the man lives in the country most of the
year. If he didn't, he would have him in his midst all the time. On
the other hand, by living in the country he generates, as it were, a
store of loopiness which expends itself with frightful violence on his
rare visits to the center of things.

What it boils down to is this—Is it better to have a loopy uncle
whose loopiness is perpetually on tap but spread out thin, so to speak,
or one who lies low in distant Hants for three hundred and sixty days
in the year and does himself proud in London for the other five?
Dashed moot, of course, and Pongo has never been able to make up
his mind on the point.

Naturally, the ideal thing would be if someone would chain the old
hound up permanently and keep him from Jan. one to Dec. thirty-
one where he wouldn't do any harm—viz. among the spuds and ten-
antry. But this, Pongo admits, is a Utopian dream. Nobody could
work harder to that end than his Aunt Jane, and she has never been
able to manage it.

Introducing

❋ *Mr. Mulliner*

That dignified regular of the Anglers' Rest whose considered judgment on any and all topics is drawn from the experiences of his innumerable relatives.

People who enjoyed a merely superficial acquaintance with my nephew Archibald (said Mr. Mulliner) were accustomed to set him down as just an ordinary pinheaded young man. It was only when they came to know him better that they discovered their mistake. Then they realized that his pinheadedness, so far from being ordinary, was exceptional. Even at his Club, where the average of intellect is not high, it was often said of Archibald that, had his brain been constructed of silk, he would have been hard put to it to find sufficient material to make a canary a pair of cami-knickers.

❀ *The Truth about George*

TWO MEN were sitting in the bar parlor of the Anglers' Rest as I entered it; and one of them, I gathered from his low, excited voice and wide gestures, was telling the other a story. I could hear nothing but an occasional "Biggest I ever saw in my life!" and "Fully as large as that!" but in such a place it was not difficult to imagine the rest; and when the second man, catching my eye, winked at me with a sort of humorous misery, I smiled sympathetically back at him.

The action had the effect of establishing a bond between us; and when the storyteller finished his tale and left, he came over to my table as if answering a formal invitation.

"Dreadful liars some men are," he said genially.

"Fishermen," I suggested, "are traditionally careless of the truth."

"He wasn't a fisherman," said my companion. "That was our local doctor. He was telling me about his latest case of dropsy. Besides"— he tapped me earnestly on the knee—"you must not fall into the popular error about fishermen. Tradition has maligned them. I am a fisherman myself, and I have never told a lie in my life."

I could well believe it. He was a short, stout, comfortable man of middle age, and the thing that struck me first about him was the extraordinary childlike candor of his eyes. They were large and round and honest. I would have bought oil stock from him without a tremor.

The door leading into the white dusty road opened, and a small man with rimless pince-nez and an anxious expression shot in like a rabbit and had consumed a gin and ginger beer almost before we knew he was there. Having thus refreshed himself, he stood looking at us, seemingly ill at ease.

"N-n-n-n-n-n—" he said.

We looked at him inquiringly.

"N-n-n-n-n-ice d-d-d-d—"

His nerve appeared to fail him, and he vanished as abruptly as he had come.

"I think he was leading up to telling us that it was a nice day," hazarded my companion.

"It must be very embarrassing," I said, "for a man with such a painful impediment in his speech to open conversation with strangers."

"Probably trying to cure himself. Like my nephew George. Have I ever told you about my nephew George?"

I reminded him that we had only just met, and that this was the first time I had learned that he had a nephew George.

"Young George Mulliner. My name is Mulliner. I will tell you about George's case—in many ways a rather remarkable one."

My nephew George (said Mr. Mulliner) was as nice a young fellow as you would ever wish to meet, but from childhood up he had been cursed with a terrible stammer. If he had had to earn his living, he would undoubtedly have found this affliction a great handicap, but fortunately his father had left him a comfortable income; and George spent a not unhappy life, residing in the village where he had been born and passing his days in the usual country sports and his evenings in doing crossword puzzles. By the time he was thirty he knew more about Eli, the prophet, Ra, the Sun God, and the bird Emu than anybody else in the county except Susan Blake, the vicar's daughter, who had also taken up the solving of crossword puzzles and was the first girl in Worcestershire to find out the meaning of "stearine" and "crepuscular."

It was his association with Miss Blake that first turned George's thoughts to a serious endeavor to cure himself of his stammer. Naturally, with this hobby in common, the young people saw a great deal of one another; for George was always looking in at the vicarage to ask her if she knew a word of seven letters meaning "appertaining to the profession of plumbing," and Susan was just as constant a caller at George's cozy little cottage—being frequently stumped, as girls will be, by words of eight letters signifying "largely used in the manufacture of poppet valves." The consequence was that one evening, just after she had helped him out of a tight place with the word "disestablishmentarianism," the boy suddenly awoke to the truth and realized that she was all the world to him—or, as he put it to himself from force of habit, precious, beloved, darling, much-loved, highly esteemed or valued.

And yet, every time he tried to tell her so, he could get no farther than a sibilant gurgle which was no more practical use than a hiccup.

Something obviously had to be done, and George went to London to see a specialist.

"I-I-I-I-I-I—" said George.

"You were saying—?"

"Woo-woo-woo-woo-woo-woo—"

"Sing it," said the specialist.

"S-s-s-s-s-s-s-s—?" said George, puzzled.

The specialist explained. He was a kindly man with moth-eaten whiskers and an eye like a meditative codfish.

"Many people," he said, "who are unable to articulate clearly in ordinary speech find themselves lucid and bell-like when they burst into song."

It seemed a good idea to George. He thought for a moment; then threw his head back, shut his eyes, and let it go in a musical baritone.

"I love a lassie, a bonny, bonny lassie," sang George. "She's as pure as the lily in the dell."

"No doubt," said the specialist, wincing a little.

"She's as sweet as the heather, the bonny purple heather—Susan, my Worcestershire bluebell."

"Ah!" said the specialist. "Sounds a nice girl. Is this she?" he asked, adjusting his glasses and peering at the photograph which George had extracted from the interior of the left side of his under-vest.

George nodded, and drew in breath.

"Yes, sir," he caroled, "that's my baby. No, sir, don't mean maybe. Yes, sir, that's my baby now. And, by the way, by the way, when I meet that preacher I shall say—'Yes, sir, that's my—' "

"Quite," said the specialist hurriedly. He had a sensitive ear. "Quite, quite."

"If you knew Susie like I know Susie," George was beginning, but the other stopped him.

"Quite. Exactly. I shouldn't wonder. And now," said the specialist, "what precisely is the trouble? No," he added hastily, as George inflated his lungs, "don't sing it. Write the particulars on this piece of paper."

George did so.

"H'm!" said the specialist, examining the screed. "You wish to woo, court, and become betrothed, engaged, affianced to this girl, but you find yourself unable, incapable, incompetent, impotent, and powerless. Every time you attempt it, your vocal cords fail, fall short, are insufficient, wanting, deficient, and go blooey."

George nodded.

"A not unusual case. I have had to deal with this sort of thing before. The effect of love on the vocal cords of even a normally elo-quent subject is frequently deleterious. As regards the habitual stam-merer, tests have shown that in ninety-seven point five six nine recurring of cases the divine passion reduces him to a condition where he sounds like a soda-water siphon trying to recite 'Gunga Din.' There is only one cure."

"W-w-w-w-w—?" asked George.

"I will tell you. Stammering," proceeded the specialist, putting the tips of his fingers together and eying George benevolently, "is mainly mental and is caused by shyness, which is caused by the inferiority complex, which in its turn is caused by suppressed desires or introverted inhibitions or something. The advice I give to all young men who come in here behaving like soda-water siphons is to go out and make a point of speaking to at least three perfect strangers every day. Engage these strangers in conversation, persevering no matter how priceless a chump you may feel, and before many weeks are out you will find that the little daily dose has had its effect. Shyness will wear off, and with it the stammer."

And, having requested the young man—in a voice of the clearest timbre, free from all trace of impediment—to hand over a fee of five guineas, the specialist sent George out into the world.

The more George thought about the advice he had been given, the less he liked it. He shivered in the cab that took him to the station to catch the train back to East Wobsley. Like all shy young men, he had never hitherto looked upon himself as shy—preferring to attribute his distaste for the society of his fellows to some subtle rareness of soul. But now that the thing had been put squarely up to him, he was compelled to realize that in all essentials he was a perfect rabbit. The thought of accosting perfect strangers and forcing his conversation upon them sickened him.

But no Mulliner has ever shirked an unpleasant duty. As he reached the platform and strode along it to the train, his teeth were set, his eyes shone with an almost fanatical light of determination, and he intended before his journey was over to conduct three heart-to-heart chats if he had to sing every bar of them.

The compartment into which he had made his way was empty at the moment, but just before the train started a very large, fierce-looking man got in. George would have preferred somebody a little less formidable for his first subject, but he braced himself and bent forward. And, as he did so, the man spoke.

"The wur-wur-wur-wur-weather," he said, "sus-sus-seems to be ter-ter-taking a tur-tur-turn for the ber-ber-better, der-doesn't it?"

George sank back as if he had been hit between the eyes. The train had moved out of the dimness of the station by now, and the sun was shining brightly on the speaker, illuminating his knobbly shoulders, his craggy jaw, and, above all, the shockingly choleric look in his eyes. To reply "Y-y-y-y-y-y-y-yes" to such a man would obviously be madness.

But to abstain from speech did not seem to be much better as a policy. George's silence appeared to arouse this man's worst passions. His face had turned purple and he glared painfully.

"I uk-uk-asked you a sus-sus-civil quk-quk-quk," he said irascibly. "Are you d-d-d-d-deaf?"

All we Mulliners have been noted for our presence of mind. To open his mouth, point to his tonsils, and utter a strangled gurgle was with George the work of a moment.

The tension relaxed. The man's annoyance abated.

"D-d-d-dumb?" he said commiseratingly. "I beg your p-p-p-p-pup. I t-t-trust I have not caused you p-p-p-p-pup. It m-must be tut-tut-tut-tut-tut not to be able to sus-sus-speak fuf-fuf-fuf-fuf-fluently."

He then buried himself in his paper, and George sank back in his corner, quivering in every limb.

To get to East Wobsley, as you doubtless know, you have to change at Ippleton and take the branch line. By the time the train reached this junction, George's composure was somewhat restored. He deposited his belongings in a compartment of the East Wobsley train, which was waiting in a glued manner on the other side of the platform, and, finding that it would not start for some ten minutes, decided to pass the time by strolling up and down in the pleasant air.

It was a lovely afternoon. The sun was gilding the platform with its rays, and a gentle breeze blew from the west. A little brook ran tinkling at the side of the road; birds were singing in the hedgerows; and through the trees could be discerned dimly the noble façade of the County Lunatic Asylum. Soothed by his surroundings, George began to feel so refreshed that he regretted that in this wayside station there was no one present whom he could engage in talk.

It was at this moment that the distinguished-looking stranger entered the platform.

The newcomer was a man of imposing physique, simply dressed in pajamas, brown boots, and a mackintosh. In his hand he carried a top hat, and into this he was dipping his fingers, taking them out, and then waving them in a curious manner to right and left. He nodded so affably to George that the latter, though a little surprised at the other's costume, decided to speak. After all, he reflected, clothes do not make the man, and, judging from the other's smile, a warm heart appeared to beat beneath that orange-and-mauve striped pajama jacket.

"N-n-n-n-nice weather," he said.

"Glad you like it," said the stranger. "I ordered it specially."

George was a little puzzled by this remark, but he persevered.

"M-might I ask wur-wur-what you are dud-doing?"

"Doing?"

"With that her-her-her-her-hat?"

"Oh, with this hat? I see what you mean. Just scattering largess to the multitude," replied the stranger, dipping his fingers once more and waving them with a generous gesture. "Devil of a bore, but it's expected of a man in my position. The fact is," he said, linking his arm in George's and speaking in a confidential undertone, "I'm the Emperor of Abyssinia. That's my palace over there," he said, pointing through the trees. "Don't let it go any farther. It's not supposed to be generally known."

It was with a rather sickly smile that George now endeavored to withdraw his arm from that of his companion, but the other would have none of this aloofness. He seemed to be in complete agreement with Shakespeare's dictum that a friend, when found, should be grappled to you with hoops of steel. He held George in a viselike grip and drew him into a recess of the platform. He looked about him and seemed satisfied.

"We are alone at last," he said.

This fact had already impressed itself with sickening clearness on the young man. There are few spots in the civilized world more deserted than the platform of a small country station. The sun shone on the smooth asphalt, on the gleaming rails, and on the machine which, in exchange for a penny placed in the slot marked "Matches," would supply a package of wholesome butterscotch—but on nothing else.

What George could have done with at the moment was a posse of police armed with stout clubs, and there was not even a dog in sight.

"I've been wanting to talk to you for a long time," said the stranger genially.

"Huh-huh-have you?" said George.

"Yes. I want your opinion of human sacrifices."

George said he didn't like them.

"Why not?" asked the other, surprised.

George said it was hard to explain. He just didn't.

"Well, I think you're wrong," said the Emperor. "I know there's a school of thought growing up that holds your views, but I disapprove of it. I hate all this modern advanced thought. Human sacrifices have always been good enough for the Emperors of Abyssinia, and they're good enough for me. Kindly step in here, if you please."

He indicated the lamp-and-mop room, at which they had now arrived. It was a dark and sinister apartment, smelling strongly of oil and porters, and was probably the last place on earth in which George would have wished to be closeted with a man of such peculiar views. He shrank back.

"You go in first," he said.

"No larks," said the other suspiciously.

"L-l-l-l-larks?"

"Yes. No pushing a fellow in and locking the door and squirting water at him through the window. I've had that happen to me before."

"Sus-certainly not."

"Right!" said the Emperor. "You're a gentleman and I'm a gentleman. Both gentlemen. Have you a knife, by the way? We shall need a knife."

"No. No knife."

"Ah, well," said the Emperor, "then we'll have to look about for something else. No doubt we shall manage somehow."

And with the debonair manner which so became him, he scattered another handful of largess and walked into the lamp room.

It was not the fact that he had given his word as a gentleman that kept George from locking the door. There is probably no family on earth more nicely scrupulous as regards keeping its promises than the Mulliners, but I am compelled to admit that, had George been able to find the key, he would have locked the door without hesitation. Not being able to find the key, he had to be satisfied with banging it. This done, he leaped back and raced away down the platform. A confused noise within seemed to indicate that the Emperor had become involved with some lamps.

George made the best of the respite. Covering the ground at a high rate of speed, he flung himself into the train and took refuge under the seat.

There he remained, quaking. At one time he thought that his uncongenial acquaintance had got upon his track, for the door of the compartment opened and a cool wind blew in upon him. Then, glancing along the floor, he perceived feminine ankles. The relief was enormous, but even in his relief George, who was the soul of modesty, did not forget his manners. He closed his eyes.

A voice spoke.

"Porter!"

"Yes, ma'am?"

"What was all that disturbance as I came into the station?"

"Patient escaped from the asylum, ma'am."

"Good gracious!"

The voice would undoubtedly have spoken further, but at this moment the train began to move. There came the sound of a body descending upon a cushioned seat, and some little time later the rustling of a paper.

George had never before traveled under the seat of a railway carriage; and, though he belonged to the younger generation, which is supposed to be so avid of new experiences, he had no desire to do so now. He decided to emerge, and, if possible, to emerge with the minimum of ostentation. Little as he knew of women, he was aware that as a sex they are apt to be startled by the sight of men crawling out from under the seats of compartments. He began his maneuvers by poking out his head and surveying the terrain.

All was well. The woman, in her seat across the way, was engrossed in her paper. Moving in a series of noiseless wriggles, George extricated himself from his hiding place and, with a twist which would have been impossible to a man not in the habit of doing Swedish exercises daily before breakfast, heaved himself into the corner seat. The woman continued reading her paper.

The events of the past quarter of an hour had tended rather to drive from George's mind the mission which he had undertaken on leaving the specialist's office. But now, having leisure for reflection, he realized that, if he meant to complete his first day of the cure, he was allowing himself to run sadly behind schedule. Speak to three strangers, the specialist had told him, and up to the present he had spoken to only one. True, this one had been a pretty considerable stranger, and a less conscientious young man than George Mulliner might have considered himself justified in chalking him up on the scoreboard as one and a half or even two. But George had the dogged, honest Mulliner streak in him, and he refused to quibble.

He nerved himself for action and cleared his throat.

"Ah-h'rm!" said George.

And, having opened the ball, he smiled a winning smile and waited for his companion to make the next move.

The move which his companion made was in an upwards direction, and measured from six to eight inches. She dropped her paper and regarded George with a pale-eyed horror. One pictures her a little in the position of Robinson Crusoe when he saw the footprint in the sand. She had been convinced that she was completely alone, and lo!

out of space a voice had spoken to her. Her face worked, but she made no remark.

George, on his side, was also feeling a little ill at ease. Women always increased his natural shyness. He never knew what to say to them.

Then a happy thought struck him. He had just glanced at his watch and found the hour to be nearly four-thirty. Women, he knew, loved a drop of tea at about this time, and fortunately there was in his suitcase a full thermos flask.

"Pardon me, but I wonder if you would care for a cup of tea?" was what he wanted to say, but, as so often happened with him when in the presence of the opposite sex, he could get no farther than a sort of sizzling sound like a cockroach calling to its young.

The woman continued to stare at him. Her eyes were now about the size of regulation standard golf balls, and her breathing suggested the last stages of asthma. And it was at this point that George, struggling for speech, had one of those inspirations which frequently came to Mulliners. There flashed into his mind what the specialist had told him about singing. Say it with music—that was the thing to do.

He delayed no longer.

"Tea for two and two for tea and me for you and you for me—"

He was shocked to observe his companion turning Nile green. He decided to make his meaning clearer.

"I have a nice thermos. I have a full thermos. Won't you share my thermos, too? When skies are gray and you feel you are blue, tea sends the sun smiling through. I have a nice thermos. I have a full thermos. May I pour out some for you?"

You will agree with me, I think, that no invitation could have been more happily put, but his companion was not responsive. With one last agonized look at him, she closed her eyes and sank back in her seat. Her lips had now turned a curious gray-blue color, and they were moving feebly. She reminded George, who, like myself, was a keen fisherman, of a newly gaffed salmon.

George sat back in his corner, brooding. Rack his brain as he might, he could think of no topic which could be guaranteed to interest, elevate, and amuse. He looked out of the window with a sigh.

The train was now approaching the dear old familiar East Wobsley country. He began to recognize landmarks. A wave of sentiment poured over George as he thought of Susan, and he reached for the bag of buns which he had bought at the refreshment room at Ippleton. Sentiment always made him hungry.

He took his thermos out of the suitcase, and, unscrewing the top, poured himself out a cup of tea. Then, placing the thermos on the seat, he drank.

He looked across at his companion. Her eyes were still closed, and she uttered little sighing noises. George was half inclined to renew his offer of tea, but the only tune he could remember was "Hard-Hearted Hannah, the Vamp from Savannah," and it was difficult to fit suitable words to it. He ate his bun and gazed out at the familiar scenery.

Now, as you approach East Wobsley, the train, I must mention, has to pass over some points; and so violent is the sudden jerking that strong men have been known to spill their beer. George, forgetting this in his preoccupation, had placed the thermos only a few inches from the edge of the seat. The result was that, as the train reached the points, the flask leaped like a live thing, dived to the floor, and exploded.

Even George was distinctly upset by the sudden sharpness of the report. His bun sprang from his hand and was dashed to fragments. He blinked thrice in rapid succession. His heart tried to jump out of his mouth and loosened a front tooth.

But on the woman opposite the effect of the untoward occurrence was still more marked. With a single piercing shriek, she rose from her seat straight into the air like a rocketing pheasant; and, having clutched the communication cord, fell back again. Impressive as her previous leap had been, she excelled it now by several inches. I do not know what the existing record for the Sitting High-Jump is, but she undoubtedly lowered it; and if George had been a member of the Olympic Games Selection Committee, he would have signed this woman up immediately.

It is a curious thing that, in spite of the railway companies' sporting willingness to let their patrons have a tug at the extremely moderate price of five pounds a go, very few people have ever either pulled a communication cord or seen one pulled. There is, thus, a widespread ignorance as to what precisely happens on such occasions.

The procedure, George tells me, is as follows: First there comes a grinding noise, as the brakes are applied. Then the train stops. And finally, from every point of the compass, a seething mob of interested onlookers begins to appear.

It was about a mile and a half from East Wobsley that the affair had taken place, and as far as the eye could reach the countryside was totally devoid of humanity. A moment before nothing had been visible but smiling cornfields and broad pasturelands; but now from east, west, north, and south running figures began to appear. We must remember that George at the time was in a somewhat over-wrought frame of mind, and his statements should therefore be accepted with caution; but he tells me that out of the middle of a single empty meadow, entirely devoid of cover, no fewer than twenty-seven distinct rustics suddenly appeared, having undoubtedly shot up through the ground.

The rails, which had been completely unoccupied, were now thronged with so dense a crowd of navvies that it seemed to George absurd to pretend that there was any unemployment in England. Every member of the laboring classes throughout the country was so palpably present. Moreover, the train, which at Ippleton had seemed sparsely occupied, was disgorging passengers from every door. It was the sort of mob scene which would have made David W. Griffith scream with delight; and it looked, George says, like Guest Night at the Royal Automobile Club. But, as I say, we must remember that he was overwrought.

It is difficult to say what precisely would have been the correct behavior of your polished man of the world in such a situation. I think myself that a great deal of sang-froid and address would be required even by the most self-possessed in order to pass off such a contretemps. To George, I may say at once, the crisis revealed itself immediately as one which he was totally incapable of handling. The one clear thought that stood out from the welter of his emotions was the reflection that it was advisable to remove himself, and to do so without delay. Drawing a deep breath, he shot swiftly off the mark.

All we Mulliners have been athletes; and George, when at the University, had been noted for his speed of foot. He ran now as he had never run before. His statement, however, that as he sprinted across the first field he distinctly saw a rabbit shoot an envious glance at him as he passed and shrug its shoulders hopelessly, I am inclined to discount. George, as I have said before, was a little over-excited.

Nevertheless, it is not to be questioned that he made good going. And he had need to, for after the first instant of surprise, which had enabled him to secure a lead, the whole mob was pouring across country after him; and dimly, as he ran, he could hear voices in the throng informally discussing the advisability of lynching him. More-over, the field through which he was running, a moment before a bare expanse of green, was now black with figures, headed by a man with a beard who carried a pitchfork. George swerved sharply to the right, casting a swift glance over his shoulder at his pursuers. He disliked them all, but especially the man with the pitchfork.

It is impossible for one who was not an eye-witness to say how long the chase continued and how much ground was covered by the interested parties. I know the East Wobsley country well, and I have checked George's statements; and, if it is true that he traveled east as far as Little-Wigmarsh-in-the-Dell and as far west as Higgleford-cum-Wortlebury-beneath-the-Hill, he must undoubtedly have done a lot of running.

But a point which must not be forgotten is that, to a man not in a condition to observe closely, the village of Higgleford-cum-Wortlebury-beneath-the-Hill might easily not have been Higgleford-cum-Wortlebury-beneath-the-Hill at all, but another hamlet which in many respects closely resembles it. I need scarcely say that I allude to Lesser-Snodsbury-in-the-Vale.

Let us assume, therefore, that George, having touched Little-Wigmarsh-in-the-Dell, shot off at a tangent and reached Lesser-Snodsbury-in-the-Vale. This would be a considerable run. And, as he remembers flitting past Farmer Higgins's pigsty and the Dog and Duck at Pondlebury Parva and splashing through the brook Wipple at the point where it joins the River Wopple, we can safely assume that, wherever else he went, he got plenty of exercise.

But the pleasantest of functions must end, and, just as the setting sun was gilding the spire of the ivy-covered church of St. Barnabas the Resilient, where George as a child had sat so often, enlivening the tedium of the sermon by making faces at the choirboys, a damp and bedraggled figure might have been observed crawling painfully along the High Street of East Wobsley in the direction of the cozy little cottage known to its builder as Chatsworth and to the village tradesmen as "Mulliner's."

It was George, home from the hunting field.

Slowly George Mulliner made his way to the familiar door, and, passing through it, flung himself into his favorite chair. But a moment later a more imperious need than the desire to rest forced itself upon his attention. Rising stiffly, he tottered to the kitchen and mixed himself a revivifying whisky and soda. Then, refilling his glass, he returned to the sitting room, to find that it was no longer empty. A slim, fair girl, tastefully attired in tailor-made tweeds, was leaning over the desk on which he kept his Dictionary of English Synonyms.

She looked up as he entered, startled.

"Why, Mr. Mulliner!" she exclaimed. "What has been happening? Your clothes are torn, rent, ragged, tattered, and your hair is all disheveled, untrimmed, hanging loose or negligently, at loose ends!"

George smiled a wan smile.

"You are right," he said. "And, what is more, I am suffering from extreme fatigue, weariness, lassitude, exhaustion, prostration, and languor."

The girl gazed at him, a divine pity in her soft eyes.

"I'm so sorry," she murmured. "So very sorry, grieved, distressed, afflicted, pained, mortified, dejected, and upset."

George took her hand. Her sweet sympathy had effected the cure for which he had been seeking so long. Coming on top of the violent emotions through which he had been passing all day, it seemed to work on him like some healing spell, charm, or incantation. Suddenly, in a flash, he realized that he was no longer a stammerer. Had he wished at that moment to say, "Peter Piper picked a peck of pickled peppers," he could have done it without a second thought.

But he had better things to say than that.

"Miss Blake—Susan—Susie." He took her other hand in his. His voice rang out clear and unimpeded. It seemed to him incredible that he had ever yammered at this girl like an overheated steam radiator. "It cannot have escaped your notice that I have long entertained toward you sentiments warmer and deeper than those of ordinary friendship. It is love, Susan, that has been animating my bosom. Love, first a tiny seed, has burgeoned in my heart till, blazing into flame, it has swept away on the crest of its wave my diffidence, my doubt, my fears, and my foreboding, and now, like the topmost topaz of some ancient tower, it cries to all the world in a voice of thunder: 'You are mine! My mate! Predestined to me since Time first began!' As the star guides the mariner when, battered by boiling billows, he hies him home to the haven of hope and happiness, so do you gleam upon me along life's rough road and seem to say, 'Have courage, George! I am here!' Susan, I am not an eloquent man—I cannot speak fluently as I could wish—but these simple words which you have just heard come from the heart, from the unspotted heart of an English gentleman. Susan, I love you. Will you be my wife, married woman, matron, spouse, helpmeet, consort, partner or better half?"

"Oh, George!" said Susan. "Yes, yea, ay, aye! Decidedly, unquestionably, indubitably, incontrovertibly, and past all dispute!"

He folded her in his arms. And, as he did so, there came from the street outside—faintly, as from a distance—the sound of feet and voices. George leaped to the window. Rounding the corner, just by the Cow and Wheelbarrow public house, licensed to sell ales, wines, and spirits, was the man with the pitchfork, and behind him followed a vast crowd.

"My darling," said George. "For purely personal and private reasons, into which I need not enter, I must now leave you. Will you join me later?"

"I will follow you to the ends of the earth," replied Susan passionately.

"It will not be necessary," said George. "I am only going down to the coal cellar. I shall spend the next half-hour or so there. If anybody calls and asks for me, perhaps you would not mind telling them that I am out."

"I will, I will," said Susan. "And, George, by the way. What I really came here for was to ask you if you knew a word of nine letters, ending in k and signifying an implement employed in the pursuit of agriculture."

"Pitchfork, sweetheart," said George. "But you may take it from me, as one who knows, that agriculture isn't the only thing it is used in pursuit of."

And since that day (concluded Mr. Mulliner) George, believe me or believe me not, has not had the slightest trace of an impediment in his speech. He is now the chosen orator at all political rallies for miles around; and so offensively self-confident has his manner become that only last Friday he had his eye blacked by a hay-corn-and-feed merchant of the name of Stubbs. It just shows you, doesn't it?

✸ *A Slice of Life*

THE CONVERSATION in the bar parlor of the Anglers' Rest had drifted round to the subject of the Arts; and somebody asked if that film serial, "The Vicissitudes of Vera," which they were showing down at the Bijou Dream, was worth seeing.

"It's very good," said Miss Postlethwaite, our courteous and efficient barmaid, who is a prominent first-nighter. "It's about this mad professor who gets this girl into his toils and tries to turn her into a lobster."

"Tries to turn her into a lobster?" echoed we, surprised.

"Yes, sir. Into *a* lobster. It seems he collected thousands and thousands of lobsters and mashed them up and boiled down the juice from their glands and was just going to inject it into this Vera Dalrymple's spinal column when Jack Frobisher broke into the house and stopped him."

"Why did he do that?"

"Because he didn't want the girl he loved to be turned into a lobster."

"What we mean," said we, "is why did the professor want to turn the girl into a lobster?"

"He had a grudge against her."

This seemed plausible, and we thought it over for a while. Then one of the company shook his head disapprovingly.

"I don't like stories like that," he said. "They aren't true to life."

"Pardon me, sir," said a voice. And we were aware of Mr. Mulliner in our midst.

"Excuse me interrupting what may be a private discussion," said Mr. Mulliner, "but I chanced to overhear the recent remarks, and you, sir, have opened up a subject on which I happen to hold strong views—to wit, the question of what is and what is not true to life. How can we, with our limited experience, answer that question? For all we know, at this very moment hundreds of young women all over the country may be in the process of being turned into lobsters. Forgive my warmth, but I have suffered a good deal from this skeptical attitude of mind which is so prevalent nowadays. I have even met people who refused to believe my story about my brother Wilfred, purely because it was a little out of the ordinary run of the average man's experience."

Considerably moved, Mr. Mulliner ordered a hot Scotch with a slice of lemon.

"What happened to your brother Wilfred? Was he turned into a lobster?"

"No," said Mr. Mulliner, fixing his honest blue eyes on the speaker, "he was not. It would be perfectly easy for me to pretend that he was turned into a lobster; but I have always made it a practice —and I always shall make it a practice—to speak nothing but the bare truth. My brother Wilfred simply had rather a curious adventure."

My brother Wilfred (said Mr. Mulliner) is the clever one of the family. Even as a boy he was always messing about with chemicals, and at the University he devoted his time entirely to research. The result was that while still quite a young man he had won an established reputation as the inventor of what are known to the trade as Mulliner's Magic Marvels—a general term embracing the Raven Gypsy Face Cream, the Snow of the Mountains Lotion and many other preparations, some designed exclusively for the toilet, others of a curative nature, intended to alleviate the many ills to which the flesh is heir.

Naturally, he was a very busy man; and it is to this absorption in his work that I attribute the fact that, though—like all the Mulliners —a man of striking personal charm, he had reached his thirty-first year without ever having been involved in an affair of the heart. I remember him telling me once that he simply had no time for girls.

But we all fall sooner or later, and these strong concentrated men harder than any. While taking a brief holiday one year at Cannes, he met a Miss Angela Purdue, who was staying at his hotel, and she bowled him over completely.

She was one of these jolly, outdoor girls; and Wilfred had told me that what attracted him first about her was her wholesome, sunburned complexion. In fact, he told Miss Purdue the same thing when, shortly after he had proposed and been accepted, she asked him in her girlish way what it was that had first made him begin to love her.

"It's such a pity," said Miss Purdue, "that sunburn fades so soon. I do wish I knew some way of keeping it."

Even in his moments of holiest emotion Wilfred never forgot that he was a businessman.

"You should try Mulliner's Raven Gypsy Face Cream," he said. "It comes in two sizes—the small, or half-crown, jar and the large jar at seven shillings and sixpence. The large jar contains three and a half times as much as the small jar. It is applied nightly with a small sponge before retiring to rest. Testimonials have been received from numerous members of the aristocracy and may be examined at the office by any bona-fide inquirer."

"Is it really good?"

"I invented it," said Wilfred simply.

She looked at him adoringly.

"How clever you are! Any girl ought to be proud to marry you."

"Oh, well," said Wilfred, with a modest wave of his hand.

"All the same, my guardian is going to be terribly angry when I tell him we're engaged."

"Why?"

"I inherited the Purdue millions when my uncle died, you see, and my guardian has always wanted me to marry his son, Percy."

Wilfred kissed her fondly, and laughed a defiant laugh.

"Jer mong feesh der selar," he said lightly.

But, some days after his return to London, whither the girl had preceded him, he had occasion to recall her words. As he sat in his study, musing on a preparation to cure the pip in canaries, a card was brought to him.

"Sir Jasper ffinch-ffarrowmere, Bart.," he read. The name was strange to him.

"Show the gentleman in," he said. And presently there entered a very stout man with a broad pink face. It was a face whose natural expression should, Wilfred felt, have been jovial, but at the moment it was grave.

"Sir Jasper Finch-Farrowmere?" said Wilfred.

"ffinch-ffarrowmere," corrected the visitor, his sensitive ear detecting the capital letters.

"Ah, yes. You spell it with two small f's."

"Four small f's."

"And to what do I owe the honor—"

"I am Angela Purdue's guardian."

"How do you do? A whiskey-and-soda?"

"I thank you, no. I am a total abstainer. I found that alcohol had a tendency to increase my weight, so I gave it up. I have also given up butter, potatoes, soups of all kinds, and— However," he broke off, the fanatic gleam which comes into the eyes of all fat men who are describing their system of diet fading away, "this is not a social call, and I must not take up your time with idle talk. I have a message for you, Mr. Mulliner. From Angela."

"Bless her!" said Wilfred. "Sir Jasper, I love that girl with a fervor which increases daily."

"Is that so?" said the baronet. "Well, what I came to say was, it's all off."

"What?"

"All off. She sent me to say that she had thought it over and wanted to break the engagement."

Wilfred's eyes narrowed. He had not forgotten what Angela had said about this man wanting her to marry his son. He gazed piercingly at his visitor, no longer deceived by the superficial geniality of his appearance. He had read too many detective stories where the fat, jolly, red-faced man turns out a fiend in human shape to be a ready victim to appearances.

"Indeed?" he said coldly. "I should prefer to have this information from Miss Purdue's own lips."

"She won't see you. But, anticipating this attitude on your part, I brought a letter from her. You recognize the writing?"

Wilfred took the letter. Certainly, the hand was Angela's, and the meaning of the words he read unmistakable. Nevertheless, as he handed the missive back, there was a hard smile on his face.

"There is such a thing as writing a letter under compulsion," he said.

The baronet's pink face turned mauve.

"What do you mean, sir?"

"What I say."

"Are you insinuating—"

"Yes, I am."

"Pooh, sir!"

"Pooh to you!" said Wilfred. "And, if you want to know what I think, you poor ffish, I believe your name is spelled with a capital F, like anybody else's."

Stung to the quick, the baronet turned on his heel and left the room without another word.

Although he had given up his life to chemical research, Wilfred Mulliner was no mere dreamer. He could be the man of action when necessity demanded. Scarcely had his visitor left when he was on his way to the Senior Test Tubes, the famous chemists' club in St. James's. There, consulting Kelly's "County Families," he learnt that

Sir Jasper's address was ffinch Hall in Yorkshire. He had found out all he wanted to know. It was at ffinch Hall, he decided, that Angela must now be immured.

For that she was being immured somewhere he had no doubt. That letter, he was positive, had been written by her under stress of threats. The writing was Angela's but he declined to believe that she was responsible for the phraseology and sentiments. He remembered reading a story where the heroine was forced into courses which she would not otherwise have contemplated by the fact that somebody was standing over her with a flask of vitriol. Possibly this was what that bounder of a baronet had done to Angela.

Considering this possibility, he did not blame her for what she had said about him, Wilfred, in the second paragraph of her note. Nor did he reproach her for signing herself "Yrs truly, A. Purdue." Naturally, when baronets are threatening to pour vitriol down her neck, a refined and sensitive young girl cannot pick her words. This sort of thing must of necessity interfere with the selection of the *mot juste*.

That afternoon, Wilfred was in a train on his way to Yorkshire. That evening, he was in the ffinch Arms in the village of which Sir Jasper was the squire. That night, he was in the gardens of ffinch Hall, prowling softly around the house, listening.

And presently, as he prowled, there came to his ears from an upper window a sound that made him stiffen like a statue and clench his hands till the knuckles stood out white under the strain.

It was the sound of a woman sobbing.

Wilfred spent a sleepless night, but by morning he had formed his plan of action. I will not weary you with a description of the slow and tedious steps by which he first made the acquaintance of Sir Jasper's valet, who was an habitué of the village inn, and then by careful stages won the man's confidence with friendly words and beer. Suffice it to say that, about a week later, Wilfred had induced this man with bribes to leave suddenly on the plea of an aunt's illness, supplying—so as to cause his employer no inconvenience—a cousin to take his place.

This cousin, as you will have guessed, was Wilfred himself. But a very different Wilfred from the dark-haired, clean-cut young scientist who had revolutionized the world of chemistry a few months before by proving that $H_2O + b3g4z7 - m9z8 = g6f5p3x$. Before leaving London on what he knew would be a dark and dangerous enterprise, Wilfred had taken the precaution of calling in at a well-known costumier's and buying a red wig. He had also purchased a pair of blue spectacles; but for the role which he had now undertaken these were, of course, useless. A blue-spectacled valet could not but have aroused suspicion in the most guileless baronet. All that Wilfred did, therefore, in the way of preparation, was to don the wig, shave off his mustache, and treat his face to a light coating of the Raven Gypsy Face Cream. This done, he sent out for ffinch Hall.

Externally, ffinch Hall was one of those gloomy, somber country houses which seem to exist only for the purpose of having horrid crimes committed in them. Even in his brief visit to the grounds, Wilfred had noticed fully half a dozen places which seemed incomplete without a cross indicating spot where body was found by the police. It was the sort of house where ravens croak in the front garden just before the death of the heir, and shrieks ring out from behind barred windows in the night.

Nor was its interior more cheerful. And, as for the personnel of the domestic staff, that was less exhilarating than anything else about the place. It consisted of an aged cook who, as she bent over her caldrons, looked like something out of a traveling company of *Macbeth,* touring the smaller towns of the North, and Murgatroyd, the butler, a huge, sinister man with a cast in one eye and an evil light in the other.

Many men, under these conditions, would have been daunted. But not Wilfred Mulliner. Apart from the fact that, like all the Mulliners, he was as brave as a lion, he had come expecting something of this nature. He settled down to his duties and kept his eyes open, and before long his vigilance was rewarded.

One day, as he lurked about the dim-lit passageways, he saw Sir Jasper coming up the stairs with a laden tray in his hands. It contained a toast rack, a half bot. of white wine, pepper, salt, veg., and in a covered dish something Wilfred, sniffing cautiously, decided was a cutlet.

Lurking in the shadows, he followed the baronet to the top of the house. Sir Jasper paused at a door on the second floor. He knocked. The door opened, a hand was stretched forth, the tray vanished, the door closed, and the baronet moved away.

So did Wilfred. He had seen what he had wanted to see, discovered what he had wanted to discover. He returned to the servants' hall, and under the gloomy eyes of Murgatroyd began to shape his plans.

"Where you been?" demanded the butler suspiciously.

"Oh, hither and thither," said Wilfred, with a well-assumed airiness.

Murgatroyd directed a menacing glance at him.

"You'd better stay where you belong," he said, in his thick, growling voice. "There's things in this house that don't want seeing."

"Ah!" agreed the cook, dropping an onion in the caldron.

Wilfred could not repress a shudder.

But, even as he shuddered, he was conscious of a certain relief. At least, he reflected, they were not starving his darling. That cutlet had smelt uncommonly good; and, if the bill of fare was always maintained at this level, she had nothing to complain of in the catering.

But his relief was short-lived. What, after all, he asked himself, are cutlets to a girl who is imprisoned in a locked room of a sinister country house and is being forced to marry a man she does not love? Practically nothing. When the heart is sick, cutlets merely alleviate, they do not cure. Fiercely Wilfred told himself that, come what might, few days should pass before he found the key to that locked door and bore away his love to freedom and happiness.

The only obstacle in the way of this scheme was that it was plainly going to be a matter of the greatest difficulty to find the key. That night, when his employer dined, Wilfred searched his room thoroughly. He found nothing. The key, he was forced to conclude, was kept on the baronet's person.

Then how to secure it?

It is not too much to say that Wilfred Mulliner was nonplused. The brain which had electrified the world of Science by discovering that if you mixed a stiffish oxygen and potassium and added a splash of trinitrotoluol and a spot of old brandy you got something that could be sold in America as champagne at a hundred and fifty dollars the case, had to confess itself baffled.

To attempt to analyze the young man's emotions, as the next week dragged itself by, would be merely morbid. Life cannot, of course, be all sunshine; and in relating a story like this, which is a slice of life, one must pay as much attention to shade as to light; nevertheless, it would be tedious were I to describe to you in detail the soul torments which afflicted Wilfred Mulliner as day followed day and no solution to the problem presented itself. You are all intelligent men, and you can picture to yourselves how a high-spirited young fellow, deeply in love, must have felt; knowing that the girl he loved was languishing in what practically amounted to a dungeon, though situated on an upper floor, and chafing at his inability to set her free.

His eyes became sunken. His cheekbones stood out. He lost weight. And so noticeable was this change in his physique that Sir Jasper ffinch-ffarrowmere commented on it one evening in tones of unconcealed envy.

"How the devil, Straker," he said—for this was the pseudonym under which Wilfred was passing, "do you manage to keep so thin? Judging by the weekly books, you eat like a starving Eskimo, and yet you don't put on weight. Now I, in addition to knocking off butter and potatoes, have started drinking hot unsweetened lemon juice each night before retiring; and yet, damme," he said—for, like all baronets, he was careless in his language, "I weighed myself this morning, and I was up another six ounces. What's the explanation?"

"Yes, Sir Jasper," said Wilfred mechanically.

"What the devil do you mean, 'Yes, Sir Jasper'?"

"No, Sir Jasper."

The baronet wheezed plaintively.

"I've been studying this matter closely," he said, "and it's one of the seven wonders of the world. Have you ever seen a fat valet? Of course not. Nor has anybody else. There is no such thing as a fat valet. And yet there is scarcely a moment during the day when a valet is not eating. He rises at six-thirty, and at seven is having coffee and buttered toast. At eight, he breakfasts off porridge, cream, eggs, bacon, jam, bread, butter, more eggs, more bacon, more jam, more tea, and more butter, finishing up with a slice of cold ham and a sardine. At eleven o'clock he has his 'elevenses,' consisting of coffee, cream, more bread and more butter. At one, luncheon—a hearty meal, replete with every form of starchy food and lots of beer. If he can get at the port, he has port. At three, a snack. At four, another snack. At five, tea and buttered toast. At seven—dinner, probably with floury potatoes, and certainly with lots more beer. At nine, another snack. And at ten-thirty he retires to bed, taking with him a glass of milk and a plate of biscuits to keep himself from getting hungry in the night. And yet he remains as slender as a string bean, while I, who have been dieting for years, tip the beam at two hundred and seventeen pounds, and am growing a third and supplementary chin. These are mysteries, Straker."

"Yes, Sir Jasper."

"Well, I'll tell you one thing," said the baronet, "I'm getting down one of those indoor Turkish-bath cabinet affairs from London; and if that doesn't do the trick, I give up the struggle."

The indoor Turkish bath duly arrived and was unpacked; and it was some three nights later that Wilfred, brooding in the servants' hall, was aroused from his reverie by Murgatroyd.

"Here," said Murgatroyd, "wake up. Sir Jasper's calling you."

"Calling me what?" asked Wilfred, coming to himself with a start.

"Calling you very loud," growled the butler.

It was indeed so. From the upper regions of the house there was proceeding a series of sharp yelps, evidently those of a man in mortal stress. Wilfred was reluctant to interfere in any way if, as seemed probable, his employer was dying in agony; but he was a conscientious man, and it was his duty, while in this sinister house, to perform the work for which he was paid. He hurried up the stairs; and, entering Sir Jasper's bedroom, perceived the baronet's crimson face protruding from the top of the indoor Turkish bath.

"So you've come at last!" cried Sir Jasper. "Look here, when you put me into this infernal contrivance just now, what did you do to the dashed thing?"

"Nothing beyond what was indicated in the printed pamphlet accompanying the machine, Sir Jasper. Following the instructions, I slid Rod A into Groove B, fastening with Catch C—"

"Well, you must have made a mess of it, somehow. The thing's stuck. I can't get out."

"You can't?" cried Wilfred.

"No. And the bally apparatus is getting considerably hotter than the hinges of the Inferno." I must apologize for Sir Jasper's language, but you know what baronets are. "I'm being cooked to a crisp."

A sudden flash of light seemed to blaze upon Wilfred Mulliner.

"I will release you, Sir Jasper—"

"Well, hurry up, then."

"On one condition." Wilfred fixed him with a piercing gaze. "First, I must have the key."

"There isn't a key, you idiot. It doesn't lock. It just clicks when you slide Gadget D into Thingummybob E."

"The key I require is that of the room in which you are holding Angela Purdue a prisoner."

"What the devil do you mean? Ouch!"

"I will tell you what I mean, Sir Jasper ffinch-ffarrowmere. I am Wilfred Mulliner!"

"Don't be an ass. Wilfred Mulliner has black hair. Yours is red. You must be thinking of someone else."

"This is a wig," said Wilfred. "By Clarkson." He shook a menacing finger at the baronet. "You little thought, Sir Jasper ffinch-ffarrowmere, when you embarked on this dastardly scheme, that Wilfred

Mulliner was watching your every move. I guessed your plans from the start. And now is the moment when I checkmate them. Give me that key, you Fiend."

"ffiend," corrected Sir Jasper automatically.

"I am going to release my darling, to take her away from this dreadful house, to marry her by special licence as soon as it can legally be done."

In spite of his sufferings, a ghastly laugh escaped Sir Jasper's lips. "You are, are you!"

"I am."

"Yes, you are!"

"Give me the key."

"I haven't got it, you chump. It's in the door."

"Ha, ha!"

"It's no good saying 'Ha, ha!' It is in the door. On Angela's side of the door."

"A likely story! But I cannot stay here wasting time. If you will not give me the key, I shall go up and break in the door."

"Do!" Once more the baronet laughed like a tortured soul. "And see what she'll say."

Wilfred could make nothing of this last remark. He could, he thought, imagine very clearly what Angela would say. He could picture her sobbing on his chest, murmuring that she knew he would come, that she had never doubted him for an instant. He leapt for the door.

"Here! Hi! Aren't you going to let me out?"

"Presently," said Wilfred. "Keep cool." He raced up the stairs.

"Angela," he cried, pressing his lips against the panel. "Angela!"

"Who's that?" answered a well-remembered voice from within.

"It is I—Wilfred. I am going to burst open the door. Stand clear of the gates."

He drew back a few paces, and hurled himself at the woodwork. There was a grinding crash as the lock gave. And Wilfred, staggering on, found himself in a room so dark that he could see nothing.

"Angela, where are you?"

"I'm here. And I'd like to know why you are, after that letter I wrote you. Some men," continued the strangely cold voice, "do not seem to know how to take a hint."

Wilfred staggered, and would have fallen had he not clutched at his forehead.

"That letter?" he stammered. "You surely didn't mean what you wrote in that letter?"

"I meant every word and I wish I had put in more."

"But—but—but— But don't you love me, Angela?"

A hard, mocking laugh rang through the room.

"Love you? Love the man who recommended me to try Mulliner's Raven Gypsy Face Cream!"

"What do you mean?"

"I will tell you what I mean. Wilfred Mulliner, look at your handiwork!"

The room became suddenly flooded with light. And there, standing with her hand on the switch, stood Angela—a queenly, lovely figure, in whose radiant beauty the sternest critic would have noted but one flaw—the fact that she was piebald.

Wilfred gazed at her with adoring eyes. Her face was partly brown and partly white, and on her snowy neck were patches of sepia that looked like the thumbprints you find on the pages of books in the Free Library; but he thought her the most beautiful creature he had ever seen. He longed to fold her in his arms; and but for the fact that her eyes told him that she would undoubtedly land an uppercut on him if he tried it he would have done so.

"Yes," she went on, "this is what you have made of me, Wilfred Mulliner—you and the awful stuff you call the Raven Gypsy Face Cream. This is the skin you loved to touch! I took your advice and bought one of the large jars at seven and six, and see the result! Barely twenty-four hours after the first application, I could have walked into any circus and named my own terms as the Spotted Princess of the Fiji Islands. I fled here to my childhood home, to hide myself. And the first thing that happened"—her voice broke—"was that my favorite hunter shied at me and tried to bite pieces out of his manger, while Ponto, my little dog, whom I have reared from a puppy, caught one sight of my face and is now in the hands of the vet and unlikely to recover. And it was you, Wilfred Mulliner, who brought this curse upon me."

Many men would have wilted beneath these searing words, but Wilfred Mulliner merely smiled with infinite compassion and understanding.

"It is quite all right," he said. "I should have warned you, sweetheart, that this occasionally happens in cases where the skin is exceptionally delicate and finely textured. It can be speedily remedied by an application of the Mulliner Snow of the Mountains Lotion, four shillings the medium-sized bottle."

"Wilfred! Is this true?"

"Perfectly true, dearest. And is this all that stands between us?"

"No!" shouted a voice of thunder.

Wilfred wheeled sharply. In the doorway stood Sir Jasper ffinch-ffarrowmere. He was swathed in a bath towel, what was visible of his person being a bright crimson. Behind him, toying with a horsewhip, stood Murgatroyd, the butler.

"You didn't expect to see me, did you?"

"I certainly," replied Wilfred severely, "did not expect to see you in a lady's presence in a costume like that."

"Never mind my costume." Sir Jasper turned.

"Murgatroyd, do your duty!"

The butler, scowling horribly, advanced into the room.

"Stop!" screamed Angela.

"I haven't begun yet, miss," said the butler deferentially.

"You shan't touch Wilfred. I love him."

"What!" cried Sir Jasper. "After all that has happened?"

"Yes. He has explained everything."

A grim frown appeared on the baronet's vermilion face.

"I'll bet he hasn't explained why he left me to be cooked in that infernal Turkish bath. I was beginning to throw out clouds of smoke when Murgatroyd, faithful fellow, heard my cries and came and released me."

"Though not my work," added the butler.

Wilfred eyed him steadily.

"If," he said, "you used Mulliner's Reduc-o, the recognized specific for obesity, whether in the tabloid form at three shillings the tin, or as a liquid at five and six the flask, you would have no need to stew in Turkish baths. Mulliner's Reduc-o, which contains no injurious chemicals, but is compounded purely of health-giving herbs, is guaranteed to remove excess weight, steadily and without weakening after effects, at the rate of two pounds a week. As used by the nobility."

The glare of hatred faded from the baronet's eyes.

"Is that a fact?" he whispered.

"It is."

"You guarantee it?"

"All the Mulliner preparations are fully guaranteed."

"My boy!" cried the baronet. He shook Wilfred by the hand. "Take her," he said brokenly. "And with her my b-blessing."

A discreet cough sounded in the background.

"You haven't anything, by any chance, sir," asked Murgatroyd, "that's good for lumbago?"

"Mulliner's Ease-o will cure the most stubborn case in six days."

"Bless you, sir, bless you," sobbed Murgatroyd. "Where can I get it?"

"At all chemists."

"It catches me in the small of the back principally, sir."

"It need catch you no longer," said Wilfred.

There is little to add. Murgatroyd is now the most lissome butler in Yorkshire. Sir Jasper's weight is down under the fifteen stone and he is thinking of taking up hunting again. Wilfred and Angela are man and wife; and never, I am informed, have the wedding bells of the old church at ffinch village rung out a blither peal than they did on that June morning when Angela, raising to her love a face on which the brown was as evenly distributed as on an antique walnut table, replied to the clergyman's question, "Wilt thou, Angela, take this Wilfred?" with a shy, "I will." They now have two bonny bairns —the small, or Percival, at a preparatory school in Sussex, and the large, or Ferdinand, at Eton.

Here Mr. Mulliner, having finished his hot Scotch, bade us farewell and took his departure.

A silence followed his exit. The company seemed plunged in deep thought. Then somebody rose.

"Well, good night all," he said.

It seemed to sum up the situation.

❂ *Mulliner's Buck-U-Uppo*

THE village Choral Society had been giving a performance of Gilbert and Sullivan's "Sorcerer" in aid of the Church Organ Fund; and, as we sat in the window of the Anglers' Rest, smoking our pipes, the audience came streaming past us down the little street. Snatches of song floated to our ears, and Mr. Mulliner began to croon in unison.

" 'Ah me! I was a pa-ale you-oung curate then!' " chanted Mr. Mulliner in the rather snuffling voice in which the amateur singer seems to find it necessary to render the old songs.

"Remarkable," he said, resuming his natural tones, "how fashions change, even in clergymen. There are very few pale young curates nowadays."

"True," I agreed. "Most of them are beefy young fellows who rowed for their colleges. I don't believe I have ever seen a pale young curate."

"You never met my nephew Augustine, I think?"

"Never."

"The description in the song would have fitted him perfectly. You will want to hear all about my nephew Augustine."

At the time of which I am speaking (said Mr. Mulliner) my nephew Augustine was a curate, and very young and extremely pale. As a boy he had completely outgrown his strength, and I rather think that at his Theological College some of the wilder spirits must have bullied him; for when he went to Lower Briskett-in-the-Midden to assist the vicar, the Rev. Stanley Brandon, in his cure of souls, he was as meek and mild a young man as you could meet in a day's journey. He had flaxen hair, weak blue eyes, and the general demeanor of a saintly but timid codfish. Precisely, in short, the sort of young curate who seems to have been so common in the eighties, or whenever it was that Gilbert wrote "The Sorcerer."

The personality of his immediate superior did little or nothing to help him to overcome his native diffidence. The Rev. Stanley Brandon was a huge and sinewy man of violent temper, whose red face and glittering eyes might well have intimidated the toughest curate.

The Rev. Stanley had been a heavyweight boxer at Cambridge, and I gather from Augustine that he seemed to be always on the point of introducing into debates on parish matters the methods which had made him so successful in the roped ring. I remember Augustine telling me that once, on the occasion when he had ventured to oppose the other's views in the matter of decorating the church for the Harvest Festival, he thought for a moment that the vicar was going to drop him with a right hook to the chin. It was some quite trivial point that had come up—a question as to whether the pumpkin would look better in the apse or the clerestory, if I recollect rightly—but for several seconds it seemed as if blood was about to be shed.

Such was the Rev. Stanley Brandon. And yet it was to the daughter of this formidable man that Augustine Mulliner had permitted himself to lose his heart. Truly, Cupid makes heroes of us all.

Jane was a very nice girl, and just as fond of Augustine as he was of her. But, as each lacked the nerve to go to the girl's father and put him abreast of the position of affairs, they were forced to meet surreptitiously. This jarred upon Augustine, who, like all the Mulliners, loved the truth and hated any form of deception. And one evening, as they paced beside the laurels at the bottom of the vicarage garden, he rebelled.

"My dearest," said Augustine, "I can no longer brook this secrecy. I shall go into the house immediately and ask your father for your hand."

Jane paled and clung to his arm. She knew so well that it was not her hand but her father's foot which he would receive if he carried out this mad scheme.

"No, no, Augustine! You must not!"

"But, darling, it is the only straightforward course."

"But not tonight. I beg of you, not tonight."

"Why not?"

"Because father is in a very bad temper. He has just had a letter from the bishop, rebuking him for wearing too many orphreys on his chasuble, and it has upset him terribly. You see, he and the bishop were at school together, and father can never forget it. He said at dinner that if old Boko Bickerton thought he was going to order him about he would jolly well show him."

"And the bishop comes here tomorrow for the Confirmation services!" gasped Augustine.

"Yes. And I'm afraid they will quarrel. It's such a pity father hasn't some other bishop over him. He always remembers that he once hit this one in the eye for pouring ink on his collar, and this lowers his respect for his spiritual authority. So you won't go in and tell him tonight, will you?"

"I will not," Augustine assured her with a slight shiver.

"And you will be sure to put your feet in hot mustard and water when you get home? The dew has made the grass so wet."

"I will indeed, dearest."

"You are not strong, you know."

"No, I am not strong."

"You ought to take some really good tonic."

"Perhaps I ought. Good night, Jane."

"Good night, Augustine."

The lovers parted. Jane slipped back into the vicarage, and Augustine made his way to his cozy rooms in the High Street. And the first thing he noticed on entering was a parcel on the table, and beside it a letter.

He opened it listlessly, his thoughts far away.

"My dear Augustine."

He turned to the last page and glanced at the signature. The letter was from his Aunt Angela, the wife of my brother, Wilfred Mulliner. You may remember that I once told you the story of how these two came together. If so, you will recall that my brother Wilfred was the eminent chemical researcher who had invented, among other specifics, such world-famous preparations at Mulliner's Raven Gypsy Face Cream and the Mulliner Snow of the Mountains Lotion. He and Augustine had never been particularly intimate, but between Augustine and his aunt there had always existed a warm friendship.

My dear Augustine (wrote Angela Mulliner),

I have been thinking so much about you lately, and I cannot forget that, when I saw you last, you seemed very fragile and deficient in vitamins. I do hope you take care of yourself.

I have been feeling for some time that you ought to take a tonic, and by a lucky chance Wilfred has just invented one which he tells me is the finest thing he has ever done. It is called Buck-U-Uppo, and acts directly on the red corpuscles. It is not yet on the market, but I have managed to smuggle a sample bottle from Wilfred's laboratory, and I want you to try it at once. I am sure it is just what you need.

                                                    Your affectionate aunt,
                                                    Angela Mulliner.

P. S.—You take a tablespoonful before going to bed, and another just before breakfast.

Augustine was not an unduly superstitious young man, but the coincidence of this tonic arriving so soon after Jane had told him that a tonic was what he needed affected him deeply. It seemed to him that this thing must have been meant. He shook the bottle, uncorked it, and, pouring out a liberal tablespoonful, shut his eyes and swallowed it.

The medicine, he was glad to find, was not unpleasant to the taste. It had a slightly pungent flavor, rather like old boot soles beaten up in sherry. Having taken the dose, he read for a while in a book of theological essays, and then went to bed.

And as his feet slipped between the sheets, he was annoyed to find that Mrs. Wardle, his housekeeper, had once more forgotten his hot-water bottle.

"Oh, dash!" said Augustine.

He was thoroughly upset. He had told the woman over and over again that he suffered from cold feet and could not get to sleep unless the dogs were properly warmed up. He sprang out of bed and went to the head of the stairs.

"Mrs. Wardle!" he cried.

There was no reply.

"Mrs. Wardle!" bellowed Augustine in a voice that rattled the windowpanes like a strong nor'easter. Until tonight he had always been very much afraid of his housekeeper and had both walked and talked softly in her presence. But now he was conscious of a strange new fortitude. His head was singing a little, and he felt equal to a dozen Mrs. Wardles.

Shuffling footsteps made themselves heard.

"Well, what is it now?" asked a querulous voice.

Augustine snorted.

"I'll tell you what it is now," he roared. "How many times have I told you always to put a hot-water bottle in my bed? You've forgotten it again, you old cloth-head!"

Mrs. Wardle peered up, astounded and militant.

"Mr. Mulliner, I am not accustomed—"

"Shut up!" thundered Augustine. "What I want from you is less backchat and more hot-water bottles. Bring it up at once, or I leave tomorrow. Let me endeavor to get it into your concrete skull that you aren't the only person letting rooms in this village. Any more lip and I walk straight round the corner, where I'll be appreciated. Hot-water bottle ho! And look slippy about it."

"Yes, Mr. Mulliner. Certainly, Mr. Mulliner. In one moment, Mr. Mulliner."

"Action! Action!" boomed Augustine. "Show some speed. Put a little snap into it."

"Yes, yes, most decidedly, Mr. Mulliner," replied the chastened voice from below.

An hour later, as he was dropping off to sleep, a thought crept into Augustine's mind. Had he not been a little brusque with Mrs. Wardle? Had there not been in his manner something a shade abrupt —almost rude? Yes, he decided regretfully, there had. He lit a candle and reached for the diary which lay on the table at his bedside.

He made an entry.

The meek shall inherit the earth. Am I sufficiently meek? I wonder. This evening, when reproaching Mrs. Wardle, my worthy house-keeper, for omitting to place a hot-water bottle in my bed, I spoke quite crossly. The provocation was severe, but still I was surely to blame for allowing my passions to run riot. Mem: Must guard agst this.

But when he woke next morning, different feelings prevailed. He took his antebreakfast dose of Buck-U-Uppo; and looking at the entry in the diary, could scarcely believe that it was he who had written it. "Quite cross?" Of course he had been quite cross. Wouldn't anybody be quite cross who was for ever being persecuted by beetle-wits who forgot hot-water bottles?

Erasing the words with one strong dash of a thick-leaded pencil, he scribbled in the margin a hasty "Mashed potatoes! Served the old idiot right!" and went down to breakfast.

He felt most amazingly fit. Undoubtedly, in asserting that this tonic of his acted forcefully upon the red corpuscles, his Uncle Wilfred had been right. Until that moment Augustine had never supposed that he had any red corpuscles; but now, as he sat waiting for Mrs. Wardle to bring him his fried egg, he could feel them dancing about all over him. They seemed to be forming rowdy parties and sliding down his spine. His eyes sparkled, and from sheer joy of living he sang a few bars from the hymn for those of riper years at sea.

He was still singing when Mrs. Wardle entered with a dish.

"What's this?" demanded Augustine, eying it dangerously.

"A nice fried egg, sir."

"And what, pray, do you mean by nice? It may be an amiable egg. It may be a civil, well-meaning egg. But if you think it is fit for human consumption, adjust that impression. Go back to your kitchen, woman; select another; and remember this time that you are a cook, not an incinerating machine. Between an egg that is fried and an egg that is cremated there is a wide and substantial difference. This difference, if you wish to retain me as a lodger in these far too expensive rooms, you will endeavor to appreciate."

The glowing sense of well-being with which Augustine had begun the day did not diminish with the passage of time. It seemed, indeed, to increase. So full of effervescing energy did the young man feel that, departing from his usual custom of spending the morning crouched over the fire, he picked up his hat, stuck it at a rakish angle on his head, and sallied out for a healthy tramp across the fields.

It was while he was returning, flushed and rosy, that he observed a sight which is rare in the country districts of England—the spectacle of a bishop running. It is not often in a place like Lower Briskett-in-the-Midden that you see a bishop at all; and when you do he is either riding in a stately car or pacing at a dignified walk. This one was sprinting like a Derby winner, and Augustine paused to drink in the sight.

The bishop was a large, burly bishop, built for endurance rather than speed; but he was making excellent going. He flashed past Augustine in a whirl of flying gaiters; and then, proving himself thereby no mere specialist but a versatile all-round athlete, suddenly dived for a tree and climbed rapidly into its branches. His motive, Augustine readily divined, was to elude a rough, hairy dog which was toiling in his wake. The dog reached the tree a moment after his quarry had climbed it, and stood there, barking.

Augustine strolled up.

"Having a little trouble with the dumb friend, bish?" he asked genially.

The bishop peered down from his eyrie.

"Young man," he said, "save me!"

"Right most indubitably ho!" replied Augustine. "Leave it to me."

Until today he had always been terrified of dogs, but now he did not hesitate. Almost quicker than words can tell, he picked up a stone, discharged it at the animal, and whooped cheerily as it got home with a thud. The dog, knowing when he had had enough, removed himself at some forty-five m.p.h.; and the bishop, descending cautiously, clasped Augustine's hand in his.

"My preserver!" said the bishop.

"Don't give it another thought," said Augustine cheerily. "Always glad to do a pal a good turn. We clergymen must stick together."

"I thought he had me for a minute."

"Quite a nasty customer. Full of rude energy."

The bishop nodded.

"His eye was not dim, nor his natural force abated. Deuteronomy xxxiv. 7," he agreed. "I wonder if you can direct me to the vicarage? I fear I have come a little out of my way."

"I'll take you there."

"Thank you. Perhaps it would be as well if you did not come in. I have a serious matter to discuss with old Pieface—I mean, with the Rev. Stanley Brandon."

"I have a serious matter to discuss with his daughter. I'll just hang about the garden."

"You are a very excellent young man," said the bishop, as they walked along. "You are a curate, eh?"

"At present. But," said Augustine, tapping his companion on the chest, "just watch my smoke. That's all I ask you to do—just watch my smoke."

"I will. You should rise to great heights—to the very top of the tree."

"Like you did just now, eh? Ha, ha!"

"Ha, ha!" said the bishop. "You young rogue!"

He poked Augustine in the ribs.

"Ha, ha, ha!" said Augustine.

He slapped the bishop on the back.

"But all joking aside," said the bishop as they entered the vicarage grounds, "I really shall keep my eye on you and see that you receive the swift preferment which your talents and character deserve. I say to you, my dear young friend, speaking seriously and weighing my words, that the way you picked that dog off with that stone was the smoothest thing I ever saw. And I am a man who always tells the strict truth."

"Great is truth and mighty above all things. Esdras iv. 41," said Augustine.

He turned away and strolled toward the laurel bushes, which were his customary meeting place with Jane. The bishop went on to the front door and rang the bell.

Although they had made no definite appointment, Augustine was surprised when the minutes passed and no Jane appeared. He did not know that she had been told off by her father to entertain the bishop's wife that morning, and show her the sights of Lower Briskett-in-the-Midden. He waited some quarter of an hour with growing impatience, and was about to leave when suddenly from the house there came to his ears the sound of voices raised angrily.

He stopped. The voices appeared to proceed from a room on the ground floor facing the garden.

Running lightly over the turf, Augustine paused outside the window and listened. The window was open at the bottom, and he could hear quite distinctly.

The vicar was speaking in a voice that vibrated through the room.

"Is that so?" said the vicar.

"Yes, it is!" said the bishop.

"Ha, ha!"

"Ha, ha! to you, and see how you like it!" rejoined the bishop with spirit.

Augustine drew a step closer. It was plain that Jane's fears had been justified and that there was serious trouble afoot between these two old schoolfellows. He peeped in. The vicar, his hands behind his coattails, was striding up and down the carpet, while the bishop, his back to the fireplace, glared defiance at him from the hearth-rug.

"Who ever told you you were an authority on chasubles?" demanded the vicar.

"That's all right who told me," rejoined the bishop.

"I don't believe you know that a chasuble is."

"Is that so?"

"Well, what is it, then?"

"It's a circular cloak hanging from the shoulders, elaborately embroidered with a pattern and with orphreys. And you can argue as much as you like, young Pieface, but you can't get away from the fact that there are too many orphreys on yours. And what I'm telling you is that you've jolly well got to switch off a few of those orphreys or you'll get it in the neck."

The vicar's eyes glittered furiously.

"Is that so?" he said. "Well, I just won't, so there! And it's like your cheek coming here and trying to high-hat me. You seem to have forgotten that I knew you when you were an inky-faced kid at school, and that, if I liked, I could tell the world one or two things about you which would probably amuse it."

"My past is an open book."

"Is it?" The vicar laughed malevolently. "Who put the white mouse in the French master's desk?"

The bishop started.

"Who put jam in the dormitory prefect's bed?" he retorted.

"Who couldn't keep his collar clean?"

"Who used to wear a dickey?" The bishop's wonderful organlike voice, whose softest whisper could be heard throughout a vast cathedral, rang out in tones of thunder. "Who was sick at the house supper?"

The vicar quivered from head to foot. His rubicund face turned a deeper crimson.

"You know jolly well," he said, in shaking accents, "that there was something wrong with the turkey. Might have upset anyone."

"The only thing wrong with the turkey was that you ate too much of it. If you had paid as much attention to developing your soul as you did to developing your tummy, you might by now," said the bishop, "have risen to my own eminence."

"Oh, might I?"

"No, perhaps I am wrong. You never had the brain."

The vicar uttered another discordant laugh.

"Brain is good! We know all about your eminence, as you call it, and how you rose to that eminence."

"What do you mean?"

"You are a bishop. How you became one we will not inquire."

"What do you mean?"

"What I say. We will not inquire."

"Why don't you inquire?"

"Because," said the vicar, "it is better not!"

The bishop's self-control left him. His face contorted with fury, he took a step forward. And simultaneously Augustine sprang lightly into the room.

"Now, now, now!" said Augustine. "Now, now, now, now, now!"

The two men stood transfixed. They stared at the intruder dumbly.

"Come, come!" said Augustine.

The vicar was the first to recover. He glowered at Augustine.

"What do you mean by jumping through my window?" he thundered. "Are you a curate or a harlequin?"

Augustine met his gaze with an unfaltering eye.

"I am a curate," he replied, with a dignity that well became him. "And, as a curate, I cannot stand by and see two superiors of the cloth, who are moreover old schoolfellows, forgetting themselves. It isn't right. Absolutely not right, my dear old superiors of the cloth."

The vicar bit his lip. The bishop bowed his head.

"Listen," proceeded Augustine, placing a hand on the shoulder of each. "I hate to see you two dear good chaps quarreling like this."

"He started it," said the vicar sullenly.

"Never mind who started it." Augustine silenced the bishop with a curt gesture as he made to speak. "Be sensible, my dear fellows. Respect the decencies of debate. Exercise a little good-humored give-and-take. You say," he went on, turning to the bishop, "that our good friend here has too many orphreys on his chasuble?"

"I do. And I stick to it."

"Yes, yes, yes. But what," said Augustine soothingly, "are a few orphreys between friends? Reflect! You and our worthy vicar here were at school together. You are bound by the sacred ties of the old Alma Mater. With him you sported on the green. With him you shared a crib and threw inked darts in the hour supposed to be devoted to the study of French. Do these things mean nothing to you? Do these memories touch no chord?" He turned appealingly from one to the other. "Vicar! Bish!"

The vicar had moved away and was wiping his eyes. The bishop fumbled for a pocket handkerchief. There was a silence.

"Sorry, Pieface," said the bishop, in a choking voice.

"Shouldn't have spoken as I did, Boko," mumbled the vicar.

"If you want to know what I think," said the bishop, "you are right in attributing your indisposition at the house supper to something wrong with the turkey. I recollect saying at the time that the bird should never have been served in such a condition."

"And when you put that white mouse in the French master's desk," said the vicar, "you performed one of the noblest services to humanity of which there is any record. They ought to have made you a bishop on the spot."

"Pieface!"

"Boko!"

The two men clasped hands.

"Splendid!" said Augustine. "Everything hotsy-totsy now?"

"Quite, quite," said the vicar.

"As far as I am concerned, completely hotsy-totsy," said the bishop. He turned to his old friend solicitously. "You will continue to wear all the orphreys you want—will you not, Pieface?"

"No, no, I see now that I was wrong. From now on, Boko, I abandon orphreys altogether."

"But, Pieface—"

"It's all right," the vicar assured him. "I can take them or leave them alone."

"Splendid fellow!" The bishop coughed to hide his emotion, and there was another silence. "I think, perhaps," he went on, after a pause, "I should be leaving you now, my dear chap, and going in search of my wife. She is with your daughter, I believe, somewhere in the village."

"They are coming up the drive now."

"Ah, yes, I see them. A charming girl, your daughter."

Augustine clapped him on the shoulder.

"Bish," he exclaimed, "you said a mouthful. She is the dearest, sweetest girl in the whole world. And I should be glad, vicar, if you would give your consent to our immediate union. I love Jane with a good man's fervor, and I am happy to inform you that my sentiments are returned. Assure us, therefore, of your approval, and I will go at once and have the banns put up."

The vicar leaped as though he had been stung. Like so many vicars, he had a poor opinion of curates, and he had always regarded Augustine as rather below than above the general norm or level of the despised class.

"What!" he cried.

"A most excellent idea," said the bishop, beaming. "A very happy notion, I call it."

"My daughter!" The vicar seemed dazed. "My daughter marry a curate!"

"You were a curate once yourself, Pieface."

"Yes, but not a curate like that."

"No!" said the bishop. "You were not. Nor was I. Better for us both had we been. This young man, I would have you know, is the most outstandingly excellent young man I have ever encountered. Are you aware that scarcely an hour ago he saved me with the most consummate address from a large shaggy dog with black spots and a kink in his tail? I was sorely pressed, Pieface, when this young man came up and, with a readiness of resource and an accuracy of aim which it would be impossible to overpraise, got that dog in the short ribs with a rock and sent him flying."

The vicar seemed to be struggling with some powerful emotion. His eyes had widened.

"A dog with black spots?"

"Very black spots. But no blacker, I fear, than the heart they hid."

"And he really plugged him in the short ribs?"

"As far as I could see, squarely in the short ribs."

The vicar held out his hand.

"Mulliner," he said, "I was not aware of this. In the light of the facts which have just been drawn to my attention, I have no hesitation in saying that my objections are removed. I have had it in for that dog since the second Sunday before Septuagesima, when he pinned me by the ankle as I paced beside the river composing a sermon on Certain Alarming Manifestations of the So-called Modern Spirit. Take Jane. I give my consent freely. And may she be as happy as any girl with such a husband ought to be."

A few more affecting words were exchanged, and then the bishop and Augustine left the house. The bishop was silent and thoughtful. "I owe you a great deal, Mulliner," he said at length.

"Oh, I don't know," said Augustine. "Would you say that?"

"A very great deal. You saved me from a terrible disaster. Had you not leaped through that window at that precise juncture and intervened, I really believe I should have pasted my dear old friend Brandon in the eye. I was sorely exasperated."

"Our good vicar can be trying at times," agreed Augustine.

"My fist was already clenched, and I was just hauling off for the swing when you checked me. What the result would have been, had you not exhibited a tact and discretion beyond your years, I do not like to think. I might have been unfrocked." He shivered at the thought, though the weather was mild. "I could never have shown my face at the Athenæum again. But, tut, tut!" went on the bishop, patting Augustine on the shoulder, "let us not dwell on what might have been. Speak to me of yourself. The vicar's charming daughter— you really love her?"

"I do, indeed."

The bishop's face had grown grave.

"Think well, Mulliner," he said. "Marriage is a serious affair. Do not plunge into it without due reflection. I myself am a husband, and, though singularly blessed in the possession of a devoted helpmeet, cannot but feel sometimes that a man is better off as a bachelor. Women, Mulliner, are odd."

"True," said Augustine.

"My own dear wife is the best of women. And, as I never weary of saying, a good woman is a wondrous creature, cleaving to the right and the good under all change; lovely in youthful comeliness, lovely all her life in comeliness of heart. And yet—"

"And yet?" said Augustine.

The bishop mused for a moment. He wriggled a little with an expression of pain, and scratched himself between the shoulder blades.

"Well, I'll tell you," said the bishop. "It is a warm and pleasant day today, is it not?"

"Exceptionally clement," said Augustine.

"A fair, sunny day, made gracious by a temperate westerly breeze. And yet, Mulliner, if you will credit my statement, my wife insisted on my putting on my thick winter woollies this morning. Truly," sighed the bishop, "as a jewel of gold in a swine's snout, so is a fair woman which is without discretion. Proverbs xi. 21."

"Twenty-two," corrected Augustine.

"I should have said twenty-two. They are made of thick flannel, and I have an exceptionally sensitive skin. Oblige me, my dear fellow, by rubbing me in the small of the back with the ferrule of your stick. I think it will ease the irritation."

"But, my poor dear old bish," said Augustine sympathetically, "this must not be."

The bishop shook his head ruefully.

"You would not speak so hardily, Mulliner, if you knew my wife. There is no appeal from her decrees."

"Nonsense," cried Augustine cheerily. He looked through the trees to where the lady bishopess, escorted by Jane, was examining a lobelia through her lorgnette with just the right bend of cordiality and condescension. "I'll fix that for you in a second."

The bishop clutched at his arm.

"My boy! What are you going to do?"

"I'm just going to have a word with your wife and put the matter up to her as a reasonable woman. Thick winter woollies on a day like this! Absurd!" said Augustine. "Preposterous! I never heard such rot."

The bishop gazed after him with a laden heart. Already he had come to love this young man like a son; and to see him charging so lightheartedly into the very jaws of destruction afflicted him with a deep and poignant sadness. He knew what his wife was like when even the highest in the land attempted to thwart her; and this brave lad was but a curate. In another moment she would be looking at him through her lorgnette; and England was littered with the shriveled remains of curates at whom the lady bishopess had looked through her lorgnette. He had seen them wilt like salted slugs at the episcopal breakfast table.

He held his breath. Augustine had reached the lady bishopess, and the lady bishopess was even now raising her lorgnette.

The bishop shut his eyes and turned away. And then—years afterwards, it seemed to him—a cheery voice hailed him; and, turning, he perceived Augustine bounding back through the trees.

"It's all right, bish," said Augustine.

"All—all right?" faltered the bishop.

"Yes. She says you can go and change into the thin cashmere."

The bishop reeled.

"But—but—but wnat did you say to her? What arguments did you employ?"

"Oh, I just pointed out what a warm day it was and jollied her along a bit—"

"Jollied her along a bit!"

"And she agreed in the most friendly and cordial manner. She has asked me to call at the Palace one of these days."

The bishop seized Augustine's hand.

"My boy," he said in a broken voice, "you shall do more than call at the Palace. You shall come and live at the Palace. Become my secretary, Mulliner, and name your own salary. If you intend to marry, you will require an increased stipend. Become my secretary, boy, and never leave my side. I have needed somebody like you for years."

It was late in the afternoon when Augustine returned to his rooms, for he had been invited to lunch at the vicarage and had been the life and soul of the cheery little party.

"A letter for you, sir," said Mrs. Wardle obsequiously.

Augustine took the letter.

"I am sorry to say I shall be leaving you shortly, Mrs. Wardle."

"Oh, sir! If there's anything I can do—"

"Oh, it's not that. The fact is, the bishop has made me his secretary, and I shall have to shift my toothbrush and spats to the Palace, you see."

"Well, fancy that, sir! Why, you'll be a bishop yourself one of these days."

"Possibly," said Augustine. "Possibly. And now let me read this."

He opened the letter. A thoughtful frown appeared on his face as he read.

> *My dear Augustine,*
>
> *I am writing in some haste to tell you that the impulsiveness of your aunt has led to a rather serious mistake.*
>
> *She tells me that she dispatched to you yesterday by parcel post a sample bottle of my new Buck-U-Uppo, which she obtained without my knowledge from my laboratory. Had she mentioned what she was intending to do, I could have prevented a very unfortunate occurrence.*
>
> *Mulliner's Buck-U-Uppo is of two grades or qualities—the A and the B. The A is a mild, but strengthening, tonic designed for human invalids. The B, on the other hand, is purely for circulation*

in the animal kingdom, and was invented to fill a long-felt want throughout our Indian possessions.

As you are doubtless aware, the favorite pastime of the Indian Maharajahs is the hunting of the tiger of the jungle from the backs of elephants; and it has happened frequently in the past that hunts have been spoiled by the failure of the elephant to see eye to eye with its owner in the matter of what constitutes sport.

Too often elephants, on sighting the tiger, have turned and galloped home; and it was to correct this tendency on their part that I invented Mulliner's Buck-U-Uppo "B." One teaspoonful of the Buck-U-Uppo "B" administered in its morning bran mash will cause the most timid elephant to trumpet loudly and charge the fiercest tiger without a qualm.

Abstain, therefore, from taking any of the contents of the bottle you now possess,

> *And believe me,*
> *Your affectionate uncle,*
> *Wilfred Mulliner.*

Augustine remained for some time in deep thought after perusing this communication. Then, rising, he whistled a few bars of the psalm appointed for the twenty-sixth of June and left the room.

Half an hour later a telegraphic message was speeding over the wires.

It ran as follows:

Wilfred Mulliner,
> *The Gables,*
>> *Lesser Lossingham,*
>>> *Salop.*

Letter received. Send immediately, C.O.D., three cases of the "B." "Blessed shall be thy basket and thy store." Deuteronomy xxviii. 5.

> *Augustine.*

❁ The Reverent Wooing
of Archibald

THE CONVERSATION in the bar parlor of the Anglers' Rest, which always tends to get deepish toward closing time, had turned to the subject of the Modern Girl; and a Gin-and-Ginger-Ale sitting in the corner by the window remarked that it was strange how types die out.

"I can remember the days," said the Gin-and-Ginger-Ale, "when every other girl you met stood about six feet two in her dancing shoes, and had as many curves as a Scenic Railway. Now they are all five foot nothing and you can't see them sideways. Why is this?"

The Draught Stout shook his head.

"Nobody can say. It's the same with dogs. One moment the world is full of pugs as far as the eye can reach; the next, not a pug in sight, only Pekes and Alsatians. Odd!"

The Small Bass and the Double-Whisky-and-Splash admitted that these things were very mysterious, and supposed we should never know the reason for them. Probably we were not meant to know.

"I cannot agree with you, gentlemen," said Mr. Mulliner. He had been sipping his hot Scotch and lemon with a rather abstracted air; but now he sat up alertly, prepared to deliver judgment. "The reason for the disappearance of the dignified, queenly type of girl is surely obvious. It is Nature's method of ensuring the continuance of the species. A world full of the sort of young woman that Meredith used to put into his novels and du Maurier into his pictures in *Punch* would be a world full of permanent spinsters. The modern young man would never be able to summon up the nerve to propose to them."

"Something in that," assented the Draught Stout.

"I speak with authority on the point," said Mr. Mulliner, "because my nephew, Archibald, made me his confidant when he fell in love with Aurelia Cammarleigh. He worshiped that girl with a fervor which threatened to unseat his reason, such as it was; but the mere idea of asking her to be his wife gave him, he informed me, such a feeling of sick faintness that only by means of a very stiff brandy and soda, or some similar restorative, was he able to pull himself together on the occasions when he contemplated it. Had it not been for . . . But perhaps you would care to hear the story from the beginning?"

People who enjoyed a merely superficial acquaintance with my nephew Archibald (said Mr. Mulliner) were accustomed to set him down as just an ordinary pinheaded young man. It was only when they came to know him better that they discovered their mistake. Then they realized that his pinheadedness, so far from being ordinary, was exceptional. Even at the Drones Club, where the average of intellect is not high, it was often said of Archibald that, had his brain been constructed of silk, he would have been hard put to it to find sufficient material to make a canary a pair of cami-knickers. He sauntered through life with a cheerful insouciance, and up to the age of twenty-five had only once been moved by anything in the nature of a really strong emotion—on the occasion when, in the heart of Bond Street and at the height of the London season, he discovered that his man, Meadowes, had carelessly sent him out with odd spats on.

And then he met Aurelia Cammarleigh.

The first encounter between these two has always seemed to me to bear an extraordinary resemblance to the famous meeting between the poet Dante and Beatrice Fortinari. Dante, if you remember, exchanged no remarks with Beatrice on that occasion. Nor did Archibald with Aurelia. Dante just goggled at the girl. So did Archibald. Like Arichbald, Dante loved at first sight; and the poet's age at the time was, we are told, nine—which was almost exactly the mental age of Archibald Mulliner when he first set eyeglass on Aurelia Cammarleigh.

Only in the actual locale of the encounter do the two cases cease to be parallel. Dante, the story relates, was walking on the Ponte Vecchia, while Archibald Mulliner was having a thoughtful cocktail in the window of the Drones Club, looking out on Dover Street.

And he had just relaxed his lower jaw in order to examine Dover Street more comfortably when there swam into his line of vision something that looked like a Greek goddess. She came out of a shop opposite the club and stood on the pavement waiting for a taxi. And, as he saw her standing there, love at first sight seemed to go all over Archibald Mulliner like nettle rash.

It was strange that this should have been so, for she was not at all the sort of girl with whom Archibald had fallen in love at first sight in the past. I chanced, while in here the other day, to pick up a copy of one of the old yellowback novels of fifty years ago—the property, I believe, of Miss Postlethwaite, our courteous and erudite barmaid. It was entitled *Sir Ralph's Secret,* and its heroine, the Lady Elaine, was described as a superbly handsome girl, divinely tall, with a noble figure, the arched Montresor nose, haughty eyes beneath delicately penciled brows, and that indefinable air of aristocratic aloofness which marks the daughter of a hundred Earls. And Aurelia Cammarleigh might have been this formidable creature's double.

Yet Archibald, sighting her, reeled as if the cocktail he had just consumed had been his tenth instead of his first.

"Golly!" said Archibald.

To save himself from falling, he had clutched at a passing fellow member: and now, examining his catch, he saw that it was young Algy Wymondham-Wymondham. Just the fellow member he would have preferred to clutch at, for Algy was a man who went everywhere and knew everybody and could doubtless give him the information he desired.

"Algy, old prune," said Archibald in a low, throaty voice, "a moment of your valuable time, if you don't mind."

He paused, for he had perceived the need for caution. Algy was a notorious babbler, and it would be the height of rashness to give him an inkling of the passion which blazed within his breast. With a strong effort, he donned the mask. When he spoke again, it was with a deceiving nonchalance.

"I was just wondering if you happened to know who that girl is, across the street there. I suppose you don't know what her name is in rough numbers? Seems to me I've met her somewhere or something, or seen her, or something. Or something, if you know what I mean."

Algy followed his pointing finger and was in time to observe Aurelia as she disappeared into the cab.

"That girl?"

"Yes," said Archibald, yawning. "Who is she, if any?"

"Girl named Cammarleigh."

"Ah?" said Archibald, yawning again. "Then I haven't met her."

"Introduce you if you like. She's sure to be at Ascot. Look out for us there."

Archibald yawned for the third time.

"All right," he said, "I'll try to remember. Tell me about her. I mean, has she any fathers or mothers or any rot of that description?"

"Only an aunt. She lives with her in Park Street. She's potty."

Archibald started, stung to the quick.

"Potty? That divine. . . . I mean, that rather attractive-looking girl?"

"Not Aurelia. The aunt. She thinks Bacon wrote Shakespeare."

"Thinks who wrote what?" asked Archibald, puzzled, for the names were strange to him.

"You must have heard of Shakespeare. He's well known. Fellow who used to write plays. Only Aurelia's aunt says he didn't. She maintains that a bloke called Bacon wrote them for him."

"Dashed decent of him," said Archibald approvingly. "Of course, he may have owed Shakespeare money."

"There's that, of course."

"What was the name again?"

"Bacon."

"Bacon," said Archibald, jotting it down on his cuff. "Right."

Algy moved on, and Archibald, his soul bubbling within him like a Welsh rabbit at the height of its fever, sank into a chair and stared sightlessly at the ceiling. Then, rising, he went off to the Burlington Arcade to buy socks.

The process of buying socks eased for a while the turmoil that ran riot in Archibald's veins. But even socks with lavender clocks can only alleviate: they do not cure. Returning to his rooms, he found the anguish rather more overwhelming than ever. For at last he had leisure to think, and thinking always hurt his head.

Algy's careless words had confirmed his worst suspicions. A girl with an aunt who knew all about Shakespeare and Bacon must of necessity live in a mental atmosphere into which a lamebrained bird like himself could scarcely hope to soar. Even if he did meet her— even if she asked him to call—even if in due time their relations became positively cordial, what then? How could he aspire to such a goddess? What had he to offer her?

Money?

Plenty of that, yes, but what was money?

Socks?

Of these he had the finest collection in London, but socks are not everything.

A loving heart?

A fat lot of use that was.

No, a girl like Aurelia Cammarleigh would, he felt, demand from the man who aspired to her hand something in the nature of gifts, of accomplishments. He would have to be a man who Did Things. And what, Archibald asked himself, could he do? Absolutely nothing except give an imitation of a hen laying an egg.

That he could do. At imitating a hen laying an egg he was admittedly a master. His fame in that one respect had spread all over the West End of London. "Others abide our question. Thou art free," was the verdict of London's gilded youth on Archibald Mulliner when considered purely in the light of a man who could imitate a hen laying an egg. "Mulliner," they said to one another, "may be a pretty minus quantity in many ways, but he can imitate a hen laying an egg."

And, so far from helping him, this one accomplishment of his would, reason told him, be a positive handicap. A girl like Aurelia Cammarleigh would simply be sickened by such coarse buffoonery. He blushed at the very thought of her ever learning that he was capable of sinking to such depths.

And so, when some weeks later he was introduced to her in the paddock at Ascot and she, gazing at him with what seemed to his sensitive mind contemptuous loathing, said:

"They tell me you give an imitation of a hen laying an egg, Mr. Mulliner."

He replied with extraordinary vehemence:

"It is a lie—a foul and contemptible lie which I shall track to its source and nail to the counter."

Brave words! But had they clicked? Had she believed him? He trusted so. But her haughty eyes were very penetrating. They seemed to pierce through to the depths of his soul and lay it bare for what it was—the soul of a hen-imitator.

However, she did ask him to call. With a sort of queenly, bored disdain and only after he had asked twice if he might—but she did it. And Archibald resolved that, no matter what the mental strain, he would show her that her first impression of him had been erroneous, that, trivial and vapid though he might seem, there were in his nature depths whose existence she had not suspected.

For a young man who had been superannuated from Eton and believed everything he read in the Racing Expert's column in the morning paper, Archibald, I am bound to admit, exhibited in this crisis a sagacity for which few of his intimates would have given him credit. It may be that love stimulates the mind, or it may be that when the moment comes Blood will tell. Archibald, you must remember, was, after all, a Mulliner; and now the old canny strain of the Mulliners came out in him.

"Meadowes, my man," he said to Meadowes, his man.

"Sir," said Meadowes.

"It appears," said Archibald, "that there is—or was—a cove of the name of Shakespeare. Also a second cove of the name of Bacon. Bacon wrote plays, it seems, and Shakespeare went and put his own name on the program and copped the credit."

"Indeed, sir?"

"If true, not right, Meadowes."

"Far from it, sir."

"Very well, then. I wish to go into this matter carefully. Kindly pop out and get me a book or two bearing on the business."

He had planned his campaign with infinite cunning. He knew that, before anything could be done in the direction of winning the heart of Aurelia Cammarleigh, he must first establish himself solidly with the aunt. He must court the aunt, ingratiate himself with her—always, of course, making it clear from the start that she was not the one. And, if reading about Shakespeare and Bacon could do it, he would, he told himself, have her eating out of his hand in a week.

Meadowes returned with a parcel of forbidding-looking volumes, and Archibald put in a fortnight's intensive study. Then, discarding the monocle which had up till then been his constant companion, and substituting for it a pair of horn-rimmed spectacles which gave him something of the look of an earnest sheep, he set out for Park Street to pay his first call. And within five minutes of his arrival he had declined a cigarette on the plea that he was a nonsmoker, and had managed to say some rather caustic things about the practice, so prevalent among his contemporaries, of drinking cocktails.

Life, said Archibald, toying with his teacup, was surely given to us for some better purpose than the destruction of our brains and digestions with alcohol. Bacon, for instance, never took a cocktail in his life, and look at him.

At this, the aunt, who up till now had plainly been regarding him as just another of those unfortunate incidents, sprang to life.

"You admire Bacon, Mr. Mulliner?" she asked eagerly.

And, reaching out an arm like the tentacle of an octopus, she drew him into a corner and talked about Cryptograms for forty-seven minutes by the drawing-room clock. In short, to sum the thing up,

my nephew Archibald, at his initial meeting with the only relative of
the girl he loved, went like a sirocco. A Mulliner is always a Mulliner.
Apply the acid test, and he will meet it.

It was not long after this that he informed me that he had sown
the good seed to such an extent that Aurelia's aunt had invited him
to pay a long visit to her country house, Brawstead Towers, in
Sussex.

He was seated at the Savoy bar when he told me this, rather feverishly putting himself outside a Scotch and soda; and I was perplexed
to note that his face was drawn and his eyes haggard.

"But you do not seem happy, my boy," I said.

"I'm not happy."

"But surely this should be an occasion for rejoicing. Thrown
together as you will be in the pleasant surroundings of a country
house, you ought easily to find an opportunity of asking this girl
to marry you."

"And a lot of good that will be," said Archibald moodily. "Even
if I do get a chance I shan't be able to make any use of it. I wouldn't
have the nerve. You don't seem to realize what it means being in love
with a girl like Aurelia. When I look into those clear, soulful eyes,
or see that perfect profile bobbing about on the horizon, a sense of
my unworthiness seems to slosh me amidships like some blunt instrument. My tongue gets entangled with my front teeth, and all I can
do is stand there feeling like a piece of Gorgonzola that has been
condemned by the local sanitary inspector. I'm going to Brawstead
Towers, yes, but I don't expect anything to come of it. I know
exactly what's going to happen to me. I shall just buzz along through
life, pining dumbly, and in the end slide into the tomb of a blasted,
blighted bachelor. Another whisky, please, and jolly well make it
a double."

Brawstead Towers, situated as it is in the pleasant Weald of
Sussex, stands some fifty miles from London; and Archibald, taking
the trip easily in his car, arrived there in time to dress comfortably
for dinner. It was only when he reached the drawing room at eight
o'clock that he discovered that the younger members of the house
party had gone off in a body to dine and dance at a hospitable neighbor's, leaving him to waste the evening tie of a lifetime, to the
composition of which he had devoted no less than twenty-two minutes,
on Aurelia's aunt.

Dinner in these circumstances could hardly hope to be an unmixedly exhilarating function. Among the things which helped to

differentiate it from a Babylonian orgy was the fact that, in deference to his known prejudices, no wine was served to Archibald. And, lacking artificial stimulus, he found the aunt even harder to endure philosophically than ever.

Archibald had long since come to a definite decision that what this woman needed was a fluid ounce of weed killer, scientifically administered. With a good deal of adroitness he contrived to head her off from her favorite topic during the meal, but after the coffee had been disposed of she threw off all restraint. Scooping him up and bearing him off into the recesses of the west wing, she wedged him into a corner of a settee and began to tell him all about the remarkable discovery which had been made by applying the Plain Cipher to Milton's well-known Epitaph on Shakespeare.

"The one beginning 'What needs my Shakespeare for his honoured bones?' " said the aunt.

"Oh, that one?" said Archibald.

" 'What needs my Shakespeare for his honoured bones? The labour of an Age in piled stones? Or that his hallowed Reliques should be hid under a starry-pointing Pyramid?' " said the aunt.

Archibald, who was not good at riddles, said he didn't know.

"As in the Plays and Sonnets," said the aunt, "we substitute the name equivalents of the figure totals."

"We do what?"

"Substitute the name equivalents of the figure totals."

"The which?"

"The figure totals."

"All right," said Archibald. "Let it go. I daresay you know best."

The aunt inflated her lungs.

"These figure totals," she said, "are always taken out in the Plain Cipher, A equaling one to Z equals twenty-four. The names are counted in the same way. A capital letter with the figures indicates an occasional variation in the Name Count. For instance, A equals twenty-seven, B twenty-eight, until K equals ten is reached, when K, instead of ten, becomes one, and T instead of nineteen, is one, and R or Reverse, and so on, until A equals twenty-four is reached. The short or single Digit is not used here. Reading the Epitaph in the light of this Cipher, it becomes: 'What need Verulam for Shakespeare? Francis Bacon England's King be hid under a W. Shakespeare? William Shakespeare. Fame, what needst Francis Tudor, King of England? Francis. Francis W. Shakespeare. For Francis thy William Shakespeare hath England's King took W. Shakespeare.

Then thou our W. Shakespeare Francis Tudor bereaving Francis Bacon Francis Tudor such a tomb William Shakespeare.' "

The speech to which he had been listening was unusually lucid and simple for a Baconian, yet Archibald, his eye catching a battle-ax that hung on the wall, could not but stifle a wistful sigh. How simple it would have been, had he not been a Mulliner and a gentleman, to remove the weapon from its hook, spit on his hands, and haul off and dot this doddering old ruin one just above the imitation pearl necklace. Placing his twitching hands underneath him and sitting on them, he stayed where he was, until just as the clock on the mantelpiece chimed the hour of midnight, a merciful fit of hiccups on the part of his hostess enabled him to retire. As she reached the twenty-seventh "hic," his fingers found the door handle and a moment later he was outside, streaking up the stairs.

The room they had given Archibald was at the end of a corridor, a pleasant, airy apartment with French windows opening upon a broad balcony. At any other time he would have found it agreeable to hop out onto this balcony and revel in the scents and sounds of the summer night, thinking the while long, lingering thoughts of Aurelia. But what with all that Francis Tudor Francis Bacon such a tomb William Shakespeare count seventeen drop one knit purl and set them up in the other alley stuff, not even thoughts of Aurelia could keep him from his bed.

Moodily tearing off his clothes and donning his pajamas, Archibald Mulliner climbed in and instantaneously discovered that the bed was an apple-pie bed. When and how it had happened he did not know, but at a point during the day some loving hand had sewn up the sheets and put two hairbrushes and a branch of some prickly shrub between them.

Himself from earliest boyhood an adept at the construction of booby traps, Archibald, had his frame of mind been sunnier, would doubtless have greeted this really extremely sound effort with a cheery laugh. As it was, weighed down with Verulams and Francis Tudors, he swore for a while with considerable fervor; then, ripping off the sheets and tossing the prickly shrub wearily into a corner, crawled between the blankets and was soon asleep.

His last waking thought was that if the aunt hoped to catch him on the morrow, she would have to be considerably quicker on her pins than her physique indicated.

How long Archibald slept he could not have said. He woke some hours later with a vague feeling that a thunderstorm of unusual violence had broken out in his immediate neighborhood. But this, he realized as the mists of slumber cleared away, was an error. The noise which had disturbed him was not thunder but the sound of someone snoring. Snoring like the dickens. The walls seemed to be vibrating like the deck of an ocean liner.

Archibald Mulliner might have had a tough evening with the aunt, but his spirit was not so completely broken as to make him lie supinely down beneath that snoring. The sound filled him, as snoring fills every right-thinking man, with a seething resentment and a passionate yearning for justice, and he climbed out of bed with the intention of taking the proper steps through the recognized channels. It is the custom nowadays to disparage the educational methods of the English public school and to maintain that they are not practical and of a kind to fit the growing boy for the problems of afterlife. But you do learn one thing at a public school, and that is how to act when somebody starts snoring.

You jolly well grab a cake of soap and pop in and stuff it down the blighter's throat. And this Archibald proposed—God willing—to do. It was the work of but a moment with him to dash to the washstand and arm himself. Then he moved softly out through the French windows onto the balcony.

The snoring, he had ascertained, proceeded from the next room. Presumably this room also would have French windows; and presumably, as the night was warm, these would be open. It would be a simple task to oil in, insert the soap, and buzz back undetected.

It was a lovely night, but Archibald paid no attention to it. Clasping his cake of soap, he crept on and was pleased to discover, on arriving outside the snorer's room, that his surmise had been correct. The windows were open. Beyond them, screening the interior of the room, were heavy curtains. And he had just placed his hand upon these when from inside a voice spoke. At the same moment the light was turned on.

"Who's that?" said the voice.

And it was as if Brawstead Towers with all its stabling, outhouses and messuages had fallen on Archibald's head. A mist rose before his eyes. He gasped and tottered.

The voice was that of Aurelia Cammarleigh.

For an instant, for a single long, sickening instant, I am compelled to admit that Archibald's love, deep as the sea though it was, definitely wobbled. It had received a grievous blow. It was not simply the discovery that the girl he adored was a snorer that unmanned him; it was the thought that she could snore like that. There was something about those snores that had seemed to sin against his whole conception of womanly purity.

Then he recovered. Even though this girl's slumber was not, as the poet Milton so beautifully puts it, "airy light," but rather reminiscent of a lumber camp when the wood sawing is proceeding at its briskest, he loved her still.

He had just reached this conclusion when a second voice spoke inside the room.

"I say, Aurelia."

It was the voice of another girl. He perceived now that the question "Who's that?" had been addressed not to him but to this newcomer fumbling at the door handle.

"I say, Aurelia," said the girl complainingly, "you've simply got to do something about that bally bulldog of yours. I can't possibly get to sleep with him snoring like that. He's making the plaster come down from the ceiling in my room."

"I'm sorry," said Aurelia. "I've got so used to it that I don't notice."

"Well, I do. Put a green baize cloth over him or something."

Out on the moonlit balcony Archibald Mulliner stood shaking like a blancmange. Although he had contrived to maintain his great love practically intact when he had supposed the snores to proceed from the girl he worshiped, it had been tough going, and for an instant, as I have said, a very near thing. The relief that swept over him at the discovery that Aurelia could still justifiably remain on her pinnacle was so profound that it made him feel filleted. He seemed for a moment in a daze. Then he was brought out of the ether by hearing his name spoken.

"Did Archie Mulliner arrive tonight?" asked Aurelia's friend.

"I suppose so," said Aurelia. "He wired that he was motoring down."

"Just between us girls," said Aurelia's friend, "what do you think of that bird?"

To listen to a private conversation—especially a private conversation between two modern girls when you never know what may come next—is rightly considered an action incompatible with the claim to be a gentleman. I regret to say, therefore, that Archibald, ignoring the fact that he belonged to a family whose code is as high as that of any in the land, instead of creeping away to his room edged at this point a step closer to the curtains and stood there with his ears flapping. It might be an ignoble thing to eavesdrop, but it was apparent that Aurelia Cammarleigh was about to reveal her candid opinion of him; and the prospect of getting the true facts—straight, as it were, from the horse's mouth—held him so fascinated that he could not move.

"Archie Mulliner?" said Aurelia meditatively.

"Yes. The betting at the Junior Lipstick is seven to two that you'll marry him."

"Why on earth?"

"Well, people have noticed he's always round at your place, and they seem to think it significant. Anyway, that's how the odds stood when I left London—seven to two."

"Get in on the short end," said Aurelia earnestly, "and you'll make a packet."

"Is that official?"

"Absolutely," said Aurelia.

Out in the moonlight, Archibald Mulliner uttered a low, bleak moan rather like the last bit of wind going out of a dying duck. True, he had always told himself that he hadn't a chance, but, however much a man may say that, he never in his heart really believes it. And now from an authoritative source he had learned that his romance was definitely blue round the edges. It was a shattering blow. He wondered dully how the trains ran to the Rocky Mountains. A spot of grizzly-bear shooting seemed indicated.

Inside the room, the other girl appeared perplexed.

"But you told me at Ascot," she said, "just after he had been introduced to you, that you rather thought you had at last met your ideal. When did the good thing begin to come unstuck?"

A silvery sigh came through the curtains.

"I did think so then," said Aurelia wistfully. "There was something about him. I liked the way his ears wiggled. And I had always heard he was such a perfectly genial, cheery, merry old soul. Algy Wymondham-Wymondham told me that his imitation of a hen laying an egg was alone enough to keep any reasonable girl happy through a long married life."

"Can he imitate a hen?"

"No. It was nothing but an idle rumor. I asked him, and he stoutly denied that he had ever done such a thing in his life. He was quite stuffy about it. I felt a little uneasy then, and the moment he started calling and hanging about the house I knew that my fears had been well founded. The man is beyond question a flat tire and a wet smack."

"As bad as that?"

"I'm not exaggerating a bit. Where people ever got the idea that Archie Mulliner is a bonhomous old bean beats me. He is the world's worst monkey wrench. He doesn't drink cocktails, he doesn't smoke cigarettes, and the thing he seems to enjoy most in the world is to sit for hours listening to the conversation of my aunt, who, as you know, is pure goof from the soles of the feet to the tortoise-shell comb and should long ago have been renting a padded cell in Earlswood. Believe me, Muriel, if you can really get seven to two, you are on to the best thing since Buttercup won the Lincolnshire."

"You don't say!"

"I do say. Apart from anything else, he's got a beastly habit of looking at me reverently. And if you knew how sick I am of being looked at reverently! They will do it, these lads. I suppose it's because I'm rather an outsize and modeled on the lines of Cleopatra."

"Tough!"

"You bet it's tough. A girl can't help her appearance. I may look as if my ideal man was the hero of a Viennese operetta, but I don't feel that way. What I want is some good sprightly sportsman who sets a neat booby trap, and who'll rush up and grab me in his arms and say to me, 'Aurelia, old girl, you're the bee's roller skates!' "

And Aurelia Cammarleigh emitted another sigh.

"Talking of booby traps," said the other girl, "if Archie Mulliner has arrived he's in the next room, isn't he?"

"I suppose so. That's where he was to be. Why?"

"Because I made him an apple-pie bed."

"It was the right spirit," said Aurelia warmly. "I wish I'd thought of it myself."

"Too late now."

"Yes," said Aurelia. "But I'll tell you what I can and will do. You say you object to Lysander's snoring. Well, I'll go and pop him in at Archie Mulliner's window. That'll give him pause for thought."

"Splendid," agreed the girl Muriel. "Well, good night."

"Good night," said Aurelia.

There followed the sound of a door closing.

There was, as I have indicated, not much of my nephew Archibald's mind, but what there was of it was now in a whirl. He was stunned. Like every man who is abruptly called upon to revise his entire scheme of values, he felt as if he had been standing on top of the Eiffel Tower and some practical joker had suddenly drawn it away from under him. Tottering back to his room, he replaced the cake of soap in its dish and sat down on the bed to grapple with this amazing development.

Aurelia Cammarleigh had compared herself to Cleopatra. It is not too much to say that my nephew Archibald's emotions at this juncture were very similar to what Marc Antony's would have been had Egypt's queen risen from her throne at his entry and without a word of warning started to dance the Black Bottom.

He was roused from his thoughts by the sound of a light footstep on the balcony outside. At the same moment he heard a low woofly gruffle, the unmistakable note of a bulldog of regular habits who has been jerked out of his basket in the small hours and forced to take the night air.

> *She is coming, my own, my sweet!*
> *Were it never so airy a tread,*
> *My heart would hear her and beat,*
> *Were it earth in an earthy bed,*

whispered Archibald's soul, or words to that effect. He rose from his seat and paused for an instant, irresolute. Then inspiration descended on him. He knew what to do, and he did it.

Yes, gentlemen, in that supreme crisis of his life, with his whole fate hanging, as you might say, in the balance, Archibald Mulliner, showing for almost the first time in his career a well-nigh human intelligence, began to give his celebrated imitation of a hen laying an egg.

Archibald's imitation of a hen laying an egg was conceived on broad and sympathetic lines. Less violent than Salvini's *Othello,* it had in it something of the poignant wistfulness of Mrs. Siddons in the sleepwalking scene of *Macbeth.* The rendition started quietly, almost inaudibly, with a sort of soft, liquid crooning—the joyful yet half-incredulous murmur of a mother who can scarcely believe as yet that her union has really been blessed, and that it is indeed she who is responsible for that oval mixture of chalk and albumen which she sees lying beside her in the straw.

Then, gradually, conviction comes.

"It looks like an egg," one seems to hear her say. "It feels like an egg. It's shaped like an egg. Damme, it *is* an egg!"

And at that, all doubting resolved, the crooning changes; takes on a firmer note; soars into the upper register; and finally swells into a maternal pæan of joy—a "Charawk-chawk-chawk-chawk" of such a caliber that few had ever been able to listen to it dry-eyed. Following which, it was Archibald's custom to run round the room, flapping the sides of his coat, and then, leaping onto a sofa or some convenient chair, to stand there with his arms at right angles, crowing himself purple in the face.

All these things he had done many a time for the idle entertainment of fellow members in the smoking room of the Drones, but never with the gusto, the *brio,* with which he performed them now. Essentially a modest man, like all the Mulliners, he was compelled, nevertheless, to recognize that tonight he was surpassing himself. Every artist knows when the authentic divine fire is within him, and an inner voice told Archibald Mulliner that he was at the top of his form and giving the performance of a lifetime. Love thrilled through every "Brt-t't-t't" that he uttered, animated each flap of his arms. Indeed, so deeply did Love drive in its spur that he tells me that, instead of the customary once, he actually made the circle of the room three times before coming to rest on top of the chest of drawers.

When at length he did so he glanced toward the window and saw that through the curtains the loveliest face in the world was peering. And in Aurelia Cammarleigh's glorious eyes there was a look he had never seen before, the sort of look Kreisler or somebody like that beholds in the eyes of the front row as he lowers his violin and brushes his forehead with the back of his hand. A look of worship.

There was a long silence. Then she spoke.

"Do it again!" she said.

And Archibald did it again. He did it four times and could, he tells me, if he had pleased, have taken a fifth encore or at any rate a couple of bows. And then, leaping lightly to the floor, he advanced toward her. He felt conquering, dominant. It was his hour. He reached out and clasped her in his arms.

"Aurelia, old girl," said Archibald Mulliner in a clear, firm voice, "you are the bee's roller skates."

And at that she seemed to melt into his embrace. Her lovely face was raised to his.

"Archibald!" she whispered.

There was another throbbing silence, broken only by the beating of two hearts and the wheezing of the bulldog, who seemed to suffer a good deal in his bronchial tubes. Then Archibald released her.

"Well, that's that," he said. "Glad everything's all settled and hotsy-totsy. Gosh, I wish I had a cigarette. This is the sort of moment a bloke needs one."

She looked at him, surprised.

"But I thought you didn't smoke."

"Oh, yes, I do."

"And do you drink as well?"

"Quite as well," said Archibald. "In fact, rather better. Oh, by the way."

"Yes?"

"There's just one other thing. Suppose that aunt of yours wants to come and visit us when we are settled down in our little nest, what, dearest, would be your reaction to the scheme of soaking her on the base of the skull with a stuffed eelskin?"

"I should like it," said Aurelia warmly, "above all things."

"Twin souls," cried Archibald. "That's what we are, when you come right down to it. I suspected it all along, and now I know. Two jolly old twin souls." He embraced her ardently. "And now," he said, "let us pop downstairs and put this bulldog in the butler's pantry, where he will come upon him unexpectedly in the morning and doubtless get a shock which will do him as much good as a week at the seaside. Are you on?"

"I am," whispered Aurelia. "Oh, I am!"

And hand in hand they wandered out together onto the broad staircase.

❃ *The Ordeal of Osbert Mulliner*

THE unwonted gravity of Mr. Mulliner's demeanor had struck us all directly he entered the bar parlor of the Anglers' Rest; and the silent, moody way in which he sipped his hot Scotch and lemon convinced us that something was wrong. We hastened to make sympathetic inquiries.

Our solicitude seemed to please him. He brightened a little.

"Well, gentlemen," he said, "I had not intended to intrude my private troubles on this happy gathering, but, if you must know, a young second cousin of mine has left his wife and is filing papers of divorce. It has upset me very much."

Miss Postlethwaite, our warmhearted barmaid, who was polishing glasses, introduced a sort of bedside manner into her task.

"Some viper crept into his home?" she asked.

Mr. Mulliner shook his head.

"No," he said. "No vipers. The whole trouble appears to have been that, whenever my second cousin spoke to his wife, she would open her eyes to their fullest extent, put her head on one side like a canary, and say 'What?' He said he had stood it for eleven months and three days, which he believes to be a European record, and that the time had now come, in his opinion, to take steps."

Mr. Mulliner sighed.

"The fact of the matter is," he said, "marriage today is made much too simple for a man. He finds it so easy to go out and grab some sweet girl that when he has got her he does not value her. I am convinced that that is the real cause of this modern boom in divorce. What marriage needs, to make it a stable institution, is something in the nature of obstacles during the courtship period. I attribute the solid happiness of my nephew Osbert's union, to take but one instance, to the events which preceded it. If the thing had been a walkover, he would have prized his wife far less highly."

"It took him a long time to teach her his true worth?" we asked.

"Love burgeoned slowly?" hazarded Miss Postlethwaite.

"On the contrary," said Mr. Mulliner, "she loved him at first sight. What made the wooing of Mabel Petherick-Soames so extraordinarily difficult for my nephew Osbert was not any coldness on her part, but the unfortunate mental attitude of J. Bashford Braddock. Does that name suggest anything to you, gentlemen?"

"No."

"You do not think that a man with such a name would be likely to be a toughish sort of egg?"

"He might be, now you mention it."

"He was. In Central Africa, where he spent a good deal of his time exploring, ostriches would bury their heads in the sand at Bashford Braddock's approach and even rhinoceroses, the most ferocious beasts in existence, frequently edged behind trees and hid till he had passed. And the moment he came into Osbert's life my nephew realized with a sickening clearness that those rhinoceroses had known their business."

Until the advent of this man Braddock (said Mr. Mulliner), Fortune seemed to have lavished her favors on my nephew Osbert in full and even overflowing measure. Handsome, like all the Mulliners, he possessed in addition to good looks the inestimable blessings of perfect health, a cheerful disposition and so much money that Income Tax assessors screamed with joy when forwarding Schedule D to his address. And, on top of all this, he had fallen deeply in love with a most charming girl and rather fancied that his passion was reciprocated.

For several peaceful, happy weeks all went well. Osbert advanced without a setback of any description through the various stages of calling, sending flowers, asking after her father's lumbago, and patting her mother's Pomeranian to the point where he was able, with the family's full approval, to invite the girl out alone to dinner and a theater. And it was on this night of nights, when all should have been joy and happiness, that the Braddock menace took shape.

Until Bashford Braddock made his appearance, no sort of hitch had occurred to mar the perfect tranquillity of the evening's proceedings. The dinner had been excellent, the play entertaining. Twice during the third act Osbert had ventured to squeeze the girl's hand in a warm, though of course gentlemanly, manner; and it seemed to him that the pressure had been returned. It is not surprising, therefore, that by the time they were parting on the steps of her house he had reached the conclusion that he was on to a good thing which should be pushed along.

Putting his fortune to the test, to win or lose it all, Osbert Mulliner reached forward, clasped Mabel Petherick-Soames to his bosom, and gave her a kiss so ardent that in the silent night it sounded like somebody letting off a Mills bomb.

And scarcely had the echoes died away, when he became aware that there was standing at his elbow a tall, broad-shouldered man in evening dress and an opera hat.

There was a pause. The girl was the first to speak.

"Hullo, Bashy," she said, and there was annoyance in her voice. "Where on earth did you spring from? I thought you were exploring on the Congo or somewhere."

The man removed his opera hat, squashed it flat, popped it out again and spoke in a deep, rumbling voice.

"I returned from the Congo this morning. I have been dining with your father and mother. They informed me that you had gone to the theater with this gentleman."

"Mr. Mulliner. My cousin, Bashford Braddock."

"How do you do?" said Osbert.

There was another pause. Bashford Braddock removed his opera hat, squashed it flat, popped it out again and replaced it on his head. He seemed disappointed that he could not play a tune on it.

"Well, good night," said Mabel.

"Good night," said Osbert.

"Good night," said Bashford Braddock.

The door closed, and Osbert, looking from it to his companion, found that the other was staring at him with a peculiar expression in his eyes. They were hard, glittering eyes. Osbert did not like them.

"Mr. Mulliner," said Bashford Braddock.

"Hullo?" said Osbert.

"A word with you. I saw all."

"All?"

"All. Mr. Mulliner, you love that girl."

"I do."

"So do I."

"You do?"

"I do."

Osbert felt a little embarrassed. All he could think of to say was that it made them seem like one great big family.

"I have loved her since she was so high."

"How high?" asked Osbert, for the light was uncertain.

"About so high. And I have always sworn that if ever any man came between us, if ever any slinking, sneaking, popeyed, lop-eared son of a sea cook attempted to rob me of that girl, I would . . ."

"Er—what?" asked Osbert.

Bashford Braddock laughed a short, metallic laugh.

"Did you ever hear what I did to the King of Mgumbo-Mgumbo?"

"I didn't even know there was a King of Mgumbo-Mgumbo."

"There isn't—now," said Bashford Braddock.

Osbert was conscious of a clammy, creeping sensation in the region of his spine.

"What did you do to him?"

"Don't ask."

"But I want to know."

"Far better not. You will find out quite soon enough if you continue to hang round Mabel Petherick-Soames. That is all, Mr. Mulliner." Bashford Braddock looked up at the twinkling stars. "What delightful weather we are having," he said. "There was just the same quiet hush and peaceful starlight, I recollect, that time out in the Ngobi desert when I strangled the jaguar."

Osbert's Adam's apple slipped a cog.

"W—what jaguar?"

"Oh, you wouldn't know it. Just one of the jaguars out there. I had a rather tricky five minutes of it at first, because my right arm was in a sling and I could only use my left. Well, good night, Mr. Mulliner, good night."

And Bashford Braddock, having removed his opera hat, squashed it flat, popped it out again and replaced it on his head, stalked off into the darkness.

For several minutes after he had disappeared Osbert Mulliner stood motionless, staring after him with unseeing eyes. Then, tottering round the corner, he made his way to his residence in South Audley Street, and, contriving after three false starts to unlock the front door, climbed the stairs to his cozy library. There, having mixed himself a strong brandy and soda, he sat down and gave himself up to meditation, and eventually, after one quick drink and another taken rather slower, was able to marshal his thoughts with a certain measure of coherence. And those thoughts, I regret to say, when marshaled, were of a nature which I shrink from revealing to you.

It is never pleasant, gentlemen, to have to display a relative in an unsympathetic light, but the truth is the truth and must be told. I am compelled, therefore, to confess that my nephew Osbert, forgetting that he was a Mulliner, writhed at this moment in an agony of craven fear.

It would be possible, of course, to find excuses for him. The thing had come upon him very suddenly, and even the stoutest are sometimes disconcerted by sudden peril. Then, again, his circumstances and upbringing had fitted him ill for such a crisis. A man who has been pampered by Fortune from birth becomes highly civilized; and the more highly civilized we are, the less adroitly do we cope with bounders of the Braddock type who seem to belong to an earlier and rougher age. Osbert Mulliner was simply unequal to the task of tackling cavemen. Apart from some slight skill at auction bridge, the only thing he was really good at was collecting old jade; and what a help that would be, he felt as he mixed himself a third brandy and soda, in a personal combat with a man who appeared to think it only sporting to give jaguars a chance by fighting them one-handed.

He could see but one way out of the delicate situation in which he had been placed. To give Mabel Petherick-Soames up would break his heart, but it seemed to be a straight issue between that and his neck, and in this black hour the voting in favor of the neck was a positive landslide. Trembling in every limb, my nephew Osbert went to the desk and began to compose a letter of farewell.

He was sorry, he wrote, that he would be unable to see Miss Petherick-Soames on the morrow, as they had planned, owing to his unfortunately being called away to Australia. He added that he was pleased to have made her acquaintance and that if, as seemed probable, they never saw each other again, he would always watch her future career with considerable interest.

Signing the letter "Yrs. truly, O. Mulliner," Osbert addressed the envelope and, taking it up the street to the post office, dropped it in the box. Then he returned home and went to bed.

The telephone, ringing by his bedside, woke Osbert at an early hour next morning. He did not answer it. A glance at his watch had told him that the time was half past eight, when the first delivery of letters is made in London. It seemed only too likely that Mabel, having just received and read his communication, was endeavoring to discuss the matter with him over the wire. He rose, bathed, shaved and dressed, and had just finished a somber breakfast when the door opened and Parker, his man, announced Major General Sir Masterman Petherick-Soames.

An icy finger seemed to travel slowly down Osbert's backbone. He cursed the preoccupation which had made him omit to instruct Parker to inform all callers that he was not at home. With some difficulty, for the bones seemed to have been removed from his legs, he rose to receive the tall, upright, grizzled and formidable old man who entered, and rallied himself to play the host.

"Good morning," he said. "Will you have a poached egg?"

"I will not have a poached egg," replied Sir Masterman. "Poached egg, indeed! Poached egg, forsooth! Ha! Tchal! Bah!"

He spoke with such curt brusqueness that a stranger, had one been present, might have supposed him to belong to some league or society for the suppression of poached eggs. Osbert, however, with his special knowledge of the facts, was able to interpret this brusqueness correctly and was not surprised when his visitor, gazing at him keenly with a pair of steely blue eyes which must have got him very much disliked in military circles, plunged at once into the subject of the letter.

"Mr. Mulliner, my niece Mabel has received a strange communication from you."

"Oh, she got it all right?" said Osbert, with an attempt at ease.

"It arrived this morning. You had omitted to stamp it. There was threepence to pay."

"Oh, I say, I'm fearfully sorry. I must . . ."

Major General Sir Masterman Petherick-Soames waved down his apologies.

"It is not the monetary loss which has so distressed my niece, but the letter's contents. My niece is under the impression that last night she and you became engaged to be married, Mr. Mulliner."

Osbert coughed.

"Well—er—not exactly. Not altogether. Not, as it were . . . I mean . . . You see . . ."

"I see very clearly. You have been trifling with my niece's affections, Mr. Mulliner. And I have always sworn that if ever a man trifled with the affections of any of my nieces, I would . . ." He broke off and, taking a lump of sugar from the bowl, balanced it absently on the edge of a slice of toast. "Did you ever hear of a Captain Walkinshaw?"

"No."

"Captain J. G. Walkinshaw? Dark man with an eyeglass. Used to play the saxophone."

"No."

"Ah? I thought you might have met him. He trifled with the affections of my niece Hester. I horsewhipped him on the steps of the Drones Club. Is the name Blenkinsop-Bustard familiar to you?"

"No."

"Rupert Blenkinsop-Bustard trifled with the affections of my niece Gertrude. He was one of the Somersetshire Blenkinsop-Bustards. Wore a fair mustache and kept pigeons. I horsewhipped him on the steps of the Junior Bird Fanciers. By the way, Mr. Mulliner, what is your club?"

"The United Jade Collectors," quavered Osbert.

"Has it steps?"

"I—I believe so."

"Good. Good." A dreamy look came into the General's eyes. "Well, the announcement of your engagement to my niece Mabel will appear in tomorrow's *Morning Post*. If it is contradicted . . . Well, good morning, Mr. Mulliner, good morning."

And, replacing in the dish the piece of bacon which he had been poising on a teaspoon, Major General Sir Masterman Petherick-Soames left the room.

The meditation to which my nephew Osbert had given himself up on the previous night was as nothing to the meditation to which he gave himself up now. For fully an hour he must have sat, his head supported by his hands, frowning despairingly at the remains of the marmalade on the plate before him. Though, like all the Mulliners, a clear thinker, he had to confess himself completely nonplused. The situation had become so complicated that after awhile he went up to the library and tried to work it out on paper, letting X equal himself. But even this brought no solution, and he was still pondering deeply when Parker came up to announce lunch.

"Lunch?" said Osbert, amazed. "Is it lunchtime already?"

"Yes, sir. And might I be permitted to offer my respectful congratulations and good wishes, sir?"

"Eh?"

"On your engagement, sir. The General happened to mention to me as I let him out that a marriage had been arranged and would shortly take place between yourself and Miss Mabel Petherick-Soames. It was fortunate that he did so, as I was thus enabled to give the gentleman the information he required."

"Gentleman?"

"A Mr. Bashford Braddock, sir. He rang up about an hour after the General had left and said he had been informed of your engagement and wished to know if the news was well founded. I assured him that it was, and he said he would be calling to see you later. He was very anxious to know when you would be at home. He seemed a nice, friendly gentleman, sir."

Osbert rose as if the chair in which he sat had suddenly become incandescent.

"Parker!"

"Sir?"

"I am unexpectedly obliged to leave London, Parker. I don't know where I am going—probably the Zambesi or Greenland—but I shall be away a long time. I shall close the house and give the staff an indefinite holiday. They will receive three months' wages in advance, and at the end of that period will communicate with my lawyers, Messrs. Peabody, Thrupp, Thrupp, Thrupp, Thrupp and Peabody of Lincoln's Inn. Inform them of this."

"Very good, sir."

"And, Parker."

"Sir?"

"I am thinking of appearing shortly in some amateur theatricals. Kindly step round the corner and get me a false wig, a false nose, some false whiskers and a good stout pair of blue spectacles."

Osbert's plans when, after a cautious glance up and down the street, he left the house an hour later and directed a taxicab to take him to an obscure hotel in the wildest and least known part of the Cromwell Road were of the vaguest. It was only when he reached that haven and had thoroughly wigged, nosed, whiskered and blue spectacled himself that he began to formulate a definite plan of campaign. He spent the rest of the day in his room, and shortly before lunch next morning set out for the secondhand-clothing establishment of the Bros. Cohen, near Covent Garden, to purchase a complete traveler's outfit. It was his intention to board the boat sailing on the morrow for India and to potter a while about the world, taking in *en route* Japan, South Africa, Peru, Mexico, China, Venezuela, the Fiji Islands and other beauty spots.

All the Cohens seemed glad to see him when he arrived at the shop. They clustered about him in a body, as if guessing by instinct that here came one of those big orders. At this excellent emporium one may buy, in addition to secondhand clothing, practically anything that exists; and the difficulty—for the brothers are all thrustful salesmen—is to avoid doing so. At the end of five minutes, Osbert was mildly surprised to find himself in possession of a smoking cap, three boxes of poker chips, some polo sticks, a fishing rod, a concertina, a ukulele and a bowl of goldfish.

He clicked his tongue in annoyance. These men appeared to him to have got quite a wrong angle on the situation. They seemed to think that he proposed to make his travels one long round of pleasure. As clearly as he was able, he tried to tell them that in the few broken years that remained to him before a shark or jungle fever put an end .

to his sorrows he would have little heart for polo, for poker, or for playing the concertina while watching the gambols of goldfish. They might just as well offer him, he said querulously, a cocked hat or a sewing machine.

Instant activity prevailed among the brothers.

"Fetch the gentleman his sewing machine, Isadore."

"And, while you're getting him the cocked hat, Lou," said Irving, "ask the customer in the shoe department if he'll be kind enough to step this way. You're in luck," he assured Osbert. "If you're going traveling in foreign parts, he's the very man to advise you. You've heard of Mr. Braddock?"

There was very little of Osbert's face visible behind his whiskers, but that little paled beneath its tan.

"Mr. B—b—b . . . ?"

"That's right. Mr. Braddock, the explorer."

"Air!" said Osbert. "Give me air!"

He made rapidly for the door, and was about to charge through when it opened to admit a tall, distinguished-looking man of military appearance.

"Shop!" cried the newcomer in a clear, patrician voice, and Osbert reeled back against a pile of trousers. It was Major General Sir Masterman Petherick-Soames.

A platoon of Cohens advanced upon him, Isadore hastily snatching up a fireman's helmet and Irving a microscope and a couple of jigsaw puzzles. The General waved them aside.

"Do you," he asked, "keep horsewhips?"

"Yes, sir. Plenty of horsewhips."

"I want a nice strong one with a medium-sized handle and lots of spring," said Major General Sir Masterman Petherick-Soames.

And at this moment Lou returned, followed by Bashford Braddock.

"Is this the gentleman?" said Bashford Braddock genially. "You're going abroad, sir, I understand. Delighted if I can be of any service."

"Bless my soul," said Major General Sir Masterman Petherick-Soames. "Bashford? It's so confoundedly dark in here, I didn't recognize you."

"Switch on the light, Irving," said Isadore.

"No, don't," said Osbert. "My eyes are weak."

"If your eyes are weak you ought not to be going to the tropics," said Bashford Braddock.

"This gentleman a friend of yours?" asked the General.

"Oh, no. I'm just going to help him to buy an outfit."

"The gentleman's already got a smoking cap, poker chips, polo sticks, a fishing rod, a concertina, a ukulele, a bowl of goldfish, a cocked hat and a sewing machine," said Isadore.

"Ah?" said Bashford Braddock. "Then all he will require now is a sun helmet, a pair of puttees, and a pot of ointment for relieving alligator bites."

With the rapid decision of an explorer who is buying things for which somebody else is going to pay, he completed the selection of Osbert's outfit.

"And what brings you here, Bashford?" asked the General.

"Me? Oh, I looked in to buy a pair of spiked boots. I want to trample on a snake."

"An odd coincidence. I came here to buy a horsewhip to horsewhip a snake."

"A bad week end for snakes," said Bashford Braddock.

The General nodded gravely.

"Of course, my snake," he said, "may prove not to be a snake. In classifying him as a snake I may have misjudged him. In that case I shall not require this horsewhip. Still, they're always useful to have about the house."

"Undoubtedly. Lunch with me, General?"

"Delighted, my dear fellow."

"Good-bye, sir," said Bashford Braddock, giving Osbert a friendly nod. "Glad I was able to be of some use. When do you sail?"

"Gentleman's sailing tomorrow morning on the *Rajputana*," said Isadore.

"What!" cried Major General Sir Masterman Petherick-Soames. "Bless my soul! I didn't realize you were going to *India*. I was out there for years and can give you all sorts of useful hints. The old *Rajputana*? Why, I know the purser well. I'll come and see you off and have a chat with him. No doubt I shall be able to get you a number of little extra attentions. No, no, my dear fellow, don't thank me. I have a good deal on my mind at the moment, and it will be a relief to do somebody a kindness."

It seemed to Osbert, as he crawled back to the shelter of his Cromwell Road bedroom, that Fate was being altogether too rough with him. Obviously, if Sir Masterman Petherick-Soames intended to come down to the boat to see him off, it would be madness to attempt to sail. On the deck of a liner under the noonday sun the General must inevitably penetrate his disguise. His whole scheme of escape must be canceled and another substituted. Osbert ordered two pots of black coffee, tied a wet handkerchief round his forehead, and plunged once more into thought.

It has been frequently said of the Mulliners that you may perplex but you cannot baffle them. It was getting on for dinnertime before Osbert finally decided upon a plan of action; but this plan, he perceived as he examined it, was far superior to the first one.

He had been wrong, he saw, in thinking of flying to foreign climes. For one who desired as fervently as he did never to see Major General Sir Masterman Petherick-Soames again in this world, the only real refuge was a London suburb. Any momentary whim might lead Sir Masterman to pack a suitcase and take the next boat to the Far East, but nothing would ever cause him to take a tram for Dulwich, Cricklewood, Winchmore Hill, Brixton, Balham or Surbiton. In those trackless wastes Osbert would be safe.

Osbert decided to wait till late at night; then go back to his house in South Audley Street, pack his collection of old jade and a few other necessaries, and vanish into the unknown.

It was getting on for midnight when, creeping warily to the familiar steps, he inserted his latch key in the familiar keyhole. He had feared that Bashford Braddock might be watching the house, but there were no signs of him. He slipped swiftly into the dark hall and closed the front door softly behind him.

It was at this moment that he became aware that from under the door of the dining room at the other end of the hall there was stealing a thin stream of light.

For an instant, this evidence that the house was not, as he had supposed, unoccupied startled Osbert considerably. Then, recovering himself, he understood what must have happened. Parker, his man, instead of leaving as he had been told to do, was taking advantage of his employer's presumed absence from London to stay on and do some informal entertaining. Osbert, thoroughly incensed, hurried to the dining room and felt that his suspicion had been confirmed. On the table were set out all the materials, except food and drink, of a cozy little supper for two. The absence of food and drink was accounted for, no doubt, by the fact that Parker and—Osbert saw only too good reason to fear—his lady friend were down in the larder, fetching them.

Osbert boiled from his false wig to the soles of his feet with a passionate fury. So this was the sort of thing that went on the moment his back was turned, was it? There were heavy curtains hiding the window, and behind these he crept. It was his intention to permit the feast to begin and then, stepping forth like some avenging Nemesis, to confront his erring manservant and put it across him in no uncertain manner. Bashford Braddock and Major General Sir Masterman Petherick-Soames, with their towering stature and whipcord muscles, might intimidate him, but with a shrimp like Parker he felt that he could do himself justice. Osbert had been through much in the last forty-eight hours, and unpleasantness with a man who, like Parker, stood a mere five feet five in his socks appeared to him rather in the nature of a tonic.

He had not been waiting long when there came to his ears the sound of footsteps outside. He softly removed his wig, his nose, his whiskers and his blue spectacles. There must be no disguise to soften the shock when Parker found himself confronted. Then, peeping through the curtains, he prepared to spring.

Osbert did not spring. Instead, he shrank back like a more than ordinarily diffident tortoise into its shell, and tried to achieve the maximum of silence by breathing through his ears. For it was no Parker who had entered, no frivolous lady friend, but a couple of plug-uglies of such outstanding physique that Bashford Braddock might have been the little brother of either of them.

Osbert stood petrified. He had never seen a burglar before, and he wished, now that he was seeing these, that it could have been arranged for him to do so through a telescope. At this close range, they gave him much the same feeling the prophet Daniel must have had on entering the lions' den, before his relations with the animals had been established on their subsequent basis of easy camaraderie. He was thankful that when the breath which he had been holding for some eighty seconds at length forced itself out in a loud gasp, the noise was drowned by the popping of a cork.

It was from a bottle of Osbert's best Bollinger that this cork had been removed. The marauders, he was able to see, were men who believed in doing themselves well. In these days when almost everybody is on some sort of diet it is rarely that one comes across the old-fashioned type of diner who does not worry about balanced meals and calories but just squares his shoulders and goes at it till his eyes bubble. Osbert's two guests plainly belonged to this nearly obsolete species. They were drinking out of tankards and eating three varieties of meat simultaneously, as if no such thing as a high blood pressure had ever been invented. A second pop announced the opening of another quart of champagne.

At the outset of the proceedings, there had been little or nothing in

the way of supper table conversation. But now, the first keen edge of
his appetite satisfied by about three pounds of ham, beef and mutton,
the burglar who sat nearest to Osbert was able to relax. He looked
about him approvingly.

"Nice little crib, this, Ernest," he said.

"R!" replied his companion—a man of few words, and those
somewhat impeded by cold potatoes and bread.

"Must have been some real swells in here one time and another."

"R!"

"Baronets and such, I wouldn't be surprised."

"R!" said the second burglar, helping himself to more champagne
and mixing in a little port, sherry, Italian vermouth, old brandy and
green chartreuse to give it body.

The first burglar looked thoughtful.

"Talking of baronets," he said, "a thing I've often wondered is—
well, suppose you're having a dinner, see?"

"R!"

"As it might be in this very room."

"R!"

"Well, would a baronet's sister go in before the daughter of the
younger son of a peer? I've often wondered about that."

The second burglar finished his champagne, port, sherry, Italian
vermouth, old brandy and green chartreuse, and mixed himself another.

"Go in?"

"Go in to dinner."

"If she was quicker on her feet, she would," said the second burglar.
"She'd get to the door first. Stands to reason."

The first burglar raised his eyebrows.

"Ernest," he said coldly, "you talk like an uneducated son of a
whatnot. Haven't you never been taught nothing about the rules and
manners of good Society?"

The second burglar flushed. It was plain that the rebuke had
touched a tender spot. There was a strained silence. The first burglar
resumed his meal. The second burglar watched him with a hostile
eye. He had the air of a man who is waiting for his chance, and it
was not long before he found it.

"Harold," he said.

"Well?" said the first burglar.

"Don't gollup your food, Harold," said the second burglar.

The first burglar stared. His eyes gleamed with sudden fury. His
armor, like his companion's, had been pierced.

"Who's golluping his food?"

"You are."

"I am?"

"Yes, you."

"Who, me?"

"R!"

"Golluping my food?"

"R! Like a pig or something."

It was evident to Osbert, peeping warily through the curtains, that the generous fluids which these two men had been drinking so lavishly had begun to have their effect. They spoke thickly, and their eyes had become red and swollen.

"I may not know all about baronets' younger sisters," said the burglar Ernest, "but I don't gollup my food like pigs or something."

And, as if to drive home the reproach, he picked up the leg of mutton and began to gnaw it with an affected daintiness.

The next moment the battle had been joined. The spectacle of the other's priggish object lesson was too much for the burglar Harold. He plainly resented tuition in the amenities from one on whom he had always looked as a social inferior. With a swift movement of the hand he grasped the bottle before him and bounced it smartly on his colleague's head.

Osbert Mulliner cowered behind the curtain. The sportsman in him whispered that he was missing something good, for ring seats to view which many men would have paid large sums, but he could not nerve himself to look out. However, there was plenty of interest in the thing, even if you merely listened. The bumps and crashes seemed to indicate that the two principals were hitting one another with virtually everything in the room except the wallpaper and the large sideboard. Now they appeared to be grappling on the floor, anon fighting at long range with bottles. Words and combinations of whose existence he had till then been unaware floated to Osbert's ears; and more and more he asked himself, as the combat proceeded: What would the harvest be?

And then, with one titanic crash, the battle ceased as suddenly as it had begun.

It was some moments before Osbert Mulliner could bring himself to peep from behind the curtains. When he did so, he seemed to be gazing upon one of those orgy scenes which have done so much to popularize the motion pictures. Scenically, the thing was perfect. All that was needed to complete the resemblance was a few attractive-looking girls with hardly any clothes on.

He came out and gaped down at the ruins. The burglar Harold was lying with his head in the fireplace; the burglar Ernest was doubled up under the table; and it seemed to Osbert almost absurd to think that these were the same hearty fellows who had come into the room to take potluck so short a while before. Harold had the appearance of a man who has been passed through a wringer. Ernest gave the illusion of having recently become entangled in some powerful machinery. If, as was probable, they were known to the police, it would take a singularly keen-eyed constable to recognize them now.

The thought of the police reminded Osbert of his duty as a citizen. He went to the telephone and called up the nearest station and was informed that representatives of the Law would be round immediately to scoop up the remains. He went back to the dining room to wait, but its atmosphere jarred upon him. He felt the need of fresh air; and, going to the front door, he opened it and stood upon the steps, breathing deeply.

And, as he stood there, a form loomed through the darkness and a heavy hand fell on his arm.

"Mr. Mulliner, I think? Mr. Mulliner, if I mistake not? Good evening, Mr. Mulliner," said the voice of Bashford Braddock. "A word with you, Mr. Mulliner."

Osbert returned his gaze without flinching. He was conscious of a strange, almost uncanny calm. The fact was that, everything in this world being relative, he was regarding Bashford Braddock at this moment as rather an undersized little pipsqueak, and wondering why he had ever worried about the man. To one who had come so recently from the society of Harold and Ernest, Bashford Braddock seemed like one of Singer's Midgets.

"Ah, Braddock?" said Osbert.

At this moment, with a grinding of brakes, a van stopped before the door and policemen began to emerge.

"Mr. Mulliner?" asked the sergeant.

Osbert greeted him affably.

"Come in," he said. "Come in. Go straight through. You will find them in the dining room. I'm afraid I had to handle them a little roughly. You had better phone for a doctor."

"Bad are they?"

"A little the worse for wear."

"Well, they asked for it," said the sergeant.

"Exactly, Sergeant," said Osbert. *"Rem acŭ tetigisti."*

Bashford Braddock had been standing listening to this exchange of remarks with a somewhat perplexed air.

"What's all this?" he said.

Osbert came out of his thoughts with a start.

"You still here, my dear chap?"

"I am."

"Want to see me about anything, dear boy? Something on your mind?"

"I just want a quiet five minutes alone with you, Mr. Mulliner."

"Certainly, my dear old fellow," said Osbert. "Certainly, certainly, certainly. Just wait till these policemen have gone and I will be at your disposal. We have had a little burglary."

"Burg—" Bashford Braddock was beginning, when there came out onto the steps a couple of policemen. They were supporting the burglar Harold, and were followed by others assisting the burglar Ernest. The sergeant, coming last, shook his head at Osbert a little gravely.

"You ought to be careful, sir," he said. "I don't say these fellows didn't deserve all you gave them, but you want to watch yourself. One of these days . . ."

"Perhaps I did overdo it a little," admitted Osbert. "But I am rather apt to see red on these occasions. One's fighting blood, you know. Well, good night, Sergeant, good night. And now," he said, taking Bashford Braddock's arm in a genial grip, "what was it you wanted to talk to me about? Come into the house. We shall be all alone there. I gave the staff a holiday. There won't be a soul except ourselves."

Bashford Braddock released his arm. He seemed embarrassed. His face, as the light of the street lamp shone upon it, was strangely pale.

"Did you—" He gulped a little. "Was that really you?"

"Really me? Oh, you mean those two fellows. Oh, yes, I found them in my dining room, eating my food and drinking my wine as cool as you please, and naturally I set about them. But the sergeant was quite right. I *do* get too rough when I lose my temper. I must remember," he said, taking out his handkerchief and tying a knot in it, "to cure myself of that. The fact is, I sometimes don't know my own strength. But you haven't told me what it is you want to see me about."

Bashford Braddock swallowed twice in quick succession. He edged past Osbert to the foot of the steps. He seemed oddly uneasy. His face had now taken on a greenish tinge.

"Oh, nothing, nothing."

"But, my dear fellow," protested Osbert, "it must have been something important to bring you round at this time of night."

Bashford Braddock gulped.

"Well, it was like this. I—er—saw the announcement of your engagement in the paper this morning, and I thought— I—er—just thought I would look in and ask you what you would like for a wedding present."

"My dear chap! Much too kind of you."

"So—er—so silly if I gave a fish slice and found that everybody else had given fish slices."

"That's true. Well, why not come inside and talk it over."

"No, I won't come in, thanks. I'd rather not come in. Perhaps you will write and let me know. *Poste Restante,* Bongo on the Congo, will find me. I am returning there immediately."

"Certainly," said Osbert. He looked down at his companion's feet. "My dear old lad, what on earth are you wearing those extraordinary boots for?"

"Corns," said Bashford Braddock.

"Why the spikes?"

"They relieve the pressure on the feet."

"I see, well, good night, Mr. Braddock."

"Good night, Mr. Mulliner."

"Good night," said Osbert.

"Good night," said Bashford Braddock.

✿ Monkey Business

A TANKARD of Stout had just squashed a wasp as it crawled on the arm of Miss Postlethwaite, our popular barmaid, and the conversation in the bar parlor of the Anglers' Rest had turned to the subject of physical courage.

The Tankard himself was inclined to make light of the whole affair, urging modestly that his profession, that of a fruit farmer, gave him perhaps a certain advantage over his fellow men when it came to dealing with wasps.

"Why, sometimes in the picking season," said the Tankard, "I've had as many as six standing on each individual plum, rolling their eyes at me and daring me to come on."

Mr. Mulliner looked up from his hot Scotch and lemon.

"Suppose they had been gorillas?" he said.

The Tankard considered this.

"There wouldn't be room," he argued, "not on an ordinary-sized plum."

"Gorillas?" said a Small Bass, puzzled.

"And I'm sure if it had been a gorilla Mr. Bunyan would have squashed it just the same," said Miss Postlethwaite, and she gazed at the Tankard with wholehearted admiration in her eyes.

Mr. Mulliner smiled gently.

"Strange," he said, "how even in these orderly, civilized days women still worship heroism in the male. Offer them wealth, brains, looks, amiability, skill at card tricks or at playing the ukulele . . . unless these are accompanied by physical courage they will turn away in scorn."

"Why gorillas?" asked the Small Bass, who liked to get these things settled.

"I was thinking of a distant cousin of mine whose life became for a time considerably complicated owing to one of these animals. Indeed, it was the fact that this gorilla's path crossed his that nearly lost Montrose Mulliner the hand of Rosalie Beamish."

The Small Bass still appeared mystified.

"I shouldn't have thought anybody's path *would* have crossed a gorilla's. I'm forty-five next birthday, and I've never so much as seen a gorilla."

"Possibly Mr. Mulliner's cousin was a big-game hunter," said a Gin Fizz.

"No," said Mr. Mulliner. "He was an assistant director in the employment of the Perfecto-Zizzbaum Motion Picture Corporation of Hollywood; and the gorilla of which I speak was one of the cast of the super film, *Black Africa,* a celluloid epic of the clashing of elemental passions in a land where might is right and the strong man comes into his own. Its capture in its native jungle was said to have cost the lives of several half-dozen members of the expedition, and at the time when this story begins it was lodged in a stout cage on the Perfecto-Zizzbaum lot at a salary of seven hundred and fifty dollars a week, with billing guaranteed in letters not smaller than those of Edmund Wigham and Luella Benstead, the stars."

In ordinary circumstances (said Mr. Mulliner) this gorilla would have been to my distant cousin Montrose merely one of a thousand fellow workers on the lot. If you had asked him, he would have said that he wished the animal every kind of success in its chosen profession but that, for all the chance there was of them ever, as it were, getting together, they were just ships that pass in the night. It is doubtful, indeed, if he would even have bothered to go down to its cage and look at it, had not Rosalie Beamish asked him to do so. As he put it to himself, if a man's duties brought him into constant personal contact with Mr. Schnellenhamer, the President of the Corporation, where was the sense of wasting time looking at gorillas? Blasé about sums up his attitude.

But Rosalie was one of the extra girls in *Black Africa* and so had a natural interest in a brother artist. And as she and Montrose were engaged to be married her word, of course, was law. Montrose had been planning to play draughts that afternoon with his friend, George Pybus, of the Press department, but he good-naturedly canceled the fixture and accompanied Rosalie to the animal's headquarters.

He was more than ordinarily anxious to oblige her today, because they had recently been having a little tiff. Rosalie had been urging him to go to Mr. Schnellenhamer and ask for a rise of salary; and this Montrose, who was excessively timid by nature, was reluctant to do. There was something about being asked to pay out money that always aroused the head of the firm's worst passions.

When he met his betrothed outside the commissary, he was relieved to find her in a more amiable mood than she had been of late. She prattled merrily of this and that as they walked along, and Montrose was congratulating himself that there was not a cloud on the sky when, arriving at the cage, he found Captain Jack Fosdyke there, prodding at the gorilla with a natty cane.

This Captain Jack Fosdyke was a famous explorer who had been engaged to superintend the production of *Black Africa*. And the fact that Rosalie's professional duties necessitated a rather close association with him had caused Montrose a good deal of uneasiness. It was not that he did not trust her, but love makes a man jealous and he knew the fascination of these lean, brown, hard-bitten adventurers of the wilds.

As they came up, the explorer turned, and Montrose did not like the chummy look in the eye which he cocked at the girl. Nor, for the matter of that, did he like the other's bold smile. And he wished that in addressing Rosalie Captain Fosdyke would not preface his remarks with the words "Ah, there, girlie."

"Ah, there, girlie," said the Captain. "Come to see the monk?"

Rosalie was staring openmouthed through the bars.

"Doesn't he look fierce!" she cried.

Captain Jack Fosdyke laughed carelessly.

"Tchah!" he said, once more directing the ferrule of his cane at the animal's ribs. "If you had led the rough, tough, slam-bang, every-man-for-himself life I have, you wouldn't be frightened of gorillas. Bless my soul, I remember once in Equatorial Africa I was strolling along with my elephant gun and my trusty native bearer, 'Mlongi, and a couple of the brutes dropped out of a tree and started throwing their weight about and behaving as if the place belonged to them. I soon put a stop to that, I can tell you. Bang, bang, left and right, and two more skins for my collection. You have to be firm with gorillas. Dining anywhere tonight, girlie?"

"I am dining with Mr. Mulliner at the Brown Derby."

"Mr. who?"

"This is Mr. Mulliner."

"Oh, that?" said Captain Fosdyke, scrutinizing Montrose in a supercilious sort of way as if he had just dropped out of a tree before him. "Well, some other time, eh?"

And, giving the gorilla a final prod, he sauntered away.

Rosalie was silent for a considerable part of the return journey. When at length she spoke it was in a vein that occasioned Montrose the gravest concern.

"Isn't he wonderful!" she breathed. "Captain Fosdyke, I mean."

"Yes?" said Montrose coldly.

"I think he's splendid. So strong, so intrepid. Have you asked Mr. Schnellenhamer for that raise yet?"

"Er—no," said Montrose. "I am—how shall I put it?—biding my time."

There was another silence.

"Captain Fosdyke isn't afraid of Mr. Schnellenhamer," said Rosalie pensively. "He slaps him on the back."

"Nor am I afraid of Mr. Schnellenhamer," replied Montrose, stung. "I would slap him on the back myself if I considered that it would serve any useful end. My delay in asking for that raise is simply due to the fact that in these matters of finance a certain tact and delicacy have to be observed. Mr. Schnellenhamer is a busy man, and I have enough consideration not to intrude my personal affairs on him at a time when he is occupied with other matters."

"I see," said Rosalie, and there the matter rested. But Montrose remained uneasy. There had been a gleam in her eyes and a rapt expression on her face as she spoke of Captain Fosdyke which he had viewed with concern. Could it be, he asked himself, that she was falling a victim to the man's undeniable magnetism? He decided to consult his friend, George Pybus, of the Press department, on the matter. George was a knowledgeable young fellow and would doubtless have something constructive to suggest.

George Pybus listened to his tale with interest and said it reminded him of a girl he had loved and lost in Des Moines, Iowa.

"She ditched me for a prize fighter," said George. "There's no getting away from it, girls do get fascinated by the strong, tough male."

Montrose's heart sank.

"You don't really think—?"

"It is difficult to say. One does not know how far this thing has gone. But I certainly feel that we must lose no time in drafting out some scheme whereby you shall acquire a glamour which will counteract the spell of this Fosdyke. I will devote a good deal of thought to the matter."

And it was on the very next afternoon, as he sat with Rosalie in the commissary sharing with her a Steak Pudding Marlene Dietrich, that Montrose noticed that the girl was in the grip of some strong excitement.

"Monty," she exclaimed, almost before she had dug out the first kidney, "do you know what Captain Fosdyke said this morning?"

Montrose choked.

"If that fellow has been insulting you," he cried, "I'll . . . Well, I shall be extremely annoyed," he concluded with a good deal of heat.

"Don't be silly. He wasn't talking to me. He was speaking to Luella Benstead. You know she's getting married again soon . . ."

"Odd how these habits persist."

". . . and Captain Fosdyke said why didn't she get married in the gorilla's cage. For the publicity."

"He did?"

Montrose laughed heartily. A quaint idea, he felt. Bizarre, even.

"She said she wouldn't dream of it. And then Mr. Pybus, who happened to be standing by, suddenly got the most wonderful idea. He came up to me and said why shouldn't you and I get married in the gorilla's cage."

Montrose's laughter died away.

"You and I?"

"Yes."

"George Pybus suggested that?"

"Yes."

Montrose groaned in spirit. He was telling himself that he might have known that something like this would have been the result of urging a member of the Press department to exercise his intellect. The brains of members of the Press department of motion-picture studios resemble soup at a cheap restaurant. It is wiser not to stir them.

"Think what a sensation it would make! No more extra work for me after that. I'd get parts, and good ones. A girl can't get anywhere in this business without publicity."

Montrose licked his lips. They had become very dry. He was thinking harshly of George Pybus. It was just loose talking like George Pybus's, he felt, that made half the trouble in this world.

"But don't you feel," he said, "that there is something a little undignified about publicity? In my opinion, a true artist ought to be above it. And I think you should not overlook another, extremely vital aspect of the matter. I refer to the deleterious effect which such an exhibition as Pybus suggests would have upon those who read about it in the papers. Speaking for myself," said Montrose, "there is nothing I should enjoy more than a quiet wedding in a gorilla's cage. But has one the right to pander to the morbid tastes of a sensation-avid public? I am not a man who often speaks of these deeper things— on the surface, no doubt, I seem careless and happy-go-lucky—but I do hold very serious views on a citizen's duties in this fevered modern age. I consider that each one of us should do all that lies in his power to fight the ever-growing trend of the public mind toward the morbid and the hectic. I have a very real feeling that the body politic can never become healthy while this appetite for sensation persists. If America is not to go the way of Babylon and Rome, we must come back to normalcy and the sane outlook. It is not much that a man in my humble position can do to stem the tide, but at least I can refrain from adding fuel to its flames by getting married in gorillas' cages."

Rosalie was gazing at him incredulously.

"You don't mean you won't do it?"

"It would not be right."

"I believe you're scared."

"Nothing of the kind. It is purely a question of civic conscience."

"You *are* scared. To think," said Rosalie vehemently, "that I should have linked my lot with a man who's afraid of a teentsy-weentsy gorilla."

Montrose could not let this pass.

"It is not a teentsy-weentsy gorilla. I should describe the animal's muscular development as well above the average."

"And the keeper would be outside the cage with a spiked stick."

"*Outside* the cage!" said Montrose thoughtfully.

Rosalie sprang to her feet in sudden passion.

"Good-bye!"

"But you haven't finished your steak pudding."

"Good-bye," she repeated. "I see now what your so-called love is worth. If you are going to start denying me every little thing before we're married, what would you be like after? I'm glad I have discovered your true character in time. Our engagement is at an end."

Montrose was pale to the lips, but he tried to reason with her.

"But, Rosalie," he urged, "surely a girl's wedding day ought to be something for her to think of all her life—to recall with dreamily smiling lips as she knits the tiny garments or cooks the evening meal for the husband she adores. She ought to be able to look back and live again through the solemn hush in the church, savor once more the sweet scent of the lilies of the valley, hear the rolling swell of the organ and the grave voice of the clergyman reading the service. What memories would you have if you carried out this plan that you suggest? One only—that of a smelly monkey. Have you reflected upon this, Rosalie?"

But she was obdurate.

"Either you marry me in the gorilla's cage, or you don't marry me at all. Mr. Pybus says it is certain to make the front page, with photographs and possibly even a short editorial on the right stuff being in the modern girl despite her surface irresponsibility."

"You will feel differently tonight, dear, when we meet for dinner."

"We shall not meet for dinner. If you are interested, I may inform you that Captain Fosdyke invited me to dine with him and I intend to do so."

"Rosalie!"

"There is a man who really is a man. When he meets a gorilla, he laughs in its face."

"Very rude."

"A million gorillas couldn't frighten him. Good-bye, Mr. Mulliner. I must go and tell him that when I said this morning that I had a previous engagement I was mistaken."

She swept out, and Montrose went on with his steak pudding like one in a dream.

It is possible (said Mr. Mulliner, taking a grave sip of his hot Scotch and lemon and surveying the company with a thoughtful eye) that what I have told you may have caused you to form a dubious opinion of my distant cousin Montrose. If so, I am not surprised. In the scene which I have just related, no one is better aware than myself that he has not shown up well. Reviewing his shallow arguments, we see through them, as Rosalie did; and, like Rosalie, we realize that he had feet of clay—and cold ones, to boot.

But I would urge in extenuation of his attitude that Montrose Mulliner, possibly through some constitutional defect such as an insufficiency of hormones, had been from childhood timorous in the extreme. And his work as an assistant director had served very noticeably to increase this innate pusillanimity.

It is one of the drawbacks to being an assistant director that virtually everything that happens to him is of a nature to create an inferiority complex—or, if one already exists, to deepen it. He is habitually addressed as "Hey, you" and alluded to in the third person as "that fathead." If anything goes wrong on the set, he gets the blame and is ticked off not only by the producer but also by the director and all the principals involved. Finally, he has to be obsequious to so many people that it is little wonder that he comes in time to resemble one of the more shrinking and respectful breeds of rabbit. Five years of assistant directing had so sapped Montrose's morale that nowadays he frequently found himself starting up and apologizing in his sleep.

It is proof, then, of the great love which he had for Rosalie Beamish that, encountering Captain Jack Fosdyke a few days later, he should have assailed him with bitter reproaches. Only love could have impelled him to act in a manner so foreign to his temperament.

The fact was, he blamed the Captain for all that had occurred. He considered that he had deliberately unsettled Rosalie and influenced her mind with the set purpose of making her dissatisfied with the man to whom she had plighted her troth.

"If it wasn't for you," he concluded warmly, "I feel sure I could have reasoned her out of what is nothing but a passing girlish whim. But you have infatuated her, and now where do I get off?"

The Captain twirled his mustache airily.

"Don't blame me, my boy. All my life I have been cursed by this fatal attraction of mine for the sex. Poor little moths, they will beat their wings against the bright light of my personality. Remind me to tell you some time of an interesting episode which occurred in the harem of the King of the 'Mbongos. There is something about me which is—what shall I say?—hypnotic. It is not my fault that this girl has compared us. It was inevitable that she should compare us. And having compared us what does she see? On the one hand, a man with a soul of chilled steel who can look his gorilla in the eye and make it play ball. On the other—I use the term in the kindliest possible sense—a crawling worm. Well, good-bye, my boy, glad to have seen you and had this little chat," said Captain Fosdyke. "I like you young fellows to bring your troubles to me."

For some moments after he had gone, Montrose remained standing motionless, while all the repartees which he might have made surged through his mind in a glittering procession. Then his thoughts turned once more to the topic of gorillas.

It is possible that it was the innuendoes uttered by Captain Fosdyke that now awoke in Montrose something which bore a shadowy resemblance to fortitude. Certainly, until this conversation, he had not intended to revisit the gorilla's cage, one sight of its occupant having been ample for him. Now, stung by the other's slurs, he decided to go and have another look at the brute. It might be that further inspection would make it seem less formidable. He had known this to happen before. The first time he had seen Mr. Schnellenhamer, for example, he had had something not unlike a fit of what our grandparents used to call the "vapors." Now, he could bear him with at least an assumption of nonchalance.

He made his way to the cage, and was presently exchanging glances with the creature through the bars.

Alas, any hope he may have had that familiarity would breed

contempt died as their eyes met. Those well-gnashed teeth, that hideous shagginess (a little reminiscent of a stockbroker motoring to Brighton in a fur coat) filled him with all the old familiar qualms. He tottered back and, with some dim idea of pulling himself together, took a banana from the bag which he had bought at the commissary to see him through the long afternoon. And, as he did so, there suddenly flashed upon him the recollection of an old saw which he had heard in his infancy—The Gorilla Never Forgets. In other words, Do the square thing by gorillas, and they will do the square thing by you.

His heart leaped within him. He pushed the banana through the bars with a cordial smile, and was rejoiced to find it readily accepted. In rapid succession he passed over the others. A banana a day keeps the gorilla away, he felt jubilantly. By standing treat to this animal regardless of cost, he reasoned, he would so ingratiate himself with it as to render the process of getting married in its cage both harmless and agreeable. And it was only when his guest had finished the last of the fruit that he realized with a sickening sense of despair that he had got his facts wrong and that his whole argument, based on a false premise, fell to the ground and became null and void.

It was the elephant who never forgot—not the gorilla. It all came back to him now. He was practically sure that gorillas had never been mentioned in connection with the subject of mnemonics. Indeed, for all he knew, these creatures might be famous for the shortness of their memory—with the result that if later on he were to put on pin-striped trousers and a top hat and enter this animal's cage with Rosalie on his arm and the studio band playing the Wedding March, all recollection of those bananas would probably have passed completely from its fat head, and it would totally fail to recognize its benefactor.

Moodily crumpling the bag, Montrose turned away. This, he felt, was the end.

I have a tender heart (said Mr. Mulliner), and I dislike to dwell on the spectacle of a human being groaning under the iron heel of Fate. Such morbid gloating, I consider, is better left to the Russians. I will spare you, therefore, a detailed analysis of my distant cousin Montrose's emotions as the long day wore on. Suffice it to say that by a few minutes to five o'clock he had become a mere toad beneath the harrow. He wandered aimlessly to and fro about the lot in the growing dusk, and it seemed to him that the falling shades of evening resembled the cloud that had settled upon his life.

He was roused from these meditations by a collision with some solid body and, coming to himself, discovered that he had been trying to walk through his old friend, George Pybus of the Press department. George was standing beside his car, apparently on the point of leaving for the day.

It is one more proof of Montrose Mulliner's gentle nature that he did not reproach George Pybus for the part he had taken in darkening his outlook. All he did was to gape and say:

"Hullo! You off?"

George Pybus climbed into the car and started the engine.

"Yes," he said, "and I'll tell you why. You know that gorilla?"

With a shudder which he could not repress Montrose said he knew the gorilla.

"Well, I'll tell you something," said George Pybus. "Its agent has been complaining that we've been throwing all the publicity to Luella Benstead and Edmund Wigham. So the boss sent out a hurry call for quick thinking. I told him that you and Rosalie Beamish were planning to get married in its cage, but I've seen Rosalie and she tells me you've backed out. Scarcely the spirit I should have expected in you, Montrose."

Montrose did his best to assume a dignity which he was far from feeling.

"One has one's code," he said. "One dislikes to pander to the morbidity of a sensation-avid . . ."

"Well, it doesn't matter, anyway," said George Pybus, "because I got another idea, and a better one. This one is a pippin. At five sharp this evening, Standard Pacific time, that gorilla's going to be let out of its cage and will menace hundreds. If that doesn't land him on the front page . . ."

Montrose was appalled.

"But you can't do that!" he gasped. "Once let that awful brute out of its cage and it may tear people to shreds."

George Pybus reassured him.

"Nobody of any consequence. The stars have all been notified and are off the lot. So are the directors. Also the executives, all except Mr. Schnellenhamer, who is cleaning up some work in his office. He will be quite safe there, of course. Nobody ever got into Mr. Schnellenhamer's office without waiting four hours in the anteroom. Well, I must be off," said George Pybus. "I've got to dress and get out to Malibu for dinner."

And, so speaking, he trod on the accelerator and was speedily lost to view in the gathering darkness.

It was a few moments later that Montrose, standing rooted to the spot, became aware of a sudden distant uproar; and, looking at his watch, he found that it was precisely five o'clock.

The spot to which Montrose had been standing rooted was in that distant part of the lot where the outdoor sets are kept permanently erected, so that a director with—let us suppose—a London street scene to shoot is able instantly to lay his hands on a back alley in Algiers, a medieval castle, or a Parisian boulevard—none of which are any good to him but which make him feel that the studio is trying to be helpful.

As far as Montrose's eye could reach, Spanish patios, thatched cottages, tenement buildings, *estaminets,* Oriental bazaars, Kaffir kraals and the residences of licentious New York clubmen stood out against the evening sky; and the fact that he selected as his haven of refuge one of the tenement buildings was due to its being both tallest and nearest.

Like all outdoor sets, it consisted of a front just like the real thing and a back composed of steps and platforms. Up these steps he raced, and on the topmost of the platforms he halted and sat down. He was still unable to think very coherently, but in a dim sort of way he was rather proud of his agility and resource. He felt that he had met a grave crisis well. He did not know what the record was for climbing a flight of steps with a gorilla loose in the neighborhood, but he would have felt surprise if informed that he had not lowered it.

The uproar which had had such a stimulating effect upon him was now increasing in volume; and, oddly, it appeared to have become stationary. He glanced down through the window of his tenement building, and was astonished to observe below him a dense crowd. And what perplexed him most about this crowd was that it was standing still and looking up.

Scarcely, felt Montrose, intelligent behavior on the part of a crowd with a savage gorilla after it.

There was a good deal of shouting going on, but he found himself unable to distinguish any words. A woman who stood in the forefront of the throng appeared particularly animated. She was waving an umbrella in a rather neurotic manner.

The whole thing, as I say, perplexed Montrose. What these people thought they were doing, he was unable to say. He was still speculating on the matter when a noise came to his ears.

It was the crying of a baby.

Now, with all these mother-love pictures so popular, the presence of a baby on the lot was not in itself a thing to occasion surprise. It is a very unambitious mother in Hollywood who, the moment she finds herself and child doing well, does not dump the little stranger into a perambulator and wheel it round to the casting office in the hope of cashing in. Ever since he had been with the Perfecto-Zizzbaum, Montrose had seen a constant stream of offspring riding up and trying to break into the game. It was not, accordingly, the fact of a baby being among those present that surprised him. What puzzled him about this particular baby was that it seemed to be so close at hand. Unless the acoustics were playing odd tricks, the infant, he was convinced, was sharing this eyrie of his. And how a mere baby, handicapped probably by swaddling clothes and a bottle, could have shinned up all those steps bewildered him to such an extent that he moved along the planks to investigate.

And he had not gone three paces when he paused, aghast. With its hairy back toward him, the gorilla was crouching over something that lay on the ground. And another bellow told him that this was the baby in person; and instantly Montrose saw what must have occurred. His reading of magazine stories had taught him that, once a gorilla gets loose, the first thing it does is to snatch a baby from a perambulator and climb to the nearest high place. It is pure routine.

This, then, was the position in which my distant cousin Montrose found himself at eight minutes past five on this misty evening. A position calculated to test the fortitude of the sternest.

Now, it has been well said that with nervous, highly strung men like Montrose Mulliner, a sudden call upon their manhood is often enough to revolutionize their whole character. Psychologists have frequently commented on this. We are too ready, they say, to dismiss as cowards those who merely require the stimulus of the desperate emergency to bring out all their latent heroism. The crisis comes, and the craven turns magically into the paladin.

With Montrose, however, this was not the case. Ninety-nine out of a hundred of those who knew him would have scoffed at the idea of him interfering with an escaped gorilla to save the life of a child, and they would have been right. To tiptoe backwards, holding his breath, was with Montrose Mulliner the work of a moment. And it was the fact that he did it so quickly that wrecked his plans. Stubbing a heel on a loose board in his haste, he fell backwards with a crash. And when the stars had ceased to obscure his vision, he found himself gazing up into the hideous face of the gorilla.

On the last occasion when the two had met, there had been iron bars between them; and even with this safeguard Montrose, as I have said, had shrunk from the creature's evil stare. Now, meeting the brute as it were socially, he experienced a thrill of horror such as had never come to him even in nightmares. Closing his eyes, he began to speculate as to which limb, when it started to tear him limb from limb, the animal would start with.

The one thing of which he was sure was that it would begin operations by uttering a fearful snarl; and when the next sound that came to his ears was a deprecating cough he was so astonished that he could keep his eyes closed no longer. Opening them, he found the gorilla looking at him with an odd, apologetic expression on its face.

"Excuse me, sir," said the gorilla, "but are you by any chance a family man?"

For an instant, on hearing the question, Montrose's astonishment deepened. Then he realized what must have happened. He must have been torn limb from limb without knowing it, and now he was in heaven. Though even this did not altogether satisfy him as an explanation, for he had never expected to find gorillas in heaven.

The animal now gave a sudden start.

"Why, it's you! I didn't recognize you at first. Before going any further, I should like to thank you for those bananas. They were delicious. A little something round about the middle of the afternoon picks one up quite a bit, doesn't it."

Montrose blinked. He could still hear the noise of the crowd below. His bewilderment increased.

"You speak very good English for a gorilla," was all he could find to say. And, indeed, the animal's diction had been remarkable for its purity.

The gorilla waved the compliment aside modestly.

"Oh, well, Balliol, you know. Dear old Balliol. One never quite forgets the lessons one learned at Alma Mater, don't you think? You are not an Oxford man, by any chance?"

"No."

"I came down in '26. Since then I have been knocking around a good deal, and a friend of mine in the circus business suggested to me that the gorilla field was not overcrowded. Plenty of room at the top, was his expression. And I must say," said the gorilla, "I've done pretty well at it. The initial expenditure comes high, of course . . . you don't get a skin like this for nothing . . . but there's virtually no overhead. Of course, to become a costar in a big feature film, as I have done, you need a good agent. Mine, I am glad to say, is a capital man of business. Stands no nonsense from these motion-picture magnates."

Montrose was not a quick thinker, but he was gradually adjusting his mind to the facts.

"Then you're not a real gorilla?"

"No, no. Synthetic, merely."

"You wouldn't tear anyone limb from limb?"

"My dear chap! My idea of a nice time is to curl up with a good book. I am happiest among my books."

Montrose's last doubts were resolved. He extended his hand cordially.

"Pleased to meet you, Mr. . . ."

"Waddesley-Davenport. Cyril Waddesley-Davenport. And I am extremely happy to meet you, Mr. . . ."

"Mulliner. Montrose Mulliner."

They shook hands warmly. From down below came the hoarse uproar of the crowd. The gorilla started.

"The reason I asked you if you were a family man," it said, "was that I hoped you might be able to tell me what is the best method of procedure to adopt with a crying baby. I don't seem able to stop the child. And all my own silly fault, too. I see now I should never have snatched it from its perambulator. If you want to know what is the matter with me, I am too much the artist. I simply had to snatch that baby. It was how I saw the scene, I *felt* it . . . felt it *here*," said the gorilla, thumping the left side of its chest. "And now what?"

Montrose reflected.

"Why don't you take it back?"

"To its mother?"

"Certainly."

"But . . ." The gorilla pulled doubtfully at its lower lip. "You have seen that crowd. Did you happen to observe a woman standing in the front row waving an umbrella?"

"The mother?"

"Precisely. Well, you know as well as I do, Mulliner, what an angry woman can do with an umbrella."

Montrose thought again.

"It's all right," he said. "I have it. Why don't you sneak down the back steps? Nobody will see you. The crowd's in front, and it's almost dark."

The gorilla's eyes lit up. It slapped Montrose gratefully on the shoulder.

"My dear chap! The very thing. But as regards the baby . . ."

"I will restore it."

"Capital! I don't know how to thank you, dear fellow," said the gorilla. "By Jove, this is going to be a lesson to me in future not to give way to the artist in me. You don't know how I've been feeling about that umbrella. Well, then, in case we don't meet again, always remember that the Lotos Club finds me when I am in New York. Drop in any time you happen to be in that neighborhood and we'll have a bite to eat and a good talk."

And what of Rosalie, meanwhile? Rosalie was standing beside the bereaved mother, using all her powers of cajolery to try to persuade Captain Jack Fosdyke to go to the rescue; and the Captain was pleading technical difficulties that stood in the way.

"Dash my buttons," he said, "if only I had my elephant gun and my trusty native bearer, 'Mlongi, here, I'd pretty soon know what to do about it. As it is, I'm handicapped."

"But you told me yesterday that you had often strangled gorillas with your bare hands."

"Not *gor*-illas, dear lady—*por*-illas. A species of South American wombat, and very good eating they make, too."

"You're afraid!"

"Afraid? Jack Fosdyke afraid? How they would laugh on the Lower Zambesi if they could hear you say that."

"You are! You, who advised me to have nothing to do with the man I love because he was of a mild and diffident nature."

Captain Jack Fosdyke twirled his mustache.

"Well, I don't notice," he sneered, "that he . . ." He broke off, and his jaw slowly fell. Round the corner of the building was walking Montrose Mulliner. His bearing was erect, even jaunty, and he carried the baby in his arms. Pausing for an instant to allow the busily clicking cameras to focus him, he advanced toward the stupefied mother and thrust the child into her arms.

"That's that," he said carelessly, dusting his fingers. "No, no, please," he went on. "A mere nothing."

For the mother was kneeling before him, endeavoring to kiss his hand. It was not only maternal love that prompted the action. That morning she had signed up her child at seventy-five dollars a week for the forthcoming picture *Tiny Fingers,* and all through these long, anxious minutes it had seemed as though the contract must be a total loss.

Rosalie was in Montrose's arms, sobbing.

"Oh, Monty!"

"There, there!"

"How I misjudged you!"

"We all make mistakes."

"I made a bad one when I listened to that man there," said Rosalie, darting a scornful look at Captain Jack Fosdyke. "Do you realize that, for all his boasting, he would not move a step to save that poor child?"

"Not a step?"

"Not a single step."

"Bad, Fosdyke," said Montrose. "Rather bad. Not quite the straight bat, eh?"

"Tchah!" said the baffled man, and he turned on his heel and strode away. He was still twirling his mustache, but a lot that got him.

Rosalie was clinging to Montrose.

"You aren't hurt? Was it a fearful struggle?"

"Struggle?" Montrose laughed. "Oh, dear no. There was no struggle. I very soon showed the animal that I was going to stand no nonsense. I generally find with gorillas that all one needs is the power of the human eye. By the way, I've been thinking it over and I realize that I may have been a little unreasonable about that idea of yours. I still would prefer to get married in some nice, quiet church, but if you feel you want the ceremony to take place in that animal's cage, I shall be delighted."

She shivered.

"I couldn't do it. I'd be scared."

Montrose smiled understandingly.

"Ah, well," he said, "it is perhaps not unnatural that a delicately nurtured woman should be of less tough stuff than the more rugged male. Shall we be strolling along? I want to look in on Mr. Schnellenhamer, and arrange about that raise of mine. You won't mind waiting while I pop in at his office?"

"My hero!" whispered Rosalie.

⚙ *The Smile That Wins*

THE CONVERSATION in thc bar parlor of the Anglers' Rest had turned to the subject of the regrettably low standard of morality prevalent among the nobility and landed gentry of Great Britain.

Miss Postlethwaite, our erudite barmaid, had brought the matter up by mentioning that in the novelette which she was reading a viscount had just thrown a family solicitor over a cliff.

"Because he had found out his guilty secret," explained Miss Postlethwaite, polishing a glass a little severely, for she was a good woman. "It was his guilty secret this solicitor had found out, so the viscount threw him over a cliff. I suppose, if one did but know, that sort of thing is going on all the time."

Mr. Mulliner nodded gravely.

"So much so," he agreed, "that I believe that whenever a family solicitor is found in two or more pieces at the bottom of a cliff, the first thing the Big Four at Scotland Yard do is make a roundup of all the viscounts in the neighborhood."

"Baronets are worse than viscounts," said a Pint of Stout vehemently. "I was done down by one only last month over the sale of a cow."

"Earls are worse than baronets," insisted a Whiskey Sour. "I could tell you something about earls."

"How about O.B.E.'s?" demanded a Mild and Bitter. "If you ask me, O.B.E.'s want watching, too."

Mr. Mulliner sighed.

"The fact is," he said, "reluctant though one may be to admit it, the entire British aristocracy is seamed and honeycombed with immorality. I venture to assert that, if you took a pin and jabbed it down anywhere in the pages of *Debrett's Peerage,* you would find it piercing the name of someone who was going about the place with a conscience as tender as a sunburned neck. If anything were needed to prove my assertion, the story of my nephew, Adrian Mulliner, the detective, would do it."

"I didn't know you had a nephew who was a detective," said the Whiskey Sour.

Oh, yes. He has retired now, but at one time he was as keen an operator as anyone in the profession. After leaving Oxford and trying his hand at one or two uncongenial tasks, he had found his niche as a member of the firm of Widgery & Boon, Investigators, of Albemarle Street. And it was during his second year with this old-established house that he met and loved Lady Millicent Shipton-Bellinger, younger daughter of the fifth Earl of Brangbolton.

It was the Adventure of the Missing Sealyham that brought the young couple together. From the purely professional standpoint, my nephew has never ranked this among his greatest triumphs of ratiocination; but, considering what it led to, he might well, I think, be justified in regarding it as the most important case of his career. What happened was that he met the animal straying in the park, deduced from the name and address on its collar that it belonged to Lady Millicent Shipton-Bellinger, of 18A, Upper Brook Street, and took it thither at the conclusion of his stroll and restored it.

"Child's play" is the phrase with which, if you happen to allude to it, Adrian Mulliner will always airily dismiss this particular investigation; but Lady Millicent could not have displayed more admiration and enthusiasm had it been the supremest masterpiece of detective work. She fawned on my nephew. She invited him in to tea, consisting of buttered toast, anchovy sandwiches, and two kinds of cake; and at the conclusion of the meal they parted on terms which, even at that early stage in their acquaintance, were something warmer than those of mere friendship.

Indeed, it is my belief that the girl fell in love with Adrian as instantaneously as he with her. On him, it was her radiant blond beauty that exercised the spell. She, on her side, was fascinated, I fancy, not only by the regularity of his features, which, as is the case with all the Mulliners, was considerable, but also by the fact that he was dark and thin and wore an air of inscrutable melancholy.

This, as a matter of fact, was due to the troublesome attacks of dyspepsia from which he had suffered since boyhood; but to the girl it naturally seemed evidence of a great and romantic soul. Nobody, she felt, could look so grave and sad, had he not hidden deeps in him.

One can see the thing from her point of view. All her life she had been accustomed to brainless juveniles who eked out their meager eyesight with monocles and, as far as conversation was concerned, were a spent force after they had asked her if she had seen the Academy or did she think she would prefer a glass of lemonade. The effect on her of a dark, keen-eyed man like Adrian Mulliner, who spoke well and easily of footprints, psychology, and the underworld, must have been stupendous.

At any rate, their love ripened rapidly. It could not have been two weeks after their first meeting when Adrian, as he was giving her lunch one day at the Senior Bloodstain, the detectives' club in Rupert Street, proposed and was accepted. And for the next twenty-four hours, one is safe in saying, there was in the whole of London, including the outlying suburban districts, no happier private investigator than he.

Next day, however, when he again met Millicent for lunch, he was disturbed to perceive on her beautiful face an emotion which his trained eye immediately recognized as anguish.

"Oh, Adrian," said the girl brokenly. "The worst has happened. My father refuses to hear of our marrying. When I told him we were engaged, he said 'Pooh!' quite a number of times, and added that he had never heard such dashed nonsense in his life. You see, ever since my Uncle Joe's trouble in nineteen-twenty-eight, Father has had a horror of detectives."

"I don't think I have met your Uncle Joe."

"You will have the opportunity next year. With the usual allowance for good conduct he should be with us again about July. And there is another thing."

"Not another?"

"Yes. Do you know Sir Jasper Addleton, O.B.E.?"

"The financier?"

"Father wants me to marry him. Isn't it awful?"

"I have certainly heard more enjoyable bits of news," agreed Adrian. "This wants a good deal of careful thinking over."

The process of thinking over his unfortunate situation had the effect of rendering excessively acute the pangs of Adrian Mulliner's dyspepsia. During the past two weeks the ecstasy of being with Millicent and deducing that she loved him had caused a complete cessation of the attacks; but now they began again, worse than ever. At length, after a sleepless night during which he experienced all the emotions of one who has carelessly swallowed a family of scorpions, he sought a specialist.

The specialist was one of those keen, modern minds who disdain the outworn formulas of the more conservative mass of the medical profession. He examined Adrian carefully, then sat back in his chair, with the tips of his fingers touching.

"Smile!" he said.

"Eh?" said Adrian.

"Smile, Mr. Mulliner."

"Did you say smile?"

"That's it. Smile."

"But," Adrian pointed out, "I've just lost the only girl I ever loved."

"Well, that's fine," said the specialist, who was a bachelor. "Come on, now, if you please. Start smiling."

Adrian was a little bewildered.

"Listen," he said. "What *is* all this about smiling? We started, if I recollect, talking about my gastric juices. Now, in some mysterious way, we seem to have got on to the subject of smiles. How do you mean—smile? I never smile. I haven't smiled since the butler tripped over the spaniel and upset the melted butter on my Aunt Elizabeth, when I was a boy of twelve."

The specialist nodded.

"Precisely. And that is why your digestive organs trouble you. Dyspepsia," he proceeded, "is now recognized by the progressive element of the profession as purely mental. We do not treat it with drugs and medicines. Happiness is the only cure. Be gay, Mr. Mulliner. Be cheerful. And, if you can't do that, at any rate smile. The mere exercise of the risible muscles is in itself beneficial. Go out now and make a point, whenever you have a spare moment, of smiling."

"Like this?" said Adrian.

"Wider than that."

"How about this?"

"Better," said the specialist, "but still not quite so elastic as one could desire. Naturally, you need practice. We must expect the muscles to work rustily for a while at their unaccustomed task. No doubt things will brighten by and by."

He regarded Adrian thoughtfully.

"Odd," he said. "A curious smile, yours, Mr. Mulliner. It reminds me a little of the Mona Lisa's. It has the same underlying note of the sardonic and the sinister. It virtually amounts to a leer. Somehow it seems to convey the suggestion that you know all. Fortunately, my own life is an open book, for all to read, and so I was not discommoded. But I think it would be better if, for the present, you endeavored not to smile at invalids or nervous persons. Good morning, Mr. Mulliner. That will be five guineas, precisely."

On Adrian's face, as he went off that afternoon to perform the duties assigned to him by his firm, there was no smile of any description. He shrank from the ordeal before him. He had been told off to guard the wedding presents at a reception in Grosvenor Square, and naturally anything to do with weddings was like a sword through his heart. His face, as he patroled the room where the gifts were laid out, was drawn and forbidding. Hitherto, at these functions, it had always been his pride that nobody could tell that he was a detective. Today, a child could have recognized his trade. He looked like Sherlock Holmes.

To the gay throng that surged about him he paid little attention. Usually tense and alert on occasions like this, he now found his mind wandering. He mused sadly on Millicent. And suddenly—the result, no doubt, of these gloomy meditations, though a glass of wedding champagne may have contributed its mite—there shot through him, starting at about the third button of his neat waistcoat, a pang of dyspepsia so keen that he felt the pressing necessity of doing something about it immediately.

With a violent effort he contorted his features into a smile. And, as he did so, a stout, bluff man of middle age, with a red face and a gray mustache, who had been hovering near one of the tables, turned and saw him.

"Egad!" he muttered, paling.

Sir Sutton Hartley-Wesping, Bart.—for the red-faced man was he —had had a pretty good afternoon. Like all baronets who attend society wedding receptions, he had been going round the various tables since his arrival, pocketing here a fish slice, there a jeweled egg boiler, until now he had taken on about all the cargo his tonnage would warrant, and was thinking of strolling off to the pawnbroker's in the Euston Road, with whom he did most of his business. At the sight of Adrian's smile, he froze where he stood, appalled.

We have seen what the specialist thought of Adrian's smile. Even to him, a man of clear and limpid conscience, it had seemed sardonic and sinister. We can picture, then, the effect it must have had on Sir Sutton Hartley-Wesping.

At all costs, he felt, he must conciliate this leering man. Swiftly removing from his pockets a diamond necklace, five fish slices, ten cigarette lighters, and a couple of egg boilers, he placed them on the table and came over to Adrian with a nervous little laugh.

"How *are* you, my dear fellow?" he said.

Adrian said that he was quite well. And so, indeed, he was. The specialist's recipe had worked like magic. He was mildly surprised at finding himself so cordially addressed by a man whom he did not remember ever having seen before, but he attributed this to the magnetic charm of his personality.

"That's fine," said the baronet heartily. "That's capital. That's splendid. Er—by the way—I fancied I saw you smile just now."

"Yes," said Adrian. "I did smile. You see—"

"Of course I see. Of course, my dear fellow. You detected the joke I was playing on our good hostess, and you were amused because you understood that there is no animus, no *arrière-pensée,* behind these little practical pleasantries—nothing but good, clean fun, at which nobody would have laughed more heartily than herself. And now, what are you doing this week end, my dear old chap? Would you care to run down to my place in Sussex?"

"Very kind of you," began Adrian doubtfully. He was not quite sure that he was in the mood for strange week ends.

"Here is my card, then. I shall expect you on Friday. Quite a small party. Lord Brangbolton, Sir Jasper Addleton, and a few more. Just loafing about, you know, and a spot of bridge at night. Splendid. Capital. See you, then, on Friday."

And, carelessly dropping another egg boiler on the table as he passed, Sir Sutton disappeared.

Any doubts which Adrian might have entertained as to accepting the baronet's invitation had vanished as he heard the names of his fellow guests. It always interests a fiancé to meet his fiancée's father and his fiancée's prospective fiancé. For the first time since Millicent had told him the bad news, Adrian became almost cheerful. If, he felt, this baronet had taken such a tremendous fancy to him at first sight, why might it not happen that Lord Brangbolton would be equally drawn to him—to the extent, in fact, of overlooking his profession and welcoming him as a son-in-law?

He packed, on the Friday, with what was to all intents and purposes a light heart.

A fortunate chance at the very outset of his expedition increased Adrian's optimism. It made him feel that Fate was fighting on his side. As he walked down the platform of Victoria Station, looking for an empty compartment in the train which was to take him to his destination, he perceived a tall, aristocratic old gentleman being assisted into a first-class carriage by a man of butlerine aspect. And in the latter he recognized the servitor who had admitted him to 18A, Upper Brook Street, when he visited the house after solving the riddle of the missing Sealyham. Obviously, then, the white-haired, dignified passenger could be none other than Lord Brangbolton. And Adrian felt that if on a long train journey he failed to ingratiate himself with the old buster, he had vastly mistaken his amiability and winning fascination of manner.

He leaped in, accordingly, as the train began to move, and the earl, glancing up from his paper, jerked a thumb at the door.

"Get out, blast you!" he said. "Full up."

As the compartment was empty but for themselves, Adrian made no move to comply with the request. Indeed, to alight now, to such an extent had the train gathered speed, would have been impossible. Instead, he spoke cordially.

"Lord Brangbolton, I believe?"

"Go to hell," said his lordship.

"I fancy we are to be fellow guests at Wesping Hall this week end."

"What of it?"

"I just mentioned it."

"Oh?" said Lord Brangbolton. "Well, since you're here, how about a little flutter?"

As is customary with men of his social position, Millicent's father always traveled with a pack of cards. Being gifted by nature with considerable manual dexterity, he usually managed to do well with these on race trains.

"Ever played Persian Monarchs?" he asked, shuffling.

"I think not," said Adrian.

"Quite simple," said Lord Brangbolton. "You just bet a quid or whatever it may be that you can cut a higher card than the other fellow, and, if you do, you win, and, if you don't, you don't."

Adrian said it sounded a little like Blind Hooky.

"It is like Blind Hooky," said Lord Brangbolton. "Very like Blind Hooky. In fact, if you can play Blind Hooky, you can play Persian Monarchs."

By the time they alighted at Wesping Parva, Adrian was twenty pounds on the wrong side of the ledger. The fact, however, did not prey upon his mind. On the contrary, he was well satisfied with the progress of events. Elated with his winnings, the old earl had become positively cordial, and Adrian resolved to press his advantage home at the earliest opportunity.

Arrived at Wesping Hall, accordingly, he did not delay. Shortly after the sounding of the dressing gong he made his way to Lord Brangbolton's room and found him in his bath.

"Might I have a word with you, Lord Brangbolton?" he said.

"You can do more than that," replied the other, with marked amiability. "You can help me find the soap."

"Have you lost the soap?"

"Yes. Had it a minute ago, and now it's gone."

"Strange," said Adrian.

"Very strange," agreed Lord Brangbolton. "Makes a fellow think a bit, that sort of thing happening. My own soap, too. Brought it with me."

Adrian considered.

"Tell me exactly what occurred," he said. "In your own words. And tell me everything, please, for one never knows when the smallest detail may not be important."

His companion marshaled his thoughts.

"My name," he began, "is Reginald Alexander Montacute James Bramfylde Tregennis Shipton-Bellinger, fifth Earl of Brangbolton. On the sixteenth of the present month—today, in fact—I journeyed to the house of my friend Sir Sutton Hartley-Wesping, Bart.—here, in short—with the purpose of spending the week end there. Knowing that Sir Sutton likes to have his guests sweet and fresh about the place, I decided to take a bath before dinner. I unpacked my soap and in a short space of time had lathered myself thoroughly from the neck upwards. And then, just as I was about to get at my right leg, what should I find but that the soap had disappeared. Nasty shock it gave me, I can tell you."

Adrian had listened to this narrative with the closest attention. Certainly the problem appeared to present several points of interest.

"It looks like an inside job," he said thoughtfully. "It could scarcely be the work of a gang. You would have noticed a gang. Just give me the facts briefly once again, if you please."

"Well, I was here, in the bath, as it might be, and the soap was here—between my hands, as it were. Next moment it was gone."

"Are you sure you have omitted nothing?"

Lord Brangbolton reflected.

"Well, I was singing, of course."

A tense look came into Adrian's face.

"Singing what?"

" 'Sonny Boy.' "

Adrian's face cleared.

"As I suspected," he said, with satisfaction. "Precisely as I had supposed. I wonder if you are aware, Lord Brangbolton, that in the singing of that particular song the muscles unconsciously contract as you come to the final 'boy'? Thus—'I still have you, Sonny BOY.' You observe? It would be impossible for anyone, rendering the number with the proper gusto, not to force his hands together at this point, assuming that they were in anything like close juxtaposition. And if there were any slippery object between them, such as a piece of soap, it would inevitably shoot sharply upwards and fall"—he scanned the room keenly—"outside the bath on the mat. As, indeed," he concluded, picking up the missing object and restoring it to its proprietor, "it did."

Lord Brangbolton gaped.

"Well, dash my buttons," he cried, "if that isn't the smartest bit of work I've seen in a month of Sundays!"

"Elementary," said Adrian with a shrug.

"You ought to be a detective."

Adrian took the cue.

"I am a detective," he said. "My name is Mulliner."

For an instant the words did not appear to have made any impression. The aged peer continued to beam through the soapsuds. Then suddenly his geniality vanished with an ominous swiftness.

"Mulliner? Did you say Mulliner?"

"I did."

"You aren't by any chance the feller—"

"—who loves your daughter Millicent with a fervor he cannot begin to express? Yes, Lord Brangbolton, I am. And I am hoping that I may receive your consent to the match."

A hideous scowl had darkened the earl's brow. His fingers, which were grasping a loofah, tightened convulsively.

"Oh?" he said. "You are, are you? You imagine, do you, that I propose to welcome a blighted footprint-and-cigar-ash inspector into my family? It is your idea, is it, that I shall acquiesce in the union of my daughter to a dashed feller who goes about the place on his hands and knees with a magnifying glass, picking up small objects and putting them carefully away in his pocketbook? I seem to see myself! Why, rather than permit Millicent to marry a bally detective—"

"What is your objection to detectives?"

"Never you mind what's my objection to detectives. Marry my daughter, indeed! I like your infernal cheek. Why, you couldn't keep her in lipsticks."

Adrian preserved his dignity.

"I admit that my services are not so amply remunerated as I could wish, but the firm hint at a rise next Christmas—"

"Tchah!" said Lord Brangbolton. "Pshaw! If you are interested in my daughter's matrimonial arrangements, she is going, as soon as he gets through with this Bramah-Yamah Gold Mines flotation of his, to marry my old friend Jasper Addleton. As for you, Mr. Mulliner, I have only two words to say to you. One is POP, the other is OFF. And do it now."

Adrian sighed. He saw that it would be hopeless to endeavor to argue with the haughty old man in his present mood.

"So be it, Lord Brangbolton," he said quietly.

And, affecting not to notice the nailbrush which struck him smartly on the back of the head, he left the room.

The food and drink provided for his guests by Sir Sutton Hartley-Wesping at the dinner which began some half-hour later were all that the veriest gourmet could have desired; but Adrian gulped them down, scarcely tasting them. His whole attention was riveted on Sir Jasper Addleton, who sat immediately opposite him.

And the more he examined Sir Jasper, the more revolting seemed the idea of his marrying the girl he loved.

Of course, an ardent young fellow inspecting a man who is going to marry the girl he loves is always a stern critic. In the peculiar circumstances Adrian would, no doubt, have looked askance at a Clark Gable or a Laurence Olivier. But, in the case of Sir Jasper, it must be admitted that he had quite reasonable grounds for his disapproval.

In the first place, there was enough of the financier to make two financiers. It was as if Nature, planning a financier, had said to itself: "We will do this thing well. We will not skimp," with the result that, becoming too enthusiastic, it had overdone it. And then, in addition to being fat, he was also bald and goggle-eyed. And, if you overlooked his baldness and the goggly protuberance of his eyes, you could not get away from the fact that he was well advanced in years. Such a man, felt Adrian, would have been better employed in pricing burial lots in Kensal Green Cemetery than in forcing his unwelcome attentions on a sweet young girl like Millicent; and as soon as the meal was concluded he approached him with cold abhorrence.

"A word with you," he said, and led him out onto the terrace.

The O.D.E., as he followed him into the cool night air, seemed surprised and a little uneasy. He had noticed Adrian scrutinizing him closely across the dinner table, and if there is one thing a financier who has just put out a prospectus of a gold mine dislikes, it is to be scrutinized closely.

"What do you want?" he asked nervously.

Adrian gave him a cold glance.

"Do you ever look in a mirror, Sir Jasper?" he asked curtly.

"Frequently," replied the financier, puzzled.

"Do you ever weigh yourself?"

"Often."

"Do you ever listen while your tailor is toiling round you with the tape measure and calling out the score to his assistant?"

"I do."

"Then," said Adrian, "and I speak in the kindest spirit of disinterested friendship, you must have realized that you are an overfed old bohunkus. And how you ever got the idea that you were a fit mate for Lady Millicent Shipton-Bellinger frankly beats me. Surely it must have occurred to you what a priceless ass you will look, walking up the aisle with that young and lovely girl at your side? People will mistake you for an elderly uncle taking his niece to the zoo."

The O.B.E. bridled.

"Ho!" he said.

"It is no use saying 'Ho!' " said Adrian. "You can't get out of it with any 'Ho's.' When all the talk and argument have died away, the fact remains that, millionaire though you be, you are a nasty-looking, fat, senile millionaire. If I were you, I should give the whole thing a miss. What do you want to get married for, anyway? You are much happier as you are. Besides, think of the risks of a financier's life. Nice it would be for that sweet girl suddenly to get a wire from you telling her not to wait dinner for you as you had just started a seven-year stretch at Dartmoor!"

An angry retort had been trembling on Sir Jasper's lips during the early portion of this speech, but at these concluding words it died unspoken. He blenched visibly and stared at the speaker with undisguised apprehension.

"What do you mean?" he faltered.

"Never mind," said Adrian.

He had spoken, of course, purely at a venture, basing his remarks on the fact that nearly all O.B.E.'s who dabble in High Finance go to prison sooner or later. Of Sir Jasper's actual affairs he knew nothing.

"Hey, listen!" said the financier.

But Adrian did not hear him. I have mentioned that during dinner, preoccupied with his thoughts, he had bolted his food. Nature now took its toll. An acute spasm suddenly ran through him, and with a brief "Ouch!" of pain he doubled up and began to walk round in circles.

Sir Jasper clicked his tongue impatiently.

"This is no time for doing the Astaire pom-pom dance," he said sharply. "Tell me what you meant by that stuff you were talking about prison."

Adrian had straightened himself. In the light of the moon which flooded the terrace with its silver beams, his clean-cut face was plainly visible. And with a shiver of apprehension Sir Jasper saw that it wore a sardonic, sinister smile—a smile which, it struck him, was virtually tantamount to a leer.

I have spoken of the dislike financiers have for being scrutinized closely. Still more vehemently do they object to being leered at. Sir Jasper reeled, and was about to press his question when Adrian, still smiling, tottered off into the shadows and was lost to sight.

The financier hurried into the smoking room, where he knew there would be the materials for a stiff drink. A stiff drink was what he felt an imperious need of at the moment. He tried to tell himself that that smile could not really have had the inner meaning which he had read into it; but he was still quivering nervously as he entered the smoking room.

As he opened the door, the sound of an angry voice smote his ears. He recognized it as Lord Brangbolton's.

"I call it dashed low," his lordship was saying in his high-pitched tenor.

Sir Jasper gazed in bewilderment. His host, Sir Sutton Hartley-Wesping, was standing backed against the wall, and Lord Brangbolton, tapping him on the shirt front with a pistonlike forefinger, was plainly in the process of giving him a thorough ticking off.

"What's the matter?" asked the financier.

"I'll tell you what's the matter," cried Lord Brangbolton. "This hound here has got down a detective to watch his guests. A dashed fellow named Mulliner. So much," he said bitterly, "for our boasted English hospitality. Egad!" he went on, still tapping the baronet round and about the diamond solitaire. "I call it thoroughly low. If I have a few of my society chums down to my little place for a visit, naturally I chain up the hairbrushes and tell the butler to count the spoons every night, but I'd never dream of going so far as to employ beastly detectives. One has one's code. *Noblesse,* I mean to say, *oblige,* what, what?"

"But, listen," pleaded the baronet. "I keep telling you. I had to invite the fellow here. I thought that if he had eaten my bread and salt, he would not expose me."

"How do you mean, expose you?"

Sir Sutton coughed.

"Oh, it was nothing. The merest trifle. Still, the man undoubtedly could have made things unpleasant for me, if he had wished. So, when I looked up and saw him smiling at me in that frightful sardonic, knowing way—"

Sir Jasper Addleton uttered a sharp cry.

"Smiling!" He gulped. "Did you say smiling?"

"Smiling," said the baronet, "is right. It was one of those smiles that seem to go right through you and light up all your inner being as if with a searchlight."

Sir Jasper gulped again.

"Is this fellow—this smiler fellow—is he a tall, dark, thin chap?"

"That's right. He sat opposite you at dinner."

"And he's a detective?"

"He is," said Lord Brangbolton. "As shrewd and smart a detective," he added grudgingly, "as I ever met in my life. The way he found that soap . . . Feller struck me as having some sort of a sixth sense, if you know what I mean, dash and curse him. I hate detectives," he said with a shiver. "They give me the creeps. This one wants to marry my daughter, Millicent, of all the dashed nerve!"

"See you later," said Sir Jasper. And with a single bound he was out of the room and on his way to the terrace. There was, he felt, no time to waste. His florid face, as he galloped along, was twisted and ashen. With one hand he drew from his inside pocket a checkbook, with the other from his trouser pocket a fountain pen.

Adrian, when the financier found him, was feeling a good deal better. He blessed the day when he had sought the specialist's advice. There was no doubt about it, he felt, the man knew his business. Smiling might make the cheek muscles ache, but it undoubtedly did the trick as regarded the pangs of dyspepsia.

For a brief while before Sir Jasper burst onto the terrace, waving fountain pen and checkbook, Adrian had been giving his face a rest. But now, the pain in his cheeks having abated, he deemed it prudent to resume the treatment. And so it came about that the financier, hurrying toward him, was met with a smile so meaning, so suggestive, that he stopped in his tracks and for a moment could not speak.

"Oh, there you are!" he said, recovering at length. "Might I have a word with you in private, Mr. Mulliner?"

Adrian nodded, beaming. The financier took him by the coat sleeve and led him across the terrace. He was breathing a little stertorously.

"I've been thinking things over," he said, "and I've come to the conclusion that you were right."

"Right?" said Adrian.

"About me marrying. It wouldn't do."

"No?"

"Positively not. Absurd. I can see it now. I'm too old for the girl."

"Yes."

"Too bald."

"Exactly."

"And too fat."

"Much too fat," agreed Adrian. This sudden change of heart puzzled him, but none the less the other's words were as music to his ears. Every syllable the O.B.E. had spoken had caused his heart to leap within him like a young lamb in springtime, and his mouth curved in a smile.

Sir Jasper, seeing it, shied like a frightened horse. He patted Adrian's arm feverishly.

"So I have decided," he said, "to take your advice and—if I recall your expression—give the thing a miss."

"You couldn't do better," said Adrian heartily.

"Now, if I were to remain in England in these circumstances," proceeded Sir Jasper, "there might be unpleasantness. So I propose to go quietly away at once to some remote spot—say, South America. Don't you think I am right?" he asked, giving the checkbook a twitch.

"Quite right," said Adrian.

"You won't mention this little plan of mine to anyone? You will keep it as just a secret between ourselves? If, for instance, any of your cronies at Scotland Yard should express curiosity as to my whereabouts, you will plead ignorance?"

"Certainly."

"Capital!" said Sir Jasper, relieved. "And there is one other thing. I gather from Brangbolton that you are anxious to marry Lady Millicent yourself. And as by the time of the wedding I shall doubtless be in—well, Callao is a spot that suggests itself offhand, I would like to give you my little wedding present now."

He scribbed hastily in his checkbook, tore out a page and handed it to Adrian.

"Remember!" he said. "Not a word to anyone!"

"Quite," said Adrian.

He watched the financier disappear in the direction of the garage, regretting that he could have misjudged a man who so evidently had much good in him. Presently the sound of a motor engine announced that the other was on his way. Feeling that one obstacle, at least, between himself and his happiness had been removed, Adrian strolled indoors to see what the rest of the party were doing.

It was a quiet, peaceful scene that met his eyes as he wandered into the library. Overruling the request of some of the members of the company for a rubber of bridge, Lord Brangbolton had gathered them together at a small table and was initiating them into his favorite game of Persian Monarchs.

"It's perfectly simple, dash it," he was saying. "You just take the pack and cut. You bet—let us say ten pounds—that you will cut a higher card than the feller you're cutting against. And, if you do, you win, dash it. And, if you don't, the other dashed feller wins. Quite clear, what?"

They settled down to their game, and Adrian wandered about the room, endeavoring to still the riot of emotion which his recent interview with Sir Jasper Addleton had aroused in his bosom. All that remained for him to do now, he reflected, was by some means or other to remove the existing prejudice against him from Lord Brangbolton's mind.

It would not be easy, of course. To begin with, there was the matter of his straitened means.

He suddenly remembered that he had not yet looked at the check which the financier had handed him. He pulled it out of his pocket.

And, having glanced at it, Adrian Mulliner swayed like a poplar in a storm.

Just what he had expected, he could not have said. A fiver, possibly. At the most, a tenner. Just a trifling gift, he had imagined, with which to buy himself a cigarette lighter, a fish slice, or an egg boiler.

The check was for a hundred thousand pounds.

So great was the shock that, as Adrian caught sight of himself in the mirror opposite to which he was standing, he scarcely recognized the face in the glass. He seemed to be seeing it through a mist. Then the mist cleared, and he saw not only his own face clearly, but also that of Lord Brangbolton, who was in the act of cutting against his left-hand neighbor, Lord Knubble of Knopp.

And, as he thought of the effect this sudden accession of wealth must surely have on the father of the girl he loved, there came into Adrian's face a sudden, swift smile.

And simultaneously from behind him he heard a gasping exclamation, and, looking in the mirror, he met Lord Brangbolton's eyes. Always a litle prominent, they were now almost prawnlike in their convexity.

Lord Knubble of Knopp had produced a banknote from his pocket and was pushing it along the table.

"Another ace!" he exclaimed. "Well, I'm dashed!"

Lord Brangbolton had risen from his chair.

"Excuse me," he said in a strange, croaking voice. "I just want to have a little chat with my friend, my dear old friend, Mulliner here. Might I have a word in private with you, Mr. Mulliner?"

There was silence between the two men until they had reached a corner of the terrace out of earshot of the library window. Then Lord Brangbolton cleared his throat.

"Mulliner," he began, "or, rather—what is your Christian name?"

"Adrian."

"Adrian, my dear fellow," said Lord Brangbolton, "my memory is not what it should be, but I seem to have a distinct recollection that, when I was in my bath before dinner, you said something about wanting to marry my daughter Millicent."

"I did," replied Adrian. "And, if your objections to me as a suitor were mainly financial, let me assure you that, since we last spoke, I have become a wealthy man."

"I never had any objections to you, Adrian, financial or otherwise," said Lord Brangbolton, patting his arm affectionately. "I have always felt that the man my daughter married ought to be a fine, warm-hearted young fellow like you. For you, Adrian," he proceeded, "are essentially warmhearted. You would never dream of distressing a father-in-law by mentioning any . . . any little . . . well, in short, I saw from your smile in there that you had noticed that I was introducing into that game of Blind Hooky—or, rather, Persian Monarchs—certain little—shall I say variations?—designed to give it additional interest and excitement, and I feel sure that you would scorn to embarrass a father-in-law by . . . Well, to cut a long story short, my boy, take Millicent and with her a father's blessing."

He extended his hand. Adrian clasped it warmly.

"I am the happiest man in the world," he said, smiling.

Lord Brangbolton winced.

"Do you mind not doing that?" he said.

"I only smiled," said Adrian.

"I know," said Lord Brangbolton.

Little remains to be told. Adrian and Millicent were married three months later at a fashionable West End church. All society was there. The presents were both numerous and costly, and the bride looked charming. The service was conducted by the Very Reverend the Dean of Bittlesham.

It was in the vestry afterwards, as Adrian looked at Millicent, and seemed to realize for the first time that all his troubles were over and that this lovely girl was indeed his, for better or worse, that a full sense of his happiness swept over the young man.

All through the ceremony he had been grave, as befitted a man at the most serious point of his career. But now, fizzing as if with some spiritual yeast, he clasped her in his arms, and over her shoulder his face broke into a quick smile.

He found himself looking into the eyes of the Dean of Bittlesham. A moment later he felt a tap on his arm.

"Might I have a word with you in private, Mr. Mulliner?" said the dean in a low voice.

❈ *Strychnine in the Soup*

FROM the moment the Draught Stout entered the bar parlor of the Anglers' Rest, it had been obvious that he was not his usual cheery self. His face was drawn and twisted, and he sat with bowed head in a distant corner by the window, contributing nothing to the conversation which, with Mr. Mulliner as its center, was in progress around the fire. From time to time he heaved a hollow sigh.

A sympathetic Lemonade and Angostura, putting down his glass, went across and laid a kindly hand on the sufferer's shoulder.

"What is it, old man?" he asked. "Lost a friend?"

"Worse," said the Draught Stout. "A mystery novel. Got halfway through it on the journey down here, and left it in the train."

"My nephew Cyril, the interior decorator," said Mr. Mulliner, "once did the very same thing. These mental lapses are not infrequent."

"And now," proceeded the Draught Stout, "I'm going to have a sleepless night, wondering who poisoned Sir Geoffrey Tuttle, Bart."

"The bart. was poisoned, was he?"

"You never said a truer word. Personally, I think it was the vicar who did him in. He was known to be interested in strange poisons."

Mr. Mulliner smiled indulgently.

"It was not the vicar," he said. "I happen to have read *The Murglow Manor Mystery*. The guilty man was the plumber."

"What plumber?"

"The one who comes in Chapter Two to mend the shower bath. Sir Geoffrey had wronged his aunt in the year '96, so he fastened a snake in the nozzle of the shower bath with glue; and when Sir Geoffrey turned on the stream the hot water melted the glue. This released the snake, which dropped through one of the holes, bit the baronet in the leg, and disappeared down the waste pipe."

"But that can't be right," said the Draught Stout. "Between Chapter Two and the murder there was an interval of several days."

"The plumber forgot his snake and had to go back for it," explained Mr. Mulliner. "I trust that this revelation will prove sedative."

"I feel a new man," said the Draught Stout. "I'd have lain awake worrying about that murder all night."

"I suppose you would. My nephew Cyril was just the same. Nothing in this modern life of ours," said Mr. Mulliner, taking a sip of his hot Scotch and lemon, "is more remarkable than the way in which the mystery novel has gripped the public. Your true enthusiast, deprived of his favorite reading, will stop at nothing in order to get it. He is like a victim of the drug habit when withheld from cocaine. My nephew Cyri—"

"Amazing the things people will leave in trains," said a Small Lager. "Bags . . . umbrellas . . . even stuffed chimpanzees, occasionally, I've been told. I heard a story the other day . . ."

My nephew Cyril (said Mr. Mulliner) had a greater passion for mystery stories than anyone I have ever met. I attribute this to the fact that, like so many interior decorators, he was a fragile, delicate young fellow, extraordinarily vulnerable to any ailment that happened to be going the rounds. Every time he caught mumps or influenza or German measles or the like, he occupied the period of convalescence in reading mystery stories. And, as the appetite grows by what it feeds on, he had become, at the time at which this narrative opens, a confirmed addict. Not only did he devour every volume of this type on which he could lay his hands, but he was also to be found at any theater which was offering the kind of drama where skinny arms come unexpectedly out of the chiffonier and the audience feels a mild surprise if the lights stay on for ten consecutive minutes.

And it was during a performance of *The Gray Vampire* at the St. James's that he found himself sitting next to Amelia Bassett, the girl whom he was to love with all the stored-up fervor of a man who hitherto had been inclined rather to edge away when in the presence of the other sex.

He did not know her name was Amelia Bassett. He had never seen her before. All he knew was that at last he had met his fate, and for the whole of the first act he was pondering the problem of how he was to make her acquaintance.

It was as the lights went up for the first intermission that he was aroused from his thoughts by a sharp pain in the right leg. He was just wondering whether it was gout or sciatica when, glancing down, he perceived that what had happened was that his neighbor, absorbed by the drama, had absent-mindedly collected a handful of his flesh and was twisting it in an ecstasy of excitement.

It seemed to Cyril a good *point d'appui*.

"Excuse me," he said.

The girl turned. Her eyes were glowing, and the tip of her nose still quivered.

"I beg your pardon?"

"My leg," said Cyril. "Might I have it back, if you've finished with it?"

The girl looked down. She started visibly.

"I'm awfully sorry," she gasped.

"Not at all," said Cyril. "Only too glad to have been of assistance."

"I got carried away."

"You are evidently fond of mystery plays."

"I love them."

"So do I. And mystery novels?"

"Oh, yes!"

"Have you read *Blood on the Banisters?*"

"Oh, *yes!* I thought it was better than *Severed Throats!*"

"So did I," said Cyril. "Much better. Brighter murders, subtler detectives, crisper clues . . . better in every way."

The two twin souls gazed into each other's eyes. There is no surer foundation for a beautiful friendship than a mutual taste in literature.

"My name is Amelia Bassett," said the girl.

"Mine is Cyril Mulliner. Bassett?" He frowned thoughtfully. "The name seems familiar."

"Perhaps you have heard of my mother. Lady Bassett. She's rather a well-known big-game hunter and explorer. She tramps through jungles and things. She's gone out to the lobby for a smoke. By the way"—she hesitated—"if she finds us talking, will you remember that we met at the Polterwoods'?"

"I quite understand."

"You see, Mother doesn't like people who talk to me without a formal introduction. And when Mother doesn't like anyone, she is so apt to hit them over the head with some hard instrument."

"I see," said Cyril. "Like the Human Ape in *Gore by the Gallon.*"

"Exactly. Tell me," said the girl, changing the subject, "if you were a millionaire, would you rather be stabbed in the back with a paper knife or found dead without a mark on you, staring with blank eyes at some appalling sight?"

Cyril was about to reply when, looking past her, he found himself virtually in the latter position. A woman of extraordinary formidableness had lowered herself into the seat beyond and was scrutinizing him keenly through a tortoise-shell lorgnette. She reminded Cyril of Wallace Beery.

"Friend of yours, Amelia?" she said.

"This is Mr. Mulliner, Mother. We met at the Polterwoods'."

"Ah?" said Lady Bassett.

She inspected Cyril through her lorgnette.

"Mr. Mulliner," she said, "is a little like the chief of the Lower Isisi—though, of course, he was darker and had a ring through his nose. A dear, good fellow," she continued reminiscently, "but inclined to become familiar under the influence of trade gin. I shot him in the leg."

"Er—why?" asked Cyril.

"He was not behaving like a gentleman," said Lady Bassett primly.

"After taking your treatment," said Cyril, awed, "I'll bet he could have written a Book of Etiquette."

"I believe he did," said Lady Bassett carelessly. "You must come and call on us some afternoon, Mr. Mulliner. I am in the telephone book. If you are interested in man-eating pumas, I can show you some nice heads."

The curtain rose on Act Two, and Cyril returned to his thoughts. Love, he felt joyously, had come into his life at last. But then so, he had to admit, had Lady Bassett. There is, he reflected, always something.

I will pass lightly over the period of Cyril's wooing. Suffice it to say that his progress was rapid. From the moment he told Amelia that he had once met Dorothy Sayers, he never looked back. And one afternoon, calling and finding that Lady Bassett was away in the country, he took the girl's hand in his and told his love.

For a while all was well. Amelia's reactions proved satisfactory to a degree. She checked up enthusiastically on his proposition. Falling into his arms, she admitted specifically that he was her Dream Man.

Then came the jarring note.

"But it's no use," she said, her lovely eyes filling with tears. "Mother will never give her consent."

"Why not?" said Cyril, stunned. "What is it she objects to about me?"

"I don't know. But she generally alludes to you as 'that pipsqueak.'"

"Pipsqueak?" said Cyril. "What *is* a pipsqueak?"

"I'm not quite sure, but it's something Mother doesn't like very much. It's a pity she ever found out that you are an interior decorator."

"An honorable profession," said Cyril, a little stiffly.

"I know; but what she admires are men who have to do with the great open spaces."

"Well, I also design ornamental gardens."

"Yes," said the girl doubtfully, "but still—"

"And, dash it," said Cyril indignantly, "this isn't the Victorian age. All that business of Mother's Consent went out twenty years ago."

"Yes, but no one told Mother."

"It's preposterous!" cried Cyril. "I never heard such rot. Let's just slip off and get married quietly and send her a picture postcard from Venice or somewhere, with a cross and a 'This is our room. Wish you were with us' on it."

The girl shuddered.

"She would be with us," she said. "You don't know Mother. The moment she got that picture postcard, she would come over to wherever we were and put you across her knee and spank you with a hairbrush. I don't think I could ever feel the same toward you if I saw you lying across Mother's knee, being spanked with a hairbrush. It would spoil the honeymoon."

Cyril frowned. But a man who has spent most of his life trying out a series of patent medicines is always an optimist.

"There is only one thing to be done," he said. "I shall see your mother and try to make her listen to reason. Where is she now?"

"She left this morning for a visit to the Winghams in Sussex."

"Excellent! I know the Winghams. In fact, I have a standing invitation to go and stay with them whenever I like. I'll send them a wire and push down this evening. I will oil up to your mother sedulously and try to correct her present unfavorable impression of me. Then, choosing my moment, I will shoot her the news. It may work. It may not work. But at any rate I consider it a fair sporting venture."

"But you are so diffident, Cyril. So shrinking. So retiring and shy. How can you carry through such a task?"

"Love will nerve me."

"Enough, do you think? Remember what Mother is. Wouldn't a good, strong drink be more help?"

Cyril looked doubtful.

"My doctor has always forbidden me alcoholic stimulants. He says they increase the blood pressure."

"Well, when you meet Mother, you will need all the blood pressure you can get. I really do advise you to fuel up a little before you see her."

"Yes," agreed Cyril, nodding thoughtfully. "I think you're right. It shall be as you say. Good-bye, my angel one."

"Good-bye, Cyril, darling. You will think of me every minute while you're gone?"

"Every single minute. Well, practically every single minute. You see, I have just got Horatio Slingsby's latest book, *Strychnine in the Soup,* and I shall be dipping into that from time to time. But all the rest of the while . . . Have you read it, by the way?"

"Not yet. I had a copy, but Mother took it with her."

"Ah? Well, if I am to catch a train that will get me to Barkley for dinner, I must be going. Good-bye, sweetheart, and never forget that Gilbert Glendale in *The Missing Toe* won the girl he loved in spite of being up against two mysterious stranglers and the entire Black Mustache gang."

He kissed her fondly, and went off to pack.

Barkley Towers, the country seat of Sir Mortimer and Lady Wingham, was two hours from London by rail. Thinking of Amelia and reading the opening chapters of Horatio Slingsby's powerful story, Cyril found the journey pass rapidly. In fact, so preoccupied was he that it was only as the train started to draw out of Barkley Regis station that he realized where he was. He managed to hurl himself onto the platform just in time.

As he had taken the five-seven express, stopping only at Gluebury Peveril, he arrived at Barkley Towers at an hour which enabled him not only to be on hand for dinner but also to take part in the life-giving distribution of cocktails which preceded the meal.

The house party, he perceived on entering the drawing room, was a small one. Besides Lady Bassett and himself, the only visitors were a nondescript couple of the name of Simpson, and a tall, bronzed, handsome man with flashing eyes who, his hostess informed him in a whispered aside, was Lester Mapledurham (pronounced Mum), the explorer and big-game hunter.

Perhaps it was the oppressive sensation of being in the same room with two explorers and big-game hunters that brought home to Cyril the need for following Amelia's advice as quickly as possible. But probably the mere sight of Lady Bassett alone would have been enough to make him break a lifelong abstinence. To her normal resemblance to Wallace Beery she appeared now to have added a distinct suggestion of Victor McLaglen, and the spectacle was sufficient to send Cyril leaping toward the cocktail tray.

After three rapid glasses he felt a better and a braver man. And so lavishly did he irrigate the ensuing dinner with hock, sherry, champagne, old brandy, and port that at the conclusion of the meal he was pleased to find that his diffidence had completely vanished. He rose from the table feeling equal to asking a dozen Lady Bassetts for their consent to marry a dozen daughters.

In fact, as he confided to the butler, prodding him genially in the ribs as he spoke, if Lady Bassett attempted to high-hat *him,* he would know what to do about it. He made no threats, he explained to the butler; he simply stated that he would know what to do about it. The butler said "Very good, sir. Thank you, sir," and the incident closed.

It had been Cyril's intention—feeling, as he did, in this singularly uplifted and dominant frame of mind—to get hold of Amelia's mother and start oiling up to her immediately after dinner. But, what with falling into a doze in the smoking room and then getting into an argument on theology with one of the underfootmen whom he met in the hall, he did not reach the drawing room until nearly half-past ten. And he was annoyed, on walking in with a merry cry of "Lady Bassett! Call for Lady Bassett!" on his lips, to discover that she had retired to her room.

Had Cyril's mood been even slightly less elevated, this news might have acted as a check on his enthusiasm. So generous, however, had been Sir Mortimer's hospitality that he merely nodded eleven times, to indicate comprehension, and then, having ascertained that his quarry was roosting in the Blue Room, sped thither with a brief "Tallyho!"

Arriving at the Blue Room, he banged heartily on the door and breezed in. He found Lady Bassett propped up with pillows. She was smoking a cigar and reading a book. And that book, Cyril saw with intense surprise and resentment, was none other than Horatio Slingsby's *Strychnine in the Soup.*

The spectacle brought him to an abrupt halt.

"Well, I'm dashed!" he cried. "Well, I'm blowed! What do you mean by pinching my book?"

Lady Bassett had lowered her cigar. She now raised her eyebrows.

"What are you doing in my room, Mr. Mulliner?"

"It's a little hard," said Cyril, trembling with self-pity. "I go to enormous expense to buy detective stories, and no sooner is my back turned than people rush about the place sneaking them."

"This book belongs to my daughter Amelia."

"Good old Amelia!" said Cyril cordially. "One of the best."

"I borrowed it to read in the train. Now will you kindly tell me what you are doing in my room, Mr. Mulliner?"

Cyril smote his forehead.

"Of course. I remember now. It all comes back to me. She told me you had taken it. And, what's more, I've suddenly recollected something which clears you completely. I was hustled and bustled at the end of the journey. I sprang to my feet, hurled bags onto the platform—in a word, lost my head. And, like a chump, I went and left my copy of *Strychnine in the Soup* in the train. Well, I can only apologize."

"You can not only apologize. You can also tell me what you are doing in my room."

"What I am doing in your room?"

"Exactly."

"Ah!" said Cyril, sitting down on the bed. "You may well ask."

"I *have* asked. Three times."

Cyril closed his eyes. For some reason, his mind seemed cloudy and not at its best.

"If you are proposing to go to sleep here, Mr. Mulliner," said Lady Bassett, "tell me, and I shall know what to do about it."

The phrase touched a chord in Cyril's memory. He recollected now his reasons for being where he was. Opening his eyes, he fixed them on her.

"Lady Bassett," he said, "you are, I believe, an explorer?"

"I am."

"In the course of your explorations, you have wandered through many a jungle in many a distant land?"

"I have."

"Tell me, Lady Bassett," said Cyril keenly, "while making a pest of yourself to the denizens of those jungles, did you notice one thing? I allude to the fact that Love is everywhere—aye, even in the jungle. Love, independent of bounds and frontiers, of nationality and species, works its spell on every living thing. So that, no matter whether an individual be a Congo native, an American song writer, a jaguar, an armadillo, a bespoke tailor, or a tsetse-tsetse fly, he will infallibly seek his mate. So why shouldn't an interior decorator and designer of ornamental gardens? I put this to you, Lady Bassett."

"Mr. Mulliner," said his roommate, "you are blotto!"

Cyril waved his hand in a spacious gesture, and fell off the bed.

"Blotto I may be," he said, resuming his seat, "but, none the less, argue as you will, you can't get away from the fact that I love your daughter Amelia."

There was a tense pause.

"What did you say?" cried Lady Bassett.

"When?" said Cyril absently, for he had fallen into a daydream and, as far as the intervening blankets would permit, was playing This Little Pig Went to Market with his companion's toes.

"Did I hear you say . . . my daughter Amelia?"

"Gray-eyed girl, medium height, sort of browny red hair," said Cyril, to assist her memory. "Dash it, you *must* know Amelia. She goes everywhere. And let me tell you something, Mrs.—I've forgotten your name. We're going to be married, if I can obtain her foul mother's consent. Speaking as an old friend, what would you say the chances were?"

"Extremely slight."

"Eh?"

"Seeing that I *am* Amelia's mother. . . ."

Cyril blinked, genuinely surprised.

"Why, so you are! I didn't recognize you. Have you been there all the time?"

"I have."

Suddenly Cyril's gaze hardened. He drew himself up stiffly.

"What are you doing in my bed?" he demanded.

"This is not your bed."

"Then whose is it?"

"Mine."

Cyril shrugged his shoulders helplessly.

"Well, it all looks very funny to me," he said. "I suppose I must believe your story, but, I repeat, I consider the whole thing odd, and I propose to institute very strict inquiries. I may tell you that I happen to know the ringleaders. I wish you a very hearty good night."

It was perhaps an hour later that Cyril, who had been walking on the terrace in deep thought, repaired once more to the Blue Room in quest of information. Running over the details of the recent interview in his head, he had suddenly discovered that there was a point which had not been satisfactorily cleared up.

"I say," he said.

Lady Bassett looked up from her book, plainly annoyed.

"Have you no bedroom of your own, Mr. Mulliner?"

"Oh, yes," said Cyril. "They've bedded me out in the Moat Room. But there was something I wanted you to tell me."

"Well?"

"Did you say I might or mightn't?"

"Might or mightn't what?"

"Marry Amelia?"

"No. You may not."

"No?"

"No!"

"Oh!" said Cyril. "Well, pip-pip once more."

It was a moody Cyril Mulliner who withdrew to the Moat Room. He now realized the position of affairs. The mother of the girl he loved refused to accept him as an eligible suitor. A dickens of a situation to be in, felt Cyril, somberly unshoeing himself.

Then he brightened a little. His life, he reflected, might be wrecked, but he still had two thirds of *Strychnine in the Soup* to read.

At the moment when the train reached Barkley Regis station, Cyril had just got to the bit where Detective Inspector Mould looks through the half-open cellar door and, drawing in his breath with a sharp hissing sound, recoils in horror. It was obviously going to be good. He was just about to proceed to the dressing table where, he presumed, the footman had placed the book on unpacking his bag, when an icy stream seemed to flow down the center of his spine and the room and its contents danced before him.

Once more he had remembered that he had left the volume in the train.

He uttered an animal cry and tottered to a chair.

The subject of bereavement is one that has often been treated powerfully by poets, who have run the whole gamut of the emotions while laying bare for us the agony of those who have lost parents, wives, children, gazelles, money, fame, dogs, cats, doves, sweethearts, horses, and even collar studs. But no poet has yet treated of the most poignant bereavement of all—that of the man halfway through a detective story who finds himself at bedtime without the book.

Cyril did not care to think of the night that lay before him. Already his brain was lashing itself from side to side like a wounded snake as it sought for some explanation of Inspector Mould's strange behavior. Horatio Slingsby was an author who could be relied on to keep faith with his public. He was not the sort of man to fob the reader off in the next chapter with the statement that what had made Inspector Mould look horrified was the fact that he had suddenly remembered that he had forgotten all about the letter his wife had given him to post. If looking through cellar doors disturbed a Slingsby detective, it was because a dismembered corpse lay there, or at least a severed hand.

A soft moan, as of something in torment, escaped Cyril. What to do? What to do? Even a makeshift substitute for *Strychnine in the Soup* was beyond his reach. He knew so well what he would find if he went to the library in search of something to read. Sir Mortimer Wingham was heavy and county-squire-ish. His wife affected strange religions. Their literature was in keeping with their tastes. In the library there would be books on Bahai-ism, volumes in old leather of the *Rural Encyclopedia, My Two Years in Sunny Ceylon,* by the Rev. Orlo Waterbury . . . but of anything that would interest Scotland Yard, of anything with a bit of blood in it and a corpse or two into which a fellow could get his teeth, not a trace.

What, then, coming right back to it, to do?

And suddenly, as if in answer to the question, came the solution. Electrified, he saw the way out.

The hour was now well advanced. By this time Lady Bassett must surely be asleep. *Strychnine in the Soup* would be lying on the table beside her bed. All he had to do was to creep in and grab it.

The more he considered the idea, the better it looked. It was not as if he did not know the way to Lady Bassett's room or the topography of it when he got there. It seemed to him as if most of his later life had been spent in Lady Bassett's room. He could find his way about it with his eyes shut.

He hesitated no longer. Donning a dressing gown, he left his room and hurried along the passage.

Pushing open the door of the Blue Room and closing it softly behind him, Cyril stood for a moment full of all those emotions which come to man revisiting some long-familiar spot. There the dear old room was, just the same as ever. How it all came back to him! The place was in darkness, but that did not deter him. He knew where the bed table was, and he made for it with stealthy steps.

In the manner in which Cyril Mulliner advanced toward the bed table there was much which would have reminded Lady Bassett, had she been an eyewitness, of the furtive prowl of the Lesser Iguanodon tracking its prey. In only one respect did Cyril and this creature of the wild differ in their technique. Iguanodons—and this applies not only to the Lesser but to the Larger Iguanodon—seldom, if ever, trip over cords on the floor and bring the lamps to which they are attached crashing to the ground like a ton of bricks.

Cyril did. Scarcely had he snatched up the book and placed it in the pocket of his dressing gown, when his foot became entangled in the trailing cord and the lamp on the table leaped nimbly into the air and, to the accompaniment of a sound not unlike that made by a hundred plates coming apart simultaneously in the hands of a hundred scullery maids, nose-dived to the floor and became a total loss.

At the same moment, Lady Bassett, who had been chasing a bat out of the window, stepped in from the balcony and switched on the lights.

To say that Cyril Mulliner was taken aback would be to understate the facts. Nothing like his recent misadventure had happened to him since his eleventh year, when, going surreptitiously to his mother's cupboard for jam, he had jerked three shelves down on his head, containing milk, butter, homemade preserves, pickles, cheese, eggs, cakes, and potted meat. His feelings on the present occasion closely paralleled that boyhood thrill.

Lady Bassett also appeared somewhat discomposed.

"You!" she said.

Cyril nodded, endeavoring the while to smile in a reassuring manner.

"Hullo!" he said.

His hostess's manner was now one of unmistakable displeasure.

"Am I not to have a moment of privacy, Mr. Mulliner?" she asked severely. "I am, I trust, a broad-minded woman, but I cannot approve of this idea of communal bedrooms."

Cyril made an effort to be conciliatory.

"I do keep coming in, don't I?" he said.

"You do," agreed Lady Bassett. "Sir Mortimer informed me, on learning that I had been given this room, that it was supposed to be haunted. Had I known that it was haunted by you, Mr. Mulliner, I should have packed up and gone to the local inn."

Cyril bowed his head. The censure, he could not but feel, was deserved.

"I admit," he said, "that my conduct has been open to criticism. In extenuation, I can but plead my great love. This is no idle social call, Lady Bassett. I looked in because I wished to take up again this matter of my marrying your daughter Amelia. You say I can't. Why can't I? Answer me that, Lady Bassett."

"I have other views for Amelia," said Lady Bassett stiffly. "When my daughter gets married it will not be to a spineless, invertebrate product of our modern hothouse civilization, but to a strong, upstanding, keen-eyed, two-fisted he-man of the open spaces. I have no wish to hurt your feelings, Mr. Mulliner," she continued, more kindly, "but you must admit that you are, when all is said and done, a pipsqueak."

"I deny it," cried Cyril warmly. "I don't even know what a pipsqueak is."

"A pipsqueak is a man who has never seen the sun rise beyond the reaches of the Lower Zambezi; who would not know what to do if faced by a charging rhinoceros. What, pray, would you do if faced by a charging rhinoceros, Mr. Mulliner?"

"I am not likely," said Cyril, "to move in the same social circles as charging rhinoceri."

"Or take another simple case, such as happens every day. Suppose you are crossing a rude bridge over a stream in Equatorial Africa. You have been thinking of a hundred trifles and are in a reverie. From this you wake to discover that in the branches overhead a python is extending its fangs toward you. At the same time, you observe that at one end of the bridge is a crouching puma; at the other are two head-hunters—call them Pat and Mike—with poisoned blowpipes to their lips. Below, half hidden in the stream, is an alligator. What would you do in such a case, Mr. Mulliner?"

Cyril weighed the point.

"I should feel embarrassed," he had to admit. "I shouldn't know where to look."

Lady Bassett laughed an amused, scornful little laugh.

"Precisely. Such a situation would not, however, disturb Lester Mapledurham."

"Lester Mapledurham!"

"The man who is to marry my daughter Amelia. He asked me for her hand shortly after dinner."

Cyril reeled. The blow, falling so suddenly and unexpectedly, had made him feel boneless. And yet, he felt, he might have expected this. These explorers and big-game hunters stick together.

"In a situation such as I have outlined, Lester Mapledurham would simply drop from the bridge, wait till the alligator made its rush, insert a stout stick between its jaws, and then hit it in the eye with a spear, being careful to avoid its lashing tail. He would then drift downstream and land at some safer spot. That is the type of man I wish for as a son-in-law."

Cyril left the room without a word. Not even the fact that he now had *Strychnine in the Soup* in his possession could cheer his mood of unrelieved blackness. Back in his room, he tossed the book moodily onto the bed and began to pace the floor. And he had scarcely completed two laps when the door opened.

For an instant, when he heard the click of the latch, Cyril supposed that his visitor must be Lady Bassett, who, having put two and two together on discovering her loss, had come to demand her property back. And he cursed the rashness which had led him to fling it so carelessly upon the bed, in full view.

But it was not Lady Bassett. The intruder was Lester Mapledurham. Clad in a suit of pajamas which in their general color scheme reminded Cyril of a boudoir he had recently decorated for a society poetess, he stood with folded arms, his keen eyes fixed menacingly on the young man.

"Give me those jewels!" said Lester Mapledurham.

Cyril was at a loss.

"Jewels?"

"Jewels!"

"What jewels?"

Lester Mapledurham tossed his head impatiently.

"I don't know what jewels. They may be the Wingham Pearls or the Bassett Diamonds or the Simpson Sapphires. I'm not sure which room it was I saw you coming out of."

Cyril began to understand.

"Oh, did you see me coming out of a room?"

"I did. I heard a crash and, when I looked out, you were hurrying along the corridor."

"I can explain everything," said Cyril. "I had just been having a chat with Lady Bassett on a personal matter. Nothing to do with diamonds."

"You're sure?" said Mapledurham.

"Oh, rather," said Cyril. "We talked about rhinoceri and pythons and her daughter Amelia and alligators and all that sort of thing, and then I came away."

Lester Mapledurham seemed only half convinced.

"H'm!" he said. "Well, if anything is missing in the morning, I shall know what to do about it." His eye fell on the bed. "Hullo!" he went on, with sudden animation. "Slingsby's latest? Well, well! I've been wanting to get hold of this. I hear it's good. The Leeds *Mercury* says: 'These gripping pages . . .'"

He turned to the door, and with a hideous pang of agony Cyril perceived that it was plainly his intention to take the book with him.

It was swinging lightly from a bronzed hand about the size of a medium ham.

"Here!" he cried vehemently.

Lester Mapledurham turned.

"Well?"

"Oh, nothing," said Cyril. "Just good night."

He flung himself face downwards on the bed as the door closed, cursing himself for the craven cowardice which had kept him from snatching the book from the explorer. There had been a moment when he had almost nerved himself to the deed, but it was followed by another moment in which he had caught the other's eye. And it was as if he had found himself exchanging glances with Lady Bassett's charging rhinoceros.

And now, thanks to this pusillanimity, he was once more *Strychnine in the Soup* -less.

How long Cyril lay there, a prey to the gloomiest thoughts, he could not have said. He was aroused from his meditations by the sound of the door opening again.

Lady Bassett stood before him. It was plain that she was deeply moved. In addition to resembling Wallace Beery and Victor Mc-Laglen, she now had a distinct look of George Bancroft.

She pointed a quivering finger at Cyril.

"You hound!" she cried. "Give me that book!"

Cyril maintained his poise with a strong effort.

"What book?"

"The book you sneaked out of my room."

"Has someone sneaked a book out of your room?" Cyril struck his forehead. "Great heavens!" he cried.

"Mr. Mulliner," said Lady Bassett coldly, "more book and less gibbering!"

Cyril raised a hand.

"I know who's got your book. Lester Mapledurham!"

"Don't be absurd."

"IIc has, I tell you As I was on my way to your room just now, I saw him coming out, carrying something in a furtive manner. I remember wondering a bit at the time. He's in the Clock Room. If we pop along there now, we shall just catch him red-handed."

Lady Bassett reflected.

"It is impossible," she said at length. "He is incapable of such an act. Lester Mapledurham is a man who once killed a lion with a sardine opener."

"The very worst sort," said Cyril. "Ask anyone."

"And he is engaged to my daughter." Lady Bassett paused. "Well, he won't be long, if I find that what you say is true. Come, Mr. Mulliner!"

Together the two passed down the silent passage. At the door of the Clock Room they paused. A light streamed from beneath it. Cyril pointed silently to this sinister evidence of reading in bed, and noted that his companion stiffened and said something to herself in an undertone in what appeared to be some sort of native dialect.

The next moment she had flung the door open and, with a spring like that of a crouching zebu, had leaped to the bed and wrenched the book from Lester Mapledurham's hands.

"So!" said Lady Bassett.

"So!" said Cyril, feeling that he could not do better than follow the lead of such a woman.

"Hullo!" said Lester Mapledurham, surprised. "Something the matter?"

"So it was you who stole my book!"

"Your book?" said Lester Mapledurham. "I borrowed this from Mr. Mulliner there."

"A likely story!" said Cyril. "Lady Bassett is aware that I left my copy of *Strychnine in the Soup* in the train."

"Certainly," said Lady Bassett. "It's no use talking, young man, I have caught you with the goods. And let me tell you one thing that may be of interest. If you think that, after a dastardly act like this, you are going to marry Amelia, forget it!"

"Wipe it right out of your mind," said Cyril.

"But listen—"

"I will not listen. Come, Mr. Mulliner."

She left the room, followed by Cyril. For some moments they walked in silence.

"A merciful escape," said Cyril.

"For whom?"

"For Amelia. My gosh, think of her tied to a man like that. Must be a relief to you to feel that she's going to marry a respectable interior decorator."

Lady Bassett halted. They were standing outside the Moat Room now. She looked at Cyril, her eyebrows raised.

"Are you under the impression, Mr. Mulliner," she said, "that, on the strength of what has happened, I intend to accept you as a son-in-law?"

Cyril reeled.

"Don't you?"

"Certainly not."

Something inside Cyril seemed to snap. Recklessness descended upon him. He became for a space a thing of courage and fire, like the African leopard in the mating season.

"Oh!" he said.

And, deftly whisking *Strychnine in the Soup* from his companion's hand, he darted into his room, banged the door, and bolted it.

"Mr. Mulliner!"

It was Lady Bassett's voice, coming pleadingly through the wood-work. It was plain that she was shaken to the core, and Cyril smiled sardonically. He was in a position to dictate terms.

"Give me that book, Mr. Mulliner!"

"Certainly not," said Cyril. "I intend to read it myself. I hear good reports of it on every side. The Peebles *Intelligencer* says: 'Vigorous and absorbing.' "

A low wail from the other side of the door answered him.

"Of course," said Cyril suggestively, "if it were my future mother-in-law who was speaking, her word would naturally be law."

There was a silence outside.

"Very well," said Lady Bassett.

"I may marry Amelia?"

"You may."

Cyril unbolted the door.

"Come—Mother," he said, in a soft, kindly voice. "We will read it together, down in the library."

Lady Bassett was still shaken.

"I hope I have acted for the best," she said.

"You have," said Cyril.

"You will make Amelia a good husband?"

"Grade A," Cyril assured her.

"Well, even if you don't," said Lady Bassett resignedly, "I can't go to bed without that book. I had just got to the bit where Inspector Mould is trapped in the underground den of the Faceless Fiend."

Cyril quivered.

"*Is* there a Faceless Fiend?" he cried.

"There are two Faceless Fiends," said Lady Bassett.

"My gosh!" said Cyril. "Let's hurry."

Introducing

❋ *Stanley Featherstonehaugh Ukridge*

The man with the big, broad, flexible outlook—together with a number of his gilt-edged schemes.

"Fortunately I had given him a false name."
"Why?"
"Just an ordinary business precaution," explained Ukridge.

❋ *Ukridge's Dog College*

"LADDIE," said Stanley Featherstonehaugh Ukridge, that much-enduring man, helping himself to my tobacco and slipping the pouch absently into his pocket, "listen to me, you son of Belial."

"What?" I said, retrieving the pouch.

"Do you want to make an enormous fortune?"

"I do."

"Then write my biography. Bung it down on paper, and we'll split the proceeds. I've been making a pretty close study of your stuff lately, old horse, and it's all wrong. The trouble with you is that you don't plumb the wellsprings of human nature and all that. You just think up some rotten yarn about some-damn-thing-or-other and shove it down. Now, if you tackled my life, you'd have something worth writing about. Pots of money in it, my boy—English serial rights and American serial rights and book rights, and dramatic rights and movie rights—well, you can take it from me that, at a conservative estimate, we should clean up at least fifty thousand pounds apiece."

"As much as that?"

"Fully that. And listen, laddie, I'll tell you what. You're a good chap and we've been pals for years, so I'll let you have my share of the English serial rights for a hundred pounds down."

"What makes you think I've got a hundred pounds?"

"Well, then, I'll make it my share of the English *and* American serial rights for fifty."

"Your collar's come off its stud."

"How about my complete share of the whole dashed outfit for twenty-five?"

"Not for me, thanks."

"Then I'll tell you what, old horse," said Ukridge, inspired. "Just lend me half a crown to be going on with."

If the leading incidents of S. F. Ukridge's disreputable career are to be given to the public—and not, as some might suggest, decently hushed up—I suppose I am the man to write them. Ukridge and I had been intimate since the days of school. Together we sported on the green, and when he was expelled no one missed him more than I. An unfortunate business, this expulsion. Ukridge's generous spirit, ever ill-attuned to school rules, caused him eventually to break the solemnest of them all by sneaking out at night to try his skill at the coconut-shies of the local village fair; and his foresight in putting on scarlet whiskers and a false nose for the expedition was completely neutralized by the fact that he absent-mindedly wore his school cap throughout the entire proceedings. He left the next morning, regretted by all.

After this there was a hiatus of some years in our friendship. I was at Cambridge, absorbing culture, and Ukridge, as far as I could gather from his rare letters and the reports of mutual acquaintances, flitting about the world like a snipe. Somebody met him in New York, just off a cattle ship. Somebody else saw him in Buenos Aires. Somebody, again, spoke sadly of having been pounced on by him at Monte Carlo and touched for a fiver. It was not until I settled down in London that he came back into my life. We met in Piccadilly one day, and resumed our relations where they had been broken off. Old associations are strong, and the fact that he was about my build and so could wear my socks and shirts drew us very close together.

Then he disappeared again, and it was a month or more before I got news of him.

It was George Tupper who brought the news. George was head of the school in my last year, and he has fulfilled exactly the impeccable promise of those early days. He is in the Foreign Office, doing well and much respected. He has an earnest, pulpy heart and takes other people's troubles very seriously. Often he had mourned to me like a father over Ukridge's erratic progress through life, and now, as he spoke, he seemed to be filled with a solemn joy, as over a reformed prodigal.

"Have you heard about Ukridge?" said George Tupper. "He has settled down at last. Gone to live with an aunt of his who owns one of those big houses on Wimbledon Common. A very rich woman. I am delighted. It will be the making of the old chap."

I suppose he was right in a way, but to me this tame subsidence into companionship with a rich aunt in Wimbledon seemed somehow an indecent, almost a tragic, end to a colorful career like that of S. F. Ukridge. And when I met the man a week later my heart grew heavier still.

It was in Oxford Street at the hour when women come up from the suburbs to shop; and he was standing among the dogs and commissionaires outside Selfridge's. His arms were full of parcels, his face was set in a mask of wan discomfort, and he was so beautifully dressed that for an instant I did not recognize him. Everything which the Correct Man wears was assembled on his person, from the silk hat to the patent-leather boots; and, as he confided to me in the first minute, he was suffering the tortures of the damned. The boots pinched him, the hat hurt his forehead, and the collar was worse than the hat and boots combined.

"She makes me wear them," he said moodily, jerking his head toward the interior of the store and uttering a sharp howl as the movement caused the collar to gouge his neck.

"Still," I said, trying to turn his mind to happier things, "you must be having a great time. George Tupper tells me that your aunt is rich. I suppose you're living off the fat of the land."

"The browsing and sluicing are good," admitted Ukridge. "But it's a wearing life, laddie. A wearing life, old horse."

"Why don't you come and see me sometimes?"

"I'm not allowed out at night."

"Well, shall I come and see you?"

A look of poignant alarm shot out from under the silk hat.

"Don't dream of it, laddie," said Ukridge earnestly. "Don't dream of it. You're a good chap—my best pal and all that sort of thing— but the fact is, my standing in the home's none too solid even now, and one sight of you would knock my prestige into hash. Aunt Julia would think you worldly."

"I'm not worldly."

"Well, you look worldly. You wear a squash hat and a soft collar. If you don't mind my suggesting it, old horse, I think, if I were you, I'd pop off now before she comes out. Good-bye, laddie."

"Ichabod!" I murmured sadly to myself as I passed on down Oxford Street. "Ichabod!"

I should have had more faith. I should have known my Ukridge better. I should have realized that a London suburb could no more imprison that great man permanently than Elba did Napoleon.

One afternoon, as I let myself into the house in Ebury Street of which I rented at that time the bedroom and sitting room on the first floor, I came upon Bowles, my landlord, standing in listening attitude at the foot of the stairs.

"Good afternoon, sir," said Bowles. "A gentleman is waiting to see you. I fancy I heard him calling me a moment ago."

"Who is he?"

"A Mr. Ukridge, sir. He—"

A vast voice boomed out from above.

"Bowles, old horse!"

Bowles, like all other proprietors of furnished apartments in the southwestern district of London, was an ex-butler, and about him, as about all ex-butlers, there clung like a garment an aura of dignified superiority which had never failed to crush my spirit. He was a man of portly aspect, with a bald head and prominent eyes of a lightish green—eyes that seemed to weigh me dispassionately and find me wanting. "H'm!" they seemed to say. "Young—very young. And not at all what I have been accustomed to in the best places." To hear this dignitary addressed—and in a shout at that—as "old horse" affected me with much the same sense of imminent chaos as would afflict a devout young curate if he saw his bishop slapped on the back. The shock, therefore, when he responded not merely mildly but with what almost amounted to camaraderie was numbing.

"Sir?" cooed Bowles.

"Bring me six bones and a corkscrew."

"Very good, sir."

Bowles retired, and I bounded upstairs and flung open the door of my sitting room.

"Great Scott!" I said blankly.

The place was a sea of Pekingese dogs. Later investigation reduced their number to six, but in that first moment there seemed to be hundreds. Goggling eyes met mine wherever I looked. The room was a forest of waving tails. With his back against the mantelpiece, smoking placidly, stood Ukridge.

"Hallo, laddie!" he said, with a genial wave of the hand, as if to make me free of the place. "You're just in time. I've got to dash off and catch a train in a quarter of an hour. Stop it, you mutts!" he bellowed, and the six Pekingese, who had been barking steadily since my arrival, stopped in mid-yap, and were still. Ukridge's personality seemed to exercise a magnetism over the animal kingdom, from ex-butlers to Pekes, which bordered on the uncanny. "I'm off to Sheep's Cray, in Kent. Taken a cottage there."

"Are you going to live there?"

"Yes."

"But what about your aunt?"

"Oh, I've left her. Life is stern and life is earnest, and if I mean to make a fortune I've got to bustle about and not stay cooped up in a place like Wimbledon."

"Something in that."

"Besides which, she told me the very sight of me made her sick and she never wanted to see me again."

I might have guessed, directly I saw him, that some upheaval had taken place. The sumptuous raiment which had made him such a treat to the eye at our last meeting was gone, and he was back in his pre-Wimbledon costume, which was, as the advertisements say, distinctly individual. Over gray flannel trousers, a golf coat and a brown sweater he wore like a royal robe a bright-yellow mackintosh. His collar had broken free from its stud and showed a couple of inches of bare neck. His hair was disordered, and his masterful nose was topped by a pair of steel-rimmed pince-nez cunningly attached to his flapping ears with ginger-beer wire. His whole appearance spelled revolt.

Bowles manifested himself with a plateful of bones.

"That's right. Chuck 'em down on the floor."

"Very good, sir."

"I like that fellow," said Ukridge as the door closed. "We had a dashed interesting talk before you came in. Did you know he had a cousin on the music halls?"

"He hasn't confided in me much."

"He's promised me an introduction to him later on. May be useful to be in touch with a man who knows the ropes. You see, laddie, I've hit on the most amazing scheme." He swept his arm round dramatically, overturning a plaster cast of the Infant Samuel at Prayer. "All right, all right, you can mend it with glue or something, and, anyway, you're probably better without it. Yessir, I've hit on a great scheme. The idea of a thousand years."

"What's that?"

"I'm going to train dogs."

"Train dogs?"

"For the music-hall stage. Dog acts, you know. Performing dogs. Pots of money in it. I start in a modest way with these six. When I've taught 'em a few tricks, I sell them to a fellow in the profession for a large sum and buy twelve more. I train those, sell 'em for a large sum, and with the money buy twenty-four more. I train those—"

"Here, wait a minute." My head was beginning to swim. I had a vision of England paved with Pekingese dogs, all doing tricks. "How do you know you'll be able to sell them?"

"Of course I shall. The demand's enormous. Supply can't cope with it. At a conservative estimate I should think I ought to scoop in four or five thousand pounds the first year. That, of course, is before the business really starts to expand."

"I see."

"When I get going properly, with a dozen assistants under me and an organized establishment, I shall begin to touch the big money. What I'm aiming at is a sort of Dogs' College out in the country somewhere. Big place with a lot of ground. Regular classes and a set curriculum. Large staff, each member of it with so many dogs under his care, me looking on and superintending. Why, once the thing starts moving it'll run itself, and all I shall have to do will be to sit back and endorse the checks. It isn't as if I would have to confine my operations to England. The demand for performing dogs is universal throughout the civilized world. America wants performing dogs. Australia wants performing dogs. Africa could do with a few, I've no doubt. My aim, laddie, is gradually to get a monopoly of the trade. I want everybody who needs a performing dog of any description to come automatically to me. And I'll tell you what, laddie. If you like to put up a bit of capital, I'll let you in on the ground floor."

"No, thanks."

"All right. Have it your own way. Only don't forget that there was a fellow who put nine hundred dollars into the Ford Car business when it was starting and he collected a cool forty million. I say, is that clock right? Great Scott! I'll be missing my train. Help me mobilize these dashed animals."

Five minutes later, accompanied by the six Pekingese and bearing about him a pound of my tobacco, three pairs of my socks, and the remains of a bottle of whisky, Ukridge departed in a taxicab for Charing Cross Station to begin his lifework.

Perhaps six weeks passed, six quiet Ukridgeless weeks, and then one morning I received an agitated telegram. Indeed, it was not so much a telegram as a cry of anguish. In every word of it there breathed the tortured spirit of a great man who has battled in vain against overwhelming odds. It was the sort of telegram which Job might have sent off after a lengthy session with Bildad the Shuhite:—

"Come here immediately, laddie. Life and death matter, old horse. Desperate situation. Don't fail me."

It stirred me like a bugle, I caught the next train.

The White Cottage, Sheep's Cray—destined, presumably, to become in future years an historic spot and a Mecca for dog-loving pilgrims—was a small and battered building standing near the main road to London at some distance from the village. I found it without difficulty, for Ukridge seemed to have achieved a certain celebrity in the neighborhood; but to effect an entry was a harder task. I rapped for a full minute without result, then shouted; and I was about to conclude that Ukridge was not at home when the door suddenly opened. As I was just giving a final bang at the moment, I entered the house in a manner reminiscent of one of the Ballet Russe practicing a new and difficult step.

"Sorry, old horse," said Ukridge. "Wouldn't have kept you waiting if I'd known who it was. Thought you were Gooch, the grocer—goods supplied to the value of six pounds three and a penny."

"I see."

"He keeps hounding me for his beastly money," said Ukridge bitterly as he led the way into the sitting room. "It's a little hard. Upon my Sam it's a little hard. I come down here to inaugurate a vast business and do the natives a bit of good by establishing a growing industry in their midst, and the first thing you know they turn round and bite the hand that was going to feed them. I've been hampered and rattled by these bloodsuckers ever since I got here. A little trust, a little sympathy, a little of the good old give-and-take spirit— that was all I asked. And what happened? They wanted a bit on account! Kept bothering me for a bit on account, I'll trouble you, just when I needed all my thoughts and all my energy and every ounce of concentration at my command for my extraordinarily difficult and delicate work. *I* couldn't give them a bit on account. Later on, if they had only exercised reasonable patience, I would no doubt have been in a position to settle their infernal bills fifty times over. But the time was not ripe. I reasoned with the men. I said, 'Here am I, a busy man, trying hard to educate six Pekingese dogs for the music-hall stage, and you come distracting my attention and impairing my efficiency by babbling about a bit on account. It isn't the pull-together spirit,' I said. 'It isn't the spirit that wins to wealth. These narrow petty-cash ideas can never make for success.' But no, they couldn't see it. They started calling here at all hours and waylaying me in the public highways till life became an absolute curse. And now what do you think has happened?"

"What?"

"The dogs."

"Got distemper?"

"No. Worse. My landlord's pinched them as security for his infernal rent! Sneaked the stock. Tied up the assets. Crippled the business at the very outset. Have you ever in your life heard of anything so dastardly? I know I agreed to pay the damned rent weekly and I'm about six weeks behind, but, my gosh! surely a man with a huge enterprise on his hands isn't supposed to have to worry about these trifles when he's occupied with the most delicate— Well, I put all that to old Nickerson, but a fat lot of good it did. So then I wired to you."

"Ah!" I said, and there was a brief and pregnant pause.

"I thought," said Ukridge meditatively, "that you might be able to suggest somebody I could touch."

He spoke in a detached and almost casual way, but his eye was gleaming at me significantly, and I avoided it with a sense of guilt. My finances at the moment were in their customary unsettled condition— rather more so, in fact, than usual, owing to unsatisfactory specula- tions at Kempton Park on the previous Saturday; and it seemed to me that, if ever there was a time for passing the buck, this was it. I mused tensely. It was an occasion for quick thinking.

"George Tupper!" I cried, on the crest of a brain wave.

"George Tupper?" echoed Ukridge radiantly, his gloom melting like fog before the sun. "The very man, by Gad! It's a most amazing thing, but I never thought of him. George Tupper, of course! Big- hearted George, the old school chum. He'll do it like a shot and won't miss the money. These Foreign Office blokes have always got a spare tenner or two tucked away in the old sock. They pinch it out of the public funds. Rush back to town, laddie, with all speed, get hold of Tuppy, lush him up, and bite his ear for twenty quid. Now is the time for all good men to come to the aid of the party."

I had been convinced that George Tupper would not fail us, nor did he. He parted without a murmur—even with enthusiasm. The consignment was one that might have been made to order for him. As a boy, George used to write sentimental poetry for the school magazine, and now he is the sort of man who is always starting sub- scription lists and getting up memorials and presentations. He listened to my story with the serious official air which these Foreign Office fellows put on when they are deciding whether to declare war on Switzerland or send a firm note to San Marino, and was reaching for his checkbook before I had been speaking two minutes. Ukridge's sad case seemed to move him deeply.

"Too bad," said George. "So he is training dogs, is he? Well, it seems very unfair that, if he has at last settled down to real work, he should be hampered by financial difficulties at the outset. We ought to do something practical for him. After all, a loan of twenty pounds cannot relieve the situation permanently."

"I think you're a bit optimistic if you're looking on it as a loan."

"What Ukridge needs is capital."

"He thinks that, too. So does Gooch, the grocer."

"Capital," repeated George Tupper firmly, as if he were reasoning with the plenipotentiary of some Great Power. "Every venture re- quires capital at first." He frowned thoughtfully. "Where can we obtain capital for Ukridge?"

"Rob a bank."

George Tupper's face cleared.

"I have it!" he said. "I will go straight over to Wimbledon tonight and approach his aunt."

"Aren't you forgetting that Ukridge is about as popular with her as a cold Welsh rabbit?"

"There may be a temporary estrangement, but if I tell her the facts and impress upon her that Ukridge is really making a genuine effort to earn a living—"

"Well, try if you like. But she will probably set the parrot on to you."

"It will have to be done diplomatically, of course. It might be as well if you did not tell Ukridge what I propose to do. I do not wish to arouse hopes which may not be fulfilled."

A blaze of yellow on the platform of Sheep's Cray Station next morning informed me that Ukridge had come to meet my train. The sun poured down from a cloudless sky, but it took more than sunshine to make Stanley Featherstonehaugh Ukridge discard his mackintosh. He looked like an animated blob of mustard.

When the train rolled in, he was standing in solitary grandeur trying to light his pipe, but as I got out I perceived that he had been joined by a sad-looking man, who, from the rapid and earnest manner in which he talked and the vehemence of his gesticulations, appeared to be ventilating some theme on which he felt deeply. Ukridge was looking warm and harassed, and, as I approached, I could hear his voice booming in reply.

"My dear sir, my dear old horse, do be reasonable, do try to cultivate the big, broad flexible outlook—"

He saw me and broke away—not unwillingly; and, gripping my arm, drew me off along the platform. The sad-looking man followed irresolutely.

"Have you got the stuff, laddie?" inquired Ukridge, in a tense whisper. "Have you got it?"

"Yes, here it is."

"Put it back, put it back!" moaned Ukridge in agony, as I felt in my pocket. "Do you know who that was I was talking to? Gooch, the grocer!"

"Goods supplied to the value of six pounds three and a penny?"

"Absolutely!"

"Well, now's your chance. Fling him a purse of gold. That'll make him look silly."

"My dear old horse, I can't afford to go about the place squander-

ing my cash simply in order to make grocers look silly. That money
is earmarked for Nickerson, my landlord."

"Oh! I say, I think the six pounds three and a penny bird is
following us."

"Then for goodness' sake, laddie, let's get a move on! If that man
knew we had twenty quid on us, our lives wouldn't be safe. He'd make
one spring."

He hurried me out of the station and led the way up a shady
lane that wound off through the fields, slinking furtively "like one that
on a lonesome road doth walk in fear and dread, and having once
looked back walks on and turns no more his head, because he knows
a frightful fiend doth close behind him tread." As a matter of fact,
the frightful fiend had given up the pursuit after the first few steps,
and a moment later I drew this fact to Ukridge's attention, for it was
not the sort of day on which to break walking records unneces-
sarily.

He halted, relieved, and mopped his spacious brow with a handkerchief which I recognized as having once been my property.

"Thank goodness we've shaken him off," he said. "Not a bad chap
in his way, I believe—a good husband and father, I'm told, and sings
in the church choir. But no vision. That's what he lacks, old horse—
vision. He can't understand that all vast industrial enterprises have
been built upon a system of liberal and cheerful credit. Won't realize
that credit is the lifeblood of commerce. Without credit commerce
has no elasticity. And if commerce has no elasticity what dam'
good is it?"

"I don't know."

"Nor does anybody else. Well, now that he's gone, you can give
me that money. Did Tuppy cough up cheerfully?"

"Blithely."

"I knew it," said Ukridge, deeply moved, "I knew it. A good fellow.
One of the best. I've always liked Tuppy. A man you can rely on. Some
day, when I get going on a big scale, he shall have this back a thousandfold. I'm glad you brought small notes."

"Why?"

"I want to scatter 'em about on the table in front of this Nickerson
blighter."

"Is this where he lives?"

We had come to a red-roofed house, set back from the road
amidst trees. Ukridge wielded the knocker forcefully.

"Tell Mr. Nickerson," he said to the maid, "that Mr. Ukridge has
called and would like a word."

About the demeanor of the man who presently entered the room into which we had been shown there was that subtle but well-marked something which stamps your creditor the world over. Mr. Nickerson was a man of medium height, almost completely surrounded by whiskers, and through the shrubbery he gazed at Ukridge with frozen eyes, shooting out waves of deleterious animal magnetism. You could see at a glance that he was not fond of Ukridge. Take him for all in all, Mr. Nickerson looked like one of the less amiable prophets of the Old Testament about to interview the captive monarch of the Amalekites.

"Well?" he said, and I have never heard the word spoken in a more forbidding manner.

"I've come about the rent."

"Ah!" said Mr. Nickerson guardedly.

"To pay it," said Ukridge.

"To pay it!" ejaculated Mr. Nickerson incredulously.

"Here!" said Ukridge, and with a superb gesture flung money on the table.

I understood now why the massive-minded man had wanted the small notes. They made a brave display. There was a light breeze blowing in through the open window, and so musical a rustling did it set up as it played about the heaped-up wealth that Mr. Nickerson's austerity seemed to vanish like breath off a razor blade. For a moment a dazed look came into his eyes and he swayed slightly; then, as he started to gather up the money, he took on the benevolent air of a bishop blessing pilgrims. As far as Mr. Nickerson was concerned, the sun was up.

"Why, thank you, Mr. Ukridge, I'm sure," he said. "Thank you very much. No hard feelings, I trust?"

"Not on my side, old horse," responded Ukridge affably. "Business is business."

"Exactly."

"Well, I may as well take those dogs now," said Ukridge, helping himself to a cigar from a box which he had just discovered on the mantelpiece and putting a couple more in his pocket in the friendliest way. "The sooner they're back with me the better. They've lost a day's education as it is."

"Why, certainly, Mr. Ukridge; certainly. They are in the shed at the bottom of the garden. I will get them for you at once."

He retreated through the door, babbling ingratiatingly.

"Amazing how fond these blokes are of money," sighed Ukridge. "It's a thing I don't like to see. Sordid, I call it. That blighter's eyes

were gleaming, positively gleaming, laddie, as he scooped up the
stuff. Good cigars these," he added, pocketing three more.

There was a faltering footstep outside, and Mr. Nickerson re-
entered the room. The man appeared to have something on his mind.
A glassy look was in his whisker-bordered eyes, and his mouth, though
it was not easy to see it through the jungle, seemed to me to be sagging
mournfully. He resembled a minor prophet who has been hit behind
the ear with a stuffed eelskin.

"Mr. Ukridge!"

"Hallo?"

"The—the little dogs!"

"Well?"

"The little dogs!"

"What about them?"

"They have gone!"

"Gone?"

"Run away!"

"Run away? How the devil could they run away?"

"There seems to have been a loose board at the back of the shed.
The little dogs must have wriggled through. There is no trace of them
to be found."

Ukridge flung up his arms despairingly. He swelled like a captive
balloon. His pince-nez rocked on his nose, his mackintosh flapped
menacingly, and his collar sprang off its stud. He brought his fist down
with a crash on the table.

"Upon my Sam!"

"I am extremely sorry—"

"Upon my Sam!" cried Ukridge. "It's hard. It's pretty hard. I come
down here to inaugurate a great business which would eventually have
brought trade and prosperity to the whole neighborhood, and I have
hardly had time to turn round and attend to the preliminary details
of the enterprise when this man comes and sneaks my dogs. And
now he tells me with a light laugh—"

"Mr. Ukridge, I assure you—"

"Tells me with a light laugh that they've gone. Gone! Gone where?
Why, dash it, they may be all over the county. A fat chance I've got
of ever seeing them again. Six valuable Pekingese, already educated
practically to the stage where they could have been sold at an enormous profit—"

Mr. Nickerson was fumbling guiltily, and now he produced from
his pocket a crumpled wad of notes, which he thrust agitatedly upon
Ukridge, who waved them away with loathing.

"This gentleman," boomed Ukridge, indicating me with a sweeping gesture, "happens to be a lawyer. It is extremely lucky that he chanced to come down today to pay me a visit. Have you followed the proceedings closely?"

I said I had followed them very closely.

"Is it your opinion that an action will lie?"

I said it seemed highly probable, and this expert ruling appeared to put the final touch on Mr. Nickerson's collapse. Almost tearfully he urged the notes on Ukridge.

"What's this?" said Ukridge loftily.

"I—I thought, Mr. Ukridge, that, if it were agreeable to you, you might consent to take your money back, and—and consider the episode closed."

Ukridge turned to me with raised eyebrows.

"Ha!" he cried. "Ha, ha!"

"Ha, ha!" I chorused dutifully.

"He thinks that he can close the episode by giving me my money back. Isn't that rich?"

"Fruity," I agreed.

"Those dogs were worth hundreds of pounds, and he thinks he can square me with a rotten twenty. Would you have believed it if you hadn't heard it with your own ears, old horse?"

"Never!"

"I'll tell you what I'll do," said Ukridge, after thought. "I'll take this money." Mr. Nickerson thanked him. "And there are one or two trifling accounts which want settling with some of the local tradesmen. You will square those—"

"Certainly, Mr. Ukridge, certainly."

"And after that—well, I'll have to think it over. If I decide to institute proceedings my lawyer will communicate with you in due course."

And we left the wretched man, cowering despicably behind his whiskers.

It seemed to me, as we passed down the tree-shaded lane and out into the white glare of the road, that Ukridge was bearing himself in his hour of disaster with a rather admirable fortitude. His stock in trade, the lifeblood of his enterprise, was scattered all over Kent, probably never to return, and all that he had to show on the other side of the balance sheet was the canceling of a few weeks' back rent and the paying off of Gooch, the grocer, and his friends. It was a situation which might well have crushed the spirit of an ordinary man, but Ukridge seemed by no means dejected. Jaunty, rather. His eyes shone behind their pince-nez and he whistled a rollicking air. When presently he began to sing, I felt it was time to create a diversion.

"What are you going to do?" I asked.

"Who, me?" said Ukridge buoyantly. "Oh, I'm coming back to town on the next train. You don't mind hoofing it to the next station, do you? It's only five miles. It might be a trifle risky to start from Sheep's Cray."

"Why risky?"

"Because of the dogs, of course."

"Dogs?"

Ukridge hummed a gay strain.

"Oh, yes. I forgot to tell you about that. I've got 'em."

"What?"

"Yes. I went out late last night and pinched them out of the shed." He chuckled amusedly. "Perfectly simple. Only needed a clear, level head. I borrowed a dead cat and tied a string to it, legged it to old Nickerson's garden after dark, dug a board out of the back of the shed, and shoved my head down and chirruped. The dogs came trickling out, and I hared off, towing old Colonel Cat on his string. Great run while it lasted, laddie. Hounds picked up the scent right away and started off in a bunch at fifty miles an hour. Cat and I doing a steady fifty-five. Thought every minute old Nickerson would hear and start blazing away with a gun, but nothing happened. I led the pack across country for a run of twenty minutes without a check, parked the dogs in my sitting room, and so to bed. Took it out of me, by gosh! Not so young as I was."

I was silent for a moment, conscious of a feeling almost of reverence. This man was undoubtedly spacious. There had always been something about Ukridge that dulled the moral sense.

"Well," I said at length, "you've certainly got vision."

"Yes?" said Ukridge, gratified.

"*And* the big, broad, flexible outlook."

"Got to, laddie, nowadays. The foundation of a successful business career."

"And what's the next move?"

We were drawing near to the White Cottage. It stood and broiled in the sunlight, and I hoped that there might be something cool to drink inside it. The window of the sitting room was open, and through it came the yapping of Pekingese.

"Oh, I shall find another cottage somewhere else," said Ukridge, eying his little home with a certain sentimentality. "That won't be hard. Lots of cottages all over the place. And then I shall buckle down to serious work. You'll be astounded at the progress I've made already. In a minute I'll show you what those dogs can do."

"They can bark all right."

"Yes. They seem excited about something. You know, laddie, I've had a great idea. When I saw you at your rooms my scheme was to specialize in performing dogs for the music halls—what you might call professional dogs. But I've been thinking it over, and now I don't see why I shouldn't go in for developing amateur talent as well. Say you have a dog—Fido, the household pet—and you think it would brighten the home if he could do a few tricks from time to time. Well, you're a busy man, you haven't the time to give up to teaching him. So you just tie a label to his collar and ship him off for a month to the Ukridge Dog College, and back he comes, thoroughly educated. No trouble, no worry, easy terms. Upon my Sam, I'm not sure there isn't more money in the amateur branch than in the professional. I don't see why eventually dog owners shouldn't send their dogs to me as a regular thing, just as they send their sons to Eton and Winchester. My golly! this idea's beginning to develop. I'll tell you what— how would it be to issue special collars to all dogs which have graduated from my college? Something distinctive which everybody would recognize. See what I mean? Sort of badge of honor. Fellow with a dog entitled to wear the Ukridge collar would be in a position to look down on the bloke whose dog hadn't got one. Gradually it would get so that anybody in a decent social position would be ashamed to be seen out with a non-Ukridge dog. The thing would become a landslide. Dogs would pour in from all corners of the country. More work than I could handle. Have to start branches. The scheme's colossal. Millions in it, my boy! Millions!" He paused with his fingers on the handle of the front door. "Of course," he went on, "just at present it's no good blinking the fact that I'm hampered and handi- capped by lack of funds and can only approach the thing on a small scale. What it amounts to, laddie, is that somehow or other I've got to get capital."

It seemed the moment to spring the glad news.

"I promised him I wouldn't mention it," I said, "for fear it might lead to disappointment, but as a matter of fact George Tupper is trying to raise some capital for you. I left him last night starting out to get it."

"George Tupper!"—Ukridge's eyes dimmed with a not unmanly emotion—"George Tupper! By Gad, that fellow is the salt of the earth. Good, loyal fellow! A true friend. A man you can rely on.

Upon my Sam, if there were more fellows about like old Tuppy, there wouldn't be all this modern pessimism and unrest. Did he seem to have any idea where he could raise a bit of capital for me?"

"Yes. He went round to tell your aunt about your coming down here to train those Pekes, and— What's the matter?"

A fearful change had come over Ukridge's jubilant front. His eyes bulged, his jaw sagged. With the addition of a few feet of gray whiskers he would have looked exactly like the recent Mr. Nickerson.

"My aunt?" he mumbled, swaying on the door handle.

"Yes. What's the matter? He thought, if he told her all about it, she might relent and rally round."

The sigh of a gallant fighter at the end of his strength forced its way up from Ukridge's mackintosh-covered bosom.

"Of all the dashed, infernal, officious, meddling, muddling, fatheaded, interfering asses," he said wanly, "George Tupper is the worst."

"What do you mean?"

"The man oughtn't to be at large. He's a public menace."

"But—"

"Those dogs *belong* to my aunt. I pinched them when she chucked me out!"

Inside the cottage the Pekingese were still yapping industriously.

"Upon my Sam," said Ukridge, "it's a little hard."

I think he would have said more, but at this point a voice spoke with a sudden and awful abruptness from the interior of the cottage. It was a woman's voice, a quiet, steely voice, a voice, it seemed to me, that suggested cold eyes, a beaky nose, and hair like gun metal.

"Stanley!"

That was all it said, but it was enough. Ukridge's eye met mine in a wild surmise. He seemed to shrink into his mackintosh like a snail surprised while eating lettuce.

"Stanley."

"Yes, Aunt Julia?" quavered Ukridge.

"Come here. I wish to speak to you."

"Yes, Aunt Julia."

I sidled out into the road. Inside the cottage the yapping of the Pekingese had become quite hysterical. I found myself trotting, and then—though it was a warm day—running quite rapidly. I could have stayed if I had wanted to, but somehow I did not want to. Something seemed to tell me that on this holy domestic scene I should be an intruder.

What it was that gave me that impression I do not know—probably vision of the big, broad, flexible outlook.

❄ *Ukridge's Accident Syndicate*

"HALF A MINUTE, Laddie," said Ukridge. And, gripping my arm, he brought me to a halt on the outskirts of the little crowd which had collected about the church door.

It was a crowd such as may be seen any morning during the London mating season outside any of the churches which nestle in the quiet squares between Hyde Park and the King's Road, Chelsea. It consisted of five women of cooklike aspect, four nursemaids, half a dozen men of the nonproducing class who had torn themselves away for the moment from their normal task of propping up the wall of the Bunch of Grapes public house on the corner, a costermonger with a barrow of vegetables, divers small boys, eleven dogs, and two or three purposeful-looking young fellows with cameras slung over their shoulders. It was plain that a wedding was in progress—and, arguing from the presence of the cameramen and the line of smart motorcars along the curb, a fairly fashionable wedding. What was not plain—to me—was why Ukridge, sternest of bachelors, had desired to add himself to the spectators.

"What," I inquired, "is the thought behind this? Why are we interrupting our walk to attend the obsequies of some perfect stranger?"

Ukridge did not reply for a moment. He seemed plunged in thought. Then he uttered a hollow, mirthless laugh—a dreadful sound like the last gargle of a dying moose.

"Perfect stranger, my number eleven foot!" he responded, in his coarse way. "Do you know who it is who's getting hitched up in there?"

"Who?"

"Teddy Weeks."

"Teddy Weeks? Teddy Weeks? Good Lord!" I exclaimed. "Not really?"

And five years rolled away.

It was at Barolini's Italian restaurant in Beak Street that Ukridge evolved his great scheme. Barolini's was a favorite resort of our little group of earnest strugglers in the days when the philanthropic restaurateurs of Soho used to supply four courses and coffee for a shilling and sixpence; and there were present that night, besides Ukridge and myself, the following men about town: Teddy Weeks, the actor, fresh from a six-week tour with the Number Three *Only a Shop-Girl* Company; Victor Beamish, the artist, the man who drew that picture of the O-So-Eesi Piano-Player in the advertisement pages of the *Piccadilly Magazine;* Bertram Fox, author of "Ashes of Remorse," and other unproduced motion-picture scenarios; and Robert Dunhill, who, being employed at a salary of eighty pounds per annum by the New Asiatic Bank, represented the sober, hardheaded commercial element. As usual, Teddy Weeks had collared the conversation, and was telling us once again how good he was and how hardly treated by a malignant fate.

There is no need to describe Teddy Weeks. Under another and a more euphonious name he has long since made his personal appearance dreadfully familiar to all who read the illustrated weekly papers. He was then, as now, a sickeningly handsome young man, possessing precisely the same melting eyes, mobile mouth, and corrugated hair so esteemed by the theatergoing public today. And yet, at this period of his career he was wasting himself on minor touring companies of the kind which open at Barrow-in-Furness and jump to Bootle for the second half of the week. He attributed this, as Ukridge was so apt to attribute his own difficulties, to lack of capital.

"I have everything," he said querulously, emphasizing his remarks with a coffee spoon. "Looks, talent, personality, a beautiful speaking voice—everything. All I need is a chance. And I can't get that because I have no clothes fit to wear. These managers are all the same, they never look below the surface, they never bother to find out if a man has genius. All they go by is his clothes. If I could afford to buy a couple of suits from a Cork Street tailor, if I could have my boots made to order by Moykoff instead of getting them ready-made and secondhand at Moses Brothers', if I could once contrive to own a decent hat, a really good pair of spats, and a gold cigarette case, all at the same time, I could walk into any manager's office in London and sign up for a West End production tomorrow."

It was at this point that Freddie Lunt came in. Freddie, like Robert Dunhill, was a financial magnate in the making and an assiduous frequenter of Barolini's; and it suddenly occurred to us that a considerable time had passed since we had last seen him in the place. We inquired the reason for this aloofness.

"I've been in bed," said Freddie, "for over a fortnight."

The statement incurred Ukridge's stern disapproval. That great man made a practice of never rising before noon, and on one occasion, when a carelessly thrown match had burned a hole in his only pair of trousers, had gone so far as to remain between the sheets for forty-eight hours; but sloth on so majestic a scale as this shocked him.

"Lazy young devil," he commented severely. "Letting the golden hours of youth slip by like that when you ought to have been bustling about and making a name for yourself."

Freddie protested himself wronged by the imputation.

"I had an accident," he explained. "Fell off my bicycle and sprained an ankle."

"Tough luck," was our verdict.

"Oh, I don't know," said Freddie. "It wasn't bad fun getting a rest. And of course there was the fiver."

"What fiver?"

"I got a fiver from the *Weekly Cyclist* for getting my ankle sprained."

"You—*what?*" cried Ukridge, profoundly stirred—as ever—by a tale of easy money. "Do you mean to sit there and tell me that some dashed paper paid you five quid simply because you sprained your ankle? Pull yourself together, old horse. Things like that don't happen."

"It's quite true."

"Can you show me the fiver?"

"No; because if I did you would try to borrow it."

Ukridge ignored this slur in dignified silence.

"Would they pay a fiver to *anyone* who sprained his ankle?" he asked, sticking to the main point.

"Yes. If he was a subscriber."

"I knew there was a catch in it," said Ukridge moodily.

"Lots of weekly papers are starting this wheeze," proceeded Freddie. "You pay a year's subscription and that entitles you to accident insurance."

We were interested. This was in the days before every daily paper in London was competing madly against its rivals in the matter of insurance and offering princely bribes to the citizens to make a fortune by breaking their necks. Nowadays papers are paying as high as two thousand pounds for a genuine corpse and five pounds a week for a mere dislocated spine; but at that time the idea was new and it had an attractive appeal.

"How many of these rags are doing this?" asked Ukridge. You could tell from the gleam in his eyes that that great brain was whirring like a dynamo. "As many as ten?"

"Yes, I should think so. Quite ten."

"Then a fellow who subscribed to them all and then sprained his ankle would get fifty quid?" said Ukridge, reasoning acutely.

"More if the injury was more serious," said Freddie, the expert. "They have a regular tariff. So much for a broken arm, so much for a broken leg, and so forth."

Ukridge's collar leaped off its stud and his pince-nez wobbled drunkenly as he turned to us.

"How much money can you blokes raise?" he demanded.

"What do you want it for?" asked Robert Dunhill, with a banker's caution.

"My dear old horse, can't you see? Why, my gosh, I've got the idea of the century. Upon my Sam, this is the giltest-edged scheme that was ever hatched. We'll get together enough money and take out a year's subscription for every one of these dashed papers."

"What's the good of that?" said Dunhill, coldly unenthusiastic.

They train bank clerks to stifle emotion, so that they will be able to refuse overdrafts when they become managers. "The odds are we should none of us have an accident of any kind, and then the money would be chucked away."

"Good heavens, ass," snorted Ukridge, "you don't suppose I'm suggesting that we should leave it to chance, do you? Listen! Here's the scheme. We take out subscriptions for all these papers, then we draw lots, and the fellow who gets the fatal card or whatever it is goes out and breaks his leg and draws the loot, and we split it up between us and live on it in luxury. It ought to run into hundreds of pounds."

A long silence followed. Then Dunhill spoke again. His was a solid rather than a nimble mind.

"Suppose he couldn't break his leg?"

"My gosh!" cried Ukridge, exasperated. "Here we are in the twentieth century, with every resource of modern civilization at our disposal, with opportunities for getting our legs broken opening about us on every side—and you ask a silly question like that! Of course he could break his leg. Any ass can break a leg. It's a little hard! We're all infernally broke—personally, unless Freddie can lend me a bit of that fiver till Saturday, I'm going to have a difficult job of pulling through. We all need money like the dickens, and yet, when I point out this marvelous scheme for collecting a bit, instead of fawning on me for my ready intelligence you sit and make objections. It isn't the right spirit. It isn't the spirit that wins."

"If you're as hard up as that," objected Dunhill, "how are you going to put in your share of the pool?"

A pained, almost a stunned, look came into Ukridge's eyes. He gazed at Dunhill through his lopsided pince-nez as one who speculates as to whether his hearing has deceived him.

"Me?" he cried. "Me? I like that! Upon my Sam, that's rich! Why, damme, if there's any justice in the world, if there's a spark of decency and good feeling in your bally bosoms, I should think you would let me in free for suggesting the idea. It's a little hard! I supply the brains and you want me to cough up cash as well. My gosh, I didn't expect this. This hurts me, by George! If anybody had told me that an old pal would—"

"Oh, all right," said Robert Dunhill. "All right, all right, all right. But I'll tell you one thing. If you draw the lot it'll be the happiest day of my life."

"I shan't," said Ukridge. "Something tells me that I shan't."

Nor did he. When, in a solemn silence broken only by the sound of a distant waiter quarreling with the cook down a speaking tube, we had completed the drawing, the man of destiny was Teddy Weeks.

I suppose that even in the springtime of Youth, when broken limbs seem a lighter matter than they become later in life, it can never be an unmixedly agreeable thing to have to go out into the public highways and try to make an accident happen to one. In such circumstances the reflection that you are thereby benefiting your friends brings but slight balm. To Teddy Weeks it appeared to bring no balm at all. That he was experiencing a certain disinclination to sacrifice himself for the public good became more and more evident as the days went by and found him still intact. Ukridge, when he called upon me to discuss the matter, was visibly perturbed. He sank into a chair beside the table at which I was beginning my modest morning meal, and, having drunk half my coffee, sighed deeply.

"Upon my Sam," he moaned, "it's a little disheartening. I strain my brain to think up schemes for getting us all a bit of money just at the moment when we are all needing it most, and when I hit on what is probably the simplest and yet ripest notion of our time, this blighter Weeks goes and lets me down by shirking his plain duty. It's just my luck that a fellow like that should have drawn the lot. And the worst of it is, laddie, that, now we've started with him, we've got to keep on. We can't possibly raise enough money to pay yearly subscriptions for anybody else. It's Weeks or nobody."

"I suppose we must give him time."

"That's what he says," grunted Ukridge morosely, helping himself to toast. "He says he doesn't know how to start about it. To listen to him, you'd think that going and having a trifling accident was the sort of delicate and intricate job that required years of study and special preparation. Why, a child of six could do it on his head at five minutes' notice. The man's so infernally particular. You make helpful suggestions, and instead of accepting them in a broad, reasonable spirit of cooperation he comes back at you every time with some frivolous objection. He's so dashed fastidious. When we were out last night, we came on a couple of navvies scrapping. Good hefty fellows, either of them capable of putting him in hospital for a month. I told him to jump in and start separating them, and he said no; it was a private dispute which was none of his business, and he didn't feel justified in interfering. Finicky, I call it. I tell you, laddie, this blighter is a broken reed. He has got cold feet. We did wrong to let him into the drawing at all. We might have known that a fellow like that would never give results. No conscience. No sense of esprit de corps. No notion of putting himself out to the most trifling extent for the benefit of the community. Haven't you any more marmalade, laddie?"

"I have not."

"Then I'll be going," said Ukridge moodily. "I suppose," he added, pausing at the door, "you couldn't lend me five bob?"

"How did you guess?"

"Then I'll tell you what," said Ukridge, ever fair and reasonable; "you can stand me dinner tonight." He seemed cheered up for the moment by this happy compromise, but gloom descended on him again. His face clouded. "When I think," he said, "of all the money that's locked up in that poor fainthearted fish, just waiting to be released, I could sob. Sob, laddie, like a litle child. I never liked that man—he has a bad eye and waves his hair. Never trust a man who waves his hair, old horse."

Ukridge's pessimism was not confined to himself. By the end of a fortnight, nothing having happened to Teddy Weeks worse than a slight cold which he shook off in a couple of days, the general consensus of opinion among his apprehensive colleagues in the Syndicate was that the situation had become desperate. There were no signs whatever of any return on the vast capital which we had laid out, and meanwhile meals had to be bought, landladies paid, and a reasonable supply of tobacco acquired. It was a melancholy task in these circumstances to read one's paper of a morning.

All over the inhabited globe, so the well-informed sheet gave one to understand, every kind of accident was happening every day to practically everybody in existence except Teddy Weeks. Farmers in Minnesota were getting mixed up with reaping machines; peasants in India were being bisected by crocodiles; iron girders from skyscrapers were falling hourly on the heads of citizens in every town from Philadelphia to San Francisco; and the only people who were not down with ptomaine poisoning were those who had walked over cliffs, driven motors into walls, tripped over manholes, or assumed on too slight evidence that the gun was not loaded. In a crippled world, it seemed, Teddy Weeks walked alone, whole and glowing with health. It was one of those grim, ironical, hopeless, gray, despairful situations which the Russian novelists love to write about, and I could not find it in me to blame Ukridge for taking direct action in this crisis. My only regret was that bad luck caused so excellent a plan to miscarry.

My first intimation that he had been trying to hurry matters on came when he and I were walking along the King's Road one evening, and he drew me into Markham Square, a dismal backwater where he had once had rooms.

"What's the idea?" I asked, for I disliked the place.

"Teddy Weeks lives here," said Ukridge. "In my old rooms." I could not see that this lent any fascination to the place. Every day and in every way I was feeling sorrier and sorrier that I had been foolish enough to put money which I could ill spare into a venture which had all the earmarks of a washout, and my sentiments toward Teddy Weeks were cold and hostile.

"I want to inquire after him."

"Inquire after him? Why?"

"Well, the fact is, laddie, I have an idea that he has been bitten by a dog."

"What makes you think that?"

"Oh, I don't know," said Ukridge dreamily. "I've just got the idea. You know how one gets ideas."

The mere contemplation of this beautiful event was so inspiring that for a while it held me silent. In each of the ten journals in which we had invested dog bites were specifically recommended as things which every subscriber ought to have. They came about halfway up the list of lucrative accidents, inferior to a broken rib or a fractured fibula, but better value than an ingrowing toenail. I was gloating happily over the picture conjured up by Ukridge's words when an exclamation brought me back with a start to the realities of life. A revolting sight met my eyes. Down the street came ambling the familiar figure of Teddy Weeks, and one glance at his elegant person was enough to tell us that our hopes had been built on sand. Not even a toy Pomeranian had chewed this man.

"Hallo, you fellows!" said Teddy Weeks.

"Hallo!" we responded dully.

"Can't stop," said Teddy Weeks. "I've got to fetch a doctor."

"A doctor?"

"Yes. Poor Victor Beamish. He's been bitten by a dog."

Ukridge and I exchanged weary glances. It seemed as if Fate was going out of its way to have sport with us. What was the good of a dog biting Victor Beamish? What was the good of a hundred dogs biting Victor Beamish? A dog-bitten Victor Beamish had no market value whatever.

"You know that fierce brute that belongs to my landlady," said Teddy Weeks. "The one that always dashes out into the area and barks at people who come to the front door." I remembered. A large mongrel with wild eyes and flashing fangs, badly in need of a haircut. I had encountered it once in the street, when visiting Ukridge, and only the presence of the latter, who knew it well and to whom all dogs were as brothers, had saved me from the doom of Victor Beamish. "Somehow or other he got into my bedroom this evening. He was waiting there when I came home. I had brought Beamish back with me, and the animal pinned him by the leg the moment I opened the door."

"Why didn't he pin you?" asked Ukridge, aggrieved.

"What I can't make out," said Teddy Weeks, "is how on earth the brute came to be in my room. Somebody must have put him there. The whole thing is very mysterious."

"Why didn't he pin you?" demanded Ukridge again.

"Oh, I managed to climb onto the top of the wardrobe while he was biting Beamish," said Teddy Weeks. "And then the landlady came and took him away. But I can't stop here talking. I must go and get that doctor."

We gazed after him in silence as he tripped down the street. We noted the careful manner in which he paused at the corner to eye the traffic before crossing the road, the wary way in which he drew back to allow a truck to rattle past.

"You heard that?" said Ukridge tensely. "He climbed onto the top of the wardrobe!"

"Yes."

"And you saw the way he dodged that excellent truck?"

"Yes."

"Something's got to be done," said Ukridge firmly. "The man has got to be awakened to a sense of his responsibilities."

Next day a deputation waited on Teddy Weeks.

Ukridge was our spokesman, and he came to the point with admirable directness.

"How about it?" asked Ukridge.

"How about what?" replied Teddy Weeks nervously, avoiding his accusing eye.

"When do we get action?"

"Oh, you mean that accident business?"

"Yes."

"I've been thinking about that," said Teddy Weeks.

Ukridge drew the mackintosh which he wore indoors and out of doors and in all weathers more closely around him. There was in the action something suggestive of a member of the Roman Senate about to denounce an enemy of the State. In just such a manner must Cicero have swished his toga as he took a deep breath preparatory to assailing Clodius. He toyed for a moment with the ginger-beer wire which held his pince-nez in place, and endeavored without success to button his collar at the back. In moments of emotion Ukridge's collar always took on a sort of temperamental jumpiness which no stud could restrain.

"And about time you *were* thinking about it," he boomed sternly.

We shifted appreciatively in our seats, all except Victor Beamish, who had declined a chair and was standing by the mantelpiece. "Upon my Sam, it's about time you were thinking about it. Do you realize that we've invested an enormous sum of money in you on the distinct understanding that we could rely on you to do your duty and get immediate results? Are we to be forced to the conclusion that you are so yellow and few in the pod as to want to evade your honorable obligations? We thought better of you, Weeks. Upon my Sam, we thought better of you. We took you for a two-fisted, enterprising, big-souled, one-hundred-per-cent he-man who would stand by his friends to the finish."

"Yes, but—"

"Any bloke with a sense of loyalty and an appreciation of what it meant to the rest of us would have rushed out and found some means of fulfilling his duty long ago. You don't even grasp at the opportunities that come your way. Only yesterday I saw you draw back when a single step into the road would have had a truck bumping into you."

"Well, it's not so easy to let a truck bump into you."

"Nonsense. It only requires a little ordinary resolution. Use your imagination, man. Try to think that a child has fallen down in the street—a little golden-haired child," said Ukridge, deeply affected.

"And a dashed great cab or something comes rolling up. The kid's mother is standing on the pavement, helpless, her hands clasped in agony. 'Dammit,' she cries, 'will no one save my darling?' 'Yes, by George,' you shout, '*I* will.' And out you jump and the thing's over in half a second. I don't know what you're making such a fuss about."

"Yes, but—" said Teddy Weeks.

"I'm told, what's more, it isn't a bit painful. A sort of dull shock, that's all."

"Who told you that?"

"I forget. Someone."

"Well, you can tell him from me that he's an ass," said Teddy Weeks with asperity.

"All right. If you object to being run over by a truck there are lots of other ways. But, upon my Sam, it's pretty hopeless suggesting them. You seem to have no enterprise at all. Yesterday, after I went to all the trouble to put a dog in your room, a dog which would have done all the work for you—all that you had to do was stand still and let him use his own judgment—what happened? You climbed onto—"

Victor Beamish interrupted, speaking in a voice husky with emotion.

"Was it you who put that damned dog in the room?"

"Eh?" said Ukridge. "Why, yes. But we can have a good talk about all that later on," he proceeded hastily. "The point at the moment is how the dickens we're going to persuade this poor worm to collect our insurance money for us. Why, damme, I should have thought you would have—"

"All I can say—" began Victor Beamish heatedly.

"Yes, yes," said Ukridge; "some other time. Must stick to business now, laddie. I was saying," he resumed, "that I should have thought you would have been as keen as mustard to put the job through for your own sake. You're always beefing that you haven't any clothes to impress managers with. Think of all you can buy with your share of the swag once you have summoned up a little ordinary determination and seen the thing through. Think of the suits, the boots, the hats, the spats. You're always talking about your dashed career, and how all you need to land you in a West End production is good clothes. Well, here's your chance to get them."

His eloquence was not wasted. A wistful look came into Teddy Weeks's eye, such a look as must have come into the eye of Moses on the summit of Pisgah. He breathed heavily. You could see that the man was mentally walking along Cork Street, weighing the merits of one famous tailor against another.

"I'll tell you what I'll do," he said suddenly. "It's no use asking me to put this thing through in cold blood. I simply can't do it. I haven't the nerve. But if you fellows will give me a dinner tonight with lots of champagne I think it will key me up to it."

A heavy silence fell upon the room. Champagne! The word was like a knell.

"How on earth are we going to afford champagne?" said Victor Beamish.

"Well, there it is," said Teddy Weeks. "Take it or leave it."

"Gentlemen," said Ukridge, "it would seem that the company requires more capital. How about it, old horses? Let's get together in a frank, businesslike, cards-on-the-table spirit, and see what can be done. I can raise ten bob."

"What!" cried the entire assembled company, amazed. "How?"

"I'll pawn a banjo."

"You haven't got a banjo."

"No, but George Tupper has, and I know where he keeps it."

Started in this spirited way, the subscriptions came pouring in. I contributed a cigarette case, Bertram Fox thought his landlady would let him owe for another week, Robert Dunhill had an uncle in Kensington who, he fancied, if tactfully approached, would be good for a quid, and Victor Beamish said that if the advertisement manager of the O-So-Eesi Piano-Player was churlish enough to refuse an advance of five shillings against future work he misjudged him sadly. Within a few minutes, in short, the Lightning Drive had produced the impressive total of two pounds six shillings, and we asked Teddy Weeks if he thought that he could get adequately keyed up within the limits of that sum.

"I'll try," said Teddy Weeks.

So, not unmindful of the fact that that excellent hostelry supplied champagne at eight shillings the quart bottle, we fixed the meeting for seven o'clock at Barolini's.

Considered as a social affair, Teddy Weeks's keying-up dinner was not a success. Almost from the start I think we all found it trying. It was not so much the fact that he was drinking deeply of Barolini's eight-shilling champagne while we, from lack of funds, were compelled to confine ourselves to meaner beverages; what really marred the pleasantness of the function was the extraordinary effect the stuff had on Teddy. What was actually in the champagne supplied to Barolini and purveyed by him to the public, such as were reckless enough to drink it, at eight shillings the bottle remains a secret between its maker and his Maker; but three glasses of it were enough to convert Teddy Weeks from a mild and rather oily young man into a truculent swashbuckler.

He quarreled with us all. With the soup he was tilting at Victor Beamish's theories of art; the fish found him ridiculing Bertram Fox's views on the future of the motion picture; and by the time the leg of chicken and dandelion salad arrived—or, as some held, string salad—opinions varied on this point—the hell-brew had so wrought on him that he had begun to lecture Ukridge on his misspent life and was urging him in accents audible across the street to go out and get a job and thus acquire sufficient self-respect to enable him to look himself in the face in a mirror without wincing. Not, added Teddy Weeks with what we all thought uncalled-for offensiveness, that any amount of self-respect was likely to do that. Having said which, he called imperiously for another eight bobs'-worth.

We gazed at one another wanly. However excellent the end toward which all this was tending, there was no denying that it was hard to bear. But policy kept us silent. We recognized that this was Teddy Weeks's evening and that he must be humored. Victor Beamish said meekly that Teddy had cleared up a lot of points which had been troubling him for a long time. Bertram Fox agreed that there was much in what Teddy had said about the future of the close-up. And even Ukridge, though his haughty soul was seared to its foundations by the latter's personal remarks, promised to take his homily to heart and act upon it at the earliest possible moment.

"You'd better!" said Teddy Weeks belligerently, biting off the end of one of Barolini's cigars. "And there's another thing—don't let me hear of your coming and sneaking people's socks again."

"Very well, laddie," said Ukridge humbly.

"If there is one person in the world that I despise," said Teddy, bending a red-eyed gaze on the offender, "it's a snock-seeker—a seek-snocker—a—well, you know what I mean."

We hastened to assure him that we knew what he meant and he relapsed into a lengthy stupor, from which he emerged three quarters of an hour later to announce that he didn't know what he intended to do, but that he was going. We said that we were going too, and we paid the bill and did so.

Teddy Weeks's indignation on discovering us gathered about him upon the pavement outside the restaurant was intense, and he expressed it freely. Among other things, he said—which was not true —that he had a reputation to keep up in Soho.

"It's all right, Teddy, old horse," said Ukridge soothingly. "We

just thought you would like to have all your old pals round you when
you did it."

"Did it? Did what?"

"Why, had the accident."

Teddy Weeks glared at him truculently. Then his mood seemed to
change abruptly, and he burst into a loud and hearty laugh.

"Well, of all the silly ideas!" he cried amusedly. "I'm not going
to have an accident. You don't suppose I ever seriously intended to
have an accident, do you? It was just my fun." Then, with another
sudden change of mood, he seemed to become a victim to an acute
unhappiness. He stroked Ukridge's arm affectionately, and a tear
rolled down his cheek. "Just my fun," he repeated. "You don't mind
my fun, do you?" he asked pleadingly. "You like my fun, don't you?
All my fun. Never meant to have an accident at all. Just wanted
dinner." The gay humor of it all overcame his sorrow once more.
"Funniest thing ever heard," he said cordially. "Didn't want accident,
wanted dinner. Dinner daxident, danner dixident," he added, driving
home his point. "Well, good night all," he said cheerily. And,
stepping off the curb onto a bananaskin, was instantly knocked
ten feet by a passing truck.

"Two ribs and an arm," said the doctor five minutes later, superintending the removal proceedings. "Gently with that stretcher."

It was two weeks before we were informed by the authorities of
Charing Cross Hospital that the patient was in a condition to receive
visitors. A whip-round secured the price of a basket of fruit, and
Ukridge and I were deputed by the shareholders to deliver it with
their compliments and kind inquiries.

"Hallo!" we said in a hushed, bedside manner when finally admitted
to his presence.

"Sit down, gentlemen," replied the invalid.

I must confess even in that first moment to having experienced a
slight feeling of surprise. It was not like Teddy Weeks to call us
gentlemen. Ukridge, however, seemed to notice nothing amiss.

"Well, well, well," he said buoyantly. "And how are you, laddie?
We've brought you a few fragments of fruit."

"I am getting along capitally," replied Teddy Weeks, still in that
odd precise way which had made his opening words strike me as
curious. "And I should like to say that in my opinion England has
reason to be proud of the alertness and enterprise of her great
journals. The excellence of their reading matter, the ingenuity of
their various competitions, and, above all, the go-ahead spirit which

has resulted in this accident insurance scheme are beyond praise. Have you got that down?" he inquired.

Ukridge and I looked at each other. We had been told that Teddy was practically normal again, but this sounded like delirium.

"Have we got what down, old horse?" asked Ukridge gently.

Teddy Weeks seemed surprised.

"Aren't you reporters?"

"How do you mean, reporters?"

"I thought you had come from one of these weekly papers that have been paying me insurance money, to interview me," said Teddy Weeks.

Ukridge and I exchanged another glance. An uneasy glance this time. I think that already a grim foreboding had begun to cast its shadow over us.

"Surely you remember me, Teddy, old horse?" said Ukridge anxiously.

Teddy Weeks knit his brow, concentrating painfully.

"Why, of course," he said at last. "You're Ukridge, aren't you?"

"That's right. Ukridge."

"Of course. Ukridge."

"Yes. Ukridge. Funny your forgetting me!"

"Yes," said Teddy Weeks. "It's the effect of the shock I got when that thing bowled me over. I must have been struck on the head, I suppose. It has had the effect of rendering my memory rather uncertain. The doctors here are very interested. They say it is a most unusual case. I can remember some things perfectly, but in some ways my memory is a complete blank."

"Oh, but I say, old horse," quavered Ukridge. "I suppose you haven't forgotten about that insurance, have you?"

"Oh, no, I remember that."

Ukridge breathed a relieved sigh.

"I was a subscriber to a number of weekly papers," went on Teddy Weeks. "They are paying me insurance money now."

"Yes, yes, old horse," cried Ukridge. "But what I mean is you remember the Syndicate, don't you?"

Teddy Weeks raised his eyebrows.

"Syndicate? What Syndicate?"

"Why, when we all got together and put up the money to pay for the subscriptions to these papers and drew lots, to choose which of us should go out and have an accident and collect the money. And you drew it, don't you remember?"

Utter astonishment, and a shocked astonishment at that, spread itself over Teddy Weeks's countenance. The man seemed outraged.

"I certainly remember nothing of the kind," he said severely. "I cannot imagine myself for a moment consenting to become a party to what from your own account would appear to have been a criminal conspiracy to obtain money under false pretenses from a number of weekly papers."

"But, laddie—"

"However," said Teddy Weeks, "if there is any truth in this story, no doubt you have documentary evidence to support it."

Ukridge looked at me. I looked at Ukridge. There was a long silence.

"Shift-ho, old horse?" said Ukridge sadly. "No use staying on here."

"No," I replied, with equal gloom. "May as well go."

"Glad to have seen you," said Teddy Weeks, "and thanks for the fruit."

The next time I saw the man he was coming out of a manager's office in the Haymarket. He had on a new Homburg hat of a delicate pearl gray, spats to match, and a new blue flannel suit, beautifully cut, with an invisible red twill. He was looking jubilant, and, as I passed him, he drew from his pocket a gold cigarette case.

It was shortly after that, if you remember, that he made a big hit as the juvenile lead in that piece at the Apollo and started on his sensational career as a matinee idol.

Inside the church the organ had swelled into the familiar music of the Wedding March. A verger came out and opened the doors. The five cooks ceased their reminiscences of other and smarter weddings at which they had participated. The cameramen unshipped their cameras. The costermonger moved his barrow of vegetables a pace forward. A disheveled and unshaven man at my side uttered a disapproving growl.

"Idle rich!" said the disheveled man.

Out of the church came a beauteous being, leading attached to his arm another being, somewhat less beauteous.

There was no denying the spectacular effect of Teddy Weeks. He was handsomer than ever. His sleek hair, gorgeously waved, shone in the sun, his eyes were large and bright; his lissome frame, garbed in faultless morning coat and trousers, was that of an Apollo. But his bride gave the impression that Teddy had married money. They paused in the doorway, and the cameramen became active and fussy.

"Have you got a shilling, laddie?" said Ukridge in a low, level voice.

"Why do you want a shilling?"

"Old horse," said Ukridge tensely, "it is of the utmost vital importance that I have a shilling here and now."

I passed it over. Ukridge turned to the disheveled man, and I perceived that he held in his hand a large rich tomato of juicy and overripe appearance.

"Would you like to earn a bob?" Ukridge said.

"Would I!" replied the disheveled man.

Ukridge sank his voice to a hoarse whisper.

The cameramen had finished their preparations. Teddy Weeks, his head thrown back in that gallant way which has endeared him to so many female hearts, was exhibiting his celebrated teeth. The cooks, in undertones, were making adverse comments on the appearance of the bride.

"Now, please," said one of the cameramen.

Over the heads of the crowd, well and truly aimed, whizzed a large juicy tomato. It burst like a shell full between Teddy Weeks's expressive eyes, obliterating them in scarlet ruin. It spattered Teddy Weeks's collar, it dripped on Teddy Weeks's morning coat. And the disheveled man turned abruptly and raced off down the street.

Ukridge grasped my arm. There was a look of deep content in his eyes.

"Shift-ho?" said Ukridge.

Arm in arm, we strolled off in the pleasant June sunshine.

❀ *A Bit of Luck for Mabel*

"LIFE, LADDIE," said Ukridge, "is very rum."

He had been lying for some time silent on the sofa, his face toward the ceiling; and I had supposed that he was asleep. But now it appeared that it was thought, not slumber, that had caused his unwonted quietude.

"Very, very rum," said Ukridge.

He heaved himself up and stared out of the window. The sitting-room window of the cottage which I had taken in the country looked upon a stretch of lawn, backed by a little spinney; and now there stole in through it from the waking world outside that first cool breeze which heralds the dawning of a summer day.

"Great Scott!" I said, looking at my watch. "Do you realize you've kept me up talking all night?"

Ukridge did not answer. There was a curious, faraway look on his face, and he uttered a sound like the last gurgle of an expiring soda-water siphon, which I took to be his idea of a sigh. I saw what had happened. There is a certain hour at the day's beginning which brings with it a strange magic, tapping wells of sentiment in the most hard-boiled. In this hour, with the sun pinking the eastern sky and the early bird chirping over its worm, Stanley Featherstonehaugh Ukridge, that battered man of wrath, had become maudlin; and, instead of being allowed to go to bed, I was in for some story of his murky past.

"Extraordinarily rum," said Ukridge. "So is Fate. It's curious to think, Corky, old horse, that if things had not happened as they did I might now be a man of tremendous importance, looked up to and respected by all in Singapore."

"Why should anyone respect you in Singapore?"

"Rolling in money," proceeded Ukridge wistfully.

"You?"

"Yes, me. Did you ever hear of one of those blokes out East who didn't amass a huge fortune? Of course you didn't. Well, think what I should have done, with my brain and vision. Mabel's father made a perfect pot of money in Singapore, and I don't suppose he had any vision whatever."

"Who was Mabel?"

"Haven't I ever spoken to you of Mabel?"

"No. Mabel who?"

"I won't mention names."

"I hate stories without names."

"You'll have this story without names—and like it," said Ukridge with spirit. He sighed again. A most unpleasant sound. "Corky, my boy," he said, "do you realize on what slender threads our lives hang? Do you realize how trifling can be the snags on which we stub our toes as we go through this world? Do you realize—"

"Get on with it."

"In my case it was a top hat."

"What was a top hat?"

"The snag."

"You stubbed your toe on a top hat?"

"Figuratively, yes. It was a top hat which altered the whole course of my life."

"You never had a top hat."

"Yes, I did have a top hat. It's absurd for you to pretend that I never had a top hat. You know perfectly well that when I go to live with my Aunt Julia in Wimbledon I roll in top hats—literally roll."

"Oh, yes, when you go to live with your aunt."

"Well, it was when I was living with her that I met Mabel. The affair of the top hat happened—"

I looked at my watch again.

"I can give you half an hour," I said. "After that I'm going to bed. If you can condense Mabel into a thirty-minute sketch, carry on."

"This is not quite the sympathetic attitude I should like to see in an old friend, Corky."

"It's the only attitude I'm capable of at half-past three in the morning. Snap into it."

Ukridge pondered.

"It's difficult to know where to begin."

"Well, to start with, who was she?"

"She was the daughter of a bloke who ran some sort of immensely wealthy business in Singapore."

"Where did she live?"

"In Onslow Square."

"Where were you living?"

"With my aunt in Wimbledon."

"Where did you meet her?"

"At a dinner party at my aunt's."

"You fell in love with her at first sight?"

"Yes."

"For a while it seemed that she might return your love?"

"Exactly."

"And then one day she saw you in a top hat and the whole thing was off. There you are. The entire story in two minutes fifteen seconds. Now let's go to bed."

Ukridge shook his head.

"You've got it wrong, old horse. Nothing like that at all. You'd better let me tell the whole thing from the beginning."

The first thing I did after that dinner (said Ukridge) was to go and call at Onslow Square. As a matter of fact, I called about three times in the first week; and it seemed to me that everything was going like a breeze. You know what I'm like when I'm staying with my Aunt Julia, Corky. Dapper is the word. Debonair. Perfectly groomed. Mind you, I don't say I enjoy dressing the way she makes me dress when I'm with her, but there's no getting away from it that it gives me an air. Seeing me strolling along the street with the gloves, the cane, the spats, the shoes, and the old top hat, you might wonder if I was a marquess or a duke, but you would be pretty sure I was one of the two.

These things count with a girl. They count still more with her mother. By the end of the second week you wouldn't be far wrong in saying that I was the popular pet at Onslow Square. And then, rolling in one afternoon for a dish of tea, I was shocked to perceive nestling in my favorite chair, with all the appearance of a cove who is absolutely at home, another bloke. Mabel's mother was fussing over him as if he were the long-lost son. Mabel seemed to like him a good deal. And the nastiest shock of all came when I discovered that the fellow was a baronet.

Now, you know as well as I do, Corky, that for the ordinary workaday bloke Barts are tough birds to go up against. There is something about Barts that appeals to the most soulful girl. And as for the average mother, she eats them alive. Even an elderly Bart with two chins and a bald head is bad enough, and this was a young and juicy specimen. He had a clean-cut, slightly pimply, patrician face; and, what was worse, he was in the Coldstream Guards. And you will bear me out, Corky, when I say that, while an ordinary civilian Bart is bad enough, a Bart who is also a Guardee is a rival the stoutest-hearted cove might well shudder at.

And when you consider that practically all I had to put up against this serious menace was honest worth and a happy disposition, you will understand why the brow was a good deal wrinkled as I sat sipping my tea and listening to the rest of the company talking about people I'd never heard of and entertainments where I hadn't been among those we also noticed.

After a while the conversation turned to Ascot.

"Are you going to Ascot, Mr. Ukridge?" said Mabel's mother, apparently feeling that it was time to include me in the chitchat.

"Wouldn't miss it for worlds," I said.

Though, as a matter of fact, until that moment I had rather intended to give it the go-by. Fond as I am of the sport of kings, to my mind a race meeting where you've got to go in a morning coat and a top hat—with the thermometer probably in the nineties—lacks fascination. I'm all for being the young duke when occasion requires, but races and toppers don't seem to me to go together.

"That's splendid," said Mabel, and I'm bound to say these kind words cheered me up a good deal. "We shall meet there."

"Sir Aubrey," said Mabel's mother, "has invited us to his house party."

"Taken a place for the week down there," explained the Bart.

"Ah!" I said. And, mark you, that was about all there was to say. For the sickening realization that this Guardee Bart, in addition to being a Bart and a Guardee, also possessed enough cash to take country houses for Ascot Week in that careless, offhand manner seemed to go all over me like nettle rash. I was rattled, Corky. Your old friend was rattled. I did some pretty tense thinking on my way back to Wimbledon.

When I got there, I found my aunt in the drawing room. And suddenly something in her attitude seemed to smite me like a blow. I don't know if you have ever had that rummy feeling which seems to whisper in your ear that Hell's foundations are about to quiver, but I got it the moment I caught sight of her. She was sitting bolt upright in a chair, and as I came in she looked at me. You know her, Corky, and you know just how she shoots her eyes at you without turning her head, as if she were a basilisk with a stiff neck. Well, that's how she looked at me now.

"Good evening," she said.

"Good evening," I said.

"So you've come in," she said.

"Yes," I said.

"Well, then, you can go straight out again," she said.

"Eh," I said.

"And never come back," she said.

I goggled at her. Mark you, I had been heaved out of the old home by my Aunt Julia many a time before, so it wasn't as if I wasn't used to it; but I had never got the boot quite so suddenly before and so completely out of a blue sky. Usually, when Aunt Julia bungs me out on my ear, it is possible to see it coming days ahead.

"I might have guessed that something like this would happen," she said.

And then all things were made plain. She had found out about the clock. And it shows what love can do to a fellow, Corky, when I tell you that I had clean forgotten all about it.

You know the position of affairs when I go to live with my Aunt Julia. She feeds me and buys me clothes, but for some reason best known to her own distorted mind it is impossible to induce her to part with a little ready cash. The consequence was that, falling in love with Mabel as I had done and needing a quid or two for current expenses, I had had to rely on my native ingenuity and resource. It was absolutely imperative that I should give the girl a few flowers and chocolates from time to time, and this runs into money. So, seeing a rather juicy clock doing nothing on the mantelpiece of the spare bedroom, I had sneaked it off under my coat and put it up the spout at the local pawnbroker's. And now, apparently, in some devious and underhand manner she had discovered this.

Well, it was no good arguing. When my Aunt Julia is standing over you with her sleeves rolled up preparatory to getting a grip on the scruff of your neck and the seat of your trousers, it has always been my experience that words are useless. The only thing to do is to drift away and trust to Time, the great healer. Some forty minutes later, therefore, a solitary figure might have been observed legging it to the station with a suitcase. I was out in the great world once more.

However, you know me, Corky. The Old Campaigner. It takes more than a knock like that to crush your old friend. I took a bed-sitting-room in Arundel Street and sat down to envisage the situation.

Undeniably things had taken a nasty twist, and many a man lacking my vision and enterprise might have turned his face to the wall and said: "This is the end!" But I am made of sterner stuff. It seemed to me that all was not yet over. I had packed the morning coat, the waistcoat, the trousers, the shoes, the spats, and the gloves, and had gone away wearing the old top hat; so, from a purely ornamental point of view, I was in precisely the position I had been before. That is to say, I could still continue to call at Onslow Square; and, what is more, if I could touch George Tupper for a fiver—which I intended to do without delay—I should have the funds to go to Ascot.

The sun, it appeared to me, therefore, was still shining. How true it is, Corky, that, no matter how the tempests lower, there is always sunshine somewhere! How true it is— Oh, all right, I was only mentioning it.

Well, George Tupper, splendid fellow, parted without a murmur. Well, no, not—to be absolutely accurate—without a murmur. Still, he parted. And the position of affairs was now as follows. Cash in hand, five pounds. Price of admission to grandstand and paddock at Ascot for first day of meeting, two pounds. Time to elapse before Ascot, ten days. Net result—three quid in my kick to keep me going till then and pay my fare down and buy flowers and so on. It all looked very rosy.

But note, Corky, how Fate plays with us. Two days before Ascot, as I was coming back from having tea at Onslow Square—not a little preoccupied, for the Bart had been very strong on the wing that afternoon—there happened what seemed at first sight an irremediable disaster.

The weather, which had been fair and warm until that evening, had suddenly broken, and a rather nippy wind had sprung up from the east. Now, if I had not been so tensely occupied with my thoughts, brooding on the Bart, I should of course have exercised reasonable precautions; but, as it was, I turned the corner into the Fulham Road in what you might call a brown study; and the first thing I knew my top hat had been whisked off my head and was tooling along briskly in the direction of Putney.

Well, you know what the Fulham Road's like. A top hat has about as much chance in it as a rabbit at a dog show. I dashed after the thing with all possible speed, but what was the use? A taxicab knocked it sideways toward a bus; and the bus, curse it, did the rest. By the time the traffic had cleared a bit, I caught sight of the ruins and turned away with a silent groan. The thing wasn't worth picking up.

So there I was, dished.

Or, rather, what the casual observer who didn't know my enterprise and resource would have called dished. For a man like me, Corky, may be down, but he is never out. So swift were my mental processes that the time that elapsed between the sight of that ruined hat and my decision to pop round to the Foreign Office and touch George Tupper for another fiver was not more than fifty seconds. It is in the crises of life that brains really tell.

You can't accumulate if you don't speculate. So, though funds were running a bit low by this time, I invested a couple of bob in a cab. It was better to be two shillings out than to risk getting to the Foreign Office and finding that Tuppy had left.

Well, late though it was, he was still there. That's one of the things I like about George Tupper, one of the reasons why I always maintain that he will rise to impressive heights in his country's service— he does not shirk; he is not a clock watcher. Many civil servants are apt to call it a day at five o'clock, but not George Tupper. That is why one of these days, Corky, when you are still struggling along turning out articles for *Interesting Bits* and writing footling short stories about girls who turn out to be the missing heiress, Tuppy will be Sir George Tupper, K.C.M.G., and a devil of a fellow among the chancelleries.

I found him up to his eyes in official-looking papers, and I came to the point with all speed. I knew that he was probably busy declaring war on Montenegro or somewhere and wouldn't want a lot of idle chatter.

"Tuppy, old horse," I said, "it is imperative that I have a fiver immediately."

"A what?" said Tuppy.

"A tenner," I said.

It was at this point that I was horrified to observe in the man's eye that rather cold, forbidding look which you sometimes see in blokes' eyes on these occasions.

"I lent you five pounds only a week ago," he said.

"And may Heaven reward you, old horse," I replied courteously.

"What do you want any more for?"

I was just about to tell him the whole circumstances when it was as if a voice whispered to me: "Don't do it!" Something told me that Tuppy was in a nasty frame of mind and was going to turn me down —yes, me, an old schoolfellow, who had known him since he was in Eton collars. And at the same time I suddenly perceived, lying on a chair by the door, Tuppy's topper. For Tuppy is not one of those civil servants who lounge into Whitehall in flannels and a straw hat. He is a correct dresser, and I honor him for it.

"What on earth," said Tuppy, "do you need money for?"

"Personal expenses, laddie," I replied. "The cost of living is very high these days."

"What you want," said Tuppy, "is work."

"What I want," I reminded him—if old Tuppy has a fault, it is that he will not stick to the point—"is a fiver."

He shook his head in a way I did not like to see.

"It's very bad for you, all this messing about on borrowed money. It's not that I grudge it to you," said Tuppy; and I knew, when I heard him talk in that pompous, Foreign Official way, that something had gone wrong that day in the country's service. Probably the draft treaty with Switzerland had been pinched by a foreign adventuress. That sort of thing is happening all the time in the Foreign Office. Mysterious veiled women blow in on old Tuppy and engage him in conversation, and when he turns round he finds the long blue envelope with the important papers in it gone.

"It's not that I grudge you the money," said Tuppy, "but you really ought to be in some regular job. I must think," said Tuppy, "I must think. I must have a look round."

"And meanwhile," I said, "the fiver?"

"No. I'm not going to give it to you."

"Only five pounds," I urged. "Five little pounds, Tuppy, old horse."

"No."

"You can chalk it up in the books to Office Expenses and throw the burden on the taxpayer."

"No."

"Will nothing move you?"

"No. And I'm awfully sorry, old man, but I must ask you to clear out now. I'm terribly busy."

"Oh, right-ho," I said.

He burrowed down into the documents again; and I moved to the door, scooped up the top hat from the chair, and passed out.

Next morning, when I was having a bit of breakfast, in rolled old Tuppy.

"I say," said Tuppy.

"Say on, laddie."

"You know when you came to see me yesterday?"

"Yes. You've come to tell me you've changed your mind about that fiver?"

"No, I haven't come to tell you I've changed my mind about that fiver. I was going to say that, when I started to leave the office, I found my top hat had gone."

"Too bad," I said.

Tuppy gave me a piercing glance.

"You didn't take it, I suppose?"

"Who, me? What would I want with a top hat?"

"Well, it's very mysterious."

"I expect you'll find it was pinched by an international spy or something."

Tuppy brooded for some moments.

"It's all very odd," he said. "I've never had it happen to me before."

"One gets new experiences."

"Well, never mind about that. What I really came about was to tell you that I think I have got you a job."

"You don't mean that!"

"I met a man at the club last night who wants a secretary. It's more a matter with him of having somebody to keep his papers in order and all that sort of thing, so typing and shorthand are not essential. You can't do shorthand, I suppose?"

"I don't know. I've never tried."

"Well, you're to go and see him tomorrow morning at ten. His name's Bulstrode, and you'll find him at my club. It's a good chance, so for Heaven's sake don't be lounging in bed at ten."

"I won't. I'll be up and ready, with a heart for any fate."

"Well, mind you are."

"And I am deeply grateful, Tuppy, old horse, for these esteemed favors."

"That's all right," said Tuppy. He paused at the door. "It's a mystery about that hat."

"Insoluble, I should say. I shouldn't worry any more about it."

"One moment it was there, and the next it had gone."

"How like life!" I said. "Makes one think a bit, that sort of thing."

He pushed off, and I was just finishing my breakfast when Mrs. Beale, my landlady, came in with a letter.

It was from Mabel, reminding me to be sure to come to Ascot. I read it three times while I was consuming a fried egg; and I am not ashamed to say, Corky, that tears filled my eyes. To think of her caring so much that she should send special letters urging me to be there made me tremble like a leaf. It looked to me as though the Bart's number was up. Yes, at that moment, Corky, I felt positively sorry for the Bart, who was in his way quite a good chap, though pimply.

That night I made my final preparations. I counted the cash in hand. I had just enough to pay my fare to Ascot and back, my entrance fee to the grandstand and paddock, with a matter of fifteen bob over for lunch and general expenses and a thoughtful ten bob to do a bit of betting with. Financially, I was on velvet.

Nor was there much wrong with the costume department. I dug out the trousers, the morning coat, the waistcoat, the shoes and the spats, and I tried on Tuppy's topper again. And for the twentieth time I wished that old Tuppy, a man of sterling qualities in every other respect, had had a slightly bigger head. It's a curious thing about old George Tupper. There's a man who you might say is practically directing the destinies of a great nation—at any rate, he's in the Foreign Office and extremely well thought of by the Nibs—and yet his size in hats is a small seven. I don't know if you've ever noticed that Tuppy's head goes up to a sort of point. Mine, on the other hand, is shaped more like a turnip, and this made the whole thing rather complex and unpleasant.

As I stood looking in the glass, giving myself a final inspection, I couldn't help feeling what a difference a hat makes to a man. Bareheaded, I was perfect in every detail; but with a hat on I looked a good deal like a bloke about to go on and do a comic song at one of the halls. Still, there it was, and it was no good worrying about it. I put the trousers under the mattress, to ensure an adequate crease; and I rang the bell for Mrs. Beale and gave her the coat to press with a hot iron. I also gave her the hat and instructed her to rub stout on it. This, as you doubtless know, gives a topper the deuce of a gloss; and when a fellow is up against a Bart, he can't afford to neglect the smallest detail.

And so to bed.

I didn't sleep very well. At about one in the morning it started to rain in buckets, and the thought suddenly struck me: what the deuce was I going to do if it rained during the day? To buy an umbrella would simply dislocate the budget beyond repair. The consequence was that I tossed pretty restlessly on my pillow.

But all was well. When I woke at eight o'clock the sun was pouring into the room, and the last snag seemed to have been removed from my path. I had breakfast, and then I dug the trouserings out from under the mattress, slipped into them, put on the shoes, buckled the spats, and rang the bell for Mrs. Beale. I was feeling debonair to a degree. The crease in the trousers was perfect.

"Oh, Mrs. Beale," I said. "The coat and the hat, please. What a lovely morning!"

Now, this Beale woman, I must tell you, was a slightly sinister sort of female, with eyes that reminded me a good deal of my Aunt Julia. And I was now somewhat rattled to perceive that she was looking at me in a rather meaning kind of manner. I also perceived that she held in her hand a paper or document. And there shot through me, Corky, a nameless fear.

It's a kind of instinct, I suppose. A man who has been up against it as frequently as I have comes to shudder automatically when he sees a landlady holding a sheet of paper and looking at him in a meaning manner.

A moment later it was plain that my sixth sense had not deceived me.

"I've brought your little account, Mr. Ukridge," said this fearful female.

"Right!" I said heartily. "Just shove it on the table, will you? And bring the coat and hat."

She looked more like my Aunt Julia than ever.

"I must ask you for the money now," she said. "Being a week overdue."

All this was taking the sunshine out of the morning, but I remained debonair.

"Yes, yes," I said. "I quite understand. We'll have a good long talk about that later. The hat and coat, please, Mrs. Beale."

"I must ask you—" she was beginning again, but I checked her with one of my looks. If there's one thing I bar in this world, Corky, it's sordidness.

"Yes, yes," I said testily. "Some other time. I want the hat and coat, please."

At this moment, by the greatest bad luck, her vampire gaze fell on the mantelpiece. You know how it is when you are dressing with unusual care—you fill your pockets last thing. And I had most unfortunately placed my little capital on the mantelpiece. Too late I saw that she had spotted it. Take the advice of a man who has seen something of life, Corky, and never leave your money lying about. It's bound to start a disagreeable train of thought in the mind of anyone who sees it.

"You've got the money there," said Mrs. Beale.

I leaped for the mantelpiece and trousered the cash.

"No, no," I said hastily. "You can't have that. I need that."

"Ho?" she said. "So do I."

"Now listen, Mrs. Beale," I said. "You know as well as I do—"

"I know as well as you do that you owe me two pounds three and sixpence ha'penny."

"And in God's good time," I said, "you shall have it. But just for the moment you must be patient. Why, dash it, Mrs. Beale," I said warmly, "you know as well as I do that in all financial transactions a certain amount of credit is an understood thing. Credit is the lifeblood of commerce. So bring the hat and coat, and later on we will thresh this matter out thoroughly."

And then this woman showed a baseness of soul, a horrible low cunning, which, I like to think, is rarely seen in the female sex.

"I'll either have the money," she said, "or I'll keep the coat and hat." And words cannot express, Corky, the hideous malignity in her voice. "They ought to fetch a bit."

I stared at her, appalled.

"But I can't go to Ascot without a top hat."

"Then you'd better not go to Ascot."

"Be reasonable!" I begged. "Reflect!"

It was no good. She stood firm on her demand for two pounds three and sixpence ha'penny, and nothing that I could say would shift her. I offered her double the sum at some future date, but no business was done. The curse of landladies as a class, Corky, and the reason why they never rise to ease and opulence is that they have no vision. They do not understand high finance. They lack the big, broad, flexible outlook which wins to wealth. The deadlock continued, and finally she went off, leaving me dished once more.

It is only when you are in a situation like that, Corky, that you really begin to be able to appreciate the true hollowness of the world. It is only then that the absolute silliness and futility of human institutions comes home to you. This Ascot business, for instance. Why in the name of Heaven, if you are going to hold a race meeting, should you make a foolish regulation about the sort of costume people must wear if they want to attend it? Why should it be necessary to wear a top hat at Ascot, when you can go to all the other races in anything you like?

Here was I, perfectly equipped for Hurst Park, Sandown, Gatwick, Ally Pally, Lingfield, or any other meeting you care to name; and, simply because a ghoul of a landlady had pinched my topper, I was utterly debarred from going to Ascot, though the price of admission was bulging in my pocket. It's just that sort of thing that makes a fellow chafe at our modern civilization and wonder if, after all, Man can be Nature's last word.

Such, Corky, were my meditations as I stood at the window and gazed bleakly out at the sunshine. And then suddenly, as I gazed, I observed a bloke approaching up the street.

I eyed him with interest. He was an elderly, prosperous bloke with a yellowish face and a white mustache, and he was looking at the numbers on the doors, as if he were trying to spot a destination. And at this moment he halted outside the front door of my house, squinted up at the number, and then trotted up the steps and rang the bell. And I realized at once that this must be Tuppy's secretary man, the fellow I was due to go and see at the club in another half-hour. For a moment it seemed odd that he should have come to call on me instead of waiting for me to call on him; and then I reflected that this was just the sort of thing that the energetic, world's-worker type of man that Tuppy chummed up with at his club would be likely to do. Time is money with these coves, and no doubt he had remembered some other appointment which he couldn't make if he waited at his club till ten.

Anyway, here he was, and I peered down at him with a beating heart. For what sent a thrill through me, Corky, was the fact that he was much about my build and was brightly clad in correct morning costume with top hat complete. And though it was hard to tell exactly at such a distance and elevation, the thought flashed across me like an inspiration from above that that top hat would fit me a dashed sight better than Tuppy's had done.

In another minute there was a knock on the door, and he came in.

Seeing him at close range, I perceived that I had not misjudged this man. He was shortish, but his shoulders were just about the same size as mine, and his head was large and round. If ever, in a word, a bloke might have been designed by Providence to wear a coat and hat that would fit me, this bloke was that bloke. I gazed at him with a gleaming eye.

"Mr. Ukridge?"

"Yes," I said. "Come in. Awfully good of you to call."

"Not at all."

And now, Corky, as you will no doubt have divined, I was, so to speak, at the crossroads. The finger-post of Prudence pointed one way, that of Love another. Prudence whispered to me to conciliate this bloke, to speak him fair, to comport myself toward him as toward one who held my destinies in his hand and who could, if well disposed, give me a job which would keep the wolf from the door while I was looking round for something bigger and more attuned to my vision and abilities.

Love, on the other hand, was shouting to me to pinch his coat and hat and leg it for the open spaces.

It was the deuce of a dilemma.

"I have called—" began the bloke.

I made up my mind. Love got the decision.

"I say," I said. "I think you've got something on the back of your coat."

"Eh?" said the bloke, trying to squint round and look between his shoulder blades—silly ass.

"It's a squashed tomato or something."

"A squashed tomato?"

"Or something."

"How would I get a squashed tomato on my coat?"

"Ah!" I said, giving him to understand with a wave of the hand that these were deep matters.

"Very curious," said the bloke.

"Very," I said. "Slip off your coat and let's have a look at it."

He slid out of the coat, and I was on it like a knife. You have to move quick on these occasions, and I moved quick. I had the coat out of his hand and the top hat off the table where he had put it, and was out of the door and dashing down the stairs before he could utter a yip.

I put on the coat, and it fitted like a glove. I slapped the top hat on to my head, and it might have been made for me. And then I went out into the sunshine, as natty a specimen as ever paced down Piccadilly.

I was passing down the front steps when I heard a sort of bellow from above. There was the bloke, protruding from the window; and, strong man though I am, Corky, I admit that for an instant I quailed at the sight of the hideous fury that distorted his countenance.

"Come back!" shouted the bloke.

Well, it wasn't a time for standing and making explanations and generally exchanging idle chatter. When a man is leaning out of window in his shirt sleves, making the amount of noise that this cove was making, it doesn't take long for a crowd to gather. And my experience has been that, when a crowd gathers, it isn't much longer before some infernal, officious policeman rolls round as well. Nothing was farther from my wishes than to have this little purely private affair between the bloke and myself sifted by a policeman in front of a large crowd.

So I didn't linger. I waved my hand as much as to say that all would come right in the future, and then I nipped at a fairly high rate of speed round the corner and hailed a taxi. It had been no part of my plans to incur the expense of a taxi, I having earmarked two-pence for a ride on the Tube to Waterloo; but there are times when economy is false prudence.

Once in the cab, whizzing along and putting more distance between the bloke and myself with every revolution of the wheels, I perked up amazingly. I had been, I confess, a trifle apprehensive until now; but from this moment everything seemed splendid. I forgot to mention it before, but this final top hat which now nestled so snugly on the brow was a gray top hat; and, if there is one thing that really lends a zip and a sort of devilish fascination to a fellow's appearance, it is one of those gray toppers. As I looked at myself in the glass and then gazed out of window at the gay sunshine, it seemed to me that God was in His Heaven and all was right with the world.

The general excellence of things continued. I had a pleasant journey; and when I got to Ascot I planked my ten bob on a horse I had heard some fellows talking about in the train, and, by Jove, it ambled home at a crisp ten to one. So there I was, five quid ahead of the game almost, you might say, before I had got there. It was with an uplifted heart, Corky, that I strolled off to the paddock to have a look at the multitude and try to find Mabel. And I had hardly emerged from that tunnel thing that you have to walk through to get from the stand to the paddock when I ran into old Tuppy.

My first feeling on observing the dear old chap was one of relief that I wasn't wearing his hat. Old Tuppy is one of the best, but little things are apt to upset him, and I was in no mood for a painful scene. I passed the time of day genially.

"Ah, Tuppy!" I said.

George Tupper is a man with a heart of gold, but he is deficient in tact.

"How the deuce did you get here?" he asked.

"In the ordinary way, laddie," I said.

"I mean, what are you doing here, dressed up to the nines like this?"

"Naturally," I replied, with a touch of stiffness, "when I come to Ascot, I wear the accepted morning costume of the well-dressed Englishman."

"You look as if you had come into a fortune."

"Yes?" I said, rather wishing he would change the subject. In spite of what you might call the perfect alibi of the gray topper, I did not want to discuss hats and clothes with Tuppy so soon after his recent bereavement. I could see that the hat he had on was a brand-new one and must have set him back at least a couple of quid.

"I suppose you've gone back to your aunt?" said Tuppy, jumping at a plausible solution. "Well, I'm awfully glad, old man, because I'm afraid that secretary job is off. I was going to write to you tonight."

"Off?" I said. Having had the advantage of seeing the bloke's face as he hung out of window at the moment of our parting, I knew it was off; but I couldn't see how Tuppy could know.

"He rang me up last night, to tell me that he was afraid you wouldn't do, as he had thought it over and decided that he must have a secretary who knew shorthand."

"Oh?" I said. "Oh, did he? Then I'm dashed glad," I said warmly, "that I pinched his hat. It will be a sharp lesson to him not to raise people's hopes and shilly-shally in this manner."

"Pinched his hat? What do you mean?"

I perceived that there was need for caution. Tuppy was looking at me in an odd manner, and I could see that the turn the conversation had taken was once more wakening in him suspicions which he ought to have known better than to entertain of an old school friend.

"It was like this, Tuppy," I said. "When you came to me and told me about that international spy sneaking your hat from the Foreign Office, it gave me an idea. I had been wanting to come to Ascot, but I had no topper. Of course, if I had pinched yours, as you imagined for a moment I had done, I should have had one; but, not having pinched yours, of course I hadn't one. So when your friend Bulstrode called on me this morning I collared his. And now that you have revealed to me what a fickle, changeable character he is, I'm very glad I did."

Tuppy gaped slightly.

"Bulstrode called on you this morning, did you say?"

"This morning at about half-past nine."

"He couldn't have done."

"Then how do you account for my having his hat? Pull yourself together, Tuppy, old horse."

"The man who came to see you couldn't have been Bulstrode."

"Why not?"

"He left for Paris last night."

"What!"

"He phoned me from the station just before his train started. He had had to change his plans."

"Then who was the bloke?" I said.

The thing seemed to me to have the makings of one of those great historic mysteries you read about. I saw no reason why posterity should not discuss for ever the problem of the bloke in the gray topper as keenly as they do the man in the iron mask. "The facts," I said, "are precisely as I have stated. At nine-thirty this morning a bird, gaily appareled in morning coat, spongebag trousers, and gray top hat, presented himself at my rooms and—"

At this moment a voice spoke behind me.

"Oh, hullo!"

I turned and observed the Bart.

"Hullo!" I said.

I introduced Tuppy. The Bart nodded courteously.

"I say," said the Bart. "Where's the old man?"

"What old man?"

"Mabel's father. Didn't he catch you?"

I stared at the man. He appeared to me to be gibbering. And a gibbering Bart is a nasty thing to have hanging about you before you have strengthened yourself with a bit of lunch.

"Mabel's father's in Singapore," I said.

"No, he isn't," said the Bart. "He got home yesterday, and Mabel sent him round to your place to pick you up and bring you down here in the car. Had you left before he arrived?"

Well, that's where the story ends, Corky. From the moment that pimply Baronet uttered those words, you might say that I faded out of the picture. I never went near Onslow Square again. Nobody can say that I lack nerve, but I hadn't nerve enough to creep into the family circle and resume acquaintance with that fearsome bloke. There are some men, no doubt, with whom I might have been able to pass the whole thing off with a light laugh, but that glimpse I had had of him as he bellowed out of the window told me that he was not one of them. I faded away, Corky, old horse, just faded away. And about a couple of months later I read in the paper that Mabel had married the Bart.

Ukridge sighed another sigh and heaved himself up from the sofa. Outside the world was blue-gray with the growing dawn, and even the later birds were busy among the worms.

"You might make a story out of that, Corky," said Ukridge.

"I might," I said.

"All profits to be shared on a strict fifty-fifty basis, of course."

"Of course."

Ukridge brooded.

"Though it really wants a bigger man to do it justice and tell it properly, bringing out all the fine shades of the tragedy. It wants somebody like Thomas Hardy or Kipling, or somebody."

"Better let me have a shot at it."

"All right," said Ukridge. "And, as regards a title, I should call it 'His Lost Romance,' or something like that. Or would you suggest simply something terse and telling, like 'Fate' or 'Destiny'?"

"I'll think of a title," I said.

❀ Buttercup Day

"LADDIE," said Ukridge, "I need capital, old horse—need it sorely."

He removed his glistening silk hat, looked at it in a puzzled way, and replaced it on his head. We had met by chance near the eastern end of Piccadilly, and the breath-taking gorgeousness of his costume told me that, since I had seen him last, there must have occurred between him and his Aunt Julia one of those periodical reconciliations which were wont to punctuate his hectic and disreputable career. For those who know Stanley Featherstonehaugh Ukridge, that much-enduring man, are aware that he is the nephew of Miss Julia Ukridge, the wealthy and popular novelist, and that from time to time, when she can bring herself to forgive and let bygones be bygones, he goes to dwell for a while in gilded servitude at her house in Wimbledon.

"Yes, Corky, my boy, I want a bit of capital."

"Oh?"

"And want it quick. The truest saying in this world is that you can't accumulate if you don't speculate. But how the deuce are you to start speculating unless you accumulate a few quid to begin with?"

"Ah," I said noncommittally.

"Take my case," proceeded Ukridge, running a large, beautifully gloved finger round the inside of a spotless collar which appeared to fit a trifle too snugly to the neck. "I have an absolutely safe double for Kempton Park on the fifteenth, and even a modest investment would bring me in several hundred pounds. But bookies, blast them, require cash down in advance, so where am I? Without capital, enterprise is strangled at birth."

"Can't you get some from your aunt?"

"Not a cent. She is one of those women who simply do not disgorge. All her surplus cash is devoted to adding to her collection of moldy snuffboxes. When I look at those snuffboxes and reflect that any single one of them, judiciously put up the spout, would set my feet on the road to Fortune, only my innate sense of honesty keeps me from pinching them."

"You mean they're locked up?"

"It's hard, laddie. Very hard and bitter and ironical. She buys me suits. She buys me hats. She buys me boots. She buys me spats. And, what is more, insists on my wearing the damned things. With what result? Not only am I infernally uncomfortable, but my exterior creates a totally false impression in the minds of any blokes I meet to whom I may happen to owe a bit of money. When I go about looking as if I owned the Mint, it becomes difficult to convince them that I am not in a position to pay them their beastly one pound fourteen and eleven, or whatever it is. I tell you, laddie, the strain has begun to weigh upon me to such an extent that the breaking point may arrive at any moment. Every day it is becoming more imperative that I clear out and start life again upon my own. But this cannot be done without cash. And that is why I look around me and say to myself: 'How am I to acquire a bit of capital?' "

I thought it best to observe at this point that my own circumstances were extremely straitened. Ukridge received the information with a sad, indulgent smile.

"I was not dreaming of biting your ear, old horse," he said. "What I require is something far beyond your power to supply. Five pounds at least. Or three, anyway. Of course, if, before we part, you think fit to hand over a couple of bob or half-a-crown as a small temporary—"

He broke off with a start, and there came into his face the look of one who has perceived snakes in his path. He gazed along the street; then, wheeling round, hurried abruptly down Church Place.

"One of your creditors?" I asked.

"Girl with flags," said Ukridge briefly. A peevish note crept into his voice. "This modern practice, laddie, of allowing females with trays of flags and collecting boxes to flood the Metropolis is developing into a scourge. If it isn't Rose Day it's Daisy Day, and if it isn't Daisy Day it's Pansy Day. And though now, thanks to a bit of quick thinking, we have managed to escape without—"

At this moment a second flag girl, emerging from Jermyn Street, held us up with a brilliant smile, and we gave till it hurt—which, in Ukridge's case, was almost immediately.

"And so it goes on," he said bitterly. "Sixpence here, a shilling there. Only last Friday I was touched for twopence at my very door. How can a man amass a huge fortune if there is this constant drain on his resources? What was that girl collecting for?"

"I didn't notice."

"Nor did I. One never does. For all we know, we may have contributed to some cause of which we heartily disapprove. And that reminds me, Corky, my aunt is lending her grounds on Tuesday for a bazaar in aid of the local Temperance League. I particularly wish you to put aside all other engagements and roll up."

"No, thanks. I don't want to meet your aunt again."

"You won't meet her. She will be away. She's going north on a lecturing tour."

"Well, I don't want to come to any bazaar. I can't afford it."

"Have no fear, laddie. There will be no expense involved. You will pass the entire afternoon in the house with me. My aunt, though she couldn't get out of lending these people her grounds, is scared that, with so many strangers prowling about, somebody might edge in and sneak her snuffboxes. So I am left on guard, with instructions not to stir out till they've all gone. And a very wise precaution, too. There is absolutely nothing which blokes whose passions have been inflamed by constant ginger beer will stick at. You will share my vigil. We will smoke a pipe or two in the study, talk of this and that, and it may be that, if we put our heads together, we shall be able to think up a scheme for collecting a bit of capital."

"Oh, well, in that case——"

"I shall rely on you. And now, if I don't want to be late, I'd better be getting along. I'm lunching with my aunt at Prince's."

He gazed malevolently at the flag girl, who had just stopped another pedestrian, and strode off.

Heath House, Wimbledon, the residence of Miss Julia Ukridge, was one of that row of large mansions which face the Common, standing back from the road in the seclusion of spacious grounds. On any normal day, the prevailing note of the place would have been a dignified calm; but when I arrived on the Tuesday afternoon a vast and unusual activity was in progress. Over the gates there hung large banners advertising the bazaar, and through these gates crowds of people were passing. From somewhere in the interior of the garden came the brassy music of a merry-go-round. I added myself to the throng, and was making for the front door when a silvery voice spoke in my ear, and I was aware of a very pretty girl at my elbow.

"Buy a buttercup?"

"I beg your pardon?"

"Buy a buttercup?"

I then perceived that, attached to her person with a strap, she carried a tray containing a mass of yellow paper objects.

"What's all this?" I inquired, automatically feeling in my pocket.

She beamed upon me like a high priestess initiating some favorite novice into a rite.

"Buttercup Day," she said winningly.

A man of greater strength of mind would, no doubt, have asked what Buttercup Day was, but I have a spine of wax. I produced the first decent-sized coin on which my fumbling fingers rested, and slipped it into her box. She thanked me with a good deal of fervor and pinned one of the yellow objects in my buttonhole.

The interview then terminated. The girl flitted off like a sunbeam in the direction of a prosperous-looking man who had just gone by, and I went on to the house, where I found Ukridge in the study gazing earnestly through the French windows which commanded a view of the grounds. He turned as I entered; and, as his eye fell upon the saffron ornament in my coat, a soft smile of pleasure played about his mouth.

"I see you've got one," he said.

"Got what?"

"One of those thingummies."

"Oh, these? Yes. There was a girl with a tray of them in the front garden. It's Buttercup Day. In aid of something or other, I suppose."

"It's in aid of me," said Ukridge, the soft smile developing into a face-splitting grin.

"What do you mean?"

"Corky, old horse," said Ukridge, motioning me to a chair, "the great thing in this world is to have a good, level business head. Many men in my position wanting capital and not seeing where they were going to get it, would have given up the struggle as a bad job. Why? Because they lacked Vision and the big, broad, flexible outlook. But what did I do? I sat down and thought. And after many hours of concentrated meditation I was rewarded with an idea. You remember that painful affair in Jermyn Street the other day—when that female bandit got into our ribs? You recall that neither of us knew what we had coughed up our good money for?"

"Well?"

"Well, laddie, it suddenly flashed upon me like an inspiration from above that nobody ever does know what they are coughing up for when they meet a girl with a tray of flags. I hit upon the great truth, old horse—one of the profoundest truths in this modern civilization of ours—that any given man, confronted by a pretty girl with a tray of flags, will automatically and without inquiry shove a coin in her box. So I got hold of a girl I know—a dear little soul, full of beans—

and arranged for her to come here this afternoon. I confidently anticipate a cleanup on an impressive scale. The outlay on the pins and bits of paper was practically nil, so there is no overhead and all that comes in will be pure velvet."

A strong pang shot through me.

"Do you mean to say," I demanded with feeling, "that that half-crown of mine goes into your beastly pocket?"

"Half of it. Naturally my colleague and partner is in on the division. Did you really give half-a-crown?" said Ukridge, pleased. "It was like you, laddie. Generous to a fault. If everyone had your lavish disposition, this world would be a better, sweeter place."

"I suppose you realize," I said, "that in about ten minutes at the outside your colleague and partner, as you call her, will be arrested for obtaining money under false pretenses?"

"Not a chance."

"After which, they will—thank God!—proceed to pinch you."

"Quite impossible, laddie. I rely on my knowledge of human psychology. What did she say when she stung you?"

"I forget. 'Buy a buttercup' or something."

"And then?"

"Then I asked what it was all about, and she said, 'Buttercup Day.' "

"Exactly. And that's all she will need to say to anyone. Is it likely, is it reasonable to suppose, that even in these materialistic days Chivalry has sunk so low that any man will require to be told more, by a girl as pretty as that, than that it is Buttercup Day?" He walked to the window and looked out. "Ah! She's come round into the back garden," he said, with satisfaction. "She seems to be doing a roaring trade. Every second man is wearing a buttercup. She is now putting it across a curate, bless her heart."

"And in a couple of minutes she will probably try to put it across a plain-clothes detective, and that will be the end."

Ukridge eyed me reproachfully.

"You persist in looking on the gloomy side, Corky. A little more of the congratulatory attitude is what I could wish to see in you, laddie. You do not appear to realize that your old friend's foot is at last on the ladder that leads to wealth. Suppose—putting it at the lowest figure—I net four pounds out of this buttercup business. It goes on Caterpillar in the two o'clock selling race at Kempton. Caterpillar wins, the odds being—let us say—ten to one. Stake and winnings go on Bismuth for the Jubilee Cup, again at ten to one. There you have a nice, clean four hundred pounds of capital, ample for a man of keen business sense to build a fortune on. For, between ourselves, Corky, I have my eye on what looks like the investment of a lifetime."

"Yes?"

"Yes. I was reading about it the other day. A cat ranch out in America."

"A cat ranch?"

"That's it. You collect a hundred thousand cats. Each cat has twelve kittens a year. The skins range from ten cents each for the white ones to seventy-five for the pure black. That gives you twelve million skins per year to sell at an average price of thirty cents per skin, making your annual revenue at a conservative estimate three hundred and sixty thousand dollars. But, you will say, what about overhead expenses?"

"Will I?"

"That has all been allowed for. To feed the cats you start a rat ranch next door. The rats multiply four times as fast as cats, so if you begin with a million rats it gives you four rats per day per cat, which is plenty. You feed the rats on what is left over of the cats after removing the skins, allowing one fourth of a cat per rat, the business thus becoming automatically self-supporting. The cats will eat the rats, the rats will eat the cats—"

There was a knock upon the door.

"Come in," bellowed Ukridge irritably. These captains of industry hate to be interrupted when in conference.

It was the butler who had broken in upon his statistics.

"A gentleman to see you, sir," said he.

"Who is he?"

"He did not give his name, sir. He is a gentleman in Holy Orders."

"Not the vicar?" cried Ukridge, in alarm.

"No, sir. The gentleman is a curate. He inquired for Miss Ukridge. I informed him that Miss Ukridge was absent, but that you were on the premises, and he then desired to see you, sir."

"Oh, all right," said Ukridge resignedly. "Show him in. Though we are running grave risks, Corky," he added, as the door closed. "These curates frequently have subscription lists up their sleeves and are extremely apt, unless you are very firm, to soak you for a donation to the Church Organ Fund or something. Still, let us hope—"

The door opened, and our visitor entered. He was a rather small size in curates, with an engaging, ingenuous face, adorned with a pair of pince-nez. He wore a paper buttercup in his coat; and, directly he began to speak, revealed himself as the possessor of a peculiar stammer.

"Pup-pup-pup—" he said.

"Eh?" said Ukridge.

"Mr. pup-pup-pup Ukridge?"

"Yes. This is my friend, Mr. Corcoran."

I bowed. The curate bowed.

"Take a seat," urged Ukridge hospitably. "You'll have a drink?"

The visitor raised a deprecatory hand.

"No, thank you," he replied. "I find it more beneficial to my health to abstain entirely from alcoholic liquids. At the University I was a moderate drinker, but since I came down I have found it better to pup-pup-pup completely. But pray do not let me stop you. I am no bigot."

He beamed for an instant in friendly fashion; then there came into his face a look of gravity. Here was a man, one perceived, who had something on his mind.

"I came here, Mr. Ukridge," he said, "on a pup-pup-pup-pup-pup—"

"Parish matter?" I hazarded, to help him out.

He shook his head.

"No, a pup-pup-pup—"

"Pleasure trip?" suggested Ukridge.

He shook his head again.

"No, a pup-pup-pup uncongenial errand. I understand that Miss Ukridge is absent and that you, as her nephew, are, therefore, the presiding genius, if I may use the expression, of these pup-pup-pup festivities."

"Eh?" said Ukridge, fogged.

"I mean that it is to you that complaints should be made."

"Complaints?"

"Of what is going on in Miss Ukridge's garden—one might say under her imprimatur."

Ukridge's classical education had been cut short by the fact that at an early age he had unfortunately been expelled from the school of which in boyhood's days we had been fellow members, and Latin small talk was not his forte. This one passed well over his head. He looked at me plaintively, and I translated.

"He means," I said, "that your aunt lent her grounds for this binge and so has a right to early information about any rough stuff that is being pulled on the premises."

"Exactly," said the curate.

"But, dash it, laddie," protested Ukridge, now abreast of the situation, "it's no good complaining of anything that happens at a charity bazaar. You know as well as I do that, when the members of a Temperance League get together and start selling things at stalls, anything goes except gouging and biting. The only thing to do is to be light on your feet and keep away."

The curate shook his head sadly.

"I have no complaint to make concerning the manner in which the stalls are being conducted, Mr. pup-pup-pup. It is only to be expected that at a bazaar in aid of a deserving cause the prices of the various articles on sale will be in excess of those charged in the ordinary marts of trade. But deliberate and calculated swindling is another matter."

"Swindling?"

"There is a young woman in the grounds extorting money from the public on the plea that it is Buttercup Day. And here is the point, Mr. Ukridge. Buttercup Day is the flag day of the National Orthopedic Institute, and is not to take place for some weeks. This young person is deliberately cheating the public."

Ukridge licked his lips, with a hunted expression.

"Probably a local institution of the same name," I suggested.

"That's it," said Ukridge gratefully. "Just what I was going to say myself. Probably a local institution. Fresh Air Fund for the poor of the neighborhood, I shouldn't wonder. I believe I've heard them talk about it, now I come to think."

The curate refused to consider the theory.

"No," he said. "If that had been so the young woman would have informed me. In answer to my questions, her manner was evasive and I could elicit no satisfactory reply. She merely smiled and repeated the words 'Buttercup Day.' I feel that the police should be called in."

"The police!" gurgled Ukridge pallidly.

"It is our pup-pup duty," said the curate, looking like a man who writes letters to the Press signed "Pro Bono Publico."

Ukridge shot out of his chair with a convulsive bound. He grasped my arm and led me to the door.

"Excuse me," he said. "Corky," he whispered tensely, dragging me out into the passage, "go and tell her to leg it—quick!"

"Right!" I said.

"You will no doubt find a constable in the road," roared Ukridge.

"I bet I will," I replied in a clear, carrying voice.

"We can't have this sort of thing going on here," bellowed Ukridge.

"Certainly not," I shouted with enthusiasm.

He returned to the study, and I went forth upon my errand of mercy. I had reached the front door and was about to open it, when it suddenly opened itself, and the next moment I was gazing into the clear blue eyes of Ukridge's Aunt Julia.

"Oh—ah—er!" I said.

There are certain people in this world in whose presence certain other people can never feel completely at their ease. Notable among the people beneath whose gaze I myself experience a sensation of extreme discomfort and guilt is Miss Julia Ukridge, author of so many widely read novels, and popular after-dinner speaker at the better class of literary reunion. This was the fourth time we had met, and on each of the previous occasions I had felt the same curious illusion of having just committed some particularly unsavory crime and—what is more—of having done it with swollen hands, enlarged feet, and trousers bagging at the knee on a morning when I had omitted to shave.

I stood and gaped. Although she had no doubt made her entry by the simple process of inserting a latchkey in the front door and turning it, her abrupt appearance had on me the effect of a miracle.

"Mr. Corcoran!" she observed, without pleasure.

"Er—"

"What are you doing here?"

An inhospitable remark; but justified, perhaps, by the circumstances of our previous relations—which had not been of the most agreeable.

"I came to see—er—Stanley."

"Oh?"

"He wanted me with him this afternoon."

"Indeed?" she said; and her manner suggested surprise at what she evidently considered a strange and even morbid taste on her nephew's part.

"We thought—we thought—we both thought you were lecturing up north."

"When I arrived at the club for luncheon I found a telegram postponing my visit," she condescended to explain. "Where is Stanley?"

"In your study."

"I will go there. I wish to see him."

I began to feel like Horatius at the Bridge. It seemed to me that, foe of the human race though Ukridge was in so many respects, it was my duty as a lifelong friend to prevent this woman winning through to him until that curate was well out of the way. I have a great belief in woman's intuition, and I was convinced that, should Miss Julia Ukridge learn that there was a girl in her grounds selling paper buttercups for a nonexistent charity, her keen intelligence would leap without the slightest hesitation to the fact of her nephew's complicity in the disgraceful affair. She had had previous experience of Ukridge's financial methods.

In this crisis I thought rapidly.

"Oh, by the way," I said. "It nearly slipped my mind. The—er—the man in charge of all this business told me he particularly wanted to see you directly you came back."

"What do you mean by the man in charge of all this business?"

"The fellow who got up the bazaar, you know."

"Do you mean Mr. Sims, the president of the Temperance League?"

"That's right. He told me he wanted to see you."

"How could he possibly know that I should be coming back?"

"Oh, in case you did, I mean." I had what Ukridge would have called an inspiration from above. "I think he wants you to say a few words."

I doubt if anything else would have shifted her. There came into her eyes, softening their steely glitter for a moment, that strange light which is seen only in the eyes of confirmed public speakers who are asked to say a few words.

"Well, I will go and see him."

She turned away, and I bounded back to the study. The advent of the mistress of the house had materially altered my plans for the afternoon. What I proposed to do now was to inform Ukridge of her arrival, advise him to eject the curate with all possible speed, give him my blessing, and then slide quietly and unostentatiously away, without any further formalities of farewell. I am not unduly sensitive, but there had been that in Miss Ukridge's manner at our recent meeting which told me that I was not her ideal guest.

I entered the study. The curate was gone, and Ukridge, breathing heavily, was fast asleep in an armchair.

The disappearance of the curate puzzled me for a moment. He was rather an insignificant little man, but not so insignificant that I would not have noticed him if he had passed me while I was standing at the front door. And then I saw that the French windows were open.

It seemed to me that there was nothing to keep me. The strong distaste for this house which I had never lost since my first entry into it had been growing, and now the great open spaces called to me with an imperious voice. I turned softly, and found my hostess standing in the doorway.

"Oh, ah!" I said; and once more was afflicted by that curious sensation of having swelled in a very loathsome manner about the hands and feet. I have observed my hands from time to time during my life and have never been struck by anything particularly hideous about them; but whenever I encounter Miss Julia Ukridge they invariably take on the appearance and proportions of uncooked hams.

"Did you tell me, Mr. Corcoran," said the woman in that quiet, purring voice which must lose her so many friends, not only in Wimbledon but in the larger world outside, "that you saw Mr. Sims and he said that he wished to speak to me?"

"That's right."

"Curious," said Miss Ukridge. "I find that Mr. Sims is confined to his bed with a chill and has not been here today."

I could sympathize with Mr. Sims's chills. I felt as if I had caught one myself. I would—possibly—have made some reply, but at this moment an enormous snore proceeded from the armchair behind me, and such was my overwrought condition that I leaped like a young ram.

"Stanley!" cried Miss Ukridge, sighting the chair.

Another snore rumbled through the air, competing with the music of the merry-go-round. Miss Ukridge advanced and shook her nephew's arm.

"I think," I said, being in the frame of mind when one does say silly things of that sort, "I think he's asleep."

"Asleep!" said Miss Ukridge briefly. Her eye fell on the half-empty glass on the table, and she shuddered austerely.

The interpretation which she obviously placed on the matter seemed incredible to me. On the stage and in motion pictures one frequently sees victims of drink keel over in a state of complete unconsciousness after a single glass, but Ukridge was surely of sterner stuff.

"I can't understand it," I said.

"Indeed!" said Miss Ukridge.

"Why, I have only been out of the room half a minute, and when I left him he was talking to a curate."

"A curate?"

"Absolutely a curate. It's hardly likely, is it, that when he was talking to a curate he would—"

My speech for the defense was cut short by a sudden, sharp noise which, proceeding from immediately behind me, caused me once more to quiver convulsively.

"Well, sir?" said Miss Ukridge.

She was looking past me; and, turning, I perceived that a stranger had joined us. He was standing in the French windows, and the noise which had startled me had apparently been caused by him rapping on the glass with the knob of a stick.

"Miss Ukridge?" said the newcomer.

He was one of those hard-faced, keen-eyed men. There clung about him, as he advanced into the room, a subtle air of authority. That he was a man of character and resolution was proved by the fact that he met Miss Ukridge's eye without a tremor.

"I am Miss Ukridge. Might I inquire—"

The visitor looked harder-faced and more keen-eyed than ever.

"My name is Dawson. From the Yard."

"What yard?" asked the lady of the house, who, it seemed, did not read detective stories.

"Scotland Yard!"

"Oh!"

"I have come to warn you, Miss Ukridge," said Mr. Dawson, looking at me as if I were a bloodstain, "to be on your guard. One of the greatest rascals in the profession is hanging about your grounds."

"Then why don't you arrest him?" demanded Miss Ukridge. The visitor smiled faintly.

"Because I want to get him good," he said.

"Get him good? Do you mean reform him?"

"I do not mean reform him," said Mr. Dawson grimly. "I mean that I want to catch him trying on something worth pulling him in for. There's no sense in taking a man like Stuttering Sam for being a suspected person."

"Stuttering Sam!" I cried, and Mr. Dawson eyed me keenly once more, this time almost as intently as if I had been the blunt instrument with which the murder was committed.

"Eh?" he said.

"Oh, nothing. Only it's curious—"

"What's curious?"

"Oh, no, it couldn't be. This fellow was a curate. A most respectable man."

"Have you seen a curate who stuttered?" exclaimed Mr. Dawson.

"Why, yes. He—"

"Hullo!" said Mr. Dawson. "Who's this?"

"That," replied Miss Ukridge, eying the armchair with loathing, "is my nephew Stanley."

"Sound sleeper."

"I prefer not to talk about him."

"Tell me about this curate," said Mr. Dawson brusquely.

"Well, he came in—"

"Came in? In here?"

"Yes."

"Why?"

"Well—"

"He must have had some story. What was it?"

I thought it judicious, in the interests of my sleeping friend, to depart somewhat from the precise truth.

"He—er—I think he said something about being interested in Miss Ukridge's collection of snuffboxes."

"Have you a collection of snuffboxes, Miss Ukridge?"

"Yes."

"Where do you keep them?"

"In the drawing room."

"Take me there, if you please."

"But I don't understand."

Mr. Dawson clicked his tongue in an annoyed manner. He seemed to be an irritable sleuth hound.

"I should have thought the thing was clear enough by this time. This man worms his way into your house with a plausible story, gets rid of this gentleman here— How did he get rid of you?"

"Oh, I just went, you know. I thought I would like a stroll."

"Oh? Well, having contrived to be alone with your nephew, Miss Ukridge, he slips knockout drops in his drink—"

"Knockout drops?"

"A drug of some kind," explained Mr. Dawson, chafing at her slowness of intelligence.

"But the man was a curate!"

Mr. Dawson barked shortly.

"Posing as a curate is the thing Stuttering Sam does best. He works the races in that character. Is this the drawing room?"

It was. And it did not need the sharp, agonized cry which proceeded from its owner's lips to tell us that the worst had happened. The floor was covered with splintered wood and broken glass.

"They've gone!" cried Miss Ukridge.

It is curious how differently the same phenomenon can strike different people. Miss Ukridge was a frozen statue of grief. Mr.

Dawson, on the other hand, seemed pleased. He stroked his short mustache with an air of indulgent complacency, and spoke of neat jobs. He described Stuttering Sam as a Tough Baby, and gave it as his opinion that the absent one might justly be considered one of the lads and not the worst of them.

"What shall I do?" wailed Miss Ukridge. I was sorry for the woman. I did not like her, but she was suffering.

"The first thing to do," said Mr. Dawson briskly, "is to find how much the fellow has got away with. Have you any other valuables in the house?"

"My jewels are in my bedroom."

"Where?"

"I keep them in a box in the dress cupboard."

"Well, it's hardly likely that he would find them there, but I'd better go and see. You be taking a look round in here and make a complete list of what has been stolen."

"All my snuffboxes are gone."

"Well, see if there is anything else missing. Where is your bedroom?"

"On the first floor, facing the front."

"Right."

Mr. Dawson, all briskness and efficiency, left us. I was sorry to see him go. I had an idea that it would not be pleasant being left alone with this bereaved woman. Nor was it.

"Why on earth," said Miss Ukridge, rounding on me as if I had been a relation, "did you not suspect this man when he came in?"

"Why, I—he—"

"A child ought to have been able to tell that he was not a real curate."

"He seemed—"

"Seemed!" She wandered restlessly about the room, and suddenly a sharp cry proceeded from her. "My jade Buddha!"

"I beg your pardon?"

"That scoundrel has stolen my jade Buddha. Go and tell the detective."

"Certainly."

"Go on! What are you waiting for?"

I fumbled at the handle.

"I don't seem able to get the door open," I explained meekly.

"Tchah!" said Miss Ukridge, swooping down. One of the rooted convictions of each member of the human race is that he or she is able without difficulty to open a door which has baffled their fellows.

She took the handle and gave it a vigorous tug. The door creaked but remained unresponsive.

"What's the matter with the thing?" exclaimed Miss Ukridge petulantly.

"It's stuck."

"I know it has stuck. Please do something at once. Good gracious, Mr. Corcoran, surely you are at least able to open a drawing-room door?"

It seemed, put in that tone of voice, a feat sufficiently modest for a man of good physique and fair general education; but I was reluctantly compelled to confess, after a few more experiments, that it was beyond my powers. This appeared to confirm my hostess in the opinion, long held by her, that I was about the most miserable worm that an inscrutable Providence had ever permitted to enter the world.

She did not actually say as much, but she sniffed, and I interpreted her meaning exactly.

"Ring the bell!"

I rang the bell.

"Ring it again!"

I rang it again.

"Shout!"

I shouted.

"Go on shouting!"

I went on shouting. I was in good voice that day. I shouted "Hi!"; I shouted "Here!"; I shouted "Help!"; I also shouted in a broad, general way. It was a performance which should have received more than a word of grateful thanks. But all Miss Ukridge said, when I paused for breath, was:

"Don't whisper!"

I nursed my aching vocal cords in a wounded silence.

"Help!" cried Miss Ukridge.

Considered as a shout, it was not in the same class as mine. It lacked body, vim, and even timbre. But, by that curious irony which governs human affairs, it produced results. Outside the door a thick voice spoke in answer.

"What's up?"

"Open this door!"

The handle rattled.

"It's stuck," said a voice, which I now recognized as that of my old friend, Stanley Featherstonehaugh Ukridge.

"I know it has stuck. Is that you, Stanley? See what is causing it to stick."

A moment of silence followed. Investigations were apparently in progress without.

"There's a wedge jammed under it."

"Well, take it out at once."

"I'll have to get a knife or something."

Another interval for rest and meditation succeeded. Miss Ukridge paced the floor with knit brows; while I sidled into a corner and stood there feeling a little like an inexperienced young animal trainer who has managed to get himself locked into the lions' den and is trying to remember what Lesson Three of his correspondence course said he ought to do in such circumstances.

Footsteps sounded outside, and then a wrenching and scratching. The door opened and we beheld on the mat Ukridge, with a carving knife in his hand, looking headachy and disheveled, and the butler, his professional poise rudely disturbed and his face stained with coal dust.

It was characteristic of Miss Ukridge that it was to the erring domestic rather than the rescuing nephew that she turned first.

"Barter," she hissed, as far as a woman, even of her intellectual gifts, is capable of hissing the word "Barter," "why didn't you come when I rang?"

"I did not hear the bell, madam. I was—"

"You must have heard the bell."

"No, madam."

"Why not?"

"Because I was in the coal cellar, madam."

"What on earth were you doing in the coal cellar?"

"I was induced to go there, madam, by a man. He intimidated me with a pistol. He then locked me in."

"What! What man?"

"A person with a short mustache and penetrating eyes. He—"

A raconteur with a story as interesting as his to tell might reasonably have expected to be allowed to finish it, but butler Barter at this point ceased to grip his audience. With a gasping moan his employer leaped past him, and we heard her running up the stairs.

Ukridge turned to me plaintively.

"What is all this, laddie? Gosh, I've got a headache. What has been happening?"

"The curate put knockout drops in your drink, and then—"

I have seldom seen anyone display such poignant emotion as Ukridge did at that moment.

"The curate! It's a little hard. Upon my Sam, it's a trifle thick.

Corky, old horse, I have traveled all over the world in tramp steamers and what not. I have drunk in waterfront saloons from Montevideo to Cardiff. And the only time anyone has ever succeeded in doctoring the stuff on me it was done in Wimbledon—and by a curate. Tell me, laddie, are all curates like that? Because, if so—"

"He has also pinched your aunt's collection of snuffboxes."

"The curate?"

"Yes."

"Golly!" said Ukridge in a low, reverent voice, and I could see a new respect for the Cloth dawning within him.

"And then this other fellow came along—his accomplice, pretending to be a detective—and locked us in and shut the butler in the coal cellar. And I rather fancy he has got away with your aunt's jewels."

A piercing scream from above rent the air.

"He has," I said briefly. "Well, old man, I think I'll be going."

"Corky," said Ukridge, "stand by me!"

I shook my head.

"In any reasonable circumstances, yes. But I will not meet your aunt again just now. In a year or so, perhaps, but not now."

Hurrying footsteps sounded on the staircase.

"Good-bye," I said, pushing past and heading for the open. "I must be off. Thanks for a very pleasant afternoon."

Money was tight in those days, but it seemed to me next morning that an outlay of twopence on a telephone call to Heath House could not be considered an unjustifiable extravagance. I was conscious of a certain curiosity to learn at long range what had happened after I had removed myself on the previous afternoon.

"Are you there?" said a grave voice in answer to my ring.

"Is that Barter?"

"Yes, sir."

"This is Mr. Corcoran. I want to speak to Mr. Ukridge."

"Mr. Ukridge is no longer here, sir. He left perhaps an hour ago."

"Oh? Do you mean left—er—for ever?"

"Yes, sir."

"Oh! Thanks."

I rang off and, pondering deeply, returned to my rooms. I was not surprised to be informed by Bowles, my landlord, that Ukridge was in my sitting room. It was this storm-tossed man's practice in times of stress to seek refuge with me.

"Hullo, laddie," said Ukridge in a graveyard voice.

"So here you are."

"Here I am."

"She kicked you out?"

Ukridge winced slightly, as at some painful recollection.

"Words passed, old horse, and in the end we decided that we were better apart."

"I don't see why she should blame you for what happened."

"A woman like my aunt, Corky, is capable of blaming anybody for anything. And so I start life again, laddie, a penniless man, with no weapons against the great world but my vision and my brain."

I endeavored to attract his attention to the silver lining.

"You're all right," I said. "You're just where you wanted to be. You have the money which your buttercup girl collected."

A strong spasm shook my poor friend, causing, as always happened with him in moments of mental agony, his collar to shoot off its stud and his glasses to fall from his nose.

"The money that girl collected," he replied, "is not available. It has passed away. I saw her this morning and she told me."

"Told you what?"

"That a curate came up to her in the garden while she was selling those buttercups and—in spite of a strong stammer—put it to her so eloquently that she was obtaining money under false pretenses that she gave him the entire takings for his Church Expenses Fund and went home, resolved to lead a better life. Women are an unstable, emotional sex, laddie. Have as little to do with them as possible. And, for the moment, give me a drink, old horse, and mix it fairly strong. These are the times that try men's souls."

❀ *Ukridge and the Old Stepper*

"CORKY, OLD HORSE," said Stanley Featherstonehaugh Ukridge, in a stunned voice, "this is the most amazing thing I have heard in the whole course of my existence. I'm astounded. You could knock me down with a feather."

"I wish I had one."

"This suit?—this shabby, worn-out suit?—you don't really mean to stand there and tell me that you actually *wanted* this ragged, seedy, battered old suit? Why, upon my honest Sam, when I came on it while rummaging through your belongings yesterday, I thought it was just something you had discarded years ago and forgotten to give to the deserving poor."

I spoke my mind. Any unbiased judge would have admitted that I had cause for warmth. Spring, coming to London in a burst of golden sunshine, was calling imperiously to all young men to rejoice in their youth, to put on their new herringbone-pattern lounge suits and go out and give the populace an eyeful; and this I had been prevented from doing by the fact that my new suit had mysteriously disappeared.

After a separation of twenty-four hours, I had just met it in Piccadilly with Ukridge inside it.

I continued to speak, and was beginning to achieve a certain eloquence, when from a taxicab beside us there alighted a small, dapper old gentleman, who might have been a duke or one of the better-class ambassadors or something of that sort. He wore a pointed white beard, a silk hat, lavender spats, an Ascot tie, and a gardenia; and if anyone had told me that such a man could have even a nodding acquaintance with S. F. Ukridge, I should have laughed hollowly. Furthermore, if I had been informed that Ukridge, warmly greeted by such a man, would have ignored him and passed coldly on, I should have declined to believe it.

Nevertheless, both these miracles happened.

"Stanley!" cried the old gentleman. "Bless my soul, I haven't seen you for years." And he spoke, what is more, as if he regretted the fact, not as if he had had a bit of luck that made my mouth water. "Come and have some lunch, my dear boy."

"Corky," said Ukridge, eying him stonily for a moment and speaking in a low, strained voice, "let us be getting along."

"But did you hear him?" I gasped, as he hurried me away. "He asked you to lunch."

"I heard him. Corky, old boy," said Ukridge gravely, "I'll tell you. That bloke is best avoided."

"Who is he?"

"An uncle of mine."

"But he seemed respectable."

"That is to say, a stepuncle. Or would you call him step-step? He married my late stepmother's stepsister. I'm not half sure," said Ukridge, pondering, "that step-step-step wouldn't be the correct description."

These were deep waters, into which I was not prepared to plunge.

"But what did you want to cut him for?"

"It's a long story. I'll tell you at lunch."

I raised a passionate hand.

"If you think that after pinching my spring suiting you're going to get so much as a crust of bread—"

"Calm yourself, laddie. You're lunching with me. Largely on the strength of this suit, I managed to get past the outer defenses of the Foreign Office just now and touch old George Tupper for a fiver. Joy will be unconfined."

"Corky," said Ukridge thoughtfully, spreading caviar on a piece of toast in the Regent grillroom some ten minutes later, "do you ever brood on what might have been?"

"I'm doing it now. I might have been wearing that suit."

"There is no need to go into that again," said Ukridge, with dignity. "I have explained that little misunderstanding—explained it fully. What I mean is, do you ever brood on the inscrutable workings of Fate and reflect how, but for this or that, you might have been— well, that or this? For instance, but for the old Stepper I would by now be the mainstay of a vast business, and in all probability happily married to a charming girl and the father of half a dozen prattling children."

"In which case, if there is anything in heredity, I should have had to keep my spring suits in a Safe Deposit."

"Corky, old horse," said Ukridge, pained, "you keep harping on this beastly suit of yours. It shows an ungracious spirit which I do not like to see. What was I saying?"

"You were babbling about Fate."

"Ah, yes."

Fate (said Ukridge) is odd. Rummy. You can't say it isn't. Lots
of people have noticed it. And one of the rummiest things about it
is the way it seems to take a delight in patting you on the head and
lulling you into security and then suddenly steering your foot onto
the banana skin. Just when things appear to be going smoothest, bang
comes the spanner into the machinery and there you are.

Take this business I'm going to tell you about. Just before it happened, I had begun to look upon myself as Fortune's favorite child.
Everything was breaking right in the most astounding fashion. My
Aunt Julia, having sailed for America on one of her lecturing tours,
had lent me her cottage at Market Deeping in Sussex till her return,
with instructions to the local tradesmen to let me have the necessaries
of life and chalk them up to her. From some source which at the
moment I cannot recollect, I had snaffled two pairs of white flannel
trousers and a tennis racket. And finally, after a rather painful scene
in the course of which I was compelled to allude to him as a pigheaded bureaucrat, I had contrived to get a couple of quid out of old
Tuppy. My position was solid. I ought to have known that luck like
that couldn't last.

Now, in a parting conversation on the platform at Waterloo while
waiting for the boat-train to start, Aunt Julia had revealed the fact
that her motive in sticking me down at her cottage had not been
simply to ensure that I had a pleasant summer. It seemed that at
Deeping Hall, the big house of the locality, there resided a certain
Sir Edward Bayliss, O.B.E., a bird deeply immersed in the jute
industry. To this day I have never quite got it clear what jute really
is, but, anyway, this Sir Edward was a man to keep in with, for his
business had ramifications everywhere and endless openings for the
bright young beginner. He was, moreover, a great admirer of my
aunt's novels, and she told me in a few and, in parts, tactless words
that what I was going down there for was to ingratiate myself with him
and land a job. Which, she said—and this was where I thought her remarks lacked taste—would give me a chance of doing something
useful and ceasing to be what she called a wastrel and an idler.

Idler! I'll trouble you! As if for a single day in my life, Corky, I had
ever not buzzed about doing the work of ten men. Why, take the mere
getting of that couple of quid from old Tuppy, for instance. Simple
as it sounds, I doubt if Napoleon could have done it. Tuppy, sterling
fellow though he is, has his bad mornings. He comes down to the
office and finds a sharp note from the President of Uruguay or some-

one on his desk, and it curdles the milk of human kindness within him. On these occasions he becomes so tight that he could carry an armful of eels up five flights of stairs and not drop one. And yet in less than a quarter of an hour I had got a couple of quid out of him.

Oh, well, women say these things.

Well, I packed a suitcase and took the next train down to Market Deeping. And the first thing for you to do, Corky, before I go on, is to visualize the general layout of the place. My aunt's cottage (Journey's End) was here, where this bit of bread is. Here, next to it, where I've put the potato, was a smallish house (Pondicherry) belonging to Colonel Bayliss, the jute-fancier's brother. The gardens adjoined, but anything in the way of neighborly fraternizing was prevented for the moment by the fact that the Colonel was away— at Harrogate, I learned later, trying to teach his liver to take a joke. All this expanse here—I'll mark it with a splash of Worcester Sauce —was the park of Deeping Hall, beyond which was the Hall itself and all the gardens, messuages, pleasaunces, and so forth that you'd expect.

Got it now? Right.

Well, as you can see from the diagram, the park of the Hall abutted—if that's the word I want—on the back garden of my cottage; and judge of my emotions when, as I smoked an after-breakfast pipe under the trees on the first morning after my arrival, I saw the most extraordinarily pretty girl riding there. Hither and thither. She came so close once that I could have hit her with an apple. Not that I did, of course.

I don't know if you have ever been in love at first sight, Corky? One moment I was looking idly through the hedge to see where the hoofbeats came from; the next I was electrified from head to foot, and in the bushes around me a million birds had begun to toot. I gathered at once that this must be the O.B.E.'s daughter, or something on those lines, and I found my whole attitude toward the jute business, which up till now had been what you might call lukewarm, changing in a flash. It didn't take me more than a second to realize that a job involving a connection with this girl was practically the ideal one.

I called at the Hall that afternoon, mentioned my name, and from the very start everything went like a breeze.

I don't want to boast, Corky—and, of course, I'm speaking now of some years ago, before Life had furrowed my brow and given my eyes that haunted look—but I may tell you frankly that at the time when these things happened I was a rather dazzling spectacle. I had just had my hair cut and the flannel bags fitted me to a nicety, and altogether I was an asset—yes, old horse, a positive asset to any social circle. The days flew by. The O.B.E. was chummy. The girl— her name was Myrtle, and I think she had found life at Market Deeping a bit on the slow side till I arrived—always seemed glad to see me. I was the petted young neighbor.

And then one afternoon in walked the Stepper.

There have been occasions in my life, Corky, when, if I had seen a strange man walking up the path to the front door of the house where I was living, I should have ducked through the back premises and remained concealed in the raspberry bushes till he had blown over. But it so happened that at this time my financial affairs were on a sound and solid basis and I hadn't a single creditor in the world. So I went down and opened the door and found him beaming on the mat.

"Stanley Ukridge?" he said.

"Yes," I said.

"I called at your aunt's house at Wimbledon the other day and they told me you were here. I'm your Uncle Percy from Australia, my boy. I married your late stepmother's stepsister Alice."

I don't suppose anybody with a pointed white beard has ever received a heartier welcome. I don't know if you have any pet day-dream, Corky, but mine had always been the sudden appearance of the rich uncle from Australia you read so much about in novels. The old-fashioned novels, I mean, the ones where the hero isn't a dope fiend. And here he was, looking as I had always expected him to look. You saw his spats just now, you observed his gardenia. Well, on the afternoon of which I'm speaking, he was just as spatted, fully as gardenia-ed, and in addition wore in his tie something that looked like a miniature Koh-i-noor.

"Well, well, well!" I said.

"Well, well, well!" he said.

He patted my back. I patted his. He said he was a lonely old man who had come back to England to spend his declining years with some congenial relative. I said I was just as keen on finding uncles as he was on spotting nephews. The thing was a love feast.

"You can put me up for a week or two, Stanley?"

"Delighted."

"Nice little place you have here."

"Glad you like it."

"Wants a bit of smartening up, though," said the Stepper, looking round at the appointments and not seeming to think a lot of them. Aunt Julia had furnished the cottage fairly sparsely.

"Perhaps you're right."

"Some comfortable chairs, eh?"

"Fine."

"And a sofa."

"Splendid."

"And perhaps a nice little summerhouse for the garden. Have you a summerhouse?"

I said: "No, no summerhouse."

"I'll be looking about for one," said the Stepper.

And everything I had read about rich uncles from Australia seemed to me to have come true. Spacious is the only word to describe his attitude. He was like some Eastern monarch giving the Court architect specifications for a new palace. This, I told myself, was how these fine, breezy, Empire-building fellows always were—generous, open-handed, gaily reckless of expense. I wished I had met him earlier.

"And now, my boy," said the old Stepper, sticking out from six to eight inches of tongue and running same round his lips, "where do you keep the drinks?"

I've always maintained, and I always will maintain, that there's nothing in this world to beat a real bachelor establishment. Men have a knack of making themselves comfortable which few women can ever achieve. My Aunt Julia's idea of a chair, for instance, was something antique made to the order of the Spanish Inquisition. The Stepper had the right conception. Men arrived in vans and unloaded things with slanting backs and cushioned seats, and whenever I wasn't over at the Hall I wallowed in these.

The Stepper wallowed in them all the time. Occasionally he put in an hour or so in the summerhouse—for he had caused a summerhouse to appear at the bottom of the garden—but mostly you would find him indoors with all the windows shut and something to drink at his elbow. He said he had had so much fresh air in Australia that what he wanted now was something he could scoop out with a spoon.

Once or twice I tried to get him over to the Hall, but he would have none of it. He said from what he knew of O.B.E.'s he wouldn't be allowed to take his boots off, and ran, moreover, a grave risk of being offered barley water. Apparently he had once met a teetotal O.B.E. in Sydney and was prejudiced. However, he was most sympathetic when I told him about Myrtle. He said that, though he wasn't any

too keen on matrimony as an institution, he was broad-minded enough
to realize that there might quite possibly be women in the world unlike his late wife. Concerning whom, he added that the rabbit was not,
as had been generally stated, Australia's worst pest.

"Tell me of this girl, my boy," he said. "You squeeze her a good
deal in dark corners, no doubt?"

"Certainly not," I said stiffly.

"Then things have changed very much since my young days. What
do you do?"

I said I looked at her quite a lot and hung on her every word and
all that sort of thing.

"Do you give her presents?"

He had touched on a subject which I had intended to bring up
myself when I could find an opening. You see, Myrtle's birthday was
approaching; and, though nothing had actually been said about any
little gift, I had sensed a certain expectation in the air. Even the best
of girls are like that, Corky. They say how old they feel with another
birthday coming along so soon, and then they look brightly at you.

"Well, as a matter of fact, Uncle Percy," I said, flicking a speck
of dust off his sleeve, "I was rather planning something of the kind,
if only I could see my way to managing it. It's her birthday next week,
Uncle Percy, and it crossed my mind that if I could stumble on somebody who could slip me a few quid, something might possibly be done
about it, Uncle Percy."

He waved his hand in an Australian sort of way.

"Leave it all to me, my boy."

"Oh, no, really!"

"I insist."

"Oh, if you insist."

"My late wife was your late stepmother's stepsister, and blood
is thicker than water. Now, let me see," mused the old Stepper,
wriggling his feet a couple of inches farther onto the table and
knitting the brow a bit. "What shall it be? Jewelry? No. Girls like
their little bit of jewelry, but perhaps it would scarcely do. I have it.
A sundial."

"A what?" I said.

"A sundial," said the old Stepper. "What could be a more pretty
and tasteful gift? No doubt she has a little garden of her own, some
sequestered nook which she tends with her own hands and where she
wanders in maiden meditation on summer evenings. If so, she needs
a sundial."

"But, Uncle Percy," I said doubtfully, "do you really think—? My idea was rather that if you could possibly let me have a fiver—or say a tenner—to make up the round sum—"

"She draws a sundial," said the old Stepper firmly, "and likes it."

I tried to reason with the man.

"But you can't get a sundial," I urged.

"I can get a sundial," said the old Stepper, waving his whisky and soda with a good deal of asperity. "I can get anything. Sundials, summerhouses, elephants if you want them. I'm noted for it. Show me the man who says that Charles Percy Cuthbertson can't get a sundial, and I'll give him the lie in his teeth. That's where I'll give it him. In his teeth!"

And, as he seemed to be warming up a bit, we left it at that. I never dreamed that he would make good, of course. You'll admit, I think, Corky, that I'm a pretty gifted fellow, but if anyone called upon me at practically a moment's notice to produce a sundial, I should be nonplused. Nevertheless, bright and early on the morning of Myrtle's birthday I heard a yodel under my window, and there he was, standing beside a wheelbarrow containing sundial complete as per invoice. It all seemed to me more like magic than anything, and I began to feel like Aladdin. Apparently my job from now on was simply to rub the lamp and the Stepper would do the rest.

"There you are, my boy," he said, dusting the thing off with a handkerchief and regarding it in a fatherly sort of way. "You give the little lady that and she'll let you cuddle her behind the front door."

This struck a slightly jarring note, of course. He seemed to me to be taking an entirely too earthy view of my great love, which was intensely spiritual. But it was not the moment to say so.

"That'll make her clap her hands prettily. That'll send her singing about the house."

"She ought to like it," I agreed.

"Of course she'll like it. She'd damn' well better like it. Show me a wholesome, sweet-minded English girl who doesn't like a sundial and I'll paste her on the nose," said the Stepper warmly. "Why, it's got a motto and everything."

And so it had. We hadn't spotted it at first, the contrivance having been more or less covered with moss; but the Stepper had worked briskly with a table knife and now you got a good view of it. Some rot, if I recollect rightly, about ye sunne and ye shoures, carved in old English letters. It seemed to alter the whole aspect of the sundial—lift it, as it were, into a higher and more dignified class; and for the first time I began to get really enthusiastic.

"This is the goods, Uncle Percy," I said. "This is the right stuff. How can I thank you enough?"

"You can't," said the Stepper.

"I'll tell you what the procedure here is," I said. "I'll take this thing over to the Hall this morning and ask Myrtle and her father to come to tea. They can't refuse when they've just been handed a sundial like this."

"Certainly," said the Stepper. "A very good idea. Ask them to tea, and I'll make the house a bower of roses."

"Can you get roses?"

"Can I get roses! Don't keep asking me if I can get things. Of course I can get roses. And eggs, too."

"We shan't want eggs."

"We shall want eggs," said the Stepper, beginning to hot up again. "If eggs are good enough for me, they're good enough for the pop-eyed daughter of a blighted O.B.E. Or don't you think so?"

"Oh, quite, Uncle Percy, quite," I said.

I would have liked to inform him that Myrtle wasn't popeyed, but he didn't seem in the mood.

Any doubts I may have had as to the acceptability of my birthday present vanished as soon as, with infinite sweat, I had wheeled it across the park in its barrow. The Stepper had had the right idea. Myrtle was all over the sundial. I sprang the tea invitation, and for the moment it looked as if there was going to be a hitch. Her Uncle Philip, the Colonel, it seemed, was due to materialize that afternoon. He always made a point of being present for his niece's birthday, however far he had to come to be there, and he would be terribly hurt if he arrived and found she had let him down. What to do?

"Bring him along," I said, of course. And we arranged it on those lines. The Colonel, on getting off the train and going to the Hall, would find a note instructing him to hoof it across the park and come and revel at Journey's End. I didn't say so to Myrtle, for the time did not seem to me ripe, but what it amounted to, I felt, was that the Colonel would come seeking a niece and would find in addition a nephew. Than which, for a bloke getting on in years and needing all the loved ones round him that could be assembled, what could be a jollier surprise? I disagree with you, Corky. It does not depend on the kind of nephew. Any nephew is a boon to a lonely bachelor like that.

So I wheeled the wheelbarrow back to the cottage, feeling that all was well. And at about half-past four the maid who came in from the village by the day to do our cooking and washing up announced Sir Edward and Miss Bayliss.

I'm an old campaigner now, Corky, and Fate has to take its coat off and spit on its hands a bit if it wants to fool me. Today, when Fate offers me something apparently gilt-edged, I look it over coldly and assume, till it has been proved otherwise, that attached to it somewhere there is a string. But at the time of which I am speaking I was younger, more buoyant, more credulous; and I honestly supposed that this tea party of mine was going to be the success it seemed at the start.

The thing had got under way without a suspicion of anything in the nature of a disaster. In the first place, the maid had responded to my coaching in the most admirable manner. A simple child of the soil, her natural disposition would have been to bung the door open and bellow: "They're here!" Instead of which, she had done the announcing with a style and polish that gave the whole proceedings a tone from the very outset. Secondly, Sir Edward had not bumped his head against the beam on the ceiling just inside the front door. And, lastly, though the Stepper's roses were present in wonderful profusion, he himself hadn't shown up. And that seemed to me the biggest stroke of luck of the lot.

You see, the old Stepper wasn't everybody's money. To begin with, he had an apparently incurable dislike of O.B.E.'s, and then he combined with a hot-blooded and imperious nature the odd belief that eggs were a suitable food for adult human beings at five o'clock in the afternoon. And he was so touchy, too, so ready to resent opposition. I had had visions of him standing over Sir Edward and shoving eggs down his throat at the point of a table knife. He was better away, and I hoped he had fallen into a ditch and couldn't get out.

From the moment the first drop of tea was poured everything went as smooth as oil. In recent years, Corky, affairs have so shaped themselves that you have had the opportunity of seeing me mainly in the capacity of a guest; but you can take it from me that, vouchsafed the right conditions, I can be a very sparkling host. Give me a roof over my head, plenty of buttered toast, and no creditors in sight, and I shine with the best of them.

On the present occasion I was at the top of my form. I handed cups. I slid the toast about. I prattled merrily. And I could see the old boy was impressed. These O.B.E.'s are silent, reserved men, and for a while he just looked at me from time to time in a meditative

way. Then, as he was dipping into his third cup of tea, out he came
into the open and began to talk turkey.

"Your aunt . . . Have you heard from her, by the way?"

"Not yet. I suppose she's very busy."

"I imagine so. An energetic woman."

"Very. All we Ukridges are energetic. We do not spare ourselves."

"Your aunt," resumed the old boy, swallowing some more tea,
"gave me the impression in one of the conversations we had before
she left England that you were looking out for an opening in the
world of commerce."

"Yes," I said. I stroked my chin thoughtfully and tried to look as
much as possible like Charles M. Schwab being approached by the
President of the United States Steel Corporation with a view to a
merger. You've got to show these birds that you've a proper sense of
your own value. Start right with them, or it's no use starting at all.
"I might accept commercial employment if the salary and prospects
were undeniable."

He cleared his throat.

"In my own business," he was beginning, "the jute business—"

Just then the door opened and the maid appeared. She was one of
those snorting girls, and she snorted something about a gentleman. I
couldn't get it.

"Who's a gentleman?" I said.

"Outside. He says he wants to see you."

"It must be Uncle Philip," said Myrtle.

"Of course," I said. "Show him in. Don't keep him waiting, my
good girl. Show him in at once."

And a moment later in came a bloke. Obviously not the Colonel,
for Myrtle and the O.B.E. gave no sign of recognition. Then who?
The man was a perfect stranger to me.

However, I played the host.

"Good afternoon," I said affably.

"Afternoon," said the bloke.

"Take a chair," I said.

"I'm going to take all the chairs," he said. "And the sofa, too.
I'm from the Mammoth Furnishing Company, and the check for the
deposit on this stuff has been returned Refer to Drawer."

It is not too much to say, Corky, that I reeled. Yes, laddie, your
old friend tottered and would have fallen had he not clutched at a
chair. And, from the look in the bloke's eye, it began to seem that
my chances of clutching at that particular chair were likely to be
very soon a thing of the past. He had one of those brooding eyes.

Two, probably, only there was a patch over the left one. I think someone must have hit him there. A fellow like that could scarcely go through life without getting punched in the eye.

"But, my dear old horse—" I began.

"It's no use arguing. We've written twice and never got an answer, and I've instructions from the firm to take the stuff."

"But we're using it."

"Not now," said the blighter. "You've finished."

I look back on that moment, Corky, old boy, as one of the worst in my career. It is always a nervous business for a fellow to entertain for the first time the girl he loves and her father; and, believe me, it doesn't help pass things off when a couple of the proletariat in shirt sleeves surge into the room and start carrying out all the chairs. Conversation during the proceedings was, you might say, at a standstill; and even after the operations were over it wasn't any too easy to get it going again.

"Some absurd mistake," I said.

"No doubt," said the O.B.E.

"I shall write those people a very stiff letter tonight."

"No doubt."

"That furniture was bought by my uncle, one of the wealthiest men in Australia. It's absurd to suppose that a man of his standing would—"

"No doubt. Myrtle, my dear, I think we will be going."

Then, Corky, I spread myself. On not a few occasions in a life that has had its ups and downs I have been compelled to do some impressive talking, but now I surpassed all previous efforts. The thought of all that was slipping away from me spurred me to heights I have never reached before or since. And gradually, little by little, I made headway. The old boy tried to shake me off and edge through the French windows, but it is pretty hard to shake me off when I am at my best. I grabbed him by the buttonhole and steered him back into the room. And when, in a dazed sort of way, he reached out and took a slice of cake, I knew the battle was won.

"The way I look at it is this," I said, getting between him and the window. "A man like my uncle would no doubt have a number of accounts in different banks. The one on which he drew this check happened to have insufficient funds in it, and the bank manager, with gross discourtesy—"

"Well, yes, possibly—"

"I shall tell my uncle of what has occurred—"

At this moment somebody behind me said "Ha!" or it may have

been "Ho!" and I spun round, and there in the French window was standing another perfect stranger.

This new addition to our little party was a long, lean, Anglo-Indian-looking individual. You know the type. Beige as to general color scheme and rather like a vulture with a white mustache.

"Uncle Philip!" cried Myrtle.

The Vulture gave a kind of nod in her direction. He seemed upset about something.

"Don't talk to me," he said. "I haven't time. Many happy returns of the day and so forth, but don't talk to me now, child. There's the man I want to talk to."

"You know Mr. Ukridge?"

"No, I don't. And I don't want to. But I know he's stolen—" He broke off with a hideous rattle in his voice, and I saw that he was staring at the table. It belonged to my aunt and was the only thing in the room that the shirt-sleeved birds had left, so it was fairly conspicuous. "Good God!" he said.

He switched an eye round and let it play on me like an oxy-acetylene blowpipe. I don't know what the treatment for liver is at Harrogate, but they ought to change it. It's ineffective. It had obviously done this man no good at all.

"Good God!" he said again.

The O.B.E. came to the surface.

"What's the matter, Philip?" he asked, annoyed. He had only just finished coughing, having swallowed a bit of cake the wrong way.

"I'll tell you what's the matter. I was in my garden just now, and I found it looted—looted! That man there has stripped it of every rose I possess. My roses! The place is a desert."

"Is this true, Mr. Ukridge?" asked the O.B.E.

"Certainly not," I said.

"Oh, it isn't?" said the Vulture. "It isn't, eh? Then where did those roses come from? There aren't any rose trees in the garden of this house. Damn it, I've been here half a dozen times and I ought to know. Where did you get those roses? Answer me that."

"My uncle gave them to me."

The O.B.E., having now disposed of the cake, uttered a nasty laugh.

"Your uncle!" he said.

"What uncle?" cried the Vulture. "Where's this uncle? Show me this uncle. Produce him."

"I'm afraid it would be a little difficult to do that, Philip," said the O.B.E., and I didn't at all like his manner. "It appears that Mr.

Ukridge possesses a mysterious uncle. Nobody has ever set eyes on him, but it would seem that he buys furniture and does not pay for it; steals roses—"

"And sundials," put in the Vulture.

"Sundials?"

"That's what I said. After I'd had a look at my garden I went over to the Hall, and there in the middle of the lawn was my sundial. They told me this fellow here had given it to Myrtle."

I wasn't in any too good shape by this time, but I collected enough of the old manly spirit to come back at him.

"How do you know it was your sundial?" I said.

"Because it had my motto on it. And, as if that wasn't enough, he's stolen my summerhouse."

The O.B.E. gulped.

"Your summerhouse?" he said in a low, almost reverent voice. The spaciousness of the thing seemed to have affected his vocal cords. "How could he have stolen a summerhouse?"

"I don't know how he did it. In sections, I suppose. It's one of those portable summerhouses. I had it sent down from the Stores last month. And there it is, standing at the bottom of his garden. I tell you the man ought not to be at large. He's a menace. Good God! When I was in Africa during the Boer War a platoon of Australians scrounged one of my cast-iron sheds one night, but I never expected that that sort of thing happened in England in peacetime."

Corky, a sudden bright light shone on me. I saw all. It was that word "scrounge" that did it. I remembered now having heard of Australia and its scroungers. They go about pinching things, Corky— No, I do *not* mean spring suits, I mean things that really matter, things of vital import like sundials and summerhouses—not beastly spring suits which nobody could tell you wanted, anyway, and you'll get it back tomorrow as good as new.

Well, be that as it may, I saw all.

"Sir Edward," I said, "let me explain. My uncle—"

But it was no use, Corky. They wouldn't listen. The O.B.E. gave me one look, the Vulture gave me another, and I rather fancy Myrtle gave me a third, and then they pushed off and I was alone.

I went over to the table and helped myself to a bit of cold buttered toast, a broken man.

About ten minutes later there was a sound of cheery whistling outside and the Stepper walked in.

"Here I am, my boy," said the Stepper. "I've got the eggs." And he began shedding them out of every pocket. It looked as if he had been looting every hen roost in the neighborhood. "Where are our guests?"

"Gone."

"Gone?"

He looked round.

"Hullo! Where's the furniture?"

"Gone."

"Gone?"

I explained.

"Tut, tut!" said the Stepper.

I sniffed a bit.

"Don't make sniffing noises at me, my boy," said the Stepper reprovingly. "The best of men have checks returned from time to time."

"And I suppose the best of men sneak eggs and roses and sundials and summerhouses?" I said. And I spoke bitterly, Corky.

"Eh?" said the Stepper. "You don't mean to say—"

"I certainly do."

"Tell me all."

I told him all.

"Too bad!" he said. "I never have been able to shake off this habit of scrounging. Wherever Charles Percy Cuthbertson is, there he scrounges. But who would have supposed that people would make a fuss about a little thing like that? I'm disappointed in the old country. Why, nobody in Australia minds a little scrounging. What's mine is yours and what's yours is mine—that's our motto out there. All this to-do about a sundial and a summerhouse! Why, bless my soul, I've scrounged a tennis lawn in my time. Oh, well, there's nothing to be done about it, I suppose."

"There's a lot to be done about it," I said. "The O.B.E. doesn't believe I've got an uncle. I thinks I pinched all those things myself."

"Does he?" said the Stepper thoughtfully. "Does he, indeed?"

"And the least you can do is to go up to the Hall and explain."

"Precisely what I was about to suggest myself. I'll walk over now and put everything right. Trust me, my boy. I'll soon fix things up."

And he trotted out, and that, Corky, is the last I ever saw of him till today. It's my belief he never went anywhere near the Hall. I am convinced that he walked straight to the station, no doubt pocketing a couple of telegraph poles and a five-barred gate or so on the way, and took the next train to London. Certainly there was nothing in the O.B.E.'s manner when I met him next day in the village to suggest that everything had been put right and things fixed up. I don't suppose a jute merchant has ever cut anybody so thoroughly.

And that's why I wish to impress it upon you, Corky, old horse, that that bloke, that snaky and conscienceless old Stepper, is best avoided. No matter how glittering the prospects he may hold out, I say to you—shun him! Looking at the thing in one way, taking the short, narrow view, I am out a lunch. Possibly a very good lunch. But do I regret? No. Who knows but that a man like that would have been called to the telephone at the eleventh hour, leaving me stuck with the bill?

And even supposing he really has got money now. How did he get it? That is the question. I shall make inquiries, and if I find that someone has pinched the Albert Memorial I shall know what to think.

✸ *Lord Emsworth*

Ruler of all he surveys at Blanding's Castle except, possibly, his sister, Lady Constance Keeble.

"*Absurd! Ridiculous! Preposterous!*" *he said hurriedly.* "*Breaking the engagement? Pooh! Tush! What nonsense! I'll have a word with this young man. If he thinks he can go about the place playing fast and loose with my niece and jilting her without so much as a—*"

"*Clarence!*"

Lord Emsworth blinked. Something appeared to be wrong, but he could not imagine what. It seemed to him that in his last speech he had struck just the right note—strong, forceful, dignified.

"*Eh?*"

"*It is Angela who has broken the engagement.*"

"*Oh, Angela?*"

"*She is infatuated with this man Belford. And the point is, what are we to do about it?*"

Lord Emsworth reflected.

"*Take a strong line,*" *he said firmly.* "*Stand no nonsense. Don't send 'em a wedding present.*"

❁ *"Pig-hoo-o-o-o-ey!"*

THANKS to the publicity given to the matter by *The Bridgnorth Shifnal, and Albrighton Argus* (with which is incorporated *The Wheat Growers' Intelligencer and Stock Breeders' Gazetteer*), the whole world today knows that the silver medal in the Fat Pigs class at the eighty-seventh annual Shropshire Agricultural Show was won by the Earl of Emsworth's black Berkshire sow, Empress of Blandings.

Very few people, however, are aware how near that splendid animal came to missing the coveted honor.

Now it can be told.

This brief chapter of Secret History may be said to have begun on the night of the eighteenth of July, when George Cyril Wellbeloved (twenty-nine), pigman in the employ of Lord Emsworth, was arrested by Police Constable Evans of Market Blandings for being drunk and disorderly in the taproom of the Goat and Feathers. On July the nineteenth, after first offering to apologize, then explaining that it had been his birthday, and finally attempting to prove an alibi, George Cyril was very properly jugged for fourteen days without the option of a fine.

On July the twentieth, Empress of Blandings, always hitherto a hearty and even a boisterous feeder, for the first time on record declined all nourishment. And on the morning of July the twenty-first, the veterinary surgeon called in to diagnose and deal with this strange asceticism, was compelled to confess to Lord Emsworth that the thing was beyond his professional skill.

Let us just see, before proceeding, that we have got these dates correct:

July 18.—Birthday Orgy of Cyril Wellbeloved.
July 19.—Incarceration of Ditto.
July 20.—Pig Lays off the Vitamins.
July 21.—Veterinary Surgeon Baffled.
Right.

The effect of the veterinary surgeon's announcement on Lord Emsworth was overwhelming. As a rule, the wear and tear of our complex modern life left this vague and amiable peer unscathed. So long as he had sunshine, regular meals and complete freedom from the society of his younger son Frederick, he was placidly happy. But there were chinks in his armor, and one of these had been pierced this morning. Dazed by the news he had received, he stood at the window of the great library of Blandings Castle, looking out with unseeing eyes.

As he stood there, the door opened. Lord Emsworth turned; and having blinked once or twice, as was his habit when confronted suddenly with anything, recognized in the handsome and imperious-looking woman who had entered his sister, Lady Constance Keeble. Her demeanor, like his own, betrayed the deepest agitation.

"Clarence," she cried, "an awful thing has happened!"

Lord Emsworth nodded dully.

"I know. He's just told me."

"What! Has he been here?"

"Only this moment left."

"Why did you let him go? You must have known I would want to see him."

"What good would that have done?"

"I could at least have assured him of my sympathy," said Lady Constance stiffly.

"Yes, I suppose you could," said Lord Emsworth, having considered the point. "Not that he deserves any sympathy. The man's an ass."

"Nothing of the kind. A most intelligent young man, as young men go."

"Young? Would you call him young? Fifty, I should have said, if a day."

"Are you out of your senses? Heacham fifty?"

"Not Heacham. Smithers."

As frequently happened to her when in conversation with her brother, Lady Constance experienced a swimming sensation in the head.

"Will you kindly tell me, Clarence, in a few simple words, what you imagine we are talking about?"

"I'm talking about Smithers. Empress of Blandings is refusing her food, and Smithers says he can't do anything about it. And he calls himself a vet!"

"Then you haven't heard? Clarence, a dreadful thing has happened. Angela has broken off her engagement to Heacham."

"And the Agricultural Show on Wednesday week!"

"What on earth has that got to do with it?" demanded Lady Constance, feeling a recurrence of the swimming sensation.

"What has it got to do with it?" said Lord Emsworth warmly. "My champion sow, with less than ten days to prepare herself for a most searching examination in competition with all the finest pigs in the county, starts refusing her food—"

"Will you stop maundering on about your insufferable pig and give your attention to something that really matters? I tell you that Angela—your niece Angela—has broken off her engagement to Lord Heacham and expresses her intention of marrying that hopeless ne'er-do-well, James Belford."

"The son of old Belford, the parson?"

"Yes."

"She can't. He's in America."

"He is not in America. He is in London."

"No," said Lord Emsworth, shaking his head sagely. "You're wrong. I remember meeting his father two years ago out on the road by Meeker's twenty-acre field, and he distinctly told me the boy was sailing for America next day. He must be there by this time."

"Can't you understand? He's come back."

"Oh? Come back? I see. Come *back?*"

"You know there was once a silly sentimental sort of affair between him and Angela; but a year after he left she became engaged to Heacham and I thought the whole thing was over and done with. And now it seems that she met this young man Belford when she was in London last week, and it has started all over again. She tells me she has written to Heacham and broken the engagement."

There was a silence. Brother and sister remained for a space plunged in thought. Lord Emsworth was the first to speak.

"We've tried acorns," he said. "We've tried skim milk. And we've tried potato peel. But, no, she won't touch them."

Conscious of two eyes raising blisters on his sensitive skin, he came to himself with a start.

"Absurd! Ridiculous! Preposterous!" he said hurriedly. "Breaking the engagement? Pooh! Tush! What nonsense! I'll have a word with that young man. If he thinks he can go about the place playing fast and loose with my niece and jilting her without so much as a—"

"Clarence!"

Lord Emsworth blinked. Something appeared to be wrong, but he could not imagine what. It seemed to him that in his last speech he had struck just the right note—strong, forceful, dignified.

"Eh?"

"It is Angela who has broken the engagement."

"Oh, Angela?"

"She is infatuated with this man Belford. And the point is, what are we to do about it?"

Lord Emsworth reflected.

"Take a strong line," he said firmly. "Stand no nonsense. Don't send 'em a wedding present."

There is no doubt that, given time, Lady Constance would have found and uttered some adequately corrosive comment on this imbecile suggestion; but even as she was swelling preparatory to giving tongue, the door opened and a girl came in.

She was a pretty girl, with fair hair and blue eyes which in their softer moments probably reminded all sorts of people of twin lagoons slumbering beneath a southern sky. This, however, was not one of those moments. To Lord Emsworth, as they met his, they looked like something out of an oxyacetylene blowpipe; and, as far as he was capable of being disturbed by anything that was not his younger son Frederick, he was disturbed. Angela, it seemed to him, was upset about something; and he was sorry. He liked Angela.

To ease a tense situation, he said:

"Angela, my dear, do you know anything about pigs?"

The girl laughed. One of those sharp, bitter laughs which are so unpleasant just after breakfast.

"Yes, I do. You're one."

"Me?"

"Yes, you. Aunt Constance says that, if I marry Jimmy, you won't let me have my money."

"Money? Money?" Lord Emsworth was mildly puzzled. "What money? You never lent me any money."

Lady Constance's feelings found vent in a sound like an overheated radiator.

"I believe this absent-mindedness of yours is nothing but a ridiculous pose, Clarence. You know perfectly well that when poor Jane died she left you Angela's trustee."

"And I can't touch my money without your consent till I'm twenty-five."

"Well, how old are you?"

"Twenty-one."

"Then what are you worrying about?" asked Lord Emsworth, surprised. "No need to worry about it for another four years. God bless my soul, the money is quite safe. It is in excellent securities."

Angela stamped her foot. An unladylike action, no doubt, but how much better than kicking an uncle with it, as her lower nature prompted.

"I have told Angela," explained Lady Constance, "that, while we naturally cannot force her to marry Lord Heacham, we can at least keep her money from being squandered by this wastrel on whom she proposes to throw herself away."

"He isn't a wastrel. He's got quite enough money to marry me on, but he wants some capital to buy a partnership in a—"

"He is a wastrel. Wasn't he sent abroad because—"

"That was two years ago. And since then—"

"My dear Angela, you may argue until—"

"I'm not arguing. I'm simply saying that I'm going to marry Jimmy, if we both have to starve in the gutter."

"What gutter?" asked his lordship, wrenching his errant mind away from thoughts of acorns.

"Any gutter."

"Now, please listen to me, Angela."

It seemed to Lord Emsworth that there was a frightful amount of conversation going on. He had the sensation of having become a mere bit of flotsam upon a tossing sea of female voices. Both his sister and his niece appeared to have much to say, and they were saying it simultaneously and fortissimo. He looked wistfully at the door.

It was smoothly done. A twist of the handle, and he was where beyond those voices there was peace. Galloping gaily down the stairs, he charged out into the sunshine.

His gaiety was not long-lived. Free at last to concentrate itself on the really serious issues of life, his mind grew somber and grim. Once more there descended upon him the cloud which had been oppressing his soul before all this Heacham-Angela-Belford business began. Each step that took him nearer to the sty where the ailing Empress resided seemed a heavier step than the last. He reached the sty; and, draping himself over the rails, peered moodily at the vast expanse of pig within.

For, even though she had been doing a bit of dieting of late, Empress of Blandings was far from being an ill-nourished animal. She resembled a captive balloon with ears and a tail, and was as nearly circular as a pig can be without bursting. Nevertheless, Lord Emsworth, as he regarded her, mourned and would not be comforted. A few more square meals under her belt, and no pig in all Shropshire could have held its head up in the Empress's presence.

And now, just for lack of those few meals, the supreme animal would probably be relegated to the mean obscurity of an "Honorably Mentioned." It was bitter, bitter.

He became aware that somebody was speaking to him; and, turning, perceived a solemn young man in riding breeches.

"I say," said the young man.

Lord Emsworth, though he would have preferred solitude, was relieved to find that the intruder was at least one of his own sex. Women are apt to stray off into side issues, but men are practical and can be relied on to stick to the fundamentals. Besides, young Heacham probably kept pigs himself and might have a useful hint or two up his sleeve.

"I say, I've just ridden over to see if there was anything I could do about this fearful business."

"Uncommonly kind and thoughtful of you, my dear fellow," said Lord Emsworth, touched. "I fear things look very black."

"It's an absolute mystery to me."

"To me, too."

"I mean to say, she was all right last week."

"She was all right as late as the day before yesterday."

"Seemed quite cheery and chirpy and all that."

"Entirely so."

"And then this happens—out of a blue sky, as you might say."

"Exactly. It is insoluble. We have done everything possible to tempt her appetite."

"Her appetite? Is Angela ill?"

"Angela? No, I fancy not. She seemed perfectly well a few minutes ago."

"You've seen her this morning, then? Did she say anything about this fearful business?"

"No. She was speaking about some money."

"It's all so dashed unexpected."

"Like a bolt from the blue," agreed Lord Emsworth. "Such a thing has never happened before. I fear the worst. According to the Wolff-Lehmann feeding standards, a pig, if in health, should consume daily nourishment amounting to fifty-seven thousand eight hundred calories, these to consist of proteins four pounds five ounces, carbohydrates twenty-five pounds—"

"What has that got to do with Angela?"

"Angela?"

"I came to find out why Angela has broken off our engagement."

Lord Emsworth marshaled his thoughts. He had a misty idea that he had heard something mentioned about that. It came back to him.

"Ah, yes, of course. She has broken off the engagement, hasn't she? I believe it is because she is in love with someone else. Yes, now that I recollect, that was distinctly stated. The whole thing comes back to me quite clearly. Angela has decided to marry someone else. I knew there was some satisfactory explanation. Tell me, my dear fellow, what are your views on linseed meal."

"What do you mean, linseed meal?"

"Why, linseed meal," said Lord Emsworth, not being able to find a better definition. "As a food for pigs."

"Oh, curse all pigs!"

"What!" There was a sort of astounded horror in Lord Emsworth's voice. He had never been particularly fond of young Heacham, for he was not a man who took much to his juniors, but he had not supposed him capable of anarchistic sentiments like this. "What did you say?"

"I said, 'Curse all pigs!' You keep talking about pigs. I'm not interested in pigs. I don't want to discuss pigs. Blast and damn every pig in existence!"

Lord Emsworth watched him, as he strode away, with an emotion that was partly indignation and partly relief—indignation that a landowner and a fellow son of Shropshire could have brought himself to utter such words, and relief that one capable of such utterance was not going to marry into his family. He had always in his woolen-headed way been very fond of his niece, Angela, and it was nice to think that the child had such solid good sense and so much cool discernment. Many girls of her age would have been carried away by the glamor of young Heacham's position and wealth; but she, divining with an intuition beyond her years that he was unsound on the subject of pigs, had drawn back while there was still time and refused to marry him.

A pleasant glow suffused Lord Emsworth's bosom, to be frozen out a few moments later as he perceived his sister Constance bearing down upon him. Lady Constance was a beautiful woman, but there were times when the charm of her face was marred by a rather curious expression; and from nursery days onward his lordship had learned that this expression meant trouble. She was wearing it now.

"Clarence," she said, "I have had enough of this nonsense of Angela and young Belford. The thing cannot be allowed to go drifting on. You must catch the two o'clock train to London."

"What! Why?"

"You must see this man Belford and tell him that, if Angela insists on marrying him, she will not have a penny for four years. I shall be greatly surprised if that piece of information does not put an end to the whole business."

Lord Emsworth scratched meditatively at the Empress's tanklike back. A mutinous expression was on his mild face.

"Don't see why she shouldn't marry the fellow," he mumbled.

"Marry James Belford?"

"I don't see why not. Seems fond of him and all that."

"You never have had a grain of sense in your head, Clarence. Angela is going to marry Heacham."

"Can't stand that man. All wrong about pigs."

"Clarence, I don't wish to have any more discussion and argument. You will go to London on the two o'clock train. You will see Mr. Belford. And you will tell him about Angela's money. Is that quite clear?"

"Oh, all right," said his lordship moodily. "All right, all right, all right."

The emotions of the Earl of Emsworth, as he sat next day facing his luncheon guest, James Bartholomew Belford, across a table in the main dining room of the Senior Conservative Club, were not of the liveliest and most agreeable. It was bad enough to be in London at all on such a day of golden sunshine. To be charged, while there, with the task of blighting the romance of two young people for whom he entertained a warm regard was unpleasant to a degree.

For, now that he had given the matter thought, Lord Emsworth recalled that he had always liked this boy Belford. A pleasant lad, with, he remembered now, a healthy fondness for that rural existence which so appealed to himself. By no means the sort of fellow who, in the very presence and hearing of Empress of Blandings, would have spoken disparagingly and with oaths of pigs as a class. It occurred to Lord Emsworth, as it has occurred to so many people, that the distribution of money in this world is all wrong. Why should a man like pig-despising Heacham have a rent roll that ran into the tens of thousands, while this very deserving youngster had nothing?

These thoughts not only saddened Lord Emsworth—they embarrassed him. He hated unpleasantness, and it was suddenly borne in upon him that, after he had broken the news that Angela's bit of capital was locked up and not likely to get loose, conversation with his young friend during the remainder of lunch would tend to be somewhat difficult.

He made up his mind to postpone the revelation. During the meal, he decided, he would chat pleasantly of this and that; and then, later, while bidding his guest good-bye, he would spring the thing on him suddenly and dive back into the recesses of the club.

Considerably cheered at having solved a delicate problem with such adroitness, he started to prattle.

"The gardens at Blandings," he said, "are looking particularly attractive this summer. My head gardener, Angus McAllister, is a man with whom I do not always find myself seeing eye to eye, notably in the matter of hollyhocks, on which I consider his views subversive to a degree; but there is no denying that he understands roses. The rose garden—"

"How well I remember that rose garden," said James Belford, sighing slightly and helping himself to Brussels sprouts. "It was there that Angela and I used to meet on summer mornings."

Lord Emsworth blinked. This was not an encouraging start, but the Emsworths were a fighting clan. He had another try.

"I have seldom seen such a blaze of color as was to be witnessed there during the month of June. Both McAllister and I adopted a very strong policy with the slugs and plant lice, with the result that the place was a mass of flourishing Damasks and Ayrshires and—"

"Properly to appreciate roses," said James Belford, "you want to see them as a setting for a girl like Angela. With her fair hair gleaming against the green leaves she makes a rose garden seem a veritable Paradise."

"No doubt," said Lord Emsworth. "No doubt. I am glad you liked my rose garden. At Blandings, of course, we have the natural advantage of loamy soil, rich in plant food and humus; but, as I often say to McAllister, and on this point we have never had the slightest disagreement, loamy soil by itself is not enough. You must have manure. If every autumn a liberal mulch of stable manure is spread upon the beds and the coarser parts removed in the spring before the annual forking—"

"Angela tells me," said James Belford, "that you have forbidden our marriage."

Lord Emsworth choked dismally over his chicken. Directness of this kind, he told himself with a pang of self-pity, was the sort of thing young Englishmen picked up in America. Diplomatic circumlocution flourished only in a more leisurely civilization, and in those energetic and forceful surroundings you learned to Talk Quick and Do It Now, and all sorts of uncomfortable things.

"Er—well, yes, now you mention it, I believe some informal

decision of that nature was arrived at. You see, my dear fellow, my sister Constance feels rather strongly—"

"I understand. I suppose she thinks I'm a sort of prodigal."

"No, no, my dear fellow. She never said that. Wastrel was the term she employed."

"Well, perhaps I did start out in business on those lines. But you can take it from me that when you find yourself employed on a farm in Nebraska belonging to an applejack-nourished patriarch with strong views on work and a good vocabulary, you soon develop a certain liveliness."

"Are you employed on a farm?"

"I was employed on a farm."

"Pigs?" said Lord Emsworth in a low, eager voice.

"Among other things."

Lord Emsworth gulped. His fingers clutched at the tablecloth.

"Then perhaps, my dear fellow, you can give me some advice. For the last two days my prize sow, Empress of Blandings, has declined all nourishment. And the Agricultural Show is on Wednesday week. I am distracted with anxiety."

James Belford frowned thoughtfully.

"What does your pigman say about it?"

"My pigman was sent to prison two days ago. Two days!" For the first time the significance of the coincidence struck him. "You don't think that can have anything to do with the animal's loss of appetite?"

"Certainly. I imagine she is missing him and pining away because he isn't there."

Lord Emsworth was surprised. He had only a distant acquaintance with George Cyril Wellbeloved, but from what he had seen of him he had not credited him with this fatal allure.

"She probably misses his afternoon call."

Again his lordship found himself perplexed. He had had no notion that pigs were such sticklers for the formalities of social life.

"His call?"

"He must have had some special call that he used when he wanted her to come to dinner. One of the first things you learn on a farm is hog calling. Pigs are temperamental. Omit to call them, and they'll starve rather than put on the nose bag. Call them right, and they will follow you to the ends of the earth with their mouths watering."

"God bless my soul! Fancy that."

"A fact, I assure you. These calls vary in different parts of America. In Wisconsin, for example, the words 'Poig, Poig, Poig' bring home—in both the literal and the figurative sense—the bacon.

In Illinois, I believe they call 'Burp, Burp, Burp,' while in Iowa the phrase 'Kus, Kus, Kus' is preferred. Proceeding to Minnesota, we find 'Peega, Peega, Peega' or, alternatively, 'Oink, Oink, Oink,' whereas in Milwaukee, so largely inhabited by those of German descent, you will hear the good old Teuton 'Komm Schweine, Komm Schweine.' Oh, yes, there are all sorts of pig calls, from the Massachusetts, 'Phew, Phew, Phew' to the 'Loo-ey, Loo-ey, Loo-ey' of Ohio, not counting various local devices such as beating on tin cans with axes or rattling pebbles in a suitcase. I knew a man out in Nebraska who used to call his pigs by tapping on the edge of the trough with his wooden leg."

"Did he, indeed?"

"But a most unfortunate thing happened. One evening, hearing a woodpecker at the top of a tree, they started shinning up it; and when the man came out he found them all lying there in a circle with their necks broken."

"This is no time for joking," said Lord Emsworth, pained.

"I'm not joking. Solid fact. Ask anybody out there."

Lord Emsworth placed a hand to his throbbing forehead.

"But if there is this wide variety, we have no means of knowing which call Wellbeloved . . ."

"Ah," said James Belford, "but wait. I haven't told you all. There is a master word."

"A what?"

"Most people don't know it, but I had it straight from the lips of Fred Patzel, the hog-calling champion of the Western States. What a man! I've known him to bring pork chops leaping from their plates. He informed me that, no matter whether an animal has been trained to answer to the Illinois 'Burp' or the Minnesota 'Oink,' it will always give immediate service in response to this magic combination of syllables. It is to the pig world what the Masonic grip is to the human. 'Oink' in Illinois or 'Burp' in Minnesota, and the animal merely raises its eyebrows and stares coldly. But go to either state and call 'Pig-hoo-oo-ey!' . . ."

The expression on Lord Emsworth's face was that of a drowning man who sees a lifeline.

"Is that the master word of which you spoke?"

"That's it."

"Pig—?"

"—hoo-oo-ey."

"Pig-hoo-o-ey?"

"You haven't got it quite right. The first syllable should be short and staccato, the second long and rising into a falsetto, high but true."

"Pig-hoo-o-o-ey."

"Pig-hoo-o-o-ey."

"Pig-hoo-o-o-ey!" yodeled Lord Emsworth, flinging his head back and giving tongue in a high, penetrating tenor which caused ninety-three Senior Conservatives, lunching in the vicinity, to congeal into living statues of alarm and disapproval.

"More body to the 'hoo,' " advised James Belford.

"Pig-hoo-oo-o-ey!"

The Senior Conservative Club is one of the few places in London where lunchers are not accustomed to getting music with their meals. White-whiskered financiers gazed bleakly at bald-headed politicians, as if asking silently what was to be done about this. Bald-headed politicians stared back at white-whiskered financiers, replying in the language of the eye that they did not know. The general sentiment prevailing was a vague determination to write to the Committee about it.

"Pig-hoo-o-o-ey!" caroled Lord Emsworth. And, as he did so, his eye fell on the clock over the mantelpiece. Its hands pointed to twenty minutes to two.

He started convulsively. The best train in the day for Market Blandings was the one which left Paddington Station at two sharp. After that there was nothing till the five-five.

He was not a man who often thought; but, when he did, to think was with him to act. A moment later he was scudding over the carpet, making for the door that led to the broad staircase.

Throughout the room which he had left, the decision to write in strong terms to the Committee was now universal; but from the mind, such as it was, of Lord Emsworth the past, with the single exception of the word "Pig-hoo-o-o-ey!" had been completely blotted.

Whispering the magic syllables, he sped to the cloakroom and retrieved his hat. Murmuring them over and over again, he sprang into a cab. He was still repeating them as the train moved out of the station; and he would doubtless have gone on repeating them all the way to Market Blandings, had he not, as was his invariable practice when traveling by rail, fallen asleep after the first ten minutes of the journey.

The stopping of the train at Swindon Junction woke him with a start. He sat up, wondering, after his usual fashion on these occasions, who and where he was. Memory returned to him, but a memory that was, alas, incomplete. He remembered his name. He remembered that he was on his way home from a visit to London. But what it was that you said to a pig when inviting it to drop in for a bite of dinner he had completely forgotten.

It was the opinion of Lady Constance Keeble, expressed verbally during dinner in the brief intervals when they were alone, and by means of silent telepathy when Beach, the butler, was adding his dignified presence to the proceedings, that her brother Clarence, in his expedition to London to put matters plainly to James Belford, had made an outstanding idiot of himself.

There had been no need whatever to invite the man Belford to lunch; but, having invited him to lunch, to leave him sitting, without having clearly stated that Angela would have no money for four years, was the act of a congenital imbecile. Lady Constance had been aware ever since their childhood days that her brother had about as much sense as a—

Here Beach entered, superintending the bringing in of the savory, and she had been obliged to suspend her remarks.

This sort of conversation is never agreeable to a sensitive man, and his lordship had removed himself from the danger zone as soon as he could manage it. He was now seated in the library, sipping port and straining a brain which Nature had never intended for hard exercise in an effort to bring back that word of magic of which his unfortunate habit of sleeping in trains had robbed him.

"Pig—"

He could remember as far as that; but of what avail was a single syllable? Besides, weak as his memory was, he could recall that the whole gist or nub of the thing lay in the syllable that followed. The "pig" was a mere preliminary.

Lord Emsworth finished his port and got up. He felt restless, stifled. The summer night seemed to call to him like some silver-voiced swineherd calling to his pig. Possibly, he thought, a breath of fresh air might stimulate his brain cells. He wandered downstairs; and, having dug a shocking old slouch hat out of the cupboard where he hid it to keep his sister Constance from impounding and burning it, he strode heavily out into the garden.

He was pottering aimlessly to and fro in the parts adjacent to the rear of the castle when there appeared in his path a slender female form. He recognized it without pleasure. Any unbiased judge would have said that his niece Angela, standing there in the soft, pale light, looked like some dainty spirit of the Moon. Lord Emsworth was not an unbiased judge. To him Angela merely looked like Trouble. The march of civilization has given the modern girl a vocabulary and an ability to use it which her grandmother never had. Lord Emsworth would not have minded meeting Angela's grandmother a bit.

"Is that you, my dear?" he said nervously.

"Yes."

"I didn't see you at dinner."

"I didn't want any dinner. The food would have choked me. I can't eat."

"It's precisely the same with my pig," said his lordship. "Young Belford tells me—"

Into Angela's queenly disdain there flashed a sudden animation. "Have you seen Jimmy? What did he say?"

"That's just what I can't remember. It began with the word 'Pig'—"

"But after he had finished talking about you, I mean. Didn't he say anything about coming down here?"

"Not that I remember."

"I expect you weren't listening. You've got a very annoying habit, Uncle Clarence," said Angela maternally, "of switching your mind off and just going blah when people are talking to you. It gets you very much disliked on all sides. Didn't Jimmy say anything about me?"

"I fancy so. Yes, I am nearly sure he did."

"Well, what?"

"I cannot remember."

There was a sharp clicking noise in the darkness. It was caused by Angela's upper front teeth meeting her lower front teeth; and was followed by a sort of wordless exclamation. It seemed only too plain that the love and respect which a niece should have for an uncle were in the present instance at a very low ebb.

"I wish you wouldn't do that," said Lord Emsworth plaintively.

"Do what?"

"Make clicking noises at me."

"I will make clicking noises at you. You know perfectly well, Uncle Clarence, that you are behaving like a bohunkus."

"A what?"

"A bohunkus," explained his niece coldly, "is a very inferior sort of worm. Not the kind of worm that you see on lawns, which you can respect, but a really degraded species."

"I wish you would go in, my dear," said Lord Emsworth. "The night air may give you a chill."

"I won't go in. I came out here to look at the moon and think of Jimmy. What are you doing out here if it comes to that?"

"I came here to think. I am greatly exercised about my pig, Empress of Blandings. For two days she has refused her food, and young Belford says she will not eat until she hears the proper call or cry. He very kindly taught it to me, but unfortunately I have forgotten it."

"I wonder you had the nerve to ask Jimmy to teach you pig calls, considering the way you're treating him."

"But—"

"Like a leper, or something. And all I can say is that, if you remember this call of his, and it makes the Empress eat, you ought to be ashamed of yourself if you still refuse to let me marry him."

"My dear," said Lord Emsworth earnestly, "if through young Belford's instrumentality Empress of Blandings is induced to take nourishment once more, there is nothing I will refuse him—nothing."

"Honor bright?"

"I give you my solemn word."

"You won't let Aunt Constance bully you out of it?"

Lord Emsworth drew himself up.

"Certainly not," he said proudly. "I am always ready to listen to your Aunt Constance's views, but there are certain matters where I claim the right to act according to my own judgment." He paused and stood musing. "It began with the word 'Pig—' "

From somewhere near at hand music made itself heard. The servants' hall, its day's labors ended, was refreshing itself with the housekeeper's gramophone. To Lord Emsworth the strains were merely an additional annoyance. He was not fond of music. It reminded him of his younger son Frederick, a flat but persevering songster both in and out of the bath.

"Yes, I can distinctly recall as much as that. Pig—Pig—"

"WHO—"

Lord Emsworth leaped in the air. It was as if an electric shock had been applied to his person.

"WHO stole my heart away?" howled the gramophone. "WHO—?"

The peace of the summer night was shattered by a triumphant shout.

"Pig-HOO-o-o-o-ey!"

A window opened. A large, bald head appeared. A dignified voice spoke.

"Who is there? Who is making that noise?"

"Beach!" cried Lord Emsworth. "Come out here at once."

"Very good, your lordship."

And presently the beautiful night was made still more lovely by the added attraction of the butler's presence.

"Beach, listen to this."

"Very good, your lordship."

"Pig-hoo-o-o-o-ey!"

"Very good, your lordship."

"Now you do it."

"I, your lordship?"

"Yes. It's a way you call pigs."

"I do not call pigs, your lordship," said the butler coldly.

"What do you want Beach to do it for?" asked Angela.

"Two heads are better than one. If we both learn it, it will not matter should I forget it again."

"By Jove, yes! Come on, Beach. Push it over the thorax," urged the girl eagerly. "You don't know it, but this is a matter of life and death. At-a-boy, Beach! Inflate the lungs and go to it."

It had been the butler's intention, prefacing his remarks with the statement that he had been in service at the castle for eighteen years, to explain frigidly to Lord Emsworth that it was not his place to stand in the moonlight practicing pig calls. If, he would have gone on to add, his lordship saw the matter from a different angle, then it was his, Beach's, painful duty to tender his resignation, to become effective one month from that day.

But the intervention of Angela made this impossible to a man of chivalry and heart. A paternal fondness for the girl, dating from the days when he had stooped to enacting—and very convincingly, too, for his was a figure that lent itself to the impersonation—the role of a hippopotamus for her childish amusement, checked the words he would have uttered. She was looking at him with bright eyes, and even the rendering of pig noises seemed a small sacrifice to make for her sake.

"Very good, your lordship," he said in a low voice, his face pale and set in the moonlight. "I shall endeavor to give satisfaction. I would merely advance the suggestion, your lordship, that we move a few steps farther away from the vicinity of the servants' hall. If I were to be overheard by any of the lower domestics, it would weaken my position as a disciplinary force."

"What chumps we are!" cried Angela, inspired. "The place to do it is outside the Empress's sty. Then, if it works, we'll see it working."

Lord Emsworth found this a little abstruse, but after a moment he got it.

"Angela," he said, "you are a very intelligent girl. Where you get your brains from, I don't know. Not from my side of the family."

The bijou residence of the Empress of Blandings looked very snug and attractive in the moonlight. But beneath even the beautiful things of life there is always an underlying sadness. This was supplied in the present instance by a long, low trough, only too plainly full to the brim of succulent mash and acorns. The fast, obviously, was still in progress.

The sty stood some considerable distance from the castle walls, so that there had been ample opportunity for Lord Emsworth to rehearse his little company during the journey. By the time they had ranged

themselves against the rails, his two assistants were letter-per-
fect.

"Now," said his lordship.

There floated out upon the summer night a strange composite sound
that sent the birds roosting in the trees above shooting off their
perches like rockets. Angela's clear soprano rang out like the voice of
the village blacksmith's daughter. Lord Emsworth contributed a reedy
tenor. And the bass notes of Beach probably did more to startle the
birds than any other one item in the program.

They paused and listened. Inside the Empress's boudoir there
sounded the movement of a heavy body. There was an inquiring
grunt. The next moment the sacking that covered the doorway was
pushed aside, and the noble animal emerged.

"Now!" said Lord Emsworth again.

Once more that musical cry shattered the silence of the night. But
it brought no responsive movement from Empress of Blandings. She
stood there motionless, her nose elevated, her ears hanging down,
her eyes everywhere but on the trough where, by rights, she should
now have been digging in and getting hers. A chill disappointment
crept over Lord Emsworth, to be succeeded by a gust of petulant
anger.

"I might have known it," he said bitterly. "That young scoundrel
was deceiving me. He was playing a joke on me."

"He wasn't," cried Angela indignantly. "Was he, Beach?"

"Not knowing the circumstances, miss, I cannot venture an
opinion."

"Well, why has it no effect, then?" demanded Lord Emsworth.

"You can't expect it to work right away. We've got her stirred up,
haven't we? She's thinking it over, isn't she? Once more will do the
trick. Ready, Beach?"

"Quite ready, miss."

"Then when I say three. And this time, Uncle Clarence, do please
for goodness' sake not yowl like you did before. It was enough to
put any pig off. Let it come out quite easily and gracefully. Now, then.
One, two—three!"

The echoes died away. And as they did so a voice spoke.

"Community singing?"

"Jimmy!" cried Angela, whisking round.

"Hullo, Angela. Hullo, Lord Emsworth. Hullo, Beach."

"Good evening, sir. Happy to see you once more."

"Thanks. I'm spending a few days at the vicarage with my father.
I got down here by the five-five."

Lord Emsworth cut peevishly in upon these civilities.

"Young man," he said, "what do you mean by telling me that my pig would respond to that cry? It does nothing of the kind."

"You can't have done it right."

"I did it precisely as you instructed me. I have had, moreover, the assistance of Beach here and my niece Angela—"

"Let's hear a sample."

Lord Emsworth cleared his throat.

"Pig-hoo-o-o-o-ey!"

James Belford shook his head.

"Nothing like it," he said. "You want to begin the 'Hoo' in a low minor of two quarter notes in four-four time. From this build gradually to a higher note, until at last the voice is soaring in full crescendo, reaching F sharp on the natural scale and dwelling for two retarded half notes, then breaking into a shower of accidental grace notes."

"God bless my soul!" said Lord Emsworth, appalled. "I shall never be able to do it."

"Jimmy will do it for you," said Angela. "Now that he's engaged to me, he'll be one of the family and always popping about here. He can do it every day till the show is over."

James Belford nodded.

"I think that would be the wisest plan. It is doubtful if an amateur could ever produce real results. You need a voice that has been trained on the open prairie and that has gathered richness and strength from competing with tornadoes. You need a manly, sunburned, wind-scorched voice with a suggestion in it of the crackling of cornhusks and the whisper of evening breezes in the fodder. Like this!"

Resting his hands on the rail before him, James Belford swelled before their eyes like a young balloon. The muscles on his cheek-bones stood out, his forehead became corrugated, his ears seemed to shimmer. Then, at the very height of the tension, he let it go like, as the poet beautifully puts it, the sound of a great Amen.

"Pig-HOOOOO-OOO-OOO-O-O-ey!"

They looked at him, awed. Slowly, fading off across hill and dale, the vast bellow died away. And suddenly, as it died, another, softer sound succeeded it. A sort of gulpy, gurgly, plobby, squishy, woffle-some sound, like a thousand eager men drinking soup in a foreign restaurant. And, as he heard it, Lord Emsworth uttered a cry of rapture.

The Empress was feeding.

Introducing

❁ *The Golf Stories*

Beginning with The Coming of Gowf, *that Beowulf of the links, and going on to four stirring sagas of the fairway as told by* The Sage *of the clubhouse,* The Oldest Member.

The thoughtful reader will be struck by the poignant depth of feeling which pervades these stories like the scent of muddy shoes in a locker room.

☸ *The Coming of Gowf*

PROLOGUE

AFTER WE HAD sent in our card and waited for a few hours in the marbled anteroom, a bell rang and the major-domo, parting the priceless curtains, ushered us in to where the editor sat writing at his desk. We advanced on all fours, knocking our head reverently on the Aubusson carpet.

"Well?" he said at length, laying down his jeweled pen.

"We just looked in," we said humbly, "to ask if it would be all right if we sent you an historical story."

"The public does not want historical stories," he said, frowning coldly.

"Ah, but the public hasn't seen one of ours!" we replied.

The editor placed a cigarette in a holder presented to him by a reigning monarch, and lit it with a match from a golden box, the gift of the millionaire president of the Amalgamated League of Working Plumbers.

"What this magazine requires," he said, "is red-blooded, one-hundred-per-cent dynamic stuff, palpitating with warm human interest and containing a strong, poignant love motive."

"That," we replied, "is us all over, Mabel."

"What I need at the moment, however, is a golf story."

"By a singular coincidence, ours is a golf story."

"Ha! say you so?" said the editor, a flicker of interest passing over his finely chiseled features. "Then you may let me see it."

He kicked us in the face, and we withdrew.

THE STORY

On the broad terrace outside his palace, overlooking the fair expanse of the Royal gardens, King Merolchazzar of Oom stood leaning on the low parapet, his chin in his hand and a frown on his noble face. The day was fine, and a light breeze bore up to him from the garden below a fragrant scent of flowers. But, for all the pleasure it seemed to give him, it might have been bone fertilizer.

The fact is, King Merolchazzar was in love, and his suit was not prospering. Enough to upset any man.

Royal love affairs in those days were conducted on the correspondence system. A monarch, hearing good reports of a neighboring princess, would dispatch messengers with gifts to her Court, beseeching an interview. The Princess would name a date, and a formal meeting would take place; after which everything usually buzzed along pretty smoothly. But in the case of King Merolchazzar's courtship of the Princess of the Outer Isles there had been a regrettable hitch. She had acknowledged the gifts, saying that they were just what she had wanted and how had he guessed, and had added that, as regarded a meeting, she would let him know later. Since that day no word had come from her, and a gloomy spirit prevailed in the capital. At the Courtiers' Club, the meeting place of the aristocracy of Oom, five to one in *pazazas* was freely offered against Merolchazzar's chances, but found no takers; while in the taverns of the common people, where less conservative odds were always to be had, you could get a snappy hundred to eight. "For in good sooth," writes a chronicler of the time on a half brick and a couple of paving stones which have survived to this day, "it did indeed begin to appear as though our beloved monarch, the son of the sun and the nephew of the moon, had been handed the bitter fruit of the citron."

The quaint old idiom is almost untranslatable, but one sees what he means.

As the King stood somberly surveying the garden, his attention was attracted by a small, bearded man with bushy eyebrows and a face like a walnut, who stood not far away on a graveled path flanked by rosebushes. For some minutes he eyed this man in silence, then he called to the Grand Vizier, who was standing in the little group of courtiers and officials at the other end of the terrace. The bearded man, apparently unconscious of the Royal scrutiny, had placed a rounded stone on the gravel, and was standing beside it making curious passes over it with his hoe. It was this singular behavior that had attracted the King's attention. Superficially it seemed silly, and yet Merolchazzar had a curious feeling that there was a deep, even a holy, meaning behind the action.

"Who," he inquired, "is that?"

"He is one of your Majesty's gardeners," replied the Vizier.

"I don't remember seeing him before. Who is he?"

The Vizier was a kindhearted man, and he hesitated for a moment.

"He is a Scotsman. One of your Majesty's invincible admirals recently made a raid on the inhospitable coast of that country at a spot known to the natives as S'nandrews and brought away this man."

"What does he think he's doing?" asked the King, as the bearded one slowly raised the hoe above his right shoulder, slightly bending the left knee as he did so.

"It is some species of savage religious ceremony, your Majesty. According to the admiral, the dunes by the seashore where he landed were covered with a multitude of men behaving just as this man is doing. They had sticks in their hands and they struck with these at small round objects. And every now and again—"

"Fo-o-ore!" called a gruff voice from below.

"And every now and again," went on the Vizier, "they would utter the strange melancholy cry which you have just heard. It is a species of chant."

The Vizier broke off. The hoe had descended on the stone, and the stone, rising in a graceful arc, had sailed through the air and fallen within a foot of where the King stood.

"Hi!" exclaimed the Vizier.

The man looked up.

"You mustn't do that! You nearly hit his serene graciousness the King!"

"Mphm!" said the bearded man nonchalantly, and began to wave his hoe mystically over another stone.

Into the King's careworn face there had crept a look of interest, almost of excitement.

"What god does he hope to propitiate by these rites?" he asked.

"The deity, I learn from your Majesty's admiral, is called Gowf."

"Gowf? Gowf?" King Merolchazzar ran over in his mind the muster roll of the gods of Oom. There were sixty-seven of them, but Gowf was not of their number. "It is a strange religion," he murmured. "A strange religion, indeed. But, by Belus, distinctly attractive. I have an idea that Oom could do with a religion like that. It has a zip to it. A sort of fascination, if you know what I mean. It looks to me extraordinarily like what the Court physician ordered. I will talk to this fellow and learn more of these holy ceremonies."

And, followed by the Vizier, the King made his way into the garden. The Vizier was now in a state of some apprehension. He was exercised in his mind as to the effect which the embracing of a new religion by the King might have on the formidable Church party. It would be certain to cause displeasure among the priesthood; and in those days it was a ticklish business to offend the priesthood, even for a monarch. And, if Merolchazzar had a fault, it was a tendency to be a little tactless in his dealings with that powerful body. Only a few mornings back the High Priest of Hec had taken the Vizier aside to complain about the quality of the meat which the King had been using lately for his sacrifices. He might be a child in worldly matters, said the High Priest, but if the King supposed that he did not know the difference between home-grown domestic and frozen imported foreign, it was time his Majesty was disabused of the idea. If, on top of this little unpleasantness, King Merolchazzar were to become an adherent of this new Gowf, the Vizier did not know what might not happen.

The King stood beside the bearded foreigner, watching him closely. The second stone soared neatly onto the terrace. Merolchazzar uttered an excited cry. His eyes were glowing, and he breathed quickly.

"It doesn't look difficult," he muttered.

"Hoots!" said the bearded man.

"I believe I could do it," went on the King, feverishly. "By the eight green gods of the mountain, I believe I could! By the holy fire that burns night and day before the altar of Belus, I'm *sure* I could! By Hec, I'm going to do it now! Gimme that hoe!"

"Toots!" said the bearded man.

It seemed to the King that the fellow spoke derisively, and his blood boiled angrily. He seized the hoe and raised it above his shoulder, bracing himself solidly on widely parted feet. His pose was an exact reproduction of the one in which the Court sculptor had depicted him when working on the life-size statue ("Our Athletic King") which stood in the principal square of the city; but it did not impress the stranger. He uttered a discordant laugh.

"Ye puir gonuph!" he cried. "Whit kin o' a staunce is that?"

The King was hurt. Hitherto the attitude had been generally admired.

"It's the way I always stand when killing lions," he said. " 'In killing lions,' " he added, quoting from the well-known treatise of Nimrod, the recognized textbook on the sport, " 'the weight at the top of the swing should be evenly balanced on both feet.' "

"Ah, weel, ye're no killing lions the noo. Ye're gowfing."

A sudden humility descended upon the King. He felt, as so many men were to feel in similar circumstances in ages to come, as though he were a child looking eagerly for guidance to an all-wise master— a child, moreover, handicapped by water on the brain, feet three sizes too large for him, and hands consisting mainly of thumbs.

"O thou of noble ancestors and agreeable disposition!" he said humbly. "Teach me the true way."

"Use the interlocking grup and keep the staunce a wee bit open and slow back, and dinna press or sway the heid and keep yer e'e on the ba'."

"My which on the what?" said the King, bewildered.

"I fancy, your Majesty," hazarded the Vizier, "that he is respectfully suggesting that your serene graciousness should deign to keep your eye on the ball."

"Oh, ah!" said the King.

The first golf lesson ever seen in the kingdom of Oom had begun.

Up on the terrace, meanwhile, in the little group of courtiers and officials, a whispered consultation was in progress. Officially, the King's unfortunate love affair was supposed to be a strict secret. But you know how it is. These things get about. The Grand Vizier tells the Lord High Chamberlain; the Lord High Chamberlain whispers it in confidence to the Supreme Hereditary Custodian of the Royal Pet Dog; the Supreme Hereditary Custodian hands it on to the Exalted Overseer of the King's Wardrobe on the understanding that it is to go no farther; and, before you know where you are, the varlets and scurvy knaves are gossiping about it in the kitchens, and the Society journalists have started to carve it out on bricks for the next issue of *Palace Prattlings*.

"The long and short of it is," said the Exalted Overseer of the King's Wardrobe, "we must cheer him up."

There was a murmur of approval. In those days of easy executions it was no light matter that a monarch should be a prey to gloom.

"But how?" queried the Lord High Chamberlain.

"I know," said the Supreme Hereditary Custodian of the Royal Pet Dog. "Try him with the minstrels."

"Here! Why us?" protested the leader of the minstrels.

"Don't be silly!" said the Lord High Chamberlain. "It's for your good just as much as ours. He was asking only last night why he never got any music nowadays. He told me to find out whether you supposed he paid you simply to eat and sleep, because if so he knew what to do about it."

"Oh, in that case!" The leader of the minstrels started nervously. Collecting his assistants and tiptoeing down the garden, he took up his stand a few feet in Merolchazzar's rear, just as that much-enduring monarch, after twenty-five futile attempts, was once more addressing his stone.

Lyric writers in those days had not reached the supreme pitch of excellence which has been produced by modern musical comedy.

The art was in its infancy then, and the best the minstrels could do was this—and they did it just as Merolchazzar, raising the hoe with painful care, reached the top of his swing and started down:—

> *"Oh, tune the string and let us sing*
> *Our godlike, great, and glorious King!*
> *He's a bear! He's a bear! He's a bear!"*

There were sixteen more verses, touching on their ruler's prowess in the realms of sport and war, but they were not destined to be sung on that circuit. King Merolchazzar jumped like a stung bullock, lifted his head, and missed the globe for the twenty-sixth time. He spun round on the minstrels, who were working pluckily through their song of praise:—

> *"Oh, may his triumphs never cease!*
> *He has the strength of ten!*
> *First in war, first in peace,*
> *First in the hearts of his countrymen."*

"Get out!" roared the King.

"Your Majesty?" quavered the leader of the minstrels.

"Make a noise like an egg and beat it!" (Again one finds the chronicler's idiom impossible to reproduce in modern speech, and must be content with a literal translation.) "By the bones of my ancestors, it's a little hard! By the beard of the sacred goat, it's tough! What in the name of Belus and Hec do you mean, you yowling misfits, by starting that sort of stuff when a man's swinging? I was just shaping to hit it right that time when you butted in, you—"

The minstrels melted away. The bearded man patted the fermenting monarch paternally on the shoulder.

"Ma mannie," he said, "ye may no' be a gowfer yet, but hoots! ye're learning the language fine!"

King Merolchazzar's fury died away. He simpered modestly at these words of commendation, the first his bearded preceptor had uttered. With exemplary patience he turned to address the stone for the twenty-seventh time.

That night it was all over the city that the King had gone crazy over a new religion, and the orthodox shook their heads.

We of the present day, living in the midst of a million marvels of a complex civilization, have learned to adjust ourselves to conditions and to take for granted phenomena which in an earlier and less advanced age would have caused the profoundest excitement and even alarm. We accept without comment the telephone, the automobile, and the wireless telegraph, and we are unmoved by the spectacle of our fellow human beings in the grip of the first stages of golf fever. Far otherwise was it with the courtiers and officials about the Palace of Oom. The obsession of the King was the sole topic of conversation.

Every day now, starting forth at dawn and returning only with the falling of darkness, Merolchazzar was out on the Linx, as the outdoor temple of the new god was called. In a luxurious house adjoining this expanse the bearded Scotsman had been installed, and there he could be found at almost any hour of the day fashioning out of holy wood the weird implements indispensable to the new religion. As a recognition of his services, the King had bestowed upon him a large pension, innumerable *kaddiz* or slaves, and the title of Promoter of the King's Happiness, which for the sake of convenience was generally shortened to The Pro.

At present, Oom being a conservative country, the worship of the new god had not attracted the public in great numbers. In fact, except for the Grand Vizier, who, always a faithful follower of his sovereign's fortunes, had taken to Gowf from the start, the courtiers held aloof to a man. But the Vizier had thrown himself into the new worship with such vigor and earnestness that it was not long before he won from the King the title of Supreme Splendiferous Maintainer of the Twenty-Four Handicap Except on Windy Days when It Goes Up to Thirty—a title which in ordinary conversation was usually abbreviated to The Dub.

All these new titles, it should be said, were, so far as the courtiers were concerned, a fruitful source of discontent. There were black looks and mutinous whispers. The laws of precedence were being disturbed, and the courtiers did not like it. It jars a man who for years has had his social position all cut and dried—a man, to take an instance at random, who, as Second Deputy Shiner of the Royal Hunting Boots, knows that his place is just below the Keeper of the Eel-Hounds and just above the Second Tenor of the Corps of Minstrels—it jars him, we say, to find suddenly that he has got to go down a step in favor of the Hereditary Bearer of the King's Number Three Iron.

But it was from the priesthood that the real, serious opposition was to be expected. And the priests of the sixty-seven gods of Oom were up in arms. As the white-bearded High Priest of Hec, who, by virtue of his office was generally regarded as leader of the guild, remarked in a glowing speech at an extraordinary meeting of the Priests' Equity Association, he had always set his face against the principle of the Closed Shop hitherto, but there were moments when every thinking man had to admit that enough was sufficient, and it was his opinion that such a moment had now arrived. The cheers which greeted the words showed how correctly he had voiced popular sentiment.

Of all those who had listened to the High Priest's speech, none had listened more intently than the King's half brother, Ascobaruch. A sinister, disappointed man, this Ascobaruch, with mean eyes and a crafty smile. All his life he had been consumed with ambition, and until now it had looked as though he must go to his grave with this ambition unfulfilled. All his life he had wanted to be King of Oom, and now he began to see daylight. He was sufficiently versed in Court intrigues to be aware that the priests were the party that really counted, the source from which all successful revolutions sprang. And of all the priests the one that mattered most was the venerable High Priest of Hec.

It was to this prelate, therefore, that Ascobaruch made his way at the close of the proceedings. The meeting had dispersed after passing a unanimous vote of censure on King Merolchazzar, and the High Priest was refreshing himself in the vestry—for the meeting had taken place in the Temple of Hec—with a small milk and honey.

"Some speech!" began Ascobaruch in his unpleasant, crafty way. None knew better than he the art of appealing to human vanity.

The High Priest was plainly gratified.

"Oh, I don't know," he said modestly.

"Yessir!" said Ascobaruch. "Considerable oration! What I can never understand is how you think up all these things to say. I couldn't do it if you paid me. The other night I had to propose the Visitors at the Old Alumni dinner of Oom University, and my mind seemed to go all blank. But you just stand up and the words come fluttering out of you like bees out of a barn. I simply cannot understand it. The thing gets past me."

"Oh, it's just a knack."

"A divine gift, I should call it."

"Perhaps you're right," said the High Priest, finishing his milk and honey. He was wondering why he had never realized before what a capital fellow Ascobaruch was.

"Of course," went on Ascobaruch, "you had an excellent subject. I mean to say, inspiring and all that. Why, by Hec, even I—though, of course, I couldn't have approached your level—even I could have done something with a subject like that. I mean, going off and worshiping a new god no one has ever heard of. I tell you, my blood fairly boiled. Nobody has a greater respect and esteem for Merolchazzar than I have, but I mean to say, what! Not right, I mean, going off worshiping gods no one has ever heard of! I'm a peaceable man, and I've made it a rule never to mix in politics, but if you happened to say to me as we were sitting here, just as one reasonable man to another—if you happened to say, 'Ascobaruch, I think it's time that definite steps were taken,' I should reply frankly, 'My dear old High Priest, I absolutely agree with you, and I'm with you all the way.' You might even go so far as to suggest that the only way out of the muddle was to assassinate Merolchazzar and start with a clean slate."

The High Priest stroked his beard thoughtfully.

"I am bound to say I never thought of going quite so far as that."

"Merely a suggestion, of course," said Ascobaruch. "Take it or leave it. I shan't be offended. If you know a superior excavation, go to it. But as a sensible man—and I've always maintained that you are the most sensible man in the country—you must see that it would be a solution. Merolchazzar has been a pretty good king, of course. No one denies that. A fair general, no doubt, and a plus man at lion hunting. But, after all—look at it fairly—is life all battles and lion-hunting? Isn't there a deeper side? Wouldn't it be better for the country to have some good orthodox fellow who has worshiped Hec all his life, and could be relied on to maintain the old beliefs—wouldn't the fact that a man like that was on the throne be likely to lead to more general prosperity? There are dozens of men of that kind simply waiting to be asked. Let us say, purely for purposes of argument, that you approached *me*. I should reply, 'Unworthy though I know myself to be of such an honor, I can tell you this. If you put me on the throne, you can bet your bottom *pazaza* that there's one thing that won't suffer, and that is the worship of Hec!' That's the way I feel about it."

The High Priest pondered.

"O thou of unshuffled features but amiable disposition!" he said, "thy discourse soundeth good to me. Could it be done?"

"Could it!" Ascobaruch uttered a hideous laugh. "Could it! Arouse me in the night watches and ask me! Question me on the matter, having stopped me for that purpose on the public highway! What I would suggest—I'm not dictating, mind you; merely trying to help you out—what I would suggest is that you took that long, sharp knife of yours, the one you use for the sacrifices, and toddled out to the Linx—you're sure to find the King there; and just when he's raising that sacrilegious stick of his over his shoulder—"

"O man of infinite wisdom," cried the High Priest warmly, "verily hast thou spoken a fullness of the mouth!"

"Is it a wager?" said Ascobaruch.

"It is a wager!" said the High Priest.

"That's that, then," said Ascobaruch. "Now, I don't want to be mixed up in any unpleasantness, so what I think I'll do while what you might call the preliminaries are being arranged is to go and take a little trip abroad somewhere. The Middle Lakes are pleasant at this time of year. When I come back, it's possible that all the formalities will have been completed, yes?"

"Rely on me, by Hec!" said the High Priest grimly, as he fingered his weapon.

The High Priest was as good as his word. Early on the morrow he made his way to the Linx, and found the King holing out on the second green. Merolchazzar was in high good humor.

"Greetings, O venerable one!" he cried jovially. "Hadst thou come a moment sooner, thou wouldst have seen me lay my ball dead —aye, dead as mutton, with the sweetest little half-mashie-niblick chip shot ever seen outside the sacred domain of S'nandrew, on whom"—he bared his head reverently—"be peace! In one under bogey did I do the hole—yea, and that despite the fact that, slicing my drive, I became ensnared in yonder undergrowth."

The High Priest had not the advantage of understanding one word of what the King was talking about, but he gathered with satisfaction that Merolchazzar was pleased and wholly without suspicion. He clasped an unseen hand more firmly about the handle of his knife, and accompanied the monarch to the next altar. Merolchazzar stooped, and placed a small round white object on a little mound of sand. In spite of his austere views, the High Priest, always a keen student of ritual, became interested.

"Why does your Majesty do that?"

"I tee it up that it may fly the fairer. If I did not, then would it be apt to run along the ground like a beetle instead of soaring like a bird, and mayhap, for thou seest how rough and tangled is the grass before us, I should have to use a niblick for my second."

The High Priest groped for his meaning.

"It is a ceremony to propitiate the god and bring good luck?"

"You might call it that."

The High Priest shook his head.

"I may be old-fashioned," he said, "but I should have thought that, to propitiate a god, it would have been better to have sacrificed one of these *kaddiz* on his altar."

"I confess," replied the King thoughtfully, "that I have often felt that it would be a relief to one's feelings to sacrifice one or two *kaddiz,* but The Pro for some reason or other has set his face against it." He swung at the ball, and sent it forcefully down the fairway. "By

Sam, the son of Snead," he cried, shading his eyes, "a bird of a drive! How truly is it written in the book of the prophet Vadun 'The left hand applieth the force, the right doth but guide. Grip not, therefore, too closely with the right hand!' Yesterday I was pulling all the time."

The High Priest frowned.

"It is written in the sacred book of Hec, your Majesty, 'Thou shalt not follow after strange gods.' "

"Take thou this stick, O venerable one," said the King, paying no attention to the remark, "and have a shot thyself. True, thou art well stricken in years, but many a man has so wrought that he was able to give his grandchildren a stroke a hole. It is never too late to begin."

The High Priest shrank back, horrified. The King frowned.

"It is our Royal wish," he said coldly.

The High Priest was forced to comply. Had they been alone, it is possible that he might have risked all on one swift stroke with his knife, but by this time a group of *kaddiz* had drifted up, and were watching the proceedings with that supercilious detachment so characteristic of them. He took the stick and arranged his limbs as the King directed.

"Now," said Merolchazzar, "slow back and keep your e'e on the ba'!"

A month later, Ascobaruch returned from his trip. He had received no word from the High Priest announcing the success of the revolution, but there might be many reasons for that. It was with unruffled contentment that he bade his charioteer drive him to the palace. He was glad to get back, for after all a holiday is hardly a holiday if you have left your business affairs unsettled.

As he drove, the chariot passed a fair open space, on the outskirts of the city. A sudden chill froze the serenity of Ascobaruch's mood. He prodded the charioteer sharply in the small of the back.

"What is that?" he demanded, catching his breath.

All over the green expanse could be seen men in strange robes, moving to and fro in couples and bearing in their hands mystic wands. Some searched restlessly in the bushes, others were walking briskly in the direction of small red flags. A sickening foreboding of disaster fell upon Ascobaruch.

The charioteer seemed surprised at the question.

"Yon's the muneecipal linx," he replied.

"The what?"

"The muneecipal linx."

"Tell me, fellow, why do you talk that way?"

"Whit way?"

"Why, like that. The way you're talking."

"Hoots, mon!" said the charioteer. "His Majesty King Merolchazzar—may his handicap decrease!—hae passit a law that a' his
soobjects shall do it. Aiblins, 'tis the language spoken by The Pro,
on whom be peace! Mphm!"

Ascobaruch sat back limply, his head swimming. The chariot drove
on, till now it took the road adjoining the royal Linx. A wall lined a
portion of this road, and suddenly, from behind this wall, there rent
the air a great shout of laughter.

"Pull up!" cried Ascobaruch to the charioteer.

He had recognized that laugh. It was the laugh of Merolchazzar.

Ascobaruch crept to the wall and cautiously poked his head over
it. The sight he saw drove the blood from his face and left him white
and haggard.

The King and the Grand Vizier were playing a foursome against
the Pro and the High Priest of Hec, and the Vizier had just laid the
High Priest a dead stymie.

Ascobaruch tottered to the chariot.

"Take me back," he muttered pallidly. "I've forgotten something!"

And so golf came to Oom, and with it prosperity unequaled in
the whole history of the land. Everybody was happy. There was no
more unemployment. Crime ceased. The chronicler repeatedly refers
to it in his memoirs as the Golden Age. And yet there remained one
man on whom complete felicity had not descended. It was all right
while he was actually on the Linx, but there were blank, dreary
stretches of the night when King Merolchazzar lay sleepless on his
couch and mourned that he had nobody to love him.

Of course, his subjects loved him in a way. A new statue had been
erected in the palace square, showing him in the act of getting out of
casual water. The minstrels had composed a whole cycle of up-to-date
songs, commemorating his prowess with the mashie. His handicap
was down to twelve. But these things are not all. A golfer needs a
loving wife, to whom he can describe the day's play through the long
evenings. And this was just where Merolchazzar's life was empty. No
word had come from the Princess of the Outer Isles, and, as he refused to be put off with just-as-good substitutes, he remained a lonely
man.

But one morning, in the early hours of a summer day, as he lay sleeping after a disturbed night, Merolchazzar was awakened by the eager hand of the Lord High Chamberlain, shaking his shoulder.

"Now what?" said the King.

"Hoots, your Majesty! Glorious news! The Princess of the Outer Isles waits without—I mean wi'oot!"

The King sprang from his couch.

"A messenger from the Princess at last!"

"Nay, sire, the Princess herself—that is to say," said the Lord Chamberlain, who was an old man and had found it hard to accustom himself to the new tongue at his age, "her ain sel'! And believe me, or rather, mind ah'm telling ye," went on the honest man joyfully, for he had been deeply exercised by his monarch's troubles, "her Highness is the easiest thing to look at these eyes hae ever seen. And you can say I said it!"

"She is beautiful?"

"Your majesty, she is, in the best and deepest sense of the word, a pippin!"

King Merolchazzar was groping wildly for his robes.

"Tell her to wait!" he cried. "Go and amuse her. Ask her riddles! Tell her anecdotes! Don't let her go. Say I'll be down in a moment. Where in the name of Zoroaster is our imperial mesh-knit underwear?"

A fair and pleasing sight was the Princess of the Outer Isles as she stood on the terrace in the clear sunshine of the summer morning, looking over the King's gardens. With her delicate little nose she sniffed the fragrance of the flowers. Her blue eyes roamed over the rosebushes, and the breeze ruffled the golden curls about her temples. Presently a sound behind her caused her to turn, and she perceived a godlike man hurrying across the terrace pulling up a sock. And at the sight of him the Princess's heart sang within her like the birds down in the garden.

"Hope I haven't kept you waiting," said Merolchazzar apologetically. He, too, was conscious of a strange, wild exhilaration. Truly was this maiden, as his Chamberlain had said, noticeably easy on the eyes. Her beauty was as water in the desert, as fire on a frosty night, as diamonds, rubies, pearls, sapphires, and amethysts.

"Oh, no!" said the princess, "I've been enjoying myself. How passing beautiful are thy gardens, O King!"

"My gardens may be passing beautiful," said Merolchazzar earnestly, "but they aren't half so passing beautiful as thy eyes. I have dreamed of thee by night and by day, and I will tell the world I was nowhere near it! My sluggish fancy came not within a hundred and fifty-seven miles of the reality. Now let the sun dim his face and the moon hide herself abashed. Now let the flowers bend their heads and the gazelle of the mountains confess itself a cripple. Princess, your slave!"

And King Merolchazzar, with that easy grace so characteristic of Royalty, took her hand in his and kissed it.

As he did so, he gave a start of surprise.

"By Hec!" he exclaimed. "What hast thou been doing to thyself? Thy hand is all over little rough places inside. Has some malignant wizard laid a spell upon thee, or what is it?"

The Princess blushed.

"If I make that clear to thee," she said, "I shall also make clear why it was that I sent thee no message all this long while. My time was so occupied, verily I did not seem to have a moment. The fact is, these sorenesses are due to a strange, new religion to which I and my subjects have but recently become converted. And O that I might make thee also of the true faith! 'Tis a wondrous tale, my lord. Some two moons back there was brought to my Court by wandering pirates a captive of an uncouth race who dwell in the north. And this man has taught us—"

King Merolchazzar uttered a loud cry.

"By Robert, the son of Jones! Can this truly be so? What is thy handicap?"

The Princess stared at him, wide-eyed.

"Truly this is a miracle! Art thou also a worshiper of the great Gowf?"

"Am I!" cried the King. "Am I!" He broke off. "Listen!"

From the minstrels' room high up in the palace there came the sound of singing. The minstrels ewere practicing a new paean of praise —words by the Grand Vizier, music by the High Priest of Hec— which they were to render at the next full moon at the banquet of the worshipers of Gowf. The words came clear and distinct through the still air:—

> *"Oh, praises let us utter*
> *   To our most glorious King!*
> *It fairly makes you stutter*
> *   To see him start his swing!*
> *Success attend his putter!*
> *   And luck be with his drive!*

> *And may he do each hole in two,*
> *Although the bogey's five!"*

The voices died away. There was a silence.

"If I hadn't missed a two-foot putt, I'd have done the long fifteenth in four yesterday," said the King.

"I won the Ladies' Open Championship of the Outer Isles last week," said the Princess.

They looked into each other's eyes for a long moment. And then, hand in hand, they walked slowly into the palace.

EPILOGUE

"Well?" we said anxiously.

"I like it," said the editor.

"Good egg!" we murmured.

The editor pressed a bell, a single ruby set in a fold of the tapestry upon the wall. The major-domo appeared.

"Give this man a purse of gold," said the editor, "and throw him out."

❀ The Awakening of Rollo Podmarsh

DOWN on the new bowling green behind the clubhouse some sort of competition was in progress. The seats about the smooth strip of turf were crowded, and the weak-minded yapping of the patients made itself plainly audible to the Oldest Member as he sat in his favorite chair in the smoking room. He shifted restlessly, and a frown marred the placidity of his venerable brow. To the Oldest Member a golf club was a golf club, and he resented the introduction of any alien element. He had opposed the institution of tennis courts; and the suggestion of a bowling green had stirred him to his depths.

A young man in spectacles came into the smoking room. His high forehead was aglow, and he lapped up a ginger ale with the air of one who considers that he has earned it.

"Capital exercise!" he said, beaming upon the Oldest Member.

The Oldest Member laid down his *Vardon on Casual Water,* and peered suspiciously at his companion.

"What did you go round in?" he asked.

"Oh, I wasn't playing golf," said the young man. "Bowls."

"A nauseating pursuit!" said the Oldest Member coldly, and resumed his reading.

The young man seemed nettled.

"I don't know why you should say that," he retorted. "It's a splendid game."

"I rank it," said the Oldest Member, "with the juvenile pastime of marbles."

The young man pondered for some moments.

"Well, anyway," he said at length, "it was good enough for Drake."

"As I have not the pleasure of the acquaintance of your friend Drake, I am unable to estimate the value of his endorsement."

"*The* Drake. The Spanish Armada Drake. He was playing bowls on Plymouth Hoe when they told him that the Armada was in sight. 'There is time to finish the game,' he replied. That's what Drake thought of bowls."

"If he had been a golfer he would have ignored the Armada altogether."

"It's easy enough to say that," said the young man, with spirit, "but can the history of golf show a parallel case?"

"A million, I should imagine."

"But you've forgotten them, eh?" said the young man satirically.

"On the contrary," said the Oldest Member. "As a typical instance, neither more nor less remarkable than a hundred others, I will select the story of Rollo Podmarsh." He settled himself comfortably in his chair, and placed the tips of his fingers together. "This Rollo Podmarsh—"

"No, I say!" protested the young man, looking at his watch.

"This Rollo Podmarsh—"

"Yes, but—"

This Rollo Podmarsh (said the Oldest Member) was the only son of his mother, and she was a widow; and like other young men in that position he had rather allowed a mother's tender care to take the edge off what you might call his rugged manliness. Not to put too fine a point on it, he had permitted his parent to coddle him ever since he had been in the nursery; and now, in his twenty-eighth year, he invariably wore flannel next his skin, changed his shoes the moment they got wet, and—from September to May, inclusive—never went to bed without partaking of a bowl of hot arrowroot. Not, you would say, the stuff of which heroes are made. But you would be wrong. Rollo Podmarsh was a golfer, and consequently pure gold at heart; and in his hour of crisis all the good in him came to the surface.

In giving you this character sketch of Rollo, I have been at pains to make it crisp, for I observe that you are wriggling in a restless manner and you persist in pulling out that watch of yours and gazing at it. Let me tell you that, if a mere skeleton outline of the man has this effect upon you, I am glad for your sake that you never met his mother. Mrs. Podmarsh could talk with enjoyment for hours on end about her son's character and habits. And, on the September evening on which I introduce her to you, though she had, as a fact, been speaking only for some ten minutes, it had seemed like hours to the girl, Mary Kent, who was the party of the second part to the conversation.

Mary Kent was the daughter of an old school friend of Mrs. Podmarsh, and she had come to spend the autumn and winter with her while her parents were abroad. The scheme had never looked particularly good to Mary, and after ten minutes of her hostess on the subject of Rollo she was beginning to weave dreams of knotted sheets and a swift getaway through the bedroom window in the dark of the night.

"He is a strict teetotaller," said Mrs. Podmarsh.

"Really?"

"And has never smoked in his life."

"Fancy that!"

"But here is the dear boy now," said Mrs. Podmarsh fondly.

Down the road toward them was coming a tall, well-knit figure in a Norfolk coat and gray flannel trousers. Over his broad shoulders was suspended a bag of golf clubs.

"Is *that* Mr. Podmarsh?" exclaimed Mary.

She was surprised. After all she had been listening to about the arrowroot and the flannel next the skin and the rest of it, she had pictured the son of the house as a far weedier specimen. She had been expecting to meet a small, slender young man with an eyebrow mustache, and pince-nez; and this person approaching might have stepped straight out of Jack Dempsey's training camp.

"Does he play golf?" asked Mary, herself an enthusiast.

"Oh, yes," said Mrs. Podmarsh. "He makes a point of going out on the links once a day. He says the fresh air gives him such an appetite."

Mary, who had taken a violent dislike to Rollo on the evidence of his mother's description of his habits, had softened toward him on discovering that he was a golfer. She now reverted to her previous opinion. A man who could play the noble game from such ignoble motives was beyond the pale.

"Rollo is exceedingly good at golf," proceeded Mrs. Podmarsh. "He scores more than a hundred and twenty every time, while Mr. Burns, who is supposed to be one of the best players in the club, seldom manages to reach eighty. But Rollo is very modest—modesty is one of his best qualities—and you would never guess he was so skillful unless you were told.

"Well, Rollo darling, did you have a nice game? You didn't get your feet wet, I hope? This is Mary Kent, dear."

Rollo Podmarsh shook hands with Mary. And at her touch the strange dizzy feeling which had come over him at the sight of her suddenly became increased a thousandfold. As I see that you are consulting your watch once more, I will not describe his emotions as exhaustively as I might. I will merely say that he had never felt

anything resembling this sensation of dazed ecstasy since the occasion
when a twenty-foot putt of his, which had been going well off the
line, as his putts generally did, had hit a worm cast sou'sou'east of
the hole and popped in, giving him a snappy six. Rollo Podmarsh,
as you will have divined, was in love at first sight. Which makes it all
the sadder to think Mary at the moment was regarding him as an
outcast and a blister.

Mrs. Podmarsh, having enfolded her son in a vehement embrace,
drew back with a startled exclamation, sniffing.

"Rollo!" she cried. "You smell of tobacco smoke."

Rollo looked embarrassed.

"Well, the fact is, mother—"

A hard protuberance in his coat pocket attracted Mrs. Podmarsh's
notice. She swooped and drew out a big-bowled pipe.

"Rollo!" she exclaimed, aghast.

"Well, the fact is, mother—"

"Don't you know," cried Mrs. Podmarsh, "that smoking is poison-
ous, and injurious to the health?"

"Yes. But the fact is, mother—"

"It causes nervous dyspepsia, sleeplessness, gnawing of the stomach,
headache, weak eyes, red spots on the skin, throat irritation, asthma,
bronchitis, heart failure, lung trouble, catarrh, melancholy, neuras-
thenia, loss of memory, impaired will power, rheumatism, lumbago,
sciatica, neuritis, heartburn, torpid liver, loss of appetite, enervation,
lassitude, lack of ambition, and falling out of hair."

"Yes, I know, mother. But the fact is, Ted Ray smokes all the
time he's playing, and I thought it might improve my game."

And it was at these splendid words that Mary Kent felt for the
first time that something might be made of Rollo Podmarsh. That
she experienced one-millionth of the fervor which was gnawing at
his vitals I will not say. A woman does not fall in love in a flash like
a man. But at least she no longer regarded him with loathing. On
the contrary, she found herself liking him. There was, she considered,
the right stuff in Rollo. And if, as seemed probable from his
mother's conversation, it would take a bit of digging to bring it up,
well—she liked rescue work and had plenty of time.

Mr. Arnold Bennett, in a recent essay, advises young bachelors
to proceed with a certain caution in matters of the heart. They should,
he asserts, first decide whether or not they are ready for love; then,
whether it is better to marry earlier or later; thirdly, whether their
ambitions are such that a wife will prove a hindrance to their career.

These romantic preliminaries concluded, they may grab a girl and go to it. Rollo Podmarsh would have made a tough audience for these precepts. Since the days of Antony and Cleopatra probably no one had ever got more swiftly off the mark. One may say that he was in love before he had come within two yards of the girl. And each day that passed found him more nearly up to his eyebrows in the tender emotion.

He thought of Mary when he was changing his wet shoes; he dreamed of her while putting flannel next his skin; he yearned for her over the evening arrowroot. Why, the man was such a slave to his devotion that he actually went to the length of purloining small articles belonging to her. Two days after Mary's arrival Rollo Podmarsh was driving off the first tee with one of her handkerchiefs, a powder puff, and a dozen hairpins secreted in his left breast pocket. When dressing for dinner he used to take them out and look at them, and at night he slept with them under his pillow. Heavens, how he loved that girl!

One evening when they had gone out into the garden together to look at the new moon—Rollo, by his mother's advice, wearing a woolen scarf to protect his throat—he endeavored to bring the conversation round to the important subject. Mary's last remark had been about earwigs. Considered as a cue, it lacked a subtle something; but Rollo was not the man to be discouraged by that.

"Talking of earwigs, Miss Kent," he said, in a low musical voice, "have you ever been in love?"

Mary was silent for a moment before replying.

"Yes, once. When I was eleven. With a conjurer who came to perform at my birthday party. He took a rabbit and two eggs out of my hair, and life seemed one grand sweet song."

"Never since then?"

"Never."

"Suppose—just for the sake of argument—suppose you ever did love anyone—er—what sort of a man would it be?"

"A hero," said Mary promptly.

"A hero?" said Rollo, somewhat taken aback. "What sort of hero?"

"Any sort. I could only love a really brave man—a man who had done some wonderful heroic action."

"Shall we go in?" said Rollo hoarsely. "The air is a little chilly."

We have now, therefore, arrived at a period in Rollo Podmarsh's career which might have inspired those lines of Henley's about "the night that covers me, black as the pit from pole to pole." What with one thing and another, he was in an almost Job-like condition of despondency. I say "one thing and another," for it was not only hopeless love that weighed him down. In addition to being hopelessly in love, he was greatly depressed about his golf.

On Rollo in his capacity of golfer I have so far not dwelt. You have probably allowed yourself, in spite of the significant episode of the pipe, to dismiss him as one of those placid, contented—shall I say dilettante?—golfers who are so frequent in these degenerate days. Such was not the case. Outwardly placid, Rollo was consumed inwardly by an ever-burning fever of ambition. His aims were not extravagant. He did not want to become amateur champion, nor even to win a monthly medal; but he did, with his whole soul, desire one of these days to go round the course in under a hundred. This feat accomplished, it was his intention to set the seal on his golfing career by playing a real money match; and already he had selected his opponent, a certain Colonel Bodger, a tottery performer of advanced years who for the last decade had been a martyr to lumbago.

But it began to look as if even the modest goal he had marked out for himself was beyond his powers. Day after day he would step on to the first tee, glowing with zeal and hope, only to crawl home in the quiet evenfall with another hundred and twenty on his card. Little wonder, then, that he began to lose his appetite and would moan feebly at the sight of a poached egg.

With Mrs. Podmarsh sedulously watching over her son's health, you might have supposed that this inability on his part to teach the foodstuffs to take a joke would have caused consternation in the home. But it so happened that Rollo's mother had recently been reading a medical treatise in which an eminent physician stated that we all eat too much nowadays, and that the secret of a happy life is to lay off the carbohydrates to some extent. She was, therefore, delighted to observe the young man's moderation in the matter of food, and frequently held him up as an example to be noted and followed by little Lettice Willoughby, her granddaughter, who was a good and consistent trencherwoman, particularly rough on the puddings. Little Lettice, I should mention, was the daughter of Rollo's sister Enid, who lived in the neighborhood. Mrs. Willoughby had been compelled to go away on a visit a few days before and had left her child with Mrs. Podmarsh during her absence.

You can fool some of the people all the time, but Lettice Willoughby was not of the type that is easily deceived. A nice, old-fashioned child would no doubt have accepted without questioning her grandmother's dictum that roly-poly pudding could not fail to hand a devastating wallop to the blood pressure, and that to take two helpings of it was practically equivalent to walking right into the family vault. A child with less decided opinions of her own would have been impressed by the spectacle of her uncle refusing sustenance, and would have received without demur the statement that he did it because he felt that abstinence was good for his health. Lettice was a modern child and knew better. She had had experience of this loss of appetitite and its significance. The first symptom which had preceded the demise of poor old Ponto, who had recently handed in his portfolio after holding office for ten years as the Willoughby family dog, had been this same disinclination to absorb nourishment. Besides, she was an observant child, and had not failed to note the haggard misery in her uncle's eyes. She tackled him squarely on the subject one morning after breakfast. Rollo had retired into the more distant parts of the garden, and was leaning forward, when she found him, with his head buried in his hands.

"Hallo, uncle," said Lettice.

Rollo looked up wanly.

"Ah, child!" he said. He was fond of his niece.

"Aren't you feeling well, uncle?"

"Far, far from well."

"It's old age, I expect," said Lettice.

"I feel old," admitted Rollo. "Old and battered. Ah, Lettice, laugh and be gay while you can."

"All right, uncle."

"Make the most of your happy, careless, smiling, halcyon childhood."

"Right-o, uncle."

"When you get to my age, dear, you will realize that it is a sad, hopeless world. A world where, if you keep your head down, you forget to let the clubhead lead; where even if you do happen by a miracle to keep 'em straight with your brassie, you blow up on the green and foozle a six-inch putt."

Lettice could not quite understand what Uncle Rollo was talking about, but she gathered broadly that she had been correct in supposing him to be in a bad state, and her warm, childish heart was filled with pity for him. She walked thoughtfully away, and Rollo resumed his reverie.

Into each life, as the poet says, some rain must fall. So much had recently been falling into Rollo's that, when Fortune at last sent along a belated sunbeam, it exercised a cheering effect out of all proportion to its size. By this I mean that when, some four days after his conversation with Lettice, Mary Kent asked him to play golf with her, he read into the invitation a significance which only a lover could have seen in it. I will not go so far as to say that Rollo Podmarsh looked on Mary Kent's suggestion that they should have a round together as actually tantamount to a revelation of undying love; but he certainly regarded it as a most encouraging sign. It seemed to him that things were beginning to move, that Rollo Preferred were on a rising market. Gone was the gloom of the past days. He forgot those sad, solitary wanderings of his in the bushes at the bottom of the garden; he forgot that his mother had bought him a new set of winter woollies which felt like horsehair; he forgot that for the last few evenings his arrowroot had tasted strange. His whole mind was occupied with the astounding fact that she had voluntarily offered to play golf with him, and he walked out on to the first tee filled with a yeasty exhilaration which nearly caused him to burst into song.

"How shall we play?" asked Mary. "I am a twelve. What is your handicap?"

Rollo was under the disadvantage of not actually possessing a handicap. He had a sort of private system of bookkeeping of his own by which he took strokes over if they did not seem to him to be up to sample, and allowed himself five-foot putts at discretion. So he had never actually handed in the three cards necessary for handicapping purposes.

"I don't exactly know," he said. "It's my ambition to get round in under a hundred, but I've never managed it yet."

"Never?"

"Never! It's strange, but something always seems to go wrong."

"Perhaps you'll manage it today," said Mary encouragingly, so encouragingly that it was all that Rollo could do to refrain from flinging himself at her feet and barking like a dog. "Well, I'll start you two holes up, and we'll see how we get on. Shall I take the honor?"

She drove off one of those fair-to-medium balls which go with a twelve handicap. Not a great length, but nice and straight.

"Splendid!" cried Rollo devoutly.

"Oh, I don't know," said Mary. "I wouldn't call it anything special."

Titanic emotions were surging in Rollo's bosom as he addressed his ball. He had never felt like this before, especially on the first tee—where as a rule he found himself overcome with a nervous humility.

"Oh, Mary! Mary!" he breathed to himself as he swung.

You who squander your golden youth fooling about on a bowling green will not understand the magic 'of those three words. But if you were a golfer, you would realize that in selecting just that invocation to breathe to himself Rollo Podmarsh had hit, by sheer accident, on the ideal method of achieving a fine drive. Let me explain. The first two words, tensely breathed, are just sufficient to take a man with the proper slowness to the top of his swing; the first syllable of the second "Mary" exactly coincides with the striking of the ball; and the final "ry!" takes care of the follow-through. The consequence was that Rollo's ball, instead of hopping down the hill like an embarrassed duck, as was its usual practice, sang off the tee with a scream like a shell, nodded in passing Mary's ball, where it lay some hundred and fifty yards down the course, and carrying on from there, came to rest within easy distance of the green. For the first time in his golfing life Rollo Podmarsh had hit a nifty.

Mary followed the ball's flight with astonished eyes.

"But this will never do!" she exclaimed. "I can't possibly start you two up if you're going to do this sort of thing."

Rollo blushed.

"I shouldn't think it would happen again," he said. "I've never done a drive like that before."

"But it must happen again," said Mary firmly. "This is evidently your day. If you don't get round in under a hundred today, I shall never forgive you."

Rollo shut his eyes, and his lips moved feverishly. He was registering a vow that, come what might, he would not fail her. A minute later he was holing out in three, one under bogey.

The second hole is the short lake hole. Bogey is three, and Rollo generally did it in four; for it was his custom not to count any balls he might sink in the water, but to start afresh with one which happened to get over, and then take three putts. But today something seemed to tell him that he would not require the aid of this ingenious system. As he took his mashie from the bag, he *knew* that his first shot would soar successfully onto the green.

"Ah, Mary!" he breathed as he swung.

These subtleties are wasted on a worm, if you will pardon the expression, like yourself, who, possibly owing to a defective education, is content to spend life's springtime rolling wooden balls across a lawn; but I will explain that in altering and shortening his soliloquy at this juncture Rollo had done the very thing any good pro would have recommended. If he had murmured, "Oh, Mary! Mary!" as before he would have overswung. "Ah, Mary!" was exactly right for a half swing with the mashie. His ball shot up in a beautiful arc, and trickled to within six inches of the hole.

Mary was delighted. There was something about this big, diffident man which had appealed from the first to everything in her that was motherly.

"Marvelous!" she said. "You'll get a two. Five for the first two holes! Why, you simply must get round in under a hundred now." She swung, but too lightly; and her ball fell in the water. "I'll give you this," she said, without the slightest chagrin, for this girl had a beautiful nature. "Let's get on to the third. Four up! Why, you're wonderful!"

And not to weary you with too much detail, I will simply remark that, stimulated by her gentle encouragement, Rollo Podmarsh actually came off the ninth green with a medal score of forty-six for the half round. A ten on the seventh had spoiled his card to some extent, and a nine on the eighth had not helped, but nevertheless here he was in forty-six, with the easier half of the course before him. He tingled all over—partly because he was wearing the new winter woollies to which I have alluded previously, but principally owing to triumph, elation, and love. He gazed at Mary as Dante might have gazed at Beatrice on one of his particularly sentimental mornings.

Mary uttered an exclamation.

"Oh, I've just remembered," she exclaimed. "I promised to write last night to Jane Simpson and give her that new formula for knitting jumpers. I think I'll phone her now from the clubhouse and then it'll be off my mind. You go on to the tenth, and I'll join you there."

Rollo proceeded over the brow of the hill to the tenth tee, and was filling in the time with practice swings when he heard his name spoken.

"Good gracious, Rollo! I couldn't believe it was you at first."

He turned to see his sister, Mrs. Willoughby, the mother of the child Lettice.

"Hallo!" he said. "When did you get back?"

"Late last night. Why, it's extraordinary!"

"Hope you had a good time. What's extraordinary? Listen, Enid. Do you know what I've done? Forty-six for the first nine! Forty-six! And holing out every putt."

"Oh, then that accounts for it."

"Accounts for what?"

"Why, your looking so pleased with life. I got an idea from Letty, when she wrote to me, that you were at death's door. Your gloom seems to have made a deep impression on the child. Her letter was full of it."

Rollo was moved.

"Dear little Letty! She is wonderfully sympathetic."

"Well, I must be off now," said Enid Willoughby. "I'm late. Oh, talking of Letty. Don't children say the funniest things! She wrote in her letter that you were very old and wretched and that she was going to put you out of your misery."

"Ha ha ha!" laughed Rollo.

"We had to poison poor old Ponto the other day, you know, and poor little Letty was inconsolable till we explained to her that it was really the kindest thing to do, because he was so old and ill. But just imagine her thinking of wanting to end *your* sufferings!"

"Ha ha!" laughed Rollo. "Ha ha h—!"

His voice trailed off into a broken gurgle. Quite suddenly a sinister thought had come to him.

The arrowroot had tasted strange!

"Why, what on earth is the matter?" asked Mrs. Willoughby, regarding his ashen face.

Rollo could find no words. He yammered speechlessly. Yes, for several nights the arrowroot had tasted very rummy. Rummy! There was no other adjective. Even as he plied the spoon he had said to himself: "This arrowroot tastes rummy!" And—he uttered a sharp yelp as he remembered—it had been little Lettice who had brought it to him. He recollected being touched at the time by the kindly act.

"What *is* the matter, Rollo?" demanded Mrs. Willoughby sharply. "Don't stand there looking like a dying duck."

"I am a dying duck," responded Rollo hoarsely. "A dying man, I mean. Enid, that infernal child has poisoned me!"

"Don't be ridiculous! And kindly don't speak of her like that!"

"I'm sorry. I shouldn't blame her, I suppose. No doubt her motives were good. But the fact remains."

"Rollo, you're too absurd."

"But the arrowroot tasted rummy."

"I never knew you could be such an idiot," said his exasperated sister with sisterly outspokenness. "I thought you would think it quaint. I thought you would roar with laughter."

"I did—till I remembered about the rumminess of the arrowroot."

Mrs. Willoughby uttered an impatient exclamation and walked away.

Rollo Podmarsh stood on the tenth tee, a volcano of mixed emotions. Mechanically he pulled out his pipe and lit it. But he found that he could not smoke. In this supreme crisis of his life tobacco seemed to have lost its magic. He put the pipe back in his pocket and gave himself up to his thoughts. Now terror gripped him; anon a sort of gentle melancholy. It was so hard that he should be compelled to leave the world just as he had begun to hit 'em right.

And then in the welter of his thoughts there came one of practical value. To wit, that by hurrying to the doctor's without delay he might yet be saved. There might be antidotes.

He turned to go and there was Mary Kent standing beside him with her bright, encouraging smile.

"I'm sorry I kept you so long," she said. "It's your honor. Fire away, and remember that you've got to do this nine in fifty-three at the outside."

Rollo's thoughts flitted wistfully to the snug surgery where Dr. Brown was probably sitting at this moment surrounded by the finest antidotes.

"Do you know, I think I ought to—"

"Of course you ought to," said Mary. "If you did the first nine in forty-six, you can't possibly take fifty-three coming in."

For one long moment Rollo continued to hesitate—a moment during which the instinct of self-preservation seemed as if it must win the day. All his life he had been brought up to be nervous about his health, and panic gripped him. But there is a deeper, nobler instinct than that of self-preservation—the instinctive desire of a golfer who is at the top of his form to go on and beat his medal-score record. And little by little this grand impulse began to dominate Rollo. If, he felt, he went off now to take antidotes, the doctor might possibly save his life; but reason told him that never again would he be likely to do the first nine in forty-six. He would have to start all over afresh.

Rollo Podmarsh hesitated no longer. With a pale, set face he teed up his ball and drove.

If I were telling this story to a golfer instead of to an excrescence— I use the word in the kindliest spirit—who spends his time messing about on a bowling green, nothing would please me better than to describe shot by shot Rollo's progress over the remaining nine holes. Epics have been written with less material. But these details would, I am aware, be wasted on you. Let it suffice that by the time his last approach trickled onto the eighteenth green he had taken exactly fifty shots.

"Three for it!" said Mary Kent. "Steady now! Take it quite easy and be sure to lay your second dead."

It was prudent counsel, but Rollo was now thoroughly above himself. He had got his feet wet in a puddle on the sixteenth, but he did not care. His winter woollies seemed to be lined with ants, but he ignored them. All he knew was that he was on the last green in ninety-six, and he meant to finish in style. No tame three putts for him! His ball was five yards away, but he aimed for the back of the hole and brought his putter down with a whack. Straight and true the ball sped, hit the tin, jumped high in the air, and fell into the hole with a rattle.

"Oo!" cried Mary.

Rollo Podmarsh wiped his forehead and leaned dizzily on his putter. For a moment so intense is the fervor induced by the game of games, all he could think of was that he had gone round in ninety-seven. Then, as one waking from a trance, he began to appreciate his position. The fever passed, and a clammy dismay took possession of him. He had achieved his life's ambition; but what now? Already he was conscious of a curious discomfort within him. He felt as he supposed Italians of the Middle Ages must have felt after dropping in to take pot luck with the Borgias. It was hard. He had gone round in ninety-seven, but he could never take the next step in the career which he had mapped out in his dreams—the money match with the lumbago-stricken Colonel Bodger.

Mary Kent was fluttering round him, bubbling congratulations, but Rollo sighed.

"Thanks," he said. "Thanks very much. But the trouble is, I'm afraid I'm going to die almost immediately. I've been poisoned!"

"Poisoned!"

"Yes. Nobody is to blame. Everything was done with the best intentions. But there it is."

"But I don't understand."

Rollo explained. Mary listened pallidly.

"Are you sure?" she gasped.

"Quite sure," said Rollo gravely. "The arrowroot tasted rummy."

"But arrowroot always does."

Rollo shook his head.

"No," he said. "It tastes like warm blotting paper, but not rummy."

Mary was sniffing.

"Don't cry," urged Rollo tenderly. "Don't cry."

"But I must. And I've come out without a handkerchief."

"Permit me," said Rollo, producing one of her best from his left breast pocket.

"I wish I had a powder puff," said Mary.

"Allow me," said Rollo. "And your hair has become a little disordered. If I may—" And from the same reservoir he drew a handful of hairpins.

Mary gazed at these exhibits with astonishment.

"But these are mine," she said.

"Yes. I sneaked them from time to time."

"But why?"

"Because I loved you," said Rollo. And in a few moving sentences which I will not trouble you with he went on to elaborate this theme.

Mary listened with her heart full of surging emotions, which I cannot possibly go into if you persist in looking at that damned watch of yours. The scales had fallen from her eyes. She had thought slightingly of this man because he had been a little overcareful of his health, and all the time he had had within him the potentiality of heroism. Something seemed to snap inside her.

"Rollo!" she cried, and flung herself into his arms.

"Mary!" muttered Rollo, gathering her up.

"I told you it was all nonsense," said Mrs. Willoughby, coming up at this tense moment and going on with the conversation where she had left off. "I've just seen Letty, and she said she meant to put you out of your misery but the chemist wouldn't sell her any poison, so she let it go."

Rollo disentangled himself from Mary.

"What?" he cried.

Mrs. Willoughby repeated her remarks.

"You're sure?" he said.

"Of course I'm sure."

"Then why did the arrowroot taste rummy?"

"I made inquiries about that. It seems that mother was worried about your taking to smoking, and she found an advertisement in one of the magazines about the Tobacco Habit Cured in Three Days by a secret method without the victim's knowledge. It was a gentle, safe, agreeable method of eliminating the nicotine poison from the system, strengthening the weakened membranes, and overcoming the craving; so she put some in your arrowroot every night."

There was a long silence. To Rollo Podmarsh it seemed as though the sun had suddenly begun to shine, the birds to sing, and the grasshoppers to toot. All Nature was one vast substantial smile. Down in the valley by the second hole he caught sight of Wallace Chesney's plus fours gleaming as their owner stooped to play his shot, and it seemed to him that he had never in his life seen anything so lovely.

"Mary," he said, in a low, vibrant voice, "will you wait here for me? I want to go into the clubhouse for a moment."

"To change your wet shoes?"

"No!" thundered Rollo. "I'm never going to change my wet shoes again in my life." He felt in his pocket, and hurled a box of patent pills far into the undergrowth. "But I *am* going to change my winter woollies. And when I've put those dashed barbed-wire entanglements into the clubhouse furnace, I'm going to phone to old Colonel Bodger. I hear his lumbago's worse than ever. I'm going to fix up a match with him for a shilling a hole. And if I don't lick the boots off him you can break the engagement!"

He kissed her, and with long, resolute steps strode to the clubhouse.

❁ *The Clicking of Cuthbert*

THE YOUNG MAN came into the smoking room of the clubhouse, and flung his bag with a clatter on the floor. He sank moodily into an armchair and pressed the bell.

"Waiter!"

"Sir?"

The young man pointed at the bag with every evidence of distaste.

"You may have these clubs," he said. "Take them away. If you don't want them yourself, give them to one of the caddies."

Across the room the Oldest Member gazed at him with a grave sadness through the smoke of his pipe. His eye was deep and dreamy—the eye of a man who, as the poet says, has seen Golf steadily and seen it whole.

"You are giving up golf?" he said.

He was not altogether unprepared for such an attitude on the young man's part, for from his eyrie on the terrace above the ninth green he had observed him start out on the afternoon's round and had seen him lose a couple of balls in the lake at the second hole after taking seven strokes at the first.

"Yes!" cried the young man fiercely. "For ever, dammit! Footling game! Blanked infernal fatheaded silly ass of a game! Nothing but a waste of time."

The Sage winced.

"Don't say that, my boy."

"But I do say it. What earthly good is golf? Life is stern and life is earnest. We live in a practical age. All round us we see foreign competition making itself unpleasant. And we spend our time playing golf! What do we get out of it? Is golf any *use?* That's what I'm asking you. Can you name me a single case where devotion to this pestilential pastime has done a man any practical good?"

The Sage smiled gently.

"I could name a thousand."

"One will do."

"I will select," said the Sage, "from the innumerable memories that rush to my mind, the story of Cuthbert Banks."

"Never heard of him."

"Be of good cheer," said the Oldest Member. "You are going to hear of him now."

It was in the picturesque little settlement of Wood Hills (said the Oldest Member) that the incidents occurred which I am about to relate. Even if you have never been in Wood Hills, that suburban paradise is probably familiar to you by name. Situated at a convenient distance from the city, it combines in a notable manner the advantages of town life with the pleasant surroundings and healthful air of the country. Its inhabitants live in commodious houses, standing in their own grounds, and enjoy so many luxuries—such as gravel soil, main drainage, electric light, telephone, baths (h. and c.), and company's own water, that you might be pardoned for imagining life to be so ideal for them that no possible improvement could be added to their lot. Mrs. Willoughby Smethurst was under no such delusion. What Wood Hills needed to make it perfect, she realized, was Culture. Material comforts are all very well, but, if the *summum bonum* is to be achieved, the Soul also demands a look in, and it was Mrs. Smethurst's unfaltering resolve that never while she had her strength should the Soul be handed the loser's end. It was her intention to make Wood Hills a center of all that was most cultivated and refined, and, golly! how she had succeeded. Under her presidency the Wood Hills Literary and Debating Society had tripled its membership.

But there is always a fly in the ointment, a caterpillar in the salad. The local golf club, an institution to which Mrs. Smethurst strongly objected, had also tripled its membership; and the division of the community into two rival camps, the Golfers and the Cultured, had become more marked than ever. This division, always acute, had attained now to the dimensions of a Schism. The rival sects treated one another with a cold hostility.

Unfortunate episodes came to widen the breach. Mrs. Smethurst's house adjoined the links, standing to the right of the fourth tee; and, as the Literary Society was in the habit of entertaining visiting lecturers, many a golfer had foozled his drive owing to sudden loud outbursts of applause coinciding with his down swing. And not long before this story opens a sliced ball, whizzing in at the open window, had come within an ace of incapacitating Raymond Parsloe Devine, the rising young novelist (who rose at that moment a clear foot and a half) from any further exercise of his art. Two inches, indeed, to the right and Raymond must inevitably have handed in his dinner pail.

To make matters worse, a ring at the front doorbell followed almost immediately, and the maid ushered in a young man of pleasing appearance in a sweater and baggy knickerbockers who apologetically but firmly insisted on playing his ball where it lay, and what with the shock of the lecturer's narrow escape and the spectacle of the intruder standing on the table and working away with a niblick, the afternoon's session had to be classed as a complete frost. Mr. Devine's determination, from which no argument could swerve him, to deliver the rest of his lecture in the coal cellar gave the meeting a jolt from which it never recovered.

I have dwelt upon this incident, because it was the means of introducing Cuthbert Banks to Mrs. Smethurst's niece, Adeline. As Cuthbert, for it was he who had so nearly reduced the muster roll of rising novelists by one, hopped down from the table after his stroke, he was suddenly aware that a beautiful girl was looking at him intently. As a matter of fact, everyone in the room was looking at him intently, none more so than Raymond Parsloe Devine, but none of the others were beautiful girls. Long as the members of Wood Hills Literary Society were on brain, they were short on looks, and, to Cuthbert's excited eye, Adeline Smethurst stood out like a jewel in a pile of coke.

He had never seen her before, for she had only arrived at her aunt's house on the previous day, but he was perfectly certain that life, even when lived in the midst of gravel soil, main drainage, and company's own water, was going to be a pretty poor affair if he did not see her again. Yes, Cuthbert was in love; and it is interesting to record, as showing the effect of the tender emotion on a man's game, that twenty minutes after he had met Adeline he did the short eleventh in one, and as near as a toucher got a three on the four-hundred-yard twelfth.

I will skip lightly over the intermediate stages of Cuthbert's courtship and come to the moment when—at the annual ball in aid of the local Cottage Hospital, the only occasion during the year on which the lion, so to speak, lay down with the lamb, and the Golfers and the Cultured met on terms of easy comradeship, their differences temporarily laid aside—he proposed to Adeline and was badly stymied.

That fair, soulful girl could not see him with a spyglass.

"Mr. Banks," she said, "I will speak frankly."

"Charge right ahead," assented Cuthbert.

"Deeply sensible as I am of—"

"I know. Of the honor and the compliment and all that. But, passing lightly over all that guff, what seems to be the trouble? I love you to distraction—"

"Love is not everything."

"You're wrong," said Cuthbert earnestly. "You're right off it. Love—" And he was about to dilate on the theme when she interrupted him.

"I am a girl of ambition."

"And very nice, too," said Cuthbert.

"I am a girl of ambition," repeated Adeline, "and I realize that the fulfillment of my ambitions must come through my husband. I am very ordinary myself—"

"What!" cried Cuthbert. "You ordinary? Why, you are a pearl among women, the queen of your sex. You can't have been looking in a glass lately. You stand alone. Simply alone. You make the rest look like battered repaints."

"Well," said Adeline, softening a trifle, "I believe I am fairly good-looking—"

"Anybody who was content to call you fairly good-looking would describe the Taj Mahal as a pretty nifty tomb."

"But that is not the point. What I mean is, if I marry a nonentity I shall be a nonentity myself for ever. And I would sooner die than be a nonentity."

"And, if I follow your reasoning, you think that that lets *me* out?"

"Well, really, Mr. Banks, *have* you done anything, or are you likely ever to do anything worth while?"

Cuthbert hesitated.

"It's true," he said, "I didn't finish in the first ten in the Open, and I was knocked out in the semifinal of the Amateur, but I won the French Open last year."

"The—what?"

"The French Open Championship. Golf, you know."

"Golf! You waste all your time playing golf. I admire a man who is more spiritual, more intellectual."

A pang of jealousy rent Cuthbert's bosom.

"Like What's-his name Devine?" he said sullenly.

"Mr. Devine," replied Adeline, blushing faintly, "is going to be a great man. Already he has achieved much. The critics say that he is more Russian than any other young American writer."

"And is that good?"

"Of course it's good."

"I should have thought the wheeze would be to be more American than any other young American writer."

"Nonsense! Who wants an American writer to be American? You've got to be Russian or Spanish or something to be a real success. The mantle of the great Russians has descended on Mr. Devine."

"From what I've heard of Russians, I should hate to have that happen to *me*."

"There is no danger of that," said Adeline scornfully.

"Oh! Well, let me tell you that there is a lot more in me than you think."

"That might easily be so."

"You think I'm not spiritual and intellectual," said Cuthbert, deeply moved. "Very well. Tomorrow I join the Literary Society."

Even as he spoke the words his leg was itching to kick himself for being such a chump, but the sudden expression of pleasure on Adeline's face soothed him; and he went home that night with the feeling that he had taken on something rather attractive. It was only in the cold, gray light of the morning that he realized what he had let himself in for.

I do not know if you have had any experience of suburban literary societies, but the one that flourished under the eye of Mrs. Willoughby Smethurst at Wood Hills was rather more so than the average. With my feeble powers of narrative, I cannot hope to make clear to you all that Cuthbert Banks endured in the next few weeks. And, even if I could, I doubt if I should do so. It is all very well to excite pity and terror, as Aristotle recommends, but there are limits. In the ancient Greek tragedies it was an ironclad rule that all the real rough stuff should take place off stage, and I shal follow this admirable principle. It will suffice if I say merely that J. Cuthbert Banks had a thin time. After attending eleven debates and fourteen lectures on *vers libre* Poetry, the Seventeenth-Century Essayists, the Neo-Scandinavian Movement in Portuguese Literature, and other subjects of a similar nature, he grew so enfeebled that, on the rare occasions when he had time for a visit to the links, he had to take a full iron for his mashie shots.

It was not simply the oppressive nature of the debates and lectures that sapped his vitality. What really got right in amongst him was the torture of seeing Adeline's adoration of Raymond Parsloe Devine. The man seemed to have made the deepest possible impression upon her plastic emotions. When he spoke, she leaned forward with parted lips and looked at him. When he was not speaking—which was seldom—she leaned back and looked at him. And when he happened to take the next seat to her, she leaned sideways and looked at him. One glance at Mr. Devine would have been more than enough for Cuthbert; but Adeline found him a spectacle that never palled. She could not have gazed at him with a more rapturous intensity if she had been a small child and he a saucer of ice cream. All this Cuthbert had to witness while still endeavoring to retain the possession of his faculties sufficiently to enable him to duck and back away if somebody suddenly asked him what he thought of the somber realism of Vladimir Brusiloff. It is little wonder that he tossed in bed, picking at the coverlet, through sleepless nights, and had to have all his waistcoats taken in three inches to keep them from sagging.

This Vladimir Brusiloff to whom I have referred was the famous Russian novelist, and, owing to the fact of his being in the country on a lecturing tour at the moment, there had been something of a boom in his works. The Wood Hills Literary Society had been studying them for weeks, and never since his first entrance into intellectual circles had Cuthbert Banks come nearer to throwing in the towel. Vladimir specialized in gray studies of hopeless misery, where nothing happened till page three hundred and eighty, when the moujik decided to commit suicide. It was tough going for a man whose deepest reading hitherto had been Vardon on the push shot, and there can be no greater proof of the magic of love than the fact that Cuthbert stuck it without a cry. But the strain was terrible and I am inclined to think that he must have cracked, had it not been for the daily reports in the papers of the internecine strife which was proceeding so briskly in Russia. Cuthbert was an optimist at heart, and it seemed to him that, at the rate at which the inhabitants of that interesting country were murdering one another, the supply of Russian novelists must eventually give out.

One morning, as he tottered down the road for the short walk which was now almost the only exercise to which he was equal, Cuthbert met Adeline. A spasm of anguish flitted through all his nerve centers as he saw that she was accompanied by Raymond Parsloe Devine.

"Good morning, Mr. Banks," said Adeline.

"Good morning," said Cuthbert hollowly.

"Such good news about Vladimir Brusiloff."

"Dead?" said Cuthbert, with a touch of hope.

"Dead? Of course not. Why should he be? No, Aunt Emily met his manager after his lecture at Queen's Hall yesterday, and he has promised that Mr. Brusiloff shall come to her next Wednesday reception."

"Oh, ah!" said Cuthbert dully.

"I don't know how she managed it. I think she must have told him that Mr. Devine would be there to meet him."

"But you said he was coming," argued Cuthbert.

"I shall be very glad," said Raymond Devine, "of the opportunity of meeting Brusiloff."

"I'm sure," said Adeline, "he will be very glad of the opportunity of meeting you."

"Possibly," said Mr. Devine. "Possibly. Competent critics have said that my work closely resembles that of the great Russian Masters."

"Your psychology is so deep."

"Yes, yes."

"And your atmosphere."

"Quite."

Cuthbert in a perfect agony of spirit prepared to withdraw from this love feast. The sun was shining brightly, but the world was black to him. Birds sang in the treetops, but he did not hear them. He might have been a moujik for all the pleasure he found in life.

"You will be there, Mr. Banks?" said Adeline, as he turned away.

"Oh, sure," said Cuthbert.

When Cuthbert had entered the drawing room on the following Wednesday and had taken his usual place in a distant corner where, while able to feast his gaze on Adeline, he had a sporting chance of being overlooked or mistaken for a piece of furniture, he perceived the great Russian thinker seated in the midst of a circle of admiring females. Raymond Parsloe Devine had not yet arrived.

His first glance at the novelist surprised Cuthbert. Doubtless with the best motives, Vladimir Brusiloff had permitted his face to become almost entirely concealed behind a dense zareba of hair, but his eyes were visible through the undergrowth, and it seemed to Cuthbert that there was an expression in them not unlike that of a cat in a strange backyard surrounded by small boys. The man looked forlorn and hopeless, and Cuthbert wondered whether he had had bad news from home.

This was not the case. The latest news which Vladimir Brusiloff had had from Russia had been particularly cheering. Three of his principal creditors had perished in the last massacre of the *bourgeoisie,* and a man whom he had owed for years for a samovar and a pair of overshoes had fled the country, and had not been heard of since. It was not bad news from home that was depressing Vladimir. What was wrong with him was the fact that this was the eighty-second suburban literary reception he had been compelled to attend since he had landed in the country on his lecturing tour, and he was sick to death of it. When his agent had first suggested the trip, he had signed on the dotted line without an instant's hesitation. Worked out in rubles, the fees offered had seemed just about right. But now, as he peered through the brushwood at the faces round him, and realized that eight out of ten of those present had manuscripts of some sort concealed on their persons, and were only waiting for an opportunity to whip them out and start reading, he wished that he had stayed at his quiet home in Nijni-Novgorod, where the worst thing that could happen to a fellow was a brace of bombs coming in through the window and mixing themselves up with his breakfast egg.

At this point in his meditations he was aware that his hostess was looming up before him with a pale young man in horn-rimmed spectacles at her side. There was in Mrs. Smethurst's demeanor something of the unction of the master of ceremonies at the big fight who introduces the earnest gentleman who wishes to challenge the winner.

"Oh, Mr. Brusiloff," said Mrs. Smethurst, "I do so want you to meet Mr. Raymond Parsloe Devine, whose work I expect you know. He is one of our younger novelists."

The distinguished visitor peered in a wary and defensive manner through the shrubbery, but did not speak. Inwardly he was thinking how exactly like Mr. Devine was to the eighty-one other younger novelists to whom he had been introduced at various hamlets throughout the country. Raymond Parsloe Devine bowed courteously, while Cuthbert, wedged into his corner, glowered at him.

"The critics," said Mr. Devine, "have been kind enough to say that my poor efforts contain a good deal of the Russian spirit. I owe much to the great Russians. I have been greatly influenced by Sovietski."

Down in the forest something stirred. It was Vladimir Brusiloff's mouth opening, as he prepared to speak. He was not a man who prattled readily, especially in a foreign tongue. He gave the impression that each word was excavated from his interior by some up-to-date process of mining. He glared bleakly at Mr. Devine, and allowed three words to drop out of him.

"Sovietski no good!"

He paused for a moment, set the machinery working again, and delivered five more at the pithead.

"I spit me of Sovietski!"

There was a painful sensation. The lot of a popular idol is in many ways an enviable one, but it has the drawback of uncertainty. Here today and gone tomorrow. Until this moment Raymond Parsloe Devine's stock had stood at something considerably over par in Wood Hills intellectual circles, but now there was a rapid slump. Hitherto he had been greatly admired for being influenced by Sovietski, but it appeared now that this was not a good thing to be. It was evidently a rotten thing to be. The law could not touch you for being influenced by Sovietski, but there is an ethical as well as a legal code, and this it was obvious that Raymond Parsloe Devine had transgressed. Women drew away from him slightly, holding their skirts. Men looked at him censoriously. Adeline Smethurst started violently, and dropped a teacup. And Cuthbert Banks, doing this popular imitation of a sardine in his corner, felt for the first time that life held something of sunshine.

Raymond Parsloe Devine was plainly shaken, but he made an adroit attempt to recover his lost prestige.

"When I say I have been influenced by Sovietski, I mean, of course, that I was once under his spell. A young writer commits many follies. I have long since passed through that phase. The false glamor of Sovietski has ceased to dazzle me. I now belong wholeheartedly to the school of Nastikoff."

There was a reaction. People nodded at one another sympathetically. After all, we cannot expect old heads on young shoulders, and a lapse at the outset of one's career should not be held against one who has eventually seen the light.

"Nastikoff no good," said Vladimir Brusiloff coldly. He paused, listening to the machinery.

"Nastikoff worse than Sovietski."

He paused again.

"I spit me of Nastikoff!" he said.

This time there was no doubt about it. The bottom had dropped out of the market, and Raymond Parsloe Devine Preferred were down in the cellar with no takers. It was clear to the entire assembled company that they had been all wrong about Raymond Parsloe Devine. They had allowed him to play on their innocence and sell them a pup. They had taken him at his own valuation, and had been cheated into admiring him as a man who amounted to something, and all the while he had belonged to the school of Nastikoff. You never can tell. Mrs. Smethurst's guests were well-bred, and there was consequently no violent demonstration, but you could see by their faces what they felt. Those nearest Raymond Parsloe jostled to get further away. Mrs. Smethurst eyed him stonily through a raised lorgnette. One or two low hisses were heard, and over at the other end of the room somebody opened the window in a marked manner.

Raymond Parsloe Devine hesitated for a moment, then, realizing his situation, turned and slunk to the door. There was an audible sigh of relief as it closed behind him.

Vladimir Brusiloff proceeded to sum up.

"No novelists any good except me. Sovietski—yah! Nastikoff— bah! I spit me of zem all. No novelists anywhere any good except me. P. G. Wodehouse and Tolstoi not bad. Not good, but not bad. No novelists any good except me."

And, having uttered this dictum, he removed a slab of cake from a nearby plate, steered it through the jungle, and began to champ.

It is too much to say that there was a dead silence. There could never be that in any room in which Vladimir Brusiloff was eating cake. But certainly what you might call the general chitchat was pretty well down and out. Nobody liked to be the first to speak. The members of the Wood Hills Literary Society looked at one another timidly. Cuthbert, for his part, gazed at Adeline; and Adeline gazed into space. It was plain that the girl was deeply stirred. Her eyes were opened wide, a faint flush crimsoned her cheeks, and her breath was coming quickly.

Adeline's mind was in a whirl. She felt as if she had been walking gaily along a pleasant path and had stopped suddenly on the very brink of a precipice. It would be idle to deny that Raymond Parsloe Devine had attracted her extraordinarily. She had taken him at his own valuation as an extremely hot potato, and her hero worship had gradually been turning into love. And now her hero had been shown to have feet of clay. It was hard, I consider, on Raymond Parsloe Devine, but that is how it goes in this world. You get a following as a celebrity, and then you run up against another bigger celebrity and your admirers desert you. One could moralize on this at considerable length, but better not, perhaps. Enough to say that the glamor of Raymond Devine ceased abruptly in that moment for Adeline, and her most coherent thought at this juncture was the resolve, as soon as she got up to her room, to burn the three signed photographs he had sent her and to give the autographed presentation set of his books to the grocer's boy.

Mrs. Smethurst, meanwhile, having rallied somewhat, was endeavoring to set the feast of reason and flow of soul going again.

"And how do you like America, Mr. Brusiloff?" she asked.

The celebrity paused in the act of lowering another segment of cake.

"Dam good," he replied cordially.

"I suppose you have traveled all over the country by this time?"

"You said it," agreed the Thinker.

"Have you met many of our great public men?"

"Yais— Yais— Quite a few of the nibs—the President, I meet him. But—" Beneath the matting a discontented expression came into his face, and his voice took on a peevish note. "But I not meet your *real* great men—your Volterragin, your Veener Sirahzen—I not meet them. That's what gives me the pipovitch. Have *you* ever met Volterragin and Veener Sirahzen?"

A strained, anguished look came into Mrs. Smethurst's face and was reflected in the faces of the other members of the circle. The eminent Russian had sprung two entirely new ones on them, and they felt that their ignorance was about to be exposed. What would Vladimir Brusiloff think of the Wood Hills Literary Society? The reputation of the Wood Hills Literary Society was at stake, trembling in the balance, and coming up for the third time. In dumb agony Mrs. Smethurst rolled her eyes about the room searching for someone capable of coming to the rescue. She drew blank.

And then, from a distant corner, there sounded a deprecating cough, and those nearest Cuthbert Banks saw that he had stopped twisting his right foot around his left ankle and his left foot round his right ankle and was sitting up with a light of almost human intelligence in his eyes.

"Er—" said Cuthbert, blushing as every eye in the room seemed to fix itself on him, "I think he means Walter Hagen and Gene Sarazen."

"Walter Hagen and Gene Sarazen?" repeated Mrs. Smethurst blankly. "I never heard of—"

"Yais! Yais! Most! Very!" shouted Vladimir Brusiloff enthusiastically. "Volterragin and Veener Sirahzen. You know them, yes, what, no, perhaps?"

"I've played with Walter Hagen often, and I was partnered with Gene Sarazen in last year's Open."

The great Russian uttered a cry that shook the chandelier.

"You play in ze Open? Why," he demanded reproachfully of Mrs. Smethurst, "was I not been introduced to this young man who play in opens?"

"Well, really," faltered Mrs. Smethurst. "Well, the fact is, Mr. Brusiloff—"

She broke off. She was unequal to the task of explaining, without hurting anyone's feelings, that she had always regarded Cuthbert as a piece of cheese and a blot on the landscape.

"Introduct me!" thundered the Celebrity.

"Why, certainly, certainly, of course. This is Mr.—" She looked appealingly at Cuthbert.

"Banks," prompted Cuthbert.

"Banks!" cried Vladimir Brusiloff. "Not Cootaboot Banks?"

"*Is* your name Cootaboot?" asked Mrs. Smethurst faintly.

"Well, it's Cuthbert."

"Yais! Yais! Cootaboot!" There was a rush and swirl, as the effervescent Muscovite burst his way through the throng and rushed to where Cuthbert sat. He stood for a moment eying him excitedly, then, stooping swiftly, kissed him on both cheeks before Cuthbert could get his guard up. "My dear young man, I saw you win ze French Open. Great! Great! Grand! Superb! Hot stuff, and you can say I said so! Will you permit one who is but eighteen at Nijni-Novgorod to salute you once more?"

And he kissed Cuthbert again. Then, brushing aside one or two intellectuals who were in the way, he dragged up a chair and sat down.

"You are a great man!" he said.

"Oh, no," said Cuthbert modestly.

"Yais! Great. Most! Very! The way you lay your approach putts dead from anywhere!"

"Oh, I don't know."

Mr. Brusiloff drew his chair closer.

"Let me tell you one vairy funny story about putting. It was one day I play at Nijni-Novgorod with the pro against Lenin and Trotsky, and Trotsky had a two-inch putt for the hole. But, just as he addresses the ball, someone in the crowd he tries to assassinate Lenin with a rewolwer—you know that is our great national sport, trying to assassinate Lenin with rewolwers—and the bang puts Trotsky off his stroke and he goes five yards past the hole, and then Lenin, who is rather shaken, you understand, he misses again himself, and we win the hole and match and I clean up three hundred and ninety-six thousand rubles, or five dollars in your money. Some gameovitch! And now let me tell you one other vairy funny story—"

Desultory conversation had begun in murmurs over the rest of the room, as the Wood Hills intellectuals politely endeavored to conceal the fact that they realized that they were about as much out of it at this reunion of twin souls as cats at a dog show. From time to time they started as Vladimir Brusiloff's laugh boomed out. Perhaps it was a consolation to them to know that he was enjoying himself.

As for Adeline, how shall I describe her emotions? She was stunned. Before her very eyes the stone which the builders had rejected had become the main thing, the hundred-to-one shot had walked away with the race. A rush of tender admiration for Cuthbert Banks flooded her heart. She saw that she had been all wrong. Cuthbert, whom she had always treated with a patronizing superiority, was really a man to be looked up to and worshiped. A deep, dreamy sigh shook Adeline's fragile form.

Half an hour later Vladimir and Cuthbert Banks rose.

"Goot-a-bye, Mrs. Smet-thirst," said the Celebrity. "Zank you for a most charming visit. My friend Cootaboot and me we go now to shoot a few holes. You will lend me clobs, friend Cootaboot?"

"Any you want."

"The niblicksky is what I use most. Goot-a-bye, Mrs. Smet-thirst."

They were moving to the door, when Cuthbert felt a light touch on his arm. Adeline was looking up at him tenderly.

"May I come, too, and walk round with you?"

Cuthbert's bosom heaved.

"Oh," he said, with a tremor in his voice, "that you would walk round with me for life!"

Her eyes met his.

"Perhaps," she whispered softly, "it could be arranged."

"And so," (concluded the Oldest Member) "you see that golf can be of the greatest practical assistance to a man in Life's struggle. Raymond Parsloe Devine, who was no player, had to move out of the neighborhood immediately, and is now, I believe, writing scenarios out in California for the Flicker Film Company. Adeline is married to Cuthbert, and it was only his earnest pleading which prevented her from having their eldest son christened Francis Ouimet Ribbed-Faced Mashie Banks, for she is now as keen a devotee of the great game as her husband. Those who know them say that theirs is a union so devoted, so—"

The Sage broke off abruptly, for the young man had rushed to the door and out into the passage. Through the open door he could hear him crying passionately to the waiter to bring back his clubs.

❁ High Stakes

THE SUMMER DAY was drawing to a close. Over the terrace outside the clubhouse the chestnut trees threw long shadows, and such bees as still lingered in the flower-beds had the air of tired businessmen who are about ready to shut up the office and go off to dinner and a musical comedy. The Oldest Member, stirring in his favorite chair, glanced at his watch and yawned.

As he did so, from the neighborhood of the eighteenth green, hidden from his view by the slope of the ground, there came suddenly a medley of shrill animal cries, and he deduced that some belated match must just have reached a finish. His surmise was correct. The babble of voices drew nearer, and over the brow of the hill came a little group of men. Two, who appeared to be the ring-leaders in the affair, were short and stout. One was cheerful and the other dejected. The rest of the company consisted of friends and adherents; and one of these, a young man who seemed to be amused, strolled to where the Oldest Member sat.

"What," inquired the Sage, "was all the shouting for?"

The young man sank into a chair and lighted a cigarette.

"Perkins and Broster," he said, "were all square at the seventeenth, and they raised the stakes to fifty pounds. They were both on the green in seven, and Perkins had a two-foot putt to halve the match. He missed it by six inches. They play pretty high, those two."

"It is a curious thing," said the Oldest Member, "that men whose golf is of a kind that makes hardened caddies wince always do. The more competent a player, the smaller the stake that contents him. It is only when you get down into the submerged tenth of the golfing world that you find the big gambling. However, I would not call fifty pounds anything sensational in the case of two men like Perkins and Broster. They are both well provided with the world's goods. If you would care to hear the story—"

The young man's jaw fell a couple of notches.

"I had no idea it was so late," he bleated. "I ought to be—"

"—of a man who played for really high stakes—"

"I promised to—"

"—I will tell it to you," said the Sage.

"Look here," said the young man sullenly, "it isn't one of those stories about two men who fall in love with the same girl and play a match to decide which is to marry her, is it? Because if so—"

"The stake to which I allude," said the Oldest Member, "was something far higher and bigger than a woman's love. Shall I proceed?"

"All right," said the young man resignedly. "Snap into it."

It has been well said—I think by the man who wrote the subtitles for "Cage Birds of Society" (began the Oldest Member)—that wealth does not always bring happiness. It was so with Bradbury Fisher, the hero of the story which I am about to relate. One of America's most prominent tainted millionaires, he had two sorrows in life—his handicap refused to stir from twenty-four and his wife disapproved of his collection of famous golf relics. Once, finding him crooning over the trousers in which Ouimet had won his historic replay against Vardon and Ray in the American Open, she had asked him why he did not collect something worth while, like Old Masters or first editions.

Worth while! Bradbury had forgiven, for he loved the woman, but he could not forget.

For Bradbury Fisher, like so many men who have taken to the game in middle age, after a youth misspent in the pursuits of commerce, was no halfhearted enthusiast. Although he still occasionally descended on Wall Street in order to pry the small investor loose from another couple of million, what he really lived for now was golf and his collection. He had begun the collection in his first year as a golfer, and he prized it dearly. And when he reflected that his wife had stopped him purchasing J. H. Taylor's shirt stud, which he could have had for a few hundred pounds, the iron seemed to enter into his soul.

The distressing episode had occurred in London, and he was now on his way back to New York, having left his wife to continue her holiday in England. All through the voyage he remained moody and distrait; and at the ship's concert, at which he was forced to take the chair, he was heard to observe to the purser that if the alleged soprano who had just sung "My Little Gray Home in the West" had the immortal gall to take a second encore he hoped that she would trip over a high note and dislocate her neck.

Such was Bradbury Fisher's mood throughout the ocean journey, and it remained constant until he arrived at his palatial home at Goldenville, Long Island, where, as he sat smoking a moody after-dinner cigar in the Versailles drawing room, Blizzard, his English butler, informed him that Mr. Gladstone Bott desired to speak to him on the telephone.

"Tell him to go and boil himself," said Bradbury.

"Very good, sir."

"No, I'll tell him myself," said Bradbury. He strode to the telephone. "Hullo!" he said curtly.

He was not fond of this Bott. There are certain men who seem fated to go through life as rivals. It was so with Bradbury Fisher and J. Gladstone Bott. Born in the same town within a few days of one another, they had come to New York in the same week; and from that moment their careers had run side by side. Fisher had made his first million two days before Bott, but Bott's first divorce had got half a column and two sticks more publicity than Fisher's.

At Sing Sing, where each had spent several happy years of early manhood, they had run neck and neck for the prizes which that institution has to offer. Fisher secured the position of catcher on the baseball nine in preference to Bott, but Bott just nosed Fisher out when it came to the choice of a tenor for the glee club. Bott was selected for the debating contest against Auburn, but Fisher got the last place on the crossword puzzle team, with Bott merely first reserve.

They had taken up golf simultaneously, and their handicaps had remained level ever since. Between such men it is not surprising that there was little love lost.

"Hullo!" said Gladstone Bott. "So you're back? Say, listen, Fisher. I think I've got something that'll interest you. Something you'll be glad to have in your golf collection."

Bradbury Fisher's mood softened. He disliked Bott, but that was no reason for not doing business with him. And though he had little faith in the man's judgment it might be that he had stumbled upon some valuable antique. There crossed his mind the comforting thought that his wife was three thousand miles away and that he was no longer under her penetrating eye—that eye which, so to speak, was always "about his bath and about his bed and spying out all his ways."

"I've just returned from a trip down South," proceeded Bott, "and I have secured the authentic baffy used by Bobby Jones in his first important contest—the Infants' All-In Championship of Atlanta, Georgia, open to those of both sexes not yet having finished teething."

Bradbury gasped. He had heard rumors that this treasure was in existence, but he had never credited them.

"You're sure?" he cried. "You're positive it's genuine?"

"I have a written guarantee from Mr. Jones, Mrs. Jones, and the nurse."

"How much, Bott, old man?" stammered Bradbury. "How much do you want for it, Gladstone, old top? I'll give you a hundred thousand dollars."

"Ha!"

"Five hundred thousand."

"Ha, ha!"

"A million."

"Ha, ha, ha!"

"Two million."

"Ha, ha, ha, ha!"

Bradbury Fisher's strong face twisted like that of a tortured fiend. He registered in quick succession rage, despair, hate, fury, anguish, pique, and resentment. But when he spoke again his voice was soft and gentle.

"Gladdy, old socks," he said, "we have been friends for years."

"No, we haven't," said Gladstone Bott.

"Yes, we have."

"No, we haven't."

"Well, anyway, what about two million five hundred?"

"Nothing doing. Say, listen. Do you really want that baffy?"

"I do, Botty, old egg, I do indeed."

"Then listen. I'll exchange it for Blizzard."

"For Blizzard?" quavered Fisher.

"For Blizzard."

It occurs to me that, when describing the closeness of the rivalry between these two men I may have conveyed the impression that in no department of life could either claim a definite advantage over the other. If that is so, I erred. It is true that in a general way, whatever one had, the other had something equally good to counterbalance it; but in just one matter Bradbury Fisher had triumphed completely over Gladstone Bott. Bradbury Fisher had the finest English butler on Long Island.

Blizzard stood alone. There is a regrettable tendency on the part of English butlers today to deviate more and more from the type which made their species famous. The modern butler has a nasty knack of being a lissome young man in perfect condition who looks like the son of the house. But Blizzard was of the fine old school. Before coming to the Fisher home he had been for fifteen years in the service of an earl, and his appearance suggested that throughout those fifteen years he had not let a day pass without its pint of port. He radiated port and popeyed dignity. He had splay feet and three chins, and when he walked his curving waistcoat preceded him like the advance guard of some royal procession.

From the first, Bradbury had been perfectly aware that Bott coveted Blizzard, and the knowledge had sweetened his life. But this was the first time he had come out into the open and admitted it.

"Blizzard?" whispered Fisher.

"Blizzard," said Bott firmly. "It's my wife's birthday next week, and I've been wondering what to give her."

Bradbury Fisher shuddered from head to foot, and his legs wobbled like asparagus stalks. Beads of perspiration stood out on his forehead. The serpent was tempting him—tempting him grievously.

"You're sure you won't take three million—or four—or something like that?"

"No; I want Blizzard."

Bradbury Fisher passed his handkerchief over his streaming brow. "So be it," he said in a low voice.

The Jones baffy arrived that night, and for some hours Bradbury Fisher gloated over it with the unmixed joy of a collector who has secured the prize of a lifetime. Then, stealing gradually over him, came the realization of what he had done.

He was thinking of his wife and what she would say when she heard of this. Blizzard was Mrs. Fisher's pride and joy. She had never, like the poet, nursed a dear gazelle, but, had she done so, her attitude toward it would have been identical with her attitude toward Blizzard. Although so far away, it was plain that her thoughts still lingered with the pleasure she had left at home, for on his arrival Bradbury had found three cables awaiting him.

The first ran:
> "How is Blizzard? Reply."

The second:
> "How is Blizzard's sciatica? Reply."

The third:
> "Blizzard's hiccups. How are they? Suggest Doctor Murphy's Tonic Swamp-Juice. Highly spoken of. Three times a day after meals. Try for week and cable result."

It did not require a clairvoyant to tell Bradbury that, if on her return she found that he had disposed of Blizzard in exchange for a child's cut-down baffy, she would certainly sue him for divorce. And there was not a jury in America that would not give their verdict in her favor without a dissentient voice. His first wife, he recalled, had divorced him on far flimsier grounds. So had his second, third, and fourth. And Bradbury loved his wife. There had been a time in his life when, if he lost a wife, he had felt philosophically that there would be another along in a minute; but, as a man grows older, he tends to become set in his habits, and he could not contemplate existence without the company of the present incumbent.

What, therefore, to do? What, when you came right down to it, to do?

There seemed no way out of the dilemma. If he kept the Jones baffy, no other price would satisfy Bott's jealous greed. And to part with the baffy, now that it was actually in his possession, was unthinkable.

And then, in the small hours of the morning, as he tossed sleeplessly on his Louis Quinze bed, his giant brain conceived a plan.

On the following afternoon he made his way to the clubhouse, and was informed that Bott was out playing a round with another millionaire of his acquaintance. Bradbury waited, and presently his rival appeared.

"Hey!" said Gladstone Bott, in his abrupt, uncouth way. "When are you going to deliver that butler?"

"I will make the shipment at the earliest date," said Bradbury.

"I was expecting him last night."

"You shall have him shortly."

"What do you feed him on?" asked Gladstone Bott.

"Oh, anything you have yourselves. Put sulphur in his port in the hot weather. Tell me, how did your match go?"

"He beat me. I had rotten luck."

Bradbury Fisher's eyes gleamed. His moment had come.

"Luck?" he said. "What do you mean, luck? Luck has nothing to do with it. You're always beefing about your luck. The trouble with you is that you play rottenly."

"What!"

"It is no use trying to play golf unless you learn the first principles and do it properly. Look at the way you drive."

"What's wrong with my driving?"

"Nothing, except that you don't do anything right. In driving, as the club comes back in the swing, the weight should be shifted by

degrees, quietly and gradually, until, when the club has reached its
topmost point, the whole weight of the body is supported by the
right leg, the left foot being turned at the time and the left knee bent
in toward the right leg. But, regardless of how much you perfect your
style, you cannot develop any method which will not require you to
keep your head still so that you can see your ball clearly."

"Hey!"

"It is obvious that it is impossible to introduce a jerk or a sudden
violent effort into any part of the swing without disturbing the balance or moving the head. I want to drive home the fact that it is
absolutely essential to—"

"Hey!" cried Gladstone Bott.

The man was shaken to the core. From the local pro, and from
scratch men of his acquaintance, he would gladly have listened to
this sort of thing by the hour, but to hear these words from Bradbury
Fisher, whose handicap was the same as his own, and out of whom
it was his unperishable conviction that he could hammer the tar any
time he got him out on the links, was too much.

"Where do you get off," he demanded heatedly, "trying to teach
me golf?"

Bradbury Fisher chuckled to himself. Everything was working out
as his subtle mind had foreseen.

"My dear fellow," he said, "I was only speaking for your good."

"I like your nerve! I can lick you any time we start."

"It's easy enough to talk."

"I trimmed you twice the week before you sailed to England."

"Naturally," said Bradbury Fisher, "in a friendly round, with only
a few thousand dollars on the match, a man does not extend himself.
You wouldn't dare to play me for anything that really mattered."

"I'll play you when you like for anything you like."

"Very well. I'll play you for Blizzard."

"Against what?"

"Oh, anything you please. How about a couple of railroads?"

"Make it three."

"Very well."

"Next Friday suit you?"

"Sure," said Bradbury Fisher.

It seemed to him that his troubles were over. Like all twenty-four
handicap men, he had the most perfect confidence in his ability to
beat all other twenty-four handicap men. As for Gladstone Bott, he
knew that he could disembowel him any time he was able to lure him
out of the clubhouse.

Nevertheless, as he breakfasted on the morning of the fateful match, Bradbury Fisher was conscious of an unwonted nervousness. He was no weakling. In Wall Street his phlegm in moments of stress was a byword. On the famous occasion when the B. and G. crowd had attacked C. and D., and in order to keep control of L. and M. he had been compelled to buy so largely of S. and T., he had not turned a hair. And yet this morning, in endeavoring to prong up segments of bacon, he twice missed the plate altogether and on a third occasion speared himself in the cheek with his fork. The spectacle of Blizzard, so calm, so competent, so supremely the perfect butler, unnerved him.

"I am jumpy today, Blizzard," he said, forcing a laugh.

"Yes, sir. You do, indeed, appear to have the willies."

"Yes. I am playing a very important golf match this morning."

"Indeed, sir?"

"I must pull myself together, Blizzard."

"Yes, sir. And, if I may respectfully make the suggestion, you should endeavor, when in action, to keep the head down and the eye rigidly upon the ball."

"I will, Blizzard, I will," said Bradbury Fisher, his keen eyes clouding under a sudden mist of tears. "Thank you, Blizzard, for the advice."

"Not at all, sir."

"How is your sciatica, Blizzard?"

"A trifle improved, I thank you, sir."

"And your hiccups?"

"I am conscious of a slight though possibly only a temporary relief, sir."

"Good," said Bradbury Fisher.

He left the room with a firm step; and proceeding to his library, read for a while portions of that grand chapter in James Braid's *Advanced Golf* which deals with driving into the wind. It was a fair and cloudless morning, but it was as well to be prepared for emergencies. Then, feeling that he had done all that could be done, he ordered the car and was taken to the links.

Gladstone Bott was awaiting him on the first tee, in company with two caddies. A curt greeting, a spin of the coin, and Gladstone Bott, securing the honor, stepped out to begin the contest.

Although there are, of course, endless subspecies in their ranks, not all of which have yet been classified by science, twenty-four handicap golfers may be stated broadly to fall into two classes, the dashing and the cautious—those, that is to say, who endeavor to do every hole in a brilliant one and those who are content to win with a steady nine. Gladstone Bott was one of the cautious brigade. He fussed about for a few moments like a hen scratching gravel, then with a stiff quarter-swing sent his ball straight down the fairway for a matter of seventy yards, and it was Bradbury Fisher's turn to drive.

Now, normally, Bradbury Fisher was essentially a dasher. It was his habit, as a rule, to raise his left foot some six inches from the ground, and having swayed forcefully back on to his right leg, to sway sharply forward again and lash out with sickening violence in the general direction of the ball. It was a method which at times produced excellent results, though it had the flaw that it was somewhat uncertain. Bradbury Fisher was the only member of the club, with the exception of the club champion, who had ever carried the second green with his drive; but, on the other hand, he was also the only member who had ever laid his drive on the eleventh dead to the pin of the sixteenth.

But today the magnitude of the issues at stake had wrought a change in him. Planted firmly on both feet, he fiddled at the ball in the manner of one playing spilikens. When he swung, it was with a swing resembling that of Gladstone Bott; and, like Bott, he achieved a nice, steady, rainbow-shaped drive of some seventy yards straight down the middle. Bott replied with an eighty-yard brassy shot. Bradbury held him with another. And so, working their way cautiously across the prairie, they came to the green, where Bradbury, laying his third putt dead, halved the hole.

The second was a repetition of the first, the third and fourth repetitions of the second. But on the fifth green the fortunes of the match began to change. Here Gladstone Bott, faced with a fifteen-foot putt to win, smote his ball firmly off the line, as had been his practice at each of the preceding holes, and the ball, hitting a worm cast and bounding off to the left, ran on a couple of yards, hit another worm cast, bounded to the right, and finally, bumping into a twig, leaped to the left again and clattered into the tin.

"One up," said Gladstone Bott. "Tricky, some of these greens are. You have to gauge the angles to a nicety."

At the sixth a donkey in an adjoining field uttered a raucous bray just as Bott was addressing his ball with a mashie-niblick on the edge of the green. He started violently and, jerking his club with a spasmodic reflex action of the forearm, holed out.

"Nice work," said Gladstone Bott.

The seventh was a short hole, guarded by two large bunkers between which ran a narrow footpath of turf. Gladstone Bott's mashie shot, falling short, ran over the rough, peered for a moment into the depths to the left, then, winding up the path, trickled onto the green, struck a fortunate slope, acquired momentum, ran on, and dropped into the hole.

"Nearly missed it," said Gladstone Bott, drawing a deep breath.

Bradbury Fisher looked out upon a world that swam and danced before his eyes. He had not been prepared for this sort of thing. The way things were shaping, he felt that it would hardly surprise him now if the cups were to start jumping up and snapping at Bott's ball like starving dogs.

"Three up," said Gladstone Bott.

With a strong effort Bradbury Fisher mastered his feelings. His mouth set grimly. Matters, he perceived, had reached a crisis. He saw now that he had made a mistake in allowing himself to be intimidated by the importance of the occasion into being scientific. Nature had never intended him for a scientific golfer, and up till now he had been behaving like an animated illustration out of a book by Vardon. He had taken his club back along and near the turf, allowing it to trend around the legs as far as was permitted by the movement of the arms. He had kept his right elbow close to the side, this action coming into operation before the club was allowed to describe a section of a circle in an upward direction, whence it was carried by means of a slow, steady, swinging movement. He had pivoted, he had pronated the wrists, and he had been careful about the lateral hip shift.

And it had been all wrong. That sort of stuff might suit some people, but not him. He was a biffer, a swatter, and a slosher; and it flashed upon him now that only by biffing, swatting, and sloshing as he had never biffed, swatted, and sloshed before could he hope to recover the ground he had lost.

Gladstone Bott was not one of those players who grow careless with success. His drive at the eighth was just as steady and short as ever. But this time Bradbury Fisher made no attempt to imitate him. For seven holes he had been checking his natural instincts, and now he drove with all the banked-up fury that comes with release from long suppression.

For an instant he remained poised on one leg like a stork; then there was a whistle and a crack, and the ball, smitten squarely in the midriff, flew down the course and, soaring over the bunkers, hit the turf and gamboled to within twenty yards of the green.

He straightened out the kinks in his spine with a grim smile. Allowing himself the regulation three putts, he would be down in five, and only a miracle could give Gladstone Bott anything better than a seven.

"Two down," he said some minutes later, and Gladstone Bott nodded sullenly.

It was not often that Bradbury Fisher kept on the fairway with two consecutive drives, but strange things were happening today. Not only was his drive at the ninth a full two hundred and forty yards, but it was also perfectly straight.

"One down," said Bradbury Fisher, and Bott nodded even more sullenly than before.

There are few things more demoralizing than to be consistently outdriven; and when he is outdriven by a hundred and seventy yards at two consecutive holes the bravest man is apt to be shaken. Gladstone Bott was only human. It was with a sinking heart that he watched his opponent heave and sway on the tenth tee; and when the ball once more flew straight and far down the course a strange weakness seemed to come over him. For the first time he lost his morale and topped. The ball trickled into the long grass, and after three fruitless stabs at it with a niblick he picked up, and the match was squared.

At the eleventh Bradbury Fisher also topped, and his tee shot, though nice and straight, traveled only a couple of feet. He had to scramble to halve in eight.

The twelfth was another short hole; and Bradbury, unable to curb the fine, careless rapture which had crept into his game, had the misfortune to overshoot the green by some sixty yards, thus enabling his opponent to take the lead once more.

The thirteenth and fourteenth were halved, but Bradbury, driving another long ball, won the fifteenth, squaring the match.

It seemed to Bradbury Fisher, as he took his stand on the sixteenth tee, that he now had the situation well in hand. At the thirteenth and fourteenth his drive had flickered, but on the fifteenth it had come back in all its glorious vigor and there appeared to be no reason to suppose that it had not come to stay. He recollected exactly how he had done that last colossal slosh, and he now prepared to reproduce the movements precisely as before. The great thing to remember was to hold the breath on the backswing and not to release it before the moment of impact. Also, the eyes should not be closed until late in the down swing. All great golfers have their little secrets, and that was Bradbury's.

With these aids to success firmly fixed in his mind, Bradbury Fisher prepared to give the ball the nastiest bang that a golf ball had ever had since Edward Blackwell was in his prime. He drew in his breath and, with lungs expanded to their fullest capacity, heaved back on to his large, flat right foot. Then, clenching his teeth, he lashed out.

When he opened his eyes, they fell upon a horrid spectacle. Either he had closed those eyes too soon or else he had breathed too precipitately—whatever the cause, the ball, which should have gone due south, was traveling with great speed sou'-sou'-east. And, even as he gazed, it curved to earth and fell into as uninviting a bit of rough as he had ever penetrated. And he was a man who had spent much time in many roughs.

Leaving Gladstone Bott to continue his imitation of a spavined octogenarian rolling peanuts with a toothpick, Bradbury Fisher, followed by his caddie, set out on the long trail into the jungle.

Hope did not altogether desert him as he walked. In spite of its erratic direction, the ball had been so shrewdly smitten that it was not far from the green. Provided luck was with him and the lie not too desperate, a mashie would put him on the carpet. It was only when he reached the rough and saw what had happened that his heart sank. There the ball lay, half hidden in the grass, while above it waved the straggling tentacle of some tough-looking shrub. Behind it was a stone, and behind the stone, at just the elevation required to catch the backswing of the club, was a tree. And, by an ironical stroke of fate which drew from Bradbury a hollow, bitter laugh, only a few feet to the right was a beautiful smooth piece of turf from which it would have been a pleasure to play one's second.

Dully, Bradbury looked round to see how Bott was getting on. And then suddenly, as he found that Bott was completely invisible behind the belt of bushes through which he had just passed, a voice seemed to whisper to him, "Why not?"

Bradbury Fisher, remember, had spent thirty years in Wall Street.

It was at this moment that he realized that he was not alone. His caddie was standing at his side.

Bradbury Fisher gazed upon the caddie, whom until now he had not had any occasion to observe with any closeness.

The caddie was not a boy. He was a man, apparently in the middle forties, with bushy eyebrows and a walrus mustache; and there was something about his appearance which suggested to Bradbury that here was a kindred spirit. He reminded Bradbury a little of Spike Huggins, the safe blower, who had been in his freshman year at Sing

Sing. It seemed to him that this caddie could be trusted in a delicate matter involving secrecy and silence. Had he been some babbling urchin, the risk might have been too great.

"Caddie," said Bradbury.

"Sir?" said the caddie.

"Yours is an ill-paid job," said Bradbury.

"It is, indeed, sir," said the caddie.

"Would you like to earn fifty dollars?"

"I would prefer to earn a hundred."

"I meant a hundred," said Bradbury.

He produced a roll of bills from his pocket, and peeled off one of that value. Then, stooping, he picked up his ball and placed it on the little oasis of turf. The caddie bowed intelligently.

"You mean to say," cried Gladstone Bott, a few moments later, "that you were out with your second? With your second!"

"I had a stroke of luck."

"You're sure it wasn't about six strokes of luck?"

"My ball was right out in the open in an excellent lie."

"Oh!" said Gladstone Bott shortly.

"I have four for it, I think."

"One down," said Gladstone Bott.

"And two to play," trilled Bradbury.

It was with a light heart that Bradbury Fisher teed up on the seventeenth. The match, he felt, was as good as over. The whole essence of golf is to discover a way of getting out of rough without losing strokes; and with this sensible, broad-minded man of the world caddying for him he seemed to have discovered the ideal way. It cost him scarcely a pang when he saw his drive slice away into a tangle of long grass, but for the sake of appearances he affected a little chagrin.

"Tut, tut!" he said.

"I shouldn't worry," said Gladstone Bott. "You will probably find it sitting upon an India-rubber tee which someone has dropped there."

He spoke sardonically, and Bradbury did not like his manner. But then he never had liked Gladstone Bott's manner, so what of that? He made his way to where the ball had fallen. It was lying under a bush.

"Caddie," said Bradbury.

"Sir?" said the caddie.

"A hundred?"

"And fifty."

"And fifty," said Bradbury Fisher.

Gladstone Bott was still toiling along the fairway when Bradbury reached the green.

"How many?" he asked, eventually winning to the goal.

"On in two," said Bradbury. "And you?"

"Playing seven."

"Then let me see. If you take two putts, which is most unlikely, I shall have six for the hole and match."

A minute later Bradbury had picked up his ball out of the cup. He stood there, basking in the sunshine, his heart glowing with quiet happiness. It seemed to him that he had never seen the countryside looking so beautiful. The birds appeared to be singing as they had never sung before. The trees and the rolling turf had taken on a charm beyond anything he had ever encountered. Even Gladstone Bott looked almost bearable.

"A very pleasant match," he said cordially, "conducted throughout in the most sporting spirit. At one time I thought you were going to pull it off, old man, but there—class will tell."

"I will now make my report," said the caddie with the walrus mustache.

"Do so," said Gladstone Bott briefly.

Bradbury Fisher stared at the man with blanched cheeks. The sun had ceased to shine, the birds had stopped singing. The trees and the rolling turf looked pretty rotten, and Gladstone Bott perfectly foul. His heart was leaden with a hideous dread.

"Your report? Your—your report? What do you mean?"

"You don't suppose," said Gladstone Bott, "that I would play you an important match unless I had detectives watching you, do you? This gentleman is from the Quick Results Agency. What have you to report?" he said, turning to the caddie.

The caddie removed his bushy eyebrows, and with a quick gesture swept off his mustache.

"On the twelfth inst.," he began in a monotonous, singsong voice, "acting upon instructions received, I made my way to the Goldenville Golf Links in order to observe the movements of the man Fisher. I had adopted for the occasion the Number Three disguise and—"

"All right, all right," said Gladstone Bott impatiently. "You can skip all that. Come down to what happened at the sixteenth."

The caddie looked wounded, but he bowed deferentially.

"At the sixteenth hole the man Fisher moved his ball into what—from his actions and furtive manner—I deduced to be a more favorable position."

"Ah!" said Gladstone Bott.

"On the seventeenth the man Fisher picked up his ball and threw it with a movement of the wrist on to the green."

"It's a lie. A foul and contemptible lie," shouted Bradbury Fisher.

"Realizing that the man Fisher might adopt this attitude, sir," said the caddie, "I took the precaution of snapshotting him in the act with my miniature wrist-watch camera, the detective's best friend."

Bradbury Fisher covered his face with his hands and uttered a hollow groan.

"My match," said Gladstone Bott, with vindictive triumph. "I'll trouble you to deliver that butler to me f.o.b. at my residence not later than noon tomorrow. Oh, yes, and I was forgetting. You owe me three railroads."

Blizzard, dignified but kindly, met Bradbury in the Byzantine hall on his return home.

"I trust your golf match terminated satisfactorily, sir?" said the butler.

A pang, almost too poignant to be borne, shot through Bradbury.

"No, Blizzard," he said. "No. Thank you for your kind inquiry, but I was not in luck."

"Too bad, sir," said Blizzard sympathetically. "I trust the prize at stake was not excessive?"

"Well—er—well, it was rather big. I should like to speak to you about that a little later, Blizzard."

"At any time that is suitable to you, sir. If you will ring for one of the assistant underfootmen when you desire to see me, sir, he will find me in my pantry. Meanwhile, sir, this cable arrived for you a short while back."

Bradbury took the envelope listlessly. He had been expecting a communication from his London agents announcing that they had bought Kent and Sussex, for which he had instructed them to make a firm offer just before he left England. No doubt this was their cable.

He opened the envelope, and started as if it had contained a scorpion. It was from his wife.

"Returning immediately 'Aquitania,' " (it ran). "Docking Friday night. Meet without fail."

Bradbury stared at the words, frozen to the marrow. Although he had been in a sort of trance ever since that dreadful moment on the seventeenth green, his great brain had not altogether ceased to function; and, while driving home in the car, he had sketched out roughly a plan of action which, he felt, might meet the crisis. Assuming that Mrs. Fisher was to remain abroad for another month, he had practically decided to buy a daily paper, insert in it a front-page story announcing the death of Blizzard, forward the clipping to his wife, and then sell his house and move to another neighborhood. In this way it might be that she would never learn of what had occurred.

But if she was due back next Friday, the scheme fell through and exposure was inevitable.

He wondered dully what had caused her change of plans, and came to the conclusion that some feminine sixth sense must have warned her of peril threatening Blizzard. With a good deal of peevishness he wished that Providence had never endowed women with this sixth sense. A woman with merely five took quite enough handling.

"Sweet suffering soupspoons!" groaned Bradbury.

"Sir?" said Blizzard.

"Nothing," said Bradbury.

"Very good, sir," said Blizzard.

For a man with anything on his mind, any little trouble calculated to affect the *joie de vivre,* there are few spots less cheering than the Customs sheds of New York. Draughts whistle dismally there—now to, now fro. Strange noises are heard. Customs officials chew gum and lurk grimly in the shadows, like tigers awaiting the luncheon gong. It is not surprising that Bradbury's spirits, low when he reached the place, should have sunk to zero long before the gangplank was lowered and the passengers began to stream down it.

His wife was among the first to land. How beautiful she looked, thought Bradbury, as he watched her. And, alas, how intimidating. His tastes had always lain in the direction of spirited women. His first wife had been spirited. So had his second, third, and fourth. And the one at the moment holding office was perhaps the most spirited of the whole platoon. For one long instant, as he went to meet her, Bradbury Fisher was conscious of a regret that he had not married one of those meek, mild girls who suffer uncomplainingly at their husband's hands in the more hectic type of feminine novel. What he felt he could have done with at the moment was the sort of wife who thinks herself dashed lucky if the other half of the sketch does not drag her round the billiard room by her hair, kicking her the while with spiked shoes.

Three conversational openings presented themselves to him as he approached her.

"Darling, there is something I want to tell you—"

"Dearest, I have a small confession to make—"

"Sweetheart, I don't know if by any chance you remember Blizzard, our butler. Well, it's like this—"

But, in the event, it was she who spoke first.

"Oh, Bradbury," she cried, rushing into his arms, "I've done the most awful thing, and you must try to forgive me!"

Bradbury blinked. He had never seen her in this strange mood before. As she clung to him, she seemed timid, fluttering, and—although a woman who weighed a full hundred and fifty-seven pounds—almost fragile.

"What is it?" he inquired tenderly. "Has somebody stolen your jewels?"

"No, no."

"Have you been losing money at bridge?"

"No, no. Worse than that."

Bradbury started.

"You didn't sing 'My Little Gray Home in the West' at the ship's concert?" he demanded, eying her closely.

"No, no! Ah, how can I tell you? Bradbury, look! You see that man over there?"

Bradbury followed her pointing finger. Standing in an attitude of negligent dignity beside a pile of trunks under the letter V was a tall, stout, ambassadorial man, at the very sight of whom, even at this distance, Bradbury Fisher felt an odd sense of inferiority. His pendulous cheeks, his curving waistcoat, his protruding eyes, and the sequence of rolling chins combined to produce in Bradbury that instinctive feeling of being in the presence of a superior which we experience when meeting scratch golfers, headwaiters of fashionable restaurants, and traffic policemen. A sudden pang of suspicion pierced him.

"Well?" he said hoarsely. "What of him?"

"Bradbury, you must not judge me too harshly. We were thrown together and I was tempted—"

"Woman," thundered Bradbury Fisher, "who is this man?"

"His name is Vosper."

"And what is there between you and him, and when did it start, and why and how and where?"

Mrs. Fisher dabbed at her eyes with her handkerchief.

"It was at the Duke of Bootle's, Bradbury. I was invited there for the week end."

"And this man was there?"

"Yes."

"Ha! Proceed!"

"The moment I set eyes on him, something seemed to go all over me."

"Indeed!"

"At first it was his mere appearance. I felt that I had dreamed of such a man all my life, and that for all these wasted years I had been putting up with the second best."

"Oh, you did, eh? Really? Is that so? You did, did you?" snorted Bradbury Fisher.

"I couldn't help it, Bradbury. I know I have always seemed so devoted to Blizzard, and so I was. But, honestly, there is no comparison between them—really there isn't. You should see the way Vosper stood behind the Duke's chair. Like a high priest presiding over some mystic religious ceremony. And his voice when he asks you if you will have sherry or hock! Like the music of some wonderful organ. I couldn't resist him. I approached him delicately, and found that he was willing to come to America. He had been eighteen years with the Duke, and he told me he couldn't stand the sight of the back of his head any longer. So—"

Bradbury Fisher reeled.

"This man—this Vosper. Who is he?"

"Why, I'm telling you, honey. He was the Duke's butler, and now he's ours. Oh, you know how impulsive I am. Honestly, it wasn't till we were halfway across the Atlantic that I suddenly said to myself, 'What about Blizzard?' What am I to do, Bradbury? I simply haven't the nerve to fire Blizzard. And yet what will happen when he walks into his pantry and finds Vosper there? Oh, think, Bradbury, think!"

Bradbury Fisher was thinking—and for the first time in a week without agony.

"Evangeline," he said gravely, "this is awkward."

"I know."

"Extremely awkward."

"I know, I know. But surely you can think of some way out of the muddle!"

"I may. I cannot promise, but I may." He pondered deeply. "Ha! I have it! It is just possible that I may be able to induce Gladstone Bott to take on Blizzard."

"Do you really think he would?"

"He may—if I play my cards carefully. At any rate, I will try to persuade him. For the moment you and Vosper had better remain in New York, while I go home and put the negotiations in train. If I am successful, I will let you know."

"Do try your very hardest."

"I think I shall be able to manage it. Gladstone and I are old friends, and he would stretch a point to oblige me. But let this be a lesson to you, Evangeline."

"Oh, I will."

"By the way," said Bradbury Fisher, "I am cabling my London agents today to instruct them to buy J. H. Taylor's shirt stud for my collection."

"Quite right, Bradbury darling. And anything else you want in that way you will get, won't you?"

"I will," said Bradbury Fisher.

❂ *The Heel of Achilles*

ON THE young man's face, as he sat sipping his ginger ale in the clubhouse smoking room, there was a look of disillusionment.

"Never again!" he said.

The Oldest Member glanced up from his paper.

"You are proposing to give up golf once more?" he queried.

"Not golf. Betting on golf." The young man frowned. "I've just been let down badly. Wouldn't you have thought I had a good thing, laying seven to one on McTavish against Robinson?"

"Undoubtedly," said the Sage. "The odds, indeed, generous as they are, scarcely indicate the former's superiority. Do you mean to tell me that the thing came unstitched?"

"Robinson won in a walk, after being three down at the turn."

"Strange! What happened?"

"Why, they looked in at the bar to have a refresher before starting for the tenth," said the young man, his voice quivering, "and McTavish suddenly discovered that there was a hole in his trousers pocket and sixpence had dropped out. He worried so frightfully about it that on the second nine he couldn't do a thing right. Went completely off his game and didn't win a hole."

The Sage shook his head gravely.

"If this is really going to be a lesson to you, my boy, never to bet on the result of a golf match, it will be a blessing in disguise. There is no such thing as a certainty in golf. I wonder if I ever told you a rather curious episode in the career of Vincent Jopp?"

"*The* Vincent Jopp? The American multimillionaire?"

"The same. You never knew he once came within an ace of winning the American Amateur Championship, did you?"

"I never heard of his playing golf."

"He played for one season. After that he gave it up and has not touched a club since. Ring the bell and get me a small lime juice, and I will tell you all."

It was long before your time (said the Oldest Member) that the events which I am about to relate took place. I had just come down from Cambridge, and was feeling particularly pleased with myself because I had secured the job of private and confidential secretary to Vincent Jopp, then a man in the early thirties, busy in laying the foundations of his present remarkable fortune. He engaged me, and took me with him to Chicago.

Jopp was, I think, the most extraordinary personality I have encountered in a long and many-sided life. He was admirably equipped for success in finance, having the steely eye and square jaw without which it is hopeless for a man to enter that line of business. He possessed also an overwhelming confidence in himself, and the ability to switch a cigar from one corner of his mouth to the other without wiggling his ears, which, as you know, is the stamp of the true Monarch of the Money Market. He was the nearest approach to the financier on the films, the fellow who makes his jaw muscles jump when he is telephoning, that I have even seen.

Like all successful men, he was a man of method. He kept a pad on his desk on which he would scribble down his appointments, and it was my duty on entering the office each morning to take this pad and type its contents neatly in a loose-leaved ledger. Usually, of course, these entries referred to business appointments and deals which he was contemplating, but one day I was interested to note, against the date May 3rd, the entry:—

"Propose to Amelia"

I was interested, as I say, but not surprised. Though a man of steel and iron, there was nothing of the celibate about Vincent Jopp. He was one of those men who marry early and often. On three separate occasions before I joined his service he had jumped off the dock, to scramble back to shore again later by means of the Divorce Court life belt. Scattered here and there about the country there were three ex-Mrs. Jopps, drawing their monthly envelope, and now, it seemed, he contemplated the addition of a fourth to the platoon.

I was not surprised, I say, at this resolve of his. What did seem a little remarkable to me was the thorough way in which he had thought the thing out. This iron-willed man recked nothing of possible obstacles. Under the date of June 1st was the entry:—

"Marry Amelia";

while in March of the following year he had arranged to have his first-born christened Thomas Reginald. Later on, the shortcoating of Thomas Reginald was arranged for, and there was a note about sending him to school. Many hard things have been said of Vincent

Jopp, but nobody has ever accused him of not being a man who looked ahead.

On the morning of May 4th Jopp came into the office, looking, I fancied, a little thoughtful. He sat for some moments staring before him with his brow a trifle furrowed; then he seemed to come to himself. He rapped his desk.

"Hi! You!" he said. It was thus that he habitually addressed me.

"Mr. Jopp?" I replied.

"What's golf?"

I had at that time just succeeded in getting my handicap down into single figures, and I welcomed the opportunity of dilating on the noblest of pastimes. But I had barely begun my eulogy when he stopped me.

"It's a game, is it?"

"I suppose you could call it that," I said, "but it is an offhand way of describing the holiest—"

"How do you play it?"

"Pretty well," I said. "At the beginning of the season I didn't seem able to keep 'em straight at all, but lately I've been doing fine. Getting better every day. Whether it was that I was moving my head or gripping too tightly with the right hand—"

"Keep the reminiscences for your grandchildren during the long winter evenings," he interrupted abruptly, as was his habit. "What I want to know is what a fellow does when he plays golf. Tell me in as few words as you can just what it's all about."

"You hit a ball with a stick till it falls into a hole."

"Easy!" he snapped. "Take dictation."

I produced my pad.

"May the fifth, take up golf. What's an Amateur Championship?"

"It is the annual competition to decide which is the best player among the amateurs. There is also a Professional Championship, and an Open event."

"Oh, there are golf professionals, are there? What do they do?"

"They teach golf."

"Which is the best of them?"

"Sandy McHoots won both British and American Open events last year."

"Wire him to come here at once."

"But McHoots is in Inverlochty, in Scotland."

"Never mind. Get him; tell him to name his own terms. When is the Amateur Championship?"

"I think it is on September the twelfth this year."

"All right, take dictation. September twelfth, win Amateur Championship."

I stared at him in amazement, but he was not looking at me.

"Got that?" he said. "September thir— Oh, I was forgetting! Add September twelfth, corner wheat. September thirteenth, marry Amelia."

"Marry Amelia," I echoed, moistening my pencil.

"Where do you play this—what's-its-name—golf?"

"There are clubs all over the country. I belong to the Wissahicky Glen."

"That a good place?"

"Very good."

"Arrange today for my becoming a member."

Sandy McHoots arrived in due course, and was shown into the private office.

"Mr. McHoots?" said Vincent Jopp.

"Mphm!" said the Open Champion.

"I have sent for you, Mr. McHoots, because I hear that you are the greatest living exponent of this game of golf."

"Aye," said the champion cordially, "I am that."

"I wish you to teach me the game. I am already somewhat behind schedule owing to the delay incident upon your long journey, so let us start at once. Name a few of the most important points in connection with the game. My secretary will make notes of them, and I will memorize them. In this way we shall save time. Now, what is the most important thing to remember when playing golf?"

"Keep your heid still."

"A simple task."

"Na sae simple as it soonds."

"Nonsense!" said Vincent Jopp curtly. "If I decide to keep my head still, I shall keep it still. What next?"

"Keep yer ee on the ba'."

"It shall be attended to. And the next?"

"Dinna press."

"I won't. And to resume."

Mr. McHoots ran through a dozen of the basic rules, and I took them down in shorthand. Vincent Jopp studied the list.

"Very good. Easier than I had supposed. On the first tee at Wissahicky Glen at eleven sharp tomorrow, Mr. McHoots. Hi! You!"

"Sir?" I said.

"Go out and buy me a set of clubs, a cloth cap, a pair of spiked shoes, and a ball."

"One ball?"

"Certainly. What need is there of more?"

"It sometimes happens," I explained, "that a player who is learning the game fails to hit his ball straight, and then he often loses it in the rough at the side of the fairway."

"Absurd!" said Vincent Jopp. "If I set out to drive my ball straight, I shall drive it straight. Good morning, Mr. McHoots. You will excuse me now. I am busy cornering Woven Textiles."

Golf is in its essence a simple game. You laugh in a sharp, bitter, barking manner when I say this, but nevertheless it is true. Where the average man goes wrong is in making the game difficult for himself. Observe the nonplayer, the man who walks round with you for the sake of the fresh air. He will hole out with a single carefree flick of his umbrella the twenty-foot putt over which you would ponder and hesitate for a full minute before sending it right off the line. Put a driver in his hands, and he pastes the ball into the next county without a thought. It is only when he takes to the game in earnest that he becomes self-conscious and anxious, and tops his shots even as you and I. A man who could retain through his golfing career the almost scornful confidence of the nonplayer would be unbeatable. Fortunately such an attitude of mind is beyond the scope of human nature.

It was not, however, beyond the scope of Vincent Jopp, the superman. Vincent Jopp was, I am inclined to think, the only golfer who ever approached the game in a spirit of Pure Reason. I have read of men who, never having swum in their lives, studied a textbook on their way down to the swimming bath, mastered its contents, and dived in and won the big race. In just such a spirit did Vincent Jopp start to play golf. He committed McHoots's hints to memory, and then went out on the links and put them into practice. He came to the tee with a clear picture in his mind of what he had to do, and he did it. He was not intimidated, like the average novice, by the thought that if he pulled in his hands he would slice, or if he gripped too tightly with the right he would pull. Pulling in the hands was an error, so he did not pull in his hands. Gripping too tightly was a defect, so he did not grip too tightly. With that weird concentration which had served him so well in business he did precisely what he had set out to do—no less and no more. Golf with Vincent Jopp was an exact science.

The annals of the game are studded with the names of those who have made rapid progress in their first season. Colonel Quill, we read in our Vardon, took up golf at the age of fifty-six, and by devising an ingenious machine consisting of a fishing line and a sawed-down bedpost was enabled to keep his head so still that he became a scratch player before the end of the year. But no one, I imagine, except Vincent Jopp, has ever achieved scratch on his first morning on the links.

The main difference, we are told, between the amateur and the professional golfer is the fact that the latter is always aiming at the pin, while the former has in his mind a vague picture of getting somewhere reasonably near it. Vincent Jopp invariably went for the pin. He tried to hole out from anywhere inside two hundred and twenty yards. The only occasion on which I ever heard him express any chagrin or disappointment was during the afternoon round on his first day out, when from the tee on the two hundred and eighty yard seventh he laid his ball within six inches of the hole.

"A marvelous shot!" I cried, genuinely stirred.

"Too much to the right," said Vincent Jopp, frowning.

He went on from triumph to triumph. He won the monthly medal in May, June, July, August, and September. Toward the end of May he was heard to complain that Wissahicky Glen was not a sporting course. The Greens Committee sat up night after night trying to adjust his handicap so as to give other members an outside chance against him. The golf experts of the daily papers wrote columns about his play. And it was pretty generally considered throughout the country that it would be a pure formality for anyone else to enter against him in the Amateur Championship—an opinion which was borne out when he got through into the final without losing a hole. A safe man to have betted on, you would have said. But mark the sequel.

The American Amateur Championship was held that year in Detroit. I had accompanied my employer there; for, though engaged on this nerve-wearing contest, he refused to allow his business to be interfered with. As he had indicated in his schedule, he was busy at the time cornering wheat; and it was my task to combine the duties of caddy and secretary. Each day I accompanied him round the links with my notebook and his bag of clubs, and the progress of his various matches was somewhat complicated by the arrival of a stream of telegraph boys bearing important messages. He would read these between the strokes and dictate replies to me, never, however, taking more than the five minutes allowed by the rules for an interval between strokes. I am inclined to think that it was this that put the finishing touch on his opponents' discomfiture. It is not soothing for a nervous man to have the game hung up on the green while his adversary dictates to his caddy a letter beginning "Yours of the 11th inst. received and contents noted. In reply would state—" This sort of thing puts a man off his game.

I was resting in the lobby of our hotel after a strenuous day's work, when I found that I was being paged. I answered the summons, and was informed that a lady wished to see me. Her card bore the name "Miss Amelia Merridew." Amelia! The name seemed familiar. Then I remembered. Amelia was the name of the girl Vincent Jopp intended to marry, the fourth of the long line of Mrs. Jopps. I hurried to present myself, and found a tall, slim girl, who was plainly laboring under a considerable agitation.

"Miss Merridew?" I said.

"Yes," she murmured. "My name will be strange to you."

"Am I right," I queried, "in supposing that you are the lady to whom Mr. Jopp—"

"I am! I am!" she replied. "And, oh, what shall I do?"

"Kindly give me particulars," I said, taking out my pad from force of habit.

She hesitated a moment, as if afraid to speak.

"You are caddying for Mr. Jopp in the Final tomorrow?" she said at last.

"I am."

"Then could you—would you mind—would it be giving you too much trouble if I asked you to shout 'Boo!' at him when he is making his stroke, if he looks like winning?"

I was perplexed.

"I don't understand."

"I see that I must tell you all. I am sure you will treat what I say as absolutely confidential."

"Certainly."

"I am provisionally engaged to Mr. Jopp."

"Provisionally?"

She gulped.

"Let me tell you my story. Mr. Jopp asked me to marry him, and I would rather do anything on earth than marry him. But how could I say 'No!' with those awful eyes of his boring me through? I knew that if I said 'No,' he would argue me out of it in two minutes. I had an idea. I gathered that he had never played golf, so I told him that I would marry him if he won the Amateur Championship this year. And now I find that he has been a golfer all along, and, what is more, a plus man! It isn't fair!"

"He was not a golfer when you made that condition," I said. "He took up the game on the following day."

"Impossible! How could he have become as good as he is in this short time?"

"Because he is Vincent Jopp! In his lexicon there is no such word as impossible."

She shuddered.

"What a man! But I can't marry him," she cried. "I want to marry somebody else. Oh, won't you help me? Do shout 'Boo!' at him when he is starting his down swing!"

I shook my head.

"It would take more than a single 'boo' to put Vincent Jopp off his stroke."

"But won't you try it?"

"I cannot. My duty is to my employer."

"Oh, do!"

"No, no. Duty is duty, and paramount with me. Besides, I have a bet on him to win."

The stricken girl uttered a faint moan, and tottered away.

I was in our suite shortly after dinner that night, going over some of the notes I had made that day, when the telephone rang. Jopp was out at the time, taking a short stroll with his after-dinner cigar. I unhooked the receiver, and a female voice spoke.

"Is that Mr. Jopp?"

"Mr. Jopp's secretary speaking. Mr. Jopp is out."

"Oh, it's nothing important. Will you say that Mrs. Luella Mainprice Jopp called up to wish him luck? I shall be on the course tomorrow to see him win the final."

I returned to my notes. Soon afterwards the telephone rang again.

"Vincent, dear?"

"Mr. Jopp's secretary speaking."

"Oh, will you say that Mrs. Jane Jukes Jopp called up to wish him luck? I shall be there tomorrow to see him play."

I resumed my work. I had hardly started when the telephone rang for the third time.

"Mr. Jopp?"

"Mr. Jopp's secretary speaking."

"This is Mrs. Agnes Parsons Jopp. I just called up to wish him luck. I shall be looking on tomorrow."

I shifted my work nearer to the telephone table so as to be ready for the next call. I had heard that Vincent Jopp had only been married three times, but you never knew.

Presently Jopp came in.

"Anybody called up?" he asked.

"Nobody on business. An assortment of your wives were on the wire wishing you luck. They asked me to say that they will be on the course tomorrow."

For a moment it seemed to me that the man's iron repose was shaken.

"Luella?" he asked.

"She was the first."

"Jane?"

"And Jane."

"And Agnes?"

"Agnes," I said, "is right."

"H'm!" said Vincent Jopp. And for the first time since I had known him I thought that he was ill at ease.

The day of the final dawned bright and clear. At least, I was not awake at the time to see, but I suppose it did; for at nine o'clock, when I came down to breakfast, the sun was shining brightly. The first eighteen holes were to be played before lunch, starting at eleven. Until twenty minutes before the hour Vincent Jopp kept me busy taking dictation, partly on matters connected with his wheat deal and partly on a signed article dealing with the Final, entitled "How I Won." At eleven sharp we were out on the first tee.

Jopp's opponent was a nice-looking young man, but obviously nervous. He giggled in a distraught sort of way as he shook hands with my employer.

"Well, may the best man win," he said.

"I have arranged to do so," replied Jopp curtly, and started to address his ball.

There was a large crowd at the tee, and, as Jopp started his down swing, from somewhere on the outskirts of this crowd there came suddenly a musical "Boo!" It rang out in the clear morning air like a bugle.

I had been right in my estimate of Vincent Jopp. His forceful stroke never wavered. The head of his club struck the ball, dispatching it a good two hundred yards down the middle of the fairway. As we left the tee I saw Amelia Merridew being led away with bowed head by two members of the Greens Committee. Poor girl! My heart bled for her. And yet, after all, Fate had been kind in removing her from the scene, even in custody, for she could hardly have borne to watch the proceedings. Vincent Jopp made rings round his antagonist. Hole after hole he won in his remorseless, machinelike way, until when lunchtime came at the end of the eighteenth he was ten up. All the other holes had been halved.

It was after lunch, as we made our way to the first tee, that the advance guard of the Mrs. Jopps appeared in the person of Luella Mainprice Jopp, a kittenish little woman with blond hair and a Pekingese dog. I remembered reading in the papers that she had divorced my employer for persistent and aggravated mental cruelty, calling witnesses to bear out her statement that he had said he did not like her in pink, and that on two separate occasions had insisted on her dog eating the leg of a chicken instead of the breast; but Time, the great healer, seemed to have removed all bitterness, and she greeted him affectionately.

"Wassums going to win great big championship against nasty rough strong man?" she said.

"Such," said Vincent Jopp, "is my intention. It was kind of you, Luella, to trouble to come and watch me. I wonder if you know Mrs. Agnes Parsons Jopp?" he said courteously, indicating a kind-looking, motherly woman who had just come up. "How are you, Agnes?"

"If you had asked me that question this morning, Vincent," replied Mrs. Agnes Parsons Jopp, "I should have been obliged to say that I felt far from well. I had an odd throbbing feeling in the left elbow, and I am sure my temperature was above the normal. But this afternoon I am a little better. How are you, Vincent?"

Although she had, as I recalled from the reports of the case, been compelled some years earlier to request the Court to sever her marital relations with Vincent Jopp on the ground of calculated and inhuman brutality, in that he had callously refused, in spite of her pleadings, to take old Dr. Bennett's Tonic Swamp-Juice three times a day, her voice, as she spoke, was kind and even anxious. Badly as this man had treated her—and I remember hearing that several of the jury had been unable to restrain their tears when she was in the witness box giving her evidence—there still seemed to linger some remnants of the old affection.

"I am quite well, thank you, Agnes," said Vincent Jopp.

"Are you wearing your liver pad?"

A frown flitted across my employer's strong face.

"I am not wearing my liver pad," he replied brusquely.

"Oh, Vincent, how rash of you!"

He was about to speak, when a sudden exclamation from his rear checked him. A genial-looking woman in a sports coat was standing there, eying him with a sort of humorous horror.

"Well, Jane," he said.

I gathered that this was Mrs. Jane Jukes Jopp, the wife who had divorced him for systematic and ingrowing fiendishness on the ground that he had repeatedly outraged her feelings by wearing a white waistcoat with a dinner jacket. She continued to look at him dumbly, and then uttered a sort of strangled, hysterical laugh.

"Those legs!" she cried. "Those legs!"

Vincent Jopp flushed darkly. Even the strongest and most silent of us have our weaknesses, and my employer's was the rooted idea that he looked well in knickerbockers. It was not my place to try to dissuade him, but there was no doubt that they did not suit him. Nature, in bestowing upon him a massive head and a jutting chin, had forgotten to finish him off at the other end. Vincent Jopp's legs were skinny.

"You poor dear man!" went on Mrs. Jane Jukes Jopp. "What practical joker ever lured you into appearing in public in knickerbockers?"

"I don't object to the knickerbockers," said Mrs. Agnes Parsons Jopp, "but when he foolishly comes out in quite a strong east wind without his liver pad—"

"Little Tinky-Ting don't need no liver pad, he don't," said Mrs. Luella Mainprice Jopp, addressing the animal in her arms, "because he was his muzzer's pet, he was."

I was standing quite near to Vincent Jopp, and at this moment I saw a bead of perspiration spring out on his forehead, and into his steely eyes there came a positively hunted look. I could understand and sympathize. Napoleon himself would have wilted if he had found himself in the midst of a trio of females, one talking baby talk, another fussing about his health, and the third making derogatory observations on his lower limbs. Vincent Jopp was becoming unstrung.

"May as well be starting, shall we?"

It was Jopp's opponent who spoke. There was a strange, set look on his face—the look of a man whose back is against the wall. Ten down on the morning's round, he had drawn on his reserves of courage and was determined to meet the inevitable bravely.

Vincent Jopp nodded absently, then turned to me.

"Keep those women away from me," he whispered tensely. "They'll put me off my stroke!"

"Put *you* off your stroke!" I exclaimed incredulously.

"Yes, me! How the deuce can I concentrate, with people babbling about liver pads, and—and knickerbockers all round me? Keep them away!"

He started to address his ball, and there was a weak uncertainty in the way he did it that prepared me for what was to come. His club rose, wavered, fell; and the ball, badly topped, trickled two feet and sank into a cuppy lie.

"Is that good or bad?" inquired Mrs. Luella Mainprice Jopp.

A sort of desperate hope gleamed in the eye of the other competitor in the final. He swung with renewed vigor. His ball sang through the air, and lay within chip-shot distance of the green.

"At the very least," said Mrs. Agnes Parsons Jopp, "I hope, Vincent, that you are wearing flannel next your skin."

I heard Jopp give a stifled groan as he took his spoon from the bag. He made a gallant effort to retrieve the lost ground, but the ball struck a stone and bounded away into the long grass to the side of the green. His opponent won the hole.

We moved to the second tee.

"Now, *that* young man," said Mrs. Jane Jukes Jopp, indicating her late husband's blushing antagonist, "is quite right to wear knickerbockers. He can carry them off. But a glance in the mirror must have shown you that you—"

"I'm sure you're feverish, Vincent," said Mrs. Agnes Parsons Jopp, solicitously. "You are quite flushed. There is a wild gleam in your eyes."

"Muzzer's pet's got little buttons of eyes, that don't never have no wild gleam in zem because he's muzzer's own darling, he was!" said Mrs. Luella Mainprice Jopp.

A hollow groan escaped Vincent Jopp's ashen lips.

I need not recount the play hole by hole, I think. There are some subjects that are too painful. It was pitiful to watch Vincent Jopp in his downfall. By the end of the first nine his lead had been reduced to one, and his antagonist, rendered a new man by success, was playing magnificent golf. On the next hole he drew level. Then with a superhuman effort Jopp contrived to halve the eleventh, twelfth, and thirteenth. It seemed as though his iron will might still assert itself, but on the fourteenth the end came.

He had driven a superb ball, outdistancing his opponent by a full fifty yards. The latter played a good second to within a few feet of the green. And then, as Vincent Jopp was shaping for his stroke, Luella Mainprice gave tongue.

"Vincent!"

"Well?"

"Vincent, that other man—bad man—not playing fair. When your back was turned just now, he gave his ball a great bang. *I* was watching him."

"At any rate," said Mrs. Agnes Parsons Jopp, "I do hope, when the game is over, Vincent, that you will remember to cool slowly."

"Flesho!" cried Mrs. Jane Jukes Jopp triumphantly. "I've been trying to remember the name all the afternoon. I saw about it in one of the papers. The advertisements speak most highly of it. You take it before breakfast and again before retiring, and they guarantee it to produce firm, healthy flesh on the most sparsely covered limbs in next to no time. Now, *will* you remember to get a bottle tonight? It comes in two sizes, the five-shilling (or large size) and the smaller at half-a-crown."

Vincent Jopp uttered a quavering moan, and his hand, as he took the mashie from his bag, was trembling like an aspen.

Ten minutes later, he was on his way back to the clubhouse, a beaten man.

And so (concluded the Oldest Member) you see that in golf there is no such thing as a soft snap. You can never be certain of the finest player. Anything may happen to the greatest expert at any stage of the game. In a recent competition George Duncan took eleven shots over a hole which eighteen-handicap men generally do in five. No! Back horses or go down to Throgmorton Street and try to take it away from the Rothschilds, and I will applaud you as a shrewd and cautious financier. But to bet at golf is pure gambling.

⊛ *Jeeves*

Impeccable, omniscient gentleman's gentleman; the final authority on the proper fit of a morning coat and on the shape of things to come.

"Jeeves!" I shouted.

"Sir?" came a faint, respectful voice from the great open spaces.

"My man," I explained to the Right Hon. "A fellow of infinite resource and sagacity. He'll have us out of this in a minute. Jeeves!"

"Sir?"

"I'm sitting on the roof."

"Very good, sir."

"Don't say 'Very good.' It's nothing of the kind. The place is alive with swans."

"I will attend to the matter immediately, sir."

I turned to the Right Hon. I even went so far as to pat him on the back. It was like slapping a wet sponge.

"All is well," I said. "Jeeves is coming."

"What can he do?"

I frowned a trifle. The man's tone had been peevish, and I didn't like it.

"That," I replied with a touch of stiffness, "we cannot say until we see him in action. He may pursue one *course, or he may pursue another. But on one thing you can rely with the utmost confidence—Jeeves will find a way. See, here he comes stealing through the undergrowth, his face shining with the light of pure intelligence. There are no limits to Jeeves's brain power. He virtually lives on fish."*

❀ *The Purity of the Turf*

AFTER THAT, life at Twing jogged along pretty peacefully for a bit. Twing is one of those places where there isn't a frightful lot to do nor any very hectic excitement to look forward to. In fact, the only event of any importance on the horizon, as far as I could ascertain, was the annual village school treat. One simply filled in the time by loafing about the grounds, playing a bit of tennis, and avoiding young Bingo as far as was humanly possible.

This last was a very necessary move if you wanted a happy life, for the Cynthia affair had jarred the unfortunate mutt to such an extent that he was always waylaying one and decanting his anguished soul. And when, one morning, he blew into my bedroom while I was toying with a bit of breakfast, I decided to take a firm line from the start. I could stand having him moaning all over me after dinner, and even after lunch; but at breakfast, no. We Woosters are amiability itself, but there is a limit.

"Now look here, old friend," I said. "I know your bally heart is broken and all that, and at some future time I shall be delighted to hear all about it, but—"

"I didn't come to talk about that."

"No? Good egg!"

"The past," said young Bingo, "is dead. Let us say no more about it."

"Right-o!"

"I have been wounded to the very depths of my soul, but don't speak about it."

"I won't."

"Ignore it. Forget it."

"Absolutely!"

I hadn't seen him so dashed reasonable for days.

"What I came to see you about this morning, Bertie," he said, fishing a sheet of paper out of his pocket, "was to ask if you would care to come in on another little flutter."

If there is one thing we Woosters are simply dripping with, it is sporting blood. I bolted the rest of my sausage, and sat up and took notice.

"Proceed," I said. "You interest me strangely, old bird."

Bingo laid the paper on the bed.

"On Monday week," he said, "you may or may not know, the annual village school treat takes place. Lord Wickhammersley lends the Hall grounds for the purpose. There will be games, and a conjurer, and cokernut shies, and tea in a tent. And also sports."

"I know. Cynthia was telling me."

Young Bingo winced.

"Would you mind not mentioning that name? I am not made of marble."

"Sorry!"

"Well, as I was saying, this jamboree is slated for Monday week. The question is, are we on?"

"How do you mean, 'Are we on'?"

"I am referring to the sports. Steggles did so well out of the Sermon Handicap that he has decided to make a book on these sports. Punters can be accommodated at ante-post odds or starting price, according to their preference. I think we ought to look into it," said young Bingo.

I pressed the bell.

"I'll consult Jeeves. I don't touch any sporting proposition without his advice. Jeeves," I said, as he drifted in, "rally round."

"Sir?"

"Stand by. We want your advice."

"Very good, sir."

"State your case, Bingo."

Bingo stated his case.

"What about it, Jeeves?" I said. "Do we go in?"

Jeeves pondered to some extent.

"I am inclined to favor the idea, sir."

That was good enough for me. "Right," I said. "Then we will form a syndicate and bust the Ring. I supply the money, you supply the brains, and Bingo—what do you supply, Bingo?"

"If you will carry me, and let me settle up later," said young Bingo, "I think I can put you in the way of winning a parcel on the Mothers' Sack Race."

"All right. We will put you down as Inside Information. Now, what are the events?"

Bingo reached for his paper and consulted it.

"Girls' Under Fourteen Fifty-Yard Dash seems to open the proceedings."

"Anything to say about that, Jeeves?"

"No, sir. I have no information."

"What's the next?"

"Boys' and Girls' Mixed Animal Potato Race, All Ages."

This was a new one to me. I had never heard of it at any of the big meetings.

"What's that?"

"Rather sporting," said young Bingo. "The competitors enter in couples, each couple being assigned an animal cry and a potato. For instance, let's suppose that you and Jeeves entered. Jeeves would stand at a fixed point holding a potato. You would have your head in a sack, and you would grope about trying to find Jeeves and making a noise like a cat; Jeeves also making a noise like a cat. Other competitors would be making noises like cows and pigs and dogs and so on, and groping about for *their* potato holders, who would also be making noises like cows and pigs and dogs and so on—"

I stopped the poor fish.

"Jolly if you're fond of animals," I said, "but on the whole—"

"Precisely, sir," said Jeeves. "I wouldn't touch it."

"Too open, what?"

"Exactly, sir. Very hard to estimate form."

"Carry on, Bingo. Where do we go from there?"

"Mothers' Sack Race."

"Ah! that's better. This is where you know something."

"A gift from Mrs. Penworthy, the tobacconist's wife," said Bingo confidently. "I was in at her shop yesterday, buying cigarettes, and she told me she had won three times at fairs in Worcestershire. She moved to these parts only a short time ago, so nobody knows about her. She promised me she would keep herself dark, and I think we could get a good price."

"Risk a tenner each way, Jeeves, what?"

"I think so, sir."

"Girls' Open Egg and Spoon Race," said Bingo.

"How about that?"

"I doubt if it would be worth while to invest, sir," said Jeeves. "I am told it is a certainty for last year's winner, Sarah Mills, who will doubtless start an odds-on favorite."

"Good, is she?"

"They tell me in the village that she carries a beautiful egg, sir."

"Then there's the Obstacle Race," said Bingo. "Risky, in my opinion. Like betting on the Grand National. Fathers' Hat-Trimming Contest—another speculative event. That's all, except for the Choirboys' Hundred Yards Handicap, for a pewter mug presented by the vicar—open to all whose voices have not broken before the second Sunday in Epiphany. Willie Chambers won last year, in a canter, receiving fifteen yards. This time he will probably be handicapped out of the race. I don't know what to advise."

"If I might make a suggestion, sir."

I eyed Jeeves with interest. I don't know that I'd ever seen him look so nearly excited.

"You've got something up your sleeve?"

"I have, sir."

"Red-hot?"

"That precisely describes it, sir. I think I may confidently assert that we have the winner of the Choirboys' Handicap under this very roof, sir. Harold, the pageboy."

"Pageboy? Do you mean the tubby little chap in buttons one sees bobbing about here and there? Why, dash it, Jeeves, nobody has a greater respect for your knowledge of form than I have, but I'm hanged if I can see Harold catching the judge's eye. He's practically circular, and every time I've seen him he's been leaning up against something, half asleep."

"He receives thirty yards, sir, and could win from scratch. The boy is a flier."

"How do you know?"

Jeeves coughed, and there was a dreamy look in his eye.

"I was as much astonished as yourself, sir, when I first became aware of the lad's capabilities. I happened to pursue him one morning with the intention of fetching him a clip on the side of the head—"

"Great Scott, Jeeves! You!"

"Yes, sir. The boy is of an outspoken disposition, and had made an opprobrious remark respecting my personal appearance."

"What did he say about your appearance?"

"I have forgotten, sir," said Jeeves, with a touch of austerity. "But it was opprobrious. I endeavored to correct him, but he outdistanced me by yards and made good his escape."

"But, I say, Jeeves, this is sensational. And yet—if he's such a sprinter, why hasn't anybody in the village found it out? Surely he plays with the other boys?"

"No, sir. As his lordship's pageboy, Harold does not mix with the village lads."

"Bit of a snob, what?"

"He is somewhat acutely alive to the existence of class distinctions, sir."

"You're absolutely certain he's such a wonder?" said Bingo. "I mean, it wouldn't do to plunge unless you're sure."

"If you desire to ascertain the boy's form by personal inspection, sir, it will be a simple matter to arrange a secret trial."

"I'm bound to say I should feel easier in my mind," I said.

"Then if I may take a shilling from the money on your dressing table—"

"What for?"

"I propose to bribe the lad to speak slightingly of the second footman's squint, sir. Charles is somewhat sensitive on the point, and should undoubtedly make the lad extend himself. If you will be at the first floor passage window, overlooking the back door, in half an hour's time—"

I don't know when I've dressed in such a hurry. As a rule, I'm what you might call a slow and careful dresser: I like to linger over the tie and see that the trousers are just so; but this morning I was all worked up. I just shoved on my things anyhow, and joined Bingo at the window with a quarter of an hour to spare.

The passage window looked down on to a broad sort of paved courtyard, which ended after about twenty yards in an archway through a high wall. Beyond this archway you got onto a strip of the drive, which curved round for another thirty yards or so, till it was lost behind a thick shrubbery. I put myself in the stripling's place and thought what steps I would take with a second footman after me. There was only one thing to do—leg it for the shrubbery and take cover; which meant that at least fifty yards would have to be covered—an excellent test. If good old Harold could fight off the second footman's challenge long enough to allow him to reach the bushes, there wasn't a choirboy in England who could give him thirty yards in the hundred. I waited, all of a twitter, for what seemed hours, and then suddenly there was a confused noise without, and something round and blue and buttony shot through the back door and buzzed for the archway like a mustang. And about two seconds later out came the second footman, going his hardest.

There was nothing to it. Absolutely nothing. The field never had a chance. Long before the footman reached the halfway mark, Harold was in the bushes, throwing stones. I came away from the window thrilled to the marrow; and when I met Jeeves on the stairs I was so moved that I nearly grasped his hand.

"Jeeves," I said, "no discussion! The Wooster shirt goes on this boy!"

"Very good, sir," said Jeeves.

The worst of these country meetings is that you can't plunge as heavily as you would like when you get a good thing, because it alarms the Ring. Steggles, though pimpled, was, as I have indicated, no chump, and if I had invested all I wanted to he would have put two and two together. I managed to get a good solid bet down for the syndicate, however, though it did make him look thoughtful. I heard in the next few days that he had been making searching inquiries in the village concerning Harold; but nobody could tell him anything, and eventually he came to the conclusion, I suppose, that I must be having a long shot on the strength of that thirty-yard start. Public opinion wavered between Jimmy Goode, receiving ten yards, at seven-to-two, and Alexander Bartlett, wih six yards' start, at eleven-to-four. Willie Chambers, scratch, was offered to the public at two-to-one, but found no takers.

We were taking no chances on the big event, and directly we had got our money on at a nice hundred-to-twelve Harold was put into strict training. It was a wearing business, and I can understand now why most of the big trainers are grim, silent men, who look as though they had suffered. The kid wanted constant watching. It was no good talking to him about honor and glory and how proud his mother would be when he wrote and told her he had won a real cup—the moment blighted Harold discovered that training meant knocking off pastry, taking exercise, and keeping away from the cigarettes, he was all against it, and it was only by unceasing vigilance that we managed to keep him in any shape at all. It was the diet that was the stumbling block. As far as exercise went, we could generally arrange for a sharp dash every morning with the assistance of the second footman. It ran into money, of course, but that couldn't be helped. Still, when a kid has simply to wait till the butler's back is turned to have the run of the pantry, and has only to nip into the smoking room to collect a handful of the best Turkish, training becomes a rocky job. We could only hope that on the day his natural stamina would pull him through.

And then one evening young Bingo came back from the links with a disturbing story. He had been in the habit of giving Harold mild exercise in the afternoons by taking him out as a caddie.

At first he seemed to think it humorous, the poor chump! He bubbled over with merry mirth as he began his tale.

"I say, rather funny this afternoon," he said. "You ought to have seen Steggles's face!"

"Seen Steggles' face? What for?"

"When he saw young Harold sprint, I mean."

I was filled with a grim foreboding of an awful doom.

"Good heavens! You didn't let Harold sprint in front of Steggles?"

Young Bingo's jaw dropped.

"I never thought of that," he said gloomily. "It wasn't my fault. I was playing a round with Steggles and after we'd finished we went into the clubhouse for a drink, leaving Harold with the clubs outside. In about five minutes we came out, and there was the kid on the gravel practicing swings with Steggles's driver and a stone. When he saw us coming, the kid dropped the club and was over the horizon like a streak. Steggles was absolutely dumfounded. And I must say it was a revelation even to me. The kid certainly gave of his best. Of course, it's a nuisance in a way; but I don't see, on second thoughts," said Bingo, brightening up, "what it matters. We're on at a good price. We've nothing to lose by the kid's form becoming known. I take it he will start odds-on, but that doesn't affect us."

I looked at Jeeves. Jeeves looked at me.

"It affects us all right if he doesn't start at all."

"Precisely, sir."

"What do you mean?" asked Bingo.

"If you ask me," I said, "I think Steggles will try to nobble him before the race."

"Good Lord! I never thought of that," Bingo blenched. "You don't think he would really do it?"

"I think he would have a jolly good try. Steggles is a bad man. From now on, Jeeves, we must watch Harold like hawks."

"Undoubtedly, sir."

"Ceaseless vigilance, what?"

"Precisely, sir."

"You wouldn't care to sleep in his room, Jeeves?"

"No, sir, I should not."

"No, nor would I, if it comes to that. But dash it all," I said, "we're letting ourselves get rattled! We're losing our nerve. This won't do. How can Steggles possibly get at Harold, even if he wants to?"

There was no cheering young Bingo up. He's one of those birds who simply leap at the morbid view, if you give them half a chance.

"There are all sorts of ways of nobbling favorites," he said, in a sort of deathbed voice. "You ought to read some of these racing novels. In *Pipped on the Post,* Lord Jasper Mauleverer as near as a toucher outed Bonny Betsy by bribing the head lad to slip a cobra into her stable the night before the Derby!"

"What are the chances of a cobra biting Harold, Jeeves?"

"Slight, I should imagine, sir. And in such an event, knowing the boy as intimately as I do, my anxiety would be entirely for the snake."

"Still, unceasing vigilance, Jeeves."

"Most certainly, sir."

I must say I got a bit fed with young Bingo in the next few days. It's all very well for a fellow with a big winner in his stable to exercise proper care, but in my opinion Bingo overdid it. The blighter's mind appeared to be absolutely saturated with racing fiction; and in stories of that kind, as far as I could make out, no horse is ever allowed to start in a race without at least a dozen attempts to put it out of action. He stuck to Harold like a plaster. Never let the unfortunate kid out of his sight. Of course, it meant a lot to the poor old egg if he could collect on this race, because it would give him enough money to chuck his tutoring job and get back to London; but all the same, he needn't have awakened me at three in the morning twice running— once to tell me we ought to cook Harold's food ourselves to prevent doping; the other time to say that he had heard mysterious noises in the shrubbery. But he reached the limit, in my opinion, when he insisted on my going to evening service on Sunday, the day before the sports.

"Why on earth?" I said, never being much of a lad for evensong.

"Well, I can't go myself. I shan't be here. I've got to go to London today with young Egbert." Egbert was Lord Wickhammersley's son, the one Bingo was tutoring. "He's going for a visit down in Kent, and I've got to see him off at Charing Cross. It's an infernal nuisance. I shan't be back till Monday afternoon. In fact, I shall miss most of the sports, I expect. Everything, therefore, depends on you, Bertie."

"But why should either of us go to evening service?"

"Ass! Harold sings in the choir, doesn't he?"

"What about it? I can't stop him dislocating his neck over a high note, if that's what you're afraid of."

"Fool! Steggles sings in the choir, too. There may be dirty work after the service."

"What absolute rot!"

"Is it?" said young Bingo. "Well, let me tell you that in *Jenny, the Girl Jockey,* the villain kidnaped the boy who was to ride the favorite the night before the big race, and he was the only one who understood and could control the horse, and if the heroine hadn't dressed up in riding things and—"

"Oh, all right, all right. But, if there's any danger, it seems to me the simplest thing would be for Harold not to turn out on Sunday evening."

"He must turn out. You seem to think the infernal kid is a monument of rectitude, beloved by all. He's got the shakiest reputation of any kid in the village. His name is as near being mud as it can jolly well stick. He's played hooky from the choir so often that the vicar told him, if one more thing happened, he would fire him out. Nice chumps we should look if he was scratched the night before the race!"

Well, of course, that being so, there was nothing for it but to toddle along.

There's something about evening service in a country church that makes a fellow feel drowsy and peaceful. Sort of end-of-a-perfect-day feeling. Old Heppenstall was up in the pulpit, and he has a kind of regular, bleating delivery that assists thought. They had left the door open, and the air was full of a mixed scent of trees and honeysuckle and mildew and villagers' Sunday clothes. As far as the eye could reach, you could see farmers propped up in restful attitudes, breathing heavily; and the children in the congregation who had fidgeted during the earlier part of the proceedings were now lying back in a surfeited sort of coma. The last rays of the setting sun shone through the stained-glass windows, birds were twittering in the trees, the women's dresses crackled gently in the stillness. Peaceful. That's what I'm driving at. I felt peaceful. Everybody felt peaceful. And that is why the explosion, when it came, sounded like the end of all things.

I call it an explosion, because that was what it seemed like when it broke loose. One moment a dreamy hush was all over the place, broken only by old Heppenstall talking about our duty to our neighbors; and then, suddenly, a sort of piercing, shrieking squeal that got you right between the eyes and ran all the way down your spine and out at the soles of the feet.

"EE-ee-ee-ee-ee! Oo-ee! Ee-ee-ee-ee!"

It sounded like about six hundred pigs having their tails twisted simultaneously, but it was simply the kid Harold, who appeared to be having some species of fit. He was jumping up and down and slapping at the back of his neck. And about every other second he would take a deep breath and give out another of the squeals.

Well, I mean, you can't do that sort of thing in the middle of the sermon during evening service without exciting remark. The congregation came out of its trance with a jerk, and climbed on the pews to get a better view. Old Heppenstall stopped in the middle of a sentence and spun round. And a couple of vergers with great presence of mind bounded up the aisle like leopards, collected Harold, still squealing, and marched him out. They disappeared into the vestry, and I grabbed my hat and legged it round to the stage door, full of apprehension and what not. I couldn't think what the deuce could have happened, but somewhere dimly behind the proceedings there seemed to me to lurk the hand of the blighter Steggles.

By the time I got there and managed to get someone to open the door, which was locked, the service seemed to be over. Old Heppenstall was standing in the middle of a crowd of choirboys and vergers and sextons and what not, putting the wretched Harold through it with no little vim. I had come in at the tail end of what must have been a fairly fruity oration.

"Wretched boy! How dare you—"

"I got a sensitive skin!"

"This is no time to talk about your skin—"

"Somebody put a beetle down my back!"

"Absurd!"

"I felt it wriggling—"

"Nonsense!"

"Sounds pretty thin, doesn't it?" said someone at my side.

It was Steggles, dash him. Clad in a snowy surplice or cassock, or whatever they call it, and wearing an expression of grave concern, the blighter had the cold, cynical crust to look me in the eyeball without a blink.

"Did you put a beetle down his neck?" I cried.

"Me!" said Steggles. "Me!"

Old Heppenstall was putting on the black cap.

"I do not credit a word of your story, wretched boy! I have warned you before, and now the time has come to act. You cease from this moment to be a member of my choir. Go, miserable child!"

Steggles plucked at my sleeve.

"In that case," he said, "those bets, you know—I'm afraid you lose your money, dear old boy. It's a pity you didn't put it on S.P. I always think S.P.'s the only safe way."

I gave him one look. Not a bit of good, of course.

"And they talk about the Purity of the Turf!" I said. And I meant it to sting, by Jove!

Jeeves received the news bravely, but I think the man was a bit rattled beneath the surface.

"An ingenious young gentleman, Mr. Steggles, sir."

"A bally swindler, you mean."

"Perhaps that would be a more exact description. However, these things will happen on the Turf, and it is useless to complain."

"I wish I had your sunny disposition, Jeeves!"

Jeeves bowed.

"We now rely, then, it would seem, sir, almost entirely on Mrs. Penworthy. Should she justify Mr. Little's encomiums and show real class in the Mothers' Sack Race, our gains will just balance our losses."

"Yes; but that's not much consolation when you've been looking forward to a big win."

"It is just possible that we may still find ourselves on the right side of the ledger after all, sir. Before Mr. Little left, I persuaded him to invest a small sum for the syndicate of which you were kind enough to make me a member, sir, on the Girls' Egg and Spoon Race."

"On Sarah Mills?"

"No, sir. On a long-priced outsider. Little Prudence Baxter, sir, the child of his lordship's head gardener. Her father assures me she has a very steady hand. She is accustomed to bring him his mug of beer from the cottage each afternoon, and he informs me she has never spilled a drop."

Well, that sounded as though young Prudence's control was good. But how about speed? With seasoned performers like Sarah Mills entered, the thing practically amounted to a classic race, and in these big events you must have speed.

"I am aware that it is what is termed a long shot, sir. Still, I thought it judicious."

"You backed her for a place, too, of course?"

"Yes, sir. Each way."

"Well, I suppose it's all right. I've never known you to make a bloomer, yet."

"Thank you very much, sir."

I'm bound to say that, as a general rule, my idea of a large afternoon would be to keep as far away from a village school treat as possible. A sticky business. But with such grave issues toward, if you know what I mean, I sank my prejudices on this occasion and rolled up. I found the proceedings about as scaly as I had expected. It was a warm day, and the Hall grounds were a dense, practically liquid mass of peasantry. Kids seethed to and fro. One of them, a small girl of sorts, grabbed my hand and hung on to it as I clove my way through the jam to where the Mothers' Sack Race was to finish. We hadn't been introduced, but she seemed to think I would do as well as anyone else to talk to about the rag doll she had won in the Lucky Dip, and she rather spread herself on the topic.

"I'm going to call it Gertrude," she said. "And I shall undress it every night and put it to bed, and wake it up in the morning and dress it, and put it to bed at night, and wake it up next morning and dress it—"

"I say, old thing," I said, "I don't want to hurry you and all that, but you couldn't condense it a bit, could you? I'm rather anxious to see the finish of this race. The Wooster fortunes are by way of hanging on it."

"I'm going to run in a race soon," she said, shelving the doll for the nonce and descending to ordinary chitchat.

"Yes?" I said. Distrait, if you know what I mean, and trying to peer through the chinks in the crowd. "What race is that?"

"Egg'n Spoon."

"No, really? Are you Sarah Mills?"

"Na-ow!" Registering scorn. "I'm Prudence Baxter."

Naturally this put our relations on a different footing. I gazed at her with considerable interest. One of the stable. I must say she didn't look much of a flier. She was short and round. Bit out of condition, I thought.

"I say," I said, "that being so, you mustn't dash about in the hot sun and take the edge off yourself. You must conserve your energies, old friend. Sit down here in the shade."

"Don't want to sit down."

"Well, take it easy, anyhow."

The kid flitted to another topic like a butterfly hovering from flower to flower.

"I'm a good girl," she said.

"I bet you are. I hope you're a good egg-and-spoon racer, too."

"Harold's a bad boy. Harold squealed in church and isn't allowed to come to the treat. I'm glad," continued this ornament of her sex, wrinkling her nose virtuously, "because he's a bad boy. He pulled my hair Friday. Harold isn't coming to the treat! Harold isn't coming to the treat! Harold isn't coming to the treat!" she chanted, making a regular song of it.

"Don't rub it in, my dear old gardener's daughter," I pleaded. "You don't know it, but you've hit on rather a painful subject."

"Ah, Wooster, my dear fellow! So you have made friends with this little lady?"

It was old Heppenstall, beaming pretty profusely. Life and soul of the party.

"I am delighted, my dear Wooster," he went on, "quite delighted at the way you young men are throwing yourselves into the spirit of this little festivity of ours."

"Oh, yes?" I said.

"Oh, yes! Even Rupert Steggles. I must confess that my opinion of Rupert Steggles has materially altered for the better this afternoon."

Mine hadn't. But I didn't say so.

"I have always considered Rupert Steggles, between ourselves, a rather self-centered youth, by no means the kind who would put himself out to further the enjoyment of his fellows. And yet twice within the last half-hour I have observed him escorting Mrs. Penworthy, our worthy tobacconist's wife, to the refreshment tent."

I left him standing. I shook off the clutching hand of the Baxter kid and hared it rapidly to the spot where the Mothers' Sack Race was just finishing. I had a horrid presentiment that there had been more dirty work at the crossroads. The first person I ran into was young Bingo. I grabbed him by the arm.

"Who won?"

"I don't know. I didn't notice." There was bitterness in his voice. "It wasn't Mrs. Penworthy, dash her! Bertie, that hound Steggles is nothing more nor less than one of our leading snakes. I don't know how he heard about her, but he must have got on to it that she was dangerous. Do you know what he did? He lured that miserable woman into the refreshment tent five minutes before the race, and brought her out so weighed down with cake and tea that she blew up in the first twenty yards. Just rolled over and lay there! Well, thank goodness, we still have Harold!"

I gaped at the poor chump.

"Harold! Haven't you heard?"

"Heard?" Bingo turned a delicate green. "Heard what? I haven't heard anything. I arrived only five minutes ago. Came here straight from the station. What has happened? Tell me!"

I slipped him the information. He stared at me for a moment in a ghastly sort of way, then with a hollow groan tottered away and was lost in the crowd. A nasty knock, poor chap. I didn't blame him for being upset.

They were clearing the decks now for the Egg and Spoon Race, and

I thought I might as well stay where I was and watch the finish. Not that I had much hope. Young Prudence was a good conversationalist, but she didn't seem to me to be the build for a winner.

As far as I could see through the mob, they got off to a good start. A short, red-haired child was making the running with a freckled blonde second, and Sarah Mills lying up an easy third. Our nominee was straggling along with the field, well behind the leaders. It was not hard even as early as this to spot the winner. There was a grace, a practiced precision, in the way Sarah Mills held her spoon that told its own story. She was cutting out a good pace, but her egg didn't even wobble. A natural egg-and-spooner, if ever there was one.

Class will tell. Thirty yards from the tape, the red-haired kid tripped over her feet and shot her egg onto the turf. The freckled blonde fought gamely, but she had run herself out halfway down the straight, and Sarah Mills came past and home on a tight rein by several lengths, a popular winner. The blonde was second. A sniffing female in blue gingham beat a pie-faced kid in pink for the place money, and Prudence Baxter, Jeeves's long shot, was either fifth or sixth, I couldn't see which.

And then I was carried along with the crowd to where old Heppenstall was going to present the prizes. I found myself standing next to the man Steggles.

"Hallo, old chap!" he said, very bright and cheery. "You've had a bad day, I'm afraid."

I looked at him with silent scorn. Lost on the blighter, of course.

"It's not been a good meeting for any of the big punters," he went on. "Poor old Bingo Little went down badly over that Egg and Spoon Race."

I hadn't been meaning to chat with the fellow, but I was startled.

"How do you mean badly?" I said. "We—he had only a small bet on."

"I don't know what you call small. He had thirty quid each way on the Baxter kid."

The landscape reeled before me.

"What!"

"Thirty quid at ten to one. I thought he must have heard something, but apparently not. The race went by the formbook all right."

I was trying to do sums in my head. I was just in the middle of working out the syndicate's losses when old Heppenstall's voice came sort of faintly to me out of the distance. He had been pretty fatherly and debonair when ladling out the prizes for the other events, but now he had suddenly grown all pained and grieved. He peered sorrowfully at the multitude.

"With regard to the Girls' Egg and Spoon Race, which has just concluded," he said, "I have a painful duty to perform. Circumstances have arisen which it is impossible to ignore. It is not too much to say that I am stunned."

He gave the populace about five seconds to wonder why he was stunned, then went on.

"Three years ago, as you are aware, I was compelled to expunge from the list of events at this annual festival the Fathers' Quarter-Mile, owing to reports coming to my ears of wagers taken and given on the result at the village inn and a strong suspicion that on at least one occasion the race had actually been sold by the speediest runner. That unfortunate occurrence shook my faith in human nature, I admit —but still there was one event at least which I confidently expected to remain untainted by the miasma of professionalism. I allude to the Girls' Egg and Spoon Race. It seems, alas, that I was too sanguine."

He stopped again, and wrestled with his feelings.

"I will not weary you with the unpleasant details. I will merely say that before the race was run a stranger in our midst, the manservant of one of the guests at the Hall—I will not specify with more particularity—approached several of the competitors and presented each of them with five shillings on condition that they— er—finished. A belated sense of remorse has led him to confess to me what he did, but it is too late. The evil is accomplished, and retribution must take its course. It is no time for half measures. I must be firm. I rule that Sarah Mills, Jane Parker, Bessie Clay, and Rosie Jukes, the first four to pass the winning post, have forfeited their amateur status and are disqualified, and this handsome workbag, presented by Lord Wickhammersley, goes, in consequence, to Prudence Baxter. Prudence, step forward!"

❋ *The Great Sermon Handicap*

AFTER GOODWOOD'S over, I generally find that I get a bit restless. I'm not much of a lad for the birds and the trees and the great open spaces as a rule, but there's no doubt that London's not at its best in August, and rather tends to give me the pip and make me think of popping down into the country till things have bucked up a trifle. London, about a couple of weeks after that spectacular finish of young Bingo's which I've just been telling you about, was empty and smelled of burning asphalt. All my pals were away, most of the theaters were shut, and they were taking up Piccadilly in large spadefuls.

It was most infernally hot. As I sat in the old flat one night trying to muster up energy enough to go to bed, I felt I couldn't stand it much longer; and when Jeeves came in with the tissue-restorers on a tray I put the thing to him squarely.

"Jeeves," I said, wiping the brow and gasping like a stranded goldfish, "it's beastly hot."

"The weather *is* oppressive, sir."

"Not all the soda, Jeeves."

"No, sir."

"I think we've had about enough of the metrop. for the time being, and require a change. Shift-ho, I think, Jeeves, what?"

"Just as you say, sir. There is a letter on the tray, sir."

"By Jove, Jeeves, that was practically poetry. Rhymed, did you notice?" I opened the letter. "I say, this is rather extraordinary."

"Sir?"

"You know Twing Hall?"

"Yes, sir."

"Well, Mr. Little is there."

"Indeed, sir?"

"Absolutely in the flesh. He's had to take another of those tutoring jobs."

After that fearful mix-up at Goodwood, when young Bingo Little, a broken man, had touched me for a tenner and whizzed silently off into the unknown, I had been all over the place, lately, asking mutual friends if they had heard anything of Bingo Little, but nobody had. And all the time he had been at Twing Hall. Rummy. And I'll tell you why it was rummy. Twing Hall belongs to old Lord Wickhammersley, a great pal of my guv'nor's when he was alive, and I have a standing invitation to pop down there when I like. I generally put in a week or two some time in the summer, and I was thinking of going there before I read the letter.

"And, what's more, Jeeves, my cousin Claude, and my cousin Eustace—you remember them?"

"Very vividly, sir."

"Well, they're down there, too, reading for some exam or other with the vicar. I used to read with him myself at one time. He's known far and wide as a pretty hot coach for those of fairly feeble intellect. Well, when I tell you he got *me* through Smalls, you'll gather that he's a bit of a hummer. I call this most extraordinary."

I read the letter again. It was from Eustace. Claude and Eustace are twins, and more or less generally admitted to be the curse of the human race.

> The Vicarage,
> Twing, Glos.
>
> DEAR BERTIE—Do you want to make a bit of money? I hear you had a bad Goodwood, so you probably do. Well, come down here quick and get in on the biggest sporting event of the season. I'll explain when I see you, but you can take it from me it's all right.
>
> Claude and I are with a reading party at old Heppenstall's. There are nine of us, not counting your pal Bingo Little, who is tutoring the kid up at the Hall.
>
> Don't miss this golden opportunity, which may never occur again. Come and join us.
>
> Yours,
> EUSTACE.

I handed this to Jeeves. He studied it thoughtfully.

"What do you make of it? A rummy communication, what?"

"Very high-spirited young gentlemen, sir, Mr. Claude and Mr. Eustace. Up to some game, I should be disposed to imagine."

"Yes. But what game, do you think?"

"It is impossible to say, sir. Did you observe that the letter continues over the page?"

"Eh, what?" I grabbed the thing. This was what was on the other side of the last page:

SERMON HANDICAP

RUNNERS AND BETTING

PROBABLE STARTERS.

Rev. Joseph Tucker (Badgwick), scratch.

Rev. Leonard Starkie (Stapleton), scratch.

Rev. Alexander Jones (Upper Bingley), receives three minutes.

Rev. W. Dix (Little Clickton-in-the-Wold), receives five minutes.

Rev. Francis Heppenstall (Twing), receives eight minutes.

Rev. Cuthbert Dibble (Boustead Parva), receives nine minutes.

Rev. Orlo Hough (Boustead Magna), receives nine minutes.

Rev. J. J. Roberts (Fale-by-the-Water), receives ten minutes.

Rev. G. Hayward (Lower Bingley), receives twelve minutes.

Rev. James Bates (Gandle-by-the-Hill), receives fifteen minutes.

(*The above have arrived.*)

PRICES.—5–2, Tucker, Starkie; 3–1, Jones; 9–2, Dix; 6–1, Heppenstall, Dibble, Hough; 100–8, any other.

It baffled me.

"Do you understand it, Jeeves?"

"No, sir."

"Well, I think we ought to have a look into it, anyway, what?"

"Undoubtedly, sir."

"Right-o, then. Pack our spare dickey and a toothbrush in a neat brown-paper parcel, send a wire to Lord Wickhammersley to say we're coming, and buy two tickets on the five-ten at Paddington tomorrow."

The five-ten was late as usual, and everybody was dressing for dinner when I arrived at the Hall. It was only by getting into my evening things in record time and taking the stairs to the dining room in a couple of bounds that I managed to dead-heat with the soup. I slid into the vacant chair, and found that I was sitting next to old Wickhammersley's youngest daughter, Cynthia.

"Oh, hallo, old thing," I said.

Great pals we've always been. In fact, there was a time when I had an idea I was in love with Cynthia. However, it blew over. A dashed pretty and lively and attractive girl, mind you, but full of ideals and all that. I may be wronging her, but I have an idea that she's the sort of girl who would want a fellow to carve out a career and what not. I know I've heard her speak favorably of Napoleon. So what with one thing and another the jolly old frenzy sort of petered out, and now we're just pals. I think she's a topper, and she thinks me next door to a loony, so everything's nice and matey.

"Well, Bertie, so you've arrived?"

"Oh, yes, I've arrived. Yes, here I am. I say, I seem to have plunged into the middle of quite a young dinner party. Who are all these coves?"

"Oh, just people from round about. You know most of them. You remember Colonel Willis, and the Spencers—"

"Of course, yes. And there's old Heppenstall. Who's the other clergyman next to Mrs. Spencer?"

"Mr. Hayward, from Lower Bingley."

"What an amazing lot of clergymen there are round here. Why, there's another, next to Mrs. Willis."

"That's Mr. Bates, Mr. Heppenstall's nephew. He's an assistant master at Eton. He's down here during the summer holidays, acting as locum tenens for Mr. Spettigue, the rector of Gandle-by-the-Hill."

"I thought I knew his face. He was in his fourth year at Oxford when I was a fresher. Rather a blood. Got his rowing-blue and all that." I took another look round the table, and spotted young Bingo. "Ah, there he is," I said. "There's the old egg."

"There's who?"

"Young Bingo Little. Great pal of mine. He's tutoring your brother, you know."

"Good gracious! Is he a friend of yours?"

"Rather! Known him all my life."

"Then tell me, Bertie, is he at all weak in the head?"

"Weak in the head?"

"I don't mean simply because he's a friend of yours. But he's so strange in his manner."

"How do you mean?"

"Well, he keeps looking at me so oddly."

"Oddly? How? Give an imitation."

"I can't in front of all these people."

"Yes, you can. I'll hold my napkin up."

"All right, then. Quick. There!"

Considering that she had only about a second and a half to do it in, I must say it was a jolly fine exhibition. She opened her mouth and eyes pretty wide and let her jaw drop sideways, and managed to look so like a dyspeptic calf that I recognized the symptoms immediately.

"Oh, that's all right," I said. "No need to be alarmed. He's simply in love with you."

"In love with me. Don't be absurd."

"My dear old thing, you don't know young Bingo. He can fall in love with *anybody*."

"Thank you!"

"Oh, I didn't mean it that way, you know. I don't wonder at his taking to you. Why, I was in love with you myself once."

"Once? Ah! And all that remains now are the cold ashes? This isn't one of your tactful evenings, Bertie."

"Well, my dear sweet thing, dash it all, considering that you gave me the bird and nearly laughed yourself into a permanent state of hiccups when I asked you—"

"Oh, I'm not reproaching you. No doubt there were faults on both sides. He's very good-looking, isn't he?"

"Good-looking? Bingo? Bingo good-looking? No, I say, come now, really!"

"I mean, compared with some people," said Cynthia.

Some time after this, Lady Wickhammersley gave the signal for the females of the species to leg it, and they duly stampeded. I didn't get a chance of talking to young Bingo when they'd gone, and later, in the drawing room, he didn't show up. I found him eventually in his room, lying on the bed with his feet on the rail, smoking a toofah. There was a notebook on the counterpane beside him.

"Hallo, old scream," I said.

"Hallo, Bertie," he replied, in what seemed to me rather a moody, distrait sort of manner.

"Rummy finding you down here. I take it your uncle cut off your allowance after that recent racing binge and you had to take this tutoring job to keep the wolf from the door?"

"Correct," said young Bingo tersely.

"Well, you might have let your pals know where you were."

He frowned darkly.

"I didn't want them to know where I was. I wanted to creep away and hide myself. I've been through a bad time, Bertie, these last weeks. The sun ceased to shine—"

"That's curious. We've had gorgeous weather in London."

"The birds ceased to sing—"

"What birds?"

"What the devil does it matter what birds?" said young Bingo, with some asperity. "Any birds. The birds round about here. You don't expect me to specify them by their pet names, do you? I tell you, Bertie, it hit me hard at first, very hard."

"What hit you?" I simply couldn't follow the blighter.

"Charlotte's calculated callousness."

"Oh, ah!" I've seen poor old Bingo through so many unsuccessful love affairs that I'd almost forgotten there was a girl mixed up with that Goodwood business. Of course! Charlotte Corday Rowbotham. And she had given him the raspberry, I remembered, and gone off with one Comrade Butt.

"I went through torments. Recently, however, I've—er—bucked up a bit. Tell me, Bertie, what are you doing down here? I didn't know you knew these people."

"Me? Why, I've known them since I was a kid."

Young Bingo put his feet down with a thud.

"Do you mean to say you've known Lady Cynthia all that time?"

"Rather! She can't have been seven when I met her first."

"Good Lord!" said young Bingo. He looked at me for the first time as though I amounted to something, and swallowed a mouthful of smoke the wrong way. "I love that girl, Bertie," he went on, when he'd finished coughing.

"Yes. Nice girl, of course."

He eyed me with pretty deep loathing.

"Don't speak of her in that horrible, casual way. She's an angel. An angel! Was she talking about me at all at dinner, Bertie?"

"Oh, yes."

"What did she say?"

"I remember one thing. She said she thought you good-looking."

Young Bingo closed his eyes in a sort of ecstasy. Then he picked up the notebook.

"Pop off now, old man, there's a good chap," he said, in a hushed, faraway voice. "I've got a bit of writing to do."

"Writing?"

"Poetry, if you must know. I wish the dickens," said young Bingo, not without some bitterness, "she had been christened something except Cynthia. There isn't a dam' word in the language it rhymes with. Ye gods, how I could have spread myself if she had only been called Jane!"

Bright and early next morning, as I lay in bed blinking at the sunlight on the dressing table and wondering when Jeeves was going to show up with a cup of tea, a heavy weight descended on my toes, and the voice of young Bingo polluted the air. The blighter had apparently risen with the lark.

"Leave me," I said, "I would be alone. I can't see anybody till I've had my tea."

"When Cynthia smiles," said young Bingo, "the skies are blue; the world takes on a roseate hue: birds in the garden trill and sing, and Joy is king of everything, when Cynthia smiles." He coughed, changing gears. "When Cynthia frowns—"

"What the devil are you talking about?"

"I'm reading you my poem. The one I wrote to Cynthia last night. I'll go on, shall I?"

"No!"

"No?"

"No. I haven't had my tea."

At this moment Jeeves came in with the good old beverage, and I sprang on it with a glad cry. After a couple of sips things looked a bit brighter. Even young Bingo didn't offend the eye to quite such an extent. By the time I'd finished the first cup I was a new man, so much so that I not only permitted but encouraged the poor fish to read the rest of the bally thing, and even went so far as to criticize the scansion of the fourth line of the fifth verse. We were still arguing the point when the door burst open and in blew Claude and Eustace. One of the things which discourage me about rural life is the frightful earliness with which events begin to break loose. I've stayed at places in the country where they've jerked me out of the dreamless at about six-thirty to go for a jolly swim in the lake. At Twing, thank heaven, they knew me, and let me breakfast in bed.

The twins seemed pleased to see me.

"Good old Bertie!" said Claude.

"Stout fellow!" said Eustace. "The Rev. told us you had arrived. I thought that letter of mine would fetch you."

"You can always bank on Bertie," said Claude. "A sportsman to the finger tips. Well, has Bingo told you about it?"

"Not a word. He's been—"

"We've been talking," said Bingo hastily, "of other matters."

Claude pinched the last slice of thin bread and butter, and Eustace poured himself out a cup of tea.

"It's like this, Bertie," said Eustace, settling down cozily. "As I told you in my letter, there are nine of us marooned in this desert spot, reading with old Heppenstall. Well, of course, nothing is jollier than sweating up the Classics when it's a hundred in the shade, but there does come a time when you begin to feel the need of a little relaxation; and, by Jove, there are absolutely no facilities for relaxation in this place whatever. And then Steggles got this idea. Steggles is one of our reading party, and, between ourselves, rather a worm as a general thing. Still, you have to give him credit for getting this idea."

"What idea?"

"Well, you know how many parsons there are round about here.

There are about a dozen hamlets within a radius of six miles, and each hamlet has a church and each church has a parson and each parson preaches a sermon every Sunday. Tomorrow week—Sunday the twenty-third—we're running off the great Sermon Handicap. Steggles is making the book. Each parson is to be clocked by a reliable steward of the course and the one that preaches the longest sermon wins. Did you study the race card I sent you?"

"I couldn't understand what it was all about."

"Why, you chump, it gives the handicaps and the current odds on each starter. I've got another one here, in case you've lost yours. Take a careful look at it. It gives you the thing in a nutshell. Jeeves, old son, do you want a sporting flutter?"

"Sir?" said Jeeves, who had just meandered in with my breakfast.

Claude explained the scheme. Amazing the way Jeeves grasped it right off. But he merely smiled in a paternal sort of way.

"Thank you, sir, I think not."

"Well, you're with us, Bertie, aren't you?" said Claude, sneaking a roll and a slice of bacon. "Have you studied that card? Well, tell me, does anything strike you about it?"

Of course it did. It had struck me the moment I looked at it.

"Why, it's a sitter for old Heppenstall," I said. "He's got the event sewed up in a parcel. There isn't a parson in the land who could give him eight minutes. Your pal Steggles must be an ass, giving him a handicap like that. Why, in the days when I was with him, old Heppenstall never used to preach under half an hour, and there was one sermon of his on Brotherly Love which lasted forty-five minutes if it lasted a second. Has he lost his vim lately, or what is it?"

"Not a bit of it," said Eustace. "Tell him what happened, Claude."

"Why," said Claude, "the first Sunday we were here, we all went to Twing church, and old Heppenstall preached a sermon that was well under twenty minutes. This is what happened. Steggles didn't notice it, and the Rev. didn't notice it himself, but Eustace and I both spotted that he had dropped a chunk of at least half a dozen pages out of his sermon case as he was walking up to the pulpit. He sort of flickered when he got to the gap in the manuscript, but carried on all right, and Steggles went away with the impression that twenty minutes or a bit under was his usual form. The next Sunday we heard Tucker and Starkie, and they both went well over the thirty-five minutes, so Steggles arranged the handicapping as you see on the card. You must come into this, Bertie. You see, the trouble is that I haven't a bean, and Eustace hasn't a bean, and Bingo Little hasn't a bean, so you'll have to finance the syndicate. Don't weaken!

It's just putting money in all our pockets. Well, we'll have to be getting back now. Think the thing over, and phone me later in the day. And, if you let us down, Bertie, may a cousin's curse— Come on, Claude, old thing."

The more I studied the scheme, the better it looked.

"How about it, Jeeves?" I said.

Jeeves smiled gently and drifted out.

"Jeeves has no sporting blood," said Bingo.

"Well, I have. I'm coming into this. Claude's quite right. It's like finding money by the wayside."

"Good man!" said Bingo. "Now I can see daylight. Say I have a tenner on Heppenstall, and cop; that'll give me a bit in hand to back Pink Pill with in the two o'clock at Gatwick the week after next: cop on that, put the pile on Musk-Rat for the one-thirty at Lewes, and there I am with a nice little sum to take to Alexandra Park on September the tenth, when I've got a tip straight from the stable."

It sounded like a bit out of "Smiles's Self-Help."

"And then," said young Bingo, "I'll be in a position to go to my uncle and beard him in his lair somewhat. He's quite a bit of a snob, you know, and when he hears that I'm going to marry the daughter of an earl—"

"I say, old man," I couldn't help saying, "aren't you looking ahead rather far?"

"Oh, that's all right. It's true nothing's actually settled yet, but she practically told me the other day she was fond of me."

"What!"

"Well, she said that the sort of man she liked was the self-reliant, manly man with strength, good looks, character, ambition, and initiative."

"Leave me, laddie," I said. "Leave me to my fried egg."

Directly I'd got up I went to the phone, snatched Eustace away from his morning's work, and instructed him to put a tenner on the Twing flier at current odds for each of the syndicate; and after lunch Eustace rang me up to say that he had done business at a snappy seven-to-one, the odds having lengthened owing to a rumor in knowledgeable circles that the Rev. was subject to hay fever, and was taking big chances strolling in the paddock behind the Vicarage in the early mornings. And it was dashed lucky, I thought next day, that we had managed to get the money on in time, for on the Sunday morning old Heppenstall fairly took the bit between his teeth and gave us thirty-six solid minutes on Certain Popular Superstitions. I was sitting next to Steggles in the pew, and I saw him blench visibly. He was a little, rat-faced fellow, with shifty eyes and a suspicious nature. The first thing he did when we emerged into the open air was to announce, formally, that anyone who fancied the Rev. could now be accommodated at fifteen-to-eight on, and he added, in a rather nasty manner, that if he had his way, this sort of in-and-out running would be brought to the attention of the Jockey Club, but that he supposed that there was nothing to be done about it. This ruinous price checked the punters at once, and there was little money in sight. And so matters stood till just after lunch on Tuesday afternoon, when, as I was strolling up and down in front of the house with a cigarette, Claude and Eustace came bursting up the drive on bicycles, dripping with momentous news.

"Bertie," said Claude, deeply agitated, "unless we take immediate action and do a bit of quick thinking, we're in the cart."

"What's the matter?"

"G. Hayward's the matter," said Eustace morosely. "The Lower Bingley starter."

"We never even considered him," said Claude. "Somehow or other, he got overlooked. It's always the way. Steggles overlooked him. We all overlooked him. But Eustace and I happened by the merest fluke to be riding through Lower Bingley this morning, and there was a wedding on at the church, and it suddenly struck us that it wouldn't be a bad move to get a line on G. Hayward's form, in case he might be a dark horse."

"And it was jolly lucky we did," said Eustace. "He delivered an address of twenty-six minutes by Claude's stop watch. At a village wedding, mark you! What'll he do when he really extends himself!"

"There's only one thing to be done, Bertie," said Claude. "You must spring some more funds, so that we can hedge on Hayward and save ourselves."

"But—"

"Well, it's the only way out."

"But I say, you know, I hate the idea of all that money we put on Heppenstall being chucked away."

"What else can you suggest? You don't suppose the Rev. can give you this absolute marvel a handicap and win, do you?"

"I've got it!" I said.

"What?"

"I see a way by which we can make it safe for our nominee. I'll pop over this afternoon, and ask him as a personal favor to preach that sermon of his on Brotherly Love on Sunday."

Claude and Eustace looked at each other, like those bozos in the poem, with a wild surmise.

"It's a scheme," said Claude.

"A jolly brainy scheme," said Eustace. "I didn't think you had it in you, Bertie."

"But even so," said Claude, "fizzer as that sermon no doubt is, will it be good enough in the face of a four-minute handicap?"

"Rather!" I said. "When I told you it lasted forty-five minutes, I was probably understating it. I should call it—from my recollection of the thing—nearer fifty."

"Then carry on," said Claude.

I toddled over in the evening and fixed the thing up. Old Heppenstall was most decent about the whole affair. He seemed pleased and touched that I should have remembered the sermon all these years, and said he had once or twice had an idea of preaching it again, only it had seemed to him, on reflection, that it was perhaps a trifle long for a rustic congregation.

"And in these restless times, my dear Wooster," he said, "I fear that brevity in the pulpit is becoming more and more desiderated by even the bucolic churchgoer, who one might have supposed would be less afflicted with the spirit of hurry and impatience than his metropolitan brother. I have had many arguments on the subject with my nephew, young Bates, who is taking my old friend Spettigue's cure over at Gandle-by-the-Hill. His view is that a sermon nowadays should be a bright, brisk, straight-from-the-shoulder address, never lasting more than ten or twelve minutes."

"Long?" I said. "Why, my goodness! you don't call that Brotherly Love sermon of yours *long,* do you?"

"It takes fully fifty minutes to deliver."

"Surely not?"

"Your incredulity, my dear Wooster, is extremely flattering—far more flattering, of course, than I deserve. Nevertheless, the facts are as I have stated. You are sure that I would not be well advised to make certain excisions and eliminations? You do not think it would be a good thing to cut, to prune? I might, for example, delete the rather exhaustive excursus into the family life of the early Assyrians?"

"Don't touch a word of it, or you'll spoil the whole thing," I said earnestly.

"I am delighted to hear you say so, and I shall preach the sermon without fail next Sunday morning."

What I have always said, and what I always shall say, is, that this ante-post betting is a mistake, an error, and a mug's game. You never can tell what's going to happen. If fellows would only stick to the good old S.P., there would be fewer young men go wrong. I'd hardly finished my breakfast on the Saturday morning when Jeeves came to my bedside to say that Eustace wanted me on the telephone.

"Good Lord, Jeeves, what's the matter, do you think?"

"Mr. Eustace did not confide in me, sir."

"Has he got the wind up?"

"Somewhat vertically, sir, to judge by his voice."

"Do you know what I think, Jeeves? Something's gone wrong with the favorite."

"Which is the favorite, sir?"

"Mr. Heppenstall. He's gone to odds on. He was intending to preach a sermon on Brotherly Love which would have brought him home by lengths. I wonder if anything's happened to him."

"You could ascertain, sir, by speaking to Mr. Eustace on the telephone. He is holding the wire."

"By Jove, yes!"

I shoved on a dressing gown and flew downstairs like a mighty, rushing wind. The moment I heard Eustace's voice I knew we were in for it. It had a croak of agony in it.

"Bertie?"

"Here I am."

Bertie, we're sunk. The favorite's blown up."

"No!"

"Yes. Coughing in his stable all last night."

"What!"

"Absolutely! Hay fever."

"Oh, my sainted aunt!"

"The doctor is with him now, and it's only a question of minutes before he's officially scratched. That means the curate will show up at the post instead, and he's no good at all. He is being offered at a hundred-to-six, but no takers. What shall we do?"

I had to grapple with the thing for a moment in silence.

"Eustace."

"Hallo?"

"What can you get on G. Hayward?"

"Only four-to-one now. I think there's been a leak, and Steggles has heard something. The odds shortened late last night in a significant manner."

"Well, four-to-one will clear us. Put another fiver all round on

G. Hayward for the syndicate. That'll bring us out on the right side of the ledger."

"If he wins."

"What do you mean? I thought you considered him a cert., bar Heppenstall."

"I'm beginning to wonder," said Eustace gloomily, "if there's such a thing as a cert. in this world. I'm told the Rev. Joseph Tucker did an extraordinary fine trial gallop at a mothers' meeting over at Badgwick yesterday. However, it seems our only chance. So long."

Not being one of the official stewards, I had my choice of churches next morning, and naturally I didn't hesitate. The only drawback to going to Lower Bingley was that it was ten miles away, which meant an early start, but I borrowed a bicycle from one of the grooms and tooled off. I had only Eustace's word for it that G. Hayward was such a stayer, and it might have been that he had showed too flattering form at that wedding where the twins had heard him preach; but any misgivings I may have had disappeared the moment he got into the pulpit. Eustace had been right. The man was a trier. He was a tall, rangy-looking graybeard, and he went off from the start with a nice, easy action, pausing and clearing his throat at the end of each sentence, and it wasn't five minutes before I realized that here was the winner. His habit of stopping dead and looking round the church at intervals was worth minutes to us, and in the home stretch we gained no little advantage owing to his dropping his pince-nez and having to grope for them. At the twenty-minute mark he had merely settled down. Twenty-five minutes saw him going strong. And when he finally finished with a good burst, the clock showed thirty-five minutes fourteen seconds. With the handicap which he had been given, this seemed to me to make the event easy for him, and it was with much bonhomie and good will to all men that I hopped on to the old bike and started back to the Hall for lunch.

Bingo was talking on the phone when I arrived.

"Fine! Splendid! Topping!" he was saying. "Eh? Oh, we needn't worry about him. Right-o, I'll tell Bertie." He hung up the receiver and caught sight of me. "Oh, hallo, Bertie; I was just talking to Eustace. It's all right, old man. The report from Lower Bingley has just got in. G. Hayward romps home."

"I knew he would. I've just come from there."

"Oh, were you there? I went to Badgwick. Tucker ran a splendid race, but the handicap was too much for him. Starkie had a sore throat and was nowhere. Roberts, of Fale-by-the-Water, ran third. Good old

G. Hayward!" said Bingo affectionately, and we strolled out onto the terrace.

"Are all the returns in, then?" I asked.

"All except Gandle-by-the-Hill. But we needn't worry about Bates. He never had a chance. By the way, poor old Jeeves loses his tenner. Silly ass!"

"Jeeves? How do you mean?"

"He came to me this morning, just after you had left, and asked me to put a tenner on Bates for him. I told him he was a chump and begged him not to throw his money away, but he would do it."

"I beg your pardon, sir. This note arrived for you just after you had left the house this morning."

Jeeves had materialized from nowhere, and was standing at my elbow.

"Eh? What? Note?"

"The Reverend Mr. Heppenstall's butler brought it over from the Vicarage, sir. It came too late to be delivered to you at the moment."

Young Bingo was talking to Jeeves like a father on the subject of betting against the formbook. The yell I gave made him bite his tongue in the middle of a sentence.

"What the dickens is the matter?" he asked, not a little peeved.

"We're dished! Listen to this!"

I read him the note:

> The Vicarage,
> Twing, Glos.

MY DEAR WOOSTER,—As you may have heard, circumstances over which I have no control will prevent my preaching the sermon on Brotherly Love for which you made such a flattering request. I am unwilling, however, that you shall be disappointed, so, if you will attend divine service at Gandle-by-the-Hill this morning, you will hear my sermon preached by young Bates, my nephew. I have lent him the manuscript at his urgent desire, for, between ourselves, there are wheels within wheels. My nephew is one of the candidates for the headmastership of a well-known public school, and the choice has narrowed down between him and one rival.

Late yesterday evening James received private information that the head of the Board of Governors of the school proposed to sit under him this Sunday in order to judge of the merits of his preaching, a most important item in swaying the Board's choice. I acceded to his plea that I lend him my sermon on Brotherly Love, of which,

like you, he apparently retains a vivid recollection. It would have
been too late for him to compose a sermon of suitable length in
place of the brief address which—mistaken, in my opinion—he
had designed to deliver to his rustic flock, and I wished to help the
boy.

Trusting that his preaching of the sermon will supply you with as
pleasant memories as you say you have of mine, I remain,

Cordially yours,

F. HEPPENSTALL.

P.S.—The hay fever has rendered my eyes unpleasantly weak
for the time being, so I am dictating this letter to my butler, Brookfield, who will convey it to you.

I don't know when I've experienced a more massive silence than
the one that followed my reading of this cheery epistle. Young Bingo
gulped once or twice, and practically every known emotion came and
went on his face. Jeeves coughed one soft, low, gentle cough like a
sheep with a blade of grass stuck in its throat, and then stood gazing
serenely at the landscape. Finally young Bingo spoke.

"Great Scott!" he whispered hoarsely. "An S.P. job!"

"I believe that is the technical term, sir," said Jeeves.

"So you had inside information, dash it!" said young Bingo.

"Why, yes, sir," said Jeeves. "Brookfield happened to mention the
contents of the note to me when he brought it. We are old friends."

Bingo registered grief, anguish, rage, despair and resentment.

"Well, all I can say," he cried, "is that it's a bit thick! Preaching
another man's sermon! Do you call that honest? Do you call that
playing the game?"

"Well, my dear old thing," I said, "be fair. It's quite within the
rules. Clergymen do it all the time. They aren't expected always to
make up the sermons they preach."

Jeeves coughed again, and fixed me with an expressionless eye.

"And in the present case, sir, if I may be permitted to take the
liberty of making the observation, I think we should make allow-
ances. We should remember that the securing of this headmastership
meant everything to the young couple."

"Young couple! What young couple?"

"The Reverend James Bates, sir, and Lady Cynthia. I am informed
by her ladyship's maid that they have been engaged to be married
for some weeks—provisionally, so to speak; and his lordship made
his consent conditional on Mr. Bates securing a really important and
remunerative position."

Young Bingo turned a light green.

"Engaged to be married!"

"Yes, sir."

There was a silence.

"I think I'll go for a walk," said Bingo.

"But, my dear old thing," I said, "it's just lunchtime. The gong will be going any minute now."

"I don't want any lunch!" said Bingo.

❖ *The Metropolitan Touch*

NOBODY is more alive than I am to the fact that young Bingo Little is in many respects a sound old egg. In one way and another he has made life pretty interesting for me at intervals ever since we were at school. As a companion for a cheery hour I think I would choose him before anybody. On the other hand, I'm bound to say that there are things about him that could be improved. His habit of falling in love with every second girl he sees is one of them; and another is his way of letting the world in on the secrets of his heart. If you want shrinking reticence, don't go to Bingo, because he's got about as much of it as a soap advertisement.

I mean to say—well, here's the telegram I got from him one evening in November, about a month after I'd got back to town from my visit to Twing Hall:

> I say Bertie old man I am in love at last. She is the most wonderful girl Bertie old man. This is the real thing at last Bertie. Come here at once and bring Jeeves. Oh I say you know that tobacco shop in Bond Street on the left side as you go up. Will you get me a hundred of their special cigarettes and send them to me here? I have run out. I know when you see her you will think she is the most wonderful girl. Mind you bring Jeeves. Don't forget the cigarettes.
> —BINGO.

It had been handed in at Twing Post Office. In other words, he had submitted that frightful rot to the goggling eye of a village post-mistress who was probably the mainspring of local gossip and would have the place ringing with the news before nightfall. He couldn't have given himself away more completely if he had hired the town crier. When I was a kid, I used to read stories about knights and Vikings and that species of blighter who would get up without a blush in the middle of a crowded banquet and loose off a song about how perfectly priceless they thought their best girl. I've often felt that those days would have suited young Bingo down to the ground.

Jeeves had brought the thing in with the evening drink, and I slung it over to him.

"It's about due, of course," I said. "Young Bingo hasn't been in love for at least a couple of months. I wonder who it is this time?"

"Miss Mary Burgess, sir," said Jeeves, "the niece of the Reverend Mr. Heppenstall. She is staying at Twing Vicarage."

"Great Scott!" I knew that Jeeves knew practically everything in the world, but this sound like second sight. "How do you know that?"

"When we were visiting Twing Hall in the summer, sir, I formed a somewhat close friendship with Mr. Heppenstall's butler. He is good enough to keep me abreast of the local news from time to time. From his account, sir, the young lady appears to be a very estimable young lady. Of a somewhat serious nature, I understand. Mr. Little is very *épris,* sir. Brookfield, my correspondent, writes that last week he observed him in the moonlight at an advanced hour gazing up at his window."

"Whose window! Brookfield's?"

"Yes, sir. Presumably under the impression that it was the young lady's."

"But what the deuce is he doing at Twing at all?"

"Mr. Little was compelled to resume his old position as tutor to Lord Wickhammersley's son at Twing Hall, sir, owing to having been unsuccessful in some speculations at Hurst Park at the end of October."

"Good Lord, Jeeves! Is there anything you don't know?"

"I could not say, sir."

I picked up the telegram.

"I suppose he wants us to go down and help him out a bit?"

"That would appear to be his motive in dispatching the message, sir."

"Well, what shall we do? Go?"

"I would advocate it, sir. If I may say so, I think that Mr. Little should be encouraged in this particular matter."

"You think he's picked a winner this time?"

"I hear nothing but excellent reports of the young lady, sir. I think it is beyond question that she would be an admirable influence for Mr. Little, should the affair come to a happy conclusion. Such a union would also, I fancy, go far to restore Mr. Little to the good graces of his uncle, the young lady being well connected and possessing private means. In short, sir, I think that if there is anything we can do we should do it."

"Well, with you behind him," I said, "I don't see how he can fail to click."

"You are very good, sir," said Jeeves. "The tribute is much appreciated."

Bingo met us at Twing station next day, and insisted on my sending Jeeves on in the car with the bags while he and I walked. He started in about the female the moment we had begun to hoof it.

"She is very wonderful, Bertie. She is not one of these flippant, shallow-minded modern girls. She is sweetly grave and beautifully earnest. She reminds me of—what is the name I want? Saint Cecilia," said young Bingo. "She reminds me of Saint Cecilia. She makes me yearn to be a better, nobler, deeper, broader man."

"What beats me," I said, following up a train of thought, "is what principle you pick them on. The girls you fall in love with, I mean. I mean to say, what's your system? As far as I can see, no two of them are alike. First it was Mabel the waitress, then Honoria Glossop, then that fearful blister Charlotte Corday Rowbotham—"

I own that Bingo had the decency to shudder. Thinking of Charlotte always made me shudder, too.

"You don't seriously mean, Bertie, that you are intending to compare the feeling I have for Mary Burgess, the holy devotion, the spiritual—"

"Oh, all right, let it go," I said. "I say, old lad, aren't we going rather a long way round?"

Considering that we were supposed to be heading for Twing Hall, it seemed to me that we were making a longish job of it. The Hall is about two miles from the station by the main road, and we had cut off down a lane, gone across country for a bit, climbed a stile or two, and were now working our way across a field that ended in another lane.

"She sometimes takes her little brother for a walk round this way," explained Bingo. "I thought we would meet her and bow, and you could see her, you know, and then we would walk on."

"Of course," I said, "that's enough excitement for anyone, and undoubtedly a corking reward for tramping three miles out of one's way over plowed fields with tight boots, but don't we do anything else? Don't we tack on to the girl and buzz along with her?"

"Good Lord!" said Bingo, honestly amazed. "You don't suppose I've got nerve enough for that, do you? I just look at her from afar and all that sort of thing. Quick! Here she comes! No, I'm wrong!"

It was like that song of Harry Lauder's where he's waiting for the girl and says "This is her-r-r. No, it's a rabbut." Young Bingo made me stand there in the teeth of a nor'east half gale for ten minutes, keeping me on my toes with a series of false alarms, and I was just thinking of suggesting that we should lay off and give the rest of the proceedings a miss, when round the corner there came a fox terrier, and Bingo quivered like an aspen. Then there hove in sight a small boy, and he shook like a jelly. Finally, like a star whose entrance has been worked up by the *personnel* of the *ensemble,* a girl appeared, and his emotion was painful to witness. His face got so red that, what with his white collar and the fact that the wind had turned his nose blue, he looked more like a French flag than anything else. He sagged from the waist upwards, as if he had been filleted.

He was just raising his fingers limply to his cap when he suddenly saw that the girl wasn't alone. A citizen in clerical costume was also among those present, and the sight of him didn't seem to do Bingo a bit of good. His face got redder and his nose bluer, and it wasn't till they had nearly passed that he managed to get hold of his cap.

The girl bowed, the curate said, "Ah, Little. Rough weather," the dog barked, and then they toddled on and the entertainment was over.

The curate was a new factor in the situation to me. I reported his movements to Jeeves when I got to the hall. Of course, Jeeves knew all about it already.

"That is the Reverend Mr. Wingham, Mr. Heppenstall's new curate, sir. I gathered from Brookfield that he is Mr. Little's rival, and at the moment the young lady appears to favor him. Mr. Wingham has the advantage of being on the premises. He and the young lady play duets after dinner, which acts as a bond. Mr. Little on these occasions, I understand, prowls about in the road, chafing visibly."

"That seems to be all the poor fish is able to do, dash it. He can chafe all right, but there he stops. He's lost his pep. He's got no dash. Why, when we met her just now, he hadn't the common manly courage to say 'Good evening'!"

"I gather that Mr. Little's affection is not unmingled with awe, sir."

"Well, how are we to help a man when he's such a rabbit as that? Have you anything to suggest? I shall be seeing him after dinner, and he's sure to ask first thing what you advise."

"In my opinion, sir, the most judicious course for Mr. Little to pursue would be to concentrate on the young gentleman."

"The small brother? How do you mean?"

"Make a friend of him, sir—take him for walks and so forth."

"It doesn't sound one of your red-hottest ideas. I must say I expected something fruitier than that."

"It would be a beginning, sir, and might lead to better things."

"Well, I'll tell him. I liked the look of her, Jeeves."

"A thoroughly estimable young lady, sir."

I slipped Bingo the tip from the stable that night, and was glad to observe that it seemed to cheer him up.

"Jeeves is always right," he said. "I ought to have thought of it myself. I'll start in tomorrow."

It was amazing how the poor fish bucked up. Long before I left for town it had become a mere commonplace for him to speak to the girl. I mean he didn't simply look stuffed when they met. The brother was forming a bond that was a dashed sight stronger than the curate's duets. She and Bingo used to take him for walks together. I asked Bingo what they talked about on these occasions, and he said Wilfred's future. The girl hoped that Wilfred would one day become a curate, but Bingo said no, there was something about curates he didn't quite like.

The day we left, Bingo came to see us off with Wilfred frisking about him like an old college chum. The last I saw of them, Bingo was standing him chocolates out of the slot machine. A scene of peace and cheery good will. Dashed promising, I thought.

Which made it all the more of a jar, about a fortnight later, when his telegram arrived. As follows:—

> Bertie old man I say Bertie could you possibly come down here at once. Everything gone wrong hang it all. Dash it Bertie you simply must come. I am in a state of absolute despair and heartbroken. Would you mind sending another hundred of those cigarettes? Bring Jeeves when you come Bertie. You simply must come Bertie. I rely on you. Don't forget to bring Jeeves.—BINGO.

For a chap who's perpetually hard up, I must say that young Bingo is the most wasteful telegraphist I ever struck. He's got no notion of condensing. The silly ass simply pours out his wounded soul at twopence a word, or whatever it is, without a thought.

"How about it, Jeeves?" I said. "I'm getting a bit fed. I can't go chucking all my engagements every second week in order to biff down to Twing and rally round young Bingo. Send him a wire telling him to end it all in the village pond."

"If you could spare me for the night, sir, I should be glad to run down and investigate."

"Oh, dash it! Well, I suppose there's nothing else to be done. After all, you're the fellow he wants. All right, carry on."

Jeeves got back late the next day.

"Well?" I said.

Jeeves appeared perturbed. He allowed his left eyebrow to flicker upwards in a concerned sort of manner.

"I have done what I could, sir," he said, "but I fear Mr. Little's chances do not appear bright. Since our last visit, sir, there has been a decidedly sinister and disquieting development."

"Oh, what's that?"

"You may remember Mr. Steggles, sir—the young gentleman who was studying for an examination with Mr. Heppenstall at the Vicarage?"

"What's Steggles got to do with it?" I asked.

"I gather from Brookfield, sir, who chanced to overhear a conversation, that Mr. Steggles is interesting himself in the affair."

"Good Lord! What, making a book on it?"

"I understand that he is accepting wagers from those in his immediate circle, sir. Against Mr. Little, whose chances he does not seem to fancy."

"I don't like that, Jeeves."

"No, sir. It is sinister."

"From what I know of Steggles there will be dirty work."

"It has already occurred, sir."

"Already?"

"Yes, sir. It seems that, in pursuance of the policy which he had been good enough to allow me to suggest to him, Mr. Little escorted Master Burgess to the church bazaar, and there met Mr. Steggles, who was in the company of young Master Heppenstall, the Reverend Mr. Heppenstall's second son, who is home from Rugby, just now, having recently recovered from an attack of mumps. The encounter took place in the refreshment room, where Mr. Steggles was at that moment entertaining Master Heppenstall. To cut a long story short, sir, the two gentlemen became extremely interested in the hearty manner in which the lads were fortifying themselves; and Mr. Steggles offered to back his nominee in a weight-for-age eating contest against Master Burgess for a pound a side. Mr. Little admitted to me that he was conscious of a certain hesitation as to what the upshot might be, should Miss Burgess get to hear of the matter, but his sporting blood was too much for him and he agreed to the contest. This was duly carried out, both lads exhibiting the utmost willingness and enthusiasm, and eventually Master Burgess justified Mr. Little's confidence by winning, but only after a bitter struggle. Next day both contestants were in considerable pain; inquiries were made and confessions extorted, and Mr. Little—I learn from Brookfield, who happened to be near the door of the drawing room at the moment—had an extremely unpleasant interview with the young lady, which ended in her desiring him never to speak to her again."

There's no getting away from the fact that, if ever a man required watching, it's Steggles. Machiavelli could have taken his correspondence course.

"It was a put-up job, Jeeves!" I said. "I mean, Steggles worked the whole thing on purpose. It's his old nobbling game."

"There would seem to be no doubt about that, sir."

"Well, he seems to have dished poor old Bingo all right."

"That is the prevalent opinion, sir. Brookfield tells me that down in the village at the Cow and Horses seven to one is being freely offered on Mr. Wingham and finding no takers."

"Good Lord! Are they betting about it down in the village, too?"

"Yes, sir. And in adjoining hamlets also. The affair has caused widespread interest. I am told that there is a certain sporting reaction in even so distant a spot as Lower Bingley."

"Well, I don't see what there is to do. If Bingo is such a chump—"

"One is fighting a losing battle, I fear, sir, but I did venture to indicate to Mr. Little a course of action which might prove of advantage. I recommended him to busy himself with good works."

"Good works?"

"About the village, sir. Reading to the bedridden—chatting with the sick—that sort of thing, sir. We can but trust that good results will ensue."

"Yes, I suppose so," I said doubtfully. "But, by gosh, if I was a sick man I'd hate to have a looney like young Bingo coming and gibbering at my bedside."

"There *is* that aspect of the matter, sir," said Jeeves.

I didn't hear a word from Bingo for a couple of weeks, and I took it after a while that he had found the going too hard and had chucked in the towel. And then, one night not long before Christmas, I came back to the flat pretty latish, having been out dancing at the Embassy. I was fairly tired, having swung a practically nonstop shoe from shortly after dinner till two A.M., and bed seemed to be indicated. Judge of my chagrin and all that sort of thing, therefore, when, tottering to my room and switching on the light, I observed the foul features of young Bingo all over the pillow. The blighter had appeared from nowhere and was in my bed, sleeping like an infant with a sort of happy, dreamy smile on his map.

A bit thick I mean to say! We Woosters are all for the good old medieval hosp. and all that, but when it comes to finding fellows collaring your bed, the thing becomes a trifle too moldy. I hove a shoe, and Bingo sat up, gurgling.

" 's matter? 's matter?" said young Bingo.

"What the deuce are you doing in my bed?" I said.

"Oh, hallo, Bertie! So there you are!"

"Yes, here I am. What are you doing in my bed?"

"I came up to town for the night on business."

"Yes, but what are you doing in my bed?"

"Dash it all, Bertie," said young Bingo querulously, "don't keep harping on your beastly bed. There's another made up in the spare room. I saw Jeeves make it with my own eyes. I believe he meant it for me, but I knew what a perfect host you were, so I just turned in here. I say, Bertie, old man," said Bingo, apparently fed up with the discussion about sleeping quarters, "I see daylight."

"Well, it's getting on for three in the morning."

"I was speaking figuratively, you ass. I meant that hope has begun to dawn. About Mary Burgess, you know. Sit down and I'll tell you all about it."

"I won't. I'm going to sleep."

"To begin with," said young Bingo, settling himself comfortably against the pillows and helping himself to a cigarette from my special private box, "I must once again pay a marked tribute to good old Jeeves. A modern Solomon. I was badly up against it when I came to him for advice, but he rolled up with a tip which has put me—I use the term advisedly and in a conservative spirit—on velvet. He may have told you that he recommended me to win back the lost ground by busying myself with good works? Bertie, old man," said young Bingo earnestly, "for the last two weeks I've been comforting the sick to such an extent that, if I had a brother and you brought him to me on a sickbed at this moment, by Jove, old man, I'd heave a brick at him. However, though it took it out of me like the deuce, the scheme worked splendidly. She softened visibly before I'd been at it a week. Started to bow again when we met in the street, and so forth. About a couple of days ago she distinctly smiled—in a sort of faint, saintlike kind of way, you know—when I ran into her outside the Vicarage. And yesterday—I say, you remember that curate chap, Wingham? Fellow with a long nose."

"Of course I remember him. Your rival."

"Rival?" Bingo raised his eyebrows. "Oh, well. I suppose you could have called him that at one time. Though it sounds a little far-fetched."

"Does it?" I said, stung by the sickening complacency of the chump's manner. "Well, let me tell you that the last I heard was that at the Cow and Horses in Twing village and all over the place as far as Lower Bingley they were offering seven to one on the curate and finding no takers."

Bingo started violently, and sprayed cigarette ash all over my bed. "Betting!" he gargled. "Betting! You don't mean that they're betting on this holy, sacred— Oh, I say, dash it all! Haven't people any sense of decency and reverence? Is nothing safe from their beastly, sordid graspingness? I wonder," said young Bingo thoughtfully, "if there's a chance of my getting any of that seven-to-one money? Seven to one! What a price! Who's offering it, do you know? Oh, well, I suppose it wouldn't do. No, I suppose it wouldn't be quite the thing."

"You seem dashed confident," I said. "I'd always thought that Wingham—"

"Oh, I'm not worried about him," said Bingo. "I was just going to tell you. Wingham's got the mumps, and won't be out and about for weeks. And, jolly as that is in itself, it's not all. You see, he was producing the Village School Christmas Entertainment, and now I've taken over the job. I went to old Heppenstall last night and clinched the contract. Well, you see what that means. It means that I shall be absolutely the center of the village life and thought for three solid weeks, with a terrific triumph to wind up with. Everybody looking up to me and fawning on me, don't you see, and all that. It's bound to have a powerful effect on Mary's mind. It will show her that I am capable of serious effort; that there is a solid foundation of worth in me; that, mere butterfly as she may once have thought me, I am in reality—"

"Oh, all right, let it go!"

"It's a big thing, you know, this Christmas Entertainment. Old Heppenstall is very much wrapped up in it. Nibs from all over the countryside rolling up. The Squire present, with family. A big chance for me, Bertie, my boy, and I mean to make the most of it. Of course, I'm handicapped a bit by not having been in on the thing from the start. Will you credit it that that uninspired doughnut of a curate wanted to give the public some rotten little fairy play out of a book for children published about fifty years ago without one good laugh or the semblance of a gag in it? It's too late to alter the thing entirely, but at least I can jazz it up. I'm going to write them in something zippy to brighten the thing up a bit."

"You can't write."

"Well, when I say write, I mean pinch. That's why I've popped up to town. I've been to see that revue, *Cuddle Up!* at the Palladium, tonight. Full of good stuff. Of course, it's rather hard to get anything in the nature of a big spectacular effect in the Twing Village Hall, with no scenery to speak of and a chorus of practically imbecile kids of ages ranging from nine to fourteen, but I think I see my way. Have you seen *Cuddle Up!?*"

"Yes. Twice."

"Well, there's some good stuff in the first act, and I can lift practically all the numbers. Then there's that show at the Palace. I can see the matinee of that tomorrow before I leave. There's sure to be some decent bits in that. Don't you worry about my not being able to write a hit. Leave it to me, laddie, leave it to me. And now, my dear old chap," said young Bingo, snuggling down cozily, "you mustn't keep me up talking all night. It's all right for you fellows who have nothing to do, but I'm a busy man. Good night, old thing. Close the door quietly after you and switch out the light. Breakfast about ten tomorrow, I suppose, what? Right-o. Good night."

For the next three weeks I didn't see Bingo. He became a sort of Voice Heard Off, developing a habit of ringing me up on long distance and consulting me on various points arising at rehearsal, until the day when he got me out of bed at eight in the morning to ask whether I thought "Merry Christmas!" was a good title. I told him then that this nuisance must now cease, and after that he cheesed it, and practically passed out of my life, till one afternoon when I got back to the flat to dress for dinner and found Jeeves inspecting a whacking big poster sort of thing which he had draped over the back of an armchair.

"Good Lord, Jeeves!" I said. I was feeling rather weak that day, and the thing shook me. "What on earth's that?"

"Mr. Little sent it to me, sir, and desired me to bring it to your notice."

"Well, you've certainly done it!"

I took another look at the object. There was no doubt about it, it caught the eye. It was about seven feet long, and most of the lettering in about as bright-red ink as I ever struck.

This was how it ran:

TWING VILLAGE HALL,
Friday, December 23rd,
RICHARD LITTLE
presents
A New and Original Revue

Entitled
WHAT HO, TWING!!
Book by
RICHARD LITTLE
Lyrics by
RICHARD LITTLE
Music by
RICHARD LITTLE.
With the Full Twing Juvenile
Company and Chorus.
Scenic effects by
RICHARD LITTLE
Produced by
RICHARD LITTLE.

"What do you make of it, Jeeves?" I said.

"I confess I am a little doubtful, sir. I think Mr. Little would have done better to follow my advice and confine himself to good works about the village."

"You think the thing will be a frost?"

"I could not hazard a conjecture, sir. But my experience has been that what pleases the London public is not always so acceptable to the rural mind. The metropolitan touch sometimes proves a trifle too exotic for the provinces."

"I suppose I ought to go down and see the dashed thing?"

"I think Mr. Little would be wounded were you not present, sir."

The Village Hall at Twing is a smallish building, smelling of apples. It was full when I turned up on the evening of the twenty-third, for I had purposely timed myself to arrive not long before the kickoff. I had had experience of one or two of these binges, and didn't want to run any risk of coming early and finding myself shoved into a seat in one of the front rows where I wouldn't be able to execute a quiet sneak into the open air halfway through the proceedings, if the occasion seemed to demand it. I secured a nice strategic position near the door at the back of the hall.

From where I stood I had a good view of the audience. As always on these occasions, the first few rows were occupied by the Nibs— consisting of the Squire, a fairly mauve old sportsman with white whiskers, his family, a platoon of local parsons and perhaps a couple of dozen prominent pewholders. Then came a dense squash of what you might call the lower middle classes. And at the back, where I was, we came down with a jerk in the social scale, this end of the hall being given up almost entirely to a collection of frankly Tough Eggs, who had rolled up not so much for any love of the drama as because there was a free tea after the show. Take it for all in all, a representative gathering of Twing life and thought. The Nibs were whispering in a pleased manner to each other, the Lower Middles were sitting up very straight, as if they'd been bleached, and the Tough Eggs whiled away the time by cracking nuts and exchanging low rustic wheezes. The girl, Mary Burgess, was at the piano playing a waltz. Beside her stood the curate, Wingham, apparently recovered. The temperature, I should think, was about a hundred and twenty-seven.

Somebody jabbed me heartily in the lower ribs, and I perceived the man Steggles.

"Hallo!" he said. "I didn't know you were coming down."

I didn't like the chap, but we Woosters can wear the mask. I beamed a bit.

"Oh, yes," I said. "Bingo wanted me to roll up and see his show."

"I hear he's giving us something pretty ambitious," said the man Steggles. "Big effects and all that sort of thing."

"I believe so."

"Of course, it means a lot to him, doesn't it? He's told you about the girl, of course?"

"Yes. And I hear you're laying seven to one against him," I said, eying the blighter a trifle austerely.

He didn't even quiver.

"Just a little flutter to relieve the monotony of country life," he said. "But you've got the facts a bit wrong. It's down in the village that they're laying seven to one. I can do you better than that, if you feel in a speculative mood. How about a tenner at a hundred to eight?"

"Good Lord! Are you giving that?"

"Yes. Somehow," said Steggles meditatively, "I have a sort of feeling, a kind of premonition that something's going to go wrong tonight. You know what Little is. A bungler, if ever there was one. Something tells me that this show of his is going to be a frost. And if it is, of course, I should think it would prejudice the girl against him pretty badly. His standing always was rather shaky."

"Are you going to try and smash up the show?" I said sternly.

"Me!" said Steggles. "Why, what could I do? Half a minute, I want to go and speak to a man."

He buzzed off, leaving me distinctly disturbed. I could see from the fellow's eye that he was meditating some of his customary rough stuff, and I thought Bingo ought to be warned. But there wasn't time and I couldn't get at him. Almost immediately after Steggles had left me the curtain went up.

Except as a prompter, Bingo wasn't much in evidence in the early part of the performance. The thing at the outset was merely one of those weird dramas which you dig out of books published around Christmastime and entitled "Twelve Little Plays for the Tots," or something like that. The kids drooled on in the usual manner, the booming voice of Bingo ringing out from time to time behind the scenes when the fatheads forgot their lines; and the audience was settling down into the sort of torpor usual on these occasions, when the first of Bingo's interpolated bits occurred. It was that number which What's-her-name sings in that revue at the Palace—you would recognize the tune if I hummed it, but I can never get hold of the dashed thing. It always got three encores at the Palace, and it went well now, even with a squeaky-voiced child jumping on and off the key like a chamois of the Alps leaping from crag to crag. Even the Tough Eggs liked it. At the end of the second refrain the entire house was shouting for an encore, and the kid with the voice like a slate pencil took a deep breath and started to let it go once more.

At this point all the lights went out.

I don't know when I've had anything so sudden and devastating happen to me before. They didn't flicker. They just went out. The hall was in complete darkness.

Well, of course, that sort of broke the spell, as you might put it. People started to shout directions, and the Tough Eggs stamped their feet and settled down for a pleasant time. And, of course, young Bingo had to make an ass of himself. His voice suddenly shot at us out of the darkness.

"Ladies and gentlemen, something has gone wrong with the lights—"

The Tough Eggs were tickled by this bit of information straight from the stable. They took it up as a sort of battle cry. Then, after about five minutes, the lights went up again, and the show was resumed.

It took ten minutes after that to get the audience back into its state of coma, but eventually they began to settle down, and everything was going nicely when a small boy with a face like a turbot edged out in front of the curtain, which had been lowered after a pretty painful scene about a wishing ring or a fairy's curse or something of that sort, and started to sing that song of George Thingummy's out of *Cuddle Up!* You know the one I mean. "Always

Listen to Mother, Girls!" it's called, and he gets the audience to join in and sing the refrain. Quite a ripeish ballad, and one which I myself have frequently sung in my bath with not a little vim; but by no means—as anyone but a perfect saphead prune like young Bingo would have known—by no means the sort of thing for a children's Christmas entertainment in the old village hall. Right from the start of the first refrain the bulk of the audience had begun to stiffen in their seats and fan themselves, and the Burgess girl at the piano was accompanying in a stunned, mechanical sort of way, while the curate at her side averted his gaze in a pained manner. The Tough Eggs, however, were all for it.

At the end of the second refrain the kid stopped and began to sidle toward the wings. Upon which the following brief dialogue took place:

YOUNG BINGO (*Voice heard off, ringing against the rafters*): "Go on!"

THE KID (*coyly*): "I don't like to."

YOUNG BINGO (*still louder*): "Go on, you little blighter, or I'll slay you!"

I suppose the kid thought it over swiftly and realized that Bingo, being in a position to get at him, had better be conciliated, whatever the harvest might be; for he shuffled down to the front and, having shut his eyes and giggled hysterically, said: "Ladies and gentlemen, I will now call upon Squire Tressidder to oblige by singing the refrain!"

You know, with the most charitable feelings toward him, there are moments when you can't help thinking that young Bingo ought to be in some sort of a home. I suppose, poor fish, he had pictured this as the big punch of the evening. He had imagined, I take it, that the Squire would spring jovially to his feet, rip the song off his chest, and all would be gaiety and mirth. Well, what happened was simply that old Tressidder—and, mark you, I'm not blaming him—just sat where he was, swelling and turning a brighter purple every second. The Lower Middle Classes remained in frozen silence, waiting for the roof to fall. The only section of the audience that really seemed to enjoy the idea was the Tough Eggs, who yelled with enthusiasm. It was jam for the Tough Eggs.

And then the lights went out again.

When they went up, some minutes later, they disclosed the Squire marching stiffly out at the head of his family, fed up to the eyebrows; the Burgess girl at the piano with a pale, set look; and the curate gazing at her with something in his expression that seemed to suggest that, although all this was no doubt deplorable, he had spotted the silver lining.

The show went on once more. There were great chunks of Plays-for-the-Tots dialogue, and then the girl at the piano struck up the prelude to that Orange-Girl number that's the big hit of the Palace revue. I took it that this was to be Bingo's smashing act-one finale. The entire company was on the stage, and a clutching hand had appeared round the edge of the curtain, ready to pull at the right moment. It looked like the finale all right. It wasn't long before I realized that it was something more. It was the finish.

I take it you know that Orange number at the Palace? It goes:

> *Oh, won't you something something oranges,*
>   *My something oranges,*
>   *My something oranges;*
> *Oh, won't you something something something I forget,*
> *Something something something tumty tumty yet:*
> *Oh—*

or words to that effect. It's a dashed clever lyric, and the tune's good, too; but the thing that made the number was the business where the girls take oranges out of their baskets, you know, and toss them lightly to the audience. I don't know if you've ever noticed it, but it always seems to tickle an audience to bits when they get things thrown at them from the stage. Every time I've been to the Palace the customers have simply gone wild over this number.

But at the Palace, of course, the oranges are made of yellow wool, and the girls don't so much chuck them as drop them limply into the first and second rows. I began to gather that the business was going to be treated rather differently tonight when a dashed great chunk of pips and mildew sailed past my ear and burst on the wall behind me. Another landed with a squelch on the neck of one of the Nibs in the third row. And then a third took me right on the tip of the nose, and I kind of lost interest in the proceeding for a while.

When I had scrubbed my face and got my eye to stop watering for a moment, I saw that the evening's entertainment had begun to resemble one of Belfast's livelier nights. The air was thick with shrieks and fruit. The kids on the stage with Bingo buzzing distractedly to and fro in their midst were having the time of their lives. I suppose they realized that this couldn't go on forever, and were making the most of their chances. The Tough Eggs had begun to pick up all the oranges that hadn't burst and were shooting them back, so that the audience got it both coming and going. In fact, take it all round, there was a certain amount of confusion; and, just as things had begun really to hot up, out went the lights again.

It seemed to me about my time for leaving, so I slid for the door. I was hardly outside when the audience began to stream out. They surged about me in twos and threes, and I've never seen a public body so dashed unanimous on any point. To a man—and to a woman —they were cursing poor old Bingo; and there was a large and rapidly growing school of thought which held that the best thing to do would be to waylay him as he emerged and splash him about in the village pond a bit.

There were such a dickens of a lot of these enthusiasts and they looked so jolly determined that it seemed to me that the only matey thing to do was to go behind and warn young Bingo to turn his coat collar up and breeze off snakily by some side exit. I went behind, and found him sitting on a box in the wings, perspiring pretty freely and looking more or less like the spot marked with a cross where the accident happened. His hair was standing up and his ears were hanging down, and one harsh word would undoubtedly have made him burst into tears.

"Bertie," he said hollowly, as he saw me, "it was that blighter Steggles! I caught one of the kids before he could get away and got it all out of him. Steggles substituted real oranges for the balls of wool which with infinite sweat and at a cost of nearly a quid I had specially prepared. Well, I will now proceed to tear him limb from limb. It'll be something to do."

I hated to spoil his daydreams, but it had to be.

"Good heavens, man," I said, "you haven't time for frivolous amusements now. You've got to get out. And quick!"

"Bertie," said Bingo, in a dull voice, "she was here just now. She said it was all my fault and that she would never speak to me again. She said she had always suspected me of being a heartless practical joker, and now she knew. She said— Oh, well, she ticked me off properly."

"That's the least of your troubles," I said. It seemed impossible to rouse the poor zib to a sense of his position. "Do you realize that about two hundred of Twing's heftiest are waiting for you outside to chuck you into the pond?"

"No!"

"Absolutely!"

For a moment the poor chap seemed crushed. But only for a moment. There has always been something of the good old English bulldog breed about Bingo. A strange, sweet smile flickered for an instant over his face.

"It's all right," he said. "I can sneak out through the cellar and climb over the wall at the back. They can't intimidate *me!*"

It couldn't have been more than a week later when Jeeves, after he had brought me my tea, gently steered me away from the sporting page of the *Morning Post* and directed my attention to an announcement in the engagements and marriages column.

It was a brief statement that a marriage had been arranged and would shortly take place between the Hon. and Rev. Hubert Wingham, third son of the Right Hon. the Earl of Sturridge, and Mary, only daughter of the late Matthew Burgess, of Weatherly Court, Hants.

"Of course," I said, after I had given it the east-to-west, "I expected this, Jeeves."

"Yes, sir."

"She would never forgive him what happened that night."

"No, sir."

"Well," I said, as I took a sip of the fragrant and steaming brew, "I don't suppose it will take old Bingo long to get over it. It's about the hundred and eleventh time this sort of thing has happened to him. You're the man I'm sorry for."

"Me, sir?"

"Well, dash it all, you can't have forgotten what a deuce of a lot of trouble you took to bring the thing off for Bingo. It's too bad that all your work should have been wasted."

"Not entirely wasted, sir."

"Eh?"

"It is true that my efforts to bring about the match between Mr. Little and the young lady were not successful, but still I look back upon the matter with a certain satisfaction."

"Because you did your best, you mean?

"Not entirely, sir, though of course that thought also gives me pleasure. I was alluding more particularly to the fact that I found the affair financially remunerative."

"Financially remunerative? What do you mean?"

"When I learned that Mr. Steggles had interested himself in the contest, sir, I went shares with my friend Brookfield and bought the book which had been made on the issue by the landlord of the Cow and Horses. It has proved a highly profitable investment. Your breakfast will be ready almost immediately, sir. Kidneys on toast and mushrooms. I will bring it when you ring."

⚙ Jeeves and the Song of Songs

ANOTHER DAY dawned all hot and fresh and, in pursuance of my unswerving policy at that time, I was singing "Sonny Boy" in my bath, when Jeeves's voice filtered through the woodwork.

"I beg your pardon, sir."

I had just got to that bit about the angels being lonely, where you need every ounce of concentration in order to make the spectacular finish, but I signed off courteously.

"Yes, Jeeves? Say on."

"Mr. Glossop, sir."

"What about him?"

"He is in the sitting room, sir."

"Young Tuppy Glossop?"

"Yes, sir."

"You say that he is in the sitting room?"

"Yes, sir."

"Desiring speech with me?"

"Yes, sir."

"H'm!"

"Sir?"

"I only said 'H'm.'"

And I'll tell you why I said "H'm." It was because the man's story had interested me strangely. And I'll tell you why the man's story had interested me strangely. Owing to a certain episode that had occurred one night at the Drones Club, there had sprung up recently a coolness, as you might describe it, between this Glossop and myself. The news, therefore, that he was visiting me at my flat, especially at an hour when he must have known that I would be in my bath and consequently in a strong strategic position to heave a wet sponge at him, surprised me considerably.

I hopped out with some briskness and, slipping a couple of towels about the torso, made for the sitting room. I found young Tuppy at the piano, playing "Sonny Boy" with one finger.

"What ho!" I said, not without hauteur.

"Oh, hullo, Bertie," said Tuppy. "I say, Bertie, I want to see you about something important."

It seemed to me that the bloke was embarrassed. He had moved to the mantelpiece, and now he broke a vase in a constrained way.

"The fact is, Bertie, I'm engaged."

"Engaged?"

"Engaged," said young Tuppy, coyly dropping a photograph frame upon the fender. "Practically, that is."

"Practically?"

"Yes. You'll like her, Bertie. Her name is Cora Bellinger. She's studying for opera. Wonderful voice she has. Also dark, flashing eyes and a great soul."

"How do you mean, 'practically'?"

"Well, it's this way. Before ordering the trousseau there is one little point she wants cleared up. You see, what with her great soul and all that, she has a rather serious outlook on life, and the one thing she absolutely bars is anything in the shape of hearty humor. You know, practical joking and so forth.

"She said if she thought I was a practical joker she would never speak to me again. And unfortunately she appears to have heard about that little affair at the Drones. . . . I expect you have forgotten all about that, Bertie?"

"I have not!"

"No, no, not forgotten exactly. What I mean is, nobody laughs more heartily at the recollection than you. And what I want you to do, old man, is to seize an early opportunity of taking Cora aside and categorically denying that there is any truth in the story. My happiness, Bertie, is in your hands, if you know what I mean."

Well, of course, if he put it like that, what could I do? We Woosters have our code.

"Oh, all right," I said, but far from brightly.

"Splendid fellow!"

"When do I meet this blighted female?"

"Don't call her 'this blighted female,' Bertie, old man. I have planned all that out. I will bring her around here today for a spot of lunch."

"What!"

"At one-thirty. Right. Good. Fine. Thanks. I knew I could rely on you."

He pushed off, and I turned to Jeeves, who had shimmered in with the morning meal.

"Lunch for three today, Jeeves," I said.

"Very good, sir."

"You know, Jeeves, it's a bit thick. You remember my telling you about what Mr. Glossop did to me that night at the Drones?"

"Yes, sir."

"For months I have been cherishing dreams of a hideous vengeance. And now, so far from crushing him into the dust, I've got to fill him and fiancée with rich food, and generally rally round and be the good angel."

"Life is like that, sir."

"True, Jeeves. What have we here?" I asked, inspecting the tray.

"Kippered herrings, sir."

"And I shouldn't wonder," I said, for I was in thoughtful mood, "if even herrings haven't troubles of their own."

"Quite possibly, sir."

"I mean, apart from getting kippered."

"Yes, sir."

"And so it goes on, Jeeves, so it goes on."

I can't say I saw exactly eye to eye with young Tuppy in his admiration for the Bellinger female. Delivered on the mat at one-twenty-five, she proved to be an upstanding light-heavyweight of some thirty summers with a commanding eye and a square chin which I, personally, would have steered clear of.

She seemed to me a good deal like what Cleopatra would have been after going in too freely for the starches and cereals. I don't know why it is, but women who have anything to do with opera, even if they're only studying for it, always appear to run to surplus poundage.

Tuppy, however, was obviously all for her. His whole demeanor, both before and during luncheon, was that of one striving to be worthy of a noble soul. When Jeeves offered him a cocktail he practically recoiled as from a serpent. It was terrible to see the change which love had effected in the man. The spectacle put me off my food.

At half past two the Bellinger left to go to a singing lesson. Tuppy trotted after her to the door, bleating and frisking a goodish bit, and then came back and looked at me in a marked manner.

"Well, Bertie?"

"Well, what?"

"I mean, isn't she?"

"Oh, rather," I said, humoring the poor fish.

"Wonderful eyes?"

"Oh, rather."

"Wonderful figure?"

"Oh, quite."

"Wonderful voice?"

Here I was able to intone the response with a little more heartiness. The Bellinger, at Tuppy's request, had sung us a few songs before digging in at the trough, and nobody could have denied that her pipes were in great shape. The plaster was still falling from the ceiling.

"Terrific," I said.

Tuppy sighed, and, having helped himself to about four inches of whisky and one of soda, took a deep, refreshing draft.

"Ah!" he said. "I needed that."

"Why didn't you have it at lunch?"

"Well, it's this way," said Tuppy. "I have not actually ascertained what Cora's opinions are on the subject of the taking of slight snorts from time to time, but I thought it more prudent to lay off. The view I took was that laying off would seem to indicate the serious mind. It is touch and go, as you might say, at the moment, and the smallest thing may turn the scale."

"What beats me is how on earth you expect to make her think you've got a mind at all—let alone a serious one."

"I have my own methods."

"I bet they're rotten."

"You do, do you?" said Tuppy warmly. "Well, let me tell you, my lad, that that's exactly what they're anything but. I am handling this affair with consummate generalship. Do you remember Beefy Bingham who was at Oxford with us?"

"I ran into him only the other day. He's a parson now."

"Yes. Down in the East End. Well, he runs a lads' club for the local toughs—you know the sort of thing—cocoa and backgammon in the reading room and occasional clean, bright entertainments in the Oddfellows' Hall; and I've been helping him. I don't suppose I've passed an evening away from the backgammon board for weeks.

"Cora is extremely pleased. I've got her to promise to sing on Tuesday at Beefy's next clean, bright entertainment."

"You have?"

"I absolutely have. And now mark my devilish ingenuity, Bertie. I'm going to sing, too."

"Why do you suppose that's going to get you anywhere?"

"Because the way I intend to sing the song I intend to sing will prove to her that there are great deeps in my nature, whose existence she has not suspected. She will see that rough, unlettered audience wiping the tears out of its bally eyes and she will say to herself, 'What ho! The old egg really has a soul!'

"For it is not one of your moldy comic songs, Bertie. No low buffoonery of that sort for me. It is all about angels being lonely and what not."

I uttered a sharp cry. "You can't mean you're going to sing 'Sonny Boy'?"

"I jolly well do."

I was shocked. Yes, dash it, I was shocked. You see, I held strong views on "Sonny Boy." I considered it a song only to be attempted by a few of the elect in the privacy of the bathroom. And the thought of its being murdered in open Oddfellows' Hall by a bloke who could treat a pal as young Tuppy had treated me that night at the Drones sickened me. Yes, sickened me.

I hadn't time, however, to express my horror and disgust, for at this juncture Jeeves came in.

"Mrs. Travers has just rung up on the telephone, sir. She desired me to say that she will be calling to see you in a few minutes."

"Contents noted, Jeeves," I said. "Now listen, Tuppy—"

I stopped. The fellow wasn't there.

"Mr. Glossop has left, sir."

"Left? How can he have left? He was sitting there."

"That is the front door closing now, sir."

"But what made him shoot off like that?"

"Possibly Mr. Glossop did not wish to meet Mrs. Travers, sir."

"Why not?"

"I could not say, sir. But undoubtedly at the mention of Mrs. Travers' name he rose very swiftly."

"Strange, Jeeves."

"Yes, sir."

I turned to a subject of more moment.

"Jeeves," I said, "Mr. Glossop proposes to sing 'Sonny Boy' at an entertainment down in the East End next Tuesday before an audience consisting mainly of costermongers, with a sprinkling of whelk-stall owners, purveyors of blood oranges, and minor pugilists."

"Indeed, sir?"

"Make a note to remind me to be there. He will infallibly get the bird, and I want to witness his downfall."

"Very good, sir."

"And when Mrs. Travers arrives I shall be in the sitting room."

Those who know Bertram Wooster best are aware that in his

journey through life he is impeded and generally snootered by about as scaly a collection of aunts as was ever assembled. But there is one exception to the general ghastliness—viz. my Aunt Dahlia. She married old Tom Travers the year Bluebottle won the Cambridge-shire, and is one of the best. It is always a pleasure to me to chat with her, and it was with a courtly geniality that I rose to receive her as she sailed over the threshold at about two-fifty-five.

She seemed somewhat perturbed, and plunged into the agenda without delay. Aunt Dahlia is one of those big, hearty women. She used to go in a lot for hunting, and she generally speaks as if she had just sighted a fox on a hillside half a mile away.

"Bertie," she cried, in the manner of one encouraging a platoon of hounds to renewed efforts, "I want your help."

"And you shall have it, aged relative," I replied suavely. "I can honestly say that there is no one to whom I would more readily do a good turn, no one to whom I am more delighted to be—"

"Less of it," she begged, "less of it. You know that friend of yours, young Glossop?"

"He's just been lunching here."

"He has, has he? Well, I wish you'd poisoned his soup."

"We didn't have soup. And when you describe him as a 'friend of mine,' I wouldn't quite say the term absolutely squared with the facts. Some time ago, one night when we had been dining together at the Drones—"

At this point Aunt Dahlia—a little brusquely, it seemed to me—said that she would rather wait for the story of my life till she could get it in book form. I could see now that she was definitely not her usual sunny self, so I shelved my personal grievances and asked what was biting her.

"It's that young hound Glossop," she said.

"What's he been doing?"

"Breaking Angela's heart."

(Angela. Daughter of above. My cousin. Quite a good egg.)

"What!"

"I say he's—breaking—Angela's—*heart!*"

"You say he's breaking Angela's heart?"

She begged me to suspend the vaudeville cross-talk stuff.

"How's he doing that?" I asked.

"With his neglect. With his low, callous, double-crossing duplicity."

" 'Duplicity' is the word, Aunt Dahlia," I said. "In treating of young Tuppy Glossop, it springs naturally to the lips. Let me tell you what he did to me one night at the Drones. We had finished dinner—"

"Ever since the beginning of the season, up to about three weeks ago, he was all over Angela. The sort of thing which, when I was a girl, we should have described as courting."

"Or wooing?"

"Wooing or courting, whichever you like."

"Whichever *you* like, Aunt Dahlia," I said courteously.

"Well, anyway, he haunted the house, lapped up daily lunches, took her out dancing half the night, and so on, till naturally the poor kid, who's quite off her oats about him, took it for granted that it was only a question of time before he suggested that they should feed for life out of the same crib. And now he's gone and dropped her like a hot brick, and I hear he's infatuated with some girl he met at a Chelsea tea party—a girl named—now, what was it?"

"Cora Bellinger."

"How do you know?"

"She was lunching here today."

"He brought her?"

"Yes."

"What's she like?"

"Pretty massive. In shape, a bit on the lines of the Albert Hall."

"Did he seem very fond of her?"

"Couldn't take his eyes off the chassis."

"The modern young man," said Aunt Dahlia, "is a pot of poison and wants a nurse to lead him by the hand and some strong attendant to kick him regularly at intervals of a quarter of an hour."

I tried to point out the silver lining.

"If you ask me, old egg," I said, "I think Angela is well out of it. This Glossop is a tough baby. One of London's toughest. I was trying to tell you just now what he did to me one night at the Drones.

"First, having got me in sporting mood with a bottle of the ripest, he bet me that I wouldn't swing myself across the swimming pool by the ropes and rings. I knew I could do it on my head, so I took him on, exulting in the fun, so to speak. And when I'd done half the trip, and was going strong, I found he had looped the last rope back against the rail, leaving me no alternative but to drop into the depths and swim ashore in correct evening costume."

"He did?"

"He certainly did. It was months ago, and I haven't got really dry yet. You wouldn't want your daughter to marry a man capable of a thing like that!"

"On the contrary, you restore my faith in the young hound. I see that there must be lots of good in him, after all. And I want this Bellinger business broken up, Bertie."

"How?"

"I don't care how. Any way you please."

"But what can I do?"

"Do? Why, put the whole thing before your man Jeeves. Jeeves will find a way. One of the most capable fellers I ever met. Put the thing squarely up to Jeeves and let Nature take its course."

"There may be something in what you say."

"Of course there is. A little thing like this will be child's play to Jeeves. Get him working on it right away, and I'll look in tomorrow to hear the result."

With which, she biffed off, and I summoned Jeeves to the presence.

"Jeeves," I said, "you have heard all?"

"Yes, sir."

"I thought you would. The recent aunt has what you might call a carrying voice. Has it ever occurred to you that, if all other sources of income failed, she could make a good living calling the cattle home across the sands of Dee?"

"I had not considered the point, sir, but no doubt you are right."

"Well, how do we go? What is your reaction? I think we should do our best to help and assist."

"Yes, sir."

"I am fond of Aunt Dahlia, and I am fond of Angela. Fond of them both, if you get my drift. What the misguided girl finds to attract her in young Tuppy, I cannot say, Jeeves, and you cannot say. But apparently she loves the man—which shows it can be done, a thing I wouldn't have believed myself—and is pining away like—"

"Patience on a monument, sir."

"Like Patience, as you very shrewdly remark, on a monument. So we must cluster round. Bend your brain to the problem, Jeeves. It is one that will tax you to the uttermost."

Aunt Dahlia blew in on the morrow, and I rang the bell for Jeeves. He appeared, looking brainier than one could have believed possible —sheer intellect shining from every feature—and I could see at once that the engine had been turning over.

"Speak, Jeeves," I said.

"Very good, sir."

"You have brooded?"

"Yes, sir."

"With what success?"

"I have a plan, sir, which I fancy may produce satisfactory results."

"Let's have it," said Aunt Dahlia.

"In affairs of this description, madam, the first essential is to study the psychology of the individual."

"The what?"

"The psychology, madam."

"He means the psychology," I said.

"Oh, ah," said Aunt Dahlia.

"And by psychology, Jeeves," I went on, to help the thing along, "you imply—?"

"The natures and dispositions of the principals in the matter, sir."

"You mean, what they're like?"

"Precisely, sir."

"Does he talk like this when you're alone, Bertie?" asked Aunt Dahlia.

"Sometimes. Occasionally. And on the other hand, sometimes not. Proceed, Jeeves."

"Well, sir, if I may say so, the thing that struck me most forcibly about Miss Bellinger when she was under my observation was that hers was a somewhat imperious nature. I could envisage Miss Bellinger applauding success. I could not so easily see her pitying and sympathizing with failure.

"Possibly you will recall, sir, her attitude when Mr. Glossop endeavored to light her cigarette with his automatic lighter? I thought I detected a certain impatience at his inability to produce the necessary flame."

"True, Jeeves. She ticked him off."

"Precisely, sir."

"Let me get this straight," said Aunt Dahlia. "You think if he goes on trying to light her cigarette with his automatic lighter long enough, she will eventually get fed up and hand him the mitten?"

"I merely mentioned the episode, madam, as an indication of Miss Bellinger's somewhat ruthless nature."

"Ruthless," I said, "is right. The Bellinger is hard-boiled. Those eyes. That chin. I could read them. A vicious specimen, if ever there was one."

"Precisely, sir. I think, therefore, that, should Miss Bellinger be a witness of Mr. Glossop's appearing to disadvantage in public, she would cease to entertain affection for him. In the event, for instance, of his failing to entertain the audience on Tuesday with his singing—"

I saw daylight.

"By Jove, Jeeves! You mean if he gets the bird all will be off?"

"I shall be greatly surprised if such is not the case, sir."

I shook my head.

"We cannot leave this thing to chance, Jeeves. Young Tuppy sing-ing 'Sonny Boy' is the likeliest prospect for the bird that I can think of—but no . . . You see for yourself that we must do more than simply trust to luck."

"We need not trust to luck, sir. I would suggest that you approach your friend Mr. Bingham and volunteer your services at his forth-coming entertainment. It could readily be arranged to have you sing immediately before Mr. Glossop. I fancy, sir, that if Mr. Glossop were to sing 'Sonny Boy' directly after you had sung 'Sonny Boy' the audience would respond satisfactorily. By the time Mr. Glossop began to sing they would have lost their taste for that particular song and would express their feelings warmly."

"Jeeves," said Aunt Dahlia, "you're a marvel!"

"Thank you, madam."

"Jeeves," I said, "you're an ass!"

"What do you mean, he's an 'ass'?" said Aunt Dahlia hotly. "I think it's the greatest scheme I ever heard."

"Me sing 'Sonny Boy' at Beefy Bingham's clean, bright entertain-ment? I can see myself!"

"You sing it daily in your bath, sir. Mr. Wooster," said Jeeves, turning to Aunt Dahlia, "has a pleasant, light baritone."

"I bet he has," said Aunt Dahlia.

I checked the man with one of my looks.

"Between singing 'Sonny Boy' in one's bath, Jeeves, and singing it before a hall full of assorted blood-orange merchants and their young, there is a substantial difference."

"Bertie," said Aunt Dahlia, "you'll sing, and like it!"

"I will not."

"Bertie!"

"Nothing will induce—"

"Bertie," said Aunt Dahlia firmly, "you will sing 'Sonny Boy' on Tuesday, the third *prox.*, or may an aunt's curse—"

"I won't!"

"Think of Angela!"

"Dash Angela!"

"Bertie!"

"No, I mean, hang it all!"

"You won't?"

"No, I won't."

"That is your last word, is it?"

"It is. Once and for all, Aunt Dahlia, nothing will induce me to let out so much as a single note."

And so that afternoon I sent a prepaid wire to Beefy Bingham, offering my services in the cause, and by nightfall the thing was fixed up. I was billed to perform next but one after the intermission. Following me, came Tuppy. And immediately after him, Miss Cora Bellinger, the well-known operatic soprano.

How these things happen, I couldn't say. The chivalry of the Woosters, I suppose.

"Jeeves," I said that evening, and I said it coldly, "I shall be glad if you will pop round to the nearest music shop and procure me a copy of 'Sonny Boy.' It will now be necessary for mc to learn both verse and refrain. Of the trouble and nervous strain which this will involve, I say nothing."

"Very good, sir."

"But this I do say—"

"I had better be starting immediately, sir, or the shop will be closed."

"Ha!" I said.

And I meant it to sting.

Although I had steeled myself to the ordeal before me and had set out full of the calm, quiet courage which makes men do desperate deeds with proud, set faces, I must admit that there was a moment, just after I had entered the Oddfellows' Hall at Bermondsey East and run an eye over the assembled pleasure seekers, when it needed all the bulldog pluck of the Woosters to keep me from calling it a day and taking a cab back to civilization.

The clean, bright entertainment was in full swing when I arrived, and somebody who looked as if he might be the local undertaker was reciting "Gunga Din." And the audience, though not actually chiyiking in the full technical sense of the term, had a grim look which I didn't like at all.

As I scanned the multitude it seemed to me that they were for the nonce suspending judgment. Did you ever tap on the door of one of those New York speak-easy places and see the grille snap back and a Face appear? There is one long, silent moment when its eyes are fixed on yours and all your past life seems to rise up before you.

Then you say that you are a friend of Mr. Zinzinheimer and he told you they would treat you right if you mentioned his name, and the strain relaxes.

Well, these costermongers and whelk stallers appeared to me to be looking just like that Face. Start something, they seemed to say, and they would know what to do about it. And I couldn't help feeling that my singing "Sonny Boy" would come, in their opinion, under the head of Starting Something.

"A nice, full house, sir," said a voice at my elbow.

It was Jeeves, watching the proceedings with an indulgent eye.

"You here, Jeeves?" I said coldly.

"Yes, sir. I have been present since the commencement."

"Oh?" I said. "Any casualties yet?"

"Sir?"

"You know what I mean, Jeeves," I said sternly, "and don't pretend you don't. Anybody got the bird yet?"

"Oh, no, sir."

"I shall be the first, you think?"

"No, sir, I see no reason to expect such a misfortune. I anticipate that you will be well received."

A sudden thought struck me. "And you think everything will go according to plan?"

"Yes, sir."

"Well, I don't," I said. "I've spotted a flaw in your beastly scheme."

"A flaw, sir?"

"Yes. Do you suppose for a moment that when Mr. Glossop hears me singing that dashed song he'll come calmly on a minute after me and sing it, too? Use your intelligence, Jeeves. He will perceive the chasm in his path and pause in time. He will back out and refuse to go on at all."

"Mr. Glossop will not hear you sing, sir. At my advice he has stepped across the road to the Jug and Bottle, an establishment immediately opposite the hall, and he intends to remain there until it is time for him to appear on the platform."

"Oh!" I said.

"If I might suggest it, sir, there is another house named the Goat and Grapes only a short distance down the street. I think it might be a judicious move—"

"If I were to put a bit of custom in their way?"

"It would ease the nervous strain of waiting, sir."

I had not been feeling any too pleased with the man for having let me in for this ghastly binge, but at these words I'm bound to say my austerity softened a trifle. He was undoubtedly right.

He had studied the psychology of the individual, if you see what I mean, and it had not led him astray. A quiet ten minutes at the Goat and Grapes was exactly what my system required. To buzz off there and inhale a couple of swift whisky and sodas was with Bertram Wooster the work of a moment.

The treatment worked like magic. What they had put into the stuff, besides vitriol, I could not have said; but it completely altered my outlook on life. That curious, gulpy feeling passed. I was no longer conscious of the sagging sensation at the knees. The limbs ceased to quiver gently, the tongue became loosened in its socket, and the backbone stiffened.

Pausing merely to order and swallow another of the same, I bade the barmaid a cheery good-night, noodcd affably to one or two fellows in the bar whose faces I liked, and came prancing back to the hall, ready for anything.

And shortly afterward I was on the platform with about a million bulging eyes goggling up at me. There was a rummy sort of buzzing in my ears, and then through the buzzing I heard the sound of a piano starting to tinkle; and, commending my soul to God, I took a good long breath and charged in.

Well, it was a close thing. If ever my grandchildren cluster about my knee and want to know what I did in the Great War, I shall say, "Never mind about the Great War. Ask me about the time I sang 'Sonny Boy' at the Oddfellows' Hall at Bermondsey East."

The whole incident is a bit blurred, but I seem to recollect a kind of murmur as I hit the refrain. I thought at the time it was an attempt on the part of the many-headed to join in the chorus, and at the moment it rather encouraged me.

I passed the thing over the larynx with all the vim at my disposal, hit the high note, and off gracefully into the wings. I didn't come on again to take a bow. I just receded and oiled round to where Jeeves awaited me among the standees at the back.

"Well, Jeeves," I said, anchoring myself at his side and brushing the honest perspiration from the brow. "They didn't rush the platform."

"No, sir."

"But you can spread it about that that's the last time I perform outside my bath. My swan song, Jeeves. Anybody who wants to hear me in future must present himself at the bathroom door and shove his ear against the keyhole. I may be wrong, but it seemed to me that toward the end they were hotting up a trifle. The bird was hovering in the air. I could hear the beating of its wings."

"I did detect a certain restlessness, sir, in the audience. I fancy they had lost their taste for that particular melody. I should have informed you earlier, sir, that the song had already been sung twice before you arrived."

"What!"

"Yes, sir. Once by a lady and once by a gentleman. It is a very popular song, sir."

I gaped at the man. That, with this knowledge, he could calmly have allowed the young master to step straight into the jaws of death, so to speak, paralyzed me. It seemed to show that the old feudal spirit had passed away altogether. I was about to give him my views on the matter in no uncertain fashion, when I was stopped by the spectacle of young Tuppy lurching onto the platform.

Young Tuppy had the unmistakable air of a man who has recently been round to the Jug and Bottle. A few cheery cries of welcome, presumably from some of his backgammon-playing pals who felt that blood was thicker than water, had the effect of causing the genial smile on his face to widen till it nearly met at the back.

He was plainly feeling about as good as a man can feel and still remain on his feet. He waved a kindly hand to his supporters and bowed in a regal sort of manner, rather like an Eastern monarch acknowledging the plaudits of the mob.

Then the female at the piano struck up the opening bars of "Sonny Boy," and Tuppy swelled like a balloon, clasped his hands together, rolled his eyes up at the ceiling in a manner denoting Soul, and began.

I think the populace was too stunned for the moment to take immediate steps. It may seem incredible, but I give you my word that young Tuppy got right through the verse without so much as a murmur. Then they seemed to pull themselves together.

A costermonger roused is a terrible thing. I have never seen the proletariat really stirred before, and I'm bound to say it rather awed me. I mean, it gave you some idea of what it must have been like during the French Revolution.

From every corner of the hall there proceeded simultaneously the sort of noise you hear at one of those East End boxing places when the referee disqualifies the popular favorite and makes the quick dash for life. And then they passed beyond mere words and began to introduce the vegetable motif.

I don't know why, but somehow I had got it into my head that the first thing thrown at Tuppy would be a potato. One gets these fancies. It was, however, as a matter of fact, a banana, and I saw in an instant that the choice had been made by wiser heads than mine. These blokes who have grown up from childhood in the knowledge of how to treat a dramatic entertainment that doesn't please them are aware by a sort of instinct just what is best to do, and the moment I saw that banana splash on Tuppy's shirt front I realized how infinitely more effective and artistic it was than any potato could have been.

Not that the potato school of thought had not also its supporters. As the proceedings warmed up I noticed several intelligent-looking fellows who threw nothing else.

The effect on young Tuppy was rather remarkable. His eyes bulged and his hair seemed to stand up, and yet his mouth went on opening and shutting, and you could see that in a dazed, automatic way he was still singing "Sonny Boy."

Then, coming out of his trance, he began to pull for the shore with some rapidity. The last seen of him, he was beating a tomato to the exit by a short head.

Presently the tumult and the shouting died. I turned to Jeeves.

"Painful, Jeeves," I said. "But what would you?"

"Yes, sir."

"The surgeon's knife, what?"

"Precisely, sir."

"Well, with this happening beneath her eyes, I think that we may definitely consider the Glossop-Bellinger romance off."

"Yes, sir."

At this point old Beefy Bingham came out upon the platform.

I supposed that he was about to rebuke his flock for the recent expression of feeling. But such was not the case. No doubt he was accustomed by now to the wholesome give-and-take of these clean, bright entertainments and had ceased to think it worth while to make any comment when there was a certain liveliness.

"Ladies and gentlemen," said old Beefy. "The next item on the program was to have been songs by Miss Cora Bellinger, the well-known operatic soprano. I have just received a telephone message from Miss Bellinger, saying that her car has broken down. She is, however, on her way here in a cab and will arrive shortly. Meanwhile, our friend Mr. Enoch Simpson will recite 'The Charge of the Light Brigade.' "

I clutched at Jeeves. "Jeeves! You heard?"

"Yes, sir."

"She wasn't here!"

"No, sir."

"She saw nothing of Tuppy's Waterloo."

"No, sir."

"The whole bally scheme has blown a fuse."

"Yes, sir."

"Come, Jeeves," I said, and those standing by wondered, no doubt, what had caused that clean-cut face to grow so pale and set. "I have been subjected to a nervous strain unparalleled since the days of the early martyrs. I have lost pounds in weight and permanently injured my entire system. I have gone through an ordeal which will make me wake up screaming in the night for months to come. And all for nothing. Let us go."

"If you have no objection, sir, I would like to witness the remainder of the entertainment."

"Suit yourself, Jeeves," I said moodily. "Personally, my heart is dead and I am going to look in at the Goat and Grapes for another of their cyanide specials and then home."

It must have been about half past ten, and I was in the old sitting room somberly sucking down a more or less final restorative, when the front doorbell rang, and there on the mat was young Tuppy. He looked like a man who has passed through some great experience and stood face to face with his soul. He had the beginnings of a black eye.

"Oh, hullo, Bertie," said young Tuppy.

He came in and hovered about the mantelpiece, as if he were looking for things to fiddle with and break.

"I've just been singing at Beefy Bingham's entertainment," he said after a pause. "You weren't there, by any chance?"

"Oh, no," I said. "How did you go?"

"Like a breeze," said young Tuppy. "Held them spellbound."

"Knocked 'em, eh?"

"Cold," said young Tuppy. "Not a dry eye."

And this, mark you, a man who had had a good upbringing and had, no doubt, spent years at his mother's knee being taught to tell the truth.

"I suppose Miss Bellinger is pleased?" I said.

"Oh, yes. Delighted."

"So now everything's all right?"

"Oh, quite." Tuppy paused. "On the other hand, Bertie—"

"Yes?"

"Well, I've been thinking things over. Somehow, I don't believe Miss Bellinger is the mate for me, after all."

"What!"

"No, I don't."

"What makes you think that?"

"Oh, I don't know. These things sort of flash on you. I respect Miss Bellinger, Bertie. I admire her. But—er—well, I can't help feeling now that a sweet, gentle girl—er—like your cousin Angela, Bertie—would—er—in fact— Well, what I came round for was to ask if you would phone Angela and find out how she reacts to the idea of coming out with me tonight to the Berkeley for a bit of supper and a spot of dancing."

"Go ahead. There's the phone."

"No; I'd rather you asked her, Bertie. What with one thing and another, if you paved the way— You see, there's just a chance that she may be—I mean, you know how misunderstandings occur— and— Well, what I'm driving at, Bertie, old man, is that I'd rather you surged round and did a bit of paving, if you don't mind."

I went to the phone and called up Angela.

"She says come right round," I said.

"Tell her," said Tuppy, in a devout sort of voice, "that I will be with her in something under a couple of ticks."

He had barely biffed when I heard a click in the keyhole and a soft padding in the passage without.

"Jeeves," I called.

"Sir," said Jeeves, manifesting himself.

"Jeeves, a remarkably rummy thing has happened. Mr. Glossop has just been here. He tells me all is off between him and Miss Bellinger."

"Yes, sir."

"You don't seem surprised."

"No, sir. I confess I had anticipated some such eventuality."

"Eh? What gave you that idea?"

"It came to me, sir, when I observed Miss Bellinger strike Mr. Glossop in the eye."

"Strike him!"

"Yes, sir."

"In the eye?"

"The right eye, sir."

I clutched the brow. "What on earth made her do that?"

"I fancy she was a little upset, sir, at the reception accorded her singing."

"Great Scott! Don't tell me she got the bird, too?"

"Yes, sir."

"But why? She's got a red-hot voice."

"Yes, sir. But I think the audience resented her choice of a song."

"Jeeves!" Reason was beginning to do a bit of tottering on its throne. "You aren't going to stand there and tell me that Miss Bellinger sang 'Sonny Boy,' too!"

"Yes, sir. And—mistakenly, in my opinion—brought a large doll onto the platform to sing it to. The audience affected to mistake it for a ventriloquist's dummy, and there was some little disturbance."

"But, Jeeves, what a coincidence!"

"Not altogether, sir. I ventured to take the liberty of accosting Miss Bellinger on her arrival at the hall and recalling myself to her recollection. I then said that Mr. Glossop had asked me to request her that as a particular favor to him—the song being a favorite of his—she would sing 'Sonny Boy.'

"And when she found that you and Mr. Glossop had also sung the song immediately before her, I rather fancy that she supposed that she had been made the victim of a practical pleasantry by Mr. Glossop. Will there be anything further, sir?"

"No, thanks."

"Good night, sir."

"Good night, Jeeves," I said reverently.

❈ *Jeeves and the Impending Doom*

IT WAS the morning of the day on which I was slated to pop down to my Aunt Agatha's place at Woollam Chersey in the county of Herts for a visit of three solid weeks; and, as I seated myself at the breakfast table, I don't mind confessing that the heart was singularly heavy. We Woosters are men of iron, but beneath my intrepid exterior at that moment there lurked a nameless dread.

"Jeeves," I said, "I am not the old merry self this morning."

"Indeed, sir?"

"No, Jeeves. Far from it. Far from the old merry self."

"I am sorry to hear that, sir."

He uncovered the fragrant eggs and b., and I pronged a moody forkful.

"Why—this is what I keep asking myself, Jeeves—why has my Aunt Agatha invited me to her country seat?"

"I could not say, sir."

"Not because she is fond of me."

"No, sir."

"It is a well-established fact that I give her a pain in the neck. How it happens I cannot say, but every time our paths cross, so to speak, it seems to be a mere matter of time before I perpetrate some ghastly floater and have her hopping after me with her hatchet. The result being that she regards me as a worm and an outcast and would gladly drop something on me from a high window. Am I right or wrong, Jeeves?"

"Perfectly correct, sir."

"And yet now she has absolutely insisted on my scratching all previous engagements and buzzing down to Woollam Chersey. She must have some sinister reason of which we know nothing. Can you blame me, Jeeves, if the heart is heavy?"

"No, sir. Excuse me, sir, I fancy I heard the front doorbell."

He shimmered out, and I took another listless stab at the e. and bacon.

"A telegram, sir," said Jeeves, reentering the presence.

"Open it, Jeeves, and read contents. Who is it from?"

"It is unsigned, sir."

"You mean there's no name at the end of it?"

"That is precisely what I was endeavoring to convey, sir."

"Let's have a look."

I scanned the thing. It was a rummy communication. Rummy. No other word.

As follows:

REMEMBER WHEN YOU COME HERE ABSOLUTELY VITAL MEET PERFECT STRANGERS

We Woosters are not very strong in the head, particularly at breakfast time; and I was conscious of a dull ache between the eyebrows.

"What does it mean, Jeeves?"

"I could not say, sir."

"It says 'come here.' Where's 'here'?"

"You will notice that the message was handed in at Woollam Chersey, sir."

"You're absolutely right. At Woollam, as you very cleverly spotted, Chersey. This tells us something, Jeeves."

"What, sir?"

"I don't know. It couldn't be from my Aunt Agatha, do you think?"

"Hardly, sir."

"No, you're right again. Then all we can say is that some person unknown, resident at Woollam Chersey, considers it absolutely vital for me to meet perfect strangers. But why should I meet perfect strangers, Jeeves?"

"I could not say, sir."

"And yet, looking at it from another angle, why shouldn't I?"

"Precisely, sir."

"Then what it comes to is that the thing is a mystery which time alone can solve. We must wait and see, Jeeves."

"The very expression I was about to employ, sir."

I hit Woollam Chersey at about four o'clock and found Aunt Agatha in her lair, writing letters. And, from what I know of her, probably offensive letters, with nasty postscripts. She regarded me with not a fearful lot of joy.

"Oh, there you are, Bertie."

"Yes, here I am."

"There's a smut on your nose."

I plied the handkerchief.

"I am glad you have arrived so early. I want to have a word with you before you meet Mr. Filmer."

"Who?"

"Mr. Filmer, the cabinet minister. He is staying in the house. Surely even you must have heard of Mr. Filmer?"

"Oh, rather," I said, though as a matter of fact the bird was completely unknown to me. What with one thing and another, I'm not frightfully well up in the personnel of the political world.

"I particularly wish you to make a good impression on Mr. Filmer."

"Right ho."

"Don't speak in that casual way, as if you supposed that it was perfectly natural that you would make a good impression upon him. Mr. Filmer is a serious-minded man of high character and purpose, and you are just the type of vapid and frivolous wastrel against which he is most likely to be prejudiced."

Hard words, of course, from one's own flesh and blood, but well in keeping with past form.

"You will endeavor, therefore, while you are here, not to display yourself in the role of a vapid and frivolous wastrel. In the first place, you will give up smoking during your visit."

"Oh, I say!"

"Mr. Filmer is president of the Anti-Tobacco League. Nor will you drink alcoholic stimulants."

"Oh, dash it!"

"And you will kindly exclude from your conversation all that is suggestive of the bar, the billiard room, and the stage door. Mr. Filmer will judge you largely by your conversation."

I rose to a point of order.

"Yes, but why have I got to make an impression on this—on Mr. Filmer?"

"Because," said the old relative, giving me the eye, "I particularly wish it."

Not, perhaps, a notably snappy comeback as comebacks go; but it was enough to show me that that was more or less that, and I beetled out with an aching heart.

I headed for the garden, and I'm dashed if the first person I saw wasn't young Bingo Little.

Bingo Little and I have been pals practically from birth. Born in the same village within a couple of days of one another, we went through kindergarten, Eton, and Oxford together; and, grown to riper years, we have enjoyed in the old metrop. full many a first-class binge in each other's society. If there was one fellow in the world, I felt, who could alleviate the horrors of this blighted visit of mine, that bloke was young Bingo Little.

But how he came to be there was more than I could understand. Some time before, you see, he had married the celebrated authoress Rosie M. Banks, and the last I had seen of him he had been on the point of accompanying her to America on a lecture tour. I distinctly remembered him cursing rather freely because the trip would mean his missing Ascot.

Still, rummy as it might seem, here he was. And, aching for the sight of a friendly face, I gave tongue like a bloodhound.

"Bingo!"

He spun round; and, by Jove, his face wasn't friendly, after all. It was what they call contorted. He waved his arms at me like a semaphore.

"*Sh!*" he hissed. "Would you ruin me?"

"Eh?"

"Didn't you get my telegram?"

"Was that your telegram?"

"Of course it was my telegram."

"Then why didn't you sign it?"

"I did sign it."

"No you didn't. I couldn't make out what it was all about."

"Well, you got my letter."

"What letter?"

"My letter."

"I didn't get any letter."

"Then I must have forgotten to post it. It was to tell you that I was down here, tutoring your cousin Thomas, and that it was essential that, when we met, you should treat me as a perfect stranger."

"But why?"

"Because, if your aunt supposed that I was a pal of yours she would naturally sack me on the spot."

"Why?"

Bingo raised his eyebrows.

"Why? Be reasonable, Bertie. If you were your aunt, and you knew the sort of chap you were, would you let a fellow you knew to be your best pal tutor your son?"

This made the old lemon swim a bit, but I got his meaning after awhile and I had to admit that there was much rugged good sense in what he said. Still, he hadn't explained what you might call the nub or gist of the mystery.

"I thought you were in America," I said.

"Well, I'm not."

"Why not?"

"Never mind why not. I'm not."

"But why have you taken a tutoring job?"

"Never mind why. I have my reasons. And I want you to get it into your head, Bertie—get it right through the concrete—that you and I must not be seen hobnobbing. Your blighted cousin was caught smoking in the shrubbery the day before yesterday, and that has made my position pretty tottery because your aunt said that, if I had exercised an adequate surveillance over him, it couldn't have happened. If, after that, she finds out I'm a friend of yours, nothing can save me from being shot out on my ear. And it is vital that I am not shot out."

"Why?"

"Never mind why."

At this point he seemed to think he heard somebody coming, for he suddenly leaped with incredible agility into a laurel bush. And I toddled along to consult Jeeves about these rummy happenings.

"Jeeves," I said, repairing to the bedroom where he was unpacking my things, "you remember that telegram?"

"Yes, sir."

"It was from Mr. Little. He's here, tutoring my young cousin Thomas."

"Indeed, sir?"

"I can't understand it. He appears to be a free agent, if you know what I mean; and yet would any man who was a free agent wantonly come to a house which contained my Aunt Agatha?"

"It seems peculiar, sir."

"Moreover, would anybody of his own free will and as a mere pleasure seeker tutor my cousin Thomas, who is notoriously a tough egg and a fiend in human shape?"

"Most improbable, sir."

"These are deep waters, Jeeves."

"Precisely, sir."

"And the ghastly part of it all is that he seems to consider it necessary, in order to keep his job, to treat me like a long-lost leper. Thus killing my only chance of having anything approaching a decent time in this abode of desolation. For do you realize, Jeeves, that my aunt says I mustn't smoke while I'm here?"

"Indeed, sir?"

"Nor drink."

"Why is this, sir?"

"Because she wants me—for some dark and furtive reason which she will not explain—to impress a fellow named Filmer."

"Too bad, sir. However, many doctors, I understand, advocate such abstinence as the secret of health. They say it promotes a freer circulation of the blood and insures the arteries against premature hardening."

"Oh, do they? Well, you can tell them next time you see them that they are silly asses."

"Very good, sir."

And so began what, looking back along a fairly eventful career, I think I can confidently say was the scaliest visit I have ever experienced in the course of my life. What with the agony of missing the lifegiving cocktail before dinner; the painful necessity of being obliged, every time I wanted a quiet cigarette, to lie on the floor in my bedroom and puff the smoke up the chimney; the constant discomfort of meeting Aunt Agatha round unexpected corners; and the fearful strain on the morale of having to chum with the Right Hon. A. B. Filmer—it was not long before Bertram was up against it to an extent hitherto undreamed of.

I played golf with the Right Hon. every day, and it was only by biting the Wooster lip and clenching the fists till the knuckles stood out white under the strain that I managed to pull through. The Right Hon. punctuated some of the ghastliest golf I have even seen with a flow of conversation which, as far as I was concerned, went completely over the top; and, all in all, I was beginning to feel pretty sorry for myself when, one night as I was in my room listlessly donning the soup-and-fish in preparation for the evening meal, in trickled young Bingo and took my mind off my own troubles.

For when it is a question of a pal being in the soup we Woosters no longer think of self; and that poor old Bingo was knee-deep in the bisque was made plain by his mere appearance, which was that of a cat which has just been struck by a half brick and is expecting another shortly.

"Bertie," said Bingo, having sat down on the bed and diffused silent gloom for a moment, "how is Jeeves's brain these days?"

"Fairly strong on the wing, I fancy. How is the gray matter, Jeeves? Surging about pretty freely?"

"Yes, sir."

"Thank heaven for that!" said young Bingo, "for I require your soundest counsel. Unless right-thinking people take strong steps through the proper channels, my name will be mud."

"What's wrong, old thing?" I asked sympathetically.

Bingo plucked at the coverlet.

"I will tell you," he said. "I will also now reveal why I am staying in this pesthouse, tutoring a kid who requires not education in the Greek and Latin languages but a swift slosh on the base of the skull with a blackjack. I came here, Bertie, because it was the only thing I could do. At the last moment before she sailed to America, Rosie decided that I had better stay behind and look after the Peke. She left me a couple of hundred quid to see me through till her return. This sum, judiciously expended over the period of her absence, would have been enough to keep the Peke and myself in moderate affluence. But you know how it is."

"How what is?"

"When someone comes slinking up to you in the club and tells you that some cripple of a horse can't help winning even if it develops lumbago and the botts ten yards from the starting post. I tell you, I regarded the thing as a cautious and conservative investment."

"You mean you planked the entire capital on a horse?"

Bingo laughed bitterly.

"If you could call the thing a horse. If it hadn't shown a flash of speed in the straight it would have got mixed up with the next race. It came in last, putting me in a dashed delicate position. Somehow or other I had to find the funds to keep me going, so that I could win through till Rosie's return without her knowing what had occurred. Rosie is the dearest girl in the world; but if you were a married man, Bertie, you would be aware that the best of wives is apt to cut up rough if she finds that her husband has dropped six weeks' housekeeping money on a single race. Isn't that so, Jeeves?"

"Yes, sir. Women are odd in that respect."

"It was a moment for swift thinking. There was enough left from the wreck to board the Peke out at a comfortable home. I signed him up for six weeks at the Kozy Komfort Kennels at Kingsbridge, Kent, and tottered out, a broken man, to get a tutoring job. I landed the kid Thomas. And here I am."

It was a sad story, of course, but it seemed to me that, awful as it might be to be in constant association with my Aunt Agatha and young Thos., he had got rather well out of a tight place.

"All you have to do," I said, "is to carry on here for a few weeks more, and everything will be oojah-cum-spiff."

Bingo barked bleakly.

"A few weeks more! I shall be lucky if I stay two days. You remember I told you that your aunt's faith in me as a guardian of her blighted son was shaken a few days ago by the fact that he was caught smoking. I now find that the person who caught him smoking was the man Filmer. And ten minutes ago young Thomas told me that he was proposing to inflict some hideous revenge on Filmer for having reported him to your aunt. I don't know what he is going to do, but if he does it, out I inevitably go on my left ear. Your aunt thinks the world of Filmer, and would sack me on the spot. And three weeks before Rosie gets back!"

I saw all.

"Jeeves," I said.

"Sir?"

"I see all. Do you see all?"

"Yes, sir."

"Then flock round."

"I fear, sir . . ."

Bingo gave a low moan.

"Don't tell me, Jeeves," he said brokenly, "that nothing suggests itself."

"Nothing at the moment, I regret to say, sir."

Bingo uttered a stricken *woofle* like a bulldog that has been refused cake.

"Well, then, the only thing I can do, I suppose," he said somberly, "is not to let the pie-faced little thug out of my sight for a second."

"Absolutely," I said. "Ceaseless vigilance, eh, Jeeves?"

"Precisely, sir."

"But meanwhile, Jeeves," said Bingo in a low, earnest voice, "you will be devoting your best thought to the matter, won't you?"

"Most certainly, sir."

"Thank you, Jeeves."

"Not at all, sir."

I will say for young Bingo that, once the need for action arrived, he behaved with an energy and determination which compelled respect. I suppose there was not a minute during the next two days when the kid Thos. was able to say to himself, "Alone at last!" But on the evening of the second day Aunt Agatha announced that some people were coming over on the morrow for a spot of tennis, and I feared that the worst must now befall.

Young Bingo, you see, is one of those fellows who, once their fingers close over the handle of a tennis racket, fall into a sort of trance in which nothing outside the radius of the lawn exists for them. If you came up to Bingo in the middle of a set and told him that panthers were devouring his best friend in the kitchen garden, he would look at you and say, "Oh, ah?" or words to that effect. I knew that he would not give a thought to young Thos. and the Right Hon. till the last ball had bounced, and, as I dressed for dinner that night, I was conscious of an impending doom.

"Jeeves," I said, "have you ever pondered on Life?"

"From time to time, sir, in my leisure moments."

"Grim, isn't it, what?"

"Grim, sir?"

"I mean to say, the difference between things as they look and things as they are."

"The trousers perhaps a half inch higher, sir. A very slight adjustment on the braces will effect the necessary alteration. You were saying, sir?"

"I mean, here at Woollam Chersey we have apparently a happy, carefree country-house party. But beneath the glittering surface, Jeeves, dark currents are running. One gazes at the Right Hon. wrapping himself round the salmon mayonnaise at lunch, and he seems a man without a care in the world. Yet all the while a dreadful fate is hanging over him, creeping nearer and nearer. What exact steps do you think the kid Thomas intends to take?"

"In the course of an informal conversation which I had with the young gentleman this afternoon, sir, he informed me that he had been reading a romance entitled *Treasure Island* and had been much struck by the character and actions of a certain Captain Flint. I gathered that he was weighing the advisability of modeling his own conduct on that of the captain."

"But, good heavens, Jeeves! If I remember *Treasure Island,* Flint was the bird who went about hitting people with a cutlass. You don't think young Thomas would bean Mr. Filmer with a cutlass?"

"Possibly he does not possess a cutlass, sir."

"Well, with anything."

"We can but wait and see, sir. The tie, if I might suggest it, sir, a shade more tightly knotted. One aims at the perfect butterfly effect. If you will permit me . . ."

"What do ties matter, Jeeves, at a time like this? Do you realize that Mr. Little's domestic happiness is hanging in the scale?"

"There is no time, sir, at which ties do not matter."

I could see the man was pained, but I did not try to heal the wound. What's the word I want? Preoccupied. I was too preoccupied, don't you know. And distrait. Not to say careworn.

I was still careworn when, next day at half past two, the revels commenced on the tennis lawn. It was one of those close, baking days with thunder rumbling just round the corner; and it seemed to me that there was a brooding menace in the air.

"Bingo," I said, as we pushed forth to do our bit in the first doubles, "I wonder what young Thos. will be up to this afternoon, with the eye of authority no longer on him?"

"Eh?" said Bingo absently. Already the tennis look had come into his face, and his eye was glazed. He swung his racket and snorted a little.

"I don't see him anywhere," I said.

"You don't what?"

"See him."

"Who?"

"Young Thos."

"What about him?"

I let it go.

The only consolation I had in the black period of the opening of the tourney was the fact that the Right Hon. had taken a seat among the spectators and was wedged in between a couple of females with parasols. Reason told me that even a kid so steeped in sin as young Thos. would hardly perpetrate any outrage on a man in such a strong strategic position. Considerably relieved, I gave myself up to the game, and was in the act of putting it across the local curate with a good deal of vim when there was a roll of thunder and the rain started to come down in buckets.

We all stampeded for the house, and had gathered in the drawing room for tea when suddenly Aunt Agatha, looking up from a cucumber sandwich, said:

"Has anybody seen Mr. Filmer?"

It was one of the nastiest jars I have ever experienced. What with my fast serve zipping sweetly over the net and the man of God utterly unable to cope with my slow bending return down the center line, I had for some little time been living, as it were, in another world. I now came down to earth with a bang; and my slice of cake, slipping from my nerveless fingers, fell to the ground and was wolfed by Aunt Agatha's terrier, McIntosh. Once more I seemed to become conscious of an impending doom.

For this man Filmer, you must understand, was not one of those men who are lightly kept from the tea table. A hearty trencherman and particularly fond of his five o'clock couple of cups and bite of muffin, he had until this afternoon always been well up among the leaders in the race for the food trough. If one thing was certain, it was that only the machinations of some enemy could be keeping him from being in the drawing room now, complete with nose bag.

"He must have got caught in the rain and be sheltering somewhere in the grounds," said Aunt Agatha. "Bertie, go out and find him. Take a raincoat to him."

"Right ho!" I said. And I meant it. My only desire in life now was to find the Right Hon. And I hoped it wouldn't be merely his body.

I put on a raincoat and tucked another under my arm, and was sallying forth, when in the hall I ran into Jeeves.

"Jeeves," I said, "I fear the worst. Mr. Filmer is missing."

"Yes, sir."

"I am about to scour the grounds in search of him."

"I can save you the trouble, sir. Mr. Filmer is on the island in the middle of the lake."

"In this rain? Why doesn't the chump row back?"

"He has no boat, sir."

"Then how can he be on the island?"

"He rowed there, sir. But Master Thomas rowed after him and set his boat adrift. He was informing me of the circumstances a moment ago, sir. It appears that Captain Flint was in the habit of marooning people on islands, and Master Thomas felt that he could pursue no more judicious course than to follow his example."

"But, good Lord, Jeeves! The man must be getting soaked."

"Yes, sir. Master Thomas commented upon that aspect of the matter."

It was a time for action.

"Come with me, Jeeves!"

"Very good, sir."

I buzzed for the boathouse.

My Aunt Agatha's husband, Spenser Gregson, who is on the Stock Exchange, had recently cleaned up to an amazing extent in Sumatra Rubber; and Aunt Agatha, in selecting a country estate, had lashed out on an impressive scale. There were miles of what they call rolling parkland, trees in considerable profusion well provided with doves and what not cooing in no uncertain voice, gardens full of roses, and also stables, outhouses, and messuages, the whole forming a rather fruity *tout ensemble*. But the feature of the place was the lake.

It stood to the east of the house, beyond the rose garden, and covered several acres. In the middle of it was an island. In the middle of the island was a building known as the Octagon. As we drew nearer, striking a fast clip with self at the oars and Jeeves handling the tiller ropes, we heard cries of gradually increasing volume, if that's the expression I want; and presently, up aloft, looking from a distance as if he were perched on top of the bushes, I located the Right Hon. He was in the middle of the Octagon, seated on the roof and spouting water like a public fountain. It seemed to me that even a cabinet minister ought to have had more sense than to stay right out in the open like that, when there were trees to shelter under.

"A little more to the right, Jeeves."

"Very good, sir."

I made a neat landing.

"Wait here, Jeeves."

"Very good, sir. The head gardener was informing me this morning, sir, that one of the swans had recently nested on this island."

"This is no time for natural-history gossip, Jeeves," I said, a little severely, for the rain was coming down harder than ever and the Wooster trouser legs were already considerably moistened.

"Very good, sir."

I pushed my way through the bushes. The going was sticky and took about eight and elevenpence off the value of my Sure-grip tennis shoes in the first two yards; but I persevered and presently came out in the open and found myself in a sort of clearing facing the Octagon.

This building was run up somewhere in the last century, I have been told, to enable the grandfather of the late owner to have some quiet place out of earshot of the house where he could practice the fiddle. From what I know of fiddlers, I should imagine that he had produced some fairly frightful sounds there in his time; but they can have been nothing to the ones that were coming from the roof of the place now. The Right Hon., not having spotted the arrival of the rescue party, was apparently trying to make his voice carry across the waste of waters to the house; and I'm not saying it was not a good sporting effort. He had one of those highish tenors, and his yowls seemed to screech over my head like shells.

I thought it about time to slip him the glad news that assistance had arrived, before he strained a vocal cord.

"Hi!" I shouted, waiting for a lull.

He poked his head over the edge.

"Hi!" he bellowed, looking in every direction but the right one, of course.

"Hi!"

"Hi!"

"Hi!"

"Hi!"

"Oh!" he said, spotting me at last.

"What ho!" I replied, sort of clinching the thing.

I suppose the conversation can't be said to have touched a frightfully high level up to this moment, but probably we should have got a good deal brainier very shortly—only just then, at the very instant when I was getting ready to say something good, there was a hissing noise like a tire bursting in a nest of cobras, and out of the bushes to my left there popped something so large and white and active that, thinking quicker than I have ever done in my puff, I rose like a rocketing pheasant and, before I knew what I was doing, had begun the climb for life. Something slapped against the wall about an inch below my right ankle, and any doubts I may have had about remaining below vanished. The lad who bore 'mid snow and ice the banner with the strange device "Excelsior!" was the model for Bertram.

"Be careful!" yipped the Right Hon.

I was.

Whoever built the Octagon might have constructed it especially for this sort of crisis. Its walls had grooves at regular intervals which were just right for the hands and feet, and it wasn't very long before I was parked up on the roof beside the Right Hon., gazing down at one of the largest and shortest-tempered swans I had ever seen. It was standing below, stretching up a neck like a hose pipe, just where a bit of brick, judiciously bunged, would catch it amidships.

I bunged the brick and scored a bull's-eye.

The Right Hon. didn't seem any too well pleased.

"Don't tease it!" he said.

"It teased me," I said.

The swan extended another eight feet of neck and gave an imitation of steam escaping from a leaky pipe. The rain continued to lash down with what you might call indescribable fury, and I was sorry that in the agitation inseparable from shinning up a stone wall at practically a second's notice I had dropped the raincoat which I had been bringing with me for my fellow rooster. For a moment I thought of offering him mine, but wiser counsels prevailed.

"How near did it come to getting you?" I asked.

"Within an ace," replied my companion, gazing down with a look of marked dislike. "I had to make a very rapid spring."

The Right Hon. was a tubby little chap who looked as if he had been poured into his clothes and had forgotten to say "When!" and the picture he conjured up, if you know what I mean, was rather pleasing.

"It is no laughing matter," he said, shifting the look of dislike to me.

"Sorry."

"I might have been seriously injured."

"Would you consider bunging another brick at the bird?"

"Do nothing of the sort. It will only annoy him."

"Well, why not annoy him? He hasn't shown such a dashed lot of consideration for our feelings."

The Right Hon. now turned to another aspect of the matter.

"I cannot understand how my boat, which I fastened securely to the stump of a willow tree, can have drifted away."

"Dashed mysterious."

"I begin to suspect that it was deliberately set loose by some mischievous person."

"Oh, I say, no, hardly likely, that. You'd have seen them doing it."

"No, Mr. Wooster. For the bushes form an effective screen. Moreover, rendered drowsy by the unusual warmth of the afternoon, I dozed off for some little time almost immediately I reached the island."

This wasn't the sort of thing I wanted his mind dwelling on, so I changed the subject.

"Wet, isn't it, what?" I said.

"I had already observed it," said the Right Hon. in one of those nasty, bitter voices. "I thank you, however, for drawing the matter to my attention."

Chitchat about the weather hadn't gone with much of a bang, I perceived. I had a shot at Bird Life in the Home Counties.

"Have you ever noticed," I said, "how a swan's eyebrows sort of meet in the middle?"

"I have had every opportunity of observing all that there is to observe about swans."

"Gives them a sort of peevish look, what?"

"The look to which you allude has not escaped me."

"Rummy," I said, rather warming to my subject, "how bad an effect family life has on a swan's disposition."

"I wish you would select some other topic of conversation than swans."

"No, but, really, it's rather interesting. I mean to say, our old pal down there is probably a perfect ray of sunshine in normal circumstances. Quite the domestic pet, don't you know. But purely and simply because the little woman happens to be nesting . . ."

I paused. You will scarcely believe me, but until this moment, what with all the recent bustle and activity, I had clean forgotten that, while we were treed up on the roof like this, there lurked all the time in the background one whose giant brain, if notified of the emergency and requested to flock round, would probably be able to think up in a couple of minutes half a dozen schemes for solving our little difficulties.

"Jeeves!" I shouted.

"Sir?" came a faint, respectful voice from the great open spaces.

"My man," I explained to the Right Hon. "A fellow of infinite resource and sagacity. He'll have us out of this in a minute. Jeeves!"

"Sir?"

"I'm sitting on the roof."

"Very good, sir."

"Don't say 'Very good.' Come and help us. Mr. Filmer and I are treed, Jeeves."

"Very good, sir."

"Don't keep saying 'Very good.' It's nothing of the kind. The place is alive with swans."

"I will attend to the matter immediately, sir."

I turned to the Right Hon. I even went so far as to pat him on the back. It was like slapping a wet sponge.

"All is well," I said. "Jeeves is coming."

"What can he do?"

I frowned a trifle. The man's tone had been peevish, and I didn't like it.

"That," I replied with a touch of stiffness, "we cannot say until we see him in action. He may pursue one course, or he may pursue another. But on one thing you can rely with the utmost confidence— Jeeves will find a way. See, here he comes stealing through the undergrowth, his face shining with the light of pure intelligence. There are no limits to Jeeves's brain power. He virtually lives on fish."

I bent over the edge and peered into the abyss.

"Look out for the swan, Jeeves."

"I have the bird under close observation, sir."

The swan had been uncoiling a further supply of neck in our direction, but now he whipped round. The sound of a voice speaking in his rear seemed to affect him powerfully. He subjected Jeeves to a short, keen scrutiny; and then, taking in some breath for hissing purposes, gave a sort of jump and charged ahead.

"Look out, Jeeves!"

"Very good, sir."

Well, I could have told that swan it was no use. As swans go, he may have been well up in the ranks of the intelligentsia, but when it came to pitting his brains against Jeeves he was simply wasting his time. He might just as well have gone home at once.

Every young man starting life ought to know how to cope with an angry swan, so I will briefly relate the proper procedure. You start by picking up the raincoat which somebody has dropped; and then, judging the distance to a nicety, you simply shove the raincoat over the bird's head; and, taking the boathook which you have prudently brought with you, you insert it underneath the swan and heave. The swan goes into a bush and starts trying to unscramble itself; and you saunter back to your boat, taking with you any friends who happen at the moment to be sitting on roofs in the vicinity. That was Jeeves's method, and I cannot see how it could have been improved upon.

The Right Hon. showing a turn of speed of which I would not have believed him capable, we were in the boat in considerably under two ticks.

"You behaved very intelligently, my man," said the Right Hon. as we pushed away from the shore.

"I endeavor to give satisfaction, sir."

The Right Hon. appeared to have said his say for the time being. From that moment he seemed to sort of huddle up and meditate. Dashed absorbed he was. Even when I caught a crab and shot about a pint of water down his neck he didn't seem to notice it.

It was only when we were landing that he came to life again.

"Mr. Wooster."

"Oh, ah?"

"I have been thinking of that matter of which I spoke to you some time back—the problem of how my boat can have got adrift."

I didn't like this.

"The dickens of a problem," I said. "Insoluble, I should call it. Better not bother about it any more."

"On the contrary, I have arrived at a solution, and one which I think is the only feasible solution. I am convinced that my boat was set adrift by the boy Thomas, my hostess's son."

"Oh, I say, no! Why?"

"He had a grudge against me. And it is the sort of thing only a boy or one who is practically an imbecile would have thought of doing."

He legged it for the house, and I turned to Jeeves, aghast. Yes, you might say aghast.

"You heard, Jeeves?"

"Yes, sir."

"What's to be done?"

"Perhaps Mr. Filmer, on thinking the matter over, will decide that his suspicions are unjust."

"But they aren't unjust."

"No, sir."

"Then what's to be done?"

"I could not say, sir."

I pushed off rather smartly to the house and reported to Aunt Agatha that the Right Hon. had been saved; and then I toddled upstairs to have a hot bath, being considerably soaked from stem to stern as the result of my rambles. While I was enjoying the grateful warmth, a knock came at the door.

It was Purvis, Aunt Agatha's butler.

"Mrs. Gregson desires me to say, sir, that she would be glad to see you as soon as you are ready."

"But she has seen me."

"I gather that she wishes to see you again, sir."

"Oh, right ho."

I lay beneath the surface for another few minutes, then, having dried the frame, went along the corridor to my room. Jeeves was there, fiddling about with underclothing.

"Oh, Jeeves," I said, "I've just been thinking. Oughtn't somebody to go and give Mr. Filmer a spot of quinine or something? Errand of mercy, what?"

"I have already done so, sir."

"Good. I wouldn't say I liked the man frightfully, but I don't want him to get a cold in the head." I shoved on a sock. "Jeeves," I said, "I suppose you know that we've got to think of something pretty quick? I mean to say, you realize the position? Mr. Filmer suspects young Thomas of doing exactly what he did do, and if he brings home the charge Aunt Agatha will undoubtedly fire Mr. Little, and then Mrs. Little will find out what Mr. Little has been up to, and what will be the upshot and outcome, Jeeves? I will tell you. It will mean that Mrs. Little will secure the goods on Mr. Little to an extent to which, though only a bachelor myself, I should say that no wife ought to secure the goods on her husband if the proper give-and-take of married life—what you might call the essential balance, as it were—is to be preserved. Women bring these things up, Jeeves. They do not forget and forgive."

"Very true, sir."

"Then how about it?"

"I have already attended to the matter, sir."

"You have?"

"Yes, sir. I had scarcely left you when the solution of the affair presented itself to me. It was a remark of Mr. Filmer's that gave me the idea."

"Jeeves, you're a marvel!"

"Thank you very much, sir."

"What was the solution?"

"I conceived the notion of going to Mr. Filmer and saying that it was you who had stolen his boat, sir."

The man flickered before me. I clutched a sock in a feverish grip.

"Saying—what?"

"At first Mr. Filmer was reluctant to credit my statement. But I pointed out to him that you had certainly known that he was on the island—a fact which he agreed was highly significant. I pointed out, furthermore, that you were a light-hearted young gentleman, sir, who might well do such a thing as a practical joke. I left him quite convinced, and there is now no danger of his attributing the action to Master Thomas."

I gazed at the blighter, spellbound.

"And that's what you consider a neat solution?" I said.

"Yes, sir. Mr. Little will now retain his position as desired."

"And what about me?"

"You are also benefited, sir."

"Oh, I am, am I?"

"Yes, sir. I have ascertained that Mrs. Gregson's motive in inviting you to this house was that she might present you to Mr. Filmer with a view to your becoming his private secretary."

"What!"

"Yes, sir. Purvis, the butler, chanced to overhear Mrs. Gregson in conversation with Mr. Filmer on the matter."

"Secretary to that super-fatted bore! Jeeves, I could never have survived it."

"No, sir. I fancy you would not have found it agreeable. Mr. Filmer is scarcely a congenial companion for you. Yet, had Mrs. Gregson secured the position for you, you might have found it embarrassing to decline to accept it."

" 'Embarrassing' is right!"

"Yes, sir."

"But, I say, Jeeves, there's just one point which you seem to have overlooked. Where exactly do I get off?"

"Sir?"

"I mean to say, Aunt Agatha sent word by Purvis just now that she wanted to see me. Probably she's polishing up her hatchet at this very moment."

"It might be the most judicious plan not to meet her, sir."

"But how can I help it?"

"There is a good, stout water pipe running down the wall immediately outside this window, sir. And I could have the two-seater waiting outside the park gates in twenty minutes."

I eyed him with reverence.

"Jeeves," I said, "you are always right. You couldn't make it five, could you?"

"Let us say ten, sir."

"Ten it is. Lay out some raiment suitable for travel, and leave the rest to me. Where is this water pipe of which you speak so highly?"

Quick Service

The Complete Novel

❖ *Quick Service*

❖ CHAPTER 1

IN SPITE OF the invigorating scent of coffee which greeted him as he opened the door it was with drawn face and dull eye that the willowy young man with the butter-colored hair and rather prominent Adam's apple entered the breakfast room of Claines Hall, the Tudor mansion in Sussex recently purchased by Mrs. Howard Steptoe of Los Angeles. He yielded to no one in his appreciation of coffee, and a couple of cups would unquestionably go down all right, but nothing could alter the fact that on the previous evening he had got engaged to be married to a girl without a bean and was going to London this morning to break the news to his trustee. Even in the most favorable circumstances he did not enjoy meeting his trustee; and when compelled to vex and agitate that human snapping turtle, as he feared would be the case today, he always found himself regretting that his late father had not placed his financial affairs in the hands of some reasonably genial soul like Jack the Ripper.

The breakfast room was bright and cheerful. Its French windows caught the morning sun. One of its walls displayed an old Flemish tapestry of boors reveling, another an old Flemish tapestry of boors taking it easy for a bit. Silver dishes warmed by little flames smiled from the sideboard, and beside them, as yet untouched by knife, the eye detected a large new ham. Over the fireplace there hung a striking portrait of a majestic woman in the early forties, who stared haughtily from the frame as if surprised and displeased by something she had seen in the middle distance. It was the work of a young artist named Jocelyn Weatherby, and its subject was Mrs. Chavender, widow of Mrs. Steptoe's brother Otis.

Mrs. Steptoe herself, a wiry little person with hard blue eyes, sat at the head of the table, instructing Sally Fairmile in her duties for the day. Sally was a poor relation, and as such always had plenty to occupy her time. When Mrs. Steptoe gave the orphan daughters of distant cousins a home she liked them to earn their board and keep.

"Good morning, Lord Holbeton," she said absently.

"Good morning," said Sally, giving him a quick smile. This was the first she had seen of him since last night, when they had become engaged.

"Oh, good morning, good morning," said Lord Holbeton. "Good morning," he added, driving the thing home, and made for the sideboard in the hope of finding something there that would fortify the spirit.

"I'm sort of wondering," Mrs. Steptoe went on as her guest seated himself after dishing out a moody portion of scrambled eggs, "how to fit everybody in today. About the cars, I mean. You're going to London, you told me."

Lord Holbeton winced.

"Yes," he said with a quiver in his voice. "Got to see a man about something."

"And Beatrice has to go to Brighton to present those prizes. She will want the Rolls. And the Packard is having something done to it. You'll have to have the two-seater. It's kind of rattly, but it moves. Sally can drive you. She's going in to get another valet for Howard."

Although he was aware that his hostess possessed the stuff in large quantities and denied her husband nothing, this surprised Lord Holbeton. It seemed to him to strike a note of almost wanton luxury, the sort of thing that causes French Revolutions and Declines and Falls of Roman Empires.

"How many does he have?" he asked, startled.

"Only one at a time," said Sally. "But he sort of runs through them."

"They don't like his manner," explained Mrs. Steptoe.

Lord Holbeton could sympathize with the honest fellows. He did not like Mr. Steptoe's manner himself. There had been something in the nature of an informal understanding, when he had come to stay at Claines Hall, that he should take his host in hand and give him a much-needed spot of polish. But so unpleasant had been the spirit in which the other had received his ministrations that he had soon abandoned this missionary work. Mr. Steptoe, when you tried to set his feet on the path that led to elegance and refinement, had a way of narrowing his eyes and saying, "Ah, nerts!" out of the corner of his mouth, which would have discouraged Emily Post.

"When that last fellow quit," said Mrs. Steptoe, stirring her coffee grimly and looking a little like a rattlesnake, if one can imagine a rattlesnake stirring coffee, "he thought he had finally fought off the challenge. But he's living in a fool's paradise. As long as there's a valet left in England Howard gets him. I've been telling Sally to hire a real tough specimen this time, the sort that'll stand no nonsense. I intend to smarten him up, if it's the last thing I do."

Mr. Steptoe came in as she spoke, an enormous mass of a man with a squashed nose and ears like the handles of an old Greek vase. He had been in once before, as a matter of fact, but Mrs. Steptoe had sent him out again to go and put a collar on. His air, which was sullen, made it plain that both in neck and spirit he was chafing under this treatment. Directing a lowering glance of dislike at Lord Holbeton, whom he considered a palooka of the first water and suspected of putting these ideas into his wife's head, he went to the sideboard and helped himself largely to fish.

The only member of the party still absent was Mrs. Chavender, the lady of the portrait. She entered a moment later, looking like Mrs. Siddons in one of her more regal roles. She would have made a good subject for the brush of Sir Peter Lely or Sir Joshua Reynolds. Indeed, both Sir Joshua and Sir Peter would probably have made even a better job of her than Joss Weatherby had done—as Joss would have been the first to admit, for he was quite free from artistic jealousy.

Sweeping into the room with an air, she got a big reception.

"Good morning, Beatrice," said Mrs. Steptoe, beaming.

"Good morning, Mrs. Chavender," said Sally.

"Oh, hullo, hullo," said Lord Holbeton.

Mr. Steptoe said nothing. He had cocked an eye at the newcomer. That was as far as he was prepared to go. A simple child of nature, he believed, when at meals, in digging in and getting his. He reached out a hairy hand for the butter, and started lathering another slice of toast.

Lord Holbeton had sprung to his feet, a thing Mr. Steptoe would not have done in a million years, and was heading gallantly for the sideboard. It was those perfect manners of his, combined with his delicate good looks and the way he had of sitting down at the piano after dinner and singing such songs as "Trees" in a soft, quivery tenor voice, that had first attracted Sally Fairmile.

"What can I get you, Mrs. Chavender? Eggs? Fish? Ham?"

It was a moment big with fate. On this woman's answer hung the destinies not only of all those present but in addition of J. B. Duff, managing director of the firm of Duff and Trotter, London's leading provision merchants; of Joss Weatherby, the artist; of Chibnall, Mrs. Steptoe's butler; and of Vera Pym, barmaid at the Rose and

Crown in the neighboring town of Loose Chippings, Chibnall's fiancée.

If she had said "Eggs," nothing would have happened. Had she replied "Fish," the foundations of this little world would have remained unrocked.

"Ham," said Mrs. Chavender.

Lord Holbeton carved the ham with the polished elegance which marked all his actions, and silence fell upon the room, broken only by a crackling sound like a forest fire as Mr. Steptoe champed his toast. This gorilla-jawed man could get a certain amount of noise-response even out of mashed potatoes, but it was when eating toast that you caught him at his best.

The conversational ball was eventually set rolling again by Mrs. Chavender. She had lowered her knife and fork, and was staring at her plate with a sort of queenly disgust, like Mrs. Siddons inspecting a caterpillar in her salad.

"This ham," she said, "is uneatable."

Mrs. Steptoe looked up in quick concern. Wealthy though she was herself, the moods of this still more opulent sister-in-law were of urgent importance to her. Like Ben Bolt's Alice, she trembled with fear at her frown. Mrs. Chavender was understood to have a weak heart, and Mrs. Steptoe was her only relative.

"Is there something wrong with it, Beatrice?"

"Considering that I have just described it as uneatable, you may take it that it is not wholly without blemish."

"You bought it, Sally," said Mrs. Steptoe accusingly.

Sally was unable to deny the charge.

"I thought it was bound to be all right," she pleaded in defense. "It came from the best people in London."

"The question of their morals," said Mrs. Chavender, "does not arise. They may, as you say, be the best people in London, though that isn't saying much. My point is that they sell inferior ham. And let me tell you that I know ham. Before I married my late husband, I was engaged to a Ham King—though at that stage in his career I suppose one would have described him as a Ham Prince—and he talked of nothing else from morning till night. So I have had a thorough grounding. I shall go and see these crooks and lodge a strong complaint. Who are the swindling hounds?"

"Duff and Trotter," said Sally. "They are supposed to be the absolute final word in breakfast foodings. I must say I'm surprised that they should have taken advantage of a young girl's inexperience."

At the mention of that name a sharp exclamation had escaped

Lord Holbeton. He was sitting staring, apparently aghast, the scrambled eggs frozen upon his lips.

"Duff and Trotter?" he quavered.

"Duff and Trotter?" echoed Mrs. Chavender. It seemed to Sally that there was elation and triumph in her handsome eyes. She was looking like a Roman matron who has unexpectedly backed the winning chariot at the Circus Maximus. "Are you telling me, my child, that this loathsome substance is one of Jimmy Duff's Paramount Hams?"

"Yes, that's what they're called."

Mrs. Chavender drew a deep breath.

"It's too good to be true," she said. "I didn't know that righteous retribution like this ever happened outside moral stories for children. Jimmy Duff is the man I was speaking of, Mabel—the one who sold hams and talked of nothing else. Words cannot describe the agonies of boredom he used to inflict on me. Jimmy Duff! James by golly Buchanan Duff! Well, well, well! I haven't seen Jimmy in fifteen years, and by the time I'm through with him he'll hope that our next get-together won't be for another thirty."

"What do you mean?"

"I propose to call on him this morning and let him know what a decent-minded woman thinks of his ghastly hams."

"But you are going to Brighton."

"I can take Jimmy en route."

"Wouldn't it be better to write?"

"Write? You don't seem to understand the position. Fifteen years ago, when I met Jimmy Duff and fell for his smooth city ways, I was a young, idealistic girl, all sentiment and romance. This sentiment and romance he blunted forever with these foul hams of his. He used to take me out in the moonlight and tell me what gave them that nutty flavor. He would wait till the band was playing 'Träumerei' and then describe the process of curing. And now, when after all these weary years I've a chance to get my own back, you tell me to write. Write indeed! I'm going to call at his office and look him in the eye and slap this ham down on his desk and watch him curl up at the edges. Ring for Chibnall."

The butler entered. A lissome, athletic young butler of the modern type. Dignified but sinewy.

"Chibnall, will you pack half a dozen slices of this ham in a cardboard box and put them in the car? And I'd better have the car a little earlier, if I'm to go to Brighton via London."

"Tell Purkis, Sally," said Mrs. Steptoe resignedly.

Sally rose obligingly. It was not till she was halfway to the garage that a bleating noise behind her told her that she had been followed by her betrothed.

"I say, Sally!"

"Oh, hullo, George," she said, turning quickly, like a startled kitten. She was conscious of a certain embarrassment. They had not been alone together since the emotional scene on the previous night, and she was thinking that it might not be easy to strike exactly the right note.

She need have had no concern. Lord Holbeton was far too agitated to be critical about right notes. His eye was wild; his mouth hung ajar; and his Adam's apple was gamboling like a lamb in springtime.

"I say, Sally, this is absolutely frightful!"

"What?"

"This Chavender woman and the ham business."

"I thought it rather funny."

"Funny? Ha!" said Lord Holbeton, doing a bitter dance step. "You won't think it so bally funny when you hear the facts in the case." He paused for an instant to overcome his feelings. The position of affairs which he was about to outline was one that had frequently caused the iron to enter into his soul.

"I didn't tell you last night, but my guv'nor, when he died, left me a pot of money."

Sally was perplexed. She was not a mercenary girl, but she had served quite a long sentence as a Steptoe poor relation, and she could see nothing in this fact to depress the spirits.

"Well, surely that's fine? I love the stuff."

"Yes, but there's a catch. He left it in trust. Having got it into his head that I wasn't fit to have a pot of money—"

"What made him think that?"

Actually, what had given the first Baron this poor opinion of a once-adored son had been that unfortunate breach-of-promise case at Oxford, but Lord Holbeton felt that it might be injudicious to mention this.

"Oh, I don't know. Guv'nors get these ideas. Anyway, he left the stuff in trust. I can't finger a fiver except by showing good and substantial cause to my trustee. And do you know who he is—this blighted trustee? Old Duff. The fellow this woman's going to slap down slices of ham in front of."

"But how does he come to be mixed up with you?"

"My guv'nor was his partner. His name was Trotter before he got his title. He always thought a lot of old Duff, so he made him my trustee. And I was planning to tackle him this morning and tell him about us and try to get some cash out of him. And now this happens."

"I see what you mean," said Sally thoughtfully. "You think he won't be in melting mood after Mrs. Chavender's visit?"

"Well, is it likely?"

"I suppose it isn't."

"If," said Lord Holbeton, "the old blister has consistently refused to cough up hitherto, will he unbelt at a moment when his soul is all gashed by this frightful female's taunts and sneers? He loves those hams of his like sons. What are those things sheep have?"

"Lambs?"

"Yes, but some special breed of lambs."

"Ewe lambs?"

"That's right. The Paramount Ham is old Duff's ewe lamb. He started out with it, and the rest of the business means nothing to him. A nice frame of mind he'll be in to listen to the voice of reason after seeing Mrs. Chavender."

It is the woman's part at times like this to stimulate and encourage.

"Oh, you'll be able to talk him round," said Sally hopefully.

"You think so?"

"Yes."

"I don't," said Lord Holbeton. "And I'll tell you why. Because I'm not going within fifty ruddy miles of him."

"Oh, George!"

"And," added Lord Holbeton, "it's no good saying 'Oh, George.' I'd rather hobnob with a wounded puma."

"But he isn't as terrible as all that."

"You've never seen him."

"I've seen his picture. When you buy a Paramount Ham you get it thrown in, on the wrapper. I thought he looked an old pet."

Lord Holbeton blinked.

"An old pet?"

"Yes."

"An old *pet?*" said Lord Holbeton, still not quite sure that he had heard aright. "What about those eyebrows?"

"Rather dressy. I admired them."

Lord Holbeton decided to abandon a fruitless discussion. On the subject of J. Buchanan Duff it was plain that this girl and he were poles apart and could never hope to find a formula.

"Well, if that's how you feel," he said, "why don't *you* go and tackle him?"

"All right," said Sally. "I will."

Lord Holbeton stared. His question had been intended in a purely satirical spirit, and her literal acceptance of it stunned him. For an instant compunction gripped him. She seemed so young, so frail to go up against one who even on his good mornings resembled something out of the Book of Revelations.

Then there swept over him the thought of what a lot of unpleasantness this would save him. If somebody had to go over Niagara Falls in a barrel how much more agreeable if it were not he.

"You don't mean that?"

"I do."

"Will you really?"

"Certainly. Who's afraid?"

"Be prepared for those eyebrows."

"I'm looking forward to them."

"You might be able to get to him before Mrs. Chavender."

"Not if she's in the Rolls and I'm in the two-seater."

"No, that's true. Then we must just hope for the best."

"That's what we must hope for."

"And all this," said Lord Holbeton, "could have been avoided if only the woman had taken scrambled eggs. That's Life, I suppose."

"That's Life," agreed Sally.

❀ CHAPTER 2

THE PREMISES of Duff and Trotter, those human benefactors at the mention of whose name every discriminating Londoner raises a reverent hat, occupy an island site in the neighborhood of Regent Street. The patron enters through a swing door and, having done so, finds himself in a sort of cathedral given over to a display of the merchandise which has made the firm famous. Here are pies; there fruit; over yonder soups and groceries; further on, jams, marmalades, caviars and potted meats. The Paramount Ham, in its capacity of ewe lamb to the managing director, has a shrine to itself.

Most of the Duff and Trotter business being conducted over the telephone, one finds here none of the squash and bustle of baser establishments. Only a sprinkling of duchesses with watering mouths and a few earls licking their lips were present at eleven o'clock that morning when Joss Weatherby came in and started to thread his way through the groves of eatables.

Joss Weatherby did the posters for Paramount Ham, a lean, cheerful, loose-limbed young man who bore up extraordinarily well under a task which might easily have soured one of a less ebullient temperament. This was probably due to the fact that he ate well, slept well and enjoyed a perfect digestion—in which respect he differed from his employer, whose alimentary canal gave him a good deal of trouble.

His course, as he headed for Mr. Duff's private office on the second floor, took him past the fruits and vegetables, and though hampered by a large portfolio under one arm he was able with his free hand to collect a bunch of grapes and a custard apple while flitting by. The disposal of the last of the grapes synchronized with his arrival at the outer cubbyhole occupied by Miss Daphne Hesseltyne, Mr. Duff's secretary.

"Good morning, young Lollipop," he said courteously.

"Good evening," said Miss Hesseltyne, who had a great gift for repartee. "This is a nice time for coming in. You were supposed to be here at ten."

"I unfortunately overslept myself this morning. A man took me to one of those charity gambling places last night. You will be glad to hear that I cleaned up big in a crap game. Have a custard apple? It's on the house. The fruit and veg. department has just given of its plenty."

"Have you been pinching fruit again? You remember how Mr. Duff told you off last time."

"But this time I defied detection. My fingers just flickered."

"Well, you'd better go in. He's waiting for you. And let me tell you he's as cross as two sticks. He's got indigestion again."

"Poor, unhappy wreck. I sometimes feel the best thing he could do would be to throw himself away and start afresh. But he won't be cross with me. Not with lovable old Weatherby. Did I ever tell you that I once saved him from drowning back in America? Stick your head through the transom and watch how his face lights up when I appear."

The inner office was, however, empty when Joss entered. It was only after he had banged cheerily on the desk with a paperweight, at the same time shouting a jovial "Bring out your dead," that Mr. Duff came in from the little balcony outside the window, where he had been attempting to alleviate his dyspepsia by deep breathing.

"Aha, J. B.," said Joss sunnily. "Good morrow."

"Oh, you're there, are you?" said Mr. Duff, making no attempt to emulate his junior's effervescence.

The managing director of Duff and Trotter was a large man who, after an athletic youth, had allowed himself to put on weight. In his college days he had been a hammer thrower of some repute, and he was looking as if he wished he had a hammer now and could throw it at Joss. The eyebrows of which Lord Holbeton had spoken so feelingly were drawn together in a solid line, and the eyes beneath them glared malignantly. They seemed to light up the room, and only a young man with the nerve of an Army mule, which Joss was fortunate enough to possess, could have met them without quailing.

"You're late!" he boomed.

"Not really," said Joss.

"What the devil do you mean, not really?"

"A man like me always seems to be later than he is. That is because people sit yearning for him. They get all tense, listening for his footstep, and every minute seems an hour. Well, J. B., they tell me you've got the collywobbles again. If true, too bad."

"You were supposed to be here at ten."

"As I was just explaining to the Hesseltyne half portion, I overslept myself. I got into a crap game last night, and swept through the opposition like a devouring flame. You would have been proud of me."

"So you gamble, do you?"

"Only once in a blue moon. I wish you wouldn't talk as if I were a Greek Syndicate. Well, now to business. I've brought you my sketches for the new posters of ye Ham Paramount. I don't know if they're any good."

"They aren't."

"You've not seen them."

"I don't have to."

Joss eyed him coldly. He was extremely fond of his employer, but he inclined to the view that it would do him all the good in the world if somebody occasionally kicked him in the stomach.

"I don't know if *you* know it, J. B., but you're the sort of fellow who causes hundreds to fall under suspicion when he's found stabbed in his library with a paper knife of oriental design."

Mr. Duff stiffened.

"I don't know if *you* know it, young man, but you get fresher and fresher every time I see you. And you were fresh enough to start with. If this sort of thing goes on I shall fire you."

"Nonsense. Why, I saved your life."

"Yes, and the way I'm feeling this morning, I'd like to sue you. Well?"

The question was addressed to Miss Hesseltyne, who had entered from her outer lair.

"There's a lady to see you, Mr. Duff."

"Heavily veiled and diffusing a strange, exotic scent," said Joss. "I suppose they're in and out of here all the time."

"Could you shut your trap for a moment?" asked Mr. Duff.

"I suppose so, if it's absolutely necessary," said Joss.

"Who is she?"

"Her name is Mrs. Chavender."

"What!"

It was as if Miss Hesseltyne had struck her overlord with a meat ax. He rocked back on his heels and seemed to give at every joint.

Joss was frowning thoughtfully.

"Chavender? Chavender? I know a Mrs. Chavender. I wonder if it's the same. Tell her to come right up."

Mr. Duff barked like a sea lion.

"Don't you do anything of the sort. What do you mean, giving orders in my office? Say I'm out."

"Yes, sir."

Joss was surprised.

"Why this coyness, J. B.? If it's the Mrs. Chavender I know, you'll like her. She's a terrific old sport. I painted her portrait at Palm Beach two years ago."

Miss Hesseltyne re-entered.

"I couldn't get the lady, sir, to tell her. She was on her way up."

Mr. Duff had begun to exhibit all the mannerisms of a trapped creature of the wild.

"I'm off!"

"You'll meet her in the passage," said Joss, and Mr. Duff paused with his fingers on the door handle. Joss, though still at a loss, felt a pang of compassion.

"Well, I can't follow your thought processes, J. B., but if you really wish to elude this very charming lady you'd better hop out onto the balcony. I'll close the window behind you."

The advice seemed admirable to Mr. Duff. He shot out like a rabbit. He had scarcely disappeared when there was a brisk bang upon the door and the visitor sailed into the room. In her right hand, like the banner with the strange device, she bore a cardboard box.

Expecting to see Mr. Duff and finding in his stead a beardless stripling, Mrs. Chavender seemed taken aback.

"Hullo, where's Jimmy?"

"He has had to step out for a moment."

"And who are you?"

"His best friend and severest critic. My name is Weatherby. I'm afraid you have forgotten me, Mrs. Chavender."

Mrs. Chavender had produced a lorgnette.

"Well, I'll be darned. You're the boy who painted my portrait."

"That's right. Have you still got it?"

"I gave it to my sister-in-law's husband, Howard Steptoe. I live with them. It's hanging in the breakfast room."

"I'll bet it gives the household a rare appetite. One look at it, and they're in among the eggs and bacon like wolves."

"I see you're still as fresh as ever."

"It's odd how people persist in describing me as fresh. I should have said that I just had a sort of easy affability of manner. Mr. Duff was complaining of my freshness only this morning. It seemed to be spoiling his day."

"Do you work for him?"

"He would tell you I didn't, but I do, like a beaver. I'm one of the staff artists."

"From what you say, it sounds as if he had become a grouch. Is he married?"

"No."

"Then that's the trouble. That's what's made him curdle. Every man ought to be married."

"You never spoke a truer word."

"Are you?"

"Not yet. I'm still waiting for the right girl. When she comes along you will see quick service."

Mrs. Chavender regarded him critically.

"You're not a bad-looking young hound."

"Surely a conservative way of putting it."

"What's Jimmy like these days? He had his moments, when I knew him."

"Traces of the old fascination remain. In a dim light he still casts a spell. I'll draw you a picture of him, shall I?"

The sketch which Joss dashed off on a piece of Duff and Trotter note paper was a hasty one and leaned somewhat in the direction of caricature, but Mrs. Chavender greeted it with appreciative cries.

"That's Jimmy, all right. But you've made him happier looking than he will be when I see him."

"I beg your pardon?"

"He'll be dancing with tears in his eyes, believe me. Cast a glance at this."

Joss peered into the cardboard box.

"It looks like ham."

"Yes, let's be fair. I suppose there is a sort of superficial resemblance. It's a clipping from one of Jimmy's Paramounts. I've come to complain about it."

Joss looked swiftly at the ceiling. It had not fallen, but he felt that it must have been a near thing.

"Complain? About Paramount Ham?"

"It's a disgrace to a proud industry and an imposition on a trusting public. Nine tenths of it is flabby fat. The remainder appears to be composed of pink elastic."

"You weren't intending to tell J. B. that? You'll break his heart."

"I want to."

"Thank heaven he's out."

"How long is he going to be out?"

"It may be for years or it may be forever."

"And I can't wait, darn it. I've got to get to Brighton. I'm presenting the prizes at a girls' school. You'll have to act as my agent. Call me up and tell me how he took it. Loose Chippings 803 is the number. Or, if you prefer to write, the address is Claines Hall, Loose Chippings, Sussex. Well, I must be getting along. Nice to have seen you again. Listen, what do I say to a bunch of schoolgirls?"

" 'Hullo, girls,' or something like that?"

"That would be fine, if my speech hadn't got to last three quarters of an hour and inspire them to become good wives and mothers. Oh, well, I guess I'll think of something on the way down."

Joss, returning from escorting her to the elevator, found that Mr. Duff had emerged from hiding. He was sitting at the desk, mopping his brow.

"Phew!" he said. "That was a narrow escape. Get me a glass of sherry."

"Sherry?"

"There's some in that cupboard over there."

"So you keep sherry in your cupboard, do you?" said Joss, interested. "Secret drinker, eh? Tell me, J. B., why didn't you want to meet Mrs. Chavender?"

A glassy, hunted look came into Mr. Duff's eyes.

"We were engaged to be married once."

"Ah!" said Joss, understanding. He knew his employer to be as sturdy a bachelor as ever shivered at the sound of a wedding bell. Sturdy bachelors, he was aware, are often averse from reunions with their old loves.

"I don't like this business of her calling at my office," said Mr.

Duff, restoring himself with sherry. "It's sinister. What did she want? I couldn't hear a thing out there."

Joss decided to be humane. No need to break this portly butterfly on the wheel by revealing the truth.

"She just wanted to see you and say hullo."

"We haven't met in fifteen years."

"Ah, but you're like thc chewing gum. The taste lingers."

"She looks just the same."

"You saw her?"

"Yes, I peeked in. Not changed a scrap. Same eyes. Same curling lip. Well, never mind that," said Mr. Duff, recalling himself to the present. His eye took on its office-hours expression. "Let's see those sketches."

Joss opened the portfolio and tilted its contents onto the desk. There were half a dozen sketches, each showing a saucer-eyed girl, her face split by a wide grin. He arranged them in a row before his employer.

"You remind me of an oriental monarch surrounded by his harem," he said genially. "The sultan looks them over."

Mr. Duff was scanning the drawings with a captious eye.

"Awful," he said.

"Lovely line work," Joss pointed out. "Who is this man Weatherby? He's good."

Mr. Duff continued peevish.

"It's these damned girls. I'm sick of them."

"Now there," said Joss, sitting on the corner of the desk and rising immediately at his employer's request, "I am with you, J. B., heart and soul. The whole trouble is, I am hampered and shackled by the Mandarins of the Art Department. They won't allow me to fulfill myself. I don't know if you have ever seen a glorious eagle spreading its wings for a flight into the empyrean only to discover that it is tied by the leg to a post, but that's me. 'Girls!' say the Mandarins. 'Let us have girls with big eyes and lots of teeth, radiantly full of Paramount Ham,' and I have to do it. Personally, I have never been able to see why the fact that a goggle-eyed girl with buck teeth likes the stuff should carry the slightest weight with an intelligent public. But there it is."

There had been slowly dawning on Mr. Duff's face during this harangue a sort of Soul's Awakening look. It was not unfamiliar to Joss. Combined with the portentous waggling of his eyebrows and the general swelling of his person, it told him that the other had been seized by one of the bright thoughts that came to him from time to time. Mr. Duff, he perceived, was now the Napoleon of Commerce, the man with the lightning mind who gets things done.

"Hey!"

"Yes, J. B."

"I've had an idea."

"I thought I noticed something fermenting."

"These girls. The public is sick of them. They want something different."

"Just what I tell the Mandarins."

"New note."

"Exactly."

"Do you know what I'm going to do?"

"Sack the lot and make me head of the Art Department."

"You'll be doing well if you hold the job you've got."

"Oh, I don't think we need have any uneasiness about that."

"Don't you? Well, listen. Here's what I'm going to do. Came to me all in a flash. Instead of a fatheaded flapper saying, 'Hurrah! It's Paramount Ham!' I'm going to give them Beatrice Chavender curling her lip and saying: 'Take this damned stuff away. I want *Paramount!*' "

Loath though he was to encourage his employer in any way lest he get above himself, Joss was forced to drop a word of approval.

"It's a thought," he agreed.

"Sninspiration," corrected Mr. Duff.

"Yes, I see what you mean. I've been thinking along those lines myself. Somebody like Mrs. Chavender—"

"I didn't say somebody like Mrs. Chavender, I said Mrs. Chavender. You say you painted a portrait of her. Was it good?"

"My dear J. B., need you ask?"

"It got that expression of hers?"

"Perfectly."

"Then it would make a great poster?"

"No question about that. It would send every thinking housewife in England rushing to her grocer like a stampeding mustang, screaming for the stuff."

"Well, that's what I'm saying. That portrait is our new poster."

Joss regarded him with frank astonishment. When Mr. Duff came over all executive and began to get bright ideas for gingering up the business, he was apt to be startling, but hitherto he had never touched quite these heights.

"You aren't serious?"

"Of course I'm serious."

"You can't do it."

"Why can't I?"

"Well, for one thing, she would bring an action and mulct you in sensational damages."

"Let her. I'll charge it off to advertising expenses."

"And then, of course, there are the ordinary human decencies to be thought of."

Mr. Duff declined to consider these.

"Has she still got that portrait?"

"She tells me she gave it to the husband of her sister-in-law, with whom she lives—a Mrs. Steptoe of Claines Hall, Loose Chippings, Sussex."

"Have Miss Hesseltyne find out the number."

"I know it. Loose Chippings 803."

"Then I'll call up this Steptoe from the club, and see if we can do a deal. I'm going to my osteopath now. He may be able to do something for this indigestion of mine."

"That's the spirit. Up the Duffs! But, listen, J. B.—"

"If I'm wanted, his name's Clunk."

"You won't be wanted whatever his name is. You won't be missed for a minute. Nobody'll know you've gone."

"Fresher and fresher and fresher," sighed Mr. Duff.

"But listen, J. B.—about this portrait."

"I don't want any argument."

"I was merely going to say—"

"Well, don't. That's the trouble with you—always has been—you talk too much."

Joss shrugged his shoulders. To attempt to reason further would, he saw, be a waste of time. His companion had spoken of this project of his as an idea, but J. B. Duff did not get ideas, he got obsessions, and on these occasions was like the gentleman in the poem who on honeydew had fed and drunk the milk of Paradise. You just said: "Beware, beware! His flashing eyes, his floating hair!" and wove a circle round him thrice, and that was practically all you could do about it.

"Well, all right," he said. "Carry on, carry on. But don't forget I told you."

"Told me what?"

"I don't know. Something, probably."

Mr. Duff fell into a momentary reverie. He emerged from it with a rumbling chuckle. A random thought seemed to have pleased him.

"Shall I tell *you* something?"

"Do."

"Here's where the joke comes in. Beatrice never liked those hams."

"No?"

"No. That's what we split up about. Gosh, how it all comes back to me. It was a summer night, and we were walking by the seashore. There was a moon, I remember, and everything was very still, except for a fellow in the distance singing some old love song to the guitar. And I was just telling her how the sales of the Paramount in New York State compared with those in Illinois, when she suddenly turned on me like a tigress and shouted: 'You and your darned old hams!' and swept off and married Otis Chavender, Import and Export. Thank God!" said Mr. Duff piously.

Joss, as we have seen, held decided views on romance. Though he had never yet met a girl on whom he could feel justified in pouring out the full ardor of a richly emotional nature, he was a modern troubadour. It was with a good deal of abhorrence that he stared at this earthy man.

"I don't want to hurt your feelings, J. B.," he said, "but you have the soul of a wart hog. And not a very nice wart hog, either."

"You're fired."

"No, I'm not. Don't start clowning now. The trouble with you is that it's anything for a laugh. Do you mean you really like being a bachelor?"

"I love it."

"You must be crazy. Me," said Joss softly, "I dream all the time of some sweet girl who will someday come into my life like a tender goddess and gaze into my eyes and put a hand on each cheek and draw my face down to hers and whisper: 'My man!' "

"Brrh!" said Mr. Duff. "Don't talk of such things. You give me the creeps."

Left alone, Joss moved over to the chair whose soft cushions were pressed as a rule only by the sacred Duff trouser seat. Having reclined there for some moments, thinking of this and that, he touched the bell sharply, and was pleasantly entertained when Miss Hesseltyne came bursting in, all zeal and notebook.

"Merely a practice alarm to test your efficiency, young Lollipop," he explained. "You may withdraw."

He nestled into the chair again, and placed his feet on the desk. It was becoming increasingly apparent to him that the head of the firm of Duff and Trotter had one of those jobs which may be grouped for purposes of convenience under the general heading of velvet.

Nearly a quarter of an hour had passed since the big chief had left him, and absolutely nothing had come up in the way of delicate problems calling for instant decision. He had always had a suspicion that these tycoons earned their money easily.

It was as he was beginning to feel a little bored by inaction that Miss Hesseltyne appeared in the doorway, causing him to raise his eyebrows sternly.

"I didn't ring."

"I know you didn't."

"Then why are you here? Go back, and I'll press the bell, and then you come in again. We must have system."

Miss Hesseltyne seemed stirred and excited.

"I told you so!" she said.

"What did you tell me?"

"The store detective saw you pinch that fruit."

"A murrain on the luck!"

"And he's going to report you to Mr. Duff directly he gets back."

Joss's face darkened.

"This is monstrous. Am I to swoon at my work for want of an occasional custard apple? Any doctor will tell you that a man needs a little something round about the middle of the morning. What is technically known as his elevenses. Otherwise the machine breaks down. I shall talk very straight to J. B. about this, when I see him. Am I in a provision bin or a concentration camp?"

He would have spoken further, but at this moment the bell rang in the outer office.

"See who that is," he said curtly. He had not meant to be curt, but the spiritual influence of J. B. Duff's chair was strong upon him.

"It's a lady to see Mr. Duff," said Miss Hesseltyne, returning.

"What, another? All right, show her in," said Joss, leaning back and putting the tips of his fingers together. "I can give her five minutes."

"Miss Fairmile," announced Miss Hesseltyne.

"Good morning," said Sally.

Joss shot from his chair like a jumping bean and came to earth, quivering.

"Good morning," he said, speaking with some difficulty. For he was in love, and the thing had come upon him as a complete surprise.

❀ CHAPTER 3

JOSS WEATHERBY, as has been shown, was a young man a good deal given to dreaming of the girl who would one day come into his life and make it a thing of moonshine and roses, and for some little while past he had made a practice of keeping an eye fixed on the horizon in case she should appear. But he had never expected her to pop up out of a trap like this. He was conscious of a tingling of the limbs and a strange inability to breathe.

Resilience, however, was one of the leading features of his interesting character. He began to recover. The mists cleared from before his eyes, and the sensation of having been hit on the head by a blunt instrument passed. If not yet actually back in midseason form, he was at least more himself and able to scrutinize Sally carefully and in detail.

Odd, he was feeling, that she should be so small and slight. He had always pictured this girl of his as rather on the tall side. And her eyes, he had fancied, would be hazel. Why, he could not have said. Just an idea.

Sally's, like Mrs. Steptoe's, were blue. But whereas the blue eyes of Mrs. Steptoe were light and gave the impression of being constructed of some sort of chinaware, those of Sally Fairmile were dark, like the sky on a summer night. Mrs. Steptoe's eyes were capable of dinting armor plate, and in the case of more yielding substances such as the soul of Howard Steptoe could go right through and come out on the other side. Sally's were soft and appealing. At least, they appealed to Joss.

He was able to observe this the more readily because at the moment she seemed all eyes. Now that she was so nearly face to face with Lord Holbeton's formidable trustee, Sally had been gripped by a sharp attack of panic.

She fought down the ignoble weakness. After all, she reminded herself, on the wrapper of that ham he had looked an old pet.

"I wanted to see Mr. Duff," she said.

Joss drew a deep breath. He remembered now that she had spoken before, as she came into the room, but he had been so dazed just then that he had scarcely heard her. The discovery that in addition to her other perfections she had a musical voice filled him with a profound relief. The way things are in this world, he was telling himself, anyone as lovely as this girl would be sure to talk like a rasping file. Joss Weatherby had lived a hard and testing life, in which most of the things which looked good at first sight had proved to have a string attached to them.

He closed his eyes.

"Say that again."

"What?"

" 'I wanted to see Mr. Duff.' "

"Why?"

"You have such an amazingly attractive speaking voice. It reminds me of springtime and daffodils and young birds chirping on dewy lawns."

"Oh?" It was beginning to be borne in upon Sally that she was in the presence of an eccentric. "Well, that's fine, isn't it?"

"It suits me," said Joss.

There was a pause. Joss's eyes were still closed. His air was that of a music lover savoring the strains of some beautiful melody. Sally, regarding him, came to the conclusion that he looked rather nice. Crazy, apparently, but quite nice.

"Well, can I?"

Joss opened his eyes.

"I beg your pardon?"

"See Mr. Duff."

"He's out at the moment. Could I help you?"

"No, thanks."

"I am his right-hand man. If you've come to buy a game pie, I think I have sufficient influence to swing it for you."

"I'm afraid a right-hand man won't do. You see, it's a personal matter."

"He has no secrets from me."

"He's going to have this one," said Sally and smiled a sudden smile which sent Joss rocking back on his heels as if the old blunt instrument had been applied again.

"You shouldn't do that without warning," he said reproachfully. "You ought to blow a horn or something. Are you really resolved to see J. B.?"

"Yes, really."

"He's a bit fretful this morning. Teething, I think. Well, in that case you ought to fortify yourself. Would you like a glass of sherry?"

"Thank you," said Sally gratefully.

"Unless the mice have been at it," said Joss, "it should be in this cupboard."

He filled the glasses. A sip satisfied him that J. B. Duff, that old tippler, was sound on sherry. This was a nice, nutty brand.

"Skin off your nose," he said politely.

"Skin off yours," said Sally. "What a perfect host you are."

"One has one's humane instincts. I couldn't let you go up against old Battler Duff without a bracer."

"Is he really so terrible?"

"Did you ever read *Pilgrim's Progress?*"

"As a child."

"Remember Apollyon straddling across the way?"

"Yes."

"Duff. More sherry?"

"Thank you."

"Mud in your eye."

"The same in yours. You've saved my life. I've had an exhausting morning."

"Shopping?"

"Trying to engage a valet."

"Any luck?"

"No. I shall have to go back after lunch."

"It shouldn't be so difficult to get a valet, if you try the right place. You went to a valetorium, I presume?"

"Yes, but I had been told to get a specially ferocious one. You see, Mr. Steptoe isn't easy to get on with."

"Did you say Steptoe?"

"Yes, I live with a Mrs. Steptoe. She's a sort of cousin."

"Not Mrs. Steptoe of Claines Hall, Loose Chippings, Sussex—telephone number Loose Chippings 803?"

"Yes. How odd that you should know."

"I've just been having a pleasant reunion with Mrs. Chavender. She and I are old buddies. Well, this is the most extraordinary thing. For years I have jogged along without so much as hearing of Claines Hall, and today—suddenly—without the slightest warning—I hear of nothing else. This must mean something. One seems to detect the hand of fate."

Sally was not interested in the hand of fate. She was anxious to be reassured on an important point.

"Did Mrs. Chavender see Mr. Duff?"

"No."

"Good!"

"Why? Not that I'm inquisitive, of course."

"No, I noticed that. It's just that there were reasons why I didn't want them to meet."

"Which were?"

"How nice it is that you're not inquisitive."

"I never have been, from a child. More sherry?"

"I have some, thanks."

"Then hey, hey!"

"Hey, hey!"

"HEY!" cried Mr. Duff, joining in the chorus from the doorway. Clunk, the osteopath, did his torso twisting at an address not very distant from the Duff and Trotter headquarters, and he had been able to get there and back in nice quick time.

The mood in which J. B. Duff surveyed the scene before him was not a frolicsome one. Clunk, the old reliable, had given him a certain amount of physical relief, but this had been offset by the fact that his soul was feeling as if it had been churned up by an egg whisk. It was no kindly purveyor of hams and groceries who now stood brooding over the revels, but to all intents and purposes a fiend with a hatchet.

To the stormy darkness of spirit from which he was suffering what had contributed most was the recent uncompromising rejection of his offer for the Chavender portrait. Establishing communication with Loose Chippings 803, he had been informed by a cold, metallic voice that Mrs. Steptoe was speaking, and a few moments later this voice, now colder and even more metallic, had said, "Certainly not!" adding that it had never heard of such a thing. The receiver at the Loose Chippings end had then been replaced with a good deal of wristy follow-through.

On top of this had come the store detective's conscientious report concerning Joss and the fruit. And now, hastening to the office to work off his pent-up venom on his erring employee, the first thing he saw as he opened the door was that young man presiding at what had all the appearance of an orgy. And simultaneously it dawned upon him that the basis of the orgy—what was making the party go—was his own personal sherry. Little wonder that he emitted that tempestuous "Hey!" Many men in his place would have said something stronger.

The ejaculation, shattering the momentary silence, affected the two occupants of the room disagreeably. Sally, whose back was to the door and who had been unaware of this addition to the festivities, leaped as if a bomb had been touched off beneath her, while Joss, rising more slowly, stood contemplating his employer with an alert eye.

It was clear to him that a situation had arisen which called for the promptest action. Miss Hesseltyne's communication had left him in no doubt as to the nature of the harangue which would follow that preliminary "Hey!" Once before, as she had reminded him, Mr. Duff had spoken with a breezy frankness on the subject of wage slaves who helped themselves to the store's fruit. And it was the recollection of what he had said on that occasion that decided Joss to act swiftly.

To approach Mr. Duff, and seize Mr. Duff by the shoulders and give Mr. Duff what is familiarly known as the bum's rush was with him the work of a moment.

"How dare you come in here and shout at me like that?" he demanded sternly. "Upon my soul, the discipline in this place gets worse every day. Excuse me," he said. "One of my staff. Wants to see me about something. Back in a minute."

He strode from the room, propelling Mr. Duff before him, and closed the door.

❁ CHAPTER 4

THE CONVERSATION that took place in the passage outside was not an extended one. Mr. Duff was temporarily incapable of speech, and Joss wanted to get back to Sally.

"J. B.," said Joss, "would you care to be torn limb from limb?"

Mr. Duff had begun to feel alarmed. He had never heard of a staff artist assaulting his employer, but everything has to have a beginning and Joss, he knew, had an original mind and would not allow himself to be deterred by mere lack of precedent.

"Because I'll tell you how you can work it. By going into that room and saying what you were intending to say. That girl in there is the most wonderful girl in the world, and if you think that I shall just stand saying 'Yes, sir' and 'No, sir' while you tick me off in her presence you are mistaken, J. B., grievously mistaken. If you so much as shove your nose inside that door till you're sent for, I'll break your spine in eight places. You'll think you're back at the osteopath's."

He turned away with a severe glance, and Mr. Duff found speech.

"Hey!"

"Yes, Duff?"

"You're fired!"

"All right."

"Really fired, I mean."

"All right, all right," said Joss impatiently. "I haven't time to talk shop now."

He went back into the office.

"I'm so sorry," he said. "The trouble is, these fellows have no initiative. The least trifle that goes wrong, they lose their heads and come running to me. It's 'Ask Mr. Weatherby,' 'Put it up to Mr. Weatherby,' 'Mr. Weatherby will know,' all the time. I suppose it's the penalty one pays for having a certain grip of things, but it can be very annoying. I had to be a little terse with poor old Wapshott."

"Wapshott?"

"That was Wapshott. P. P. Wapshott, head of the pressed beef and *pâté de foie gras* department."

"How odd."

"Why odd?"

"He looked to me just like Mr. Duff."

"But I gathered you had not met Mr. Duff."

"His picture is on the wrapper of Paramount Ham."

"Ah? I had forgotten that. Yes, you are quite right. It was Mr. Duff."

"What happened?"

"He fired me. And, do you know, I had a premonition that he would. I suppose I'm psychic."

Sally had been principally concerned with the probable effect of the recent activities on her own fortunes, reasoning correctly that a J. B. Duff who had just been bundled out of his office by the shoulder blades would be in no mood to listen with sympathy to a tale of young love. She now forgot self. This pleasant, if half-witted, young man was in trouble, and she grieved for him.

"Oh, I am sorry."

"The loss is his."

"Why did you do it?"

"I had no option. A little unpleasantness has arisen this morning in connection with my habit of helping myself to samples from the fruit and veg. department, and I saw that he was about to deliver a set speech on the subject, coupled with the name of sherry. I naturally couldn't have him doing that in front of you. He's an outspoken old bird, and it would have been impossible for you, listening to him, to have retained the high opinion you have formed of me. At the moment when he entered the room you were just saying to yourself, 'What a splendid fellow this Mr. Weatherby is, to be sure! I can't remember ever meeting a man I admired more.' Two minutes of J. B. Duff's coarse abuse, and my glamour would have wilted like a salted snail."

"But what will you do?"

"You mean in the way of securing other employment? That's all right. I'm going to be Mr. Steptoe's valet."

"What?"

"You said the place was open."

"But you can't be a valet."

"Why not?"

"How can you?"

"By presenting myself at Claines Hall this afternoon in that capacity. You aren't going to tell me that you refuse to give me the nomination? If it hadn't been for you I wouldn't be out of a job. There are such things as moral obligations. Do have some more sherry, won't you? This may be our last chance of enjoying J. B. Duff's hospitality."

Sally shook her head. She was thinking. If she was to secure something special in the way of gentlemen's personal gentlemen, as Mrs. Steptoe had enjoined upon her, this did seem an admirable opportunity of doing it.

It seemed, indeed, the only opportunity. The registry office that morning had been able to produce none but the softer and more fragile type of valet. Wispy young men with spaniel eyes and deferential manners had been paraded before her in large numbers, all probably admirable at folding, brushing and pressing, but all obviously unfitted for the stern task of making Howard Steptoe see reason in the matter of stiff-bosomed shirts for evening wear. If she went back there after lunch, it would, she knew, be merely to inspect a further procession of human rabbits.

Moreover, though now a little subdued by the thought of her coming interview with Mr. Duff, she was a lighthearted girl and enjoyed simple, wholesome comedy. The prospect of watching Mr. Steptoe's reactions when confronted with Joss made a strong appeal to her.

"Well, if you're really serious."

"Of course I'm serious," said Joss. As an alternative to having this girl pass from his life he would have accepted office as the Claines Hall scullery maid. When love came to them the Weatherbys did not count the cost.

"You haven't forgotten what I told you about Mr. Steptoe?"

"Yes, I have. What did you tell me about Mr. Steptoe?"

"He's rather a difficult man."

"Tough, eh?"

"Very tough!"

"I understand. One of these twenty-minute eggs. That's quite all right. To one who has been in the entourage of J. B. Duff all other eggs seem ludicrously soft-boiled. Steptoe will be a nice rest. Well, now that that's settled how about a bite of lunch?"

"I can't, I'm afraid. I must see Mr. Duff."

"Of course, yes. I was forgetting. I'll send him in."

Mr. Duff was leaning against the wall in a daydream. There had just floated into his mind like drifting thistledown the thought of how pleasant it would be to skin Joss.

"Hey!" said Joss. "You're to go in."

"Well, don't forget you're fired," said Mr. Duff, who wished to leave no loophole for misunderstanding on this point.

❈ CHAPTER 5

As Mr. Duff came into the office she realized that the fateful interview was about to begin. Sally gave a quick gasp, as if iced water had been poured down her back. She felt like a very small Christian in the arena watching the approach of an outsize lion.

Then, as he advanced and she was able to see him steadily and see him whole, her nervousness left her, giving place to a maternal tenderness. J. B. Duff's features were working in what had the appearance of agony.

The fact was that Mr. Duff, a devil of a fellow among his own sex, was terrified of women. He avoided them if possible, and when cornered by one without hope of escape always adopted the shrewd tactics of the caterpillar of the puss moth—which, we are told by an eminent authority, "not satisfied with Nature's provisions for its safety, makes faces at young birds and alarms them considerably." That was why Mr. Duff's features were working. Nature, making provision for his safety, had given him bushy eyebrows and piercing eyes, and he threw in the faces as an extra.

But to Sally he seemed in pain and, being a nice girl, she became the little mother.

"Won't you have some sherry?" she said, remembering what a tonic it had been to her.

This hospitable offer, coming on top of all the other disturbing events of the morning, had the effect of unmanning Mr. Duff for a moment. But he was practical. You have to be to build up a world-famous hammery. He needed sherry, so he accepted it.

"Thanks," he said gruffly.

"Drink that, and you'll feel better."

"How do you know I'm not feeling fine?"

"I thought Mr. Weatherby might have upset you."

"Young thug!"

"I liked him."

"You can have him."

"He's funny."

"He doesn't amuse me."

"Who is he?"

"Look," said Mr. Duff, whom this topic of conversation was afflicting with a rising nausea. "Suppose we don't talk about him any more." It occurred to him that he had not yet been informed to what he owed the honor of this visit. "Who are you?"

"My name is Fairmile."

"You want to see me?"

"Yes."

"What about?"

Sally took the plunge.

"Lord Holbeton asked me to come and see you. I . . . He . . . He's staying at the house where I live."

"Where's that? I haven't heard from him in months. Began to hope he was dead."

A coldness crept into Sally's manner. She decided that she had been wrong in thinking this man an old pet.

"Claines Hall," she said shortly. "It's in Sussex."

"Claines Hall? That's curious. Do you know Mrs. Chavender?"

"Of course."

"Seen that portrait of her that's there?"

"Of course."

"What's it like?"

"It's good."

"It really gets that snooty expression of hers?"

"Oh, yes."

Mr. Duff sighed wistfully.

"But who told you about it?"

"Young Weatherby. He painted it."

"Is he an artist?"

"Yes."

"I was wondering what he was."

"I could tell you what I think he is."

"He must be very clever."

"Now we're back to him again!" said Mr. Duff disgustedly. "I thought you told me you had come to talk about George Trotter."

"George Holbeton."

"Well, George Holbeton, if you prefer it. His father was Percy Trotter till he started going around under an alias. I suppose he sent you to try to get money out of me?"

"Yes," said Sally, startled at this clairvoyance.

"Why didn't he come himself?"

It was a question which Sally had anticipated.

"He isn't well."

"What's the matter with him?"

"He—er—he's got a sore throat."

"I don't wonder. Does he still sing all the time?"

"He sings quite a lot."

"If you can call it singing. Sounds like gas escaping from a pipe. 'But only God can make a tree.' Bah! In a really civilized community crooners would be shot on sight. Well, I won't give him a penny. How do you come to be mixing yourself up in this?"

"We're engaged."

"What! You've gone and got engaged to George Holbeton?"

"Yes."

"Then you ought to have your head examined," said Mr. Duff.

Sally stiffened. Her manner became colder.

"I'm sorry now," she said, "that I gave you that sherry."

"What do you mean, gave me that sherry?" retorted Mr. Duff warmly. "It's my sherry."

The point was one which Sally had overlooked, and she found herself unable to frame a telling reply.

"Engaged to George Holbeton?" said Mr. Duff, marveling. An idea seemed to strike him. "Are you rich?"

"No."

"Then how on earth can you be engaged to George Holbeton?" said Mr. Duff, plainly bewildered.

"I think I'll go," said Sally.

It seemed that Mr. Duff was quite willing that she should do so. He allowed her to reach the door without speaking. Then suddenly, as her fingers were on the handle, there passed through his portly frame a sort of spasm, causing it to quiver like a jelly. He had the appearance of a man whose brow a thought has flushed.

"Wait!" he cried.

Sally paused, cold and hostile. Her nose was small, but she tilted it with an almost Chavenderesque hauteur.

"Why? I've said all I came to say."

"I've a proposition I'd like to put up to you."

"You've refused to give George his money."

"Yes, but I think we can do a deal."

"What do you mean?"

"Come and sit down."

Sally returned to her seat.

"Well?"

Mr. Duff was frowning at the desk, as if wondering how to begin. His eye fell on the picture of himself which Joss had drawn for Mrs. Chavender, and he stared at it unpleasantly for a moment. Then he crumpled it up and threw it in the wastepaper basket. The action seemed to have the effect of clearing his mind. He had found the right approach, and in a business conference the right approach is everything.

"Listen," he said. "Lemme tell you a little story."

✸ CHAPTER 6

SINCE EARLY MORNING the summer sun had been shining down from a cloudless sky on Claines Hall and neighborhood. Birds had twittered, bees buzzed and insects tootled. But despite these agreeable weather conditions the day had been for George, second Baron Holbeton, one of gloom and mental unrest. The strain of waiting for news from the front had brought him within measurable distance of a fit of the vapors.

Mrs. Steptoe's announcement during luncheon that Mr. Duff had been on the telephone, offering extravagant sums for the portrait of Mrs. Chavender, had done nothing to diminish his anxiety. Seeming as it did to indicate that the custodian of his affairs had gone definitely off his onion, it caused him to fear the worst. It is hard enough to get money out of a sane trustee. Let loopiness set in, and the difficulties become immeasurably enhanced.

All through the afternoon his agitation increased. Unaware of the numerous commissions which Mrs. Steptoe had given Sally to execute in the metropolis, he could not understand why she did not appear. By half-past four, as he paced the drive by the main gate, his frame of mind resembled in almost equal proportions that of Mariana in the Moated Grange and of those priests of Baal who gashed themselves with knives.

The sound of a car caused him to spin round with eyes aglow. A natty two-seater was turning in at the gate. Then the glow faded. Its occupant was not Sally but a pleasant-faced young man, a stranger to him, who gave him a genial wave of the hand and passed on toward the house.

The fact that there were suitcases in the rumble seat of the car diverted his thoughts for a while. He had heard of no guest who was expected. Then he dismissed the matter from his mind and resumed his pacing.

Shadows had begun to creep across the drive before Sally made her appearance. She found him querulous.

"At last!"

"Were you expecting me earlier?"

"Of course I was."

"I had a lot to do."

There was a gaiety in her manner which suddenly caused his spirits to rise. Hope began to dawn. No girl, he reasoned, who had recently got the bird from a provision merchant could be as chirpy as this.

"Well?"

"It's all right."

"You got the money?"

"Not exactly."

"How do you mean?"

"He didn't actually give it to me."

"He's sending it?"

"No. But it's all right. I'd better tell you what happened."

"Yes," said Lord Holbeton, who was anxious to know.

Sally looked about her. Her manner seemed to Lord Holbeton furtive.

"Do you think anyone can hear us?"

"No."

"They might. Get in, and we'll drive along the road."

"What's all the bally mystery about?"

"You'll understand."

She backed the car, and they drove in the direction of Loose Chippings. At the corner by Higgins's duck pond, where there is open country and no facilities for eavesdropping, she halted.

"I've had the weirdest day, George. I met the most extraordinary young man."

Lord Holbeton was not interested in extraordinary young men.

"What happened when you saw old Duff?"

"Well, he started by being very rude. I don't think he likes you much."

"He doesn't like anybody."

"Doesn't he? You little know!"

"What do you mean?"

"Though like isn't the right word. Not nearly strong enough. Well, as I say, he started by being very rude. In fact, I was just sweeping

out of the room with my nose in the air when he suddenly said 'Wait!'
So I waited."

"And then?"

"He sat waggling his eyebrows for a while, and then he said: 'Let
me tell you a little story.'"

"Yes?"

"Well, then he told me it. He said that years ago he had been a
young fellow chock full of romance, and he used to dream all the time
of some sweet girl who would come into his life like a tender
goddess—"

Lord Holbeton was staring blankly.

"Old Duff said that?"

"Yes."

"You're sure it *was* old Duff?"

"Of course."

"He must have been tight."

"Not a bit, though we had been quaffing sherry. As a matter of fact,
sherry flowed like water all the time. Mr. Weatherby found it in a
cupboard."

"Who the dickens is Mr. Weatherby?"

"He's the extraordinary young man I told you about. He's done the
craziest thing—"

Lord Holbeton's lack of interest in extraordinary young men extended to their unbalanced actions.

"Well, go on. What about my money?"

"Where was I? Oh, yes, about Mr. Duff dreaming of this girl who
would come into his life. Well, she came. But unfortunately they
quarreled and she went right out again. And he still loves her! After
fifteen years, George. It was the most pathetic thing I ever heard.
That poor, lonely old man. My heart just bled for him. Buckets. You
know who she is, of course?"

"How on earth should I know?"

"Of course you do. You heard what she was saying at breakfast
about having been engaged to him. Mrs. Chavender."

"Oh?" said Lord Holbeton. Except for the fact that this had cleared
up the mystery of why Mr. Duff wanted Mrs. Chavender's portrait he
found little in it to interest him. If he had a fault it was that he was a
little self-centered. "Well, how about my money?"

"I'm coming to that. I've got to tell you the whole story, or you
won't understand. Mr. Duff still loves Mrs. Chavender. You've got
that? Well, he's found out about that portrait of her in the breakfast
room, and he's dying to have it. He says he wants to hang it up and

gaze at it and think of the old days. So he telephoned Mrs. Steptoe and asked her to sell it to him."

"And about my money?"

"Of course she refused. Mrs. Chavender gave Mr. Steptoe the portrait, and Mrs. Steptoe wouldn't dare sell it for fear of offending her. Mr. Duff was brokenhearted."

"What did he say about my money?"

"His voice trembled as he told me."

Her own voice trembled. In any girl who is capable of falling beneath the spell of a man who sings "Trees" there must of necessity be a strong vein of sentiment, and J. B. Duff's desire to possess a concrete reminder of the dear old days had affected Sally deeply.

"And then he took my breath away. Do you know what he said?"

"About my money?"

"No, about this portrait. He said he had got to have it somehow. He just had to, he said. And when I said I was afraid I didn't see how it was to be managed, he said you would steal it for him."

A sound like the wind going out of a dying duck escaped Lord Holbeton.

"Steal it?"

"And I said: 'Why, Mr. Duff! What a splendid idea!' "

Lord Holbeton swallowed.

"You said: 'What a splendid idea'?"

"Yes. Because, you see, he says he will give you your money if you do. And it will be quite easy, he pointed out. He said he wasn't asking you to break into the strong room of the Bank of England and get away with a ton of gold bars. All you will have to do is wait till there's no one about and snip it out of its frame and hide it under your coat."

"Oh?" said Lord Holbeton. He was aware that the remark was a weak one, but at the moment he could think of nothing better.

"One thing I was very firm about though. His idea was that you should take the thing to him in London, and I absolutely refused to dream of it. I said you were very highly strung and that I wasn't going to have you subjected to any nervous strain. So we left it that he was to come and stay at the Rose and Crown in Loose Chippings, and you will take the portrait to him there."

"Oh?" said Lord Holbeton again.

"So now all you've got to do is to find a good opportunity. We mustn't fail the poor old man. He's too touching for words. You should have seen his face light up when I said I thought it was a splendid idea."

Lord Holbeton did not speak. It might have been supposed that what kept him silent was horror at finding the ethical standards of provision merchants so low. This, however, was not the case. He had just begun to wonder whether in plighting his troth to a girl who considered it a splendid idea that he should snip portraits out of their frames and hide them under his coat he might not have acted a little rashly.

✸ CHAPTER 7

THE TWO-SEATER which had passed Lord Holbeton in the drive continued its progress toward the house, and a few moments later Chibnall, the butler, brooding in his pantry over tea and buttered toast, was roused from a somber reverie by the sound of the front-door bell.

Chibnall, though of a sedate exterior, was a man of strong passions, and what was causing him to brood was the fact that, looking in at the Rose and Crown that morning for a quick one, he had found his fiancée, Vera Pym, flirting with a commercial traveler. She had, indeed, been in the very act of straightening the latter's tie, and the sight had given him an unpleasant shock. This was not the first time he had observed in her conduct a levity which he deplored; and though he had said nothing at the time, merely withdrawing in a rather marked manner, it was his intention before the day was done to write her a pretty nasty note and send it round by the knives-and-boots boy.

The bell reminded him that there are other things in life besides woman's faithlessness. It was Chibnall, the lover, who had sat down to the tea and toast, but the individual who rose and wiped the butter from his lips and went and opened the front door was Chibnall, the slave of duty.

"Good afternoon," said the pleasant-faced young man whom he found standing on the mat.

"Good afternoon, sir," said Chibnall.

That there are other ways for a new valet to report to G.H.Q. than by driving up to the front door in a sports-model car had not occurred to Joss Weatherby. He was fond of motoring, and his first act on leaving Sally had been to go round to the garage and collect the old machine. The stimulating drive through rural England, which was looking its best on this fine afternoon, together with the still more stimulating thought that he was about to take up his residence beneath the same roof as the girl he loved, had lent a sparkle to his eyes and increased the always rather noticeable affability of his manner.

He looked upon Claines Hall and found it good. The whole setup appealed to him enormously. He liked its mellow walls, its green lawns, its gay flower beds, its twittering birds, its buzzing bees and its tootling insects. And when Chibnall appeared he beamed at him as if he loved him like a brother. The butler could not remember when he had opened the door to a sunnier visitor.

"Is Mrs. Steptoe at home?"

"Yes sir."

"Beautiful day."

"Yes sir."

"Nice place, this. Tudor, isn't it?"

"Yes sir."

"You don't happen to know what the bird would be that I met as I came along the drive, do you? Reddish, with a yellow head."

"No sir."

"A pity," said Joss. "I liked its looks."

Chibnall descended the steps and removed the suitcases from the car. Like Lord Holbeton, he found himself puzzled by them, but it was not for him to comment. In God's good time, no doubt, all would be explained.

"Oh, thanks."

"I will have your car taken round to the stables, sir."

"Will you really?"

To Joss, in his uplifted mood, this seemed so extraordinarily decent of the man that he had no hesitation in taking a five-pound note from his pocket and handing it to him. He was glad that his successful speculation at the charity gambling place had put him in a position to be able to do so.

"Why, thank you, sir!" ejaculated Chibnall, and blushed to think how near he had come to saying "Coo." Here, he told himself, was the real thing in guests. Too many of those who had enjoyed Mrs. Steptoe's hospitality during his term of office had been content to discharge their obligations with ten bob and a bright smile. "It is extremely kind of you, sir."

"Not at all."

"If you would come this way, sir. Mrs. Steptoe is in the drawing room."

They proceeded thither, chatting amiably of this and that.

Mrs. Steptoe had gone to the drawing room not to relax but to concentrate. She was on the eve of giving her first garden party, a social event of the greatest importance, certain to have wide repercussions in the County, and she wanted to go through the list of guests again. She could not rid herself of an uneasy suspicion that she had left out somebody of substance, whose reaction to the slight would be like that of the Bad Fairy who was not invited to the royal christening. Nothing, she knew, more surely gives an aspiring newcomer a social black eye in English County circles than the omission to include in her tea-and-strawberries beano the big shot of the neighborhood.

Chibnall's smooth "Mr. Weatherby" from the doorway told her how well-founded her fears had been. There was nobody of that name among the "*W*s," and the quiet distinction of Joss's costume and the carefree jauntiness of his manner made it plain that here was the son of some noble house. And she could not ask him flatly who he was and where he lived, for that way lay the raised eyebrow and the bleak British stare.

She was too forceful a woman actually to flutter, but her voice as she addressed him distinctly shook.

"Oh, how do you do?"

"How do you do?"

"What a lovely day!"

"Delightful."

"So nice of you to call. Do sit down."

She motioned her visitor to a chair, and resumed her own. She was conscious that this was not going to be easy.

The curse of English life, the thing about it that makes strangers put straws in their hair and pick at the coverlet, is, of course, the fact that the best type of father so often has sons with totally different names. You get the Earl of Thingummy, for instance. Right. So far, so good. But his heir is Lord Whoosis, and if his union has been still further blessed, the result will be anything from the Hon. Algernon Whatisit to the Hon. Lionel Umph. To ascertain this young man's identity, so that he could be bidden to the garden party, Mrs. Steptoe realized that she might have to uncover layer after layer of nomenclature, like a dancer removing the seven veils.

"Have you come far?" she asked, feeling that here might be a clue on which she could work.

"From London."

"Oh?" said Mrs. Steptoe, baffled.

There was a pause. Joss looked about him, admiring the cozy opulence of his surroundings. A man, he felt, might make himself very snug in a place like this. The reflection that during his stay at

Claines Hall he was not likely to be given the run of the drawing room had not yet suggested itself.

"It must have been warm in London today."

"There were moments when things got very warm."

"So pleasant getting back to the country."

"Oh, most."

"Sussex is so lovely at this time of year."

"At any time of year."

"Which part of it do you like best?" asked Mrs. Steptoe, hoping for an outburst of local patriotism.

"All of it. Hullo," said Joss, whose eye, roving along the opposite wall, had been suddenly arrested, "isn't that a Corot over there?"

"I beg your pardon?"

"That picture," said Joss, rising. "A Corot, surely?"

"Is it?" said Mrs. Steptoe, who was not really an authority on Art, though she knew what she liked.

"Yes, that's right. His Italian period. Very plastic."

"Oh yes?"

"Very, ve-ry plastic. I like the structure. Interesting. Calmly stated. Strong, but not bombastic. The values are close and the colors finely related."

"Perhaps you would care for a cup of tea?" said Mrs. Steptoe.

It may have been a slight asperity in her tone that gave him the feeling, but there came over Joss at this point a sense of something being wrong. Though nothing could have been more enjoyable than this exchange of views on the Barbizon school he was conscious that in some way he had been remiss. And then he saw what had happened. He had allowed *joie de vivre* to impair his technique. It was all very well to love everybody on this happy day, but he must not forget that he was a gentleman's personal gentleman. Long ere this, he should have been scattering "Madams" like birdseed.

"Thank you, madam," he said, rectifying the error.

Mrs. Steptoe blinked, but came back strongly.

"Tea's one of your English customs I've taken to in a big way," she said. "My husband doesn't like it, but I never miss my cup at five o'clock."

"Indeed, madam?"

"So refreshing."

"Extremely, madam."

Mrs. Steptoe's embarrassment expressed itself in an uneasy titter. She was beginning to feel unequal to the situation. Her residence in Great Britain had done much to put her abreast of the customs of the country—for weeks she had been eating her boiled eggs out of the shell instead of mashed up in a glass, and Howard was never allowed to fasten the bottom button of his waistcoat—but she knew that there were still weak spots in her equipment, and one of these was that she had not yet quite got the hang of English humor. Sometimes she could grab it off the bat, but sometimes—as now—it got past her.

"Is that the latest gag?" she asked, with what she hoped was adequate sprightliness.

"Madam?"

"Yes, calling women that, like men in the old novels saying 'Dear Lady.' It's kind of cute," said Mrs. Steptoe musingly, "but I'm not sure I really like it. It makes you sound as if you were a valet or something."

"I am, madam."

There came to Mrs. Steptoe an unworthy suspicion. Joss still looked like the son of some noble house, but she now found herself regarding him as the son of a noble house who has had a couple.

"I'm afraid you will think me very dumb," she said coldly, "but I don't quite see the joke."

"No joke, madam. I am Mr. Steptoe's new valet."

"What!"

"Yes, madam. Miss Fairmile engaged me this morning."

There is no anguish so acute as that experienced by a woman of strong views on class distinctions, who, having lavished all the charm of her best manner on a supposed scion of the nobility, discovers that he is the latest addition to her domestic staff. And Mrs. Steptoe would undoubtedly have given eloquent expression to her feelings had she not, just as she was about to begin, caught Joss's eye. It was a strong, steady eye, the eye of a man who for two years had given J. B. Duff look for look, and if not actually made him wilt at least confined him reasonably closely to the decencies of debate. It impressed Mrs. Steptoe. She could recognize personality when she saw it.

Hard, keen, practical woman though she was, the chatelaine of Claines Hall had a wistful, castles-in-the-air-building side to her nature. Ever since she had landed in England she had dreamed of one day securing a valet of the right sort, a gentleman's personal gentleman of blood and iron, capable of sticking his chin out at her Howard and making him play ball. And here, unless she had been totally deceived by a promising exterior, he was.

Her glance softened. An instant before she could have been mistaken for a rattlesnake about to strike. Her air now became that of a rattlesnake which is prepared to reserve its judgment till it has heard all the facts.

"Oh?" she said.

"Yes, madam."

"Chibnall should have taken you to the servants' hall."

"Yes, madam."

"Still, now you are here—"

"Precisely, madam. No doubt you wish to give me certain hints and instructions with regard to my duties." Joss coughed discreetly. "I understand from Miss Fairmile, madam, that Mr. Steptoe is inclined to be a little difficult."

It was the very point which Mrs. Steptoe was anxious to discuss.

"That's right," she said. "He gets rough with his valets."

"Indeed, madam?"

"He throws a scare into them, and they quit. The only one so far that's stayed as long as two weeks was the fellow before you. I had hopes of him, but Mr. Steptoe finally got him down. He didn't like Mr. Steptoe rubbing his nose on his shirt front."

This interested Joss. He had not known that he was taking service under a man with an India-rubber neck.

"Is Mr. Steptoe a contortionist?"

"You don't get me. It was the fellow before you's nose that Mr. Steptoe rubbed on Mr. Steptoe's shirt front. The fellow before you had laid out a stiff-bosomed shirt for him to wear at dinner, and Mr. Steptoe doesn't like stiff-bosomed shirts. So he rubbed the fellow before you's nose on it."

"I see, madam."

"So there you are. That's what you're up against."

"I quite appreciate the situation, madam. But I view it without concern. This will not be the first time I have been in the employment of a difficult gentleman."

"And you made out all right?"

"Entirely satisfactorily, madam."

Mrs. Steptoe's last lingering doubts were removed. If she still bore any resemblance to a rattlesnake it was to one which has heard the voice of conscience and decided to simmer down and spend a quiet evening with the boys. This was the superman she had dreamed of. She resolved to conceal nothing from him, but to give him the low-down in overflowing measure.

"Well, that's fine," she said. "You've taken a weight off my mind. I'm beginning to think you'll be able to swing this job. It's not everybody that can handle Mr. Steptoe when he's going good, but you seem to have what it takes. You see, the whole trouble is this. Mind you, this is strictly off the record. I wouldn't want to be quoted."

"I quite understand, madam."

"Between ourselves, then, for your guidance, Mr. Steptoe is a hick."

"Indeed, madam."

"He has no natural sense of dignity. I can't seem to drive it into his nut that he's got a position to keep up. Only the other day I caught him in the stable yard, shooting craps with my chauffeur."

"Tut, madam."

"Yes. I heard a voice yelling, 'Baby needs new shoes!' and there he was."

"Dear, dear, madam."

"And he hates dressing for dinner. He says collars scratch his neck and he can't stand for the way stiff-bosomed shirts go pop when he breathes. You see, he was raised all wrong. He was a boxer.

"Preliminary bouts on the Pacific coast. The first time I ever saw him was at the American Legion stadium in Hollywood. He was getting the tar whaled out of him by a fellow called Wildcat Wix."

This relieved Joss somewhat. He was prepared to take the rough with the smooth, but it was nice to feel that he was not coming up against an irritable world's champion.

"Well, you know what smalltime box-fighters are. They get the pork-and-beans outlook and don't seem able to shake it off. So I'm relying on you to be very firm with him. Tonight particularly. There's one or two really nice people expected to dinner, and I wouldn't put it past Mr. Steptoe, if left to his own unbridled instincts to show up in a turtle-neck sweater. And now I'll ring for Chibnall to take you to your room. I hope you'll be comfortable."

"Thank you, madam."

"Watch Mr. Steptoe's shoes. Take your eye off him for a second, and he'll be coming down to dinner in sneakers."

"I will be very vigilant, madam."

"I'm sure you will. Oh, Chibnall," said Mrs. Steptoe, "this is Weatherby, Mr. Steptoe's new valet. Will you show him to his room?"

In stating that there is no anguish so acute as that which is experienced by a hostess who mistakes a member of her staff for a scion of the nobility, we were guilty of an error. It is equaled, if not surpassed, by that of a butler of haughty spirit who finds that he has been calling a fellow toiler "sir." It was with burning eyes and resentment in every feature that Chibnall turned on Joss as the door closed behind them. Only the fact that Joss's five-pound note was nestling in his trousers pocket restrained him from the most violent form of rebuke.

"Why didn't you tell me who you were?" he demanded.

"You never asked me," said Joss.

"Bowling up to the front door in your car as if you had bought the place!"

"The wrong note, you think? Yes, I suppose you're right. Here, where are we going?"

"I was instructed to show your lordship your lordship's room," said Chibnall, whose satire, though good, was always inclined to be a little on the heavy side. "Perhaps your lordship will be so obliging as to pick up your lordship's feet and follow me."

They had left behind the soft rugs and Chippendale furniture of the ruling classes and had come into a barren land of uncarpeted stairs and passages smelling of yellow soap. Joss found his spirits sinking. He felt like Dante being shown through the Inferno by Virgil. And when Virgil threw open a door in the very heart of the yellow-soap zone, revealing a small bedroom with an iron bedstead and a cracked pitcher standing in a chipped bowl, he shook his head decidedly.

"Oh, no, no, no," he said. "Oh, no, no, no, no, no."

"I beg your pardon?"

"This will never do. Haven't you something better than this?"

"Perhaps you'd like a private bath?"

"A private bath, of course," said Joss. "And a few good prints on the walls and a decent armchair. Two armchairs, in fact, because I am hoping that you will often look in on me for a smoke and a chat when we are off duty."

A sharp, whistling intake of breath at his side told him that he had been too abrupt. He felt that he should have remembered that preliminaries are essential to these negotiations.

"I wonder," he said, taking a five-pound note from his pocket, "if you would be interested in another of these? Perhaps you are a collector?"

There was a long pause, during which Chibnall, the man, wrestled with Chibnall, the butler. The man wished to fling the five-pound note in Joss's face, the butler was in favor of trousering it. The latter won.

"Thanks," he said.

"You see," Joss explained, "Mrs. Steptoe made such a point of telling me to be comfortable. I wouldn't like to disappoint her. And I ought to tell you that I have not always been as you see me now. Until recently I lived in an atmosphere of refinement, even luxury. In fact, I dwelt in marble halls with vassals and serfs at my side. I can't mention names, even to you, but if I were to reveal the identity of the titled father who cut me off with a shilling for refusing to marry the girl he had chosen for me you would be staggered."

It was as if Chibnall had suddenly seen light in the darkness. Subconsciously, he realized now, some such explanation of these peculiar goings-on had already begun to suggest itself. He was a great reader of novelettes and had often argued their merits with Miss Pym, who preferred thrillers. The situation which Joss had outlined was not a new one to him. He had come across it not only in *Hyacinth* but in *Mark Delamere, Gentleman,* and *The World Well Lost.*

"Indeed, sir?"

"That's what makes me a little fussy."

"I quite understand, sir."

"Who arranges about the bedrooms here?"

"The housekeeper, sir."

"She should be able to find me something suitable?"

"Unquestionably, sir. There are a number of unoccupied guest rooms."

"Then lead me to her. In fact, you had better assemble the whole staff. I should like to address them on an important point of policy."

It was some half-hour later, as Joss sat in the servants' hall enjoying a pleasant rubber of bridge with Mrs. Barlow, the housekeeper, Mrs. Ellis, the cook, and Chibnall, that there pealed through the regions below stairs the sound of a bell. It gave the impression that somebody with a powerful thumb had placed that thumb on the button and kept it there.

"Mr. Steptoe," said Chibnall, who was dummy.

Joss sighed. Enthusiastically supported by his partner, he had just bid little slam in hearts and looked like making it.

"A nuisance," he said. "But inevitable, I suppose. Perhaps you would come and show me the way."

The door of Mr. Steptoe's bedroom, when they reached it, was ajar, and from within there came the restless movement of some heavy body, suggesting either that an elephant had got loose or that Mr. Steptoe was pacing the floor. It was a sinister sound, and Chibnall's eyes, as they met Joss's, were alive with respectful pity. Chibnall had seen so many valets enter that room, only to totter out shaking in every limb and groping their way blindly, like guests coming away from a Lord Mayor's Banquet—or even, as in the case of the fellow before you, bleeding profusely at the nose.

Quickly shaking Joss's hand, he tiptoed off.

Joss pushed the door open and went in. It seemed to him that the early stages of his first interview with his new employer might be marked by a little friction. Nor was he mistaken. One glance at the latter was enough to show him that Mr. Steptoe was not at his sunniest.

As a matter of fact, nobody who had known him only since his arrival in England had ever seen Howard Steptoe sunny. He was, as has already been indicated by his demeanor at the breakfast table, a soured and disillusioned man.

When a wealthy widow, infatuated by his robust charms, had removed him from the pork-and-beans surroundings in which he had passed his formative years Howard ("Mugsy") Steptoe had supposed that he was about to sit on top of the world. And here he was in a hell of valets, starched collars, tea parties, County society and companions who were so good for him, like Lord Holbeton. A rude awakening.

Today he had been hotting up ever since lunch. It was over the luncheon table, it will be remembered, that Mrs. Steptoe had told him of Mr. Duff's offer for the portrait of Mrs. Chavender. And when a man, sorely in need of ready cash, hears that his wife has turned down a dazzling offer for a portrait, belonging to himself, on which he would have put an outside price of thirty cents, he is apt, even if of a mild and equable temperament, to chafe pretty considerably. Mr. Steptoe, who was not mild and equable, had chafed like a gumboil.

And about half an hour ago he had met Sally and learned from her that a new valet had arrived at Claines Hall. Just when he had been congratulating himself on having stamped this evil out.

Howard Steptoe was waiting for this valet.

"Good evening, sir," said Joss. "You rang?"

He found himself impressed by the other's physique and was surprised that it had never carried him beyond preliminary bouts on the Pacific coast. Faulty footwork, he presumed.

There was a snowy shirt lying on the bed. Mr. Steptoe pointed a bananalike finger at it—emotionally, for it represented to him the last straw.

"You!"

"Sir?"

"See that shirt?"

"Yes sir."

"Stiff."

"Precisely, sir."

"Well, take it away, or I'll make you eat it."

Joss felt that the moment had come to be firm. There was a compelling steadiness in the eye which he fixed on the fermenting man. "Steptoe," he said quietly, "you will wear your nice shirt."

❀ CHAPTER 8

THERE WAS A SILENCE. Mr. Steptoe's vast frame had become afflicted by what looked like a palsy. He moved; he stirred; he seemed to feel the thrill of life along his keel. His hands had bunched themselves into fists, and he breathed tensely through his squashed nose.

"What?" he muttered throatily. "Wassat you said?"

Joss repeated his observation. He had shifted his position slightly, so as to place a substantial chair between them, and had taken from the mantelpiece a stout and serviceable vase—just in case. He was pretty confident of being able to settle this dispute through the channels of diplomacy, but there was no harm in being prepared.

"I'll break you into little bits."

"Don't be silly. What use would I be in little bits?"

A bitter smile disturbed for an instant the tenseness of Mr. Steptoe's lips.

"Ha!" he said. "Smart guy, huh?"

Joss slapped his thigh.

"I knew you were going to say that."

"Is that so?"

"Either that or 'Wise guy, huh?' I was as sure of it as I am that I have in my pocket the IOUs for the money you lost to the cook at craps."

"Cheese!" said Mr. Steptoe, tottering on his base.

It was about a week since Howard Steptoe, in the hope of picking up a little pocket money, had started teaching the domestic staff this fascinating game and in a black hour had come up against Mrs Ellis, the cook, who possessed a natural aptitude for it. This very evening he had been compelled to ask her to accept another promissory note for sixteen shillings, bringing his obligations up to the colossal figure of six pounds, eight and twopence.

"And when I think what Mrs. Steptoe is going to say when show them to her," said Joss, "I shudder."

So did Mr. Steptoe. He shuddered from stem to stern.

The fear lest this evidence of his sinning might some day fin

way to Mrs. Steptoe had haunted Mugsy's dreams for a week. He knew so well what the harvest would be.

In the main, though despotic, his wife's rule was benevolent, and the love she bore him enabled him to rub valets' noses in shirt fronts without exciting anything worse than a pained "Oh, Howard!" She had even been reasonably mild when she had found him rolling the bones with the chauffeur.

But there was one point on which he knew that she would tolerate no funny business. Let her discover that he had been trying to skin the best cook in Sussex, thus sowing in that cook's mind possible thoughts of giving her notice, and the tigress that slept in her would be unchained.

"Anticipating a spot of toughness on your part," said Joss, "I leaped at the opportunity offered to me just now of buying up your paper. It may interest you to know that I got it dirt cheap. Confidence in your financial stability is very low in the servants' hall, and sacrifice prices prevailed." He paused. "Steptoe," he said, "you will wear your stiff-bosomed shirt and like it."

Mr. Steptoe had sunk into a chair and was supporting his head on his hands. Joss felt a pang of pity for the stricken man.

"Cheer up," he said. "You have only to show a docile and reasonable spirit, and I shall not proceed to the last awful extreme. How on earth," he asked sympathetically, "did you come to get in the red to that extent? You must have been rolling them all wrong. You'd better let me give you a few lessons."

Mr. Steptoe raised his head, staring.

"Do you play craps?"

"Do I play craps?" said Joss with a light laugh. "That's good. The dicers of a dozen cities would smile if they heard you ask that. You, I take it, are a novice."

"No, I'm not," said Mr. Steptoe hotly.

"Then there must be something seriously wrong with your methods. The whole science of craps consists in saying the right thing to the bones at the right time. And that, I suspect, is where you have slipped. You suggest to me the ultraconservative, hidebound personality. What you learned at your mother's knee is good enough for you. I understand that you still say, 'Baby needs new shoes.'"

"Well, why not?"

"All wrong. Dice aren't going to respond to outmoded stuff like that. But I'll go into all that later. For the moment, Steptoe, let me urge upon you never again to play with cooks. Practically all of them have an uncanny skill. Your future as a crapshooter, as I see it,

lies among the nobility and gentry. If I were you I would reserve myself for this garden party of which I hear so much."

"How do you mean?"

"Wait till the garden party, and then detach a contingent of the best element in the County from the tea and buns and take them behind the stables and give them the works."

"I never thought of that."

"I see no reason why you should not make a substantial killing."

"It can't be too substantial for me."

"You require the money for some special purpose?"

"Do I!" Although they were alone, behind closed doors, Mr. Steptoe looked nervously over his shoulder. "I want to raise enough to buy my transportation back to Hollywood."

"Your heart is still there, is it? But I was given to understand that your career there was not an unmixedly successful one. Suppose you ran into Wildcat Wix again?"

"Say, listen, I could eat that guy for breakfast."

"I was told that he whaled the tar out of you."

"Who said that?"

"Mrs. Steptoe."

"Women don't understand these things. I was robbed of the decision by a venal referee. And, anyway, I'm not planning to go back to being a box-fighter. When I left there I was doing swell in pictures."

"I don't remember seeing you."

"Well, it was extra work till just at the end. Then I was in one where I had three good speeches."

"You had?"

"That's what I had. It was one of these tough stories, where everybody's all the time slapping somebody else's face. I was one of these gangsters. A guy comes up to me and says, 'Oh yeah?' and I say, 'Oh yeah?' and slap his face. Then another guy comes up to me and says, 'Oh yeah?' and I say, 'Oh yeah?' and slap his face. And then a third guy comes up to me and says, 'Oh yeah?' and I say, 'Oh yeah?' and I slap him on the kisser too."

"I suppose they couldn't get Clark Gable?"

"And then Mrs. Steptoe goes and marries me. Wouldn't that jar you? Just as I'm starting to break in."

"Many people say that the artist should not marry."

"It bust my career. There's a rising demand in pictures for fellows with maps like mine. Look at Wallace Beery. Look at Edward G. Robinson. How about Maxie Rosenbloom? There's a case for you. Started out as a box-fighter like me, and now look at him."

"Maxie was a champion."

"Well, so would I of been a champion if it hadn't of been for jealousy in high places. I tell you, I was being groomed for stardom when Mrs. Steptoe comes along and takes me away from it all. And all that stands between me and it now is not having the dough for my transportation."

"A lesson or two from me, and we'll soon adjust that. You'll send those dukes and earls back from the garden party in their shirts."

"I cert'ny will. Say, listen," said Mr. Steptoe, regarding Joss with affection and respect. "You're all right!"

"I'm one of the nicest fellows you ever met. In proof of which take these."

"Cheese!"

"I merely needed them at the outset of our acquaintance to ensure the establishing of our relations on a chummy basis. And now," said Joss briskly, "as time is getting on, climb into that shirt."

The joyous light died out of the other's eyes.

"Must I?"

"I'm afraid so. People are coming to dinner."

"Just a bunch of stiffs."

"The stiffer the stiffs, the stiffer the shirt front. That is the fundamental law on which society rests. So upsy-daisy, Steptoe, and get it over."

"Well, if you say so."

"That's my brave little man. And now," said Joss, who had been looking out of the window, "I must leave you. There's somebody down in the garden that I want to see."

❀ CHAPTER 9

SALLY HAD DRESSED for dinner early, in order to be able to enjoy a stroll in the garden before the guests should arrive. Claines Hall was one of the moated houses of England, and a walk beside those still waters always refreshed her after one of her visits to London.

Her thoughts, as she leaned over the low wall, looking down at the fish darting in and out of the weeds, had turned to Joss. As his social sponsor she felt herself concerned in his fortunes. She wondered how he was settling down in the servants' hall and hoped that that exuberance of his had not led him into the perpetration of one of those *gaffes* which are so rightly resented in such places.

It was nice, at any rate, to find that he had been an outstanding success with Mrs. Steptoe. That autocrat's enthusiastic responses to her rather apprehensive inquiries had astonished Sally. Mrs. Steptoe had unhesitatingly stamped Joss with the seal of her approval as the goods. She had spoken in no measured terms of the quiet forcefulness of his personality, giving it as her opinion that this time the master of the house had come up against something red-hot. If this new fellow was as good as he seemed, said Mrs. Steptoe, not mincing her words, it was quite within the bounds of possibility that Howard might make his appearance at the garden party looking halfway human.

A cheery "Hoy!" broke the stillness, and she turned to see the very person she had been thinking about. Valets did not as a rule saunter about the gardens of Claines Hall in the quiet evenfall, but nobody had told Joss Weatherby that.

"So there you are," he said. "Do you know, in this uncertain light I mistook you for a wood nymph."

"Do you always shout 'Hoy!' at wood nymphs?"

"Nearly always."

"I suppose you know that valets aren't supposed to shout 'Hoy!' at people?"

"You must open a conversation somehow."

"Well, if you want to attract, for instance, Mrs. Steptoe's attention, it would be more suitable to say 'Hoy, madam.' "

"Or 'Hoy, dear lady!' "

"Yes, that would be friendlier."

"Thanks. I'll remember it." He joined her at the wall and stood scrutinizing the fish for a moment in silence. The evening was very still. Somewhere in the distance sheep bells were tinkling, and from one of the windows of the house there came the sound of a raucous voice rendering the *Lambeth Walk*. Despite the shirt, Joss had left Mr. Steptoe happy, even gay. "This is a lovely place," he said.

"I'm glad you like it."

"An earthly Paradise, absolutely. Though mark you," said Joss, who believed in coming to the point, "a gasworks in Jersey City would be all right with me, so long as you were there. 'A book of verses underneath the bough—' "

The quotation was familiar to Sally, and she felt it might be better to change the subject.

"How are you getting on?"

"Fine. Couldn't be better. I was hoping to run across you, and here you are. And as I was saying, 'a jug of wine, a loaf of bread and thou beside me, singing in the wilderness—' "

"I didn't mean in the wilderness. I meant in the servants' hall."

"Oh, the servants' hall? I'm its pet."

"Chibnall, of course, is the man you have to conciliate. His word can make or break."

"I have Chibnall in my pocket."

"Really?"

"We're like Cohen and Corcoran. One of those beautiful friendships. We hadn't known each other half an hour before he was taking his hair down and confiding in me. Did you know he was engaged to the barmaid at the local pub?"

"No."

"Perhaps it hasn't been given out yet. And he was a good deal upset because he found her this morning straightening a commercial traveler's tie. Oh, curse of marriage, he said to himself, that we can call these delicate creatures ours but not their appetites. His impulse was to write her a stinker."

"And did you approve?"

"No. I was against it. I pointed out to him that it is of the essence of a barmaid's duties that she be all things to all men and that it had probably been a mere professional gesture, designed purely to stimulate trade. I am a close enough student of human nature to be aware that a commercial traveler who has had his tie straightened by a pretty girl with copper-colored hair is far more likely to order a second beer than one to whom such girl has been distant and aloof."

"That's true. He must have found you a great comfort."

"Oh, he did. He's going to introduce me to her tomorrow."

"You seem to have comforted Mr. Steptoe too. That sounds like him singing."

"Yes. I found him rather moody, but I dropped a few kindly words, and they cheered him up like a noggin of J. B. Duff's sherry. I forgot to ask about that, by the way. Did you and he finish the bottle after I had left?"

"Not quite."

"Was the interview satisfactory?"

"Very, thanks."

"Let me see, I forget what it was you were seeing him about."

"You should take one of those memory courses. How do you get on with the others?"

"They eat out of my hand."

"Has Mrs. Barlow given you a nice room?"

"Terrific."

"Then you think you will be happy here?"

"Ecstatically."

"How are you going to manage about looking after Mr. Steptoe? Can you valet?"

"You have touched on my secret sorrow. I can't. But it's all arranged. Immediately upon arrival I summoned the staff and addressed them. I said that if they were prepared to take my work off my hands I was prepared to pay well for good service. I had the meeting with me from the start, and the details were speedily fixed up. Charles, the footman, will see to the technical side of Mr. Steptoe's valeting. The matter of my morning cup of tea is in the capable hands of the kitchen maid. The cook has contracted to see that a few sandwiches shall be beside my bed last thing at night, in case I get peckish in the small hours. The whisky and soda to accompany them will, of course, be in Chibnall's department."

Sally stared. For one disloyal moment she found herself regretting that Lord Holbeton had not more of this spirit of enterprise. It might have been purely her fancy, but she thought she had detected in the latter's manner, when she broached the idea of stealing Mrs. Chavender's portrait, a certain listlessness and lack of enthusiasm.

"You're quite an organizer."

"I like to get working smoothly."

"What used you to be before this? A captain of industry? But I was forgetting. Mr. Duff said you were an artist."

"Yes."

"Then what were you doing in his office? When I came in, I thought you must be a partner or something."

"That is a mistake lots of people used to make. My air of quiet dignity was misleading. I was a kind of tame artist employed by the firm to do illustrations for advertisements and so on. Among other things I did the posters for Paramount Ham."

"Oh no!"

"All right, I don't like them myself."

"But Mr. Duff told me you painted that portrait of Mrs. Chavender that's in the breakfast room."

"Quite true."

"Then why—?"

"The whole trouble was," said Joss, "that the necessity for eating thrust itself into the foreground of my domestic politics. When I painted that portrait I was in the chips. I had a private income—the young artist's best friend. It was later converted to his own use by the lawyer who had charge of it, he getting the feeling one day that his need was greater than mine. When you're faced by the pauper's home you have to take what you can get."

"Yes," said Sally, who had had the same experience. "But what a shame! I'm sorry."

"Thanks," said Joss. "Thanks for being sorry. Well, I struggled along for a while, getting thinner and thinner, and finally did what I ought to have had the sense to do at the start. I saved J. B. Duff from a watery grave. We were at Easthampton at the time, he on his yacht, I holding an executive post in a local soda fountain, and we met in mid-ocean. I got him to shore, and in a natural spasm of gratitude he added me to his London staff. He was just leaving for London to take charge. I have an idea he has regretted it since. Thinking it over, I believe he wishes occasionally that he had gone down for the third time."

"I can see how you might not be everybody's dream employee."

"Too affable, you think?"

"A little, perhaps. Well, it's a shame."

"Oh, all in the day's work. Some day I hope to be able to be a portrait painter again. The difficulty is, of course, that in order to paint portraits you have to have sitters, and you can't get sitters till you've made a name, and you can't make a name till you've painted portraits. It is what is known as a vicious circle."

"Very vicious."

"Almost a menace. But let's not waste time talking about me. Let's go on to that dress you're wearing. It's stupendous."

"Thank you."

"It looks as if it were woven of mist and moonbeams. Mist and moonbeams, and you inside. Beat that for a combination. It's a most extraordinary thing. You seem to go from strength to strength. When you came into the office this morning in that blue frock I thought it was the last word in woman's wear. And now you knock my eye out with this astounding creation. But of course it isn't the upholstery; it's you. You would look wonderful in anything. Tell me," said Joss, "there's a thing I've been wanting to discuss with you ever since we met. Do you believe in love at first sight?"

Once more Sally had the feeling that the conversation might be changed.

"The ducks nest on that island over there," she said, pointing at a dim mass that loomed amid the shadows of the moat.

"Let them," said Joss cordially. "Do you?"

"Do I what?"

"Believe in love at first sight? Chibnall does."

A car rounded the corner of the drive and came raspingly to a halt at the front door.

"I must go," said Sally.

"Oh no, don't."

"People are arriving."

"Just a bunch of stiffs. I have this on Mr. Steptoe's authority. Pay no attention to them."

"Good night."

"You are really going?"

"Yes."

"Then I shall look forward to seeing you tomorrow, and we will take up this subject where we left off. There was some famous fellow who fell in love at first sight. Not Chibnall. Somebody else. Where do you stroll in the mornings?"

"I don't stroll. I work."

"Work?"

"Yes. I see the cook—"

"Don't take her on at craps."

"And I do the flowers and I brush the dog—"

"I'll help you brush the dog."

"No, you won't."

"Why not?"

"It would excite remark."

"I being a humble valet?"

"You being a humble valet."

"What a curse these social distinctions are. They ought to be abolished. I remember saying that to Karl Marx once, and he thought there might be an idea for a book in it. Romeo! That's the name I was trying to think of."

"What about him?"

"He fell in love at first sight, like Chibnall and—"

"Good night," said Sally.

❂ CHAPTER 10

IT WAS ON A TUESDAY that Mr. Duff had conferred with Sally in his office. Wednesday morning found him in the bar parlor of the Rose and Crown, sipping a small gin and ginger.

J. B. Duff was not a man who procrastinated. He thought on his feet and let no grass grow under them. Sally had returned to Claines

Hall at half-past four on the previous afternoon, charged with the task of opening negotiations with Lord Holbeton for the removal of Mrs. Chavender's portrait. At seven Mr. Duff was alighting at Loose Chippings station, all ready to be on the spot the moment anything broke. But one glance out of the window, as his cab rolled up the High Street, had been enough to tell him that this was not the place of his dreams. As he sipped his gin and ginger he was feeling homesick.

Towns like Loose Chippings (Population 4916) are all right if you are fond of towns with Populations of 4916, but Mr. Duff's tastes had always been metropolitan. And now, although it was so brief a time ago that his arrival had made the Population 4917, it seemed to him that he had been here ever since he was a small boy, getting more bored every minute. Like some minstrel of Tin Pan Alley, he was wishing that he could go back, back, back to the place where he was born, which was Greater New York—or, failing that, to his adopted city of London.

There is never a great deal doing in the bar parlor of a country inn at eleven o'clock in the morning. It is only later in the day that it becomes the hub of the neighborhood's social life, attracting all that is gayest and wittiest for miles around. The only other occupant of the room at this moment was the girl with copper-colored hair who sat behind the counter reading a mystery story. Vera Pym, barmaid, the affianced of Chibnall, the butler.

The first thing any regular client would have noticed, had he entered, was that Miss Pym was strangely silent. As a rule when she found herself alone with a customer she felt it her duty to be the hostess, and it was her practice to chat with great freedom, ranging vivaciously from politics and the weather to darts gossip and the new films. But now she had not spoken for nearly ten minutes. She sat reading her book and from time to time shooting quick, sidelong glances in Mr. Duff's direction. There was nervousness in these glances and a sort of shocked horror.

This, as we say, would have mystified the regular client. But her taciturnity may be readily explained. What was causing it was the fact that Mr. Duff was wearing on his upper lip a large mustache of the soup-strainer type. It lent to his aspect a strange and rather ghastly menace. Who knew, the observer felt as he saw it, what sinister things might not be lurking within that undergrowth, waiting to spring out and pounce?

That was what Miss Pym was feeling as she eyed it with those quick, sidelong glances. She had a complex about mustaches. So many of the worst bounders in the crime fiction to which she was addicted had affected them. The mysterious leper and the man with the missing toe were examples that leaped to her mind. In both these instances the shrubbery had proved to be as false as its wearer's heart, and the more she eyed Mr. Duff's the surer she became that it was not a natural disfigurement but had been stuck on with glue.

It was no idle whim that had led Mr. Duff to bar his features to the general public in this manner. Prudence and foresight had guided his actions. In coming to Loose Chippings, only a stone's throw from the residence of Mrs. Chavender, he had never lost sight of the fact that he was entering a danger zone. At any moment he might run into his old love, and the thought of such an encounter was one that froze the grand old bachelor's blood. False mustaches cost money, but he had considered it money well spent.

He finished his gin and ginger and got up.

"Say," he said, and Miss Pym leaped like a rising trout. A most impossible outsider, who went about shooting people with a tommy gun, had just said "Say" in the story she was reading.

"Sir?" she faltered.

"How do you get to a place called Claines Hall?"

"Turn to the left as you leave the inn and straight along the road," said Miss Pym faintly.

"Thanks," said Mr. Duff and, making for the door, collided with Chibnall, who was entering at the moment, accompanied by Joss.

"Pardon," said Chibnall.

"Grrh," said Mr. Duff.

Joss looked after him, puzzled. Mr. Duff reminded him in an odd sort of way of someone he had met somewhere, possibly in a nightmare. He found himself, however, unable to place him and came back to the present to find that Chibnall was presenting him to his betrothed.

"Mr. Weatherby is Mr. Steptoe's new personal attendant."

"How do you do, Mr. Weatherby?"

"How do you do?" said Joss. He submitted Miss Pym to a quick inspection and was able to assure Chibnall with a swift lift of the right eyebrow that in his opinion the other's judgment had been sound. A girl well fitted to be the butler's bride was Joss's verdict.

Gratified by this, Chibnall talked easily and well, and for some minutes it seemed that a perfect harmony was to prevail. Then he struck what was to prove to be a discordant note.

"Who was the walrus?" he asked, for he was always interested in new faces in the bar parlor.

Miss Pym polished a glass thoughtfully. Her manner, which had been animated, had become grave.

"I've never seen him before."

"I thought I had," said Joss. "His face seemed somehow familiar."

"He's staying at the inn," said Miss Pym. "And if you want to know what I think, Sidney—"

Chibnall laughed amusedly, as one who has heard this before and knows what is coming. To Joss, who had a sensitive ear, it seemed that there was far too strong a note of "Silly little woman," for she bridled visibly.

"All right. You can laugh as much as you like, but if you want to know what I think, I believe he's a crook."

Chibnall laughed again, once more with offensive masculine superiority.

"You and your crooks. What's gone and put that idea into your head?"

"I think it's suspicious, him being at the inn. He's not an artist; he's not a commercial; and he hasn't come for the fishing, because he's not brought any rods and things."

"He may be one of these writers, come down here to work where it's quiet."

"Well, what's he wearing a false mustache for?"

"How do you know it's false?"

"I have a feeling."

"Pooh!"

"Pooh to you!" retorted Miss Pym.

It seemed to Joss that he was becoming involved in a lovers' quarrel. This, and the fact that he had promised to meet Mr. Steptoe in the stable yard at noon and give him a craps lesson, decided him to finish his half of bitter and leave. He excused himself and went out, and Chibnall, lighting a cigarette, took up the discussion where it had been broken off.

"If you want to know what's the matter with you, my girl, you read too many of these trashy detective stories."

"Better than reading silly novelettes."

"May I ask why you call novelettes silly?"

"Because they are."

"Mere abuse is no criticism."

"Well, they're full of things happening that don't happen."

"Such as?"

"Well, what we were talking about the other day. Whoever heard of a young fellow being buzzed out of his home because his father wanted him to marry somebody and he wouldn't?"

Chibnall blew an airy smoke ring. With subtle cunning he had contrived to work the conversation round to the exact point where he wanted it. His love, deep though it was, had never blinded him to the fact that what the modern young woman needed, for the discipline of her soul, was to be properly scored off and put in her place from time to time.

"You will doubtless be surprised to learn," he said with quiet satisfaction, "that a case of that very nature has come under my own personal notice. I allude to Mr. Weatherby, who has just left us."

"I suppose he's the son of a duke, who gave him the push for not marrying the girl he had picked out for him?"

"He did not specify a duke—he merely referred to a titled father —but that, substantially, was the story he told."

"He was pulling your leg."

"Not at all. I had spotted already that he was no ordinary valet. You should have seen him turning up his nose at his room and insisting on something more like what he'd been accustomed to."

"What cheek! Didn't you tell him off?"

"Certainly not. I wouldn't have taken the liberty."

Miss Pym polished a glass, derision in every flick of the cloth.

"And then, of course, he tried to borrow money from you?"

"On the contrary, he tipped me ten pounds. A little more of that sort of thing and I'll have enough saved to buy that pub I've got my eye on, and we'll be able to put up the banns."

Miss Pym had lowered the glass. There was horror in her eyes.

"Ten pounds?"

"Ten pounds."

"Ten *pounds?*"

"I thought you'd be surprised."

"Surprised? I'm scared stiff. I suppose you know what this fellow is?"

"Is he a crook too?"

"Of course he is. He must be. Don't you ever go to the pictures? He's one of these gangsters that's just pulled off a big thing and is using the Hall as a hide-out. Where would a chap whose father had bunged him out get ten pounds to tip people with?"

Chibnall frowned. He did not like this feverish imagination of hers. He thought it unwholesome.

"Pooh!" he said.

"Pooh to you!" said Miss Pym. "Oh well, I don't suppose there's a hope of opening your eyes to the realities of life, but everybody except you knows that that sort of thing is happening all the time.

You read your *News of the World,* don't you? You've heard of Mayfair Men, haven't you? But you can talk to some people till you're blue
in the face."

"Don't you go getting blue in the face. It wouldn't suit you. Oh
well," said Chibnall, looking at his watch, "back to the old job, I
suppose. You'll be round for tea tomorrow?"

The question was purely a perfunctory one. Tomorrow was Miss
Pym's afternoon off, and on these occasions she always came to his
pantry for a cozy cup of tea. To his amazement she was evasive.

"I'll ring you up."

"How do you mean, ring me up?"

"Just possible," said Miss Pym, who had been deeply piqued by
her loved one's skepticism, "that I may be engaged."

The butler froze.

"Oh, very well," he said aloofly. "If I'm not in, leave a message."

He stalked out, hurt and offended. As he made his way along the
road all those old doubts which Joss's soothing reasoning had dispelled
came back to gnaw at his heart. The image of that commercial traveler
rose before his eyes. In speaking of this butler we must speak of one
that loved not wisely but too well, of one not easily jealous but being
wrought perplexed in the extreme. Dark suspicions came flooding in
on Sidney Chibnall as he walked, and he writhed freely.

Mr. Duff, meanwhile, was approaching Claines Hall.

In the light of what has been said about his apprehensions concerning a chance meeting with Mrs. Chavender it might seem that a madness had fallen upon this ham distributor, robbing him of his usual
calm judgment. But he had the situation well in hand. It was not his
intention to penetrate to the Hall's front door—he was not so reckless
as that—he merely intended to prowl about in the vicinity on the
chance of getting a word with Lord Holbeton.

He was intensely anxious to establish contact with that young man
at the first possible moment, in order to learn from him how prospects
looked for an early delivery of the portrait. The sooner he could get
away from the Rose and Crown, whose eccentric cooking had already
begun to give him the feeling that sinister things were happening inside
him, the better he would be pleased.

The distance from the inn door to the main entrance of the Hall
was just under a mile, and he had covered the greater part of it when
he perceived that this was his lucky morning. Just ahead of him, turning in at the gate, was the very man he sought. Though not fond of

active exercise, he broke into a clumsy gallop, at the same time shouting that favorite word of his—"Hey!"

It was in order to ponder over the future that Lord Holbeton had gone for his solitary walk. He found in this future much food for meditation.

Sally, in assigning to him the task of snipping portraits out their frames in a house where he was an honored guest, had seemed to take it for granted that he would leap at it without hesitation. He found himself unable to share her sunny enthusiasm.

All crooners are nervous men—the twiddly bits seem to affect their moral stamina—and Lord Holbeton was no exception. Only the reflection of how much he needed the money had enabled him even to contemplate the venture as a possibility. And the more he contemplated it the less of a possibility did it seem. As he started to walk up the drive he had just begun to toy with the thought of what would happen if Mrs. Steptoe caught him in the act.

The shout and the sound of pursuing footsteps in his rear came to him, consequently, at a moment when he was not feeling at the peak of his form. He turned and was aware of a densely mustached stranger galloping up, shouting, "Hey!"

The attitude of people toward densely mustached strangers who are galloping up, shouting, "Hey!" varies a good deal according to the individual. Joss Weatherby in such circumstances would have stood his ground and investigated the phenomenon. So, probably, would Napoleon, Joe Louis and Attila the Hun. Lord Holbeton was made of more neurotic stuff. The spectacle, acting upon his already enfeebled morale, was too much for him. Directing at the other a single, horrified glance, he was off up the drive with a briskness which would have put him immediately out of range of anything that was not a jack rabbit. And even a jack rabbit would have been extended.

J. B. Duff gave up the chase and came to a halt, panting. He mopped his forehead, and broken words, unworthy of a leading provision merchant, fell from his trembling lips.

He felt profoundly discouraged. He had never thought highly of Lord Holbeton as an agent, and this extraordinary behavior on his part convinced him that the fellow was a broken reed. Like so many heavily mustached men, Mr. Duff was unaware of the spiritual shock, akin to that experienced by Macbeth on witnessing the approach of the forest of Dunsinane, which the fungus had on nervous persons who saw it suddenly on its way toward them. All he felt was that, in hoping that a total loss like the sprinter who had just left him would be capable of the dashing act of purloining the Chavender portrait, he had been guilty of wishful thinking of the worst type.

Yet, failing him, to whom could he look for assistance?

Just when it was that a voice whispered in his ear that homely saw: "If you want a thing well done do it yourself," he could not have said. One moment the idea was not there; the next it was, and he was examining it carefully with a growing feeling that he had got something.

It is possible, however, that he might have been unable to screw his courage to the sticking point had there not come along at this moment from the direction of the house a two-seater car, containing in addition to the very pretty girl at the wheel, in whom he recognized his visitor of yesterday, two passengers, one human, the other canine. Mrs. Chavender's Pekingese, Patricia, had woken up that morning a little below par, and Sally was driving her and it to the veterinary surgeon in Lewes.

Mrs. Chavender gave Mr. Duff an uninterested glance in passing, evidently taking him for just another of the strange fauna which are always drifting up and down the drives of country houses. He, on his side, gasped quickly and reeled a little, like an African explorer who sees a rhinoceros pass by without having had its attention drawn to him. The luck of the Duffs, he felt, was in the ascendant. The coast was now clear, and he could carry on with an easy mind.

Ten minutes later, after one or two false starts, he had located the breakfast room and was peering through its open French windows at the fireplace and what hung above it.

Even now, though twenty-four hours had elapsed since they had had their little unpleasantness, Mr. Duff's feelings toward Joss Weatherby were not cordial. The desire to skin him still lingered. But he had to admit that the young hound, in painting that portrait, had done a good job. It was all he had said it was, and more, and it drew Mr. Duff like a magnet. He was inside the room, creeping across the floor like a leopard, when his concentration was disturbed by the falling on his shoulder of a heavy hand, and he found himself gazing into the eyes of an enormous man with a squashed nose and ears that seemed to be set at right angles to his singularly unprepossessing face.

"What's the idea?" inquired this person.

Mr. Duff's heart, which had been dashing about in his mouth like an imprisoned rabbit, returned slowly to its base. He swallowed once or twice, and his mustache trembled gently, like a field of daffodils stirred by a March wind.

"It's all right," he said ingratiatingly.

He had endeavored to inject into the words all the charm of which he was capable, and it was with a pang that he saw that his effort had been wasted.

"You go spit up a rope," retorted his companion. "It's not all right. What you doing in my house?"

"Are you Mr. Steptoe?"

"I am."

The situation was unquestionably a difficult one, but Mr. Duff persevered.

"Pleased to meet you," he said.

"You won't be long," predicted the other.

"I guess it seems funny to you, finding me here."

"A scream. I'm laughing my head off."

"I can explain everything."

"I'm listening."

"Lemme tell you a little story."

"It better be good."

"My name is Duff."

Mr. Steptoe started. It was plain that the name had touched a chord.

"Duff? The guy that was on the phone yesterday, making an offer for that portrait?"

"That's right."

There was no need for the little story. Mr. Steptoe was not a highly intelligent man, but he could put two and two together.

"Now I got it. So when Mrs. Steptoe turned you down you think to yourself you'll gumshoe in and swipe the thing?"

"No, no. I—er—just wanted to look at it."

"Oh yeah?"

"Well, I'll tell you."

"You don't have to. Listen. How bad do you want that portrait?"

"Listen. I've just got to have it. Can you," asked Mr. Duff, his voice trembling emotionally, "understand a man pining for a woman he's loved and lost and wanting to have her portrait so that he can sit and look at it and dream of what might have been?"

"Sure," said Mr. Steptoe cordially. "I've seen somebody doing that in the pictures. I've an idea it was Lionel Barrymore. Either him or Adolph Menjou. I guessed it must be something like that when Mrs. Steptoe told me about you phoning. Listen. Was it right what she said, that you're willing to pay good money for it?"

"Listen," said Mr. Duff. "The sky's the limit."

"You mean that?"

"Well, within reason," said Mr. Duff, his native prudence jogging his elbow.

"Then let's go," said Mr. Steptoe. "You need the old portrait. I need the old money. Got a knife?"

"No."

"Nor me. I'll go fetch one," said Mr. Steptoe and, bounding to the door, checked himself just in time to avoid a collision with the lady of the house. He recovered his balance, which he had lost by tripping over his large feet, a constant habit of his pugilistic days and one which had done much to prevent him rising to great heights in his profession. "Oh, hello, honey," he said, giggling girlishly. "Meet Mr. Duff."

It seemed to Mr. Duff, as it would have seemed to any sensitive man, that at this woman's entrance a chill had crept into the warmth of the summer day. He fingered his mustache nervously.

Mrs. Steptoe's eyes were roaming over his person with a distressing effect on his equanimity. They were at their coldest and hardest. Like her husband she could put two and two together, and she found no difficulty in accounting for Mr. Duff's presence. He had come, she concluded, to plead in person for the boon which had been denied him over the telephone. Her lights tightened. She disapproved of these follow-up campaigns. When she announced a decision, she liked to have it accepted.

"Duff?"

"I spoke to you on the telephone yesterday, Mrs. Steptoe—"

"Yes. And I have nothing to add to what I said then. The portrait is not for sale. Howard, show Mr. Duff out."

"Yes, honey."

In the aspect of the two men, as they shambled through the French windows, there was a crushed defeatism which would have reminded Napoleon, had he been present, of the old days at Moscow. Neither spoke until they were out of sight and hearing of the room they had left. Then Mr. Steptoe, producing a handkerchief and passing it over his brow, said, "Cheese!" adding the words: "No dice!"

"Brother," he went on, clarifying his meaning beyond all chance of misunderstanding, "it's off!"

"What!"

"It's cold."

"You mean you won't get it?"

"I haven't the nerve."

"Think of the money," pleaded Mr. Duff.

Mr. Steptoe was thinking of the money, and it was as if wildcats were clawing his vitals. His face was drawn with anguish.

Then abruptly, it brightened, and Mr. Duff, startled by his sudden look of animation, wondered what had caused it. It seemed absurd to suppose that the other had had an idea, yet something was unmistakably stirring behind that concrete brow.

"Oi!" cried Mr. Steptoe.

"Yes?" said Mr. Duff. "Yes?"

"Listen. What's that thing fellows have to have? You know, when they're up against a stiff proposition and get cold feet."

"Grit?"

"Something to give them grit. Moral support! That's it. If I'm to put this deal through I got to have moral support. And I know where to get it. My new valet. We'll bring him in on this."

"Your valet?"

"Wait till you see him. He's a wonder. Come along to the stable yard and we'll put it up to him. He's waiting there to give me a craps lesson."

Joss was not only waiting but getting tired of waiting. He was, indeed, on the point of giving his pupil up and leaving in dudgeon, when he observed him approaching. And with him, he saw with surprise, was the mustached stranger of the inn who had reminded him of something he had seen in a nightmare.

And now that the latter was close enough to be examined in detail recognition came.

"J. B.!"

"Weatherby!"

"Well, for Pete's sake," said Mr. Steptoe, marveling. "Do you guys know each other?"

"Do we know each other?" said Joss. "Why, I look on J. B. Duff as a grandfather. Who ran to catch me when I fell and would some pretty story tell and kiss the place to make it well? J. B. Duff."

"Well, say, that's swell," said Mr. Steptoe. "If you're that way there's no need for me to hang around, explaining things. I'm going to go get me a little drink. I kind of need it."

His departure was scarcely noticed. Joss was staring at Mr. Duff. Mr. Duff was staring at Joss.

"Weatherby!" gasped Mr. Duff at length. "What the devil are you doing here?"

There was a stern look on Joss's face.

"Don't go into side issues, J. B.," he said. "I demand an explanation. Of the growth on the upper lip," he added. "It's frightful. Ghastly."

"Never mind—"

"There must be a certain code in these matters. Either a man is Grover Whalen or he is not Grover Whalen. If he is not he has no right to wear a mustache like that."

"Never mind about my mustache. I asked you what you were doing here."

Joss raised his eyebrows.

"My dear J. B., when you madly dispensed with my services you surely did not expect that a man of my gifts would be out of employment long? I was snapped up immediately. I have a sort of general commission to look after things here. You might call me the Claines Hall Führer."

"Steptoe said you were his valet."

"Yes, that's another way of putting it."

"There's something behind this."

"I see it's hopeless to try to conceal anything from one of your penetration. If you really want to know, J. B., I took on the job so that I could be with Miss Fairmile. You may possibly recall that I spoke of her with some warmth at our last meeting. Since then my feelings have, if such a thing were possible, deepened. If you would like it in words of one syllable, J. B., I'm in love."

"Oh?"

"A rather chilly comment on a great romance, but let it go. And now about the mustache. Explain fully, if you please."

Mr. Duff had begun to see that all things were working together for good.

"Listen," he said. "Do you want your job back?"

"I am prepared to hear what you have to say on the point."

"Then listen," said Mr. Duff.

Mr. Steptoe reappeared, looking refreshed.

"Told him?" he asked.

"I was just going to," said Mr. Duff. "Listen."

"Listen," said Mr. Steptoe.

"Now I've got it," said Joss. "You want me to listen. Why didn't you say so before?"

He stood in thoughtful silence while Mr. Duff placed the facts in the case before him.

"Well?" said Mr. Steptoe.

"I beg your pardon? You spoke?"

"Will you?"

"Will I what? Oh, pinch the portrait? Of course, of course. I'm sorry I was distrait. I was just wondering how J. B. gets his food past the

zareba. I suppose it works on a hinge or something. Yes, of course,
I shall be delighted."

"When? Tonight?"

"Tonight's the night," said Joss. "And now away with trivialities.
Take these bones, Steptoe, and I'll show you how to roll them right."

⊛ CHAPTER 11

NIGHT HAD FALLEN on Claines Hall, terminating a day which had
been fraught with no little interest for many of those beneath its roof.
But to only a limited number of these had it brought restful slumber.
Lord Holbeton was awake. Chibnall was awake. Mr. Steptoe was
awake. Joss was awake. Mrs. Chavender, also, had found it impossible
to start getting her eight hours.

As a rule this masterful woman shared with Napoleon the ability
to sleep the moment the head touched the pillow. Others might count
sheep, but she had no need for such adventitious aids to repose. She
just creamed her face, basketed her Pekingese, climbed into bed,
switched the light out and there she was.

Yet tonight she lay wakeful.

Ever since her return from Brighton there had been noticeable in
Mrs. Chavender's manner a strange moodiness. There was not a
great deal of rollicking gaiety at Claines Hall, but from what there
was she had held herself aloof. And if an observer could have seen
her now as she lay staring into the darkness, he would have remarked
that this moodiness still prevailed.

It was as she heaved a weary sigh and fell to wondering whether to
get up and go to the library for the book which she had been reading
after dinner or to stay where she was and give the sandman another
chance that a faint whoofle from the direction of the door and a
scratching of delicate paws on the woodwork told her that Patricia,
her Peke, was up and about and wished to leave the room.

"Okay," said Mrs. Chavender, rather pleased that the problem had
been settled for her. "Just a minute. Hold the line."

She turned on the light and rose and donned a dressing gown.

"Grass?" she said.

The Peke nodded briefly.

"I thought as much," said Mrs. Chavender. A slight disorder of
the digestive tract, due to a surfeit of cheese, had been the cause of

that visit to the vet, and on these occasions the dumb chum was apt to want to head for the lawn and nibble.

The French windows of the breakfast room suggested themselves as the quickest way to the great outdoors. She proceeded thither and threw back the heavy curtains. The cool fragrance of the night, pouring in, seemed to bring momentary relief from the cares which were gnawing at her.

"There you are," she said. "Push along and help yourself. You'll find me in the library."

Patricia pottered out and for some minutes roamed the dewy lawn, sniffing at this blade of grass and that like a connoisseur savoring rival vintages of brandy. Presently she found some excellent stuff and became absorbed in it. Perhaps a quarter of an hour passed before she was at liberty to turn her attention elsewhere. When she did she beheld a sight which brought her up with a sharp turn. She looked again to make sure that she had not been mistaken. But her eyes had not deceived her. The light in the breakfast room was on, and a man was standing in the window. He remained there for an instant, then drew the curtains.

Patricia stood staring. She was uncertain what to make of this. It might be all right, or it might not be all right. Time alone could tell. Offhand she was inclined to think it fishy.

Lord Holbeton, having drawn the curtains, took a knife from the pocket of his dressing gown and walked to the fireplace. There for a while he stood, exchanging glances with the portrait which hung above it.

It was in no mood of gay adventure that Lord Holbeton had embarked upon this midnight raid. He definitely did not like the job. Sally had urged him to it with girlish eagerness, but if it had been merely a question of obliging Sally he would have been in bed. The motivating force behind his actions was the lust for gold.

Pondering over that disturbing encounter in the drive, he had suddenly realized that the mustached stranger must have been Mr. Duff, whom he knew to be established at the local inn, and he was able to understand now why Mr. Duff had shouted "Hey!" and come charging up at the double. Obviously he had been anxious for a conference. It was the thought of how he had avoided that conference and an accurate estimate of what the effects of that avoidance on his always rather easily annoyed trustee would be that had spurred Lord Holbeton on to take action. Only by securing the portrait and delivering it at the earliest possible moment could he hope to wipe out the bad impression he must have made and bring the other to a frame of mind where he would reach for his fountain pen and start writing checks.

That was what had made him creep to the breakfast room in the watches of the night. But it could not make him like it.

Oddly enough, the discovery that the window was open had not caused him any additional concern. The inference he drew was not that others beside himself were abroad in the darkness but that whoever was supposed to lock up had been negligent. As a matter of fact, he had been intending to open it himself, for Sally, showing an easy familiarity with criminal procedure which he privately felt a really nice girl should not have possessed, had impressed it upon him that this must be made to look like an outside job.

He wrenched his gaze from that of the portrait, which he was beginning to find hypnotic, and opened his knife. If 'twere done, he felt, then 'twere well 'twere done quickly.

At this moment the door flew open and there entered at a brisk pace a gentleman with a battle-ax. He advanced upon Lord Holbeton like a Danish warrior of the old school coming ashore from his galley, and the latter, dropping the knife, made an energetic attempt to get through the wall backwards. Not even on the occasion when he had called upon Mr. Duff and asked him for a thousand pounds so that he could go to Italy and have his voice trained had he been conscious of so urgent a desire to be elsewhere.

His disintegration was, however, only momentary. A second glance showed him that martial figure was merely Chibnall.

Chibnall, like Mrs. Chavender, had found himself unable, on retiring for the night, to fall into a refreshing slumber. Airily, even mockingly, though he had received them at the time, Miss Pym's alarmist theories regarding Joss Weatherby had been sinking in throughout the day, and bedtime found him so entirely converted to them that sleep was out of the question.

Her remorseless reasoning had had its effect. Odd, he felt, that he had not spotted for himself that palpable flaw in the new valet's story to which she had directed his attention. A young fellow, getting the bird from his father, gets it good and proper. The father, just before administering the boot, does not say, "Oh, by the way, you will be needing cash for expenses. Take these few hundreds." Where, then, as Miss Pym had asked, had Joss obtained the money in which he rolled?

And that stuff about Mayfair Men. That made you think a bit. Suave, presentable chaps they were, he had always been given to understand—just like this Weatherby.

At the moment when Lord Holbeton was entering the breakfast room Chibnall, too restless to remain between the sheets, had risen from his bed and gone to the window. And as Claines Hall was an L-shaped house, and his room in the smaller part of the L, he had been admirably placed to see the light when it flashed on. It confirmed his worst fears. Two minutes later he was on the spot, armed with the weapon which he had picked up while passing through the hall.

His disappointment at finding Lord Holbeton was great.

"Oh, it's you, m'lord," he said dejectedly.

Lord Holbeton, though a crooner, was not without a certain sagacity. Some explanation of his presence would, he realized, be required, and he had thought one up.

"I say, Chibnall, I saw a light in here."

"So did I, m'lord."

"It was still on when I got here."

"Indeed, m'lord?"

"And I found the window open. Did you lock it tonight? You did? Well, it was open when I arrived. Odd."

"Very odd, m'lord."

"In fact, a bit rummy."

"Yes, m'lord."

At this moment, just when their conversation promised to develop along interesting lines, it seemed to both men that the end of the world had suddenly come. It was, as a matter of fact, only Patricia barking, but that was the impression they got.

If there was one thing this Pekingese prided herself on it was her voice. She might not be big; she might look like a section of hearthrug, but she could bark. She was a coloratura soprano who thought nothing of starting at A in alt and going steadily higher, and when she went off unexpectedly under their feet like a bomb strong men were apt to lose their poise and skip like the high hills.

Until this moment what had kept her silent was the fact that the man she had seen had been inside the house, looking out, and not outside the house, looking in. This had decided her to suspend judgment until she could investigate further. But as she made for the breakfast room she had been feeling extremely dubious, and what had finally turned the scale was the sight of Lord Holbeton's dressing gown. It was of a pattern so loud and vivid that it seemed absurd to suppose that it could encase an honest man. Patricia threw her head back, allowed her eyes to bulge to their extremest limit and went into a trill of accidental grace notes. And simultaneously Mrs. Chavender, in the library, and Mrs. Steptoe, in her bedroom, started up and hurried to the spot.

Mrs. Chavender, being nearer, got there first and was just in time to see Patricia, a dog of action as well as words, bite Lord Holbeton shrewdly on the ankle.

The sight woke all the mother in her.

"What do you mean," she demanded sternly, snatching the Pekingese to her bosom, "by teasing the poor little thing when you know she's not well?"

It was while Lord Holbeton was endeavoring to select the most acid of the six replies which had suggested themselves to him that Mrs. Steptoe entered.

"What the heck?" inquired Mrs. Steptoe.

"Why, hullo, Mabel," said Mrs. Chavender. "You here? Doesn't anyone sleep in this joint?"

"I shouldn't think so," said Mrs. Steptoe tartly, "unless they're deaf."

"The dear old place has been a little on the noisy side tonight," admitted Mrs. Chavender. "Plenty of life and movement."

"I thought there had been a murder."

"I don't believe blood has actually been spilled, unless Lord Holbeton has lost a drop or two. From motives which she has not yet explained to me, though I assume they were sound, Patricia made a light supper off his leg."

"Chewed me to the bally bone," said Lord Holbeton morosely. "Get hydrophobia as likely as not."

Mrs. Steptoe addressed herself to the butler, appearing to consider him, in spite of the battle-ax, the most responsible party present.

"What is all this, Chibnall?"

"There was a light in the window, madam. I saw it from my room and felt it my duty to descend and investigate. On arrival I found his lordship here. He, too, had observed the light. And he informs me that when he entered he found the window open."

"I opened it," said Mrs. Chavender, "to let Patricia out."

"Indeed, madam? I was not aware of that."

"She wanted to go and eat grass."

"I quite understand, madam."

"Her tummy was upset."

"Precisely, madam. Grass in such circumstances is a recognized specific."

Whether Mrs. Steptoe was pleased or disappointed at this tame explanation of the affair it would have been difficult to say. Her

manner, when she spoke, was brusque, but then it always tended to
be a little on that side.

"Well, if your dog is sure it has had all the grass it requires,
Beatrice," she said, "perhaps we might all go back to bed and try to
get a little sleep."

Mrs. Chavender intimated that that was just what she was thinking,
and Lord Holbeton said he thought so, too, adding a little frostily that
this would enable him to bathe his ankle in cold water and get in
touch with the iodine bottle, thus possibly saving a human life.

"Shut that window, Chibnall."

"Very good, madam."

"Well, good night, all," said Mrs. Chavender. "No, Patricia, no
second helping."

She passed from the room, followed by Lord Holbeton, limping reproachfully. Patricia gave a final shrill comment on the dressing gown
before signing off.

Mrs. Steptoe clicked her tongue impatiently. Chibnall was standing
at the window, peering out as if rapt by the beauty of the night, and
she disapproved. When she told butlers to close windows she expected
an imitation of forked lightning.

"Chibnall!"

"Madam?"

"Be quick."

"Excuse me, madam."

"Well, what is it?"

The butler had closed the window and withdrawn into the room.
There was an urgency in his manner.

"I fancied I saw dim figures stealing across the lawn, madam."

"What?"

"Yes, madam. Two dim figures. They appeared to be coming in this
direction."

"What on earth," asked Mrs. Steptoe, not unreasonably, "would
dim figures be doing on the lawn at this time of night?"

"Burglars, no doubt, madam. If I might—"

He moved to the switch, and the next moment the room was in
darkness, a fact that seemed to make an unfavorable impression on
Mrs. Steptoe.

"You poor fish," she cried, forgetting in her agitation the respect
due to butlers, "what on earth are you doing?"

"I thought it advisable to extinguish the light, madam, in order not
to alarm these persons."

To a sentimentalist it would have seemed a kindly, rather pretty thought, but the exclamation that proceeded from the darkness suggested that Mrs. Steptoe found such consideration for the nervous systems of the criminal classes hypersensitive.

"I am in favor, if it can be contrived, madam, of catching the miscreants red-handed. I have closed the window. If they break the glass that will be proof of their unlawful intentions. As they enter the room I will switch the light on and confront them."

"Oh, I see. Well, don't let go of that battle-ax."

"I have it in readiness, madam. If I might make the suggestion, it would be best if we now preserved a complete silence."

They did so. There was a long moment of suspense. Then something tinkled in the darkness. Glass had fallen to the floor.

The light flashed on. It shone on Mr. Steptoe blinking, and behind him Joss, whose air was one of courteous interest.

If Joss had been aware that the idea of lending to the night's proceedings the aspect of an outside job had occurred independently to Sally he would have taken it as additional proof, if such were needed, that she and he were twin souls, for it was what he had thought of himself. Mr. Steptoe, a blunt, direct man, had been unable to see the point of getting out of the house merely in order to get into it again, but Joss had overruled him. These things, he had explained, should be done properly or not at all.

"Well!" said Mrs. Steptoe.

"Oh, there you are," said Joss heartily.

"Weatherby!"

"Madam? Ah, good evening, Chibnall," said Joss, not wishing to leave him out of the conversation.

"What the heck do you think you're doing? And you, Howard," demanded Mrs. Steptoe, turning on her mate, "what do you think *you're* doing?"

It was a question which Mr. Steptoe could see was prompted by a genuine desire for information, and he was in a position to answer it. But he shrank from doing so. He seemed to swallow something which his thorax was not quite wide enough to accommodate with comfort and cast at Joss the look of a drowning man anxious to be thrown a lifeline.

Joss did not fail him.

"I am afraid, madam," he said smoothly, "that I am wholly to blame for this untimely intrusion. Lying awake in bed just now, I happened to hear the nightingale and, feeling that Mr. Steptoe ought not to miss this treat, I woke him and suggested that he should accompany me into the garden."

"Oh!"

"Yes, madam. We could not see what flowers were at our feet, nor what soft incense hung upon the boughs, but we managed to catch a glimpse of the bird, did we not, sir?"

"Yeah," said Mr. Steptoe. "It was a whopper."

"Quite well developed," assented Joss. "And vocally in tremendous form. We listened, entranced. 'Thou wast not made for death, immortal bird,' said Mr. Steptoe, and I agreed with him. I often say that there is no melody quite like the song of the nightingale. Mr. Steptoe feels the same."

"Yeah," said Mr. Steptoe.

"He put forward the rather interesting theory that this was quite possibly the selfsame song that found a path through the sad heart of Ruth when, sick for home, she stood in tears amid the alien corn. I thought there might be something in it."

"Weatherby," said Mrs. Steptoe, "have you been drinking?"

"Only of the Pierian fount, madam."

The intellectual pressure of the conversation was becoming too much for Mrs. Steptoe.

"All this," she said, "doesn't explain why you come busting in through windows."

"In his anxiety to reach the garden, madam, Mr. Steptoe unfortunately omitted to take his latchkey with him, and we found ourselves shut out. Not wishing to disturb the house, I suggested that we should make an unobtrusive entrance through a window."

"Oh," said Mrs. Steptoe. She stood awhile in thought, then jerked an imperious hand toward the door. "Howard, go to bed."

"Yes, honey," said Mr. Steptoe obediently and shambled out. His mind was in a whirl, but there emerged from the welter one coherent thought. Like the poet Keats on a similar occasion, he wanted a drink. Oh, he was saying to himself as he mounted the stairs, for a beaker full of the warm South, full of the true, the blushful Hippocrene, and by a singular piece of good fortune he had the makings in a flask on the table beside his bed. His rather careworn manner softened, and he sucked in his lips in pleasant anticipation.

"Shut that window," said Mrs. Steptoe.

"Very good, madam," said Joss.

"Though it's hardly worth while after you've been punching holes in it," said Mrs. Steptoe, and left the room stiffly.

She was surprised to discover, as she reached the foot of the stairs, that she had been accompanied by her butler and paused to ascertain the reason for this matiness on his part.

"Yes, Chibnall?"

"I wonder if I might speak to you for a moment, madam?"

"You've picked a swell time for chatting. I need my beauty sleep. Well, all right, make it snappy."

"It is with reference to the young man Weatherby, madam."

"What about him?"

"I am not easy in my mind about his *bona fides,* madam. I find his behavior suspicious. Were you aware, madam, that he arrived at the Hall in his personal automobile."

"Did he?"

"Yes, madam. That was my reason for showing him to the drawing room. I naturally supposed him to be a guest."

Mrs. Steptoe pursed her lips. In her native California, of course, the incident would have been without significance. It is a very impoverished valet in the Golden State who does not dash up to the door in his private car. But in England, she knew, different conditions prevailed.

"Odd," she said.

"Yes, madam. It is also unusual for a young fellow in his position to give the butler in the establishment where he is taking service a present of ten pounds."

"Did he do that?"

"Yes, madam."

"H'm."

"A suggestion which has been advanced by a friend of mine to whom I confided the circumstances is that he is one of these Mayfair Men who, having recently pulled off a big job, is using the Hall for what is termed a hide-out."

"Nonsense."

"Just as you say, madam. But he seems a very peculiar valet to me. I certainly think it would be advisable to notify the police and have them institute inquiries into his antecedents."

"No, that's out," said Mrs. Steptoe decidedly. Chibnall had agitated her, but even in her agitation she did not lose sight of the fact that Joss, if a peculiar—and possibly a criminal—valet, was an extremely efficient one. By what magic he had wrought the miracle she could not say, but he had sent the hick Howard down to dinner on the previous night looking not merely respectable but refulgent. His shirt had shown like a lighthouse, so that baronets gaped at the sight of it. So had his shoes. And as for his collar and tie, they could have been used as exhibits in a lecture on what the smart dresser should wear. It would be madness to put the police on the trail of this wonder man.

On the other hand, she did not want to wake up one morning and find the place looted.

"I'm not going to have the house littered up with cops. You had better watch him."

"Very good, madam. I was about to suggest that, if the idea meets with your approval, I should pass the remainder of the night in the breakfast room. This would enable me to guard the tapestries."

"He can't be after those."

"They are extremely valuable."

"Yes, but if he had been trying to swipe them would he have taken Mr. Steptoe with him?"

"There is that, of course, madam."

"Still, I'm all for your spending the night in the breakfast room. I don't like leaving that broken window. Snap into it."

"Very good, madam."

In the breakfast room, meanwhile, Joss, having closed the window, had been standing in a train of thought. What had started this train of thought had been the sight of the knife which Lord Holbeton had dropped on the floor. He was at a loss to account for its presence there, but it seemed to him to come under the head of manna from heaven. Two things are essential to the purloining of a portrait from a country house—the first, opportunity; the second, some implement for removing the thing from its frame. He now had both.

He picked up the knife and, like Lord Holbeton, crossed to the fireplace. There, also like Lord Holbeton, he stood gazing at the portrait, thinking—though this Lord Holbeton had not done—what a remarkably good bit of work it was. Then, bringing up a chair and standing on it, he was about to start carving when a voice, speaking in his rear, brought him to the ground as if he had been lassoed.

"Ah!" said the voice.

Mrs. Chavender was standing in the doorway.

❀ CHAPTER 12

MRS. CHAVENDER'S APPEARANCE was always striking. It was now rendered additionally so by the circumstances that she, like himself, was armed to the teeth. There was a large knife in her hand. It made her look like Lady Macbeth.

Too well-bred to comment on this, Joss opened the conversation with a civil "Good evening."

"We meet again, Mrs. Chavender."

"We do, young Weatherby."

"You are doubtless surprised—"

"No, I'm not. Sally Fairmile told me you were here. And I know—Sh!" said Mrs. Chavender, breaking off her remarks. "There's someone coming."

"There always is in this house. It's the Claines Hall curse."

"Meet me in the library."

"Where is it?"

"Along the passage. I want to talk with you, young man. Yes, Chibnall?"

The butler was entering, bowed down beneath the weight of blankets and pillows. Though all enthusiasm to begin this vigil of his, he had taken time out to go to his room and collect the materials for making himself as comfortable as possible.

"Mrs. Steptoe desired me to pass the remainder of the night in here, madam."

"Why on earth?"

"One of the windows has become broken, madam, and Mrs. Steptoe is uneasy about having it left. It is possible," said Chibnall darkly, "that there may be suspicious characters about."

"Oh! Well, sooner you than me. Good night."

"Good night, madam."

Mrs. Chavender sailed from the room, and Chibnall looked at Joss coldly.

"Still here?"

"Just going. Tell me, my dear Chibnall, would you describe this as one of Claines Hall's ordinary nights? I merely want to know what to expect."

"Took you quite a time to close that window."

"No, no. I did it like a flash. But I was then engaged in conversation by the lady who has just left us. Are you really going to sleep in here?"

"I am."

"I'll bet you're not. You won't get a wink. I've tried dossing in chairs myself. No, what you ought to do, my dear fellow," said Joss winningly, "is to toddle back to your little bed and curl up your pink toes. Nobody will know."

"Thank you. I prefer to do my duty."

"Oh. Well, in that case, good night."

"Good night."

As Joss made his way to the library he was finding the atmosphere too heavily charged with mystery for comfort. Chibnall had been mysterious. So had Mrs. Chavender. Mrs. Chavender's mysteriousness would no doubt shortly be explained, but there seemed no hope of penetrating the inscrutability of the butler. At the Rose and Crown that morning and right through the day Chibnall had been all that was cordial and friendly, and now he was a changed man, curt in his speech and showing a tendency to shoot sharp, sidelong glances. Joss found it puzzling.

The enigmatic attitude of Chibnall, however, could wait. The immediate subject on the agenda paper was the enigmatic attitude of Mrs. Chavender. It was with a lively desire for enlightenment that he entered the library.

"Oh, there you are," said Mrs. Chavender. "Shut the door."

Joss shut the door.

"Sit down."

Joss sat down.

"Now where were we?" said Mrs. Chavender.

Joss was able to refresh her memory.

"You had begun by saying that you were not surprised to find me on the premises because Miss Fairmile had told you I was here. Is her name really Sally? Capital, capital. A delightful name. One of my favorites. It's positively amazing," said Joss, warming to his subject, "how everything seems to be working out, as if I had had it done to my specifications. She's beautiful. She has a lovely voice. And her name's Sally. Not a flaw in the setup as far as I can see."

Mrs. Chavender seemed perplexed.

"Would you mind telling me what, if anything, you're talking about?"

"I should have mentioned," Joss explained, "that I love this young Fairmile. It hit me like the kick of a mule the instant I saw her. Romeo had the same experience. And Chibnall."

"Oh. Well, we can go into that later."

"Any time that suits you," said Joss courteously. "Well, after saying that you were not surprised to find me here you added the words: 'And I know . . .' At that point you heard Chibnall coming and switched off. You never did get around to telling me what it was that you knew."

"Well, I'll tell you now. I know why you're here. Jimmy Duff sent you to swipe that portrait."

"What an extraordinary idea."

"Is it? Well, let me tell you I've had the whole story from an authoritative source. Mrs. Steptoe told me that Jimmy had made an offer for the thing and she had turned him down. And the next thing that happens is that you sneak into the place."

"Not sneak. I bowled up to the front door in my car."

"You being Jimmy's—what did you say you were?"

"Best friend and severest critic?"

"That was it. Well, it's all pretty plain, isn't it? Can you beat it?" said Mrs. Chavender, her voice softening. "After fifteen years Jimmy's still that way about me. I'm darned if I'd have thought he had that much sentiment in him. It looks as if I'd been getting him wrong all this time. When you told me he was still a bachelor I supposed he had stayed one because he liked it. And all the time it was because he was so crazy about me that he couldn't look at anybody else. And the way he figures it out is that even if he has lost me he can still have my portrait to remember me by. If you don't think that's sweet and lovely and touching and wonderful maybe you'll tell me what is."

It was not for Joss to destroy this gossamer fabric of romance with the acid cleaning fluid of truth. He nodded sympathetically.

"Yes, he's a rare soul. He reminds me a little of Sir Galahad. But he didn't send me down here. At the moment when I signed on at Claines Hall there existed between J. B. and myself a slight coolness. He had fired me."

"What did you do to him?"

"Not a thing, except sling him out of his office."

"I don't get this. You aren't going to tell me that when I came into that room just now you weren't starting to cut the portrait out of its frame."

"Quite true, I was."

"Well, then?"

"But J. B. had got in touch with me since my arrival here. This affair is a lot more complicated than you think it. All sorts of dark currents are running beneath the quiet surface of life at Claines Hall. May I speak confidentially?"

"Shoot."

"This will go no further?"

"Not through me."

"Well, then, I am acting not only for J. B. but for Mr. Steptoe."

"Howard Steptoe?"

"Yes. It was he who brought J. B. and me together. He needs cash, and it was his original intention to put the deal through by himself. Finding, however, that he required moral support, he called me in."

"Well, listen," said Mrs. Chavender vehemently. "I'm in on this too. I don't mind giving Howard Steptoe his cut, but when Jimmy starts paying out five hundred pounds has got to be earmarked for me. You say Howard Steptoe needs cash. Well, take a look at someone else who does."

Joss was astounded.

"You?"

"Me."

"But I thought you were a millionairess."

"So I was till about a year ago. Remember the Battersby crash?"

"Were you in that?"

"Up to the eyebrows. I lost my chemise. When the accountants had finished raking over the ashes I found I'd just about enough left to pay Patricia's license and a modest annual dress bill."

"Well, well, well," said Joss. "Well, well, well, well, well."

There was a silence. Mrs. Chavender was wrestling with an obviously powerful emotion.

"Got a cigarette?" she said.

"I'm afraid not."

"Then I'll have to have one of my own. And I hate them. I was hoping you might have something better."

Joss was adjusting his faculties to this sensational revelation.

"You've kept it pretty dark. The servants' hall knows nothing of this. Mrs. Barlow was saying to me only this evening that you were a female creosote."

Mrs. Chavender puffed at her cigarette in silence for a moment. Then she showed that she was her old self again by emitting a deep chuckle.

"You bet I kept it dark. And I'll tell you why. You've met Mabel?"

"You mean Sally?"

"I don't mean Sally. I mean Mabel. Mabel Steptoe."

"Oh, Mrs. Steptoe, yes, of course. A delightful woman. She held me spellbound with her views on Corot."

"Did she mention her views on poor relations?"

"No, we didn't get around to those."

"Well, keep your eye on young Sally Fairmile, and you'll soon know what they are. She believes in treating them rough. Talk about oppressed minorities."

The library swam before Joss.

"You mean she bullies that sweet girl?"

"Well, she doesn't beat her and she doesn't starve her, but that's about all you can say. No, that's not fair. She's quite kind to her really,

I suppose. Put it this way. Young Sally's position in the home is about that of an unpaid lady's maid."

"Monstrous!"

"What mine would be, if it ever came out that I was broke, I don't know. A sort of female butler without portfolio, I guess. Mabel has her points—I'm very fond of her—but she's one of those women who can't help taking it out of the underdog. You daren't let her get on top of you. You've got to keep her under your thumb. That's what I've been doing this last year since I came to live with her. Thank God for giving me a curling lip and a commanding eye. Not that they would be any good if she didn't think I had a weak heart and all the money in the world and was going to hand in my dinner pail at any moment and leave my millions to her."

"The woman is a ghoul."

"No, she's not. She's all right, provided you're in a position to sit on her head. And so far I have been. But, oh baby, if I can't raise that five hundred pounds!"

This second mention of that specific sum interested Joss.

"Why do you want that exact amount?"

"It's a debt I've got to pay. One of these debts of honor. And if I can't get the money any other way I shall have to ask Mabel for it, and then the whole facts about my financial position will come out and I shall sink to the level of a fifth-rate power. Say, have you ever presented the prizes at a girls' school?"

Joss said that he had never had that experience.

"Well, don't," said Mrs. Chavender and relapsed into a pensive silence. She seemed to be reliving a scene which, if the frown on her fine forehead was to be taken as evidence, had not been an agreeable one. Her eyes, as she drew at her cigarette, were clouded.

"Don't you do it," she said at length. "There's something about the atmosphere that does something to you. There they are, all those shining young faces looking eagerly up at you, and you think of the time when you were that age, with the world before you, and it's as if you had gone on a bender and got full to the gills of vintage champagne. I presented the prizes at a girls' school yesterday."

"Yes, I remember you telling me that you were going to. You wanted something to say to the inmates, and I suggested, 'Hullo, girls,' which you seemed to feel would be inadequate. Did you think of something better on the way down?"

"Did I! I made the speech of a lifetime. I had them tearing up the seats and rolling in the aisles."

"Good," said Joss.

"Not so good," said Mrs. Chavender. "Because I hadn't the sense to stop there and take a bow and get off. I had to go and overdo it. Shall I tell you what happened?"

"I'm all agog."

"Well, I must begin by mentioning that the warden of this sea-shore Sing Sing, in her few words of introduction, had spoken of a new gymnasium or some damn thing which they were planning to build and had hoped that all parents would contribute generously to this very deserving cause, as the school expected to be punched in the pocketbook for at least two thousand of the best and brightest. She then said that Mrs. Chavender would now address you on Ideals and the Future Life, and I spat out my lozenge and advanced to the footlights. And, as I say, I wowed them. And then, when the applause had died down and I could hear myself speak, I heard myself speak. And do you know what I was saying? I was saying that I would give five hundred pounds toward their blasted gymnasium if three others would do the same."

"Ah!" said Joss.

"You may well say 'Ah!' Mark you, even though my eloquence had reduced me to a condition where I could have walked straight into any inebriates' home and no questions asked, I thought I was playing it pretty safe. I remembered the gloomy silence which had greeted that gag about contributing generously, and while the room re-echoed to the salvos of applause and the dust went up from the stamping of six hundred girlish feet I kept saying to myself: 'All may yet be well, old sport. I think so. I hope so.' And would you believe it, a couple of minutes later two nitwits with criminal faces had sprung forward with tears in their eyes, shouting that they were with me. And a moment later another certifiable idiot had said the same. So there I was. The best I could do, which wasn't much, was to say I had left my checkbook at home but that they would hear from me in due course. So now, young Weatherby, you know why I want five hundred pounds."

Her admirably clear exposition of the facts had left Joss in no doubt on that point.

"You must certainly have it," he said. "As I see it, we form a syndicate. About how much do you think J. B. would go to?"

"Apparently Mabel didn't let him get as far as talking figures. But I think a thousand pounds would be cheap in the circumstances, don't you?"

"Dirt cheap. An absolutely authentic Weatherby—his Palm Beach period—should fetch that and more."

"Would five hundred be enough for you and Howard Steptoe to split?"

"Don't worry about me. I don't come in on the money end of it. What I want is my job back, or possibly I may stand out for being made head of the art department. I shall have to think it over."

"I'd stand out."

"Yes, perhaps I will. I'm not thinking of myself. It would be such a grand thing for the firm to have a head of the art department like me."

"Then what's the procedure? Do I run up to London and see Jimmy?"

"He's at the inn at Loose Chippings."

"That's convenient. I'll look in there."

"And now to form a plan of campaign. How do we act for the best? It's not going to be easy. Did you notice anything about Chibnall just now?"

"His pajamas?"

"No, though I agree that they were striking. Somehow one always pictures a butler in a nightshirt. I was referring to his manner. I didn't like it. He's stopped calling me 'Sir.' Also, his eye was cold."

"You think he suspects?"

"I'm convinced of it."

"You can outsmart him. Just choose a time when he isn't prowling. And I'll tell you when that'll be. During the garden party."

"Of course. I suppose a butler has to buttle like nobody's business during a garden party."

"He won't have a free minute. And there's another thing. All the nobility and gentry for miles around will be at the garden party. The place will become practically a thieves' kitchen. This will distribute suspicion."

"You think of everything."

From somewhere in the distance there sounded a shrill, impatient bark. Mrs. Chavender rose hurriedly.

"I must go. That's Patricia what-the-helling. She dooon't like being left alone."

"Your bloodhound?"

"My Peke, God bless her."

"Is that the one Miss Fairmile brushes?"

"It's one of the ones she brushes. She's an admirable dog brusher. Tactful and soothing. All right, my angel rabbit, mother's coming. By the way," said Mrs. Chavender, pausing at the door, "did I understand you to say you loved Sally?"

"That's right."

"Well, I don't know how it's going to affect your plans, but she told me this morning, when we were driving to Lewes, that she was engaged to this Lord Holbeton you may have seen pottering about the place. All right, all right, all right," said Mrs. Chavender, as the imperious summons sounded once more from above. "I'm coming, I tell you. The way these darned Pekes keep you on the jump you'd think they thought you went around in spiked shoes and running shorts."

❀ CHAPTER 13

IT WAS NOT UNTIL LATE on the following morning that Sally learned from Lord Holbeton of the stirring doings which had enlivened the watches of the previous night. She had breakfasted early and he, nature having taken its toll of the tired frame, had breakfasted late. He found her eventually in the stable yard, preparing to set out for London in the two-seater, and proceeded to pour forth his tale, omitting no detail, however slight. In particular, he stressed more than was perhaps actually essential what might be termed the Pekingese motif. Women love men for the dangers they have passed, but Sally could not help feeling that there was no need for him to show her the sore place on his leg three times.

Having already observed that the portrait of Mrs. Chavender was still in its frame, she had, of course, been prepared for a record of failure, and she was fair-minded enough, now that the circumstances had been placed before her, to recognize that the failure had been an honorable one. A man can but do his best, and in enterprises of the type which her betrothed had undertaken privacy is the first essential. She quite realized that he could not have been expected to operate successfully with butlers popping in all the time.

Nevertheless, though she tried to fight against it, she could not check a certain sense of disappointment. Perhaps it was that other story which he had told her yesterday, of his race for life in the drive, that colored her view. At any rate, she was left with the feeling, coming to her now for the first time and giving her an uncomfortable shock as if scales had fallen from her eyes, that Lord Holbeton, though svelte and willowy and unquestionably good at singing "Trees," was not quite the man she had thought him. "Feet of clay" was the distasteful phrase that forced itself on the mind.

Having sympathized with her loved one's sore leg and declined, though cordially invited to do so, to look at it for the fourth time, she applied herself to the problem of what was to be done next. Her immediate impulse was to seek out Mr. Duff and make a report. After that unfortunate affair in the drive, she felt, he must be needing reassurance that his interests were being looked after. But her time was not her own. Mrs. Steptoe having suddenly decided that in the matter of extra help for the garden party it would be madness to trust to local talent, she was being dispatched to London to engage metropolitan waiters, hard-bitten and experienced veterans who could be relied on.

The quest for these occupied the whole of the early afternoon, and the hands of the church clock were pointing to half-past four as she entered Loose Chippings on her homeward journey. And she was just speculating on the chances of Mr. Duff being at the Rose and Crown at this hour when she saw him in the High Street. He was standing in a sort of trance, staring at the statue of the late Anthony Briggs.

To those who find themselves marooned in Loose Chippings about the only thing offered in the way of mental stimulus is the privilege of looking at the statue erected by a few friends and admirers to the memory of the late Anthony Briggs, J. P., for many years Parliamentary representative for the local division. You can walk up the High Street and look at it from the front, or you can walk down the High Street and look at it from the back. (By standing in the middle of the High Street you can also look at it sideways, but this is a technicality which need not detain us.)

Mr. Duff at the moment was looking at it from the front but without any sensation of uplift. Even if you are interested in statues of members of Parliament their fascination tends to relax its grip after you have seen them forty or fifty times. For Mr. Duff the late Anthony Briggs had definitely lost his magic. He was also feeling that he had seen all that he wanted to of Loose Chippings.

And he was just thinking what a real pleasure it would be to touch off a stick of dynamite under the late Anthony Briggs and—more generally—that it would be all right with him if the entire town of Loose Chippings were to be submerged in molten lava like the Cities of the Plain, when he heard his name called by a feminine voice, and the hideous thought that it was Mrs. Chavender who had spoken brought him out of his meditations, quivering in every limb.

"Oh, it's you," he said, relieved.

"Can I talk to you, Mr. Duff?" said Sally.

"Sure," said Mr. Duff. He did not like talking to girls, but it was something to do.

"Will you give me some tea?"

"If you like."

"There's a place just along here. The Gardenia."

Mr. Duff was familiar with it or at least with its exterior. The Gardenia Tea Shoppe stood almost immediately opposite the Rose and Crown, and many a time had he shied like a startled horse at the sight of the tiers of disgusting, bilious-looking pastry displayed in its window. Left to himself, he would have avoided an establishment the mere appearance of which made him feel that his indigestion was coming on again, but he supposed that if his companion wanted to go there he must humor her. He climbed into the car, and they drove off.

Like all tea shoppes in English country towns the Gardenia was hermetically sealed. No crevice in its walls allowed fresh air to steal in and dilute its peculiar atmosphere. A warm, sickly scent of buns and cake and hot bread and chocolate seemed to Mr. Duff to twine itself about him as he entered, and he closed his eyes with a faint shudder. Coming back to this world after an interval of semiconsciousness, he found that the ladylike waitress had set their repast before them.

"I ordered buns," said Sally, who had the healthy appetite of youth. "Do you like buns?"

"I do not like buns," said Mr. Duff.

"I'm sorry. Some fancy cakes, please."

"Fancy cakes, right," said the ladylike waitress.

"Couldn't touch 'em," moaned Mr. Duff.

"Oh, but you must," urged Sally, "now they're here. I can't eat alone. Just one."

"Well, one," said Mr. Duff weakly. "You like to hear what this is going to do to me? Just going to kill me, that's all."

He picked feebly at the gruesome lump of cream and pastry which had been placed before him, then, catching the waitress's eye, attacked it with more animation. She was a tall, severe young woman with pince-nez, and there was something about her that reminded him of a strong-willed nurse of childhood days who had always made him eat his fat.

They sat for some moments in silence. Sally, though consumed with curiosity about the mustache, forbore to make any reference to it. Deciding that it was one of those painful disfigurements to which one cannot allude, she finished her tea and came to business.

"Well," she said brightly, for she had determined to be bright, "I suppose you are wondering what has been happening?"

Mr. Duff, before replying, sent a questing tongue in search of a piece of the fancy cake which had adhered to the outskirts of the foliage. He secured it at length, but the struggle had been a hard one and had deepened the moroseness of his mood.

"I know what's been happening," he said with a snort. "That young loafer you say you want to marry has been running like a rabbit every time I get near him."

"Yes, he told me about that. But, you see—"

"I've said it before, and I'll say it again. If George Holbeton had two ounces more brain, just two ounces more, he would be half-witted. The poor wet smack!"

Not for the first time Sally found this man's conversation an irritant.

"Don't call him a poor wet smack!"

"If you only knew what I'd like to call him."

"Of course he ran away. Who wouldn't, with people bounding out at him on every side with false mustaches on? He thought you were a homicidal maniac. George is very high-strung."

"You couldn't string him too high for me."

Sally was silent for a space. Prudence had whispered to her that it were wiser not to say what she would have liked to say. Whatever his spiritual defects, J. B. Duff was the man who signed the checks and must at all costs be conciliated. She wrestled with her better self and finally succeeded in bringing it to the surface by the scruff of its neck.

"Well, anyway," she said with the strained sweetness of a girl of spirit who is keeping that spirit under with an effort almost too great for her frail strength, "he hasn't just been sitting around, doing nothing. He's full of zeal. He had a try for the portrait last night."

"And didn't get it, I'll bet."

"It wasn't his fault. The butler came in with a battle-ax. He is going to try again."

"He needn't. You can tell him it's off. I've made other arrangements."

"What do you mean?"

"What I say. I've put the matter in other hands."

"Whose?"

"Never mind."

Sally gave a little jump.

"Not Mr. Weatherby's?"

"Yes. He's attending to the whole thing."

Sally sat biting her lip. Her face was grave. This, she could not but feel, was serious. Brief though her acquaintance with Joss had been, she had seen enough of him to be aware that he would be a formidable rival.

"Now there," proceeded Mr. Duff, "is a young fellow that amounts to something. I don't say he isn't as fresh as an April breeze. He is. I don't say I haven't often wanted to hit him with a brick. I have. But I do say he's got getup in him. Enterprise. Resource. Look," said Mr. Duff in a sort of ecstasy, "at the way he bounced me out of my office that time, just because he didn't want me giving him hell in front of you. Quick as a flash. Why you don't marry him, instead of fooling around with your string bean of a Holbeton, beats me."

Sally smiled a wintry smile.

"He hasn't asked me."

"He will."

"And if he did I should remind him that we are practically strangers."

"He says he's crazy about you."

"And if that wasn't enough I should add that I love George."

"Now why?" mused Mr. Duff, mystified. "I can't understand how you get that idea. I wonder if in the whole of England there is a fatter-headed chump than George Holbeton. Maybe. Somewhere. Take a bit of finding though."

It is not often that a girl has occasion to grind her teeth, but Sally did so now. With a stupendous effort she once more forced herself to remain courteous. Her better self had made a dive for freedom, but she grabbed it just in time and dragged it back, kicking and struggling.

"But, Mr. Duff, you must be fair. If George gets the portrait—"

"He won't."

"Well, suppose I do?"

"You?"

"Yes. If I do will you keep your promise and give George his money?"

Her words had opened up new vistas to Mr. Duff. He saw no objection whatever to a little competition. A corps of assistants is better than a single assistant. Quite possibly, he reflected, this enterprise might be one of those things which require the woman's touch.

"Sure," he said. "A bargain's a bargain."

"Then you can expect it tomorrow."

"As soon as that?"

"Tomorrow evening at about this time."

"You seem pretty certain of yourself."

"I am."

"Don't forget young Weatherby will be working against you."

"I don't care who's working against me. And now I must be going. Mrs. Steptoe is giving a big garden party tomorrow, and she will be wanting me."

It was in a somewhat more optimistic mood that Mr. Duff left the Gardenia Tea Shoppe and crossed the street to the Rose and Crown. In the lounge he found Joss waiting for him. To Joss, as well as to Sally, it had occurred that his principal ought to be informed at an early date of the night's doings. Mr. Duff, as he saw it, was rather in the position of a mastermind of the criminal world directing a gang of pock-marked Mexicans, and such persons like to keep in touch.

"Oh, it's you," said Mr. Duff, regarding his young friend without enthusiasm. The fancy cake had begun to put in its deadly work, and that brief spurt of happiness had already died away, leaving behind it a leaden despondency.

This despondency was not lessened by the fact that his companion was looking as disgustingly fit and cheerful as ever. In spite of last night's bit of bad news there was nothing of the heartbroken lover about Joss. He was, as has been indicated before, a resilient young man, and though Mrs. Chavender's sensational revelation had given him an unpleasant jolt at the moment, he had quickly recovered from the blow. He had seen Lord Holbeton here and there about the place since his arrival at Claines Hall, and he declined to believe that a girl like Sally could really love a man like that. Just one of those absurd misunderstandings, he felt, over which they would have a good laugh later.

"Come to give you the latest news, J. B.," he said. "I thought you would like to have it. Let's step into the bar parlor. It's quieter there, and you look as if you could do with a quick shot."

It being Miss Pym's afternoon off, the bar parlor was being presided over by a potboy; and though this robbed it of much of its social glitter, Joss was not sorry that the future Mrs. Chibnall was absent. There are moments when one likes to sit exchanging light nothings with charming women, others when the business note must be stressed. He ordered a small draught ale for himself and for his companion, whom he saw to be in need of something more authoritative, a double brandy and split soda. This done, he delivered his report.

"In a word," he concluded, "fortune did not smile. But you will be glad to learn that I propose to make another attempt tomorrow.

News may have reached you of a garden party that will break out at the Hall in the afternoon. That will be my hour, J. B. Not a soul around. Everybody out on the lawn, swilling tea and sucking down strawberries. I shall be able to saunter in and help myself at my leisure."

Mr. Duff seemed to think well of the idea. It occurred to him that Sally, speaking so confidently of delivering the portrait on the morrow, must also have had in her mind the strategic possibilities offered by a garden party.

"I suppose that's what that girl was planning," he said. "She seemed pretty sure of delivering the goods."

"What girl?"

"The one you're stuck on. I've forgotten her name. Little shrimp with blue eyes."

Joss raised his eyebrows.

"Are you by any chance alluding to Miss Fairmile?"

"That's right. Fairmile. That's the name."

"Then, for your information, she is not a little shrimp."

"She is too."

"She is not. I've seen shrimps, and I've seen Miss Fairmile, and there is no resemblance whatever. If what you are trying to say in your uncouth way is that she is as tiny and graceful as a Tanagra figurine then I am with you. But this loose talk about shrimps must cease and cease immediately. What do you mean about her saying she would deliver the goods?"

"I met her just now. She yoo-hooed at me from her car, and we got to talking. She's engaged to a fellow I'm trustee for. Young chap named Holbeton."

"So I hear. Damned silly idea, isn't it? Of course she'll have to break it off. We can't have that sort of thing going on."

"And she said that if I would give him his money, so that they could get married, she would swipe that portrait for me."

"To which you very properly replied that the matter was in the hands of your accredited agent?"

"No, I didn't. I told her to go right ahead."

Joss was shocked.

"You mean you encouraged her in this mad scheme? You weren't appalled at the thought of that lovely girl marrying a bird who looks as if he were trying to swallow a tennis ball?"

"Matter of fact, I told her she was a fool to have anything to do with him. I said she ought to marry you."

"You did? Then I'm sorry I called you a louse."

"You didn't."

"Well, I was just going to. So you advised her to marry me, eh?" said Joss, laying an affectionate hand on his companion's knee. "You advised her to marry me, did you, old pal?"

"Sooner than him," said Mr. Duff, moving the knee. "Personally, if I was a girl I'd rather be dead in a ditch than marry either of you."

"Another double brandy for this gentleman," said Joss to the pot-boy. "And slip a shot of some little-known Asiatic poison in it. You're a hard nut, J. B. I suppose there *is* a heart of gold beneath that rugged exterior of yours, but I should require more than a verbal assurance on the point."

Mr. Duff regarded his glass dubiously.

"I don't know if I ought to have another. If I'm not in for one of my dyspeptic attacks the signs have got me fooled. It's the cooking in this joint. Passes belief. You'd think they'd have learned to fry an egg by now. Well, all right, since it's here."

He sat sipping it after Joss had left him, and his dubiousness increased. Too late he remembered that his medical adviser had warned him against spirits. By the time Joss was nearing the Hall (walking pensively, for Mr. Duff's words had given him food for thought) he had come definitely to the conclusion that he had better go to his room and lie down awhile.

And he had just pushed open the main door of the Rose and Crown with that end in view when there came to his ears, speaking from within, a feminine voice. It was fifteen years since he had heard it, but he had not forgotten those rich contralto notes.

"Well, when he comes back," it was saying, "tell him that Mrs. Chavender called and wants to see him right away."

For one agelong instant Mr. Duff stood frozen in his tracks. Then life returned to the rigid limbs, and he darted back into the High Street, looking about him in a panic for a place of refuge.

It was only too evident that this old love of his would be out in next to no time, and whatever haven he might select must be selected immediately. His eye, in a fine frenzy rolling, was caught by the window of the Gardenia Tea Shoppe across the way. And so keen was the sense of peril that gripped him that it now seemed to have a kindly and a welcoming look.

There is this to be said for tea shoppes, no matter how revolting to a dyspeptic man the wares in which they deal, that in extending their hospitality they do not keep their eye on the clock. At a bespoke tailor's, to take an instance at random, the cry is all for rapid action. You dash in, bespeak your bit of tailoring and dash out again. You can't make it too quick for the tailor. If you take a seat and show signs of settling down for the evening he raises his eyebrows. But in a tea shoppe you can linger. And Mr. Duff's primary requisite was a place where he could linger till the All Clear had been blown. He was across the street and through the door and panting in a wickerwork chair almost before he knew he had started.

The ladylike waitress greeted him with surprise.

"Hello! Forgotten something?"

"Gimme some tea."

"Tea?"

"And buns."

"Yes, sir," said the waitress with a new respect and approval in her voice. There had been a time when she had looked a little askance at Mr. Duff, not liking his offhand manner toward that fancy cake, but now all was forgiven. A man of the right sort, obviously. She could recall no previous case of a client liking his meal so much that he immediately returned for another. A notable compliment for the Gardenia's catering.

She went off to give the order in a modest flutter of excitement, and Mr. Duff, with a sigh of relief, leaned back in his chair.

But even now his troubled spirit was not to be at rest. There spoke from behind him a feminine voice, and he swung around, blinking. It seemed to him that life this afternoon had been just one damned feminine voice after another.

"Why, how do you do?" said the voice, and he perceived, sitting at the next table, Vera Pym, the Rose and Crown's efficient barmaid.

Vera Pym had come to the Gardenia Tea Shoppe to brood and ponder. Pique at his aggravating behavior had, of course, been partly responsible for her calling Chibnall up on the telephone that morning and regretting her inability to take tea with him in his pantry owing to an unfortunate previous engagement, but in any case she would have preferred to be alone. She wanted to give her whole mind to the problem of Mr. Duff's mustache. There must, she felt, if she thought long enough, be some way of discovering once and for all if it was false or genuine.

His abrupt incursion had for an instant alarmed her. Then she had fought down her momentary panic with a barmaid's splendid resolution. There is good stuff in Britain's barmaids, and the Motherland points at them with justifiable pride. This, she told herself, was just what a conscientious investigator would have wished to happen. To fraternize as much as possible with suspects, thus lulling them to a

false security and learning their secrets, is the aim of every detective
whose heart is really in his work.

So, he said, "Why, how do you do?" and tried not to shudder. The
mustache, seen close to, looked more villainous than ever; and in
addition to this the man's features were working violently, as if in
almost ungovernable rage. As always when in the presence of the
other sex, Mr. Duff had started making faces.

"Well, you're just in time to give me tea," she said with the bright-
ness which her professional training enabled her to put on at will like
a garment. "I'll come over to your table, shall I?"

In normal circumstances Mr. Duff would have answered this question with an unhesitating negative. But now he found himself at a
loss. Short of rising and leaving the tea shoppe, it seemed to him that
he was helpless against this woman's advances. And a glance out of
the window showed him how Utopian any dream of rising and leaving
would be. Mrs. Chavender had just come out of the Rose and Crown
and was standing on the pavement waiting for her Pekingese to finish
sniffing at a banana skin.

"They're getting me some tea and buns," said Miss Pym.

"They're getting *me* some tea and buns," said Mr. Duff.

"Well, that's splendid, isn't it?" said Miss Pym.

"Great," said Mr. Duff and sat back, feeling like somebody in one
of his companion's favorite works of fiction who has been trapped by
one-eyed Chinamen in a ruined mill.

Conversation flagged for a while. It is never easy to know just what
to say to the criminal classes, and Miss Pym found herself short of
small talk. But presently the return of the waitress, preceded by a
revolting smell of hot buns, emboldened her to continue. She poured
out tea for herself and host and moved her own cup as far away from
him as was possible. She had known too many men who dropped
mysterious white pellets in teacups to take any chances.

"Lovely day," she said.

"Ur," said Mr. Duff.

"I expect you were surprised to find me in here, weren't you?"

"Ur," said Mr. Duff.

"It's my afternoon off," explained Miss Pym.

"Ur," said Mr. Duff.

"It's nice to get away from that old bar once and again," proceeded Miss Pym, beginning to hit her stride. "Apart from the hard
work of it all there's the society. It gets very mixed, specially in the
evenings, when the proletariat come in and play darts. I've often
thought I'd sooner be a waitress in a place like this. More refine-

ment. They give you a good tea here. Nice, these buns, aren't they?"

"Sure," said Mr. Duff, who had absent-mindedly swallowed one and could feel it fighting with the fancy cake and the double brandies preparatory to turning to lead inside him.

The monosyllable gave Miss Pym a cue. Your good detective is always on the alert to seize these opportunities of keeping the conversation going.

"You're an American gentleman, aren't you?"

"Yes."

"I thought so. The way you said 'Sure.' I can always tell Americans. But," said Miss Pym, who had had a good grounding in vaudeville comedy, "I can't tell them much. Ha, ha."

"Ha, ha," echoed Mr. Duff despondently. He looked out of the window again. Mrs. Chavender was still there. The Pekingese was now sniffing at a piece of paper.

"Mr. Chibnall sometimes talks of going to America. He says the salaries butlers get over there are literally fantastic."

"Mr. Chibnall?"

"My fiancé."

Mr. Duff perked up amazingly. In another distrait moment, not realizing what he was doing, he had swallowed a second bun, and it had teamed up with its predecessor, forming a solid *anschluss,* but the relief of discovering that this young woman was not, as he had supposed, an unattached siren, ready for any excesses, overcame his physical discomfort.

"Going to be married, are you?"

"When we've saved enough to buy a pub."

"They're expensive, I guess."

"They run into money. But Sidney's a saving man, and I've put by a bit. Some of these commercials that come into my bar sometimes give you a good tip for the races. I had Westinghouse for the Ascot Gold Cup. A hundred to eight. That was ten pounds right away."

"Well, well, well. You'll be a Hetty Green before you know where you are."

As is so often the way with a shy man, once the ice has been broken, Mr. Duff was beginning quite to enjoy this little adventure. Mrs. Chavender and Pekingese had now disappeared, but he felt no inclination to leave. He even ate another bun with something of a devil-may-care flourish.

"Who's she?"

"She was one of the richest women in America."

"I suppose everybody makes tons of money there."

"Yes, and when they've made it what happens? Does Mister Whiskers let 'em keep it? Not a hope. Listen," said Mr. Duff, beginning to swell, "lemme—"

He paused. He had been about to speak freely and forcefully of some of the defects of the existing administration in his native country, but he felt that a tête-à-tête with a charming woman was not the occasion for it. Better to wait till he was back with the boys at the Union League Club.

"Plenty taxes in America these days," he said, condensing the gist of it into a sentence. He became aware that his guest was eying him intently. "S'matter?" he asked, puzzled.

"Pardon?"

"You seem to be looking at me pretty hard."

Miss Pym simpered coyly.

"You'll think I'm awful, but I was admiring your mustache."

"Oh."

"You don't often see American gentlemen with mustaches. Not big ones. Must have taken a lot of growing, if you don't mind me being personal."

"Oh well," said Mr. Duff with something of the air of a modest hero protesting that any man could have done what he had done.

"Mind if I look at it?"

"Go right ahead," said Mr. Duff, now not so much the modest hero as the big shot presenting some favored visitor with the freedom of the city.

Miss Pym leaned forward. Her heart was thumping. She passed a shapely hand over the growth. And Chibnall, who had just arrived outside the window, halted abruptly and stood staring, a dark flush spreading slowly over his face.

That telephone call, with its airy allusions to previous engagements, had left Chibnall in a frenzy of doubt and suspicion. A bystander who had heard his careless "Oh? Right ho. Well, see you some time" would not have divined it, but his soul had seethed like a cistern struck by a thunderbolt. Something, he felt, was up. And it was in order to ascertain, if possible, what this something was that he had hastened to Loose Chippings.

Hoping against hope that the woman he loved was merely taking tea with the wife of the Rose and Crown's landlord, as she did from time to time, he had first gone there to inquire and had been informed that Miss Pym had been seen stepping across the way to the Gardenia. And here in the Gardenia she was, carousing with the mustached visitor at the inn whom she had so cunningly affected to distrust and dislike—and not only carousing, but actually patting his face.

It was, in short, the black business of the commercial traveler over again, only worse, far worse. There could be no question here of professional gestures designed to stimulate trade. And it was a long step from straightening ties to patting faces. This, felt Chibnall, was a straight orgy, and something like it, he told himself, was precisely what he had been expecting.

Clenching his fists till the knuckles stood out white under the strain, Sidney Chibnall drew back into the doorway of a ham-and-beef shop to think it over.

Inside the Gardenia Miss Pym had concluded her investigations. It was just as she had suspected. Her fingers, roaming lightly through the jungle, had touched a hard substance which could be nothing but glue or spirit gum or whatever it was that the underworld employed when disguising its upper lip with hair.

She rose. It was imperative that she telephone Chibnall about this immediately. All that a woman could do she had done, and it was now time for the tougher male to take over.

"Yes, it's beautiful," she said, panting a little like a girl who has discovered a dismembered corpse in the attic. "Lovely. Well, I must be shoving along. Ta for the tea."

She hurried out, it seemed to Mr. Duff a trifle abruptly and, after pausing to pay the bill, he also left. And he had scarcely set foot on the pavement when he had the identical experience which had happened to him on the previous morning. There fell suddenly upon his shoulder a heavy hand.

The only detail which differentiated the two episodes was the circumstance that this second heavy-hander was a good deal better looking than his predecessor had been. Yesterday Mr. Duff had found himself staring at a squashed nose and airplane ears. Today it was on a handsome, clean-cut face that his attention was riveted. But this was not really so much of an improvement as it sounds, for the face was suffused with violent emotion and only the dullest observer could have failed to note that the glitter in the eyes was homicidal.

It would have shocked Mrs. Steptoe profoundly could she have known that her butler was capable of looking like that. She would also have disapproved of the way he spoke.

"Oi!" he said.

"Ouch!" said Mr. Duff.

"Just a minute," said Chibnall.

"What the devil are you doing?" said Mr. Duff.

"I'll tell you what I'm going to do," said Chibnall, swift with the effective repartee. "I'm going to knock your ugly fat head off and dance on it."

"Why?" asked Mr. Duff, not unreasonably.

"You don't know, do you?" said Chibnall and brought his teeth together with an unpleasant click. "Ha! He doesn't know!"

There had been a time, in the hammer-throwing days of his youth, when J. B. Duff would have had a short way with this sort of thing. But the years, bringing with them surplus material about the waistline, had brought also pusillanimity and the instinct for self-preservation. He found himself with little appetite for a vulgar brawl. This apparent lunatic had a hard, athletic look, and he himself had not only allowed his muscles to grow flaccid but was at the moment full to the brim with tea and buns.

The ladylike waitress was beginning to get used to Mr. Duff. She showed scarcely any surprise as he now re-entered the Gardenia Tea Shoppe, moving extraordinarily well for a man of his years. He had become an old customer, a sort of foundation member, and she beamed on him as such.

"More tea?" she said brightly.

Mr. Duff sank into a chair with a corroborative nod.

"And buns?"

"Yup."

The waitress was looking like a preacher at a revival meeting who watches the sinners' bench filling up. If there were more men in it like Mr. Duff, her eye seemed to say, the world would be a better place.

"Very good, sir. Is this gentleman with you?" she asked, looking past him. "Why, it's Mr. Chibnall. Good evening, Mr. Chibnall."

"Good evening."

"Lovely weather."

"Beautiful," said the butler absently. He had halted at Mr. Duff's table and was glowering down at him in a hostile and intimidating manner. It was with considerable relief that Mr. Duff realized that for the moment he proposed to go no further than glowering. He applauded the decent respect for the amenities which restrained the other from defiling these refined premises with anything in the nature of a roughhouse.

The waitress continued chatty.

"Your young lady's only just left, Mr. Chibnall."

"I saw her."

"She was having tea with this gentleman."

"I saw her."

His unresponsiveness had its effect.

"Well, I'll go and get your tea and buns," said the waitress and went off to do so.

Chibnall leaned on the table. His aspect, in addition to being homicidal, now betrayed baffled fury. He was blaming himself for having relaxed his grip on Mr. Duff's shoulder, thus enabling the latter to get away and seek sanctuary. What he had popped in for now was to point out that this sanctuary must not be regarded as permanent.

"I'll be waiting for you outside," he said to make this clear.

Mr. Duff did not speak. His intelligent mind, assisted by the waitress's recent remarks, had gathered now the reason for this man's at first inexplicable behavior, and his heart sank as he realized how impossible it would be to explain. Nothing could alter the fact that he had been entertaining the other's fiancée to a dish of tea, and in this world one is judged by one's actions, not by one's purity of heart.

"Understand?"

"There," said the waitress in a motherly way, returning with a laden tray. "There you are."

"You won't see me," said Chibnall, "but I'll be there."

He strode from the shop. The waitress's eyes followed him admiringly.

"That was Mr. Chibnall," she said. "The butler at the Hall."

"Oh?" said Mr. Duff.

"Fine, strapping fellow, isn't he? It's funny, I always used to think of butlers as fat old men, always drinking port, but Mr. Chibnall is a mass of muscle."

"Ah?" said Mr. Duff.

"And the best boxer round these parts, they tell me. He beats them all at the Lads' Club. Strong as a lion, I'm told, and as quick on his feet as a panther. You aren't eating your buns."

"I'm not so sure I want them."

"Then I'll bring you some French pastry and assorted cakes," said the waitress indulgently, like one humoring a spoiled child at a school treat. "Those ones with the cream and pink sugar on the top are the sort you like, aren't they?"

Vera Pym was coming away from the telephone booth, annoyed to learn that the man she sought was not on the premises of Claines Hall, when Chibnall entered the Rose and Crown. She saw him and ran to him, her copper-colored hair dancing with excitement.

"There you are! I've just been trying to get you on the phone."

She looked about her and saw that they were alone. "Sidney, it's true!"

"A fat lot more than you are," said Chibnall morosely.

"What do you mean?"

"I saw you."

"When?"

"Just now. In the tea shoppe. With that fellow."

Miss Pym's attractive eyes widened.

"You don't mean you didn't understand?"

"I certainly did," said Chibnall. "Only too well." He laughed a hollow laugh. "And you pretending he was a crook!"

"But he is. That's why I was having tea with him. I wanted to make sure. I was in there by myself, thinking everything over, and suddenly there he was at the next table. Well, I knew I should never have such a good chance again, so I went and sat with him."

"You patted his face."

"I never. I was feeling his mustache."

"It's the same thing."

"It's not. Sidney, it's fastened on with glue!"

"What!"

"Yes."

"You really mean that?"

"I felt it."

"I mean, you weren't flirting with him?"

"Well, the idea! I was detecting him."

Chibnall relaxed. He had been looking like King Arthur interviewing Guinevere in the monastery. He now looked merely like a butler who has had a weight taken off his mind.

"So that was it!"

"Of course it was. Sidney, I've just remembered something. Sidney, do you know what? Yesterday morning, before you came into my bar, he had been asking the way to the Hall!"

"You don't mean it?"

"That's what he had. And didn't you hear that Weatherby fellow say his face was familiar? And didn't Weatherby leave just after he did? I see it all. They're pals. It's as plain as the nose on your face. Weatherby worms his way into the house, and then he lets this chap in at dead of night to burgle all the valuables."

"I wonder."

"It's what's known as working the inside stand."

"I believe you're right, Vera. I was thinking things over last night, and I came round to your view that there's something very fishy about that Weatherby. I don't like the way he's acting. He was prowling last night. Looking for nightingales, *he* said. But I don't know about him and this fellow with the mustache being pals. Wouldn't he have known him?"

"Not if he's put the mustache on since they plotted together, he wouldn't. You take my advice, Sidney, and watch Weatherby like a hawk. Pretty silly you'd look if you suddenly found him murdering you in your bed."

Chibnall flushed. His pride was touched.

"I'd like to catch him murdering me in my bed. Feel that," he said, directing her attention to a biceps strengthened to steely hardness by morning exercises and evening boxing at the Lads' Club.

"A lot of use that would be against a tommy gun."

"He hasn't got a tommy gun."

"How do you know he hasn't? You didn't see him unpack. You be careful, that's what I say."

"I will."

"And if he offers you any more of his tainted gold you refuse it."

"Would you go so far as that?" said Chibnall dubiously.

In the Gardenia Tea Shoppe J. B. Duff had unfastened the last three buttons of his waistcoat and was leaning back in his chair, breathing stertorously. Under the vigilant eye of the waitress he had long since finished the French pastry, and she was now bringing him some more fancy cakes. He stared bleakly into a dark future. There would be a heavy price to pay for this—physical as well as financial.

But you cannot go into a tea shoppe and just sit. Nor, if a berserk butler is waiting for you outside, can you leave.

The waitress came back with the fancy cakes. It was plain from her somewhat abstracted manner that she had now come to look upon herself rather in the light of an experimental scientist and upon her customer as a guinea pig.

"I'll tell you what," she said, struck with an idea. "After you've finished those I'll get the cook to do you up some of her pancakes. Shall I?"

"Okay," said Mr. Duff in a low voice, but not so low that his stomach was not able to overhear the word. It gave an apprehensive leap and cowered miserably. Nothing could surprise it now. It had long since given up trying to understand what was going on in the front office.

❂ CHAPTER 14

THE AFTERNOON of the garden party, that red-letter day for the nobility and gentry of Sussex, found Sidney Chibnall groaning in spirit.

There are moments in the life of every butler when he is compelled to wonder if flesh and blood can stand the demands made upon them or if they will not be forced to crack beneath the strain, and one of these comes when he holds office under a nervous hostess who is about to give her first important garden party. Chibnall was a man who took a pride in not sparing himself, but by lunchtime on the day of Mrs. Steptoe's colossal binge the constant ringing of the bell and the agitated inquiries of his employer as to whether all was well concerning the band, the refreshments, the extra help and the like had begun to take their toll.

These, however, were but the normal anxieties unavoidable at such a time. In addition to them there weighed upon his mind the dark menace of the man Weatherby. Joss, he was convinced, intended to start something. And it was the thought of what an admirable opportunity he would have of doing so, with everybody in the place busy out in the grounds, that was causing Chibnall to groan in spirit. It is only when he has a big garden party on his hands and knows that during that garden party a Mayfair Man will be roaming the house with no check upon his movements that a butler really drains the bitter cup.

The comparative relaxation afforded by luncheon and a couple of quick ones in his pantry at the conclusion of the meal enabled his active brain to hit on a solution of his difficulties. It was with a clever and well-formulated scheme in his mind that he approached Mrs. Steptoe as she stood fidgeting on the terrace, watching the sky. Mrs. Steptoe had just discovered that she did not like the look of that sky.

"Well, Chibnall?"

"Might I have a word, madam?"

"There's a cloud over those trees there."

"Yes, madam."

"Oh gosh!" cried Mrs. Steptoe emotionally. "And in another minute, I suppose, one might as well be standing under Niagara Falls. I'd like to find the man who invented this English climate and tell him what I think of him. Well, what is it?"

"It is with reference to the young man Weatherby, madam."

"What's he done now?"

"It is rather what he may do in the course of the afternoon that is causing me uneasiness, madam. I confess that I feel dubious about leaving him in occupation of the house while I and my staff are away from it."

His quiet impressiveness was not without its effect. Mrs. Steptoe removed a troubled eye from the cloud, which was now spreading across the sky like an inkstain.

"You really think he's a crook?"

"I am convinced of it, madam."

"Then what's to be done?"

"What I would advise, madam, is that you instruct me to go to him and inform him that you wish him to help with the service at the garden party. He will thus fully be occupied under my personal eye."

"Bright," said Mrs. Steptoe. "Very bright. More," she added, relapsing into gloom again, "than the weather is. It's going to pour in a minute. Then what?"

"I fear you will be compelled to receive your guests in the drawing room, madam."

"And a nice flop that will be. Not that I suppose anyone'll come if the county's under water. You ever been in California, Chibnall?"

"No, madam. I have never visited the United States of America, though I have often felt a desire to do so."

"What a Paradise!"

"So I was given to understand, madam, by a California gentleman whom I once met in a milk bar in London. He spoke extremely highly of his native state."

"You know what happens in California? You say to yourself: 'I feel like throwing a party. I'll have it in my garden two weeks from next Tuesday,' and you send out the invitations. You don't say: 'Will it be fine?' You know it'll be fine. You don't even have to wonder about it. But there . . . All right, go tell Weatherby."

The process of telling Weatherby occupied three minutes of the butler's time. At the end of that period he was back on the terrace.

"I have seen the young man, madam."

"Then everything's all right?"

"No, madam. He refuses to assist with the service."

"What!"

"Yes, madam. I informed him of your wishes, but he merely made some frivolous reply about the rules of the valets' union. No such organization exists."

"Well, of all the . . . Listen, you go right back and tell him from me—"

Mrs. Steptoe broke off. She had been on the point of requesting her butler to tell Joss from her that his term of service beneath the roof of Claines Hall was at an end and that he could get out and stay out, but even as she started to speak there emerged from the house a Vision. It was as if one of those full-page colored advertisements of what the well-dressed man is wearing had detached itself from a monthly magazine and come onto the terrace.

From the suède shoes on his large, flat feet to the jaunty hat on his pumpkin-shaped head Howard Steptoe was correct in every detail. Birds twittered in admiration of his quiet gray suit; bees drew in their breath sharply as they eyed that faultless shirt; beetles directed one another's attention to the gardenia in the buttonhole. And Mrs. Steptoe, who had been expecting something that looked like a tramp cyclist, revised her views about dispensing with Joss's services. He might be a criminal and as fresh a criminal as ever wisecracked with one hand while pocketing the spoons with the other, but to a man who could turn Howard Steptoe out like that all must be forgiven.

"No, never mind," she said.

At this moment it began to rain.

Joss was in the servants' hall, whiling away the time with a crossword puzzle. If Chibnall had been gifted with second sight he could not have predicted more exactly this young man's plans for the afternoon. It was his intention to wait till the house was empty and then carry through the commission he had undertaken on Mr. Duff's behalf. He realized now that in attempting that night foray he had been foolishly blind to the advantages offered to the young portrait-stealer by a garden party.

It was as he sat wondering what was the earliest hour at which he might reasonably expect the residents and guests of Claines Hall to have become stupefied by tea and cucumber sandwiches that he became aware of Chibnall brooding over him like a thundercloud.

"Ah, Chibnall," he said genially.

The butler's manner was cold.

"Mr. Steptoe wants you."

"You mean Mrs. Steptoe?"

"I mean Mr. Steptoe. He's in his room."

"Or rather on the lawn?"

"In his *room*," said Chibnall, raising his voice. "If you'd bothered to look out of window you'd have seen it's raining cats and dogs."

Joss directed his gaze at the window and found the statement correct.

"Egad, so it is. I'm afraid this has messed up the garden party to some extent."

Chibnall had not intended to be chatty, but the topic which had been broached was one on which he felt so strongly that he was forced to say a word or two.

"Ruined. Half the guests have telephoned to say they aren't coming, and the ones that have come are squashed into the drawing room. And is Mrs. Steptoe in a state!"

"I can readily imagine it," said Joss sympathetically. "It must have stuck the gaff into her up to the hilt. The heart bleeds. So Pop Steptoe has sneaked off to his room, has he? That won't do. His place is in the forefront of the battle. I'll go and shoo him back."

Complete though his confidence had been both in Charles the footman's judgment in the matter of gala wear and in Mr. Steptoe's docile acceptance of the clothes laid out for him, his employer's appearance smote Joss like a blow.

"Steptoe!" he cried, stunned with admiration. "My God! You look like Great Lovers through the Ages!"

Mr. Steptoe was in no mood for compliments, however deserved. "Listen," he said.

"I was wondering when you were going to say that."

"Listen," said Mr. Steptoe. "I'm in a spot." His manner was agitated in the extreme. He plucked nervously at his gardenia. "Listen," he said. "Aren't you ever going to get around to swiping that portrait?"

"I'm biding my time."

"Well, don't. Do it now. I'm in a spot."

"So I understood you to say. What has happened?"

Mr. Steptoe advanced his lips to Joss's ear and spoke in a hissing whisper.

"Listen," he said.

"Well?" said Joss, removing the ear and drying it.

"Listen. I did as you said. I grab me a bunch of those guys, and I take them around the corner and we shoot craps."

"Excellent."

"What do you mean, excellent? They cleaned me out."

"Cleaned you out?"

"That's what they did. There was a little bozo with pimples—a baronet or something like that—that never stopped pulling out sevens and elevens. I couldn't get started. He come away all loaded down with my IOUs, and I've told him I'll send over the dough tomorrow. And if I don't come through, then what? He spreads it around among his gang, and the first thing you know Mrs. Steptoe has got the story. Cheese!" said Mr. Steptoe, shivering.

"What would she do?"

"Plenty."

"Then I agree with you. There must be no delay. I confess I had anticipated doing the job at a moment when the house was empty, but I don't suppose anyone will come into the breakfast room."

"They're all having tea."

"That'll hold them. May I borrow your manicure set?"

"Eh?"

"I shall need scissors."

"I haven't any scissors."

"Then give me a razor blade."

A razor blade is not the ideal instrument for removing a canvas from its frame, but Joss made it serve. His task completed, he stood for a moment wondering whether to leave by the door and go to his room or by the French windows and make straight for the Rose and Crown. A rattle of rain against the glass decided him in favor of the former course. He looked up and down the passage. Nothing was stirring. He ran silently up the stairs, and Sally, who had been sent by Mrs. Steptoe to her bedroom to fetch her wrist watch, came out onto the landing just as he reached it.

"Oh!" said Sally.

"Ah!" said Joss.

"You made me jump."

"It was your guilty conscience that made you jump," said Joss sternly. "You're just the girl I was looking for, young S. Fairmile. I've been wanting a word with you for days. One very serious drawback to this place is that it's so difficult to get hold of you for a chat."

"Was there something particular you wanted to chat about?"

"There was. The time has come for a frank round-table conference. In here, if you please."

"But this is Mrs. Steptoe's bedroom."

"That's fine," said Joss. "Nice and quiet."

❀ CHAPTER 15

HE SHUT the door.

"Now, then," he said, "what's all this nonsense I hear about you being engaged?"

If a criticism could have been made of the tone in which he spoke it was that it resembled rather too closely that of a governess of rigid ethical views addressing one of her young charges upon whom suspicion of stealing jam has rested, and Sally gave a little gasp. Her full height was not much but, such as it was, she drew herself to it. She had decided that cold dignity was what the situation demanded.

"I beg your pardon?"

"And well you may, if it's true. Is it true?"

"Perfectly true. May I ask what business it is of yours?"

"That," said Joss, more like a governess than ever, "is one of the silliest questions I ever heard. Considering that I'm going to marry you myself."

"Oh. I didn't know that."

"Well, you know it now. Why, good lord, we were made for each other. I spotted it the minute you came into J. B. Duff's office. You don't mean you didn't get it too? Why, it stuck out a mile. There were you and there was I, and there we were, so to speak. My poor young fathead, I should have thought you would have got onto it right away."

Sally, who had relaxed, for it is a strain on the muscles drawing yourself to your full height, drew herself to her full height again.

"We are not amused," she said coldly.

"I beg your pardon?"

"I was merely trying to point out that you are not being a bit funny." Joss stared.

"Funny? Of course I'm not being funny. What on earth would I want to be funny for?"

"Do you really want me to believe that you are serious?"

"Of course I'm serious."

"You realize, I suppose, that you've only seen me twice in your life?"

"Three times—and once would have been ample. What did you think I meant by all those hints I dropped about falling in love at first sight? People do fall in love at first sight, don't they? Look at Romeo. Look at Chibnall. He went into the Rose and Crown one morning, a carefree butler with not a thing on his mind except the thought of the pot of beer he was going to order, and there was a girl with copper-colored hair behind the bar, and their eyes met, and it seemed to Chibnall as if something had gone all over him like. 'That's the one!' he said to himself, and that's what I said when you came into J. B. Duff's office. I knew in an instant that we had been destined for one another since the beginning of time. I loved you the moment I saw you. I worshiped you. I had been dreaming about you for years. I knew you would be along sooner or later. And in you came."

Sally was conscious of a strange breathlessness. This man might have a peculiar way of laying bare his heart, but she did not question his sincerity. Not even the fact that he had just wandered to Mrs. Steptoe's dressing table and was absently drawing a face on the mirror with lipstick caused her to revise this opinion. Romeo and Chibnall might not have chosen this moment for drawing faces on mirrors, but this was Joss Weatherby, an incalculable being, for whom she was suddenly aware that she felt a very warm affection—of, she was careful to tell herself, a purely maternal nature.

"You'd better rub that out," she said.

"True," said Joss, doing so. "Well, that's the setup."

There was a silence. Joss had found a jar of cold cream and was applying it thoughtfully to the tip of his nose.

"I'm sorry," said Sally.

"Nothing to be sorry about. It's wonderful. When you consider what the odds are against your meeting the one person in the world who's intended for you the thing's a miracle. Suppose you hadn't come to J. B.'s office that morning. Suppose I hadn't been there. Why, it's a pure fluke that I happen to be in England at all."

"I mean I'm sorry you feel like that."

"Why?"

Something of her maternal warmth left Sally, to be replaced by a touch of the resentment she had felt at the beginning of the interview. At times such as this a girl likes to be helped out.

"Well, if you think I enjoy having to tell you that I'm in love with someone else—"

Joss gaped.

"You don't mean—"

"You've got cold cream all over your nose."

"You don't mean you're taking this engagement of yours seriously?"

"Don't you think engagements ought to be taken seriously?"

"Not this one."

"Oh."

"Certainly not. The whole thing's absurd. It stands to reason that you can't really love this fellow."

"Do you know George?"

"Is his name George? No, I don't. But I know all about him. I've made inquiries in the servants' hall. He's a crooner. This is a known fact. He sings 'Trees.' It's sheer nonsense to say you love him."

There had been a moment, when she had woken to the realization that she was engaged to be married, when Sally had been conscious of misgivings on this point herself. Lord Holbeton, as Joss had said, was addicted to singing "Trees," and he had been doing it just before he proposed. Like so many "Trees" singers, he always extracted the last drop of sirup from words and music, and that night he had let it go in a manner that might have melted a Medusa. Even Mr. Steptoe had seemed affected. And some malignant imp of doubt had whispered to her, as she lay thinking in bed next morning, that her acceptance of his proposal might have been merely an impulsive girl's natural reaction to a tenor voice that sounded like a swooning mosquito.

These misgivings had passed as quickly as they had come, but the fact that she had entertained them, if only for an instant, lent vehemence to her statement of faith now.

"I do!"

Joss was telling himself that he must be very tactful, very diplomatic.

"But the man's a mess," he said in pursuance of this policy.

"He is not!"

"Well, no," said Joss, ever fair-minded, "I oughtn't to have said that. I know nothing against him, except that he sings 'Trees.' I suppose it's just the idea of the girl you love even considering anyone else that's so revolting. It seems to go right against one's better nature. Very well, we'll let it go that he's quite a good chap in his way, and if he marries somebody else I am perfectly willing to send him a fish slice. But it's ridiculous to think of him marrying you. The thing doesn't make sense. And you're utterly mistaken in supposing that you love him. Dismiss that notion absolutely. Of course," said Joss, "one can see how you got the idea."

"Do tell me that."

"It's obvious. You were having a rotten time here. You were crushed and oppressed by old Ma Steptoe. It was 'Sally this' and 'Sally that,' 'Comb this dog! See that cook—' "

"That sounds like a bit out of 'Old Man River.' "

"You are familiar with 'Old Man River'?"

"I am."

"I sing it a good deal."

"It must sound wonderful."

"It does. And there," said Joss, seizing on the point with the skill of a practical debater, "you have in a nutshell the essential difference between this George of yours and me. When I sing I sing openly and honestly, starting from the soles of the feet, very deep and loud and manly, so that anyone can see that my heart is in the right place. He gives it out from the eyebrows in an effeminate trickle. The State rests."

"You were saying something about dogs and cooks."

"Oh yes. I was just pointing out that your lot in the home was such a hard one that quite naturally you said to yourself, 'Oh hell! Anything to get out of this.' With the result that when George came along you kidded yourself that you were in love with him."

This was so true that it stung Sally like the flick of a whip. However, long training as a poor relation had given her the ability to curb her temper in trying circumstances.

"I must be going," she said.

"Where?"

"Back to the drawing room."

"Not before we've got all this threshed out. We can't leave it hanging in the air. It beats me why I can't make you see how things are between us. You must believe in affinities."

"Like George and me?"

"Don't," pleaded Joss, "be funny at a moment like this. It clouds the issue. It isn't possible, I repeat, that you love this bird Holbeton. We know him in the servants' hall as That Bloke with the Adam's Apple."

Sally had long since come to the conclusion that cold dignity was too difficult. She now found resentment equally hard to achieve. From their first meeting she had been strangely drawn to this extraordinary young man, and her subconscious self was even now trying rather austerely to draw her attention to the fact that she was deriving far too much pleasure from his society at this moment.

Of course it was abominable what he was saying about poor George, but there was no getting away from it that That Bloke with the Adam's Apple was an admirable description of him—terse, neat and telling the story in a sentence.

"Watch that Adam's apple. That's all I say. Watch it. And in the privacy of your chamber reflect what it would be like to spend the remainder of your life with it."

Nor was there any getting away from the fact that in Joss's company she felt stimulated and happy, as if she were a child watching a three-ring circus. That was how she had felt directly she had seen him, that first morning when they had drunk sherry together in the office of J. B. Duff.

A sudden, uncontrollable giggle escaped her.

"No laughing matter," said Joss reprovingly. "It would drive you nuts."

"I was thinking," Sally explained, "of Mr. Duff and the sherry."

Joss's stern face relaxed into a smile.

"Quite a party, that."

"Quite."

"When he suddenly appeared from nowhere, shouting, 'Hey!' I wonder if you experienced the same odd sensation that I did, as if the top of the head had parted abruptly from its moorings?"

"Yes, that's just how I felt."

"Twin souls," said Joss. "Twin souls. Two minds with but a single thought. But let us not diverge from the main theme. By Jove, though," he went on, "we haven't. J. B. Duff. We will now speak of him. I saw him yesterday."

"I did too."

"So he said. And he told me something that shocked me. It appears that this delusion of yours that you love George Holbeton persists so strongly that you are prepared to steal portraits in order to get money for him so that he can marry you."

"Quite true."

"Well, thank heaven, I can block that punt."

"You think so?"

"I know so."

"Oh?"

"Yes."

"Well, we needn't wrangle about it. He told me you were after the portrait too. Let the best man win."

"He has. I've got it."

"What!"

"Under my waistcoat at this very moment, like a chest protector."

"I don't believe you."

"Well, look."

Sally uttered a wailing cry.

"Mr. Weatherby!"

"You may call me Joss."

"Give it to me!"

"Thereby enabling you to marry a man who sings 'Trees' at the drop of the hat? No, no. This is not the true Sally Fairmile speaking. This is a Sally Fairmile who has not yet come out from under the ether and is not responsible for what she says. Gosh, you'll thank me for this someday."

Desperation came upon Sally. She flung herself at him, like Mrs. Chavender's Pekingese attacking Mrs. Steptoe's Alsatian. Her fingers clawed at his waistcoat, and he caught her wrists. And then, so true is it that one thing leads to another and that you can try a good man just so high, he suddenly found that she was in his arms. After that he hardly knew what he was doing. Chibnall, however, could have told him. Chibnall, with his intimate knowledge of the Nosegay Novelette series, would have recognized the procedure immediately. He was clasping Sally to his bosom and showering burning kisses on her upturned face.

This sort of thing went on for some time. It might have gone on longer had not Lord Holbeton entered the room. Mrs. Steptoe, wearying of waiting for Sally to bring her that wrist watch, had asked him if he would be kind enough to go and see what he could do about it.

⊛ CHAPTER 16

THE SPECTACLE at which Lord Holbeton found himself gazing was one which could not have been viewed with indifference by any fiancé. Owing to the noiseless manner in which he had opened the door, neither of the other two principals in the scene had become aware of his presence, and for some moments after his arrival what might be called the *status quo ante* continued to prevail. Joss was still kissing Sally, and Sally, who in the opening stages had kicked him on the shin, had just begun to realize that she was feeling disgracefully happy about it all.

That this was not the right attitude she was well aware. Her better self was being rather critical. Nevertheless, that was how she felt. In a curious sort of way this seemed to her something that ought to have happened long ago, something to which she had been looking forward without knowing it ever since that morning in Mr. Duff's office.

Lord Holbeton coughed.

"I say," he said.

The comment was one which to some might have seemed lacking in fire and spirit. It was not the sort of thing Othello would have said in similar circumstances. But the truth was that only with the greatest difficulty had the speaker managed to keep out of his voice a note of wholehearted relief. The problem of how to find a way of canceling his commitments without offending against the code of an English gentleman had been putting dark circles under his eyes. And now he perceived that it had been handed to him on a plate. Normally the troth of a Holbeton, once plighted, would have had to stay plighted. But this altered everything.

In the time which had elapsed since he had proposed in the scented garden of Claines Hall Lord Holbeton had been putting in some very intensive thinking, and he had come definitely to the conclusion that in becoming engaged to Sally Fairmile he had made a mistake. He liked Sally. He admired Sally. He wished her well and would watch her future career with considerable interest. But, while still vague as to what exactly were the qualities which he demanded in a wife, he was very clear in his mind that she must not be the sort of girl who routs a man out at midnight to go and pinch portraits and gets him bitten in the leg by Pekingese.

"Look here," said Lord Holbeton.

Joss had released Sally. He would have preferred to go on showering burning kisses on her upturned face, but one has to do the civil thing. Now that her betrothed had put in an appearance he could not be ignored. He must be drawn into their little circle.

"Oh, hullo," he said.

"Who are you?" said Lord Holbeton.

"Weatherby is the name."

"Why, dash it, you're Steptoe's man!"

"Yes."

"Well, I'm dashed. This won't do," said Lord Holbeton, for the first time addressing his remarks directly to Sally. "You can't do this sort of thing, you know. Go about hugging and kissing the domestic staff, I mean. I mean to say, dash it! Well, after this, of course, everything's off. This is official."

He strode from the room without Mrs. Steptoe's wrist watch.

On the part of at least one of the two occupants of the apartment the silence which he left behind him was a thoughtful one. Joss, as he returned to Mrs. Steptoe's dressing table and started to draw a mustache on his upper lip with her mascara, was frowning meditatively. He realized now what before had escaped his notice, that his recent behavior was in certain respects open to criticism.

"I'm sorry," he said.

Sally did not speak. He peered into the mirror, hesitated whether to add a small imperial to the mustache, decided not to.

"You shouldn't have grappled with me. It put ideas into my head. Shall I go after him and explain?"

"No, don't bother."

Joss turned quickly. Sally gave a little squeal of laughter.

"Your face!"

"There is something wrong with it?"

"No, no. It's an improvement."

Joss was looking at her incredulously. He felt that he must have misunderstood her.

"Did you say, 'Don't bother'?"

"I did."

"You don't want me to explain?"

"No, thanks."

"But I've ruined your romance."

"I prefer it that way."

"You said you loved him."

"One changes one's mind."

Joss nodded understandingly.

"I see. So you took my advice and studied that Adam's apple? Very agile, was it not? Like some creature of the wild struggling to escape from a trap or snare. You see now how right I was?"

"You're always right."

"I wonder."

"That's very modest of you. What makes you doubtful?"

"Well, you see, I thought . . . I had an idea . . . There was a time, if you remember, when I thought it might be possible that you would marry me. But, of course, after what has occurred . . . after this loathsome exhibition I've just been making of myself . . . now that you realize that I'm the sort of man who—"

"—takes advantage of a helpless girl?"

"Exactly! Did you notice? I grabbed you—hugged you—"

"—kissed me."

"Yes," cried Joss, his voice vibrating with indignation and abhorrence, "and kissed you. What a cad! What a hound! We don't want anything more to do with J. P. Weatherby after that."

"What does the P. stand for?"

"Parmalee."

"How frightful!"

"Named after a godfather, and not a penny to show for it. No," said

Joss, resuming his remarks, "that will be about all we shall require from J. P. Weatherby, I fancy. We wash him out. We dismiss him."

"So you can be wrong after all."

"What do you mean?"

"If you don't know what I mean—"

"I do know what you mean, but I don't see how you can mean it. Sally, will you?"

"Parmalee, I will."

He clasped her in his arms and went into his routine. Practice makes perfect. It was some time before he spoke again.

"This," he said, "is heaven!"

"Is it?"

"Yes," said Joss, "I do not mince my words. It's heaven." He paused. "Heaven," he repeated. "And yet—"

"—you wish it hadn't happened?"

"No, no, no, no, no, no, no, no," said Joss with all the emphasis at his disposal. "What I was about to say was— And yet I am weighed down by a sense of unworthiness."

"I thought you thought rather highly of J. P. Weatherby."

"I do. I do. A splendid fellow. Nevertheless, I have this crushing sense of unworthiness. If someone came along at this moment and said, 'Tell me, Weatherby, to settle a bet, what have you done to deserve this?' I should be nonplused. I shouldn't know what to answer. I should just go all red and shuffle my feet. Because we've got to face it, I'm not fit to button your shoes."

"They lace."

"I've put up a front. Probably I have struck you as, if anything, a little on the brash side. But really I'm a crawling, creeping chunk of humility. I look at you and I look at myself, and I feel like a swineherd in a fairy story who finds himself loved by a princess. What you see in me I can't imagine."

"Why, your looks. Your character. Your bright future."

"Is my future bright?"

"Glittering. You're going to take that portrait to Mr. Duff and get your job back."

"Better than that. It was a rotten job. All right for a young bachelor, but we men who are planning to marry and settle down have got to look ahead. I intend to stand out for being made head of the art department. Those are my terms," said Joss, and his voice was strong and resolute. "If J. B. won't meet them not a smell of this portrait does he get."

"Oh, Joss, are you sure?"

"Sure?"

"That he wants it as much as that? It would be awful to spoil everything by asking too much."

"You wait. He'll come across. I know J. B. He's one of those men whose legs you have to count to be sure they aren't mules. When he gets an idea into his head you couldn't dig it out with a chisel. He has set his heart on having this portrait, and the thing has become an obsession."

Sally was looking thoughtful.

"Something on your mind?" asked Joss.

"I was thinking that I ought to go and see him."

"Instead of me?"

"Yes. I can do it much better than you. You're not very tactful."

"Me? Not tactful?"

"You might throw him out of the room or something."

"But you don't understand. This is a very intricate business deal, and I doubt if a slip of a girl is capable of handling it. It isn't only a question of my end of the thing. I represent a syndicate whose interests must be borne in mind throughout the negotiations."

"I don't understand."

"I told you you didn't. Can you keep a secret?"

"I don't think so."

"Well, try to keep this one. Money, and substantial money, has got to pass between J. B. Duff and self. Mr. Steptoe needs his little bit. He wants to return to Hollywood and resume what appears to have been a highly promising career in the pictures."

"I didn't know he was in pictures."

"Extra work till just at the end, and then he was in one where he had three good speeches. Get him to tell you about it sometime. And then . . . I wish I knew how good you were at giving an imitation of the silent tomb."

"Why?"

"Because what I am about to say must go no further, if that. Mrs. Chavender."

"What about her?"

"She wants her cut."

"Mrs. Chavender? But she has all the money there is."

"No. She had but hasn't any longer. Lemme, as J. B. would say, tell you a little story."

"Have you heard him say that?"

"Dozens of times."

"He said it to me that day in his office."

"Oh. Well, to get back to it, lemme."

He held his audience. There was no question about that. Sally listened, absorbed, as the story of Mrs. Chavender's unfortunate circumstances unfolded itself.

"The poor old thing!"

" 'Poor' is the exact word."

"I see what she means. If Mrs. Steptoe knew she would trample all over her."

"With spiked shoes."

"Of course she must have her money. I'll be very firm with Mr. Duff."

"You're sure you can manage it? You won't weaken?"

"Of course not."

"Very well. Here's the portrait. Tuck it into your little shirt front, and be very careful not to let anyone get you into a game of strip poker. Are you going to the Rose and Crown in your car?"

"Yes. I'll be back in no time."

"It will seem like hours. Where do we meet?"

"At the gate?"

"Right. Skin off your nose, Sally."

"Skin off yours, Joss."

The door closed. Joss sank into a chair. He drew up a small table and put his feet on it. He took out his pipe and lit it. This wonderful thing that had happened to him demanded quiet, steady meditation. He had to go over all that had occurred since he had met Sally, taking each moment by itself and savoring it like the leaf of an artichoke before going on to the next.

And he had just reached the point where he had found her in his arms and was in the process of dwelling on this phase of their relationship with a tender, reminiscent smile when his attention was attracted by a noise in his rear like the explosion of an ammunition dump, and he looked round to see Mrs. Steptoe. Like J. B. Duff on a similar occasion, equally historic, she was standing in the doorway, spellbound.

Although in Joss's demeanor, as he rose, an observer would have noted only a rather charming, old-world courtliness, he was not without a certain apprehensiveness, a sort of nebulous feeling that this was not so good and that the going in the immediate future promised to be sticky. He had just discovered—or rediscovered—with so many other things to think about it had temporarily slipped his mind—that this room in which he had been enjoying his reverie was Mrs. Steptoe's bedroom. Hard words, he feared, might be spoken and black looks be looked.

Nor had his intuition deceived him. If Fate had wished to cement a lasting friendship between this woman and himself it could hardly have brought them together under less favorable conditions.

Even before opening the door Mrs. Steptoe had been feeling a little edgy. The rain had ruined her garden party. She had had to spend the afternoon cooped up in a stuffy drawing room with some of the dullest people she had ever met. The pimpled baronet, laughing amusedly like one telling a good story which he knows is sure to be well received, had just revealed to her that her Howard had been yielding to his lower instincts and trying to take money off his guests at craps. And the more messengers she dispatched to fetch wrist watches for her the fewer wrist watches did she get.

It just needed the sight of her husband's valet in her bedroom, wreathed in tobacco smoke, with his feet on the table, to complete her day.

"*Well!*" she said.

There is really very little that a man can do at a moment like this, but something, Joss felt, might be accomplished by an apologetic smile. He released one accordingly, and his companion quivered from head to foot as if he had struck her with a sandbag. There are certain situations, one of which had now arisen in Mrs. Steptoe's life, when a smile, however apologetic, seems to a woman the ultimate payoff.

"Grinning!" she said in a strangled voice, not getting the spirit behind the smile at all. "I find him in my bedroom," she went on more loudly, as if confiding her grievances to a slightly deaf friend on whose sympathy she knew she could rely. "I find him right plumb spang in the middle of my bedroom . . . smoking a pipe . . . his feet on the table . . . and he ger-RINS!"

"I assure you, madam—"

"GRINS!" said Mrs. Steptoe. "Like a half-witted ape," she added, specifying more exactly.

There seemed to Joss nothing to do in the circumstances but make wounded noises. He made them.

"Listen!" said Mrs. Steptoe, having probably picked up the expression from her mate.

She began to speak again, and now her voice, which at first had been hushed as if by a sort of awe, rang out like a clarion. And for some time Joss listened with bowed head as she touched on the numerous aspects of his character which did not appeal to her. Exactly when he began to feel that this nuisance must cease he could not have said. But when the thought did come it took root.

"Madam," he said, taking advantage of the fact that even an angry woman has sometimes to pause for breath. "I should be glad if you would accept my resignation. Dating from tomorrow."

"Resignation my foot!" said Mrs. Steptoe, a puff of flame coming from her nostrils. "You're fired. Dating from today."

"Very good, madam. And now," said Joss, "if you will excuse me, I must be leaving you. I have an appointment."

Time, what with his thoughts and Mrs. Steptoe's conversation, had passed on such fleeting wings that he anticipated, as he made his way down the drive, that he might have to wait some little while at the tryst before Sally made her appearance. To his surprise she was already there.

She seemed agitated.

"What a time you've been!"

"I'm sorry. I was chatting with Mrs. Steptoe. Difficult to get away. Well, everything all straight?"

"Joss, an awful thing has happened!"

"Eh?"

"I saw Mr. Duff."

"Well?"

"Joss, he doesn't want the portrait!"

"What!"

"He told me to take it back," said Sally, her voice rising to a wail. Her stout heart failed her. She burst into tears.

❀ CHAPTER 17

It is not the easiest of tasks to scoop a crying girl out from behind a steering wheel and hoist her over the side and fold her in your arms and stanch her tears, but Joss managed it at length. The sobs became gurgles. The gurgles faded into silence.

"Now, then," he said. "Tell me all."

Sally gulped.

"I'm sorry. I was a fool."

"No, no. Nothing like a good cry. What seems to be the trouble?"

"I told you. He doesn't—"

"Yes, but there must be some mistake. You probably misunderstood him."

"I didn't. It's quite simple, really, I suppose."

"Not to me."

"I mean, now that he's going to marry Mrs. Chavender—"

"What!"

"Yes. She went to see him at the inn this morning, and they arranged it then. He's been in love with her for years. Didn't he tell you?"

"No, he didn't mention that."

"And now that they are going to be married of course he doesn't need her portrait. He only wanted it when he thought he had lost her forever, so that he could have something to remember her by. I'm surprised he didn't tell you."

"Probably slipped his mind."

"But why did you think he wanted it?"

"Wouldn't anyone want a genuine Weatherby? But let's begin at the beginning. You arrived at the Rose and Crown and found him—"

"Sitting in the lounge. He looked very ill. Apparently he ate something that disagreed with him and had a bad attack of indigestion last night."

"Ah!"

"He told me he thought he was going to die. And this morning Mrs. Chavender came to see him."

"I'm beginning to understand. There he was, weak and wan after his night of suffering, and in walks Mrs. Chavender and gives aid and comfort. Is that right?"

"Yes. He says she was like a ministering angel."

"He swiped that from me. I once wrote a poem about woman being not so hot in our hours of ease but coming across in a big way when pain and anguish rack the brow. I suppose he got hold of a copy. Yes, I begin to follow the continuity. Mrs. Chavender comes into the sickroom and starts being the ministering angel. He thinks of the old days and what might have been. She places a cool hand on his fevered forehead, and he takes it in his and says: 'Why did we ever part? Why, when we were on to a good thing, did we not push it along? Can we not make a new start?' She thinks the idea sound, and they fix it up. Something on those lines was what happened, I imagine."

"I suppose so."

"Indigestion is an amazing thing. It softens the toughest."

"But he had always loved her."

"I was forgetting that."

"It's sweet, of course."

"Oh, most sweet."

"But rather awkward for us."

"Yes, one was rather relying on delivery of that portrait to solve our little perplexities. Did you touch on me and my job?"

"Of course. I told him we were engaged."

"How did he seem to take it?"

"He said I was crazy and advised me to break it off."

"The lovable old gentleman!"

"He said he had understood that I wanted to marry George and that he had been thinking it over and had decided that he had misjudged George all these years. He said there was a lot of good in him."

"He must have been on an absolute toot last night. No ordinary attack of indigestion would sap the brain to that extent."

"He has given George his money."

"That's splendid news. I was worrying myself sick about George. And my job?"

"No."

"Off?"

"Yes. He said he had been thinking—"

"He thinks too much."

"—and he had come to the conclusion that it was having you around that gave him indigestion. He said he couldn't explain, but you did something to him."

"The old devil. I saved his life."

"Yes, I reminded him of that, and he said that he had put up with you for two years and he considered that that squared it. Did you make him drink brandy yesterday?"

"I didn't make him. I offered it, and he lapped it up. Why?"

"He said it was that that upset him. It seemed to rankle, rather."

"The mind of a man like J. B. Duff is unfathomable. I think that long association with hams must have unhinged his reason. Well, if he won't give me my job back I'm afraid we may have to wait a little before we get married. I have nothing against love in a cottage, but just at the moment I don't see how it would even run to that. My capital is about fifteen pounds, and I am asking myself a little dubiously how it is to be augmented. Who wants an artist?"

"I do."

"Bless you. You're sure you wouldn't prefer to switch back to George now that he has the stuff?"

"No, thanks."

"My God!" said Joss, struck by an unnerving thought. "Do you realize that if I hadn't overslept myself that morning we should never have met?"

"Shouldn't we?"

"No. I was supposed to be at the office at ten. If I had got there on time I should have been gone long before you arrived. But owing to having stayed up late, shooting craps, I didn't clock in till eleven. What a lesson this should teach to all of us."

"To shoot craps?"

"That, of course. But what I was really thinking of was how one ought never to be punctual. From now on I shall make a point of always being late, at least an hour late, for everything."

"Including the wedding?"

"The wedding. Ah! Now we're back to it. What do we do about that?"

"It's difficult, isn't it?"

"There must be some way. People are getting married every day. They can't all be millionaires. I'll tell you what. Give me the canvas, and I'll hide it in my room, and then I'll go for a long walk and think things over. I get rather bright after I've been walking a mile or two. Expect to hear from me shortly."

The evening was well advanced when Joss returned to Claines Hall. The rain had stopped, and a belated sun was shining brightly. It had brought Lord Holbeton out into the grounds for a saunter before dinner.

Lord Holbeton was feeling in the pink. As he made his way down the drive he walked on air. He was honorably free from an alliance which, as has been shown, he had come to recognize as entangling, and he had in his pocket a check bearing his trustee's signature. If that was not a pretty goodish day's work George, second Baron Holbeton, would have been vastly interested to know what was.

He sang as he floated along, naturally selecting his favorite melody, and he had just got as far as the line about nests of robins in the hair and was rendering it with even more than his customary *brio* when there impinged upon his ears one of the gloomier passages of "Old Man River," and he perceived coming toward him the bowed figure of the chap Weatherby.

When a man singing "Trees" meets a man singing "Old Man River" something has to give. They cannot both continue to function. Lord Holbeton generously decided to be the one to yield. It gave him a slight pang not to be able to do the high, wobbly note on the "hair," but a man learns to take the rough with the smooth.

"Hullo," he said. "What ho."

In normal circumstances he might not have been so expansive. But this evening he was the friend of all mankind.

For a moment it seemed as if Joss, like Old Man River, would just keep rolling along. He was walking with bent head, his manner preoccupied. Then he appeared to realize that he had been addressed, and he halted.

"Oh, hullo."

It seemed to Lord Holbeton that the blighter looked a bit dejected, and he was not mistaken. His walk had brought Joss no solution of the problems confronting him. It had, indeed, merely deepened and intensified that unpleasant feeling, which comes to all of us at times, that he was in the soup and liable at any moment to sink without trace. He had endeavored to be gay and debonair while discussing the future with Sally, but not for an instant had he lost sight of the fact that his future was a murky one.

"I say," said Lord Holbeton, "Sally's been telling me about you."

"Oh yes?"

"She says you're not a man. I mean, not really a man. I mean," said Lord Holbeton, determined to make his meaning clear, "you only signed on with old Steptoe so as to be near her."

"Yes."

"Very creditable," said Lord Holbeton handsomely.

There was a pause. Joss, who had now been able to bring his mind to bear on these exchanges, was feeling somewhat embarrassed.

"She tells me you know old Duff."

"Yes."

"Served under his banner and so forth."

"Yes."

"What an egg!"

"Yes."

"Rummy, if you come to think of it, that we never met. I mean, you constantly popping in and out of the office and self repeatedly dropping in to try to gouge the old boy for a bit of the stuff, you'd have thought we'd have run into one another."

"Yes."

"Still, there it is."

"Yes."

It occurred to Joss that up to the present all this cordiality had been a little one-sided and that it was time for him to do his bit.

"I hear I have to congratulate you," he said.

"Eh?"

"Duff has given you your money, I'm told."

"Oh, I see. Yes, yes, oh yes. I couldn't think what you meant for a moment. Yes, I've got the check on my person now. I'm going to London after dinner, so as to be right on the spot tomorrow morning for paying-in purposes in case he changes his mind. I've had that happen before."

"Oh yes?"

"Yes. When the old blister gets these spells of his that's how it works. While weakened by the pangs he's all mellowness and loving kindness. But comes a time when the reaction sets in, and then he's his old self again. And that's when you want to watch out. I remember a couple of years ago he went to a city dinner, and next morning he sent for me and told me he'd come to the conclusion that he had been misjudging me all these years and that there was really a lot of good in me. And, to cut a long story short, he tottered to his desk and wrote me out a check for the full amount. And like an ass I wasted the rest of the day going round and showing it to chaps and having my health drunk, and by the time I got to the bank next morning I found he'd had the bally thing stopped. Taught me a lesson, that, I can tell you. If anyone happens to ask you my whereabouts at 9 A.M. tomorrow you can reply with perfect confidence that I'm standing on the steps of the City and Home Counties Bank, waiting for the establishment to open."

Joss was staring, openmouthed.

"You don't mean that?"

"I do. Right on the top step."

"I mean, is that really what happens with J. B.?"

"Invariably."

"Then you think . . . Well, take a case. If, while under the influence, he thought he was in love with someone—"

"Old Duff?" said Lord Holbeton incredulously.

"I'm just taking the first instance that comes into my mind."

"I should be vastly surprised if even after a city dinner—"

"Just for the sake of argument. You think that later on, when he was feeling better, remorse would supervene?"

"Super what?"

"You think he would regret?"

"Oh, bitterly, beyond a question."

Something seemed to go off inside Joss like a spring. It was hope dawning.

"I must ponder on this," he said. "You have opened up a new line of thought."

"You going?"

"If you don't mind. I should like to meditate."

"Oh, rather," said Lord Holbeton with a spacious wave of his hand, as if to indicate that he was free to do so wherever he pleased, all over the grounds. "Go ahead. Give my regards to Sally if you see her."

Again there was a pause. Once more Joss felt embarrassed. He could not forget that this was the man whom he had deprived of the only girl who could possibly matter to any man. True, the second Baron was not looking notably depressed, but that, he presumed, merely signified that he was wearing the mask, biting the bullet and keeping a stiff upper lip.

"I'm sorry," he said awkwardly.

"Sorry?"

"About Sally and me."

"What, already?" said Lord Holbeton, surprised.

"I mean . . . I can understand how you must be feeling . . ."

"Oh, that?" said Lord Holbeton, comprehending. "My dear chap, don't give it another thought. I'm all right. I'm feeling fine. Once I've got that check safely deposited I shan't have a care in the world. I shall go to Italy and have my voice trained. Best thing that could have happened, is my view of the matter. Nice girl, of course. None better. But personally I consider that a man's an ass to get married. Silly business altogether, I've decided."

It was a point which Joss would have liked to debate hotly, but he was unable to give his mind to it. Was that, he was asking himself, what J. B. Duff was feeling or shortly about to feel? He walked back to the house and, reaching the staff quarters, found Chibnall at the telephone.

"Yes?" he was saying. " 'Oo? Weatherby? Yes, here he is. You're wanted on the telephone," said Chibnall, speaking coldly.

Joss took the instrument.

"Hullo?"

"Weatherby?"

"Yes."

"Listen. Can anybody hear?"

Joss looked round. He was alone.

"No."

"Then listen. Can you come here right away?"

"I dare say I could fit it in."

"Then listen. Go find that girl of yours and get that portrait from her and bring it with you."

"You want it?"

"Of course I want it."

"You said you didn't."

"I've changed my mind."

"Oh."

"Understand?"

"Perfectly."

"Then come along. And listen," said Mr. Duff, "make it snappy."

❀ CHAPTER 18

IN FANCYING that he had sensed in Chibnall's manner at their recent encounter a certain coldness, Joss had not erred. The sound of Mr. Duff's voice over the wire had shocked the butler to his foundations. Brief though their conversation in the Gardenia Tea Shoppe had been, he had recognized it immediately; and it was with a feeling that now was the time for all good men to come to the aid of the party that he had handed over the instrument. The thought that two of the underworld are using his employer's telephone for the hatching of their low plots can never be an agreeable one to a zealous butler.

As always when he had solid thinking to do, he had made his way to the cell-like seclusion of his pantry. The servants' hall, with its flow of merry quip and flashing badinage, he reserved for his more convivial moments when he was in the mood for a gay whirl. He poured himself out a glass of port and sat down to ponder.

Stern though his determination was to foil whatever foul designs this precious pair might be meditating, there was mingled with it a touch of resentment. It seemed unjust to him that a man who was paid for buttling should be compelled to throw in gratis, as a sort of bonus to his employer, the unremitting efforts of a secret service man and a highly trained watchdog. It was quite possible that the man Weatherby and his associate were planning some lightning stroke in the night, and that would mean sitting up again. Reflecting how much he liked his sleep and how cramped he had felt after that last vigil, Chibnall almost regretted that he was so conscientious.

He had finished his glass of port and was considering the advisability of stimulating his brain further through this medium when the hallboy entered to say that he was wanted on the telephone. The voice that spoke in his ear as he adjusted the receiver was that of Miss Pym.

"Sidney!"

"Hullo."

"Are you there?"

"I am."

"Sidney!"

"Hullo."

Miss Pym, who was plainly much stirred, now proceeded to utter about two hundred and fifty words in the space of time more customarily reserved for uttering ten, and Chibnall felt obliged to remonstrate.

"Who is this speaking?"

"Me, of course, Vera."

"Then don't talk like Donald Duck, my girl. You're fusing the wire."

Thus rebuked, Miss Pym applied the brakes.

"Sidney, it's those two men."

Chibnall started. This was more interesting. He had supposed, when the conversation began, that he was merely about to listen to one of those rambling addresses to which his loved one, in common with so many of her sex, was so addicted when she took the receiver in hand.

"Eh? What about them?"

"They're here."

"Where?"

"In my bar. Plotting."

"Then get back there and listen. Haven't you any sense?"

Miss Pym said that Chibnall needn't bite a girl's head off. Chibnall said that he had not bitten a girl's head off but that every instant was precious. Miss Pym conceded this but said that, be that as it might, there was no necessity to go biting a girl's head off.

"I'm going to listen," she said, wounded. "I've been listening."

"What did they say?"

"Nothing much. Well, they wouldn't, would they, with me there?"

"You said they were plotting."

"I meant they were going to plot as soon as I was out of the way. So far they've been talking about marriage."

"Marriage?"

"Yes. The thin one seemed to like it. The stout one didn't. Oh, Sid-*nee!*"

"Well?"

"The stout one's taken his mustache off!"

"What!"

"Yes. Not a trace of it left. Well, I'm going to listen now. I had to ring you up first and tell you. They're sitting right under that little sliding-panel thing that you send the drinks into the lounge through by, and I'm going to open it an inch or two. I'll be able to hear all."

"Go on, then, and ring me the moment you have."

"All right, all right, all right, all right, all right," said Miss Pym, once more giving evidence that she was not her usual calm self. "What did you think I was going to do?"

She hung up the receiver and darted to the panel with rapid, silent footsteps, like Drexdale Drew in the *Limehouse Mystery* that time when he listened in on the conversation in the steel-paneled room at the Blue Chicken. Cautiously she slid it open, and through the aperture there came a snatch of dialogue so significant that it was all she could do to stop herself giving a long, low whistle of astonishment. (Drexdale Drew, it will be remembered, was guilty of this imprudence on the occasion to which we have referred, and it was that that led to all the subsequent unpleasantness with the Faceless Fiend and the Thing in the Cellar.)

The dialogue ran as follows:

The Stout One: Then where is it?

The Thin One: Hidden in my room.

The Stout One: Well, go fetch it.

The Thin One: No, J. B. Before letting you get your hooks on it I wish to talk turkey.

Miss Pym clung to the shelf below the little sliding-panel thing that you send the drinks into the lounge through by, her ears standing straight up from the side of her head. This, she was telling herself, or the whole trend of the conversation had deceived her, was the real ginger.

The example of this girl in dismissing lightly, as if devoid of interest, the earlier portion of the interview between Joss Weatherby and Mr. Duff is one that cannot be followed by a conscientious historian. When two such minds are discussing a subject of such universal concern as the holy state of marriage one must not scamp and abridge. It is not enough merely to say that the thin one seemed to like it and the stout one didn't. Their actual words must be placed on the record.

The conversation began in the lounge, where Joss, hastening to the Rose and Crown, had found Mr. Duff huddled in a chair, looking like an Epstein sculpture. The young man's opening remark, as that of anybody else in his place would have done, dealt with the new and improved conditions prevailing on his elder's upper lip.

"Thank God!"

"Eh?"

"You've removed it."

"She made me."

"Who?"

"Beatrice Chavender," said Mr. Duff glumly. He had not particularly valued the mustache, but his proud spirit chafed at coercion.

The mention of that name enabled Joss to bring up without further delay the main subject on the agenda paper.

"Tell me, J. B., arising from that, is it true what they say about Dixie?"

"Eh?"

"It's correct, is it, this story I hear about you being engaged?"

"That's what I wish someone would tell me."

"You are reported to have said you were."

"She acts as if I was."

"But you aren't sure?"

"No."

"I don't get you, J. B. You speak in riddles. Why aren't you sure?"

"I don't seem able to figure out whether I really committed myself or not."

"Come, come, J. B. You must know if you proposed to her."

"Oh, I didn't do that."

"Then what did you do?"

"Well, lemme tell you," said Mr. Duff.

He paused for a moment before proceeding. It was only too plain that it cost him an effort to delve into the past.

"Well, listen," he said at length. "It was like this. There I was in bed after the worst siege I've ever had. If I attempted to describe to you the agonies I'd been suffering through the night you wouldn't believe me."

"But came the dawn, and you perked up?"

"No, I didn't. I felt like the devil. The pain had gone but—"

"—it left you weak. You were white and shaken. Like a sidecar. All right, push along."

"Don't bustle me."

"I want to get on to the sex interest. I'm waiting for the entrance of the female star. Did Mrs. Chavender come to you as you lay there?"

"Yes. And when the door suddenly opened and there she was, did it nearly slay me!"

"Whereupon—"

"She said, 'Gosh, Jimmy, you look like a rainy Sunday in Pittsburgh!' And I said, 'I feel like a rainy Sunday in Pittsburgh.' And she said, 'Have you been eating something that disagreed with you?' And I said, 'And how!' And she said, 'Poor old slob, your stomach always was weak, wasn't it? A king among men, but a pushover for the gastric juices, even in the old days.' "

"These were the first words you had exchanged in fifteen years?"

"Yes. Why?"

"I had often wondered what lovers said to one another when they met again after long parting. Now I know."

"I wish you wouldn't call us lovers."

"Well, aren't you?"

"I tell you that's what I'm trying to figure out."

"Did she smooth your pillow?"

"No."

"What did she do?"

"She went around to the drugstore and bought me some stuff that tasted like weed killer. I'm not saying it didn't do me good. It did. But I'm still feeling as if someone had started a sewage plant in my mouth."

"And then—"

"She sat down, and we kidded back and forth for a while."

"Along what lines?"

"Well, she said this, and I said that."

"That's a lot of help."

"What I mean, we talked of old times. Picking up the threads, as it were. 'Remember this?' 'Remember that?' 'Whatever became of old So-and-so?' You know the sort of thing. And then she asked me how I had got that way and I told her."

"How did you get that way?"

"Well, it's a long story."

"Then don't tell it. Save it up for some evening when I'm head of the art department and you've asked me to drop in for dinner and a chat on general policy."

"Head of the art department?"

"That's what I said."

"Oh yeah?" said Mr. Duff with some spirit.

Joss forbore to press the point. It could wait.

"Well, so far," he said, "you seem to have come out of the thing with reasonable credit. If that was all that happened—"

"It wasn't."

"I thought the probe would dig up something sooner or later. What did happen?"

"Well, I'd finished telling her how I got that way, and she put her hand on my forehead—"

"I thought as much."

"—and said something about I ought to have a wife to look after me. And I said I guessed she was about right."

"Well, then! Well, there you are!"

"You think that committed me?" said Mr. Duff anxiously.

"Of course it committed you."

"I didn't mean anything personal," urged Mr. Duff. "I was just speaking in general terms."

"You need say no more, J. B. Order the wedding cake."

"Oh gosh!"

"Buy the tickets for the honeymoon trip. Get measured for the hymeneal trousers. Sign up a good minister and make all the arrangements for conscripting the ushers. Good heavens," said Joss, "you go to infinite pains to spread the story that you wanted that portrait because you had been pining for this woman for fifteen years—"

"She hasn't heard that?"

"Of course she has heard it. The whole neighborhood is ringing with it. Your fidelity is being held up as a mark for the male sex to shoot at by every female in the county. Do you really suppose that on top of a blast of propaganda like that you can tell Mrs. Chavender that you need a wife to look after you and expect to carry on with your bachelor existence as if nothing had happened? You astound me, J. B. You're as good as brushing the rice out of your hair at the Niagara Falls Hotel already."

Mr. Duff rose. His face was drawn. He moved heavily.

"Come into the bar," he said. "I think I'd like a drink."

It seemed to Joss that Miss Pym, presiding at the fount of supply, was a little nervous in her manner as they stepped up to give their order. Her attractive eyes were large and round, and she showed a disposition to giggle in a rather febrile way. It occurred to him as a passing thought that something in the nature of a spiritual upheaval was taking place inside this puller of beer handles. But neither he nor his companion was in a mood to inquire too closely into the soul states of barmaids. They withdrew with their tankards to a table at the side of the room—a table which, as Miss Pym was so swift to observe, was situated immediately below the little sliding-panel thing.

It was Joss who resumed the conversation, opening it now on a cheerier and more encouraging note.

"What beats me, J. B., is why you are making all this heavy weather about a situation which should, one would have imagined, have set you twining flowers in your hair and doing buck-and-wing dances all over Loose Chippings. Can't you see how lucky you are? She's a wonderful woman. Looks. Brains. A delightful sense of humor. What more do you want? If you ask me, this is a far, far better thing that you do than you have ever done. This is where you begin to live."

Mr. Duff was not in the frame of mind to respond to pep talks. He continued somber. His resemblance to something carved by Epstein on the morning after a New Year's party had increased rather than diminished.

"It's the whole idea of marriage that gives me that sinking feeling," he said. "It always did. When I proposed I was thinking all the time what a sap I was making of myself. And when she bust our engagement I went around singing like a lark."

It was not merely the nauseating thought of the other singing like a lark that caused Joss to shudder so violently that he spilled his beer. His whole soul was revolted by the man's mental outlook.

"Marriage is the most wonderful thing in the world," he cried warmly, "and only a subhuman cretin with a diseased mind could argue to the contrary. I appeal to you, Miss Pym," he said, arriving at the counter to have his tankard refilled.

"Pardon?" said Miss Pym, starting. She had been distrait.

"Isn't marriage a terrific institution?"

"Oo!" said Miss Pym, pouring beer in a flutter.

"Nothing like it, is there?"

"Coo!" said Miss Pym. "Excuse me," she added, and withdrew hastily. Joss returned to the table, feeling that he had made his point.

"You heard her reply to my question? 'Oo!' she said, and 'Coo!' Those words, straight from a barmaid's unspotted heart, are as complete an endorsement of my views as you could wish to have. You should take that soul of yours around the corner, J. B., and have it thoroughly cleaned and pressed."

"Look," said Mr. Duff, as impervious to honest scorn as he had been to encouragement. "When you get married, what happens? I'll tell you what happens. Government of the people, by the people, for the people perishes from the earth. That's what happens. You get bossed. You can't call your soul your own. Look at the way she made me take off that mustache. It was a false one and I don't like mustaches anyway, but that shows you. And it's that sort of thing all the time, once you've let them poison-needle you and get you into the church. I like to smoke a mild cigar in bed before dropping off. That'll be out. Same with reading the evening paper at dinner. And what happens when I come back from the office, all tired out, and start reaching for my slippers? It'll be, 'Snap into it and get dressed, Jimmy. Have you forgotten we're dining with the Wilburflosses?' Don't talk to me about marriage."

Joss shook his head.

"You paint a gloomy picture, J. B. I look at it in a different way. Let me sketch for you a typical day in my married life. I wake up, feeling like a giant refreshed. I spring under the cold shower. I climb merrily into my clothes, and down I go to a breakfast daintily served by loving hands and rendered additionally palatable by that smiling face peeping over the coffeepot. Off to work, buoyed up by the thought that at last I've got something worth working for. Perhaps we meet for a bite of lunch. Back to work again, right on my toes once more, with her gentle encouragement ringing in my ears. And then the long, restful evening, listening to the radio and discussing the day's doings, or possibly—"

"Look," said Mr. Duff, who had been wrapped in thought. "I've had an idea. Seems to me there's a way out."

"I wish you wouldn't interrupt when I'm talking," said Joss, annoyed. "Now you've made me forget what I was going to say."

"Look."

"And another thing. Generally, when I meet you, you say 'Listen,' and now you're started saying 'Look.' I wish you would decide on some settled policy. One doesn't know where one is."

"Look," said Mr. Duff. "That time when we were engaged before she called it off just because I happened to mention Paramount Ham once or twice. Well, look. What's she going to do when she finds out I'm using her portrait as a poster for the good old P. H.?"

Joss stared.

"You aren't going ahead with that scheme now?"

"I certainly am."

"I don't envy you when you tell her."

"I shan't tell her. I'll simply rush the thing through, and one fine morning she'll see the walls and billboards plastered with her face. And then what? I'll tell you what. She'll throw fifty-seven fits, and then she'll be on the phone to my office, asking what the hell. And I'll just raise my eyebrows—"

"Over the phone?"

"Over the phone. And I'll say, 'Once and for all, I will not be dictated to. If I want to use your face to advertise Paramount Ham I'll use it—see? If you don't like it you know what you can do about it—see?' Just like that."

"Over the phone?"

"Over the phone. Well, I'm here to tell you that if I know Beatrice that'll be the finish. You brought the portrait with you?"

"No."

"But I told you to. Don't I get any cooperation? I distinctly said, 'Go find that girl of yours'—I keep forgetting her name—that little shrimp—"

"I have had to speak to you before about this practice of yours of alluding to Miss Fairmile as a—"

" '—and get it from her,' I said."

"I did get it from her."

"Then where is it?"

"Hidden in my room."

"Well, go fetch it."

"No, J. B. Before letting you get your hooks on it I wish to talk turkey. You will now accompany me to Claines Hall, and on the way I will state my terms. I warn you in advance that they will be stiff."

At the address mentioned Chibnall, too impatient to wait in his pantry till the summons should come which he was expecting every moment, stood tensely beside the telephone. The bell shrilled in his ear.

"Hullo."

"Sidney?"

"Speaking."

"Are you there?"

"Of course I'm here. Where did you think I was? Riding a bicycle across Africa?"

"You needn't be a crosspatch."

"I am not a crosspatch."

"Yes, you are a crosspatch."

"I am sorry," said Chibnall, bringing to bear all the splendid Chibnall self-restraint, "if I appear to be exasperated, but I am anxious to hear your news with as little delay as possible."

"Oo. Well—"

"Well?"

"Oo, Sid-nee, it's thrilling!"

"You heard something?"

"Did I? Coo! Talk about plotters!"

"Did they plot?"

"You bet they plotted. Sidney, that Weatherby has got something valuable hidden in his room. And the stout one wants it. And they're coming to the Hall now."

"What!"

"I heard them say so. Weatherby is stating his terms on the way. They haven't arranged yet how to divide the swag. What are you going to do?"

Chibnall's jaw muscles were working menacingly.

"I'll tell you what I'm going to do. I'm going straight to that Weatherby's room and search it from top to bottom. And when they get there they'll find me waiting for them."

"Oo! Sid-nee!"

"Yes?"

"They'll murder you."

"They won't. Because if they so much as start trying to I'll jolly well murder them first. I'm going to get a gun from the gun room."

"Oo!"

"I'll hide behind the curtains."

"Coo!"

"And pop out at 'em."

"Well, mind you're careful."

"I'll be careful."

"I don't want to be rung up from the Hall by Mrs. Ellis or someone and told that you've been found weltering in your blood."

Chibnall laughed lightly. He found these girlish tremors engaging. He liked women to be feminine.

"I shan't welter in my blood."

"Well, mind you don't," said Miss Pym.

✿ CHAPTER 19

THE HOUR of nine-thirty found Claines Hall, dinner over, settled down to what Joss had described to Mr. Duff as the long, restful evening. Curtains had been drawn, lamps lit, the radio switched on to an organ recital, and Mrs. Steptoe and her Alsatian, Mrs. Chavender and her Pekingese and Mr. Steptoe and a cat which liked his looks, which seemed odd, but cats are cats, and had attached itself to him in close comradeship, were seated about the library, occupied in their various ways.

Mrs. Steptoe was glancing through the morning paper, which until now she had had neither the leisure nor the inclination to peruse. The

Alsatian was staring unpleasantly at the cat. The cat was sneering at the Alsatian. Mrs. Chavender was reading a novel and scratching her Pekingese's stomach. Mr. Steptoe, still practically a stretcher case after hearing what his wife had to say about men who shot craps with the flower of the county, was lying slumped in a chair, thinking of Hollywood.

Sally was not present. She had gone for a walk in the garden. And Lord Holbeton, unswerving in his resolve to be on the top step of the City and Home Counties Bank when that institution opened its doors for the transaction of business on the morrow, had already left for London.

Mrs. Steptoe, refreshed by cocktails and one of Mrs. Ellis's admirable dinners, was feeling better. The agony of that ruined garden party had abated, and the loathing for the human species which had animated her throughout the afternoon and evening had gradually dwindled, until now about the only member of it whom she would have disemboweled with genuine relish was Joss. She could not forgive his behavior at their last meeting. In fact, she was not trying to.

She had just read in her paper a paragraph containing the hot news that Albert Philbrick (39) of Acacia Grove, Fulham, had been removed to hospital, suffering from a broken rib and scalp wounds owing to falling down an excavation in the King's Road, Chelsea, and was just thinking in a dreamy way what a capital thing it would be if something like that could happen to the last of her husband's long line of valets, now presumably back in the metropolis, when the door opened and Chibnall appeared.

Supposing that he had merely flitted in, as butlers do flit in at about nine-thirty, to remove the coffee cups, she was surprised when, instead of buckling down to this domestic duty, he advanced and took his stand before her, coughing portentously.

"Could I speak to you, madam?"

"Yes, Chibnall?"

A closer student of the Greek drama than Mrs. Steptoe would have been reminded of a messenger bringing news from Troy, but even now she sensed nothing ominous in the atmosphere.

"It is with reference to the young man Weatherby, madam."

Mrs. Steptoe's tranquil mood was shot through by a quick twinge of irritation. She respected Chibnall. She had always thought him an excellent butler. But she found his conversation annoyingly limited in its range. It seemed to her that her recent life had been one long series of interviews with him which began with this preamble. She had a feeling that when she died the words, "It is with reference to the young man Weatherby, madam," would be found graven on her heart.

"Weatherby? Hasn't he gone?"

"Not yet, madam."

"Then get him out of here immediately," snapped Mrs. Steptoe, going briskly into her rattlesnake imitation. "I never heard of such a thing. When I fire someone—"

Mr. Steptoe came out of his coma with a start.

"Did you fire Weatherby, honey?"

"Yes, I did. And when I fire someone I expect them to act like they were fired. So he's still here, is he, lounging about the place just as if—"

"No, madam. He is in the coal cellar."

"What?"

"I apprehended him and an associate burgling the house this evening, madam, and thought it advisable to lock them in the coal cellar."

It was a sensational announcement, and Chibnall knew it. It gratified him accordingly to note that it had gone over with solid effect. Apart from his own, and excluding those of the Pekingese, the Alsatian and the cat, there were three lower jaws in the room, and each had fallen to its farthest extent. In addition to this Mr. Steptoe had uttered a low, choking cry.

"Burgling the house?"

"Yes, madam."

"Why was I not told about this before?"

"I thought it best to wait until after dinner, madam, in order not to interfere with your enjoyment of the meal."

This was obviously very decent and considerate of a man, and Mrs. Steptoe recognized it as such. She suspended that line of inquiry.

"Had they taken anything?" she asked in a softer voice.

"Yes, madam. The portrait of Mrs. Chavender that hangs in the breakfast room."

The Pekingese raised its head with a frown. The loving fingers which were kneading its stomach had administered an unpleasantly sharp jab.

"You don't say?" said Mrs. Steptoe.

"Yes, madam. I received information from a reliable source that the young man Weatherby was concealing something of value in his bedchamber, and I proceeded thither and instituted a rigorous search. I discovered the canvas hidden in a drawer and deposited it in my pantry. I then took up my station behind the curtain in the room, armed with a shotgun, and waited. Eventually Weatherby arrived with his associate, and I apprehended them and conducted them to the coal cellar."

He paused modestly, like an orator waiting for the round of applause. It came in the shape of a marked tribute from Mrs. Steptoe.

"Nice work, Chibnall."

"Thank you, madam."

"Have you phoned the police?"

"Not yet, madam. I was awaiting your instructions."

"Go do it."

"Yes, madam. Should I bring Weatherby to you?"

"Why?"

"I gather that he wishes to make a statement."

"All right. Fetch him along."

"Very good, madam."

The stage wait which followed the butler's exit was filled in by a masterly résumé of the affair by Mrs. Steptoe who, like the detective in the final chapter of a thriller, proceeded to sum up and strip the case of its last layers of mystery.

There had been a time, Mrs. Steptoe frankly confessed, when the machinations of the man Weatherby had perplexed her. She had guessed, of course, that he was up to some kind of phonus-bolonus, but if you had asked her what particular kind of phonus-bolonus she would not have been able to tell you. Everything was now crystal clear. This bimbo Weatherby was obviously a hireling in the pay of the bozo Duff, whom she had distrusted the moment she saw him. (You remember, Howard, when you found him sneaking around the place that time.) And it was her intention after shipping Weatherby off to a dungeon, to bring an action against Duff for whatever it was— any good lawyer would tell her—and soak him for millions. This, in Mrs. Steptoe's view, would teach him.

All this took the form of a monologue, for neither Mr. Steptoe nor Mrs. Chavender seemed in the mood to contribute the remarks which would have turned it into a symposium. Mrs. Chavender was still scratching the Pekingese's stomach meditatively, while Mr. Steptoe paced the floor, his habit at times of mental unrest.

It seemed to Howard Steptoe that the curse had come upon him. Already he was solidly established in the doghouse as the result of that craps business. Into what inferno he would be plunged when this bird Weatherby arrived and started spilling the beans he shuddered to think.

His reverie was interrupted by the entrance of the bird Weatherby, escorted by Chibnall.

Joss was not looking his best. You cannot spend several hours in a coal cellar and be spruce. There was grime both on his hands and on his face. His cheerfulness, however, remained undiminished.

"Good evening," he said. "I must apologize for appearing before you like this, but my suggestion of a wash and a brush up was vetoed by our good friend here. He seemed to think that speed was of the essence."

"You'll get a bath in prison," Mrs. Steptoe pointed out, possibly wishing to be consoling, though this was not suggested by her manner.

"Oh, we hope it won't come to that."

"Will we?"

"Statement," said Chibnall in a curt aside. Throughout these exchanges he had contrived with admirable skill to combine in his manner the inexorable rigidity of the G-man with the demure respectfulness of the butler. He was now for the moment pure G-man.

"Eh?"

"You told me you wished to make a statement."

"And I do wish to make a statement," said Joss heartily. "First, however, I would like to acquit my roommate of the coal cellar of any complicity in this affair. He was merely a crony I had brought in for a smoke and a chat and nobody more surprised than himself when he discovered that he was being held up with guns and placed among the anthracite. Dismiss him without a stain on his character is my advice."

"Madam."

"Yes?"

"This is not true. My informant heard these two men plotting together. Their words left no room for doubt that they were in this game together up to the neck. Accomplices," said Chibnall, correcting with a slight blush this lapse from the purer English.

"Well, never mind about the other fellow," said Mrs. Steptoe "What do you want to say?"

"This," said Joss. "I admit that I removed that portrait. But why did I?"

"I'll tell you."

"No, let me tell you. I painted that portrait myself. It was my own unaided work and my masterpiece. Well, you know how artists feel when they paint masterpieces. They hate to let them go. If they let them go they want them back. It was thus with me. The moment I parted with that portrait I felt an irresistible urge to get it into my possession again. I had to have it. So I took it. Blame me if you will—"

"I will."

"You will? I had hoped," said Joss reproachfully, "that a woman as sound on Corot as Mrs. Steptoe would understand and sympathize."

"Well, she doesn't."

"I shouldn't be surprised if Corot hadn't frequently done the same thing in his time. We artists are like that."

"And we Steptoes are like this. When we catch smooth young thugs looting the joint we put them in the cooler. And that's what's going to happen to you, my friend. I don't believe a word of your story."

"But it's *good*," protested Joss.

"Go phone the police, Chibnall."

Howard Steptoe had stopped pacing the room. He was standing propped up against the table, trying to nerve himself to speak. The cat sprang onto the top of his head, unheeded.

The amazing discovery that this Weatherby, so far from spilling beans, intended to take the rap and go in silence to a prison cell had first stunned Howard Steptoe, then aroused all the latent nobility in his nature. Not normally a very emotional man, he found himself stirred to his depths. He saw that he must reveal all. To say that he liked the idea would be an overstatement, but he felt that he must do it.

And he was on the point of starting to do it when Mrs. Chavender spoke.

"Just a minute, Mabel."

"Yes, Beatrice?"

"Mr. Weatherby did paint that portrait."

"Is that any reason why he should steal it?"

"That wasn't the reason why he stole it. He did it for me."

"No, no," cried Joss. "Don't listen to her. The woman's potty."

Mrs. Steptoe's china-blue eyes were wide with astonishment.

"For you?"

"Yes. I had to raise some money in a hurry, and I'm busted. I'm afraid I have misled you a little about my finances, Mabel. I lost practically all I had a couple of years ago."

"Delirium," said Joss. "Pay no attention."

Mrs. Steptoe blinked.

"You," she said, and paused.

"Are," she said, and paused again.

"Busted?" she said, her voice breaking in an incredulous squeak. "Is this a joke, Beatrice?"

"Not for me."

Mrs. Steptoe's face had been slowly turning bright red.

"Well!" she said.

"Still, after all," said Joss, "what's money?"

"Well!"

"You can't take it with you."

"Well!"

"It isn't money that counts; it's—"

"Well!" said Mrs. Steptoe. "I must say!" She had sprung to her feet. The Alsatian, who came between her and the carpet, uttered a yelp which drew a quiet smile from the cat.

"Well, I must say I wouldn't have expected you to be so deceitful, Beatrice. After this . . . Of course this makes everything very different. . . . Of course, for poor Otis' sake, you can always have a home with me—"

"I knew you would be sweet about it, Mabel."

"But—"

"But," said Mrs. Chavender, "I expect my husband will want me to make my home with him.

"Your husband?"

"I'm going to marry Jimmy Duff."

"Oh!" said Mrs. Steptoe. She paused, disconcerted.

"He's very rich, isn't he?"

"Very."

"I should estimate J. B.'s annual income," said Joss, putting in his oar in his helpful way, "at around two hundred thousand dollars. It will be larger, of course, if he employs me."

Mrs. Steptoe eyed him coldly. The thought that she had been so injudicious as to treat as a poor relation a woman who was about to marry a millionaire was a bitter one, and she accepted thankfully this opportunity of working off some of her chagrin.

"If he's going to employ you," she said, "he'll have to wait a while. Your time's going to be occupied elsewhere for quite a spell. Chibnall, phone the police."

"Mabel, you can't do this."

"Can't I?"

"But, Mabel—"

Whatever appeal Mrs. Chavender had been intending to make to her sister-in-law's better nature was checked abruptly at its source. The air had suddenly become vocal with canine yelps and feline spittings.

Ever since he had been trodden on by Mrs. Steptoe the Alsatian had been thinking things over and trying to fix the responsibility. It had now become plain to him that all the evidence pointed to the cat. He had never liked the cat. He had disapproved all along of admitting her to the library. But he had been prepared to tolerate her presence, provided she started no phonus-bolonus. This, by hypnotizing women into treading on his sore foot and smiling superciliously after it had occurred, she had done, and it was time, he felt, to act.

The cat, at the moment when he reached this decision, was still on top of Mr. Steptoe's head. It was consequently with something of a shock that the latter, whose attention had been riveted on his wife and Mrs. Chavender, became aware that a dog whom he had never liked was leaping up and scrabbling at his face. Nothing could actually affect his face, for better or for worse, but it was the principle of the thing that mattered. He resented being used by this animal as a steppingstone by which it could rise to higher things.

Nature had bestowed upon Howard Steptoe one gift of which he was modestly proud—his right uppercut. In the days when he had battled among the pork-and-beaners he had too often been restricted in its use by the evasiveness of his opponents; but now, at last, confronted by an antagonist who seemed willing to mix it, he was able to express himself. There was a dull, chunky sound, and the Alsatian, flying through the air, descended on an occasional table covered with china. Picking himself up, he sat surrounded by the debris, like Marius among the ruins of Carthage, and began licking himself. As far as the Alsatian was concerned the war was over.

"How-WERD!" said Mrs. Steptoe.

There had been a time, and that recently, when the sound of his name, spoken by this woman in that tone of voice, would have been amply sufficient to reduce Mr. Steptoe to a shambling protoplasm. But now his eye was steady, his chin firm. He looked like a statue of Right Triumphing Over Wrong.

A man cannot have all the nobility aroused in him by the splendid behavior of chivalrous valets and on top of that win a notable one-punch victory over one of the animal kingdom and still retain the old, crushed outlook. It was a revised and improved edition of Howard Steptoe that now stood tickling the cat behind the ear with one hand and making wide, defiant gestures with the other. Just after he has kayoed an Alsatian that is the moment when a henpecked husband is to be feared.

"Listen," he said, "what's all this about fetching cops?"

"I intend to send this man to prison."

"Do you?" said Mr. Steptoe, red about the eyes and bulging in the torso. "Is that a fact? Well, listen while I tell you something. This guy Weatherby is a right guy, and he doesn't go to any hoosegow, not while I have my strength."

"Well spoken, Steptoe," said Joss.

"The boy's good," said Mrs. Chavender.

"A fine fellow," said Joss. "I liked him from the first."

This excellent Press emboldened Mr. Steptoe to continue.

"Who does this portrait belong to? Me. Who's the interested party then? Me. So who's got to prosecute if guys are to be slapped in the cooler for swiping it? Me. M-e," said Mr. Steptoe, who was all right at words of one syllable. "And I'm not going to prosecute—see? You know what I'm going to do? I'm going to hunt up Duff and sell him the thing."

"You won't have to hunt far," said Joss. "You will find him in the cellar."

"What!" said Mr. Steptoe.

"*What!*" said Mrs. Chavender.

"And I'm sure he will be charmed to do a deal."

Mrs. Chavender had risen, Peke in hand, and seldom in a long career of looking like Mrs. Siddons in *Macbeth* had she looked more like Mrs. Siddons in *Macbeth* than now. It is not given to many people to see an English butler cower, but that is what Chibnall did as her fine eyes scorched their way through him.

"What's that? Have you been shutting my Jimmy in your filthy coal cellar?"

Until this moment Chibnall's attitude had been that of a detached and interested spectator. Basking in the background, he had been storing up in his mind every detail of this priceless scene in high life in order to be able to give Miss Pym a full eye-witness's description later. He had pictured her hanging on his lips as he reeled out sentences beginning with "He said" and "She said." That he might be swept into the swirl of the battle had not occurred to him, and now that this disaster had befallen he was unable to meet it with the old poise. He gave at the knees and looked sheepish.

"Er—yes, madam," he said in a soft, meek voice.

There was an instant when it seemed as if Mrs. Chavender would strike him with the Pekingese. But she mastered her emotion.

"Take me to him immediately."

"Very good, madam. If you will come this way, madam."

The door closed. Mr. Steptoe resumed.

"Listen."

"Lemme tell you something," prompted Joss.

"Lemme tell you something," said Mr. Steptoe. "The moment I've got Duff's dough in my jeans this joint has seen the last of me. I'm going back to Hollywood; that's what I'm going to do; and if you've a morsel of sense you'll come with me. What you want wasting your time in this darned place beats me. Nobody but stiffs for miles around. And look what happens today. You give this lawn party, and what do you get? Cloudbursts and thunderstorms. Where's the sense in sticking around in a climate like this? If you like being rained on come to Hollywood and stand under the shower bath."

"That's telling her," said Joss, awed. "That's talking."

Mrs. Steptoe, who had resumed her seat, was leaning forward with her chin in her hands, thinking. Like Joss, she had been profoundly stirred by this silver-tongued orator. Not if he had sat up at night for weeks, pruning and polishing and searching for the convincing argument, could Howard Steptoe have struck the right note more surely. He had put in a nutshell her very inmost thoughts.

"Listen," proceeded Mr. Steptoe, his voice now gentle and winning. "Just throw your mind back to Hollywood, honey. Think of that old sun. Think of that old surf at Malibu."

"That old Catalina," suggested Joss.

"That old Catalina," said Mr. Steptoe. "Say, you been to Hollywood?"

"Yes, I was there three years ago."

"Some place!"

"Considerable."

"You were a sap to come away."

"I'm glad I did."

"You're crazy."

"No. You see, Steptoe," said Joss, "love has found me. Which it wouldn't have done in that old Hollywood. Apropos of which, do you happen by any chance to know where Miss Fairmile is?"

"Said she was going out in the garden."

"Then I will be leaving you," said Joss. "Keep working," he added in an encouraging whisper. "I think she's weakening."

For some moments after the door had closed Mrs. Steptoe maintained her pensive reserve. Mr. Steptoe watched her anxiously. Presently she looked up.

"You know something, Howard?"

"Yes, honey?"

"I believe you're about right."

"You'll come?"

"I guess so."

" 'At-a-girl!" said Mr. Steptoe. " 'At-a-baby! 'At's the way to talk. 'At's the stuff I like to hear."

He clasped her to his bosom and showered burning kisses on her upturned face. Not even Joss, who was good at this, could have done it better.

❂ CHAPTER 20

SALLY'S WALK in the garden had taken her to the wall of the moat, and when Joss found her she was leaning on it dejectedly, feeling out of tune with the lovely English twilight. Weeping skies would have been more in keeping with her mood. The weather is always in the wrong. This afternoon Mrs. Steptoe had blamed it for being wet. This evening Sally was reproaching it with being so fine.

The sound of Joss's footsteps made her turn, and at the sight of him she felt a faint flicker of hope. Her acquaintance with him, short though it had been, had given her considerable confidence in his ability to solve difficult problems.

"Well?"

He halted beside her.

"So here you are at my favorite spot. This is like old times. Remember?"

"I remember."

"You look more like a wood nymph than ever. It just shows."

"What?"

"I was thinking how utterly mistaken a man can be on matters outside his own business. J. B. Duff, for instance. He thinks you're a shrimp. One of these days, if the funds will run to it, I shall buy a pint of shrimps and show them to him. It seems the only way of convincing him. He repeated the monstrous statement this evening."

Sally started.

"You haven't seen him again?"

It came to Joss with a shock that this girl knew nothing of the tidal waves and earthquakes which had been giving his former employer the run-around and rocking Claines Hall to its foundations and would have to be informed of what had occurred from the beginning. He paused, appalled at the immensity of the task. It was like finding someone who had never heard of the Great War.

"Oh gosh!" he said.

Sally's worst forebodings were confirmed.

"Bad news?"

"Yes."

"Well, go on."

It was not a pleasant tale to have to tell, but he told it courageously, omitting nothing. When he had finished he heard her teeth come together with a little click. There was a silence before she spoke.

"Then that's that?"

"I'm afraid so."

"You think Mrs. Steptoe is going back to Hollywood?"

"It looks like it."

"That means I shall have to go too."

"Yes. I never thought of that at the time. I abetted and encouraged Steptoe in his insane scheme. I ought to be kicked."

"Are you sure Mr. Duff won't give you back your job?"

"Quite sure. He was peevish all through our sojourn in the cellar. He seemed to blame me for what had occurred."

Sally was silent again.

"Can't we get married and chance it?"

"On a capital of fifteen pounds and no job?"

"You'll get a job."

"Of course I shall," cried Joss. It was unlike him to remain despondent even for so long as this. His resilient nature reacted to her words like a horse that feels the spur. Nobody who had had the privilege of his acquaintance had ever mistaken him for anything but an optimist.

"There are lots of jobs."

"Millions of them, all over the place, just waiting to be got. I see now," said Joss, "where we have made our mistake. We have been looking on this Weatherby purely as an artist, forgetting how versatile he is. With you behind me I don't see that there's anything I can't do. So everything's all right. I'm glad that's settled."

"What were you thinking of doing?"

"I can't tell you that till I have glanced through the Classified Telephone Directory."

"The only thing I can remember in the Classified Telephone Directory is Zinc Spelters."

"That may be what I shall decide on. Pots of money in it, I expect. Can't you see us in our little home—you shaking up the cocktails, me lying back in the armchair with my tongue out? 'You look tired tonight, darling.' 'I am a little. This new consignment of zinc seems to take quite a bit of spelting. Not like the last lot.' "

"Oh, Joss!"

"Hullo."

"I suppose you know I'm just going to commit suicide in the moat. I'm utterly miserable."

"Me, too, if you probe beneath the debonair exterior. I'm feeling like hell. I hope I haven't seemed too bright. When the bottom's dropped out of the world I never know whether to try to keep up a shallow pretense that everything's grand or to let myself go and break down. But, honestly, why shouldn't I get something? I'm young and strong and willing for anything. Also—a point I was nearly forgetting —two can live as cheap as one."

"And money doesn't bring happiness."

"True. But, on the other hand, happiness doesn't bring money. You've got to think of that too."

"I suppose so."

"Still, good lord, when you look at some of the people who have got the stuff in sackfuls you feel it must be pie to become rich. Take J. B. Duff. There's a case. Wears bank notes next the skin winter and summer and yet, apart from a certain rude skill in the selling of ham, probably instinctive, as complete a fathead as ever drank bicarbonate of soda."

"Hey!"

The voice that spoke proceeded from a shadowy figure which had approached them unperceived. The visibility was now far from good, but the monosyllabic exclamation with which it had announced its presence rendered identification simple.

"Ah, J. B.," said Joss genially. "Torn yourself away from the little woman?"

Mr. Duff came to a halt, wheezing. His manner was not cordial.

"What was that you were saying about me?"

"I was telling Miss Fairmile here how rich you were."

"You said I was a fathead."

"And whom have you to blame for that, J. B.?" said Joss sternly. "Only yourself. Would anyone but a fathead have let a man like me go? If you would give me back my old job—"

Mr. Duff sighed heavily.

"It's worse than that. She says—"

"Who says?"

"Beatrice Chavender. We've just been chewing the fat, and she says I've got to make you head of the art department."

"Eek!" cried Sally, squeaking like a mouse surprised while eating cheese.

"Don't do that!" said Mr. Duff, quivering. "I'm nervous."

Joss, who had staggered so that he had been obliged to restore his balance by placing a hand on the wall, now laid this hand on the other's shoulder. His manner was urgent.

"You wouldn't fool me, J. B.? This is true?"

"That's what She says," said Mr. Duff lugubriously. "I told you how it would be. Bossed. Right from the start."

"Head of the art department?"

"So She says."

Joss drew a deep breath.

"Did you hear that, Sally?"

"I heard, Joss."

"Head of the art department. A position that carries with it a salary beyond the dreams of avarice."

"No, it doesn't," said Mr. Duff hastily.

"Well, we can discuss that later. Meanwhile," said Joss heartily, "let me be the first to congratulate you, J. B., on this rare bit of good fortune that has befallen you. You are getting a splendid man, one who will give selfless service to the dear old firm, who will think on his feet when its interests are at stake and strain every fiber of his being to promote those interests. I shouldn't be surprised if this did not prove to be a turning point in the fortunes of Duff and Trotter."

"She says I've got to have you paint my portrait."

"Better and better."

"And give that butler a wad of money to make him keep his mouth shut."

"Of course. We mustn't have him spreading the story of your shame all over the place. 'Tycoon in Coal Cellar' . . . 'Duff Dumped in Dust' . . . That wouldn't do. Stop his mouth, J. B. It will be money well spent. Gosh!" said Joss, "you've been doing yourself proud tonight, have you not? Thanks to you, my wedding bells will ring out. Thanks to you, Chibnall will now be able to buy that pub of his and team up with the Pym. Talk about spreading sweetness and light!"

"Ur," said Mr. Duff, not with much enthusiasm.

"It's sensational. Do you know what you remind me of, J. B.? One of those fat cherubs in those seventeenth-century pictures in the Louvre who hover above the happy lovers and pour down abundance on them. Take your clothes off, fit you out with a pair of wings and a cornucopia, and nobody could tell the difference."

Another long sigh escaped Mr. Duff.

"Fresher and fresher *and* fresher," he said sadly. "Well, I got to be getting back to Her. She's waiting to walk to the inn with me."

He turned and was lost in the gathering dusk.

"Sally!" said Joss.

"Joss!" said Sally.

"My darling!" said Joss. "My angel! My own precious little blue-eyed rabbit!"

"Eh?" said Mr. Duff, reappearing.

"I wasn't talking to you," said Joss.

"Oh," said Mr. Duff and withdrew once more.

A rich contralto voice hailed him as he approached the front door.

"Is that you, Jimmy?"

"It's me."

"Did you see Weatherby?"

"I saw him."

"Then let's go," said Mrs. Chavender, chirruping to her Pekingese. "It's a lovely evening for a walk."

This was indisputably true, but to Mr. Duff, as to Sally earlier, the fact brought no balm. As they made their way along the path that skirted the lawn there rose from the wet earth like incense the fragrance of the sweet flowers of the night. All wasted on J. B. Duff. His heart continued heavy.

Mrs. Chavender, on the other hand, whose heart was light, sniffed appreciatively.

"Ah!"

"Eh?"

"Um!"

"Oh," said Mr. Duff, getting her meaning.

"Stocks," said Mrs. Chavender. "You can't beat the scent of stocks."

"Swell smell," agreed Mr. Duff.

Mrs. Chavender seemed pleased by this poetic eulogy.

"You know, you've become a lot more spiritual since I first knew you, Jimmy. There's a sort of lyrical note in your conversation which used not to be there. About now, in the old days, if I had mentioned the scent of stocks you would have been comparing it to its disadvantage with the smell of Paramount Ham in the early boiling stage."

"Ah," said Mr. Duff, sighing for the old days.

They walked on in silence for a moment.

"I want to talk to you about that, Jimmy."

"Ah?"

"Yes," said Mrs. Chavender, putting her arm through his. "I've been thinking quite a bit lately. Looking back, I can see that I must have been an awful disappointment to you in those days. I was a fool of a girl and didn't know enough to be interested in higher things.

Like ham. Do you remember me saying, 'You and your darned old hams!' and throwing the ring at you?"

"Ah!" said Mr. Duff wistfully. He was oppressed by a dull feeling that breaks like that do not happen twice in a man's life.

"I've got sense now. You'll find me a wife that takes an interest in her husband's business. Yessir!"

For an instant Mr. Duff's gloom lifted a little. Then the fog came down again. It was that operative word "husband" that was like a knell.

"Jimmy," said Mrs. Chavender, an earnest note coming into her voice, "let's talk about that portrait. Did you take a real good look at it?"

"Ah."

"Anything strike you about it?"

"How do you mean?"

"Listen, Jimmy," said Mrs. Chavender, "I was giving it the once-over before I came out, and an idea hit me like a bullet. I believe I've got something. Here's what I thought. It seems to me people must be getting tired of seeing nothing but pretty girls in the advertisements of Paramount Ham. Isn't it about time you gave them something different? You may think I'm crazy, but I can see that portrait as a poster."

Mr. Duff had halted and was swaying gently, as if he had been poleaxed and could not make up his mind which way to fall. Her words seemed to come to him from far away.

"I don't know if you get what I mean. Here's what I was thinking. Maybe it was just a passing expression that Weatherby happened to catch, but in that portrait he's given me a sort of impatient, imperious look, as if I was mad about something and didn't intend to stand for it. And what I thought was that if you took the portrait just as it is and put underneath some gag like—well, for instance: 'Take this stuff away. I ordered Paramount!' you'd have a poster that got a new angle. Any good?" said Mrs. Chavender diffidently.

Nothing could ever make Mr. Duff's face really beautiful, but at these words it went some of the way. A sudden glow of ecstasy illuminated it like a lantern.

All that he had ever heard or read about soul mates came back to him. All that he had ever thought and felt about the drawbacks of marriage surged into his mind, and it seemed incredible to him that he could have entertained such sentiments. Looking at it in its broad, general aspect, of course, he had been right. In the great majority of cases a man who married proved himself thereby a sap of the first order, and he could understand how marriage had come to be referred to as the fate that is worse than death.

But where he had made his error was in not allowing for the special case. Grab the right partner, as he had so cleverly done, and you were sitting pretty. There lay before him in the years to come, he estimated, some nine thousand, two hundred and twenty-five breakfasts, and at each of these breakfasts he would see this woman's face across the table. And he liked it. He was heart and soul in favor of the thing. By careful attention to his health he hoped to make the total larger.

"Listen," he said huskily.

"Yes?"

"Will you do something for me?"

"Sure. What?"

"No, nothing," said Mr. Duff.

He had been about to ask her if she would gaze into his eyes and put a hand on each cheek and draw his face down to hers and whisper, "My man!" but though feeling fine, he was not feeling quite fine enough for that. Later on perhaps.

He drew her arm against his side with a loving pressure.

"Listen," he said. "Lemme tell you something about Paramount Ham. All through the slump years, when every other ham on the market was taking it on the chin and yelling for help, good old Paramount—"

The night covered them up.